Exploring the Gospel of John

D. Moody Smith

Exploring the Gospel of John

In Honor of D. Moody Smith

Edited by

R. ALAN CULPEPPER *and* C. CLIFTON BLACK

Westminster John Knox Press
Louisville, Kentucky

Book design by Jennifer K. Cox
Cover design by Kevin Darst

First edition

Published by Westminster John Knox Press
Louisville, Kentucky

This book is printed on acid-free paper that meets the American National Standards Institute Z39.48 standard. ♾

PRINTED IN THE UNITED STATES OF AMERICA
96 97 98 99 00 01 02 03 04 05 — 10 9 8 7 6 5 4 3 2 1

Library of Congress Cataloging-in-Publication Data

Exploring the Gospel of John : in honor of D. Moody Smith / edited by
    R. Alan Culpepper and C. Clifton Black. — 1st ed.
        p.   cm.
    Includes bibliographical references and index.
    ISBN 0-664-22083-5 (alk. paper)
    1. Bible. N.T. John—Criticism, interpretation, etc.   I. Smith,
D. Moody (Dwight Moody)   II. Culpepper, R. Alan.   III. Black, Carl
Clifton.
BS2615.2.E96   1996
226.5'06—dc20
                                                        95-46685

Contents

Preface

Dear Moody,

We could not allow your sixty-fifth year to pass without acknowledging this birthday with a special gift. Knowing your zeal for a particular sport—to which some of this volume's contributors can offer firsthand testimony—we might have considered tickets for you and Jane at Wimbledon's Centre Court. Nevertheless, we decided firmly in favor of this book: for though you occasionally swing the tennis racket with bravura, you constantly wield the scholar's pen with love.

The title of the volume you are holding has not been adopted on impulse. This book is most certainly prompted by our aspiration to honor you. That one so modest as you would stand in the limelight without flinching is probably too much to expect. We do hope, however, that the reading of this work may distract you from discomfiture, that from its perusal you may derive some measure of the immense satisfaction we have enjoyed in preparing it.

Equally obvious, this book is concentrated on the Fourth Gospel, to whose study and elucidation you have dedicated so much of your professional life—to the enrichment of countless students and teachers, scholars and pastors, around the world. In this volume's focus on the biblical text from diverse critical perspectives, we trust that you recognize the center and range of your own learned interests over three decades, as well as the immeasurable influence that your scholarship has exerted on the ways that all of us now approach and interpret the Gospel of John. Thanks to the expert guidance of our collaborators gathered here, this book, we hope, will offer its readers a reliable map of the liveliest issues in Johannine study of the twentieth century, with some directional signs for the advancement of that research into the twenty-first. Alongside their service as kudos for you, nothing would give us greater gratification than for these essays to galvanize the intelligence and imagination of the next generation of Johannine interpreters.

Finally, as its title indicates, this is a book of explorations: provisional surveys of forested terrain, soundings of the depths. No one has counseled us more wisely than you in that affable, equanimous doubt with which "the assured results of biblical scholarship" should be regarded. From you we have learned that prudence in biblical interpretation is invariably appropriate—not because timidity is virtuous or the quest for meaning futile, whether in the study of texts or in other important enterprises of life. Far from it. Your unswerving devotion to truth's pursuit; your kindhearted discernment of the foibles of all interpreters and the finitude of all interpretations; your reverence for the radiant mystery to which scripture points and under which all should stand who would ultimately understand—these are the reasons, you have taught us, for discipline in our exegesis, friendliness toward others' insights, and genuine humility before the biblical word.

In realizing this tribute to you, many companions have given generously of their talents, time, and experience. Readily apparent among these are the book's contributors, your celebrated colleagues and longstanding friends. As a gifted *Übersetzer* of theological German, you will surely appreciate the erudite contribution of Douglas W. Stott, who translated into English the essay written for this volume by Hans Weder. Laura H. Randall, Senior Reference Librarian at the Bridwell Library of Southern Methodist University, ran to earth many a bibliographical hare with remarkable adroitness. Robert Baker, Stan Harstine, and Freda Virnau of Baylor University, Sarah Freedman of Duke Divinity School, and Mary Ann Marshall of Perkins School of Theology rendered uncommon editorial and secretarial assistance. Cynthia Thompson, now of Augsburg Fortress, warmly welcomed our plans into Westminster John Knox; Jon L. Berquist, her successor at WJK, has spared no effort to produce a volume worthy of you. Over the years of its preparation we have received encouragement and help, in various forms, from Dennis M. Campbell, Beverly R. Gaventa, Harriet F. Black, Jacque Culpepper, and Jane Allen Smith.

Mention of Jane reminds us that a book like this can never be more than a token of that widespread circle of esteem that enfolds you — including not only Cynthia, Catherine, David, and Allen, but also a host within the church and the academy. A number of those within that extended family wished that they could have participated more tangibly in this volume, but for different reasons were unable to do so. In spirit, however, they constitute a great cloud of witnesses who join with us in saluting you, Moody, during your sixty-fifth year. With eagerness we await the ripening harvest of your exegetical labors, which to our delight show no signs of abatement; and with unalloyed affection we give thanks to God for your life among us, as our teacher and our friend.

As ever,
Clift and Alan

Contributors

C. K. Barrett, Professor Emeritus of Divinity, Department of Theology, University of Durham, Durham, England

Johannes Beutler, S.J., Professor of New Testament and Fundamental Theology, Philosophisch-Theologische Hochschule Sankt Georgen, Frankfurt am Main, Germany

C. Clifton Black, Associate Professor of New Testament, Perkins School of Theology, Southern Methodist University, Dallas, Texas

Peder Borgen, Research Professor, Department of Religious Studies, University of Trondheim, Dragvoll-Trondheim, Norway

James H. Charlesworth, George L. Collord Professor of New Testament Language and Literature, Princeton Theological Seminary, Princeton, New Jersey

R. Alan Culpepper, Dean, Mercer University School of Theology, Atlanta, Georgia

W. D. Davies, George Washington Ivey Professor Emeritus of Christian Origins, The Divinity School, Duke University, Durham, North Carolina

James D. G. Dunn, Lightfoot Professor of Divinity, Department of Theology, University of Durham, Durham, England

Beverly Roberts Gaventa, Helen H. P. Manson Professor of New Testament Literature and Exegesis, Princeton Theological Seminary, Princeton, New Jersey

Leander E. Keck, Winkley Professor of Biblical Theology, The Divinity School, Yale University, New Haven, Connecticut

Robert Kysar, Bandy Professor of Preaching and New Testament, Candler School of Theology, Emory University, Atlanta, Georgia

J. Louis Martyn, Edward Robinson Professor Emeritus of Biblical Theology, Union Theological Seminary, New York, New York

Wayne A. Meeks, Woolsey Professor of Biblical Studies, Department of Religious Studies, Yale University, New Haven, Connecticut

Paul W. Meyer, Helen H. P. Manson Professor of New Testament Literature and Exegesis Emeritus, Princeton Theological Seminary, Princeton, New Jersey

John Painter, Reader in Religious Studies, School of History, La Trobe University, Melbourne, Australia

Eduard Schweizer, Professor Emeritus of New Testament Theology and Exegesis, Theologisches Seminar, University of Zurich, Zurich, Switzerland

Fernando F. Segovia, Professor of New Testament and Early Christianity, The Divinity School, Vanderbilt University, Nashville, Tennessee

Stephen S. Smalley, Dean of Chester Cathedral, Chester, England

Marianne Meye Thompson, Associate Professor of New Testament Interpretation, Fuller Theological Seminary, Pasadena, California

Hans Weder, Professor of Theology, Institut für Hermeneutik, University of Zurich, Zurich, Switzerland

Congratulators

There follows a list of those whose doctoral dissertations at Duke University have been directed by D. Moody Smith. Each is identified by his or her current professional position, the title of the dissertation, and the year in which that work at Duke was completed. These persons join with this volume's contributors in saluting Professor Smith, with grateful appreciation of his scholarship and friendship.

David R. Beck, Assistant Professor of New Testament and Greek, Southeastern Baptist Theological Seminary, Wake Forest, North Carolina

"Readers and Anonymous Characters in the Fourth Gospel: The Discipleship Paradigm" (1994)

C. Clifton Black, Associate Professor of New Testament, Perkins School of Theology, Southern Methodist University, Dallas, Texas

"An Evaluation of the Investigative Method and Exegetical Results of Redaction Criticism of the Gospel of Mark: The Role of the Disciples as a Test-Case in Current Research" (1986)

Delbert Burkett, Assistant Professor of New Testament, Louisiana State University, Baton Rouge, Lousiana

"The Son of Man in the Gospel of John" (1989)

R. Alan Culpepper, Dean, Mercer University School of Theology, Atlanta, Georgia

"The Johannine School: An Evaluation of the Johannine Hypothesis Based on an Investigation of the Nature of Ancient Schools" (1974)

Edward F. Glusman, Jr., Rector of The Episcopal Church of the Ascension, Knoxville, Tennessee

"The Shape of Mark and John: A Primitive Gospel Outline" (1977)

Robert G. Hall, Elliott Associate Professor of Religion, Hampden-Sydney College, Hampden-Sydney, Virginia

"Revealed History: A Jewish and Christian Technique of Interpreting the Past" (1986)

Judith L. Hill, Professor, Department of New Testament, Bangui Evangelical School of Theology, Bangui, Central African Republic

"Establishing the Church in Thessalonica" (1989)

Thomas L. Hoyt, Jr., Bishop, Fourth Episcopal District (Mississippi and Louisiana), Christian Methodist Episcopal Church, Shreveport, Louisiana

"The Poor in Luke-Acts" (1974)

Thomas F. Johnson, President, University of Sioux Falls, Sioux Falls, South Dakota

"The Antitheses of the Elder: A Study of the Dualistic Language of the Johannine Epistles" (1979)

Craig S. Keener, Professor of New Testament, Hood Theological Seminary, Salisbury, North Carolina

"The Function of Johannine Pneumatology in the Context of Late First-Century Judaism" (1991)

Amy-Jill Levine, Professor of New Testament Interpretation, The Divinity School, Vanderbilt University, Nashville, Tennessee

"The Matthean Program of Salvation History: A Contextual Analysis of the Exclusivity Logia" (1984)

Gene Miller, Emeritus Professor of New Testament, Anderson University School of Theology, Mt. Carmel, Tennessee

"The Nature and Purpose of the Signs of the Fourth Gospel" (1968)

Allen F. Page, Dean of Undergraduate Instruction and Registrar, Meredith College, Raleigh, North Carolina

"Proto-Luke Reconsidered: A Study of Literary Method and Theology in the Gospel of Luke" (1968)

Dwight N. Peterson, Adjunct Instructor, North Carolina State University, Raleigh, North Carolina

"The Origins of Mark: The Marcan Community in Current Debate" (1995)

Philip Pharr, Department of Religion, Pfeiffer College, Meisenheimer, North Carolina

"The Passion Narrative of the Fourth Gospel: A Study of Sources in John 18:1–19:42" (1972)

Stephen Pogoloff, Vicar, The Prince of Peace Episcopal Church, Apex, North Carolina

"Logos and Sophia: The Rhetorical Situation of 1 Corinthians 1–4 in the Light of Greco-Roman Rhetoric" (1990)

Christopher D. Stanley, Associate Professor, Department of Religious Studies, McKendree College, Lebanon, Illinois

"Citation Technique in the Pauline Epistles and Contemporary Literature" (1990)

Keith D. Stephenson, Emeritus Professor of New Testament Studies, Fakultas Teologia, Universitas Kristen Indonesia di Tomohon

"Pierre Benoit's Contributions to New Testament Study and Their Implications for the Issue of Tradition" (1967)

Frank Thielman, Associate Professor of Divinity, Beeson Divinity School, Samford University, Birmingham, Alabama

"From Plight to Solution: A Framework for Understanding Paul's View of the Law in Romans and Galatians Against a Jewish Background" (1987)

Marianne Meye Thompson, Associate Professor of New Testament Interpretation, Fuller Theological Seminary, Pasadena, California

"The Humanity of Jesus in the Gospel of John" (1985)

Richard Bolling Vinson, Professor, Department of Religion, and Director of Institutional Research, Averett College, Danville, Virginia

"The Significance of the Minor Agreements as an Argument Against the Two-Document Hypothesis" (1984)

Dwight Moody Smith
Cursus Vitae

1931	Born in Murfreesboro, Tennessee
1950	Graduated from Spartanburg High School (Spartanburg, South Carolina, City Schools)
1953	Election to Phi Beta Kappa and Omicron Delta Kappa, Davidson College
1954	A.B., Davidson College, *magna cum laude*
	Married to Cynthia Jane Allen, November 26, 1954; Children: Cynthia Beckwith (September 30, 1959), Catherine Mitchell (August 31, 1961), David Burton and John Allen (February 17, 1966)
1957	B.D., Duke University
1957–58	Boies Fellow, Yale University
1958	Elected a Kent Fellow, The Society for Values in Higher Education (then The National Council on Religion in Higher Education)
	A.M., Yale University
	Ordained as Elder in the South Carolina Annual Conference, The Methodist Church
1958–59	Dempster Fellow of The Methodist Church, Yale University
1959–60	Fels Fellow, Yale University
	Elected Rockefeller Fellow, Yale University (declined)
1960–61	Visiting Instructor of Religion, Ohio Wesleyan University
	Instructor of New Testament, Methodist Theological School in Ohio
1961	Ph.D., Yale University
1961–65	Assistant Professor of New Testament, Methodist Theological School in Ohio
1963–64	Lilly Postdoctoral Fellow, Swiss-American Student Exchange Fellowship, Universities of Basel and Zurich
1965	Election to *Studiorum Novi Testamenti Societas*
1965–70	Associate Professor of New Testament, The Divinity School, Duke University
1968–71	Member, Faith and Order Study on Biblical Authority, World Council of Churches
1970–	Professor of New Testament Interpretation, The Divinity School, Duke University
1970–71	Major grant recipient, Duke University Research Council
	John Simon Guggenheim Fellow, Cambridge University

1973–74	Associate Dean, Duke Divinity School
	Member, Task Force to study United Methodist Theological Education on the Eastern Seaboard
1974–80	Representative of Duke University to the Council on Graduate Studies in Religion
	Director of Graduate Studies in Religion, Duke University
1977–78	Major grant recipient, Duke University Research Council
	Research Fellow, Association of Theological Schools
1980–86	Co-chairman, Johannine Seminar, *Studiorum Novi Testamenti Societas*
1981	Earle Lecturer, Nazarene Theological Seminary
1981–87	Chairperson, Johannine Section, Society of Biblical Literature
1982	Election to the American Theological Society
1983	Staley Distinguished Christian Scholar Lecturer, Emory and Henry College
1984	Erasmus Club Lecturer, Duke University
1985–88	Member, Central Committee, *Studiorum Novi Testamenti Societas*
1987–	George Washington Ivey Professor of New Testament, The Divinity School, Duke University
1990	Distinguished Professors Lecturer, Duke University
	D.Litt., *honoris causa,* Davidson College
1990–91	Resident member of the Center of Theological Inquiry, Princeton, New Jersey
1993	Distinguished Alumni Award, Duke Divinity School
	Scholar/Teacher of the Year Award, Duke University
1994	Alexander Robertson Lecturer, University of Glasgow
1996	Nadine Beacham and Charlton F. Hall, Sr., Visiting Lecturer in New Testament, University of South Carolina

Dwight Moody Smith
A Selected Bibliography of Published Works
1963–1995

Compiled by Robert Kysar

From among 186 of his publications to date, the following have been selected as representative of D. Moody Smith's work, especially his contribution to Johannine scholarship. Books, major articles, and reviews of books have been included in every case, even though some sixty-eight book notices in *Religious Studies Review* (1975–) have perforce been omitted. Publications are listed here for each year in the following order: books and translations of other works; chapters in books, *Festschriften,* and encyclopedia articles; articles in journals; videotape presentations; review articles; and reviews. Even with its omissions, this bibliography gives readers an impression of the scope and prolificacy of Smith's scholarship.

1963   "From Schweitzer to Robinson: Prolegomenon to the Current Discussion of the Problem of the Historical Jesus." *Journal: Methodist Theological School in Ohio* 2 (1963): 8–25.
"John 12:12ff. and the Question of John's Use of the Synoptics." *Journal of Biblical Literature* 82 (1963): 58–64. Reprinted in *Johannine Christianity* (1984), pp. 97–105.

1964   "The Sources of the Gospel of John: An Assessment of the Present State of the Problem." *New Testament Studies* 10 (1964): 336–51. Reprinted in *Johannine Christianity* (1984), pp. 39–61.

1965   *The Composition and Order of the Fourth Gospel: Bultmann's Literary Theory.* Yale Publications in Religion 10. New Haven, Conn., and London: Yale University Press, 1965. Pp. xx + 272.
"Theological Study in America and Europe: Some Observations and Reflections." *Journal: Methodist Theological School in Ohio* 3 (1965): 1–9.
Review of Joachim Jeremias, *The Central Message of the New Testament* (New York: Scribner's, 1965), in *The Duke Divinity School Review* 30 (1965): 211–12.

1966   "The Historical Jesus in Paul Tillich's Christology." *The Journal of Re-

ligion 46 (1966): 131–47 (with a "Rejoinder," by Paul Tillich, 184–96, especially 191–94).

Review of Howard Clark Kee, Franklin W. Young, and Karlfried Froelich, *Understanding the New Testament,* second edition (Englewood Cliffs, N.J.: Prentice–Hall, 1965), and Bruce M. Metzger, *The New Testament: Its Background, Growth, and Content* (New York: Abingdon, 1965), in *The Duke Divinity School Review* 31 (1966): 87–88.

1967   Translation of Heinrich Ott, "Das Problem des nicht-objektivierenden Denkens und Redens in der Theologie," *Zeitschrift für Theologie und Kirche* 61 (1964): 327–52 = "The Problem of Non-objectifying Speaking and Thinking in Theology," *Journal for Theology and Church* 3 (1967): 112–35.

"HO DE DIKAIOS EK PISTEOS ZESETAI." In *Studies in the History and Text of the New Testament in Honor of Kenneth Willis Clark, Ph.D.* Edited by Boyd L. Daniels and M. Jack Suggs. Studies and Documents 19. Salt Lake City, Utah: University of Utah Press, 1967, pp. 13–25.

"Jesus Christ and Mythology," *Adult Teacher* 21 (1967–68): 30–33.

"A Major New Commentary on John." Review of Raymond E. Brown, *The Gospel according to John (i–xii),* Anchor Bible 29 (Garden City, N.Y.: Doubleday, 1966), in *Interpretation* 21 (1967): 469–75.

Review of Paolo Ricca, *Die Eschatologie des vierten Evangeliums* (Zurich and Frankfurt a. M.: Gotthelf, 1966), in *Catholic Biblical Quarterly* 29 (1967): 672–74.

1968   "Comment" (on Robert E. Cushman, "Theological Education: A Reconsideration of Its Nature in Light of Its Objective," *The Duke Divinity School Review* 33 [1968]: 3–13), *The Duke Divinity School Review* 33 (1968): 18–24.

Review of Fred B. Craddock, *The Pre-Existence of Christ in the New Testament* (Nashville: Abingdon, 1968), in *The Duke Divinity School Review* 33 (1968): 213–14.

Review of W. R. Farmer, C.F.D. Moule, and R. R. Niebuhr, editors, *Christian History and Interpretation: Studies Presented to John Knox* (Cambridge: Cambridge University Press, 1967), in *The Duke Divinity School Review* 33 (1968): 125–27, and in *Theology Today* 25 (1968): 406–8.

Review of Birger Gerhardsson, *The Testing of God's Son (Matt. 4:1–11 & Par.): An Analysis of an Early Christian Midrash,* Coniectanea

Biblica, New Testament series 2:1 (Lund: Gleerup, 1966), in *Interpretation* 22 (1968): 349–50.

Review of Ernest W. Saunders, *Jesus in the Gospels* (Englewood Cliffs, N.J.: Prentice-Hall, 1967), in *Catholic Biblical Quarterly* 30 (1968): 288–89.

1969   *Anatomy of the New Testament: A Guide to Its Structure and Meaning.* With Robert A. Spivey. New York: Macmillan, 1969. Pp. xviii + 510.

"Authority, Hermeneutic, and the Church." *The Duke Divinity School Review* 34 (1969): 67–80.

"Survey of the New Testament," *New Creation* (fall 1969): 1–96. Republished in *New Creation* (fall 1971): 2–74.

"John and the Jews." Review of J. Louis Martyn, *History and Theology in the Fourth Gospel* (New York: Harper & Row, 1968), in *Interpretation* 23 (1969): 220–23.

Review of S.G.F. Brandon, *Jesus and the Zealots: A Study of the Political Factor in Primitive Christianity* (New York: Scribner's, 1968), in *The Duke Divinity School Review* 34 (1969): 128–30.

Review of Rudolf Bultmann, *Die drei Johannesbriefe,* Kritisch-exegetischer Kommentar über das Neue Testament 14 (Göttingen: Vandenhoeck & Ruprecht, 1967), in *Journal of Biblical Literature* 88 (1969): 120–21.

1970   Review of Robert T. Fortna, *The Gospel of Signs: A Reconstruction of the Narrative Source Underlying the Fourth Gospel,* Society for New Testament Studies Monograph Series 11 (Cambridge: Cambridge University Press, 1970), in *Journal of Biblical Literature* 89 (1970): 498–501.

Review of Willi Marxsen, *Mark the Evangelist: Studies on the Redaction History of the Gospel,* translated by Roy Harrisville et al. (Nashville: Abingdon, 1969), in *The Duke Divinity School Review* 35 (1970): 176–77.

Review of E. P. Sanders, *The Tendencies of the Synoptic Tradition,* Society for New Testament Studies Monograph Series 9 (Cambridge: Cambridge University Press, 1969), in *The Duke Divinity School Review* 35 (1970): 173–75.

Review of J. N. Sanders and B. A. Mastin, *A Commentary on the Gospel according to St. John,* Harper's New Testament Commentaries (New York: Harper & Row, 1968), in *Journal of the American Academy of Religion* 38 (1970): 194–98.

1971   "Political Responsibility amid Violence and Revolution: A Challenge to Biblical Authority." *The Duke Divinity School Review* 36 (1971): 163–82.

1972   "The Use of the Old Testament in the New." In *The Use of the Old Testament in the New and Other Essays: Studies in Honor of William Franklin Stinespring.* Edited by James M. Efird. Durham, N.C.: Duke University Press, pp. 3–65.

"An Unexpurgated Theological Bibliography." With Don E. Ferguson, Jr., Harriet V. Leonard, and W. Douglas Tanner, Jr. *The Duke Divinity School Review* 37 (1972): 57–129.

Review of Leander E. Keck, *A Future for the Historical Jesus: The Place of Jesus in Preaching and Theology* (Nashville: Abingdon, 1971), in *Religion in Life* 41 (1972): 278–79.

Review of Leon Morris, *The Gospel according to John: The English Text with Introduction, Exposition and Notes,* New International Commentary on the New Testament (Grand Rapids: Eerdmans, 1971), in *Journal of Biblical Literature* 91 (1972): 420–23.

Review of Jack T. Sanders, *The New Testament Christological Hymns: Their Historical Religious Background,* Society for New Testament Studies Monograph Series 15 (Cambridge: Cambridge University Press, 1971), in *The Duke Divinity School Review* 37 (1972): 53–54.

Review of Walter Schmithals, *Gnosticism in Corinth: An Investigation of the Letters to the Corinthians,* translated by John E. Steely (Nashville: Abingdon, 1971), in *The Duke Divinity School Review* 37 (1972): 174–76.

Review of David W. Wead, *The Literary Devices in John's Gospel,* Theologische Dissertationen 4 (Basel: Reinhardt, 1970), in *Interpretation* 26 (1972): 119–20.

1973   "New Testament Scholarship: The German Scene." Review of Werner Georg Kümmel, *The New Testament: The History of the Investigation of Its Problems,* translated by S. MacLean Gilmour and Howard C. Kee (Nashville: Abingdon, 1972), in *Interpretation* 27 (1973): 353–58.

1974   *Anatomy of the New Testament: A Guide to Its Structure and Meaning.* With Robert A. Spivey. Second Edition. New York: Macmillan, 1974. Pp. xviii + 539.

"Glossolalia and Other Spiritual Gifts in a New Testament Perspective." *Interpretation* 28 (1974): 307–20.

Review of Otto Merk, *Biblische Theologie des Neuen Testaments in ihrer Anfangszeit: Ihre methodischen Probleme bei Johann Philipp Gabler und Georg Lorenz Bauer und deren Nachwirkungen,* Marburger Theologische Studien 9 (Marburg: Elwert, 1972), in *Interpretation* 28 (1974): 365–66.

1975   Translation of C. K. Barrett, *Das Johannesevangelium und das Judentum* (Stuttgart and Berlin: W. Kohlhammer, 1970) = *The Gospel of John and Judaism* (Philadelphia: Fortress, 1975).

"An Exposition of Luke 1:26–38." *Interpretation* 29 (1975): 411–17.

"Johannine Christianity: Some Reflections on its Character and Delineation." *New Testament Studies* 21 (1975): 222–48. Reprinted as "Introduction: Johannine Christianity" in *Johannine Christianity* (1984), pp. 1–36.

Review of J. Terrence Forestell, *The Word of the Cross: Salvation as Revelation in the Fourth Gospel,* Analecta Biblica 57 (Rome: Pontifical Biblical Institute, 1974), in *Journal of Biblical Literature* 94 (1975): 464–66.

Review of Günter Reim, *Studien zum alttestamentlichen Hintergrund des Johannesevangeliums,* Society for New Testament Studies Monograph Series 22 (Cambridge: Cambridge University Press, 1974), in *Interpretation* 29 (1975): 320–21.

1976   *John.* Proclamation Commentaries. Edited by Gerhard Krodel. Philadelphia: Fortress, 1976. Pp. xiii + 114.

"Beloved Disciple," "Gospel of John," "Letters of John," "Paraclete," "Sign in the New Testament." In *The Interpreter's Dictionary of the Bible,* Supplementary Volume. Edited by Keith Crim et al. Nashville: Abingdon, 1976, pp. 95, 482–86, 486–87, 642–43, 824–25.

"The Milieu of the Johannine Miracle Source: A Proposal." In *Jews, Greeks and Christians: Religious Cultures in Late Antiquity. Essays in Honor of William David Davies.* Edited by Robert Hamerton-Kelly and Robin Scroggs. Studies in Judaism in Late Antiquity 21. Leiden: Brill, 1976, pp. 164–180. Reprinted in *Johannine Christianity* (1984), pp. 62–79.

"The Setting and Shape of a Johannine Narrative Source." *Journal of Biblical Literature* 95 (1976): 231–41. Reprinted in *Johannine Christianity* (1984), pp. 80–93.

Review of Fred O. Francis and J. Paul Sampley, editors, *Pauline Parallels,* Sources for Biblical Study 9 (Philadelphia and Missoula, Mont.: Fortress and Scholars, 1975), in *The Duke Divinity School Review* 41 (1976): 220–21.

Review of Martin McNamara, *Targum and New Testament: Aramaic Paraphrases of the Hebrew Bible: A Light on the New Testament* (Grand Rapids: Eerdmans, 1972), in *The Duke Divinity School Review* 41 (1976): 136–37.

Review of Robert Mahoney, *Two Disciples at the Tomb: The Background and Message of John 20:1–10,* Theologie und Wirklichkeit 6 (Bern and Frankfurt: Lang, 1974), in *Journal of Biblical Literature* 95 (1976): 492–94.

Review of D. George Vanderlip, *Christianity according to John* (Philadelphia: Westminster, 1975), in *Religion in Life* 45 (1976): 125–26.

Review of Dan O. Via, *Kerygma and Comedy in the New Testament: A Structuralist Approach to Hermeneutic* (Philadelphia: Fortress, 1975), in *The Duke Divinity School Review* 41 (1976): 132–33.

1977   "The Presentation of Jesus in the Fourth Gospel." *Interpretation* 31(1977): 367–78. Reprinted in *Interpreting the Gospels,* edited by James Luther Mays (Philadelphia: Fortress, 1981), pp. 278–90, and in *Johannine Christianity* (1984), pp. 175–89.

"Redating the New Testament." Review of John A. T. Robinson, *Redating the New Testament* (Philadelphia: Westminster, 1976), in *The Duke Divinity School Review* 42 (1977): 193–205.

Review of Oscar Cullmann, *The Johannine Circle,* translated by John Bowden (Philadelphia: Westminster, 1976), in *The Duke Divinity School Review* 42 (1977): 125–27.

Review of Richard A. Edwards, *A Theology of Q: Eschatology, Prophecy, and Wisdom* (Philadelphia: Fortress, 1976), in *Journal of the American Academy of Religion* 45 (1977): 372–74.

Review of Edgar Krentz, *The Historical-Critical Method,* Guides to Biblical Scholarship, Old Testament Series (Philadelphia: Fortress, 1975), in *The Duke Divinity School Review* 42 (1977): 124–25.

Review of Michael Lattke, *Einheit im Wort: Die spezifische Bedeutung von* Agape, Agapan *und* Filein *im Johannesevangelium,* Studien zum Alten und Neuen Testament 41 (Munich: Kösel, 1975), in *Journal of Biblical Literature* 96 (1977): 147–48.

Review of Eduard Lohse, *The New Testament Environment,* translated by John E. Steely (Nashville: Abingdon, 1976), in *The Duke Divinity School Review* 42 (1977): 56–57.

Review of Milan Machoveč, *A Marxist Looks at Jesus* (Philadelphia: Fortress, 1976), in *The Duke Divinity School Review* 42 (1977): 58–59.

Review of Francis J. Moloney, *The Johannine Son of Man,* Biblioteca di Scienze Religiose 14 (Rome: Libreria Ateneo Salesiano, 1976), in *Catholic Biblical Quarterly* 39 (1977): 440–41.

Review of Daniel Patte, *What Is Structural Exegesis?* Guides to Biblical Scholarship, New Testament Series (Philadelphia: Fortress, 1976), in *The Duke Divinity School Review* 42 (1977): 217–18.

Review of Felix Porsch, *Pneuma und Wort: Ein exegetischer Beitrag zur Pneumatologie des Johannesevangeliums,* Frankfurter Theologische Studien 16 (Frankfurt a. M.: Knecht, 1974), in *Journal of Biblical Literature* 96 (1977): 458–59.

1978   Review of Norman R. Petersen, *Literary Criticism for New Testament Critics,* Guides to Biblical Scholarship, New Testament Series (Philadelphia: Fortress, 1978), in *The Duke Divinity School Review* 43 (1978): 201–2.

1979   "John 16:1–15." *Interpretation* 33 (1979): 58–62.

Review of Virgil P. Howard, *Das Ego Jesu in den synoptischen Evangelien: Untersuchungen zum Sprachgebrauch Jesu,* Marburger Theologische Studien 14 (Marburg: Elwert, 1975), in *Catholic Biblical Quarterly* 41 (1979): 159–60.

1980   *Interpreting the Gospels for Preaching.* Philadelphia: Fortress, 1980. Pp. x + 118.

"John and the Synoptics: Some Dimensions of the Problem." *New Testament Studies* 26 (1980): 425–44. Reprinted in *Johannine Christianity* (1984), pp. 145–72.

Review of C. K. Barrett, *The Gospel according to St. John: An Introduction with Commentary and Notes on the Greek Text,* 2d edition (Philadelphia: Westminster, 1978), in *Journal of Biblical Literature* 99 (1980): 626–27.

Review of C. K. Barrett, *The Gospel according to St. John: An Introduction with Commentary and Notes on the Greek Text,* 2d edition (Philadelphia: Westminster, 1978), and J. Louis Martyn, *History and Theology in the Fourth Gospel,* 2d edition (Nashville: Abingdon, 1979), in *The Duke Divinity School Review* 45 (1980): 67–69.

Review of Raymond E. Brown, *The Community of the Beloved Disciple* (New York: Paulist, 1979), in *Catholic Biblical Quarterly* 42 (1980): 397–99.

Review of William O. Walker, Jr., editor, *The Relationships Among the Gospels: An Interdisciplinary Dialogue,* Trinity University Monograph Series in Religion 5 (San Antonio, Tex.: Trinity University Press, 1978), in *Interpretation* 34 (1980): 106–7.

1981   "The Presentation of Jesus in the Fourth Gospel." In *Interpreting the Gospels,* edited by James Luther Mays (Philadelphia: Fortress, 1981), pp. 278–90. Reprinted from *Interpretation* 31 (1977): 367–78 and included in *Johannine Christianity* (1984), pp. 175–89.

"Theology and Ministry in John." In *A Biblical Basis for Ministry.* Edited by Earl E. Shelp and Ronald Sunderland. Philadelphia: Westminster, 1981, pp. 186–228. Reprinted in *Johannine Christianity* (1984), 190–222.

"B. W. Bacon on John and Mark." *Perspectives in Religious Studies* 8 (1981): 201–18. Reprinted in *Johannine Christianity* (1984), pp. 106–27.

1982   *Anatomy of the New Testament: A Guide to Its Structure and Meaning.* With Robert A. Spivey. 3d edition. New York: Macmillan, 1982. Pp. xix + 539.

"Mark 15:46: The Shroud of Turin as a Problem of History and Faith." *Biblical Archaeologist* 46 (1983): 251–54.

"From Whence the Doctrine of the Incarnation?" Review of James D. G. Dunn, *Christology in the Making: A New Testament Inquiry into the Origins of the Doctrine of the Incarnation* (Philadelphia: Westminster, 1980), in *Interpretation* 37 (1982): 291–95.

"John and the Synoptics." Review of Bruno de Solages, *Jean et les synoptiques* (Leiden: Brill, 1979), and Frans Neirynck, with the collaboration of Joël Delobel, Thierry Snoy, Gilbert Van Belle, and Frans Van Segbroeck, *Jean et les synoptiques: Examen critique de l'exégèse de M.-É. Boismard,* Bibliotheca Ephemeridum Theologicarum Lovaniensium 49 (Leuven: Leuven University Press, 1979), in *Biblica* 63 (1982): 102–13. Reprinted as "John and the Synoptics: de Solages and Neirynck," in *Johannine Christianity* (1984), 128–44.

Review of Ellis Rivkin, *A Hidden Revolution: The Pharisees' Search for the Kingdom Within* (Nashville: Abingdon, 1978), in *The Journal of the American Oriental Society* 102 (1982): 204–5.

1983   Review of Ernst Haenchen, *Das Johannesevangelium: ein Kommentar,* edited by Ulrich Busse (Tübingen: Mohr [Siebeck], 1980), in *Journal of Biblical Literature* 102 (1983): 443–48.

1984   *Johannine Christianity: Essays on Its Setting, Sources, and Theology.* Columbia, S.C.: University of South Carolina Press, 1984. Also Edinburgh: T. & T. Clark, 1987. Pp. xix + 234.

Review of Raymond E. Brown, *The Epistles of John: Translated, with Introduction, Notes, and Commentary,* Anchor Bible 30 (Garden City, N.Y.: Doubleday, 1982), in *Journal of Biblical Literature* 103 (1984): 666–71.

1985   "The Gospel according to John" and "The Letters of John." In *Harper's Bible Dictionary.* Edited by Paul J. Achtemeier et al. San Francisco: Harper & Row, 1985, pp. 496–99 and 499–500.

Review of Kenneth Grayston, *The Johannine Epistles,* New Century Bible Commentary (Grand Rapids: Eerdmans, 1984), in *Epworth Review* 12 (May 1985): 104–6.

1986   *John.* Second Edition. Proclamation Commentaries. Edited by Gerhard Krodel. Philadelphia: Fortress, 1986. Pp. ix + 133.

"*The Rise of Christianity:* A Review." Review of W.H.C. Frend, *The Rise of Christianity* (Philadelphia: Fortress, 1984), in *Journal of the American Academy of Religion* 54 (1986): 337–42.

"Why Approaching the New Testament as Canon Matters." Review of Brevard S. Childs, *The New Testament as Canon: An Introduction* (Philadelphia: Fortress, 1985), in *Interpretation* 40 (1986): 407–11.

1987   "John the Evangelist," "Luke the Evangelist," "Mark the Evangelist," "Matthew the Evangelist." In *The Encyclopedia of Religion.* Edited by Mircea Eliade. 16 volumes. New York: Macmillan and Free Press, 1987, 8:114–15, 9:51–52, 9:208–9, 9:284–85.

"The Pauline Literature." In *It is Written: Scripture Citing Scripture. Essays in Honour of Barnabas Lindars, SSF.* Edited by D. A. Carson and H. G. M. Williamson. Cambridge: Cambridge University Press, 1987, pp. 265–91.

1988   "The Gospel of John." In *Harper's Bible Commentary.* Edited by James L. Mays et al. San Francisco: Harper & Row, 1988, pp. 1044–76.

"John, the Synoptics, and the Canonical Approach to Exegesis." In *Tradition and Interpretation in the New Testament: Essays in Honor of E. Earle Ellis.* Edited by Gerald F. Hawthorne with Otto Betz. Grand Rapids and Tübingen: Eerdmans and Mohr (Siebeck), 1988, pp. 166–80.

"The Life Setting of the Gospel of John." *Review and Expositor* 85 (1988): 433–444.

1989   *Anatomy of the New Testament: A Guide to Its Structure and Meaning.*
With Robert A. Spivey. 4th edition. New York: Macmillan, 1989.
Pp. xxiv + 501.

"Johannine Studies." In *The New Testament and Its Modern Interpreters.* Edited by Eldon Jay Epp and George W. MacRae. The Society of Biblical Literature Centennial Publications. Atlanta: Scholars, 1989, pp. 271–96.

The Gospel of John. Two volumes in "The Standard Video Bible Study:
New Testament Series." A Production of the Revised Standard Version Project, Division of Education and Ministry, National Council of
the Churches of Christ in the U.S.A. Nashville: Kerr Associates, 1989.

Review of Marcus J. Borg, *Jesus: A New Vision* (San Fancisco: Harper
& Row, 1987), in *Forum: A Journal of the Foundation and Facets
of Western Culture* 5 (December 1989): 71–82.

Review of John A. T. Robinson, *The Priority of John,* edited by J. F.
Coakley (London: SCM, 1985), in *Journal of Biblical Literature*
108 (1989): 156–58.

1990   "The Contribution of J. Louis Martyn to the Understanding of the Gospel
of John." In *The Conversation Continues: Studies in Paul and John
in Honor of J. Louis Martyn.* Edited by Robert T. Fortna and Beverly R. Gaventa. Nashville: Abingdon, 1990, pp. 275–94.

"John and the Synoptics in Light of the Problem of Faith and History."
In *Faith and History: Essays in Honor of Paul W. Meyer.* Edited by
John T. Carroll, Charles H. Cosgrove, and E. Elizabeth Johnson. At-
lanta: Scholars, 1990, pp. 74–89.

"Judaism and the Gospel of John." In *Jews and Christians: Exploring
the Past, Present, and Future.* Edited by James H. Charlesworth.
New York: Crossroad, 1990, pp. 76–99.

Review of Robert Tomson Fortna, *The Fourth Gospel and Its Predecessor: From Narrative Source to Present Gospel* (Philadelphia:
Fortress, 1988), in *Journal of Biblical Literature* 109 (1990): 352–55.

1991   *First, Second, and Third John.* Interpretation: A Bible Commentary for
Teaching and Preaching. Louisville: John Knox, 1991. Pp. viii +
164.

1992   *John among the Gospels: The Relationship in Twentieth-Century Research.* Minneapolis: Fortress, 1992. Pp. xiii + 210.

"John and the Synoptics and the Question of Gospel Genre." In *The
Four Gospels. 1992: Festschrift Frans Neirynck.* Edited by F. Van

Segbroeck, C. M. Tuckett, G. Van Belle, and J. Verheyden. Leuven: Leuven University Press, 1992, vol. 3, pp. 1783–97.

"The Problem of John and the Synoptics in Light of the Relation between Apocryphal and Canonical Gospels." In *John and the Synoptics*. Edited by Adelbert Denaux. Bibliotheca Ephemeridum Theologicarum Lovaniensium 101. Leuven: Leuven University Press, 1992, pp. 147–62.

Review of John Ashton, *Understanding the Fourth Gospel* (Oxford: Clarendon, 1991), in *The Journal of Theological Studies* 43 (1992): 594–600.

Review of Johannes Beutler and Robert T. Fortna, editors, *The Shepherd Discourse of John 10 and Its Context*, Society for New Testament Studies Monograph Series 67 (Cambridge: Cambridge University Press, 1991), in *The Journal of Theological Studies* 43 (1992): 182–84.

Review of Ed L. Miller, *Salvation History in the Prologue of John: The Significance of John 1:3/4*, Supplements to Novum Testamentum 60 (Leiden: Brill, 1989), in *Journal of Biblical Literature* 111 (1992): 542–44.

1994 Japanese translation of *First, Second, and Third John* (1991), by Mitsugu Shinmen. Tokyo: The United Church of Christ in Japan, 1994.

"Historical Issues and the Problem of John and the Synoptics." In *From Jesus to John: Essays on Jesus and New Testament Christology in Honour of Marinus de Jonge*. Edited by Martinus C. de Boer. Journal for the Study of the New Testament Supplement Series 84. Sheffield: JSOT, 1994, pp. 252–67.

1995 *Anatomy of the New Testament: A Guide to Its Structure and Meaning*. With Robert A. Spivey. 5th edition. Englewood Cliffs, New Jersey: Prentice Hall, 1995. Pp. xxviii + 513.

The Theology of the Gospel of John. New Testament Theology. Edited by James D. G. Dunn. Cambridge: Cambridge University Press, 1995. Pp. xiv + 202.

EDITORSHIPS

1975– Editor, "Christian Origins: Johannine Studies," *Religious Studies Review*

1978–81 Advisory Council, *Interpretation: A Journal of Bible and Theology*

1981–86 Editorial Board, *Journal of Biblical Literature*

1994– General Editor, "Studies on Personalities of the New Testament," Columbia, S.C.: University of South Carolina Press; including the following volumes:

C. Clifton Black, *Mark: Images of an Apostolic Interpreter* (1994). Pp. xx + 327.

R. Alan Culpepper, *John, the Son of Zebedee: The Life of a Legend* (1994). Pp. xix + 376.

Pheme Perkins, *Peter: Apostle for the Whole Church* (1994). Pp. vi + 209.

Beverly Roberts Gaventa, *Mary: Glimpses of the Mother of Jesus* (1995). Pp. xvi + 164.

Abbreviations

FB	Forschung zur Bibel
FBBS	Facet Books, Biblical Series
FFNT	Foundations and Facets: New Testament
FRLANT	Forschungen zur Religion und Literatur des Alten und Neuen Testaments
HNT	Handbuch zum Neuen Testament
HR	*History of Religions*
HSS	Harvard Semitic Studies
HTKNT	Herders theologischer Kommentar zum Neuen Testament
HTKNTSup	Herders theologischer Kommentar zum Neuen Testament, Supplement Series
HTR	*Harvard Theological Review*
HUCA	*Hebrew Union College Annual*
HUT	Hermeneutische Untersuchungen zur Theologie
IB	*Interpreter's Bible*
ICC	International Critical Commentary
IDB	G. A. Buttrick (ed.), *Interpreter's Dictionary of the Bible*
IDBSup	K. Crim (ed.), *Interpreter's Dictionary of the Bible, Supplementary Volume*
Int	*Interpretation*
IRT	Issues in Religion and Theology
JAAR	*Journal of the American Academy of Religion*
JAC	Jahrbuch für Antike und Christentum
JBL	*Journal of Biblical Literature*
JSJ	*Journal for the Study of Judaism in the Persian, Hellenistic and Roman Period*
JSNT	*Journal for the Study of the New Testament*
JSNTSup	Journal for the Study of the New Testament, Supplement Series
JSP	*Journal for the Study of the Pseudepigrapha*
JSPSup	Journal for the Study of the Pseudepigrapha, Supplement Series
JTS	*Journal of Theological Studies*
KD	*Kerygma und Dogma*
LCL	Loeb Classical Library
LD	Lectio divina
LXX	Septuagint
MeyerK	H. A. W. Meyer, Kritisch-exegetischer Kommentar über das Neue Testament
MGWJ	*Monatsschrift für Geschichte und Wissenschaft des Judentums*
MT	Masoretic Text
N.B.	*Nota bene*
NCB	New Century Bible
NEB	New English Bible

Neot	*Neotestamentica*
N.F.	Neue Folge (new series)
NIV	New International Version
NovT	*Novum Testamentum*
NovTSup	Novum Testamentum, Supplements
NRSV	New Revised Standard Version
n.s.	new series
NT	New Testament
NTAbh	Neutestamentliche Abhandlungen
NTS	*New Testament Studies*
NTTS	New Testament Tools and Studies
ÖTK	Ökumenischer Taschenbuchkommentar zum Neuen Testament
Pr.	Prologue
PTMS	Pittsburgh (Princeton) Theological Monograph Series
RAC	*Reallexikon für Antike und Christentum*
RB	*Revue biblique*
REB	Revised English Bible
RelSRev	*Religious Studies Review*
RevExp	*Review and Expositor*
RGG³	*Die Religion in Geschichte und Gegenwart,* 3d edition
RHPR	*Revue d'histoire et de philosophie religieuses*
RSV	Revised Standard Version
SBL	Society of Biblical Literature
SBLDS	Society of Biblical Literature Dissertation Series
SBLMS	Society of Biblical Literature Monograph Series
SBLSBS	Society of Biblical Literature Sources for Biblical Study
SBS	Stuttgarter Bibelstudien
SBT	Studies in Biblical Theology
ScEccl	*Sciences ecclésiastiques*
SE I	*Studia Evangelica I*
SJLA	Studies in Judaism in Late Antiquity
SJT	*Scottish Journal of Theology*
SNTSMS	Society for New Testament Studies Monograph Series
SNTU	*Studien zum Neuen Testament und seiner Umwelt*
SR	*Studies in Religion/Sciences religieuses*
ST	*Studia theologica*
STDJ	Studies on the Texts of the Desert of Judea
Str-B	[H. Strack and] P. Billerbeck, *Kommentar zum Neuen Testament*
SUNT	Studien zur Umwelt des Neuen Testaments
TDNT	G. Kittel and G. Friedrich (eds.), *Theological Dictionary of the New Testament*

TRE	*Theologische Realenzyklopädie*
TU	Texte und Untersuchungen
TZ	*Theologische Zeitschrift*
UBSGNT	United Bible Societies *Greek New Testament*
UNT	Untersuchungen zum Neuen Testament
USQR	*Union Seminary Quarterly Review*
VC	*Vigiliae christianae*
WBC	Word Biblical Commentary
WMANT	Wissenschaftliche Monographien zum Alten und Neuen Testament
WUNT	Wissenschaftliche Untersuchungen zum Neuen Testament
ZBK	Zürcher Bibelkommentare
ZNW	*Zeitschrift für die neutestamentliche Wissenschaft*
ZTK	*Zeitschrift für Theologie und Kirche*

MANUSCRIPTS OF THE NEW TESTAMENT

א	Codex Sinaiticus (fourth century)
a	Old Latin version a (fourth century)
B	Codex Vaticanus (fourth century)
e	Old Latin version e (fifth/sixth century)
p⁶⁶	Papyrus Bodmer II (second/third century)
sy^s	Sinaitic Syriac version (second/third century)
sy^p	Peshitta Syriac version (fifth/sixth century)

DEAD SEA SCROLLS AND RELATED MANUSCRIPTS

CD	Cairo (Genizah text of the) *Damascus Document*
MasShirShabb	*Songs of Sabbath Sacrifice*, or *Angelic Liturgy*, from Masada
1QH	*Hodayot* (*Thanksgiving Hymns*), from Qumran Cave 1
1QHª	Appendix to *Hodayot* (*Thanksgiving Hymns*), from Qumran Cave 1
1QM	*Milḥama* (*War Scroll*) from Qumran Cave 1
1QS	*Rule of the Community* from Qumran Cave 1
1QSa	Appendix A to 1QS
1QSb	Appendix B (*Blessings*) to 1QS
1QpHab	*Pesher on Habakkuk* from Qumran Cave 1
1Q22	*Words of Moses* (= 1QDM) from Qumran Cave 1
1Q30	*Holy Messi[ah] Fragment* from Qumran Cave 1
3Q15	*Copper Scroll* from Qumran Cave 3
4QS	*Rule of the Community* from Qumran Cave 4

4Q186	*Horoscope* from Qumran Cave 4
4Q243	*Pseudo-Daniel* (= 4QpsDan ar[a]) from Qumran Cave 4
4Q246	*Aramaic Apocalypse* (previously known as 4QpsDan A[a], 4Q243) from Qumran Cave 4
4Q317	*Cryptic Phases of the Moon* from Qumran Cave 4
4Q381	*Noncanonical (Pseudepigraphic) Psalms A* from Qumran Cave 4
4Q491	*War Scroll*[a] from Qumran Cave 4
4Q504	*Words of the Luminaries*[a] from Qumran Cave 4
4Q510	*Songs of the Sage*[a] from Qumran Cave 4
4Q521	*On Resurrection* (or *Messianic Apocalypse*) from Qumran Cave 4
4QCat[a]	Fragment a of *Catena* from Qumran Cave 4
4QFlor	*Florilegium* (or *Eschatological Midrashim*) from Qumran Cave 4
4QMess ar	*Elect of God Text* from Qumran Cave 4
4QShirShabb	*Songs of Sabbath Sacrifice*, or *Angelic Liturgy*, from Qumran Cave 4
5QS	*Rule of the Community* from Qumran Cave 5
11QTemple[a]	*Temple Scroll* from Qumran Cave 11

WRITINGS OF JOSEPHUS

Ant.	*Jewish Antiquities*
J.W.	*Jewish War*

WRITINGS OF PHILO

De Cher.	*De Cherubim*
Det. Pot. Ins.	*Quod Deterius Potiori insidiari solet*
In Flac.	*In Flaccum*
De Gig.	*De Gigantibus*
Heres	*Quis Rerum Divinarum Heres*
Leg. All.	*Legum Allegoriae*
De Legat. ad Gaium	*De Legatione ad Gaium*
De Mig. Abr.	*De Migratione Abrahami*
De Mut. Nom.	*De Mutatione Nominum*
De Opif. Mundi	*De Opificio Mundi*
Quaes. Exod.	*Quaestiones et Solutiones in Exodum*
De Somn.	*De Somniis*
De Spec. Leg.	*De Specialibus Legibus*

De Virt.	*De Virtutibus*
De Vit. Mos.	*De Vita Mosis*

OTHER GRECO-ROMAN LITERATURE

Alex.	*Rhetorica ad Alexandrum*
Eloc.	*Elocutione (On Style,* attributed to "Demetrius")
Her.	*Rhetorica ad Herennium*
Inv.	Cicero, *De Inventione*
Ion	Plato, *Ion*
De Optimo	Cicero, *De Optimo Genere Oratorum*
Or.	Cicero, *Orator*
De Or.	Cicero, *De Oratore*
Part. Or.	Cicero, *De Partitione Oratoria*
Peri ideōn	Hermogenes, *On Types of Style*
Phaedr.	Plato, *Phaedrus*
Poet.	Aristotle, *Peri Poiētikēs* (= *Poetics*)
Quintilian	Quintilian, *Institutio Oratoria*
Resp.	Plato, *Respublica* (= *Republic*)
Rhet.	Aristotle, *Technē Rhētorikē* (= *On the Art of Rhetoric*)
Soph.	Plato, *Sophista*
Subl.	*On the Sublime* (= attributed to "Longinus")

PSEUDEPIGRAPHICAL AND EARLY PATRISTIC BOOKS

Bib. Ant.	Pseudo-Philo, *Biblical Antiquities*
2 Clem.	*2 Clement*
Did.	*Didache*
De Doct. Christ.	Augustine, *De Doctrina Christiana (On Christian Doctrine)*
H. E.	Eusebius, *Historia Ecclesiastica (Ecclesiastical History)*
Ign. *Magn.*	Ignatius, *Letter to the Magnesians*
Ign. *Smyrn.*	Ignatius, *Letter to the Smyrnaeans*
Justin, *Dial.*	Justin Martyr, *Dialogue with Trypho*

MISHNAIC TRACTATES AND OTHER RABBINIC LITERATURE

b.	Babylonian Talmud (before a tractate)
m.	Mishnah, before a tractate
Ber.	*Berakot*
Ḥag.	*Ḥagiga*

Ḥal.	*Ḥalla*
Menaḥ.	*Menaḥot*
Metzi'a	*Baba Metzi'a*
Nazir	*Nazir*
Qidd.	*Qiddušin*
Sanh.	*Sanhedrin*
Sukk.	*Sukka*
Mek.	*Mekilta* (preceding abbreviation for biblical book)
Midr.	*Midrash* (preceding abbreviation for biblical book)
Rab.	*Rabbah* (following abbreviation for biblical book)
y.	Jerusalem Talmud (before a tractate)

Introduction

Robert Kysar

The Contribution of D. Moody Smith to Johannine Scholarship

In 1965 a young Ph.D. candidate struggled through Rudolf Bultmann's seminal commentary on the Gospel of John.[1] In spite of his careful reading, the budding researcher could make little sense of Bultmann's appeal to the sources employed by the fourth evangelist and was totally mystified by the commentator's rearrangement of large segments of the Gospel. Rereading the section devoted to the Gospel of John in Bultmann's *Theology of the New Testament*[2] was of no help, since the author simply footnoted his commentary!

Then the student discovered a new volume titled *The Composition and Order of the Fourth Gospel: Bultmann's Literary Theory,* authored by one Dwight Moody Smith, Jr.[3] To the student's delight, this work described and analyzed both Bultmann's theory of the evangelist's sources and his proposal for the displacement and rearrangement of the Gospel text. The description was remarkably detailed; the critical insights, probing. After a careful reading of Smith's work, the young scholar returned to his own efforts on Bultmann, now able to understand the succinct comments of *Das Evangelium des Johannes.*

This was my own introduction to the work of Moody Smith and my first taste of what was to come from his scholarship.[4] Smith's early work on Bultmann is in several ways representative of his contribution to Johannine studies. First of all, this book signaled the role he would play as an interpreter of Bultmann and, more significantly, as a participant in American Johannine scholarship's move away from European dominance.[5] Second, *Composition and Order* was a foretaste of Smith's unique contribution to the issue of the sources for the composition of the Fourth Gospel. In succeeding years his attention became more and more riveted on the possibility that the Synoptic Gospels figured in the composition of the Gospel of John. Hence, in retrospect we see how his first major work set the magnetic north of Smith's scholarly compass.

A brief survey of Smith's work demonstrates, however, that his scholarship spans the whole range of major themes of Johannine studies in the last four decades of the twentieth century. Like the branches of a mature tree, his work stretches out over each of the five sections that constitute this honorary volume.

THE HISTORY AND CHARACTER OF THE JOHANNINE COMMUNITY

North American Johannine scholarship was irreversibly transformed at the approach of the 1970s when Raymond E. Brown and J. Louis Martyn launched it on a voyage in a new direction. In separate, distinctive ways each argued for a foundational Jewish setting for the Fourth Gospel and proposed that the expulsion of the Johannine Christians from their synagogue (and the subsequent dialogue between the Johannine community and the synagogue) marked crucial events responsible for the milieu of the Fourth Gospel. With their work and that of Wayne A. Meeks, they also initiated a revitalized concern for the Johannine community.[6] North American scholarship began the tedious but exciting task of examining and developing the implications of this innovative view of the origin of the Gospel.

Smith soon became a substantial player in that movement, clarifying Brown's and Martyn's work and sometimes extending it.[7] Through the years he has tended to accept and to work from the assumption of "a polemical situation within the synagogue and later between the Johannine community and the synagogue" as the setting of the Gospel.[8] The Jewish character of John is inescapable, and the Johannine community, Smith contends, arose from a context within or on the margins of the Judaism of the first century C.E.[9] The nature of that form of Judaism is suggested to us in the medley of Jewish expressions found in the Qumran scrolls, Samaritanism, and wisdom speculation.[10] Thus Smith helped us to imagine the Gospel's setting as one of prerabbinic Judaism and distinguished the contemporary hypothesis from earlier proposals of a Jewish background for the Gospel.[11] Smith acknowledges, however, that the Gospel's text suggests a community in transition between its Jewish origin and new frontiers. The province of the community soon expanded, he believes, into a universal concern.[12]

Smith consistently nuances his endorsement of the polemical setting for the origin of the Fourth Gospel in several ways. First, he contends that there might have been a Gnostic feature of the Johannine community and that Paul's Jewish-Christian opponents in Corinth may have been "close relatives" of those responsible for the early miracle tradition embedded in the Fourth Gospel. Indeed, that Gospel may have been representative of "an early stage in the emergence of motifs that had a later flowering in Gnosticism."[13] Accordingly, he resists an easy reduction of the complexities of the origin and development of the community. The Christology of the Gospel, for instance, cannot be explained entirely on the basis of the controversy with the synagogue but emerged gradually, perhaps influenced by Gnostic modes of thought. Hellenistic and Gnostic as well as Jewish elements are found in the thought of the Fourth Gospel.[14]

Second, following Brown, Smith is careful to detect hints of different settings in portions of the Gospel. The farewell discourses of chapters 13—17 imply an inner-community controversy, which doubtless arose in a period after the conflict with the synagogue had begun to subside.[15] This suggests that the Gospel betrays a history of composition, which in turn implies the likelihood of later stages in the life of the community. "Thus, the present Gospel embodies and sets before the reader the history of the preaching, experience, theological questions, and conflicts of what we now call the Johannine Christian community."[16]

This community understood itself, Smith contends, as standing in direct continuity with the Jesus of history. That self-understanding is indicated by the role of the "disciple whom Jesus loved"[17] and by the use of the first-person plural pronoun in John 1:14. Still, the community had a distinct sense of identity apart from other Christian bodies. Most likely, it originated in a remote and isolated area. (Smith hints a preference for Syria.)[18]

The history of the Johannine community, however, can never be imagined strictly in terms of the evidence of the Gospel alone, Smith argues, but must also include inferences drawn from the Johannine epistles and the Revelation to John. He suggests an analysis of this body of literature in terms of its treatment of the Spirit's inspiration, from which one may reconstruct a plausible history of the community. Such a reconstruction gives first place, chronologically, to Revelation, in which apocalyptic eschatology figures prominently. The work of the Spirit in conveying Christ's words in Revelation has what Smith calls a "primitive character." The Gospel reflects a later period in the community's life. Apocalyptic eschatology is absent or at least subdued, and speeches are attributed to Jesus that clearly originated with Christian prophets inspired by the Spirit. Finally, 1 John urges the testing of the spirits (4:1), suggesting the need to control those who claim the inspiration of the Spirit.[19]

Smith saw the wisdom of the proposal for the setting of the Gospel and the life of the community amid the fracturing of the church and the synagogue. He has contributed to the usefulness of such a proposition by both defending and refining it in his scholarship.

THE TRADITIONS OF THE FOURTH GOSPEL

The movement toward something like Brown's and Martyn's understandings of the Gospel's setting aroused fresh interest in the history of the Johannine community. That interest quickly spread to the question of the community's peculiarly Christian traditions and the sources employed by the fourth evangelist. Working from the hypothesis of a Jewish-Christian community expelled from the synagogue, Robert T. Fortna (one of Martyn's students) boldly attempted to isolate a basic source within the Gospel text. The results were what Fortna called a "Signs Gospel," a lengthy narrative source with a passion story.[20] Fortna's courageous work evoked a firestorm of controversy, into whose draft Smith was drawn.[21]

One of the issues surrounding Fortna's theory of a Signs Gospel source was his assertion that it combined wonder stories with a passion narrative. As early as

1976 Smith made a case for a Jewish milieu for the proposed *semeia* source. Following Bultmann's suggestion, Smith demonstrates the plausibility of a collection of wonder stories without a passion narrative. Such a collection would have arisen, Smith contends, out of expectations of a miracle-working prophet.[22] Its function would have been to invite followers of John the Baptizer into the Christian community and to differentiate Jesus' ministry from that of the Baptizer (cf. John 10:41). By the very nature of his careful scholarship, Smith is less optimistic than Fortna that it is possible to reconstruct the precise text of the source. But with Fortna he acknowledges that the miracle tradition constituted the formative beginnings of the composition of the Gospel, and he recognizes the possibilities both of a *semeia* source with a passion narrative and of the later addition of the passion to the miracle source. In either case, it is likely that the role of the story of Jesus' passion was to justify Jesus' messiahship in the face of the fact that he was executed as a common criminal. A good deal of the Gospel's discourse material was founded on the signs stories and shaped by them but was equally influenced by the community's opponents. Those discourses arose, Smith argues, from prophets within the community.[23]

Beyond these proposed sources for its composition, there is considerable evidence that the Gospel has undergone redaction, both in the process of the inclusion of tradition and probably later. The use of sources did not diminish the creativity of the evangelist. Indeed, "'John' is, after all, an original thinker, whose genius shines through his writings, especially the Gospel."[24] The Gospel was composed near the turn of the first century in response to a variety of issues, including the delay of the Parousia, the historical Jesus tradition in relation to the activity of the Spirit, and the hostility of the world.[25] The purpose of this composition was not essentially evangelistic, since the bulk of its message is addressed to a Christian community or communities. Literary analysis of the Gospel demonstrates that the evangelist assumes readers who are acquainted with the essential features of the Jesus story.[26] Smith locates the most obvious evidence for later redaction of John in chapter 21, the farewell discourses, and (possibly) 6:51–58. Such redactional work on the Gospel took place, Smith contends, within the Johannine community itself.[27]

Nevertheless, Smith has made his greatest contribution to the quest for the sources behind the Fourth Gospel in another arena. He will stand tall in the history of twentieth-century Johannine research as the one who summarized and critically analyzed the relationship of the Fourth Gospel to the Synoptics. Indeed, that relationship has intrigued Smith over the last several decades.[28] While the question of other sources did not escape his microscopic criticism, he correctly saw that the first question on the agenda of source analysis of the Fourth Gospel had to be the question of "John among the Gospels."

The work of C. H. Dodd solidified the view that the fourth evangelist did not use or know any of the Synoptic Gospels. Dodd tried to show that the Fourth

Gospel reflected the influence of the oral tradition commonly held to stand behind the Synoptics.[29] His work convinced many that the similarities between the Synoptics and the Fourth Gospel could be best explained by their mutual use of a common oral tradition, and Dodd's proposal prevailed into the 1970s.[30]

Smith's attention to the issue, expressed as early as the mid-1960s, positioned him to become the most valuable of those interpreters of the discussion that was soon to ensue.[31] His collection of essays, *Johannine Christianity*, demonstrates his critical attention to continental scholars who sought to revive a hypothesis that the fourth evangelist knew and used at least one of the Synoptics.[32] In his monumental survey of investigations of the relationship between John and the Synoptics,[33] he creates the definitive conceptual and chronological map that leads us skillfully through the maze of different perspectives on the question. Laying a foundation in the early church's interpretation, the book then moves to the nineteenth century and the emergence of a theory of independence, climaxing in the work of Percival Gardner-Smith. That theory became a near consensus in the wake of Dodd's work. What begins soon after that, however, is a process of what Smith calls the "dissolution of a consensus." He treats that process in three stages. The first comprises a series of studies of the contacts between the Gospels of Luke and John. The second is centered in comparisons of the passion narratives and the implications of the hypothesis that the Markan passion narrative is the redactional work of the second evangelist. The final blow to the consensus, in Smith's scheme, comes with investigations of a number of continental scholars, especially M.-É. Boismard, Frans Neirynck, Anton Dauer, and Bruno de Solages.

Smith's careful modulation of his own point of view over the years is interesting to chronicle. In 1963 he penned the memorable pronouncement that the burden of proof is on the scholar who would argue that the fourth evangelist knew and used one or more of the Synoptics.[34] In 1980 he affirmed, on the basis of redaction criticism, that it is "less difficult" to explain similarities between the Fourth Gospel and the Synoptics from a theory of literary independence than from an assumption of literary dependence. Here, however, he raised the question of indirect ("at best secondary and perhaps in some cases even second-hand") knowledge of the Synoptics on the part of the fourth evangelist.[35] In 1982, in a review of the works of Bruno de Solages and Frans Neirynck, Smith admitted that it is not possible to *prove* that the fourth evangelist did not know and use the Synoptics. Then he observed, "John presupposes more than he narrates," whatever that "more" might have been, and concluded that the relationship is a mysterious one.[36] Finally, in 1992, he repositioned the whole question.

> The Gospel of John, whether or not it was written with the others in view, now inevitably colors the way they are received and read and in turn is colored by them. Their coexistence in the Christian canon of Scripture modifies and mollifies the sharpness of their juxtaposition, a sharpness

that has been established and perhaps accentuated by historical-critical readings. At the level of such reading and exegesis, the questions of John's knowledge and use of the Synoptics remains a vexing, critical one. At the same time, the whole question of their points of contact and the tensions between them, if it has not been resolved by their inclusion in the same New Testament, has been moved to the level of theological discussion and intertextual relationships.[37]

Johannine scholarship will for some time stand in Smith's debt for his careful attention to the question of the sources involved in the composition of the Fourth Gospel and, most especially, for his study of the relationship between the Fourth Gospel and the Synoptics. Clearly one of his contributions is in the manner in which he participates in the discussion. One could argue that Smith's own position has changed only slightly since his 1963 article. But that has not prevented his careful listening to the views of others. Progress in scholarship is sometimes retarded by the dogmatism with which individuals defend their own positions. Smith is remarkably free of such defensiveness. Instead, he carefully studies those with whom he may not agree, sensitive to new data or new perspectives on old data that might be decisive. That kind of genuine openness to the truth and respect for the work of others characterizes both the man and his scholarship. These characteristics are evident throughout his scholarship but are clearest in his interest in the source analysis of the Fourth Gospel.

LITERARY ASPECTS OF THE FOURTH GOSPEL

Smith's willingness to learn and to grow from others' work shows itself again in his appreciation of the newer literary methods in Johannine interpretation. His commitment to the literary aspects of the Fourth Gospel is already evident in his attention to the literary relationship of that Gospel and the Synoptics.[38] Moreover, he has pondered the question of the literary genre of John in new ways, teasing us, for instance, with the question, "Was John the First Apocryphal Gospel?" He suggests that the answer might be "yes." The Apocryphal Gospels diverged from the Markan order, which Matthew and Luke so carefully honored, and the Fourth Gospel shares that apocryphal feature. Along with the Apocryphal Gospels, the Gospel of John resides outside the canonical pattern of the Jesus story. Insofar as Mark's patterning of the story of Jesus was treated as canonical by the first and third evangelists, the fourth evangelist refused to be equally constrained.[39]

Smith's own interpretive approach is primarily that of historical criticism, using literary analysis as it was formulated in that tradition. Yet in recent years he has revised his work on the Gospel to reflect some of the new methods.[40] Moreover, he has mentored students who have gone on to work with those methods, not least of all the two editors of this volume.

In turn, Smith has welcomed his former students as his teachers. Hence, his understanding of the literary features of the Fourth Gospel is expressly dependent on the work of R. Alan Culpepper.[41] Following Culpepper, he affirms that the Fourth Gospel can be read as a kind of "mirror," without appeal to its historical origin and setting. The chapter "The Gospel of John as Literature" in *John* is essentially a summary of the substance of Culpepper's book, augmented by Smith's own flair for communication. He observes, for instance, "because John gives a fuller narration of the opposition's plotting, he has a more satisfactory and satisfying plot."[42]

The four Gospels, Smith thinks, lend themselves particularly to a literary interpretation, as opposed, for instance, to the Pauline letters. Methodologically, Smith seems to value the study of the literary features of the Fourth Gospel as a supplement to the more traditional or historical-critical approach and acknowledges that the document may be read both as a mirror and as a window. He seems to view the newer literary emphasis as a natural evolution of redaction criticism, concerned as it is with attention to the whole composition. Moreover, he cannot resist comparisons of the literary qualities of the Synoptics with those of the Fourth Gospel, pointing out, for instance, that characterization in the Synoptics is far less developed than in the Gospel of John.[43]

THE THEOLOGY OF THE FOURTH GOSPEL

The Gospel of John has been of interest to Smith not for historical and literary reasons alone; he sees the fourth evangelist as having dealt with theological issues in a more perceptive and subtle way than that of the other Gospel writers. Smith has persistently articulated the theological themes of the Gospel with a distinctive method. Foremost in his theological method is the treatment of the thought of the Gospel in its own structural categories. For instance, he discusses "the themes of Johannine theology" in two major parts, which are divisions that he finds in the Gospel's own structure: "The Revelation of the Glory to the World" and "The Revelation of the Glory to the Community." Another feature of his theological method is always to put Johannine thought in dialogue with other New Testament literature, especially the Synoptics and Paul, but also Hebrews. An example of this feature is his analysis of the Gospel's soteriology, which entails examination of 1 John and Revelation. Indeed, for Smith the theology of the Fourth Gospel needs to be understood canonically, because it stands in a "pivotal position" in the canon where it "guides and deeply influences the reading of the New Testament."[44]

Not surprisingly, Smith finds the heart of Johannine theology in its Christology. Such a christological Gospel cannot easily be explained solely by appeal to the community's polemical situation. It is more likely the result of a longer period of time during which the community dealt with various questions, in response to which the claims for Christ were heightened.[45] While the Gospel writer achieves a delicate balance of the human and divine in the portrayal of Christ, John's unique contribution is in identifying Jesus with God's very being. For the evangelist, Jesus reveals God's glory — "the quality of God as God" — and is the μονογενής ("only begotten") son by nature of his unique relationship with God. The Johannine christological language and conceptuality are not the result of metaphysical construction, but to reduce them to functionalist or existentialist categories is to misunderstand the evangelist. "John obviously intends to make far-reaching, extravagant, and extreme claims about who Jesus is, and the interpreter must let him."[46]

In an astute article published in 1977, Smith characterizes the Gospel's representation of Jesus as "metahistorical." Jesus in the Fourth Gospel is at the same time both the historical figure of the past and a living spiritual reality in the church (made present through the Spirit, or Paraclete). The uniqueness of the Gospel's presentation of Jesus lies in its coalescing of these temporal periods.[47]

Christology is the hub out of which emerge other themes in Johannine thought. Christology is inseparably linked with soteriology. The fourth evangelist presupposes a "primitive view of the vicarious sacrificial effect of Jesus' death" but stresses the salvific results of revelation itself.[48] Johannine pneumatology is likewise shaped by christocentricity, according to Smith. The Fourth Gospel suggests that Christ's resurrection is already his glorious return to the disciples. Yet the fourth evangelist avoids the necessity of visions of the risen Lord and maintains a connection with Jesus' historical reality by making the Spirit, and not the risen Jesus, the medium of Christ's continuing presence in the community. The Johannine community experienced the reality of Christ's presence in the words of Spirit-inspired prophets. The Paraclete sayings (John 14:15–17, 25–26; 15:26–27; 16:12–15) show that the Spirit's role is that of a witness to God's historical revelation in Jesus. But the Spirit also represents the words and person of Jesus for the community in its own day and for its own struggles.[49]

Eschatology figures prominently in Smith's understanding of the theology of the Fourth Gospel, where "the meaning of eschatology is redefined in light of the coming of Jesus."[50] This redefinition can be seen in the context of what has often been called the problem of the delay of the Parousia. While fragments of an older apocalyptic perspective are present in the Gospel, its primary emphasis is on the sense in which the final salvation has already taken place. The fourth evangelist's reinterpretation of the traditional eschatology addressed the problem of Christ's bodily absence from the community, as well as the unfulfilled expectation of his glorious appearing. To speak of the Johannine view of eschatology as a development of the older Synoptic and Pauline views would be a mistake, yet the Johannine, Synoptic, and Pauline views must be understood together.[51]

The degree to which the Gospel accurately reports historical tradition concerning Jesus and his ministry is related to a proper understanding of Johannine Christology, as well as to the implicit use of the Gospel genre. Smith argues that John's story of Jesus should not be dismissed as purely theological or symbolic, for there are features of the Johannine narrative that have a historical appeal against the Synoptic witness. Therefore, the Gospel's "statements or narratives deserve serious consideration as quite possibly historically superior to the Synoptics."[52]

APPROPRIATING THE PROCLAMATION OF THE FOURTH GOSPEL

Smith's scholarly work is never pursued for the sake of historical inquiry alone, nor solely in the interest of literary aesthetics. The goal of all such inquiry is a better, more perceptive reading of the document. Furthermore, Smith is a devout Christian, dedicated to the ministry of the church. Hence, his scholarship is rooted in his commitment to the Bible as the church's book.

This commitment is exemplified in his article "Theology and Ministry in John" (1981). The Fourth Gospel is Christian preaching. In the midst of the waning hope for the imminent Parousia, the Johannine church focused on the presence of salvation in the proclaimed Christ. Hence, for Smith, the Christology of the Gospel enables us to comprehend the nature of distinctively Christian belief and preaching. The faith of the church manifests itself in a unique lifestyle: namely, in ministry, which in the Fourth Gospel is understood as the reenactment of Jesus' love of his disciples in Christians' love for one another. "Ministry in John is self-giving sacrifice."[53]

In the case of the Fourth Gospel, the preacher's task is more complicated, since, as Smith puts it, "we interpret an interpretation." The interpretive dimension of the primitive tradition is "deeper" in the Johannine story. He speaks of the Synoptics as the embodiment of a tradition distant from the evangelists, while the Fourth Gospel adopts a perspective that is "entirely Christian," whose characters are not always early first-century Jews in Palestine. Still, Smith advises his readers to avoid a simplistic historicism, on the one hand, and the reduction of the narratives and discourses to pure symbolism or theological meditation, on the other.[54]

Smith proposes that three interpretive frames be kept in view in any reading of the Gospel of John. The first includes the "preexistent, eternal" expressions of the validity and ultimate significance of the Christian message. The second interpretive frame is "past, historical," which has to do with the continuity between the historical Jesus and the Christian community. The final structure for interpretation is the "present, Christian." In the Fourth Gospel, Christ is the present Lord, alive and active within the church.[55] Preachers are urged to note that in the hands of the fourth evangelist, Jesus himself has become a postresurrection preacher. They are counseled to keep in mind that the literary context of any passage may be larger than it is in the Synoptic Gospels and that the historical context for the whole of the Gospel is especially important. We cannot easily equate Johannine passages with Synoptic parallels, but neither can we isolate the Fourth Gospel from its canonical companions.[56]

Smith makes a case for a new canonical reading of the Fourth Gospel, arguing that there is a danger in allowing the Johannine Gospel to become a kind of canon within the canon. Instead, we need to interpret the Fourth Gospel in the context of the Synoptics and the rest of the New Testament as well.[57] The student of Smith's work can detect here a convergence of his thought. He urges preachers not to interpret the Fourth Gospel in isolation from the Synoptics. He concludes his study of *John among the Gospels* with an appeal to the canonical relationship among them. His interpretation of Johannine theology is accomplished by means of a dialogue between the views of the fourth evangelist and those of other New Testament writers. And now he counsels the general value of a canonical reading of the Fourth Gospel. For all his special interest in the Gospel of John, Smith refuses to allow it to be viewed apart from the whole body of the church's scriptures. There is a reason for the canonical positioning of John in relationship with the Synoptics: namely, the wisdom of reading the Fourth Gospel as an interpretation of the first three.[58] How fascinating that this agile mind, convinced as it may be of at least a modified independence of the Fourth Gospel from the Synoptics, leads the interpreter back to a classical view of that relationship! But his emphasis on the canonical reading of John further reflects his Christian perspective. The canon is the church's book.

In the introduction of his book on preaching the Gospels, Smith paraphrases James T. Cleland's view of preaching this way: "preaching from where the church was to where the church is."[59] That description of the homiletical task also well summarizes a cherished value in Smith's whole interpretive method. His vocation has been to illumine "where the church was" for the sake of "where the church is."

CONCLUSION

Such a brief survey as this cannot do justice to the rich work Smith has done for our benefit. Yet out of this discussion there emerges a consistent portrait. One striking feature of that portrait is Smith's openness to new ideas and movements. We have seen that aspect most clearly, perhaps, in his attentiveness to all of the theories of the possible relationship between the Synoptics and the Gospel of John. But it is also evident in his use of the newer literary methods for interpretation and in his movement toward a canonical criticism. He has allowed himself to be taught by the work of others, including the work of those whom he had formerly taught. I propose that in this way Smith is a model for the community of biblical studies — the way in which we might all better listen to and learn from one another.[60]

And yet the portrait has another feature. Let me call it a "modest caution."[61] What we see in any of Smith's writings is a careful expression of views, insights, and proposals that avoids radical claims for truth; a crafted, deliberate, nuanced care not to claim too much and not to pretend certainty when none can be had. Sometimes in reading Smith we might become impatient for stronger assertions and wish for more dogmatic propagations. But Smith is too aware of the clay feet with which we all walk our scholarly paths. He is content to make modest and qualified suggestions, rather than try to overpower us with his rhetoric. He is cautious in his proposals, for he believes that something serious is at stake, namely, the quest for truth. And his commitment to that quest is too deep for him ever to lead another away from the truth.

NOTES

1. Rudolf Bultmann, *Das Evangelium Johannes,* MeyerK (Göttingen: Vandenhoeck & Ruprecht, 1962; E.T., *The Gospel of John: A Commentary,* trans. G. R. Beasley-Murray [Philadelphia: Westminster, 1971]).

2. Rudolf Bultmann, *Theology of the New Testament,* vol. 2: *The Theology of the Gospel of John and the Johannine Epistles* (New York: Scribner's, 1955), Part 3.

3. *The Composition and Order of the Fourth Gospel: Bultmann's Literary Theory,* Yale Publications in Religion 10 (New Haven, Conn., and London: Yale University Press, 1965).

4. Smith had earlier published "The Sources of the Gospel of John: An Assessment of the Present State of the Problem," *NTS* 10 (1964): 336–51.

5. In his most recent book, Smith acknowledges Bultmann's continued influence on his thought (*The Theology of the Gospel of John,* New Testament Theology [Cambridge: Cambridge University Press, 1995], xi). See also his review of John Ashton, *Understanding the Fourth Gospel,* in *JTS* 43 (1992): 594–600.

6. Raymond E. Brown, *The Gospel according to John,* AB 29, 29A (Garden City, N.Y.: Doubleday, 1966, 1970), and idem, *The Community of the Beloved Disciple* (New York: Paulist, 1979); J. Louis Martyn, *History and Theology in the Fourth Gospel* (New York: Harper and Row, 1968; 2d ed., Nashville: Abingdon, 1979), and idem, *The Gospel of John in Christian History: Essays for Interpreters,* Theological Inquiries (New York: Paulist, 1978); Wayne A. Meeks, "The Man from Heaven in Johannine Sectarianism," *JBL* 91 (1972): 44–72, reprinted in *The Interpretation of John,* ed. John Ashton, IRT 9 (Philadelphia and London: Fortress/SPCK, 1986), 141–73. See also Robert Kysar, *The Fourth Evangelist and His Gospel: An Examination of Contemporary Scholarship* (Minneapolis: Augsburg, 1975), 149–56, and idem, "Community and Gospel: Vectors in Fourth Gospel Criticism," *Int* 31 (1977): 335–66, reprinted in *Interpreting the Gospels,* ed. James Luther Mays (Philadelphia: Fortress, 1981), 265–77.

7. See his reviews of the first volume of Brown's commentary in *Int* 21 (1967): 469–75, and the first edition of Martyn's *History and Theology* in *Int* 23 (1969): 220–23. In his most recent book Smith explicitly affirms Martyn's "two-level" reading of the Gospel (*Theology of the Gospel of John,* 73). See also the reviews by Smith of Brown's *The Community of the Beloved Disciple* and *The Epistles of John,* AB30 (Garden City, N.Y.: Doubleday, 1982), in, respectively, *CBQ* 42 (1980): 397–99 and *JBL* 103 (1984): 666–71.

8. D. Moody Smith, *Johannine Christianity: Essays on Its Setting, Sources, and Theology* (Columbia, S.C.: University of South Carolina Press, 1984), 23. Smith's most detailed discussion of Martyn's work is found in his article "The Contribution

of J. Louis Martyn to the Understanding of the Gospel of John," in *The Conversation Continues: Studies in Paul and John in Honor of J. Louis Martyn,* ed. Robert T. Fortna and Beverly R. Gaventa (Nashville: Abingdon, 1990), 275–94. Also helpful in understanding Smith's position is "Judaism and the Gospel of John," in *Jews and Christians: Exploring the Past, Present, and Future,* ed. James H. Charlesworth (New York: Crossroad, 1990), 76–99; there he expresses the value of Martyn's original linking of the expulsion from the synagogue and the Twelfth Benediction, although he carefully distances himself from any necessary connection between the two (see esp. ibid., 85 and 98). See also *Theology of the Gospel of John,* 54–56, and *John,* Proclamation Commentaries, 2d ed. (Philadelphia: Fortress, 1986), 76. Smith's commitment to this understanding of the Gospel's setting is exemplified in his discussion of John 16 in *Interpreting the Gospels for Preaching* (Philadelphia: Fortress, 1980), 83–94, as well as in the most recent edition of his introduction to the New Testament, authored with Robert A. Spivey, *Anatomy of the New Testament: A Guide to Its Structure and Meaning,* 5th ed. (Englewood Cliffs, N.J.: Prentice Hall, 1995), 165–66.

9. He writes, "we are hardly justified in looking elsewhere for the Gospel's setting, especially in view of the evidence of the Gospel itself and our knowledge of the Judaism contemporary with it. . . . [T]he closer one gets to Judaism, as well as early Christianity, the closer one is to John" (*Theology of the Gospel of John,* 56, 72).

10. *John,* 17–18; *Johannine Christianity,* 26–30; also *Anatomy,* 200–201.

11. See, for instance, the first edition of C. K. Barrett, *The Gospel according to St. John: An Introduction with Commentary and Notes on the Greek Text* (London: SPCK, 1955), esp. 16–28, although Barrett concluded that Hellenistic Judaism is "the most illuminating background of the fourth gospel" (33). Compare Smith's reviews of the second edition of Barrett's commentary in *JBL* 99 (1980): 626–27 and *Duke Divinity School Review* 43 (1980): 67–69.

12. *Johannine Christianity,* 35–36.

13. *Johannine Christianity,* 25; see also *Theology of the Gospel of John,* 12–16.

14. *Theology of the Gospel of John,* 20; *Johannine Christianity,* 34; and *John,* 17.

15. *Johannine Christianity,* 35.

16. *Interpreting the Gospels for Preaching,* 81.

17. Smith says simply that the Beloved Disciple "defies the historical investigator," so that we can never know if this figure is to be identified with a historical or purely literary character (*John,* 50). See also *Anatomy of the New Testament,* 201, and "Beloved Disciple," *IDBSup* (1976): 95.

18. *Johannine Christianity,* 20–22. In *Anatomy of the New Testament* (166) he declares that a "Palestinian origin of the Johannine tradition no longer appears out of the question."

19. *John,* 91–92. Smith believes that there is probably "an actual historical relationship of some sort underlying the traditional linking of the Apocalypse to the other Johannine writings. What that relationship is we may never know precisely" (ibid., 15; see also *Johannine Christianity,* 15–18). He contends that the Gospel, Johannine epistles, and Revelation "are related by content and perspective as well as by tradition" (*Anatomy of the New Testament,* 436). For his treatment of "the Johannine circle or school," see *John,* 74–81; on 1 John, see esp. *First, Second, and Third John,* Interpretation (Louisville, Ky.: John Knox, 1991), and *John,* 59–64. Smith has been persistent in keeping the Book of Revelation in view when speaking of the Johannine literature, while other scholars have often tended to dismiss it. Still, he has exercised

caution in how we conceive a relationship between the work of John of Patmos and the other canonical Johannine documents (e.g., *Theology of the Gospel of John*, 60–62).

20. Robert T. Fortna, *The Gospel of Signs: A Reconstruction of the Narrative Source Underlying the Fourth Gospel*, SNTSMS 11 (Cambridge: Cambridge University Press, 1970). Fortna's later work, *The Fourth Gospel and Its Predecessor: From Narrative Source to Present Gospel* (Philadelphia: Fortress, 1988), further advances his original thesis. Smith reviewed each of the volumes in, respectively, *JBL* 89 (1970): 498–501 and *JBL* 109 (1990): 352–55 (cf. Kysar, *The Fourth Evangelist and His Gospel*, 13–37). Contemporary interest in source analysis has waned but still continues; see, for instance, Urban C. von Wahlde, *The Earliest Version of John's Gospel: Recovering the Gospel of Signs*, Good News Studies 30 (Wilmington, Del.: Michael Glazier, 1989), and Thomas L. Brodie, *The Quest for the Origin of John's Gospel: A Source-Oriented Approach* (New York: Oxford University Press, 1993).

21. In the area of source analysis, Gerard Sloyan calls Smith "the dean of U.S. Johannine specialists" (*What Are They Saying about John?* [New York: Paulist, 1991], 38).

22. "The Setting and Shape of a Johannine Narrative Source," *JBL* 95 (1976): 231–41. See, further, Wayne A. Meeks, *The Prophet-King: Moses Traditions and the Johannine Christology*, NovTSup 14 (Leiden: Brill, 1967).

23. *Johannine Christianity*, 31–33, 76–78, and 89–93; also *Interpreting the Gospels for Preaching*, 88–89. In *Theology of the Gospel of John* he cites Fortna and von Wahlde with approval and writes, "Quite possibly the Gospel incorporates a primitive narrative source consisting of miracles and passion" (48 n. 28).

24. *Theology of the Gospel of John*, 74. See also Smith's discussion of eschatology in *John*, 89: "John moves boldly in reformulating Christian eschatology."

25. In this connection note Smith's reviews of J.A.T. Robinson's two works, *Redating the New Testament* and *The Priority of John*, in, respectively, *Duke Divinity School Review* 42 (1977): 193–205 and *JBL* 108 (1989): 156–58.

26. *John*, 67–68, 76, 83–86, 115. Contrast Smith's view with that of D. A. Carson, *The Gospel according to John* (Grand Rapids: Eerdmans, 1991), esp. 90–91. On the question of authorship, see Smith, *John*, 72–74; *Theology of the Gospel of John*, 3; and *Anatomy of the New Testament*, 201. In *First, Second, and Third John* Smith concludes, "The authorship of the Johannine Gospel and letters remains an enigma shrouded in mystery" (18).

27. *Johannine Christianity*, 19. Here Smith agrees with Brown's proposal of a "friendly redactor" (*The Gospel according to John (i–xii)*, 29.xxxvi), as opposed to Bultmann's "ecclesiastical redactor" (e.g., *Theology of the New Testament* 2.9).

28. See, for example, "John, the Synoptics and the Canonical Approach to Exegesis," in *Tradition and Interpretation in the New Testament: Essays in Honor of E. Earle Ellis*, ed. Gerald Hawthorne (Grand Rapids: Eerdmans, 1988), 166–80.

29. C.H. Dodd, *Historical Tradition in the Fourth Gospel* (Cambridge: Cambridge University Press, 1963). See Kysar, *The Fourth Evangelist and His Gospel*, 54–66.

30. For example, see my *John, the Maverick Gospel*, rev. ed. (Louisville, Ky.: Westminster/John Knox, 1993), 12–13.

31. "John 12:12ff. and the Question of John's Use of the Synoptics," *JBL* 82 (1963): 58–64. There Smith concludes that an oral-tradition hypothesis best accounts for the evidence.

32. Note also his provocative article, "John and the Synoptics and the Question of Gospel Genre," in *The Four Gospels: Festschrift Frans Neirynck,* ed. F. Van Segbroeck, C. M. Tuckett, G. Van Belle, and J. Verheyden, BETL 100 (Leuven: Leuven University Press, 1992), 3.1783–97.

33. *John among the Gospels: The Relationship in Twentieth-Century Research* (Minneapolis: Fortress, 1992). See my review in *Int* 48 (1994): 96.

34. *Johannine Christianity,* 105. The essay, "John 12:12ff. and the Question of John's Use of the Synoptics," was first published in 1963 (see above, n. 31).

35. *Johannine Christianity,* 105 and 169–72.

36. Ibid., 143–44. See also *John,* ix (cf. 10–11): "The work of Frans Neirynck and others on the relation of John to the synoptics has certainly demonstrated that any facile assertion of John's independence of the synoptics is no longer possible."

37. *John among the Gospels,* 193; see also "John, the Synoptics and the Canonical Approach to Exegesis."

38. See also his review of David W. Wead, *The Literary Devices in John's Gospel* (1971), in *Int* 26 (1972): 119–20.

39. "The Problem of John and the Synoptics in Light of the Relation between Apocryphal and Canonical Gospels," in *John and the Synoptics,* ed. Adelbert Denaux, BETL 101 (Leuven: Leuven University Press, 1992), 148–62.

40. Note that, unlike its first edition, the revised and enlarged edition of *John* includes a chapter on "Understanding the Gospel of John as Literature" (94–104); similarly, the Gospel's "narrative setting" is discussed in *Theology of the Gospel of John* (20–48, see esp. 32). Note also *Anatomy of the New Testament,* 203, where the authors claim that the narrative structure of John mirrors the evangelist's emphases. Helpful in understanding Smith's growing appreciation for the newer literary methods is his review of Norman R. Petersen, *Literary Criticism for New Testament Critics* (1978), in *Duke Divinity School Review* 43 (1978): 201–2.

41. R. Alan Culpepper, *Anatomy of the Fourth Gospel: A Study in Literary Design,* FFNT (Philadelphia: Fortress, 1983). Culpepper's seminal work began the effort to use the new literary criticism in the interpretation of the Fourth Gospel. Among others who have followed Culpepper's lead are these: Paul D. Duke, *Irony in the Fourth Gospel* (Atlanta: John Knox, 1985); Fernando F. Segovia, *The Farewell of the Word: The Johannine Call to Abide* (Minneapolis: Fortress, 1991); Mark W. G. Stibbe, *John as Storyteller: Narrative Criticism and the Fourth Gospel,* SNTSMS 73 (Cambridge: Cambridge University Press, 1992); and Francis J. Moloney, *Belief in the Word: Reading John 1–4* (Minneapolis: Fortress, 1993). See also "The Fourth Gospel from a Literary Perspective," ed. R. Alan Culpepper and Fernando F. Segovia, in *Semeia* 53 (Atlanta: Scholars Press, 1991).

42. *John,* 100.

43. Ibid., 94–96 and 100–101.

44. *Theology of the Gospel of John,* 1, 80–160 (esp. 116), 181–82 (quotation, 182). For examples of Smith's interpretation of John in dialogue with Paul, see ibid., 66–67, 99, and 143; and in dialogue with Matthew, see 179–81. Also note *John,* 65, and *Anatomy of the New Testament,* 166.

45. *John,* 43 and 49.

46. *Theology of the Gospel of John,* 91, 103, 121 (quotation), 129, and 130 (quotation).

47. *Johannine Christianity,* 184–87. In *Theology of the Gospel of John* Smith uses

the categories "cosmic," "postresurrection," and "historical" to make a similar point (101–102; see also 142).

48. *Theology of the Gospel of John*, 116–20.

49. *Interpreting the Gospels for Preaching*, 88–89, and *John*, 55–59 and 89–90. See also *Theology of the Gospel of John*, 141–44.

50. *Theology of the Gospel of John*, 106. Smith points out, however, that the fourth evangelist's views of the world and God are similar to those of apocalypticism (ibid., 85).

51. *John*, 86–89. On the subject of the Fourth Gospel's dualism, Smith contends that it was "almost certainly socially conditioned," as the separation of the Jewish and Christian communities widened (77). See his review of Jerome H. Neyrey, *An Ideology of Revolt: John's Christology in Social-Science Perspective* (1988), in *RelSRev* 16 (1990): 262.

52. "Historical Issues and the Problem of John and the Synoptics," in *From Jesus to John: Essays on Jesus and New Testament Christology in Honour of Marinus de Jonge*, ed. Martinus C. de Boer, JSNTSup 84 (Sheffield: JSOT, 1994), 252–67 (quotation, 267). See also "John and the Synoptics in Light of the Problem of Faith and History," in *Faith and History: Essays in Honor of Paul W. Meyer*, ed. John T. Carroll, Charles H. Cosgrove, and E. Elizabeth Johnson, Homage Series (Atlanta: Scholars Press, 1991), 74–89.

53. *Johannine Christianity*, 197–220 (quotation, 220).

54. *John*, 40–41 (quotation, 107), and *Interpreting the Gospels for Preaching*, 81–82.

55. *John*, 107–13; also *Theology of the Gospel of John*, 101–2.

56. *Interpreting the Gospels for Preaching*, 91–94 and 101.

57. "A Canonical Reading of the Fourth Gospel," unpublished paper for the Johannine Literature Section of the Society of Biblical Literature, 1992.

58. *John*, 113–14. See also his review of Brevard S. Childs, *The New Testament as Canon: An Introduction* (1985), "Why Approaching the New Testament as Canon Matters," in *Int* 40 (1986): 407–11; also see *Theology of the Gospel of John*, 181–82.

59. *Interpreting the Gospels for Preaching*, ix.

60. Smith's participation in the scholarly community, and the respect others have for him, is witnessed in the number of articles he has contributed to *Festschriften* for his senior colleagues. See the bibliography of his work, elsewhere in this volume.

61. Smith and Spivey call the views expressed in their introduction "centrist" (*Anatomy of the New Testament*, xix).

Part One

The History and Character of the Johannine Community

Marianne Meye Thompson

2

The Historical Jesus
and the Johannine Christ

Countless portraits of Jesus have been painted over the centuries, and there seems to be no end in sight to the creativity and productivity of the artists wishing to display their work. In the academic wing of the gallery, the portraits have routinely differed from one another in texture, point of view, expression, and pose. But the materials used have been markedly the same, for most of the portraits of Jesus here have used the palette of the Synoptic Gospels.[1] Although John is sometimes used, the portraits painted from the vantage point and in the style of the Fourth Gospel are usually hung off to one side of the gallery of academic scholarship, isolated as idiosyncratic or unreliable interpretations of the one who sat for the portrait. Ironically, for centuries prior to the rise of critical scholarship, this was not the case. In earlier ages the doctors of the church used and mixed the colors of the four Gospels indiscriminately, without conscious attention to the source of their pigments.

Because scholars depend on the Synoptics for the materials used to reconstruct their portraits of Jesus, "the historical Jesus" is nowadays almost synonymous with "the Synoptic Jesus." John's portrait seems to be painted in such an innovative style and with such unusual technique that critics have wondered whether the portrait better captures the subject or the artist.[2] So, whereas one studies the canvases of the Synoptic Gospels to catch a glimpse of "the historical Jesus," in the distinctive rendering of the Fourth Evangelist we have "the Johannine Christ"— almost a different subject, and certainly a unique interpretation of him. More interested in mimetic representation, the Synoptics allegedly approximate Jesus "as he really was." But John, not so interested in art imitating life, gives us "the Christ as the church confessed him."

The purpose of this chapter is to explore some dimensions of the relationship between "the historical Jesus" and "the Johannine Christ."[3] We begin, first, with a review of the substantial similarities and considerable differences between the Johannine and Synoptic traditions. Endeavors to explain this mixed evidence have produced a number of theories about John's historicity, and it will be worthwhile, second, to consider briefly the definition of "historical" operative in discussions about the Gospel of John. Following these introductory sections, we will survey, third, the attempts to uncover historical traditions in John.

There are places in which John has not interpreted the tradition in ways that we might have expected or predicted even when the opportunity seemed at hand, and other instances where the details of the Gospel strike one as historically plausible. Some elements of the Gospel's presentation of Jesus seem at once to be the stuff and substance of Johannine interpretation and yet accurately capture the conditions of first-century Palestine and the lineaments of Jesus' ministry. In fact, there are some features of John's portrayal of Jesus that are remarkably in keeping with recent scholarly reconstructions of the aims and intentions of Jesus. Thus, in light of the alleged theological and interpretive stance of the Gospel, it will be worthwhile to explore some of the "primitive" features of the Gospel of John, instances where John seems less theological, "spiritual," or interpretive than do the Synoptics.

In the light of all these observations, we will conclude with some reflections about the nature of the interpretation that we have in John, noting what distinguishes not just the content of the Gospel but the kind of interpretation of Jesus' ministry that John offers. But we begin with a comparison of the portraits of Jesus in John and the other canonical gospels.

THE PORTRAITS OF JESUS IN JOHN
AND IN THE SYNOPTIC GOSPELS

In all the Gospels, Jesus preaches and teaches, gathers disciples, performs extraordinary deeds, enters into debate and conflict with Jewish authorities, and is put to death by Roman crucifixion. Moreover, the broad outlines of the narratives are similar. Jesus' public ministry begins with the baptizing activity of John; roughly in the middle of the narrative comes a miraculous feeding and Peter's confession; there is a decisive entry into Jerusalem, a last meal with his followers, a trial, crucifixion, and burial, accounts of an empty tomb, and appearances of the risen Jesus. And yet at almost every point John's portrayal of these events stands out from the corresponding Synoptic accounts.[4]

While Jesus figures prominently as a teacher in all the Gospels, there are striking differences between John and the Synoptics in style and content. In a nutshell, the most characteristic aspect of Jesus' teaching in the Synoptic Gospels is lacking in John, and what typifies John's presentation of Jesus' teaching is absent in the Synoptics. Specifically, whereas in the Synoptic Gospels Jesus proclaims the kingdom of God in parables and aphorisms (see Mark 1:38; Luke 4:43), in the Gospel of John "kingdom of God" occurs only in 3:3 and 3:5, and none of the classic kingdom parables (the sower, the wheat and the tares, pearl of great price) or the great story parables (the good Samaritan, the prodigal son, the great banquet) are to be found. Again, in the Synoptic Gospels, Jesus is the herald of the kingdom of God, but in John he is the agent of God's gift of eternal life.[5] Finally,

John's most frequent designation for Jesus is "Son," and for God, "Father." Although both images are found in the Synoptics, again we find that what is central in John is merely alluded to or implied in the other Gospels.[6]

Rather than speaking in parables and aphorisms, the Johannine Jesus either engages in extended dialogue (chaps. 3, 4, 5, 9, 11) or speaks in long discourses (chaps. 6, 7, 8), in which are embedded the renowned "I am" sayings.[7] Thus the public discourses of Jesus become occasions in which he speaks pointedly and repeatedly of his own role and relationship to God. Disclosure and discussion of his identity are found in the Synoptic accounts, but generally in scenes set in private (Mark 8:27–31; Matt. 10:32–33, 37–39, 40), in implicit or veiled statements, and never in terms of the revelatory "I am" pronouncements.[8] Other features that characterize Jesus' speech in John are the dualism of light and darkness and of above and below, including the requirement of "birth from above"; the summons to "believe in" Jesus (John 3:16) rather than to follow (Mark 10:21), receive (Mark 9:38; 10:37 par. Matt. 10:40–41), or hear (Luke 10:16) Jesus; the characterization of Jesus' opponents as "the Jews" and "the world"; and the theme of the unity of Father and Son, and of their unity with believers. Finally, one is hard put to find statements on the lips of Jesus in the Synoptics such as "Before Abraham was I am" (8:58; cf. 17:5, 24).

In short, the Gospel of John contains such a sustained presentation of the centrality of Jesus in mediating the presence and knowledge of God and the gift of eternal life that it would be difficult to derive from John the portrait of Jesus as merely or primarily a great ethical teacher, or as a prophet of God in the tradition of the great Hebrew prophets. Such a portrait can more easily be painted using the materials of the Synoptic Gospels, where Jesus teaches regularly about the establishment of the kingdom and the human conduct that God requires, covering such matters as prayer, almsgiving, wealth, mission, forgiveness, paying taxes, retaliation, anxiety, speech, love, and discipleship. The question remains, of course: Which emphases were characteristic of the teachings of Jesus? And, if both the Johannine and Synoptic records are reliable digests of Jesus' proclamation, why is there not greater overlap between them?

The miracle tradition of John also differs from that of the other Gospels, and in two chief ways: The deeds recorded are, on the whole, found only in John, and their accompanying interpretation is not only unique to John but generally serves as the primary vehicle for John's theology and distinctive viewpoint. Although many of Jesus' deeds are of the same kind in John and the Synoptics (healing the lame, the blind, the ill) except for the feeding of the five thousand, no Johannine miracle can clearly be identified with any of the Synoptic miracles.[9] Demon exorcisms figure prominently in the Synoptics, bearing witness to Jesus' authority and the presence of God's spirit through his exorcistic activity (Mark 3:23–27; Luke 11:17–20/Matt. 12:25–28), but no exorcisms are found in John. There are no cures of those with leprosy (Mark 1:40–45; Luke 17:11–19). Although women play particularly important roles in John, both as exemplars of faith and recipients of revelation, no women are healed or cured. Even the miracles with which John frames the account of Jesus' public ministry — the changing of the water to wine, and the raising of Lazarus — are found only in John.

John interprets the miracles by labeling them "signs." That is, they are tokens of Jesus' own identity as the agent of God's salvation, whereas the Synoptic miracles are linked to the fulfillment of the messianic age (Matt. 11:4; Luke 7:22) and to the manifestation of God's kingdom.[10] Once again, the Synoptic tradition heralds Jesus as the mediator of God's kingdom, whereas the Johannine miracles acclaim him as the agent through whom God brings life to the world.

Finally, in John as in the other Gospels, Jesus is brought to trial and put to death by crucifixion. Here, too, there are differences among the various Gospel narratives. In John, and only in John, Jesus washes his disciples' feet as a model of his selfless love and sacrificial death on the cross (13:1–18), which the disciples are to imitate.[11] And in contrast with the Synoptic Gospels, at this last meal the Johannine Jesus does not institute the "Lord's Supper."[12] Additionally, the last supper becomes the occasion at which Jesus delivers a lengthy parting address, the well-known "farewell discourses." Like the eschatological discourses of the Synoptics, they warn of coming persecutions and promise the aid of the Spirit; but they also, unlike the Synoptic Gospels, include lengthy discussions of Jesus' return to God and to the preexistent heavenly glory, a return that takes place through the crucifixion, the "lifting up" on the cross.[13] John reports that a Roman cohort was sent to seize Jesus, and when he acknowledged — with a mysterious "I am he"(18:5) — that he was the one they were seeking, the arresting soldiers fell to the ground (18:6). With Pilate, Jesus carried on a lengthy discussion about kingship and power (18:33–38; 19:7–15), whereas the Synoptics report that after an initial terse response to the question, "Are you the King of the Jews?" Jesus remained silent (Mark 14:5 parr.). Jesus' mother and the beloved disciple are to be found at the foot of the cross (19:25–27); no Synoptic Gospel mentions a male disciple present at the cross. As he died, Jesus proclaimed the accomplishment of his work with the announcement, "It is finished!" (19:30), rather than quoting the words of the lament, "My God, my God, why hast thou forsaken me?" A soldier thrust a spear into Jesus' side to verify that he was dead and, in so doing, released the flow of blood and water (19:34–37), emblematic of the gift of life and the Spirit. These features of the passion narrative are unique to John. They also stand in service of that Gospel's presentation of Jesus, who acted with sovereign authority and foreknowledge, willingly and deliberately laying down his life to bring life to the world.[14]

There is other material unique to John (e.g., the encounters with Nicodemus, the Samaritan woman, the man at the pool in Jerusalem, and the man born blind). If it were merely that the individuals healed, the persons encountered, or the occasions of Jesus' discourses were different from those found in the other Gospels, one might be able to account for the discrepancies as stemming from different traditions or sources. It is, however, not simply the fact of the differences but rather the consistent recasting of the material in an idiom not characteristic of the other

Gospels that raises the question of the value of the testimony to Jesus found only in John. In other words, precisely that which makes John John—the great christological claims and discourses and the distinctive idiom in which the Johannine Jesus speaks—also raises the question of whether and in what way John's distinctive portrait of Jesus may be used in getting back to "the historical Jesus." Before investigating this quest a bit more closely, it will be useful to review what the phrase "the historical Jesus" connotes by the standards of critical scholarship.

THE "HISTORICAL" JESUS

By the conventions of academic idiom, "the historical Jesus" is a shorthand way of designating the picture of Jesus constructed by scholarly explanations of the aims, intentions, words and deeds of Jesus in the Gospels in the context of other ancient documents. The purpose of such reconstructions is to provide as good an approximation as one can of the "Jesus of history" or "Jesus as he really was." Implicit in this quest is the conviction that the Gospels give us information that can be used in getting at "the Jesus of history," but that they themselves do not give the kinds of explanations that are desirable in historical reporting. "The historical Jesus"—and sometimes simply "Jesus"—remains a cipher for the results of the scholar's reconstruction of him. The historical Jesus is the historian's Jesus. But the historian's Jesus is not the Johannine Jesus.

At issue is not whether Jesus actually lived, for that is disputed by no reputable historian. Rather, the question is whether John can be considered "historical" in the sense that it reports what "really happened," something like what we would have been able to capture on videotape had we been there.[15] To be sure, many scholars would grant that John gives us history in the sense that it contains some events that really happened or some sayings that approximate what Jesus actually said, as well as information that accurately explains customs and geography of ancient Palestine.[16] Some have gone even further in advocating the historical value of the Gospel of John, suggesting that it is to be preferred as an account for information about the historical Jesus.[17]

But on the whole, fewer scholars would be willing to label John's overall presentation of Jesus' words and deeds as "historical" in the sense that the entire presentation of Jesus could be analyzed by historical methods of study and shown to regularly provide narratives of what Jesus actually said and did and so serve as a useful source in reconstructing the historical Jesus. By this definition John's account is not accepted as historical, because its interpretation of events has overshadowed any particular interest in reporting history (what actually happened). So while many scholars would affirm that John includes historical information and that John intends to provide a meaningful narration of the significance of the events of Jesus' life and is in this sense historical and not fictional, it is also true that many, if not most, New Testament scholars find John only an occasionally useful source for developing a picture of the historical Jesus. Instead, John gives us his own distinctive portrait of Jesus, and it is a portrait heavily colored and decisively shaped by the historical circumstances of the Johannine community and later church confessions of Jesus as Messiah and Son of God. In other words, John gives us "the Christ," not the Jesus of history.

From the way that scholars have addressed the problem of John's historicity, two observations emerge. First, "history" and "theology" continue to be juxtaposed as opposing categories. Despite frequent arguments that to set history and theology against each other will do violence to the character of the Gospels and especially the Fourth Gospel, such a schema continues to inform much discussion about the differences between John and the other Gospels, and John's theological agenda continues to count against its historical value.[18] Second, it is obvious that the baseline against which John is measured is the Synoptic Gospels. While the question of the literary relationship of the Gospels is not identical with, and cannot alone settle, the problem of the historicity of John, it does have implications for the historical value of the Fourth Gospel. For if the Synoptics provide reliable information about Jesus' ministry, words, and deeds, and if John differs from them at every point, can one nevertheless detect materials in John that are not only traditional but equally as useful as those in the Synoptic Gospels? The question of John's relationship to the other Gospels thus continues to play an important role in considerations of the historicity of John.

THE QUESTION OF HISTORICAL TRADITION IN JOHN

One of the earliest explanations of the relationship of John to the other Gospels was offered in Clement of Alexandria's account of the writing of John: "Last of all, aware that the physical facts [τὰ σωματικά] had been recorded in the Gospels, encouraged by his pupils and irresistibly moved by the Spirit, John wrote a spiritual Gospel."[19] Though Clement undoubtedly did not intend to impugn the historical value of the Fourth Gospel, his statement points to an awareness of the differences between it and the other Gospels. Since these differences could be attributed to the inspired testimony of the apostle, the disparities were no cause for alarm. Such a model was useful and accepted in one form or another for many years in the church.[20] But with the rise of historical criticism, basic assumptions about John and, indeed, all the Gospels began to be called into question. Historical criticism challenged the Johannine authorship of the Gospel and its historical value because of its obvious differences from the other Gospels and its intensely "spiritual" theologizing. Eventually it was concluded that, given the significant differences, both John and the Synoptics could not be taken as equally historical accounts of Jesus' life, and one would have to choose between them.[21] Although there were those who wished to give John preference or at least equal voice, the balance tilted decisively towards the Synoptic accounts.

But in the twentieth century, two developments provoked a reconsideration of John's historical value. The discoveries of the Dead Sea Scrolls prompted a reassessment of the Gospel of John, since in the eyes of many they allowed for a first-century Jewish Palestinian context for the idiom of Jesus in the Fourth Gospel, discounting the necessity of a late "hellenizing" influence.[22] John no longer needed, it was argued, a late date or a non-Palestinian provenance, since a first-century Palestinian Jew could have spoken as the Johannine Jesus did.[23]

The unquestionably more significant trend developing in Johannine studies, however, was the inclination to regard John as literarily independent of the other Gospels. Two names figure most prominently in this discussion: P. Gardner-Smith and C. H. Dodd. Both Gardner-Smith, in a slim but suggestive volume, and Dodd, in a lengthy and detailed tome, contended that John's distinctiveness vis-à-vis the Synoptics could be explained more plausibly on the assumption that the Fourth Gospel was independent of, rather than dependent on, the other three.[24] This raised the question of the historical value of the tradition found only in John.[25] For as long as John was viewed as dependent upon the other Gospels, it was also frequently understood as a theological reflection upon them. In other words, John's dependence counted against its historical value. But if the Gospel of John could not be explained as the product of the Evangelist's ruminations and reflections on the Synoptic Gospels, then what was the source of the Gospel's peculiar material and distinctive vantage point? Dodd's investigations were a powerful argument for rooting the materials of John in historical tradition independent of the Synoptic tradition. While the independent origins of John's traditions do not necessarily imply the historicity of the events they purport to record, it was no longer so simple to assign to the Evangelist's creativity or theologizing all elements distinctive to John.

In an article on the development of the oral tradition in John, James D. G. Dunn provides a helpful and schematic overview of the data, sifted by Dodd and others, with positive implications for the historical value of John.[26] The resulting list includes geographical and narrative details, many of the events of Jesus' ministry, and quite a few sayings, including some material most typical of John (e.g., cf. John 3:8 with Mark 4:27; John 3:35 and 5:19–20a with Matt. 11:27; John 5:23 with Matt. 10:40; John 12:47 with Luke 9:56; John 13:13–16 with Matt. 10:24–25 parr.; and John 16:2 with Matt. 24:9).

Furthermore, there are items of Jesus' self-presentation in the Gospel, including some of the most characteristically Johannine features, that can plausibly be said to have a historical base in the earliest memories of Jesus' ministry. The Father-Son imagery that dominates John is paralleled in the Synoptics; "Son of Man" remains a designation used only by Jesus; Jesus acknowledges the title "Messiah," but only in private and never overtly; arguments about Jesus' authority are raised in the Synoptic accounts. Even the Johannine "I am" statements ("I am the bread of life," 6:35; or "I am the light of the world," 8:12; 9:5) have some likeness to the "I" statements of the Synoptic Gospels insofar as they focus attention on Jesus and his role ("I have come to call not the righteous but sinners," Matt. 9:13/Luke 5:32; "If it is by the Spirit of God that I cast out demons, then the kingdom of God has come upon you," Matt. 12:28/Luke 11:20).

Some material found only in John has a parallel in the Synoptics, even though it is found in different settings. There is the charge of demon possession, made in the Synoptics with respect to his exorcisms (Mark 3:22) but in John with reference to his teaching (John 7:20; 8:48; 10:21). In both John and the Synoptics, Jesus consistently distances himself from his family (Mark 3:31–35; John 2:4), and they fail to understand him (Mark 3:21; John 7:5). The table fellowship with "sinners and tax collectors," so well known from the other Gospels, has no parallel in John, but there is extended discussion about whether Jesus is a sinner (John 9:16, 24–34), and Jesus pronounces forgiveness of sins (John 5:14). Jesus twice heals on the Sabbath (John 5; 9), which raises the question of his authority and relationship to God, even as do different Sabbath violations in the Synoptics. Mary and Martha (Luke 10:38–42) appear in a completely different story in John 11, here with their brother Lazarus, who is raised from the dead (cf. Luke 16:19–31). Implicit and explicit analogies are made to Jesus as shepherd (Luke 15:4–7; John 10:1–18).

Additionally, there are items only in John that are likely to be historical and ought to be given due weight. Jesus' first disciples may once have been followers of the Baptist (cf. John 1:35–42). There is no a priori reason to reject the report of Jesus and his disciples' conducting a ministry of baptism for a time (3:22–26). That Jesus regularly visited Jerusalem, rather than merely at the time of his death, is often accepted as more realistic for a pious, first-century Jewish male (and is hinted at in the other Gospels as well: Mark 11:2; Luke 13:34; 22:8–13, 53). Martin Hengel thinks it historically likely that Annas was the figure pulling the strings behind the scenes at Jesus' arrest and trial.[27] Even John's placement of the Last Supper before Passover has struck some as likely.

Finally, the degree of verisimilitude or realism that attends John's Gospel has also been noted.[28] Thus, for example, it is precisely the extended discourses and debates of John's Gospel, rather than the brief encounters of the Synoptics, that seem to represent more plausibly the kind of interaction and debate that Jesus had with his opponents.[29]

It is difficult to doubt, in the face of such data, that the Fourth Gospel depends on traditions which are in some respects quite similar to and even identical with those of the Synoptic Gospels. Therefore, it is worth asking why more scholars have not been persuaded to admit John as a reliable witness to the historical Jesus. Probably the main issue is that it is difficult to find elements of the distinctively Johannine portrait of Jesus in the other Gospels, and this deficit is difficult to explain if John intended to chronicle the events of Jesus' life. For example, it certainly gives one pause that none of the oft-quoted "I am" sayings with predicate ("I am the bread of life"; "I am the resurrection and the life"; "I am the way, the truth, and the life") can be found in the Synoptics. It is equally odd that no true parables are found in John, especially since the parables come from multiple sources (Mark, Q, L, M). Again, if the Father-Son relationship was as central to Jesus' teaching as it is in John, why have the Synoptic traditions boiled this theme down to one or two pithy but enigmatic sayings? In short, it has generally been judged easier to explain why and how John has shaped his material into its present form if the Synoptics reflect the themes of Jesus' preaching and teaching, than to account for the Synoptic rendering of Jesus' teachings if John's rendition is deemed more literal. Thus, the historical information indisputably to be found in John and the fact that John's theological reflections and unique material often have parallels and overlap in Synoptic tradition do not, taken together, serve to convince most scholars that the preference for the Synoptics as a source for information about Jesus' life and teaching ought to be put aside in favor of the Gospel of John. Yet the picture is more complicated than it first appears.

THE PORTRAIT OF JESUS IN THE GOSPEL OF JOHN

It is widely (although sometimes rather uncritically) accepted that John's portrait is more developed towards a "higher" Christology. But a curious feature of John is that there are a number of items that strike one as more "primitive" or perhaps less theologically exploited or useful than comparable details of tradition in the Synoptic Gospels. Eugene Lemcio, for example, argues that the Synoptic Gospels, particularly Mark, portray Jesus as acting more independently of God than does John.[30] Whereas in Mark the emphasis falls on the astonishing authority and independence by which Jesus acts, in John the accent falls on the dependence and obedience to God from whom Jesus derives his authority. Similarly, although the "amen" formula, which in Mark introduces authoritative pronouncements, is solemnly doubled in John, even so the Johannine "amen" sayings seem to point to Jesus as the bearer of the Father's authority, rather than to his own independence. Finally, the mutual love of Father and Son, a cornerstone of John's presentation of Jesus, contributes to the emphasis on Jesus' dependence on God. It is, of course, debatable whether the Johannine stress on the obedience and dependence of Jesus is more or less developed than the Markan emphasis on Jesus' independent action and authority. But in a Gospel that is often understood to stress the divinity and exalted status of its central figure, such an emphasis at least causes one to reconsider what precisely is the best way to formulate Jesus' status in John and to question whether every item in the Johannine presentation of Jesus is more highly "developed."

John's Christological Witness

A similarly and surprisingly undeveloped feature of the Gospel is its decided restraint in applying to Jesus the full range of christological titles and designations. In the prologue the Word of God is explicitly spoken of as preexistent and as God, attributes that Thomas echoes in the confession "My Lord and my God!" (20:28). But the explicit confession of Jesus as God happens first and only after the resurrection. None of Jesus' disciples is portrayed as making this confession during his lifetime, nor does Jesus himself ask for it or state it explicitly. This is striking, since several of John's narratives seem to begin with confessions that are deemed inadequate (e.g., prophet) and progress to more satisfactory designations of Jesus (e.g., Savior of the world; Son of Man).[31] But in these narratives no one arrives at the confession "You are God!"

Instead, the arguments about Jesus' identity still have to do with questions of Messiahship (4:25–26; 7:26–27, 31, 40–44; 10:24; 12:34) and other messianic roles of the first century (e.g., the Prophet; 4:19; 6:14–15; 7:40).[32] Indeed, the Johannine Jesus shows a certain reserve towards using and accepting the title "Messiah." Where there is recognition of Jesus as Messiah (John 4:25–26; cf. Mark 8:27–31), the scene is set in private, and Jesus himself is portrayed as reluctant to make explicitly royal claims. Certainly Peter's confession that Jesus is "the Holy One of God" (John 6:69) strikes one as decidedly less confessional than the acknowledgment found in the Synoptic accounts, "You are the Messiah." And even as the Synoptic Jesus deflects Caiaphas's question, "Are you the Messiah?" so the Johannine Jesus parries Pilate's query, "Are you the King of the Jews?" with a counterthrust: "Do you say this of your own accord?" (18:34). While John's avowed purpose is to elicit faith in Jesus as the Christ (20:30–31), oddly enough the "Johannine Christ" does not broadcast his messianic status any more than does the "Synoptic Jesus."[33]

The case is similar with the enigmatic designation, "Son of Man." As in the Synoptic Gospels, "Son of Man" remains a self-designation on the lips of Jesus.[34] In the catalog of titles adduced in the first chapter (Lamb of God; Son of God; Rabbi; Messiah; King of Israel), the disciples do not venture to call Jesus "Son of Man" (or "Word" or "God," for that matter). When the blind man of chapter 9 is asked, "Do you believe in the Son of Man?" he does confess his faith in him, but with the assertion "Lord [or, "Sir"], I believe." John apparently opts for the puzzling "Son of Man" as a vehicle for his interpretation of Jesus, in part because Jesus himself, and only Jesus, used the title, and so it becomes a central feature of his self-revelation. John has pressed the title into service particularly to speak of the Son of Man who must be "lifted up" (ascend) even as he has "come down from heaven" (descended). So, while John uses "Son of Man" with a different accent, he does prefer it to a designation foreign to the historical Jesus, such as "Logos."

John's reserve in applying to the earthly Jesus the full range of later christological titles indicates that there are limits beyond which he does not venture.[35] His theological creativity is not unbridled but shaped by that which comes to him in his traditions, in which the question of the messianic status of Jesus no doubt loomed large. It may well be that even John's preferred designation of Jesus simply as "Son" has not lost its messianic overtones. Nathanael's initial confession—

"Rabbi, you are the Son of God! You are the King of Israel!"—not only suggests the near equivalence of these terms with each other and with Messiah, but puts them in apparently ascending order, so that the climactic confession is that Jesus is "King of Israel."[36] Here there are similarities to Jesus' trial before Pilate, where the issue of Jesus' kingship is understood to be particularly a Jewish concern (18:33–39). Indeed, in the Johannine passion narrative the royal claim and status of Jesus dominate—even as the proclamation of the kingdom of God dominates in the Synoptics, and as the question "Are you the Messiah, the Son of God?" becomes central in their trial scenes before the high priest. Finally, the possible equivalence of "Son of God" and "Messiah" is also suggested by John's statement of express purpose in 20:30–31. The designation of Jesus as "Son" in John may well be a development of and reflection on the ideal of the Messiah as the chosen and anointed King, the righteous "Son" of God.[37]

The Account of Jesus' Death

As this survey of John's titles shows, at one and the same time John has some of the most primitive as well as the most developed elements of the Gospel tradition. The same may be said of John's portrayal of Jesus' death. One of the striking features of John's account is the way in which he presents Jesus as deliberately advancing towards his death with the full knowledge that it accomplished God's salvation of the world. In no other Gospel does Jesus speak so plainly of the result of his death: "If I be lifted up, I will draw all people to myself" (John 12:32). Indeed, the theme of the gathering together of God's people becomes a hallmark of John's interpretation of Jesus' death: The good shepherd lays down his life for the sheep so that there may be one shepherd and one flock (10:10–18); a seed remains alone unless it falls into the ground and dies, in which case it bears much fruit (12:23); and one must give his life for the nation, to gather the scattered children of God together (11:45–52). Such repeated statements develop at length the idea found only tersely in Mark, "The Son of Man came to give his life a ransom for many" (10:45). The authenticity of this saying has been disputed by those who think it smacks too much of later language of atonement. But Mark and John share the (somewhat undeveloped) idea that the death of the one serves to gather many, and in neither Gospel is this gathering linked specifically to the expiation or bearing of sin. Their similarity is all the more interesting in view of one currently popular conception of Jesus as the leader of an eschatological renewal movement in Judaism, whose purpose it was to gather the faithful to enjoy the blessings of God's kingdom.[38] John insists that Jesus ultimately thought that the promise that "many shall come from east and west and sit at table in the kingdom of God" (cf. Luke 13:29) would be brought to fulfillment only through his death.

Interestingly, one event that has figured prominently in recent reconstructions of Jesus' life is the "cleansing of the Temple," which is understood to trigger Jesus' arrest and so lead to his death.[39] This incident is reported in John, but at the outset rather than at the end of Jesus' public ministry. But despite its new placement, the link between it and Jesus' death is not lost. First, the threatened destruction of the Temple prefigures Jesus' death and resurrection, and perhaps even hints at the causal link between the prophetic act against the Temple and Jesus' own death. Furthermore, only in John does the quotation of Ps. 69:9 serve to interpret Jesus' act in the Temple: "Zeal for thy house will consume me." John has substituted a future tense ("will consume") for the past tense ("consumed").[40] By moving the Temple cleansing forward and introducing the altered quotation from the Psalms, John has assigned to that act the prominent role that it has assumed in some recent hypotheses about the events that may well have triggered Jesus' arrest.[41]

John's Gospel also provides a motivation for Jesus' crucifixion—namely, political expediency—that seems credible and is more accessible historically than recourse to the theory of Jewish "jealousy." The theory that the problem facing the Jewish leaders was not merely "religious" (that is, how to deal with an idiosyncratic and upstart prophet and teacher) but political (how to explain the popularity of Jesus to their Roman overlords) seems quite likely, given the history of abortive revolts and Roman intervention in the first century.[42] Even the placement of Roman soldiers at Jesus' arrest, while perhaps exaggerated in number, does not seem inherently impossible. In short, John makes clearer than any of the other Gospels what the Roman stake in Jesus' death was and on what charges the Romans might have been persuaded to eliminate him. In thus emphasizing the political implications of Jesus' ministry and the way in which he might have been perceived or portrayed as endangering the peace, John provides a historically credible reason for Jesus' death at the hand of the Romans.[43]

What is particularly striking is that all these elements of the Johannine account of Jesus' death are both characteristic of or even unique to John, and yet they seem to embody primitive tradition, or at least tradition that has not developed along lines that are familiar from elsewhere in the New Testament. In spite of passages such as John 1:29 ("Behold the Lamb of God who takes away the sin of the world!"), the Fourth Gospel does not interpret Jesus' death primarily as an atonement for sin, as is characteristic of the Pauline understanding of the cross. Even if we want to label John's interpretation as "developed" or "Christian" or "confessional," we must admit that the interpretation has run along its own trajectory. Such passages might provide for us a window into other, perhaps early traditions about Jesus, and so ultimately aid us in reconstructions of the historical Jesus as well.

INTERPRETATION IN THE GOSPEL OF JOHN

It is time to draw together the threads of our discussion. It seems difficult to dispute the view that John gives us a more thoroughgoing, theological reworking of traditional material. This does not mean that (unlike the Synoptics) John reworks and reflects on the material that has come to him in the tradition. Rather, his interpretation takes him more decidedly in a certain direction. The tradition is, as it were, funneled through a narrower spout. So the vocabulary becomes distinctively Johannine, and the themes on which Jesus discourses are fewer. Perhaps, then, John might better be termed more "paraphrastic" than the other Gospels. The idiom of the Johannine Jesus is not the idiom characteristic of the Synoptic Jesus. The Gospel of John is also less determined by certain prominent traditions of Jesus' ministry, such as the proclamation of the kingdom of God, the exorcism of demonic forces, the primarily Galilean setting of the ministry, and so on.

The issue is not so much whether John is *more* interpretive than the other Gospels. It is whether the trajectory of John's interpretation runs counter to, parallel with, or in direct continuity from the trajectories established by the Synoptic Gospels and their various sources. I would argue that the trajectories of John and the Synoptics run parallel to each other, but John's parallel trajectory is located on a different conceptual plane than that of the Synoptics. Just how widely separated those planes are is open to debate. But it is not the question of whether Jesus was a faithful or unfaithful servant of God, a true or false prophet, the Messiah or merely a pretender, that divides John and the Synoptics. Rather, the differences between John and the Synoptics reflect different approaches to the best way to express the reality and significance of Jesus' person for those who believe. John has chosen to shape the story of Jesus in a way quite different from that of the other Evangelists.

John shapes his material in several ways. First, certain traditional motifs, such as the occasional address to God as Father or Jesus' self-designation as "Son," have become central and thematic. Such motifs or ideas are elements from the historical tradition, which, we may say with some confidence, come from Jesus' own words or actions. They would provide the stuff of a good documentary. But the total effect is more like a docudrama, a creative and dramatic interpretation of the historical material.

Second, John highlights what he regards as the major issues between Jesus and his contemporaries. On the one hand, he leaves out quite a lot of material (parables; teaching about the kingdom of God; table fellowship; demon exorcisms) otherwise key to the Synpotic accounts. On the other hand, he reorients the remaining material. Thus, for example, in controversies triggered by Sabbath healings (chaps. 5 and 9) the propriety of Jesus' violation of Sabbath law becomes transmuted to a question of Jesus' relationship to God. Whereas in the other Gospels Jesus rebuts—with arguments from the scriptures and common practice—accusations that he has violated the Sabbath, in John it is Jesus' relationship to God that is invoked as the justification for his practice.[44]

Similarly, although the discussions about purity laws (foods, washing, table fellowship) and the great commandment are missing in John, questions about the proper interpretation of the law are quite important. But again, the issue is not what the law says about eating certain food, or passing judgments about which commandment ranks above the rest. Instead, the law is about Jesus. Moses, properly understood, points to Jesus and bears testimony to him (5:39). As A. E. Harvey puts it, given that Jesus was condemned to death by men fully competent in the Law of Moses, who was right: he or they?[45] The focus is intensely personal, and the Jesus of John's Gospel does not so much refute arguments about interpretation of the law as assert his own claims. John's interest is not so much in what the arguments were about, but in Jesus' own right and authority to speak and act as he did, because of his relationship to and mission from God. E. P. Sanders' characterization of the bottom line of Jesus' ministry aptly captures what is at stake especially and explicitly in the Gospel of John: "Exegesis indicates that there were *specific issues* at stake between Jesus and the Jewish hierarchy, and that the specific issues revolved around a *basic question:* who spoke for God?"[46]

A third feature of John's interpretation of the life of Jesus is his provision for a framework that shapes a revealing portrait of Jesus, in John's estimation. And the framework that he provides can be found in Jewish traditions about agency and wisdom.[47] The wisdom category, in particular, helps to account both for the "I am" sayings and for the "descent" of the Word of God, analogous to the descent of Wisdom to the world (cf. Sir. 24; Wisd. Sol. 7:22–30; 9:16–17). Wisdom was understood as a manifestation of God's own presence; with Jesus as God's Wisdom incarnate, John understood him as "God in his self-manifestation," since Wisdom itself is "the self-expression of God."[48] The traditions of agency, with the practical identity of the one who is sent with the sender, are foundational in portraying the unity of the Father and Son. Both the categories of "agency" and "wisdom" can plausibly be traced back to Jesus himself, and each plays a role in the Synoptic traditions.[49] Neither becomes central, however, in accounting for Jesus' person and mission as they do in the Gospel of John, nor is either pressed, as in John, to betoken the heavenly origin, divine status, and preexistence of God's chosen agent.

Is the presentation of Jesus as the incarnation of God's wisdom "historical"? A. T. Hanson, among others, comments that the Jesus of the Fourth Gospel "cannot possibly be a historical representation" since he is "a divine figure, the eternal Word appearing as a man."[50] Hanson's comment—"The only way of defending the historicity of the figure is to claim that a God-man is a unique phenomenon and therefore we have no criteria by which to judge whether it could have occurred as it did or not"—shows that the issue, for him, is verifiability by historical criteria. To be sure, on those grounds it will be impossible to label John's account as historical, for how could one "verify" that Jesus was, indeed, the Word of God incarnate? But John's placement of his account of Jesus' life within a cosmological framework does not therefore render that account "unhistorical," particularly when one can sort out traditional and historical items and distinguish the contributions of that framework to the overall portrait.

John means to tell the reader what, in his view, was really going on in what went on in the life of Jesus of Nazareth.[51] John's interpretation derives from reflection upon Jesus' action and words. Perhaps it is not, by modern measures, historical reporting, but much will depend on how one defines "historical." It is too simplistic to be left only with the options of historical or unhistorical. Instead, one must specify in what way the Gospel is (or is not) historical, and what definition is at work in such assessments. Not surprisingly, many judgments about historicity will turn out to be in the eye of the beholder. But the Gospel is a meaningful narration of historical events, clearly committed to the truth of the interpretative framework in which the events are placed. In the end, perhaps, the framework—the confession of Jesus as the incarnate Word and Wisdom of God, and thus God's uniquely commissioned and supreme agent—upstages the events within them. But without the events, the frame would collapse.

George Johnston speaks of John's portrait of Jesus as an icon. An icon is not a literal representation, but a stylized depiction, with some features highlighted to bring out the true spiritual significance of its subject.[52] In John's iconic representation of Jesus, the historical Jesus is the portrait, and the confessional level, the frame. To hang the bare frame on the wall would be ludicrous. No one displays an empty frame. On the other hand, no artist paints a portrait merely to complement a previously chosen frame. But in John's case, the subject and the frame seem to have been in view from the beginning in the production of the finished product. With one eye on the frame and one eye on his subject, the evangelist produced a portrait that has struck many as the most daring of the Gospel portraits. While many will continue to dispute whether John's is a "good" likeness, this dispute may finally be as futile and irresolvable as arguing that photography is superior to Impressionism.

NOTES

1. Although each of the Synoptic Gospels has its own emphases and unique material as well, there is such a degree of commonality in their portraits of Jesus that we may speak of them together as "the Synoptic witness to Jesus." Moreover, it is precisely their similarity of outlook that makes the contrast with the Gospel of John all the more striking.

2. Of course this observation is neither peculiar nor limited to opinions about the Gospel of John. In *The Quest of the Historical Jesus,* Albert Schweitzer wrote, "There is no historical task which so reveals a man's true self as the writing of a Life of Jesus" ([New York: Macmillan, 1910], 4). More recently, John Dominic Crossan writes, perhaps a bit cynically, "It is impossible to avoid the suspicion that historical Jesus research is a very safe place . . . to do autobiography and call it biography" (*The Historical Jesus: The Life of a Mediterranean Jewish Peasant* [San Francisco: HarperSanFrancisco, 1991], xxviii).

3. Professor Smith's writings have tackled, directly and indirectly, many of the issues that are raised by a consideration of the topic of this chapter. See the collection of essays in *Johannine Christianity: Essays on Its Setting, Sources, and Theology*

(Columbia, South Carolina: University of South Carolina Press, 1984); and idem, "Historical Issues and the Problem of John and the Synoptics," in *From Jesus to John: Essays on Jesus and New Testament Christology in Honour of Marinus de Jonge*, ed. Martinus C. de Boer, JSNTSup 84 (Sheffield: JSOT, 1994), 252–67. It is gratifying to offer this chapter to his *Festschrift* inasmuch as it addresses issues that have regularly occupied his mind and pen.

4. See particularly Smith's discussion in "The Presentation of Jesus in the Fourth Gospel," reprinted in *Johannine Christianity*, 175–89.

5. There are references in the Synoptics to life and eternal life, but the motif figures thematically in John as it does not in the other Gospels. See Marianne Meye Thompson, "Eternal Life in the Gospel of John," *Ex Auditu* 5 (1989): 35–55.

6. The *locus classicus* in the Synoptics is Matt. 11:27 par. Luke 10:22. Not surprisingly, this passage has been called "the bolt from the Johannine blue."

7. In Dominic Crossan's reconstruction of Jesus (in *The Historical Jesus*) as a wisdom teacher and purveyor of aphorisms and parables, there is not one reference in the scripture index to the Gospel of John. In *The Five Gospels*, the version of the Gospels produced by the Jesus Seminar with the likely authentic sayings of Jesus printed in red type, not one saying of Jesus in the Gospel of John is so designated (Robert W. Funk, Roy W. Hoover, and the Jesus Seminar, *The Five Gospels: The Search for the Authentic Words of Jesus: New Translation and Commentary* [New York and Toronto: Macmillan/Maxwell Macmillan Canada, 1993]).

8. It was particularly characteristic of proponents of the so-called "New Quest of the Historical Jesus" in the 1950s and 1960s to argue that while Jesus made few if any explicit messianic claims, there were implicit claims to authority in Jesus' proclamation of the kingdom of God and his interpretation of the law. Thus see the classic work by Günther Bornkamm, *Jesus of Nazareth* (New York: Harper & Row, 1960). Therefore a shadow falls over the historical character of the Gospel of John precisely because Jesus' proclamation in it is marked by overt claims about his status and person. This difference between John and the other Gospels continues to be identified as the heart of the problem in accepting the historicity of the Fourth Gospel, even when Jesus' claims are understood to be more offensive and explicit than previously allowed. See, for example, the comment of E. P. Sanders, who speaks of Jesus' "extraordinary self-claim" (*Jesus and Judaism* [Philadelphia: Fortress, 1985], 305).

9. A possible exception is the healing of the official's son at Capernaum, John 4:48–52; see Matt. 8:5–13 and Luke 7:1–10.

10. However, it is also true that Mark lacks the explicit link between the demon exorcisms and the arrival of the kingdom of God (Luke 11:20/Matt. 12:28), as well as the link to the fulfillment of Old Testament prophecy (Luke 7:22/Matt. 11:4–5). In both Mark and John the miracles focus attention on Jesus. But in Mark they call attention to Jesus' authority; in John, they call attention to Jesus' obedience to God. See Eugene Lemcio's discussion of this difference in "Father and Son in the Synoptics and John: A Canonical Reading," in Robert W. Wall and Eugene E. Lemcio, *The New Testament as Canon: A Reader in Canonical Criticism*, JSNTSup 76 (Sheffield: JSOT, 1992), 78–108.

11. In Mark 10:35–45 and Luke 22:27 there are traditions in which Jesus speaks of his service and love, holds these up as a model for his disciples, and locates the supreme example of such love in Jesus' own death.

12. John 6:51–58 speaks of the necessity of "eating the flesh" and "drinking the

blood of Jesus," language which certainly echoes the traditions of the institution of the Lord's Supper as found in Paul (1 Cor. 11:23–26) and the Synoptics (Matt. 26:26–29; Mark 14:22–25; Luke 22:17–20).

13. For the parallels between the eschatological discourse of Mark 13 and the farewell discourses of John, compare the following passages: Mark 13:9 and John 15:18–27; 16:2; Mark 13:10 and John 14:10–14; 15:1–8, 12–16; Mark 13:11 and John 14:15–26; Mark 13:12 and John 15:18–27; 16:1–2. John's account has surely elaborated themes of the eschatological discourse found in Mark and the other Gospels. But one wonders whether Anthony Tyrrell Hanson does not overstate the case when he suggests that in John 14—18 "we find ourselves very . . . far removed from the sort of teaching that could ever be plausibly attributed to the earthly Jesus" (*The Prophetic Gospel: A Study of John and the Old Testament* [Edinburgh: T. & T. Clark, 1991], 263).

14. For a discussion of the Johannine passion narrative, see particularly Donald Senior, *The Passion of Jesus in Gospel of John* (Collegeville: Liturgical Press, 1991), and Marianne Meye Thompson, *The Incarnate Word: Perspectives on Jesus in the Fourth Gospel* (Peabody, Mass.: Hendrickson, 1993), 105–15. For detailed analysis and commentary, consult Raymond E. Brown, *The Death of the Messiah: From Gethsemane to the Grave: A Commentary on the Passion Narratives* (2 vols.; New York: Doubleday, 1994).

15. There is a whole body of literature that deals with questions about the philosophy of history, treating such problems as the nature, method, and purpose of historical inquiry. It is my intention here not to engage this discussion, but only to show what definitions of "historical" have been operative in discussions of the historical Jesus and of the historicity of John. The nineteenth-century German historian, Leopold von Ranke, spoke of the aim of history as laying out "what actually happened" (*wie es eigentlich gewesen ist*), a statement that has subsequently come under attack for ignoring the inevitably subjective judgments of the historian in offering explanations of limited and incomplete historical data. (For a helpful discussion of von Ranke's view, see Colin Brown, *History and Faith: A Personal Exploration* [Grand Rapids: Zondervan, 1987], 52.) But in spite of objections, it has been a foundational, if not primary, goal of studies of the historical Jesus to describe "what actually happened," what Jesus actually said and did. Scholars have attempted not only to recount what Jesus said and did, but also to suggest what degree of certainty may be attached to a particular judgment. But the Fourth Gospel is not taken as reporting the words of Jesus as he first uttered them, and in this sense it is not an account of "what Jesus actually said." There are differing judgments on the degree to which some of the deeds of Jesus in John represent "what actually happened."

16. See, for example, Raymond E. Brown, "The Problem of Historicity in John," *New Testament Essays* (London and Dublin: Geoffrey Chapman, 1965), 143–67; A.J.B. Higgins, *The Historicity of the Fourth Gospel* (London: Lutterworth, 1960); A. M. Hunter, *According to John: The New Look at the Fourth Gospel* (London: SCM, 1968); John A. T. Robinson, "The New Look on the Fourth Gospel," *Twelve New Testament Studies*, SBT 34 (London: SCM, 1962), 94–106, and idem, *The Priority of John*, ed. J. F. Coakley (London: SCM Press, 1985); Smith, "Historical Issues and the Problem of John and the Synoptics" (see above, n. 3).

17. Especially noteworthy in this regard is the monograph by J.A.T. Robinson, *The Priority of John*. In *Jesus and His Story*, Ethelbert Stauffer argued that while the

Synoptics on the whole adhered most faithfully to the language of Jesus, the Fourth
Evangelist "clarified the chronology in the story of Jesus" ([New York: Alfred Knopf,
1959], 4). But Stauffer concludes that many of the accounts of John, including accounts of Jesus' speeches, represent "what actually happened." Swimming against the
tide, Stauffer even argued that the "I am" statements, modeled on the Old Testament
theophanic formula, represent what Jesus "actually said."

18. The commentary by Edwyn Clement Hoskyns stands out as perhaps the most
consistent attempt to wed history and theology: *The Fourth Gospel,* ed. Francis Noel
Davey (London: Faber & Faber, 1940).

19. According to Eusebius, *H.E.,* 6.14.7. Here Clement presupposes that the
Gospel was written by the apostle John, that it was the last of the four canonical
Gospels to be written, and that John was well aware of the existence of the other
Gospels and their contents. There is also an acknowledged difference in the tenor of
the accounts: the Synoptics reported the "outward facts," but John wrote τὰ πνευ-
ματικά, the "spiritual matters."

20. Hans Windisch offered four models to explain the relationship of John to the
Synoptic Gospels: the supplementation, interpretation, independence, and displacement theories. The views that John tended to interpret or to supplement the other
Gospels could be linked to the apostolic authorship of the Gospel: Either John offered
his own reflections on the meaning of Jesus' life, or he added additional information
that the other Evangelists had omitted for various reasons (*Johannes und die Synoptiker: Wollte der vierte Evangelist die älteren Evangelien ergänzen oder ersetzen?*
UNT 12 [Leipzig: J. C. Hinrichs'sche Buchhandlung, 1926]).

21. David Friedrich Strauss, *The Life of Jesus Critically Examined* (Philadelphia:
Fortress, 1972 [4th German ed., 1840]), is often credited with forcing the issue of the
unhistorical character of the Fourth Gospel. See Ben F. Meyer, *The Aims of Jesus*
(London: SCM, 1979), 35, 259 n. 39; John Ashton, *Understanding the Fourth Gospel*
(Oxford: Clarendon, 1991), 36–38.

22. An early comment on the implications of the Scrolls for the historical value
of John was offered by W. F. Albright, "Recent Discoveries in Palestine and the
Gospel of John," in *The Background of the New Testament and Its Eschatology: Studies in Honour of C. H. Dodd,* ed. W. D. Davies and David Daube (Cambridge: Cambridge University Press, 1956), 153–71. See also Raymond E. Brown, "The Qumran
Scrolls and the Johannine Gospel and Epistles," in *New Testament Essays,* 102–31;
and Leon Morris, "The Dead Sea Scrolls and St. John's Gospel," in *Studies in the
Fourth Gospel* (Grand Rapids: Eerdmans, 1969), 321–58, which includes an extensive bibliography.

23. This, of course, establishes only a possibility, and a possibility that could apply equally to the author of the Gospel as to Jesus himself.

24. Percival Gardner-Smith, *Saint John and the Synoptic Gospels* (Cambridge:
Cambridge University Press, 1938); C. H. Dodd, *Historical Tradition in the Fourth
Gospel* (Cambridge: Cambridge University Press, 1963). The history of scholarship
on this issue can be read in D. Moody Smith, *John among the Gospels: The Relationship in Twentieth-Century Research* (Minneapolis: Augsburg Fortress, 1992); for discussions therein of Gardner-Smith and Dodd, see 37–62.

25. The title of Dodd's book, *Historical Tradition in the Fourth Gospel,* already
intimates how John's independence could be pressed into the service of an argument
for its historicity. As Donald A. Carson comments, "The vast majority of the book is

given over to the minute defence of John's literary independence from the synoptic gospels" ("Historical Tradition in the Fourth Gospel: After Dodd, What?" in *Gospel Perspectives*, vol. 2: *Studies of History and Tradition in the Four Gospels*, ed. R. T. France and David Wenham [Sheffield: JSOT, 1981], 89). In other words, although Dodd proceeds by endeavoring to establish the literary independence of John from the other Gospels, the purpose in doing so is to suggest that there is indeed "historical tradition in the fourth gospel." But literary independence does not necessarily either imply or impugn the historical value of the Gospel of John.

26. See James D. G. Dunn, "John and the Oral Gospel Tradition," in *Jesus and the Oral Gospel Tradition*, ed. Henry Wansbrough, JSNTSup 64 (Sheffield: JSOT, 1991), 351–79.

27. Martin Hengel, *The Johannine Question* (London and Philadelphia: SCM/ Trinity Press International, 1989), 132.

28. When Hengel calls particular features "more realistic," he seems to mean "more likely historical" (thus *The Johannine Question*, 132). N. T. Wright suggests that protracted and rambling discourses of John (such as one finds in the sixth chapter) are more likely to represent the debates of Jesus with his opponents than are the highly condensed controversy stories of the Synoptic Gospels (*The New Testament and the People of God*, vol. 1: *Christian Origins and the Question of God* [Minneapolis: Fortress, 1992], 431). Smith, in "The Presentation of Jesus in the Fourth Gospel," speaks of John as having created a Gospel "in which Jesus as the representative of the world above visits and really lives in this world without depriving it of its verisimilitude" (*Johannine Christianity*, 187–88).

29. At first it seems the ultimate scholarly perversity to argue that, while the style of Jesus' discourses and debates in John's Gospel is more likely to reflect Jesus' own historical style, nevertheless the Synoptic sayings material has greater claims to historicity. But long discourses, such as Jesus taught in public in John, are not easily memorized and passed on to subsequent generations, whereas the forms of the material in the Synoptics are good examples of material that can more easily be memorized and transmitted, and square with what we know of ancient methods of teaching. See the articles by Dunn, "John and the Oral Gospel Tradition" (352–79) and Rainer Riesner, "Jesus as Preacher and Teacher" (185–210), both in *Jesus and the Oral Gospel Tradition* (above, n. 26).

30. See "Father and Son in the Synoptics and John," in Wall and Lemcio, *The New Testament as Canon* (above, n. 10).

31. See, for example, the progression of titles in chapter 4, from prophet (4:19), to Messiah (4:25), to Savior of the world (4:42); and in chapter 9, from prophet (9:17) to Son of man (9:35), to Lord (9:38).

32. John A. T. Robinson's contention that Messiah "is the category which controls [John's] Christology in the body of the Gospel," has much to commend it ("The Destination and Purpose of St. John's Gospel," in *New Testament Issues*, ed. Richard A. Batey [London: SCM, 1970], 198). See also Ashton, *Understanding the Fourth Gospel*, 104–6.

33. Here the ninth chapter of John is an interesting study, for the issues center on the question of whether Jesus is "a sinner" or "from God." The charge is not that some are confessing that Jesus is "divine," "equal to God," or "God," but that they acknowledge him as Messiah. This is presented as the heart of the problem, the confession that some are unwilling to make (9:22–23). As Ashton (*Understanding the*

Fourth Gospel, 180) asserts, "It is important to recognize that the distinctively Johannine (high) christology is absent from this debate."

34. Only in John 12:34 do others speak of the Son of Man, and there it is simply to query Jesus about who this mysterious figure might be.

35. John's restraint in this matter is particularly striking since, in the final analysis, he does not regard titles such as "prophet," "king," or even "Messiah" as in and of themselves fully sufficient designations of Jesus. They are not wrong, but neither are they fully adequate to express the reality of his being. See also Marinus de Jonge, "Jewish Expectations about the 'Messiah' in the Fourth Gospel," in idem, *Jesus, Stranger from Heaven and Son of God: Jesus Christ and the Christians in Johannine Perspective,* SBLMS 11 (Missoula, Mont.: Scholars Press, 1977), 83.

36. Robinson ("The Destination and Purpose of St. John's Gospel," 198) alleges that Son of God is epexegetic of "the Christ." He continues, "I believe there is no other New Testament document more important for studying the Jewish sources of the term 'Son of God' than the fourth Gospel."

37. The roots of the identification of the Messiah with the Son of God are found particularly in Nathan's oracle in 2 Sam. 7:10–14, and in the Psalms, esp. 2:7 and 89:26–27. 4QFlor 1:10–13 joins together 2 Sam. 7:10–14 and Psalms 1 and 2 in a running commentary on the promised Messiah. For arguments that "Son of God" can be construed as messianic language, see Richard N. Longenecker, *The Christology of Early Jewish Christianity* (London: SCM Press, 1970; reprinted, Grand Rapids: Baker, 1981), 93–99; C.F.D. Moule, *The Origin of Christology* (Cambridge and New York: Cambridge University Press, 1977), 22–31; Martin Hengel, *The Son of God: The Origin of Christology and the History of Jewish-Hellenistic Religion* (Philadelphia: Fortress, 1976); Donald Juel, *Messianic Exegesis: Christological Interpretation of the Old Testament in Early Christianity* (Philadelphia: Fortress, 1988), 59–88. For hesitation in reading the so-called "Son of God" text (4Q246) from Qumran messianically, see Joseph A. Fitzmyer, "The Contribution of Qumran Aramaic to the Study of the New Testament," in *A Wandering Aramean: Collected Aramaic Essays,* SBLMS 25 (Chico, Calif.: Scholars Press, 1979), 90–93; and Edward M. Cook, "4Q246," *Bulletin of Biblical Research* 5 (1995): 43–66.

38. So, particularly, in the works of E. P. Sanders, *Jesus and Judaism,* and Ben F. Meyer, *The Aims of Jesus.*

39. See Sanders, *Jesus and Judaism,* 61–76. For the argument that John's early dating of the cleansing is probably correct, see Robinson, *The Priority of John,* 127–31, 185–86.

40. The MT (69:10) has a perfect and the LXX (68:10) has an aorist for the verb that John's quotation renders with the future.

41. Raymond E. Brown notes, "John interprets the Psalm to mean that zeal for the Temple will destroy Jesus and bring his death. Thus . . . his account still preserves the memory that the action led to his death" (*The Gospel according to John (i–xii),* AB 29 [New York: Doubleday, 1966], 124). Similarly, Rudolf Schnackenburg writes, "According to the evangelist, the disciples grasp the dangerous consequences of Jesus' action: his zeal for the house of God 'will cost him his life'" (*The Gospel according to St. John,* vol. 1 [New York: Seabury, 1980], 347).

42. See, for example, the accounts in Josephus about various movements of revolt and resistance and the Roman response to them: on the treatment of terrorists and false prophets by Felix and Festus, see *J.W.* 2.253–65, 271; on Pilate's treatment of a

Samaritan messianic figure, see *Ant.* 18.85–87; on Fadus's dealings with Theudas, *Ant.* 20.97–99. Josephus claims that the majority of Jews were peace-loving, while some were misguided rebels who acted inappropriately, even though understandably provoked by incompetent or intolerant Roman governors. Roman intervention restored order and preserved the peace. In *J.W.* 2.234–37 "the magistrates of Jerusalem" try to prevent reprisals for the Samaritan murder of a Galilean. They implore their fellow Jews who had rushed to avenge the death "not to bring down the wrath of the Romans on Jerusalem, but to take pity on their country and sanctuary."

43. In a fictionalized but historically responsible account, Gerd Theissen suggests that the Romans had precisely such an interest in the various individuals and movement of first-century Palestine, not only in Jesus. Theissen also cleverly suggests that it was not just the Jewish leaders but the Romans themselves who shrewdly calculated that Jesus would be the "one" sacrificed for the "many" (*The Shadow of the Galilean: The Quest of the Historical Jesus in Narrative Form* [Philadelphia: Fortress, 1987]).

44. In this regard there are particular affinities between the discourse in John 5 and the Synoptic assertion that "the Son of Man is Lord even of the Sabbath" (Mark 2:28 and parr.).

45. A. E. Harvey, *Jesus on Trial: A Study in the Fourth Gospel* (Atlanta: John Knox, 1976), 14–15.

46. Sanders, *Jesus and Judaism,* 281.

47. For a discussion of agency and its applicability to the Gospel of John, see especially Peder Borgen, "God's Agent in the Fourth Gospel," in *Religions in Antiquity: Essays in Memory of Erwin Ramsdell Goodenough,* ed. Jacob Neusner, Studies in the History of Religions 14 (Leiden: Brill, 1968), 137–48, reprinted in *The Interpretation of John,* ed. John Ashton, IRT 9 (Philadelphia and London: Fortress/SPCK, 1986), 67–78; Jan-Adolf Bühner, *Der Gesandte und sein Weg im 4. Evangelium,* WUNT 2 (Tübingen: Mohr, 1977); A. E. Harvey, *Jesus and the Constraints of History* (Philadelphia: Westminster, 1982), 161–73, and idem, "Christ as Agent," in *The Glory of Christ in the New Testament: Studies in Christology in Memory of George Bradford Caird,* ed. L. D. Hurst and N. T. Wright (Oxford and New York: Clarendon/Oxford University Press, 1987), 239–50; Wayne A. Meeks, "The Divine Agent and His Counterfeit in Philo and the Fourth Gospel," in *Aspects of Religious Propaganda in Judaism and Early Christianity,* ed. Elisabeth Schüssler Fiorenza (Notre Dame, Ind.: University of Notre Dame Press, 1976), 43–67; James D. G. Dunn, "Let John Be John: A Gospel for Its Time," in *The Gospel and the Gospels,* ed. Peter Stuhlmacher (Grand Rapids: Eerdmans, 1991), 293–322. For a more general, historical discussion that includes treatment of themes of agency and wisdom, see Larry Hurtado, *One God, One Lord: Early Christian Devotion and Ancient Jewish Monotheism* (Philadelphia: Fortress, 1988).

48. See Dunn, "Let John Be John," 332–33, and idem, *Christology in the Making: A New Testament Inquiry into the Origins of the Doctrine of the Incarnation,* 2d ed. (London: SCM, 1989), 163–212, for a vigorous argument that wisdom is to be considered as a way of speaking of God's own activity, rather than of the activity of another heavenly being. See also Hurtado, *One God, One Lord,* 42–50, and Martin Scott, *Sophia and the Johannine Jesus,* JSNTSup 71 (Sheffield: JSOT, 1992).

49. On tracing wisdom back to Jesus, see now Craig A. Evans, *Word and Glory: On the Exegetical and Theological Background of John's Prologue,* JSNTSup 89 (Sheffield: JSOT, 1993), 195–98.

50. Hanson, *The Prophetic Gospel,* 269.

51. Or, as John Ashton puts it, John's point is that "what Jesus is to the faith of the true Christian believer, he was in the flesh" (Ashton, *Understanding the Fourth Gospel,* 42). C. K. Barrett suggests that John sought to "draw out the true meaning of the life and death of one whom he believed to be the Son of God" (*The Gospel according to St. John: An Introduction with Commentary and Notes on the Greek Text,* 2d ed. [Philadelphia: Westminster, 1975], 54). Contrast Hanson, who asserts, "John is not just bringing out into the open what was always implicit. He is creating his own christology" (*The Prophetic Gospel,* 259). Hanson continues, "How did John convince himself that he was justified in putting forward a christology that he knew was more exalted than that of the early tradition?" Hanson's own answer is that, as a Christian prophet, John wrote his Gospel under the conviction that it was his duty to expound the scriptures in such a way as to show their fulfillment in Jesus (ibid., 324). However, we might well ask Hanson (1) whether John would have thought of his Christology as "more exalted" than that of the early tradition, and (2) whether he would have had to "convince himself" that putting forward such a portrait was justified.

52. "*Ecce Homo!* Irony in the Christology of the Fourth Evangelist," in *The Glory of Christ in the New Testament,* 125–38 (see above, n. 47).

W. D. Davies

3

Reflections on Aspects
of the Jewish Background
of the Gospel of John

At the time when Rudolf Bultmann was finding connections between the Fourth Gospel and Gnosticism, C. H. Dodd also turned both to Hellenistic sources, especially the *Hermetica,* and to Jewish sources, publishing his great work *The Interpretation of the Fourth Gospel* in 1953.[1] This volume can be regarded as the full flowering of the emphasis on Hellenism in New Testament study. In this sense it marks the end of an era. But *The Interpretation of the Fourth Gospel* also shows "the encroachment of the Semitic on New Testament scholarship — an encroachment that has grown ever stronger — so that it also reflects new beginnings. [Dodd's writings] are a mirror of the transition which has marked our time from a predominantly Hellenistic to a more Semitic approach to the New Testament. In him one world was already dying and another struggling to be born."[2] I now connect this transition with a young B.D. student who, in meticulous, scrupulous and comprehensive contributions, was to share in that transition — the honoree of this volume, who was among the members of my earliest classes at Duke University in the 1950s and later became for many years my colleague there. Only my personal connection with him has induced me, very temerariously, to contribute to this volume of Johannine studies in his honor. In doing so, I conjoin him with his lifelong helpmeet.

The subject assigned to me is the Jewish background of the Fourth Gospel. To be dealt with at all adequately, this theme needs to be divided into three sections. There is, first, the world of Jewish belief and practice, which formed part of the general background — that is, the cultural and religious hinterland of the author of the Fourth Gospel (henceforth called John): the inherited furniture of John's mind, the unexpressed religious and other assumptions that governed him consciously and unconsciously, the "Common Judaism" described by E. P. Sanders. Secondly, there is the immediate foreground of John's mind — the specific conditions and developments within Judaism at the time when he wrote, which we conveniently call the period of "Jamnian Judaism." This has proved to be particularly important for the understanding of the Fourth Gospel. We are justified in making this clear distinction between background and foreground because, with most scholars, we assume that John's Gospel was written around the end of the first century—the time of Jamnian Judaism—by a Jew who had become a Christian.

There is also a third aspect to the theme, that which can be called John's immediate inner "domestic" or "intimate" foreground, that is, the conditions that he faced within his own community of Jewish (and possibly other) Christians. Some of these were fully committed to Jesus and his followers and prepared to establish an existence separate from the main body of Jews and Judaism; others were not prepared to take such a step. Only scholars immersed in Johannine studies can deal adequately with this aspect; we do not feel competent to do so. Our treatment, therefore, cannot but be more generalized than this third aspect demands,[3] and must be confined to the first two backgrounds noted above. We must crave the reader's indulgence. We recognize that there is necessarily much interpenetration among background and foreground and John's domestic world. The reader will also be aware that this very brief treatment is necessarily reductionist; for example, we do not touch upon possible Samaritan influences upon John.

THE JEWISH BACKGROUND

When I first read John's Gospel, I discovered to my amazement that its Greek, which at first encounter seemed the easiest in the whole of the New Testament, was the most difficult to translate. The vocabulary of John is simple, but there is always a strange twist in the structure of his sentences, especially in his use of relative clauses, which makes translation difficult. I soon realized that this is because the Greek of John was more influenced by Semitic (Aramaic) usage than that of any other New Testament documents. C. F. Burney,[4] like C. C. Torrey, went so far as to claim that the Gospel of John was first written in Aramaic and that, as we now have it, it is a translation. Few have been convinced of this, but it is evident that John thought as a Jew. The Greek he wrote was influenced by a Hebraic-Aramaic idiom and connotation.

In the recent reaction against the overemphasis on the Hellenistic in favor of the Semitic in New Testament studies, it is easy to underestimate and, indeed, overlook the deep interpenetration of the Hellenistic and Semitic worlds to which we referred above. Jean Daniélou[5] used the term "Jewish-Christian" of those Christians who expressed their thought in terms borrowed from Judaism. In this sense, as in others recognized by Daniélou, John was a Jewish Christian. This is why the studies of Adolf Schlatter, C. H. Dodd, David Hill, George Caird, and of the contributors to Kittel's famous *Wörterbuch*—to name only a few—still illumine the vocabulary of John; they were all very sensitive to this phenomenon. To understand John it is necessary to listen to him with two pairs of ears, as it were. As every bilingual person knows, bilingualism easily deceives. And John's bilingualism does so in favor of finding either a Hellenistic or a Hebraic-Aramaic connotation (or perhaps both) in his very same words. This was what led C. H. Dodd to find the

Hermetica so ubiquitously present in John, while M. Philonenko saw Essenism in so many documents. But there can be no doubt, in the light of studies since Dodd, that by far the dominant element in the tradition John inherited was the Judaism of his people: This formed the ultimate background on which he drew.[6]

To describe this background in detail is impossible here. The first century in the history of Judaism was one of transition. By that time, Persian, Greek, and Roman influences had left their mark on Judaism to make it varied, complex, and fluid. The recognition of this has been reinforced by two developments in the scholarship of this century. First, in the past a rigid distinction was drawn between Judaism in Palestine, uncontaminated to any considerable degree by Gentile influences, and the Judaism that developed outside Palestine, which had assimilated much from the Greco-Roman culture within which it grew. A greater appreciation has now developed regarding the extent to which Judaism had been for a long period—certainly since the time of Alexander the Great—subject to Hellenistic influences. Archaeologists have revealed in the synagogues of Palestine a considerable Greek influence; Rabbis have been discovered to have tasted Greek culture, and it has been claimed that even their exegetical methods are adaptations of Greek traditions. In the realm of ideas on immortality, anthropology, and, possibly, time, and in the sphere of the institutional life of the synagogue, Greek influences and terminology are traceable. Nor must the regular intercourse between the diaspora Jews and Palestine—and especially Jerusalem—be forgotten. This meant that Palestinian Judaism was not closed to diaspora ideas and habits. On the other hand, despite the greater ease with which Greco-Roman forces could impinge upon the Judaism of the Diaspora, the real contacts that the latter maintained with Judaism at its cultural and religious center in Palestine, the maintenance of the annual half-shekel tax for the support of the Jews, and the visits from the emissaries sent from Jerusalem to the Diaspora—all these meant that Judaism everywhere preserved an unmistakable unity that found expression in the ubiquitous synagogue, which was both a sign and cause of this unity. Thus, Philo of Alexandria agreed in crucial matters with the Rabbis of Palestine, and it is strikingly significant that the Jews of the Diaspora were prepared to substitute Aquila's rough Greek translation of the Old Testament for the Septuagint, partly in order to retain a text more in accord with rabbinic exegesis. Thus, the division of first-century Judaism into distinct Palestinian and Hellenistic compartments has broken down.[7]

But there is a second development not unconnected with this. Since 1947, we have been in possession of the manuscripts called the Dead Sea Scrolls. While there is still no unanimity about their place and date of origin (and thus we must use them very cautiously), most scholars have regarded them as pre-Christian and emanating from a sect possibly akin to that of the Essenes, whose faith was an extreme form of Pharisaism. While the Dead Sea Scrolls are not as revolutionary as was at first claimed, they have reinforced what we have just written: There were Greek books discovered in the "library" of the legalistic community that was centered at

Qumran (though the presence of Greek books does not necessarily mean their acceptance). The Dead Sea Scrolls also support the recent tendency to emphasize that the Judaism of the first century was far less monolithic—and more complex and changing—than previous scholars had supposed. Like the language of the time, which the scrolls have revealed to be in process of development, so too the religion.

Can we find a common element or conjoined common elements shared by all forms of Judaism of the period? With caution we can disentangle these elements but with the caveat that, taken in isolation, they are at best abstractions. Any common element was very variously clothed upon by the several groups that constituted first-century Judaism. But there were certain basic assumptions that we can discern: belief in the one God, the one people of his choice, the one Land,[8] the one law that connected the people, The Land and God, and obedience to whose law governed the future; and a hope for the future in that Land, an eschatological hope. These assumptions constituted much of the substance of the Jewish tradition that John inherited, but they were not distinct or consciously separated. They were, rather, a cluster of assumptions, mutually interacting. Each in its turn, at different periods, could become prominent or suffer eclipse as compared with the others. Conjoined, they were the furniture of John's mind. They are here separately listed only for academic convenience: none of them was an "island." The relative importance of each of these elements has been much discussed: Was there a hierarchy of "values" in Judaism? For our immediate purpose, we emphasize again that the elements we noted separately are all integrally interrelated.[9] E. P. Sanders's definition of this Judaism as "covenantal nomism" has been widely accepted.[10] Apart from other important studies,[11] readers can now fortunately turn to Sanders's truly magisterial work[12] to give substance to the assumptions we have noted and to the activities and the hopes—messianic and other—that they engendered. In this essay we only list these fundamentals of the content of John's Jewish background, because his immediate foreground calls for more pointed attention. We can only reiterate here that John did not encounter Jesus and his movement with a *tabula rasa* but with a mind enriched by the wealth of the Jewish religious tradition. Professor Smith has himself sought to indicate how fully aware John was of that tradition.[13]

THE JEWISH FOREGROUND

What, then, of the immediate Jewish foreground of John? We have pointed to the theological complexity of that Judaism, although we did not dwell on the fissiparous, divisive sectarianism that this complexity had spawned. Apart from the Pharisees, there were the Sadducees, the Essenes, the members of the Qumran community, "apocalyptists" of various types, the Zealots, Sicarii, the Fourth Philosophy, the Samaritans, Therapeutae, Christians, and there was also diaspora

Judaism. But the events that culminated in the fall of Jerusalem in 70 C.E. and those that ensued therefrom were of crucial significance in the history of Judaism. Some have claimed that they transformed it.[14] After 70 C.E. under the initial leadership of Johannan ben Zakkai, the Pharisees became the dominant (though not the sole) surviving group, and it was they who were to lay the foundations for the more concentrated and homogeneous rabbinic Judaism of later times. Our sources do not allow us to trace and date developments with strict exactitude, but the essential characteristics, activity, and achievement of "Jamnia" are clear. We strongly emphasize that the term "Jamnia" is here used not for that location, nor for any precise definite date of any "council," but for the whole complex process of transformation to which we have referred.[15]

This process was symbolized in the character and work of R. Johannan ben Zakkai, who first gathered at Jamnia the scholars who survived the revolt of 66–70 C.E. against Rome. Owing to the paucity and confusion of our sources, there can be no complete biography of this key figure, but three forces seem to have molded him. First, under the influence of his teacher, the great and gentle Hillel, he became—in a positive, almost aggressive way—a man of peace. He opposed the policy of armed revolt against Rome from the beginning. When war finally came, his experience of it merely confirmed Johannan in his pacifism. At the appropriate moment, he decided to leave the doomed city to found a school in Jamnia, where Judaism could preserve its continuity. His attitude to the war had set Johannan over against the apocalyptic-zealot visionaries and sectarians who had plunged his people into destruction. Although it is important to note that he did not abandon apocalyptic hopes, not fiery zeal but patient attention to the immediate task of obedience to the law was always Johannan's aim. It continued to be such after 70 C.E., when he sought to lead his people away from fiery, futuristic fantasies to the actualities of the present. Thus, the study and application of the Torah, with a view to defining the task next to be done, was his policy.

Secondly, the earthly, rabbinic sobriety of R. Johannan had been probably reinforced by his early experience in Galilee, which was prone to the charismatic and the apocalyptic. Reaction against an unrealistic, uninformed enthusiasm that he encountered in Galilee[16] had increased Johannan's reverence for the learning of the schools. But there remains a third factor in his development. The relationship between Pharisaism and the priesthood in first-century Judaism can be easily misunderstood: it was one of both acceptance and rejection. On the one hand, the sacrificial system and the priesthood were ordained in the law and, therefore, were to be honored. But on the other hand, there was much in the priesthood that Pharisees could not but condemn and that created friction between the priests and the Pharisees, who were essentially purists. This was aggravated because Pharisees sometimes presumed to instruct the priesthood in their interpretation of the law. It is not surprising, therefore, that a predominantly lay Pharisaism found itself opposed to the priesthood in fact, although it accepted it in principle. Johannan ben

Zakkai shared in this opposition. Over against charisma, apocalyptic vision and priesthood, he set the Torah and the Sages; alongside, if not over against, the Temple, he set the House of Study. He carried these emphases with him to Jamnia.

Thus, both nurture and experience had determined that the leader of Judaism after 70 C.E. should be a man of the law and the synagogue and of peace, of the present duty rather than the future hope, of "study" more than "sacrifice." It was he who placed his stamp on the deliberations of the Sages after 70 C.E. as they faced the problems of reconstruction. By the time that Johannan was followed as leader by Gamaliel II, the foundations had been gradually and truly laid for the ultimate triumph of Pharisaic Judaism, and they were reinforced by the latter.

Two inextricable dangers confronted the Pharisaic leaders after 70 C.E., namely, disintegration within Judaism itself and the contemporaneous, insidious attraction of forces from without—paganism in general and especially Christianity and Gnosticism in some form or other. Under these circumstances a policy of consolidation and exclusion was the only sane one, and in the light of what we have written above, it was to be expected that this was the policy that their rabbinic sobriety dictated to both Johannan and Gamaliel. Opposing extreme apocalyptic fervor, priestly pretensions and unrealistic quietism or romanticism, they faced the present with the realism of the law to be applied: under their leadership the Torah became central.

As always, the process of consolidation also demanded certain "pruning." In the first place, serious rivals to the dominant Pharisaic elements within Jewry itself had to be eliminated. The Zealots had been largely "liquidated" by the war; so too the Essenes were decimated, and, although Essenism did not die in 70 C.E., it was not subsequently aggressive enough to constitute a menace. It was, however, necessary to deal with the Sadducees. The Sages saw to it that Sadduceanism was discredited; they made a "dogma" of the resurrection from the dead, belief in which was denied by the Sadduccees, who thus automatically became heretics (see *m. Sanh.* 10:1). The Sages, whom we assume to have been (at the least) predominantly Pharisiaic, also asserted their authority over the calendar. They gradually transferred to the synagogue a part of the ritual of the Temple in such a way that the dignity of the congregations outside the Temple was to be honored—any pretensions to priestly superiority over the congregation were denied. Legislation was passed also concerning gifts and offerings normally due to the Temple, so as to assert the authority of the Sages over that of the priests.

The Pharisees forged further links beween the actual worship of the synagogue and the defunct Temple. Whenever possible, they aimed at concentrating in the synagogue forms that were previously associated with the Temple, so that these forms would continue to evoke memories of the latter. The Temple had always been a symbol of the unity of Jewry, and thus the synagogue could constantly serve after 70 C.E. to preserve that unifying significance. Thus the Pharisees made changes in the use of the *lulav* ("palm branch") in the Feast of Tabernacles and introduced the priestly blessing from the Temple into the liturgy of the synagogue. Rabban Gamaliel II revised the Passover Haggadah to include references to the Passover sacrifice at Jerusalem and prayers for the restoration of that city and its sacrificial system. In the same spirit, the Sages standardized and unified the details of the synagogue's traditional service of worship. The same concern for unity led to a concentration on the problem of the canon, and in the same period, to the institution of the Rabbinate, which legitimized the Pharisaic leaders as the guarantors of the tradition against the excesses of sectarians and charismatics.

In the second place, the Pharisaic Sages also sought to do away with dissension among themselves, especially between the Houses of Hillel and Shammai. The Mishnah reveals the efforts of the Pharisees to minimize the differences between these two Houses. They feared that those differences, which occasioned deep personal bitterness, might lead to the creation of "two laws," a conception that would have insinuated a divided loyalty, a disastrous disunity at the very heart of Judaism. Apart from this, the interpretation of the law in the first century had been in a chaotic state, and for the sake of unity the Pharisees saw the need to codify it. The developments that culminated in the codification of the Mishnah of Rabbi Judah the Patriarch, about 220 C.E., had their insistent beginnings in the period of Jamnia; codification and modification of the legal tradition was in the Jamnian air. This was part of the Pharisaic response to the need for unity and for adaptation to changed conditions.

In the third place, the Sages were also called upon to preserve Judaism from enemies without, in addition to consolidating Judaism internally. Consolidation was inseparable from exclusion. Here, we are particularly concerned with the fear of the subversive influence of Christianity, which may have influenced the Sages. Some scholars have sought to minimize, if not to deny, any such fear on the ground that Judaism was so engrossed in its internal problems that it overlooked or deliberately ignored the incipient menace of Christianity. Others have contrasted the active opposition to the latter, which Judaism offered in the second century, with its comparative unconcern about it in the first. Thus, for example, although Christians had already in the first century interpreted the fall of the Temple as a punishment on Jewry for their rejection of Christ, it is only in the second that the Rabbis reveal a polemical interest in that event. But, while it is true that bitterness increased as the second century came, there was conflict before this, and there are unmistakable signs that the Sages were not uninfluenced by the rising significance of Christianity.

Interest in the canon was at least in part a reaction to Christianity. It is clear that the dispute as to whether the scriptures "rendered the hands unclean," that is, were to be treated as "holy," went back to the period before the war, as appears from Mishnah *Yadayim* 4:6. But the attempts at fixing a canon have been claimed to reflect the need to counteract certain influences: the heresy of the Sadducees, the futuristic fantasies of apocalyptists, the speculative aberrations of Gnosticism, and—from the Pharisaic point of view—the equally dangerous, quietistic illusions of Christianity. As Christianity produced a literature, Judaism had to look more guardedly to its own. In Mishnah *Sanhedrin* 10:1 the "external books"—the prohibition of which occurs in a context dealing with heresy—have been interpreted as "heretical," particularly early Christian writings.[17] But Ginzberg[18] urged that "external" here did not mean "heretical," but merely noncanonical, and that the prohibition applied not to private but to public reading. It is exceedingly unlikely that Jewish synagogues would have been in danger of reading Christian writings in public, so the prohibition can hardly have applied to them. Similarly, the predominant view that "the books of the *minim* [heretics]," in such passages as Tosepta *Shabbat* 13.5 and the Babylonian Talmud *Gittin* 45b, can be regarded as Christian has been challenged. The pith of the argument for the customary view— that the reference is to Christian writings—is twofold. First, the term *minim* can include Jewish Christians, and second, in the Babylonian Talmud *Shabbat* 116a, apparently an early passage, there is a specific reference to the Gospels in the phrase גליון עון ("blasphemous marginalia"), and in Tosepta *Yadayim* 2.13 and Tosepta *Shabbat* 13.5 the term גליונים again suggests the Gospels. But Kuhn's arguments[19] are convincing that the books of the *minim* refer to scriptural (that is, Old Testament) texts, written and used by heterodox Jewish groups such as that at Qumran. While the term *minim* included Jewish Christians, it only later came to denote groups outside Jews, and especially Gentile Christians. Moreover, גליונים refers quite simply to the margins of Torah-scrolls, while עון גליון cannot be a transliteration of εὐαγγέλιον ("good news"), which has a plural in α: גליונים can hardly have been formed out of εὐαγγέλια. Moreover, Babylonian Talmud *Shabbat* 116a is too late, despite its mention of early authorities, to be used for the Jamnian period. The outcome of Kuhn's work is to make us more cautious in connecting the fixation of the canon at Jamnia directly with the Christian Gospels and writings, despite the impressive list of scholars who have urged this.

Nevertheless, Kuhn's understanding of the *minim* as including Jewish Christians leaves the door open for the view that the fixation of the canon at Jamnia was not unrelated to the awareness of a growing Christianity, as was the later codification of the Mishnah to the growing authority of the New Testament. The changes in liturgy and religious practice introduced by the Sages in the Jamnian period make this clear. While the deliberate attention paid to these matters was largely stimulated by the need for liturgical and other unity within Judaism, it also revealed anti-Christian concern. One significant liturgical development was the reformulation of the chief prayer of the synagogue, called the *Tefillah* or *Amidah,* so that it came to constitute Eighteen Benedictions. A petition, the Twelfth Benediction (the *Birkath ha-Minim*)—either against heretics, including Jewish Christians, or against heretics and specifically Jewish Christians—was introduced into the *Tefillah.* The exact date we cannot ascertain, but it was probably between 85 and 90 C.E. This *Birkath ha-Minim* makes it clear that the Sages regarded Jewish

Christians as a menace sufficiently serious to warrant a liturgical innovation. It worked simply, but effectively, as follows. In the synagogue service a man was designated to lead in the reciting of the *Tefillah*. As he approached the platform where the ark containing the scrolls of the law stood, the congregation rose. The leader would recite the Benedictions and the congregation responded to these with an "Amen." Anyone called upon to recite the *Tefillah* who stumbled on the Twelfth Benediction could easily be detected. Thus, the *Birkath ha-Minim* served the purpose of making any Christian—or other "heretic" who might be present in a synagogal service—conspicuous by the way he recited or glossed over this Benediction.

Largely similar in its intent to isolate Jewish Christians was the use of the ban at Jamnia. This again involved the assumption that the *Beth Din* ("house of judgment," or court of law) in that place had taken to itself the status of the Sanhedrin, because it meant the reintroduction of a usage that had been controlled by that body before the war. There can be no doubt that Rabbi Eliezer, one of the most important figures at Jamnia after the withdrawal of Rabbi Johannan ben Zakkai, had either before or after his banishment been in such communication with Christians that their tradition was known to him. And it is also clear that the reason for the frequent use of the ban by Rabban Gamaliel was his fear of dissentients, including Jewish Christians, against whom the *Birkath ha-Minim* was aimed. In this connection, it cannot be sufficiently emphasized that the Sages were frequently in contact with Jewish Christians.[20] Justin Martyr's *Dialogue with Trypho* 16.4 refers almost certainly to the *Birkath ha-Minim,* although the reference in 138.1 cannot simply be to the *Birkath ha-Minim,* which was not strictly a law; we have no other evidence for such a law. However, the main point is clear: By the end of the first century the synagogue had adopted an attitude of isolation from and opposition to Jewish Christians in the interests of its own integrity. It did this, possibly if not probably, by the significant liturgical change of the use of the *Birkath ha-Minim,* by the use of the ban, and, possibly, by a legal enactment whose precise date and character are lost to us.[21]

In view of the data given above, it is arguable that when John was writing, the Judaism that any Jewish Christian faced was very dynamic. It was vigorously adjusting to the new conditions prevailing among Jewry after 70 C.E. It was not only a reacting Judaism, but one actively engaged in proselytizing and presenting its case against the encroachments of the Christian and other movements. The view that after 70 C.E. Judaism ceased to be missionary cannot be substantiated; it continued to be such until the fifth century.[22] John had to come to terms with a militant Judaism. The recognition of this "foreground" illuminates much in his Gospel. Are there pointers to this vigorous Jamnian Judaism in that document? We note the following four possibilities.

First, it appears from a simple glance at the demography of his Gospel that it was the Pharisaic Sages with whom John had to deal. Most of first-century Judaism had been marked by a multiplicity of sects, but gradually after 70 C.E. it was the Pharisees who best survived and, in time, became dominant. The multiplicity of the sects referred to in the Synoptic Gospels reflects the situation existing when the sources on which they drew and those Gospels themselves were written. The same is true of John; he too reflects his own historical situation. Whereas in the earlier first century there existed Pharisees, Sadducees, the scribes, Essenes, the sectarians at Qumran, Zealots, Sicarii, the members of the Fourth Philosophy, Samaritans, Therapeutae—many of whom (scribes, Sadducees, Pharisees, Herodians, Zealots) are mentioned in the Synoptics—in the Gospel of John most of these groups do not appear. They no longer existed, having been largely eliminated in the revolt against Rome, 66–70 C.E. In John's Gospel "the Jews" are usually directly equated with Pharisees. The foreground of John, then, would seem to be that of Pharisaic Jamnia.[23]

Second, in a study of the Sermon on the Mount we suggested that the Gospel of Matthew was, among other things, a response to Jamnian Judaism. That John also points to Jamnian activity was suggested by J. L. Martyn in his important study, *History and Theology in the Fourth Gospel*. He had earlier urged that the Twelfth Benediction, the *Birkath ha-Minim* of the *Tefillah* (Eighteen Benedictions), was reformulated in order to make it easier to detect Jewish Christians and other sectarians, whom the Sages wanted to exclude from the synagogue service. The version of the *Tefillah* found in the Cairo Genizah is as follows: "For apostates let there be no hope. And let the arrogant government be speedily uprooted in our days. Let the Nazareans [= Christians] the *minim* [heretics] be destroyed in a moment." The Cairo Genizah text contained only the word *minim* (heretics), but possibly Samuel the Small (80–90 C.E.) revised this older form by the addition of the word *notzrim* (Nazareans), in order to include Jewish Christians. The passage in John 9:22 (see also 12:42), Martyn urged, is to be understood in the light of the *Birkath ha-Minim*—the Twelfth Benediction. Not all have been convinced, as Martyn has recognized.[24] However, whether or not the exact form of the Twelfth Benediction was changed by the addition of "the Nazareans" in order to explicitly include "Christians" among the *minim*, it still seems to us historically probable that the Sages at Jamnia were aware of the "menace" of the Christian movement and that among the *minim* whom they sought to exclude from the synagogue were Jewish Christians who were attending those synagogues.

Assuming, then, that John at the very least was caught up in events that ultimately led to the formulation of the *Birkath ha-Minim*—even though the exact date of its formulation eludes us—can we detect other data in his Gospel that confirm his engagement with Jamnian Judaism? We can only very cursorily suggest a few pertinent aspects of the Fourth Gospel here.

Third, it has been claimed that John, in presenting the "signs" that Jesus gave through miraculous events, drew upon a special source. R. T. Fortna[25] and Martyn[26] have taken this source to have been a kind of text used in the synagogue for missionary preaching aimed at Jews—"that [they] may believe that Jesus is the

Christ, the Son of God, and that believing [they] may have life in his name" (John 20:31). However, it seems clear that the use of miracles in the original source on which John drew, if such existed, was altogether simpler than the use ascribed to them by John. The "signs" of John are not simply miraculous wonders; they are pointers to a truth beyond themselves. John makes a miracle a sign, a point of departure for a dialogue or discourse in which he sets forth a truth of the gospel. For example, in 6:1–58, the feeding of the five thousand is expounded in terms of the manna given to the people of Israel in the wilderness: Not through Moses, but in Jesus comes the eternal life, the living bread. In 11:1–53 the sign, the raising of Lazarus from the dead, is followed by the discussion of the resurrection of the dead. There are indications that John is aware of the dangers of concentrating on the merely miraculous. In 4:48, for example, in response to an officer who pleaded with him to cure his son, Jesus asks, "Will none of you ever believe without seeing signs and wonders?" Nevertheless, unlike the Synoptic writers (see Mark 8:11–12), John regards the signs as legitimate pathways to belief (2:11, 23), although they do not always achieve their aim (12:37). In 1:51 the implication is that greater signs than the one concerning Nathanael can appropriately be anticipated. We cannot enter into the intricacies of the discussion concerning the signs-source in recent scholarship here. It is pertinent that John drew upon and elaborated a written or oral tradition of miracles to provide evidence that Jesus was the expected Messiah of Judaism.

If John did elaborate and reinterpret a previously existing signs-source, written to convince Jews by interpreting the miracles, is it possible that he was aware of the rejection of "simple" miracles by the Sages? While retaining his miracles as signs, did he partly at least lend them a new, more sophisticated signification in order to undercut the Rabbis' objection to miracles? In short, does the elaboration of signs by John suggest that he has one ear open to the Sages, who, in order to counteract the Christian use of miracles to establish the claims of Jesus, rejected the validity of the miraculous? Exaggeration is easy at this point. The Rabbis may have rejected miracles because they were so commonplace as to be insignificant. But, though caution is in order, there can be little doubt that the use of miracles to legitimize Jesus as the Messiah, such as we find in John, engaged the Sages. A. Guttmann long ago made this clear.[27] The rejection of miracles and of the *bath qôl* ("daughter of a voice" = heavenly voice) by the Sages was almost certainly a reaction against their use by early Christians. The matter, however, is complex. Is it possible that John, in using the reinterpreted miracles of a possibly early, more simple "Book of Signs," was reacting at least partially to the criticisms of the Jamnian Sages, or was it that the Jamnian Sages were reacting to John and the Christian evidential use of miracles? In either case Jamnian Judaism and Johannine Christianity were mutually reacting. The full scope of their mutual reaction we cannot trace within the limits of this chapter. Here we can only note that John seems anxious to avoid specific reference to a *bath qôl* in his dealing with the

baptism of Jesus in 1:29–34, and that in 12:27–33 (see esp. vv. 30–31) his treatment of the voice out of heaven implies caution. Is he aware of the Jamnian criticism of the *bath qôl?*

Fourth, we make only one further suggestion by way of an illustration of this
possible, mutual reaction. It concerns the attitude of John to the geographic or territorial dimension of Judaism as the Jamnian Sages—like other Jews in other
ages—so emphatically embraced it. In *The Gospel and the Land: Early Christian
and Jewish Territorial Doctrine,*[28] we provided evidence that John was markedly
concerned with "holy space." The Hebrew scriptures, the Midrash, the Midrashim,
the Talmud, the liturgies that Jews have constantly celebrated and the observances
they have kept across the centuries all point to the Land of Promise, *Eretz Israel,*
"The Land," as uniquely related to the Deity, as established in Jewish tradition. A
recent study by B. Halperin-Amaru, *Rewriting the Bible: Land and Covenant in
Post-biblical Jewish Literature,*[29] gives further evidence from *Jubilees,* the *Testament of Moses,* and the works of Philo and Josephus that in their concern for the
Land of Promise, the authors of these documents, who were roughly contemporary with John, rewrote and reinterpreted the biblical sources in Genesis dealing
with the covenant and containing the references to the Promised Land. Those documents reveal how their authors were each influenced by their several historial
settings and by their contemporary interests, and how under the impact of those
settings and interests, they all reinterpreted differently the tradition they had received. The complexity and difficulty of the understanding of "The Land" in the
postexilic period we had already indicated in *The Gospel and the Land,* and
Halpern-Amaru's work has greatly increased our awareness of that complexity. It
is now clear that the question of The Land was as living a concern in the "in-
tertestamental" period as it came to be in the rabbinic period.

However, it has been suggested that after 70 C.E. many Jews were tempted to
leave The Land to escape its onerous, devastated conditions, and the Sages at Jamnia were especially concerned about opposing emigration. Thus, they initiated a
deliberate policy of extolling the virtues of The Land. The need to encourage Jews
to remain in it became urgent. The emigration of Jews to neighboring countries,
especially to Syria, threatened to depopulate The Land. For example, Rabbi Eliezer
the Great (Ben Hyrcanus, 80–120 C.E.), in order to protect Palestinian agriculture,
wanted to subject Syrian agriculture to all the requirements of tithing and of the
sabbatical year, so as to make it less attractive for Jewish farmers to emigrate to
Syria. Rabbi Gamaliel II (80–120 C.E.) shared in the same purpose, though in a less
extreme manner (see *m. Ḥal.* 4:7–8). As we have elsewhere urged, the economic
was not the only source of the glorification of The Land,[30] but the other causes for
the extolling of The Land do not directly concern us here. Suffice it to note that
many factors after 70 C.E. conjoined to enhance that glorification.

In two ways at least, we connect both the concentration on the centrality of the
law as the "portable land" of Jews in rabbinic Judaism and the simultaneous em-

phasis on The Land as the only sphere for the truly full life of Jews—their *bene esse*—with emphases in John's Gospel.

We previously referred to the exploitation by John of a possible signs-source, oral or written, to reinforce the centrality of Jesus. There were other ways in which he made clear that Jesus' Person had replaced the Torah as "the ultimate" for Jews, as for all people. From the prologue on, the christological emphasis in his Gospel is unmistakable. That emphasis was strictly "personal." But the personal bears in itself "the universal": the personal in itself challenges any form of particularism, such as that centered in the Torah and in The Land. The Jamnian Sages would find John's christological emphases a menace. Is it merely accidental that while John is careful to make Moses—as the mediator of the Torah—subordinate to Jesus as the Christ (John 1:17, etc.), *Pirqe 'Abot,* in the very first verse, makes it emphatically clear that it was through Moses that the Torah came? The first word of the *'Abot* is "Moses" ("Moses received the Law from Sinai"), just as the first verse of John points to the Logos as incarnate in Christ.

At the same time, the elevation of holy places in Judaism and of The Land by the Sages, we suggest, might have reinforced John's marked concentration on the person of Christ. Although unlike Paul he does not so freely engage in proof from scripture, and although we cannot directly pinpoint his dismissal of the Pharisaic emphasis on The Land, implicit in his christological emphasis is such a dismissal. The force of this dismissal must be measured against the background of that living engagement with The Land to which we pointed in our work and which Halpern-Amaru has further documented.

Moreover, one aspect of the doctrine of The Land is, possibly, directly countered by John. The gift of the Holy Spirit, which plays a notable part in John's Gospel, was, like the gift of prophecy and of the resurrection of the dead, connected by some Sages with The Land (*Mek. Pisḥa* 1 on Ex. 12:1–13:16). We have elsewhere tried to show how the experience of the Holy Spirit was tied to The Land and occurred, according to some, only in The Land.[31] Is it possible that in his interpretation of the Holy Spirit, John is reacting to the territorial limitation of the Spirit, which was exercised by Jamnian Pharisaism? Was his pneumatology, like his Christology, at least partly sharpened by his reaction against Jamnian influences—that is, the concentration of the Sages on the Torah and The Land? The words in 3:8 ("The wind [spirit] blows where it wills; you hear the sound of it but you do not know where it comes from, or where it is going. So is everyone who is born from spirit" [NEB]) were spoken in response to "one of the Pharisees named Nicodemus, a member of the Jewish Council" (3:1). They take on added significance when set over against the territorial boundary set to the activity of the Spirit by Pharisaism; for John that activity embraces the whole of creation and yet can dwell "in the humble heart."[32] Similarly, in the prologue at 1:11, if the term τὰ ἴδια ("his own") includes The Land, as some commentators suggest, is not its thrust sharpened in the light of the Pharisaic emphasis on the significance of The Land?

That Land had rejected the Lord of Glory. So too the theme of the replacement of holy places in John, which is unmistakable, gains force when set against the Pharisaic emphasis.[33] The poignancy of that emphasis itself must, in turn, be understood in the light of the fall of Jerusalem and the devastation of The Land in the revolt against Rome. To point to Jesus the Christ as the replacement of the fallen Temple and of the sacred holy places (like Bethel), as John does at a time when the war against Rome had deprived Jews of their Land and Temple and had desecrated their holy places so that their loss was constantly and painfully present, was to touch a most raw nerve. John lived in a postwar world, when traditional geographic and other loyalites had been violated. His theme of "replacement" was, therefore, peculiarly sensitive and challenging and could not but provoke resentment. Nor must it be overlooked that John wrote when the failure of Jewish Christians to join in the revolt against Rome had made them a source of contempt and hatred for their Jewish kinsfolk. Jewish Christians were "quislings," supplying comfort to the enemy. As Dale Allison and I have pointed out in our commentary on Matthew,[34] the emphasis on love of the enemy and on reconciliation in that Gospel, in the Sermon on the Mount and elsewhere, is partly due to its author's reaction to the atrocities of the revolt. We suggest that, likewise, John's emphasis on the gift of peace—not as "the world giveth"—in his Gospel finds its sharpest outlines when set over against the horror of that revolt. Oddly enough, both the Sages and John, opposed as they were, enjoined on their followers the same theme: the importance of unity, reconciliation, and peace. They were both children of a war-torn world, and the horror of strife had been burnt into their bones, as it had into Matthew's.

The reaction of Jewry to John's Christian challenge—its replacement of Torah and The Land by the Person of Christ—could have been nothing but sharp and bitter. Is it this that at least partly explains the antagonism towards Jews in John that has led to the charge that he was "anti-Semitic"? To examine the use of the phrase οἱ Ἰουδαῖοι, "the Jews," in John is not possible here. The view of Lowe[35] that the term means "Judaeans," the view of von Wahlde that it signifies a handful of highly placed officials,[36] and the view of Bultmann that they are an "archetypal symbol of the sinfulness of humankind,"[37] have all been examined by Ashton and found not altogether satisfactory.[38] Given the pointers that I have tried to indicate (implicit rather than unambiguously explicit though they be), does not the antagonism of Jamnian Pharisaism to the growing Christian movement provide at least in part the reason for John's pejorative use of "The Jews"? Limitations of space do not allow us to do justice to this complex question, but we can suggest that the Jamnian/Christian context needs further consideration because it constituted the foreground of John.

So far we have emphasized the Pharisaic foreground of John. John Ashton, in his very important study *Understanding the Fourth Gospel,*[39] has reminded us of the apocalyptic world to which John belonged, and since the days of Johannes Weiss and Albert Schweitzer, the eschatological (apocalyptic)[40] dimension of early Christianity—including that of John—has been fully recognized. But while Ashton's emphasis is a healthy corrective to any diminution of the apocalyptic elements in John, the dichotomy between the apocalyptic and the Pharisaic or rabbinic cannot be pressed, as it once was.[41] The Pharisees of Jamnia, despite their suspicion of "extremism" among early Christians and others, could themselves embrace the apocalyptic. Akiba found Bar-Kokhba to be the Messiah: Sage and Seer could and did coexist in the same person. Judaism was not rigidly compartmentalized between the Pharisaic and apocalyptic. John was familiar with both worlds. It was not messianism as such that the Sages objected to, but the Christian variety of it. Moreover, the Pharisees and the Christians were alike in that they were both often leery of the excesses of the apocalyptic. The eschatology of early Christianity, it might be argued, was reductionist, as was that of the Pharisees.[42] By reductionist we mean that it was not as elaborate and complex as much found in the apocalyptic sources. Moreover, the concentration of eschatology in the Person of Christ in John, to which C. H. Dodd pointed us in his emphasis on the "realized eschatology" of the Fourth Gospel, naturally led to reductionism in the sense indicated.[43] It could be claimed that in John eschatology or apocalyptic in large part has been engulfed by Christology.

Here, Gershom Scholem's understanding of the development of any radical messianic movement (such as early Christianity in its relationship to Judaism) illumines the place of John as he encountered Jamnian Judaism. It is important to recognize the stage at which John penned his Gospel in the development of Christianity in its relationship to Judaism. The Gospel created a crisis of tradition within Jewish messianism. This messianism, in which conceptions of an ideal world, of the restoration of the Davidic kingdom, of the centrality of The Land and of Jerusalem were combined with those of the Day of the Lord and the last judgment, was a recognized aspect of Jewish revelation and tradition. Belief in a future redemption had become domesticated within the tradition of Judaism with little discomfort to that tradition. Hopes for a redemption either by the restoration of Israel and the world to a primordial or primeval condition, that is, in a restorative sense, or by the advent of a kind of utopia that represents "the conception of redemption as a phenomenon in which something emerges which has never before existed, in which something totally new is unmistakably expressed," could coexist. Scholem continues:

> Of course, those restorative and utopian elements in the Messianic idea could exist side by side *as long as it was simply a hope that was projected into the distant future, an affirmation of faith that corresponded to no real experience.* As long as the Messianic hope remained abstract, not yet concretized in people's experience or demanding a concrete decision, it was possible for it to embody even what was contradictory without the latent contradiction being felt. . . . Messianism could take

over even a conservative attitude and in this way become part of the tradition. Messianic *activity,* however, could hardly do this. The moment
that Messianism moved from the realm of affirmation of faith, abstract
doctrine, and synthesizing imagination into life and took on acute forms,
it had to reach a point where the energies that lay dormant in these two
elements would emerge into conflict with each other—the conflict of the
tradition of the past version versus the presence of redemption.[44]

For Paul the conflict to which Scholem refers had not yet been resolved; it was
still brewing. It was not clear in Paul's day whether Christian "messianism" would
demand an utterly radical break with the tradition of Judaism. It could be taken as
an interpretation of the Jewish tradition, and rooted in the Jewish scriptures. This
could be the reason for Paul's constant engagement with the law. Christian messianism had initiated the crisis, but Paul had not fully resolved it. John, on the
other hand, assumes that the true meaning of the Jewish tradition—of the law—
was to be found in its witness to Jesus the Messiah. But he still engaged in the interpretation of the law in a midrashic fashion, and Martyn may be going too far in
claiming that "John employs a form of midrashic discussion in order to terminate
all midrashic discussion."[45] The temptation is to think of John as having been a
development beyond Paul. But it may be wiser to think of the differences between
Paul and John as different responses to Judaism at different points in the conflict
between early Christianity and its mother faith. Again, it was not simply that John,
a Jewish Christian, was concerned with Jews and Jewish Christians only and had
to be concerned with them, whereas Paul was the apostle to the Gentiles and,
therefore, had to focus on the law that separated Jews and Gentiles; nor simply
that the Sages, like John himself, had come to see more clearly and unambiguously than Paul that there would have to come a parting of the ways and were, at
the least, engaged in that process that eventually would lead to the *Birkath ha-
Minim.* The center of the Sages' concentration had shifted to the claims of Jesus
of Nazareth, which, now that so many Gentiles had so obviously embraced Jesus,
were taken with a new seriousness by the Sages. The Christian movement was no
longer merely speculative but had acute, tangible consequences. Until the success
of the Gentile mission—a visible fact, not merely a speculation—had emerged,
the Sages could have regarded early Christianity as a passing phenomenon. But
the church's missionary activity had changed the situation. In their response to it,
they could no longer minimize the seriousness of the Christian challenge. It was
at this particular juncture, when the Sages had come to realize more fully the importance of the Christian movement as a critical challenge, that John wrote, and
in this light are his christological and other emphases, to which we previously referred, to be understood.

The prologue of John's Gospel reveals these emphases: the counter-Pharisaic,
the christological, and the de-territorializing. For John, Christ has become the

Word, the Light, the Life—attributes that the Sages applied to the Torah, the Wisdom of God. But in a very illuminating essay, R. A. Culpepper urged that the center or pivot of the prologue is not primarily in its Christology, but in 1:12b: "And he gave them authority to become the children of God." Not even "the incarnation nor the witness of the community that 'we have behold his glory' would have enduring meaning were it not for the result of the confession of the incarnation. He gave [us] authority to become children of God." Culpepper continues, "by claiming the designation 'the children of God' the Johannine community was identifying itself (or perhaps more broadly all Christianity) as the heir to a role and standing which Israel had abdicated by her failure to receive the Son of God. This was a subject of considerable dispute between the Johannine school and 'the Jews'."[46] Again, along with Torah, The Land, and the Messiah as basic elements in Judaism, we named the People of Israel.[47] Recently Arthur Hertzberg has claimed that "The essence of Judaism is the affirmation that the Jews are the chosen people; all else is commentary."[48] Exaggerated though this may be, it was true of first-century Judaism that there was for the Sages a "privacy" in the relation of Jews to the divine that is difficult to deny. It was a challenge to this privacy that the success of the Pauline mission had raised, and which John resolved in 1:12b by redefining the term "children of God" to include among God's chosen people whosoever "believed" in Jesus.

In sum, John engaged all the essential elements in the Judaism of his day, to which we have pointed, and challenged them in the name of Christ. Unfortunately, though understandably, the challenge led to bitterness towards Christians among Jews and towards Jews among Christians. It was this bitterness that constituted the context that engendered that vivid, foreboding sense of crisis, inescapable in John to which C. H. Dodd pointed.[49] The yearning of Paul for the acceptance of Jesus by his own people (Rom. 9—11)[50] and the anxious ambiguity of Matthew about the relationship between his church and the Jewish people[51] have given way, in the Fourth Evangelist, to a more radical opposition and judgment—although John can still assert that "salvation is of the Jews" and does not include all Jews, including himself, among "The Jews."[52]

NOTES

1. Cambridge: Cambridge University Press, 1953.
2. W. D. Davies, "*In Memoriam:* Charles Harold Dodd, 1884–1973," *NTS* 20 (1973–74): i–v.
3. Raymond E. Brown, *The Community of the Beloved Disciple* (New York: Paulist, 1979), and J. Louis Martyn, *History and Theology of the Fourth Gospel,* rev. ed. (Nashville: Abingdon, 1979), are particularly important here. For a summary statement, see R. Alan Culpepper's excellent study, "The Gospel of John and the Jews," in *RevExp* 84 (1987): 273–88, esp. 281–82.

4. C. F. Burney, *The Aramaic Origin of the Fourth Gospel* (Oxford: Clarendon, 1926); so also C. C. Torrey, *The Four Gospels: A New Translation* (New York and London: Harper, 1933), and idem, *Our Translated Gospels: Some of the Evidence* (New York and London: Harper & Brothers, 1936).

5. Jean Daniélou, *The Theology of Jewish Christianity*, ed. J. A. Baker, History of Early Christian Doctrine before the Council of Nicea 1 (London: Darton, Longman & Todd, 1964), 9.

6. Dodd's treatment of the words of the Gospel of John is, for the reasons indicated, still extremely important. An example of the interpenetration to which we refer was offered by Martin Buber in a memorable seminar at Princeton University. He took the Greek words in John 3:8, πνεῦμα πνεῖ ("wind [or 'spirit'] blows") to be a direct reference to the spirit of God being "on the face [פני] of the waters" in Genesis 1:3: the πνεῖ of John, as Buber argued, being a transliteration into Greek of the Hebrew פני. Readers may find this improbable, but only a Hebrew scholar such as Buber could "hear" the text in this dual way. We all can now so hear it, but only after he had pointed this out.

7. For bibliographical details, see the introduction in W. D. Davies, *Paul and Rabbinic Judaism*, 4th ed. (Philadelphia: Fortress, 1980), v–xii. Martin Hengel's great work has abundantly confirmed and established the point of this paragraph.

8. Here and throughout, following rabbinic custom, we refer to the land of Israel as "The Land."

9. On all this, see W. D. Davies, "Reflections on the Nature of Judaism," *RHPR* 75 (1995): 85–111.

10. See his *Paul and Palestinian Judaism: A Comparison of Patterns of Religion* (Philadelphia: Fortress, 1977). We hesitate quite fully to endorse "covenantal nomism," because it perhaps needs to recognize, more clearly and sufficiently, the "territorial dimension"—the place of "The Land." Sanders' definition runs as follows (ibid., 422): "The 'pattern' or 'structure' of covenantal nomism is this: (1) God has chosen Israel and (2) given the law. The law implies both (3) God's promise to maintain the election and (4) the requirement to obey. (5) God rewards obedience and punishes transgression. (6) The law provides for means of atonement, and atonement results in (7) maintenance or re-establishment of the covenantal relationship. (8) All those who are maintained in the covenant by obedience, atonement, and God's mercy belong to the group which will be saved. An important interpretation of the first and last points is that election and ultimately salvation are considered to be by God's mercy rather than human achievement."

11. The works of Jacob Neusner have been especially important. See also the English translation of Emil Schürer, *A History of the Jewish People in the Time of Jesus Christ*, 2d ed., rev. (Edinburgh: T. & T. Clark, 1897–98; rev. and ed. G. Vermes, F. Millar, P. Vermes, and M. Black, 1973–87); *The Cambridge History of Judaism*, ed. W. D. Davies and Louis Finkelstein (Cambridge and New York: Cambridge University Press), vol. 1 (1984), vol. 2 (1989), vol. 3 (forthcoming); the brief treatment by Lawrence H. Schiffman, *From Text to Tradition: A History of Second Temple and Rabbinic Judaism* (Hoboken, N.J.: Ktav, 1991); and studies by Lee I. A. Levine ("The Age of Hellenism: Alexander the Great and the Rise and Fall of the Hasmonean Kingdom") and Shaye J. D. Cohen ("Roman Domination: The Jewish Revolt and the Destruction of the Second Temple") in *Ancient Israel: A Short History from Abraham to the Roman Destruction of the Temple*, ed. Hershel Shanks (Washington, D.C.: Bibli-

cal Archaeological Society, 1988), 177–204 and 205–35, respectively. The developments after 70 C.E., outlined above, have been questioned: the "myth" of Jamnia has been dismissed as having no historical grounds. The case against it has been brilliantly stated by Philip S. Alexander in the chapter, "'The Parting of the Ways' from the Perspective of Rabbinic Judaism," in *Jews and Christians: The Parting of the Ways A.D. 70 to 135*, ed. James D. G. Dunn, The Second Durham-Tübingen Research Symposium on Earliest Christianity and Judaism (Tübingen: Mohr [Siebeck], 1992), 1–26. However, we emphasize (see below, n. 15) that for convenience we use the term "Jamnia" of the process that eventually led to the fully developed later rabbinic Judaism. That process was gradual and not completed until the third century. It produced discussion and activity such as is adumbrated in John's Gospel: doubtless there were initial, preparatory expressions of this process, which John encountered and reflects. But scholars, accustomed to the leisurely discussions of "ideas" rather than to the more immediately demanding need for action in situations of social crisis, perhaps tend to underestimate the degree to which the kind of crisis that faced Jewry after 70 C.E. demanded immediate response, and that gradualism in such a situation can be overemphasized. See "Retrospect," in W. D. Davies and D. C. Allison, *A Critical and Exegetical Commentary on the Gospel according to St. Matthew*, vol. 3, ICC (Edinburgh: T. & T. Clark, forthcoming), and the balanced statements by Douglas R. A. Hare, *The Theme of the Persecution of Christians in the Gospel according to St. Matthew*, SNTSMS 6 (Cambridge: Cambridge University Press, 1967), 48–56, esp. 54–56. D. M. Smith refers to "the initial certainty that Johannine Christians felt threatened by expulsion from the Synagogue (9:22; 12:42; 16:2)" ("Representation of Judaism in the Gospel of John," forthcoming). We concur.

12. E. P. Sanders, *Judaism: Practice and Belief, 63 B.C.E.–66 C.E.* (London and Philadelphia: SCM/Trinity Press International, 1992).

13. Smith, "Representation of Judaism in the Gospel of John."

14. See especially Jacob Neusner, "The Formation of Rabbinic Judaism," *ANRW* 11.19.2 (1979): 3–42, and *The Cambridge History of Judaism*, ed. Davies and Finkelstein, vol. 3; also Shaye J. D. Cohen, "Yavneh Revisited: Pharisees, Rabbis, and the End of Jewish Sectarianism," in *Society of Biblical Literature 1982 Seminar Papers*, ed. K. H. Richards (Chico, Calif.: Scholars Press, 1982), 45–61, and Cohen, "The Significance of Yavneh: Pharisees, Rabbis, and the End of Jewish Sectarianism," *HUCA* 55 (1984): 27–53.

15. Failure to recognize that we use the term "Jamnian" for the whole "process" of the emergence of rabbinic Judaism, strictly so-called, has led to criticism of our position, which is beside the point. Similarly, the use of the term "council" for the deliberations among the Sages after 70 C.E. has been clouded by unconscious parallels drawn between what went on after 70 C.E. among the Sages and the more formalized and structured "councils" of later Christianity. There was no "Council of Jamnia." See Davies and Allison, "Retrospect," in *The Gospel according to Saint Matthew*, vol. 3 (forthcoming). The complexity of the transition period from 70–135 C.E. is summarized by N. T. Wright, *The New Testament and the People of God*, vol. 1: *Christian Origins and the Question of God* (Minneapolis: Fortress, 1992), 161–66 ("Judaism Reconstructed (A.D. 70–135)"). Wright's view that "early Christianity, claiming the high ground of Israel's heritage, was first and foremost a movement that defined itself in opposition to paganism and only secondarily in opposition to mainline Judaism itself" (165) needs more consideration than space allows here. Is it acceptable?

16. For the relationship between Galilean and Judaean Judaism, see Martin Goodman, in *The Cambridge History of Judaism*, vol. 3 (forthcoming); and Francis Xavier Malinowski, "Galilean Judaism and the Writings of Flavius Josephus" (Ph.D. dissertation, Duke University, 1973).

17. Mishnah *Sanhedrin* 10:1 reads as follows, in Danby's translation: "All Israelites have a share in the world to come, for it is written, *'Thy people also shall all be righteous, they shall inherit the land for ever, the branch of my planting, the work of my hands that I may be glorified'* [Isa. 60:12]. And these are they that have no share in the world to come: he that says there is no resurrection of the dead prescribed in the Law [some texts omit these last four words], and he [that says] that the Law is not from Heaven, and an Epicurean [one opposed to the rabbinical teachings]. R. Akiba says: Also he that reads the heretical books [literally, "external books," which Danby understands as "books excluded from the canon of Hebrew Scriptures"]."

18. Louis Ginzberg, "Some Observations on the Attitude of the Synagogue towards the Apocalyptic-Eschatological Writings," *JBL* 41 (1922): 115–36.

19. K. G. Kuhn, "Giljonim und sifre minim," in *Judentum, Urchristentum, Kirche: Festschrift für Joachim Jeremias*, ed. Walther Eltester, BZNW 26 (Berlin: Töpelmann, 1960), 24–61.

20. See W. D. Davies, *The Setting of the Sermon on the Mount* (Cambridge: Cambridge University Press, 1964), 276–78.

21. Whether we trace a concern to combat Christianity elsewhere in the liturgy is discussed in *The Setting of the Sermon on the Mount*, 279–82, where the Jamnian emphasis on the *Shema'* in the life of Jewry and in the synagogal service, on the *Tefillah* (phylactery), and on the *Mezuzah* (doorpost scroll) is noted as possibly having had a polemic anti-Christian intent, as had the withdrawal of the Decalogue, the *Mezuzah*, and the *Tefillah* from the synagogue service. On the *Birkath ha-Minim* see William Horbury, "The Benediction of the *Minim* and Early Jewish-Christian Controversy," *JTS* 33 (1982): 19–61; Steven T. Katz, "Issues in the Separation of Judaism and Christianity after 70 C.E.: A Reconstruction," *JBL* 103 (1984): 43–76; Reuven Kimelman, "*Birkath Ha-Minim* and the Lack of Evidence for an Anti-Jewish Prayer in Late Antiquity," in *Jewish and Christian Self-Definition*, vol. 2: *Aspects of Judaism in the Greco-Roman Period*, ed. E. P. Sanders with A. I. Baumgarten and Alan Mendelsohn (Philadelphia: Fortress, 1981), 226–44, 391–403.

22. The view that after 70 C.E. Judaism from necessity became isolationist was contested by Marcel Simon, *Verus Israel: A Study of Relations between Christians and Jews in the Roman Empire (135–425)*, Littman Library of Jewish Civilization (New York: Oxford University Press, 1985), esp. 272, and recently by L. H. Feldman, "Proselytism by Jews in the Third, Fourth, and Fifth Centuries," *JSJ* 24 (1993): 1–58. See also Robert L. Wilken, *John Chrysostom and the Jews: Rhetoric and Reality* (London and Berkeley: University of California Press, 1985).

23. See Shaye J. D. Cohen, *From the Maccabees to the Mishnah*, Library of Early Christianity (Philadelphia: Westminster, 1987), 224; and idem, "The Significance of Yavneh."

24. Martyn, *History and Theology in the Fourth Gospel* (rev. ed., passim). See also D. M. Smith, "Judaism and the Gospel of John," in *Jews and Christians: Exploring the Past, Present and Future*, ed. J. H. Charlesworth with F. X. Blisard and J. S. Siker (New York: Crossroad, 1990), 76–96, esp. 85–88.

25. Robert Tomson Fortna, *The Gospel of Signs: A Reconstruction of the Narrative Source Underlying the Fourth Gospel,* SNTSMS 11 (London: Cambridge University Press, 1970).

26. See Martyn, *History and Theology in the Fourth Gospel.*

27. See Alexander Guttmann, "The Significance of Miracles for Talmudic Judaism," *HUCA* 20 (1947), 363–406; see also Davies, *Paul and Rabbinic Judaism,* 374–75.

28. Berkeley: University of California Press, 1974, 234–88; rpt., Sheffield: JSOT, 1994.

29. Valley Forge, Pa.: Trinity Press International, 1994.

30. Davies, *The Gospel and the Land,* 56–60.

31. Idem, "Reflections on the Spirit in the Mekilta: A Suggestion," in *Jewish and Pauline Studies* (Philadelphia and New York: Fortress/S.P.C.K., 1984), 72–83.

32 See Buber's connection in n. 6, above.

33. On this see Davies, *The Gospel and the Land.* The following commentators note that τὰ ἴδια in John 1:11 may refer to the land of Israel: B. F. Westcott, Theodor Zahn, G.H.C. Macgregor, J. H. Bernard, Raymond E. Brown, and Rudolf Schnackenburg.

34. Davies and Allison, *The Gospel according to St. Matthew,* vol. 1 (1988), passim.

35. Malcom Lowe, "Who Were the ΙΟΥΔΑΙΟΙ?" *NovT* 18 (1976): 101–30 (here, 106–107).

36. Urban C. von Wahlde, "The Johannine Jews: A Critical Survey," *NTS* 28 (1982): 33–60.

37. Rudolf Bultmann, *The Gospel of John: A Commentary* (Philadelphia: Westminster, 1971), 86.

38. John Ashton, *Studying John: Approaches to the Fourth Gospel* (Oxford and New York: Clarendon, 1994), 5–36.

39. Oxford and New York: Clarendon/Oxford University Press, 1991, 381–401.

40. On the distinction between eschatology and apocalyptic we cannot here enlarge, nor on what C. H. Dodd taught us to call "realized eschatology" in John. See, on this, Dale C. Allison, *The End of the Ages Has Come: An Early Interpretation of the Passion and Resurrection of Jesus* (Philadelphia: Fortress, 1985), 51–61.

41. See Davies, *Paul and Rabbinic Judaism,* "Preface to the Fourth Edition," xxvi, and idem, "Apocalyptic and Pharisaism," in *Christian Origins and Judaism* (New York: Arno, 1973), 19–30.

42. For reductionism in Paul, see Davies, "Pauline and Jewish Christianity according to Cardinal Daniélou: A Suggestion," in *Jewish and Pauline Studies,* 164–71.

43. See again Allison, *The End of the Ages Has Come,* 51–61.

44. G. Scholem, *The Messianic Idea in Judaism and Other Essays on Jewish Spirituality* (New York: Schocken Books, 1971), 51–52 (our italics).

45. Martyn, *History and Theology in the Fourth Gospel,* 128.

46. R. A. Culpepper, "The Pivot of John's Prologue," *NTS* 27 (1980–81): 1–31 (here, 31).

47. See our discussion, above, and Davies, "Reflections on the Nature of Judaism."

48. See A. Hertzberg, in *The Condition of Jewish Belief: A Symposium Conducted by the Editors of Commentary Magazine* (New York: Macmillan, 1966), 90.

49. Dodd, *The Interpretation of the Fourth Gospel,* particularly 352–53. And see John 3:19; 5:22, 24, 27, 29, 30; 7:24; 8:16; 12:31.

50. See W. D. Davies, "Paul and the People of Israel," in *Jewish and Pauline Studies*, 123–52.

51. See Wright, *The New Testament and the People of God*, 1.98–102; R. T. France, *Matthew: Evangelist and Teacher* (Grand Rapids: Academie Books, 1989), 206–41, on "Matthew and Israel" (N.B. the last paragraph, 241); and the rich treatment by Jean-Claude Ingelaere, "Universalisme et Particularisme dans l'Évangile de Matthieu: Matthieu et le Judaïsme," *RHPR* 75 (1995): 45–59.

52. Dr. D. C. Allison, Jr., read the typescript of this chapter; I am very grateful for his helpful criticism and comments. I also thank Ms. Sarah Freedman for her unfailing competence.

James H. Charlesworth

4

The Dead Sea Scrolls
and the Gospel according to John

The Dead Sea Scrolls have certainly revolutionized our perception of Judaism before the burning of the Temple in 70 C.E.[1] They have also dramatically altered our understanding of the origins of Christianity.[2] The interpretations of Paul's letters, Hebrews, Revelation, Matthew, and Acts have all been appreciably enriched and at times significantly changed.[3] The exegesis of no document in the New Testament, however, has been so fundamentally altered by the recovery of the scrolls as the Gospel according to John: What some nineteenth-century scholars had identified as a second-century Greek composition is now perceived to be a late first-century Jewish writing. That is a shift in paradigms, and it is due in part to the assessment of archaeological discoveries, especially the Dead Sea Scrolls.

AN EARLIER CONSENSUS IN HISTORICAL CRITICISM

For the last two centuries the acids of biblical criticism have burned away many cherished perceptions regarding the Fourth Gospel. It was slowly but widely accepted that John was the latest of the Gospels and unreliable historically, since it was the product of late second-century Christianity. The founder of the Tübingen School, F. C. Baur, claimed that John could not be apostolic because it was written around 170 C.E.[4] For A. Loisy, the fourth evangelist was a theologian unacquainted with any historical preoccupation; he could not have been an eyewitness to Jesus' life and teachings, let alone an apostle. Loisy contended, moreover, that John was composed by a convert from diaspora Judaism: Influenced by Philo, the evangelist was "one of the greatest mystical theologians," his concepts were shaped by Alexandrian Judaism.[5] Thus, John was a Gospel inspired by Greek philosophy: The Logos-concept aligned John with pre-Socratics, like Heraclitus, or with the Stoics. J. Weiss concluded that Johannine dualism could not have derived from any form of Judaism; it came from Hellenism.[6] Similarly, E. J. Goodspeed claimed, "The thoroughly Greek character of the thought and interest of the Gospel, its literary (dialogue) cast, its thoroughly Greek style, its comparatively limited use of the Jewish Scriptures (roughly one-fifth of Matthew's), its definite purpose to strip Christianity of its Jewish swaddling clothes, its intense anti-Jewish feeling, and its great debt to the mystery religions—combined to show that its author was a Greek not a Jew. In the Gospel of John the Greek genius returns to religion."[7] In the 1930s not all Johannine scholars would have agreed, but Goodspeed's words do encapsulate the spirit of an earlier age and an old approach to the Fourth Gospel.[8] Thus, exactly ten years before the discovery of the scrolls, a leading New Testament expert could claim that John was composed by a Greek who was influenced by the mystery religions; the evangelist was a genius who had worked alone in his study and was influenced by Greek philosophy.

Building on nineteenth-century research, many experts once supported a scholarly consensus that John was perhaps written sometime in the second century C.E. Scholars also claimed that John was the most Greek of the Gospels. Hence, they confidently dismissed the cherished tradition that the Fourth Gospel was related—let alone written—by the apostle John.

A NEW CONSENSUS

Now, virtually all Johannine experts throughout the world have concluded that John may contain some of the oldest traditions in, and even some of the oldest sections of, the Gospels. It is also conceivable, though unprovable, that some of these oldest sections may be related in some way to an apostle, perhaps John himself. The Fourth Gospel is now judged to be Jewish, and it is studied in terms of first-century Palestinian Jewish writings, especially the Dead Sea Scrolls. M. Hengel, a leading specialist on Judaism and Christian origins, rightly states, "The Qumran discoveries are a landmark for a new assessment of the situation of the Fourth Gospel in the history of religion."[9] How is this possible? What has led us to such a marked shift?

THE DATE OF THE GOSPEL OF JOHN

The discovery of Papyrus 52, preserved in Manchester's John Rylands Library, closed the door to the possibility that John postdates 125 C.E.[10] This fragment is not from a source utilized by the Gospel's author. It represents a codex of John, which contains 18:31–33 and 18:37–38 and dates no later than 125 C.E. A late second-century date for the Gospel is now impossible, since a fragment of a book can hardly predate its composition by almost a century.

It now seems safe to report that no scholar dates the Fourth Gospel after the first decade of the second century C.E., and most experts agree that it dates from around 100 C.E. or perhaps a decade earlier. Hence, John is now perceived to be a late first-century composition in its present, edited form. Moreover, the Gospel shows signs of being a "second edition," with at least 1:1–18 and chapters 15–17 added by the evangelist himself; hence, the "first edition" would have to antedate the present gospel (chaps. 1—20), and that may take us to a time near to the composition of the Gospel of Mark, or perhaps even earlier.[11]

The evangelist used sources, and some of these are very early. One of them, the signs-source, apparently predates the Gospel of Mark, or 70 C.E.; it may have been composed in ancient Palestine by a Jew living within a decade or two of Jesus of Nazareth.[12]

THE HISTORICITY OF THE GOSPEL OF JOHN

For decades scholars thought it obvious that John contained false or, at least, historically misleading information. The evangelist referred to a monumental pool inside the Sheep Gate, but no ancient description—in the Old Testament Pseudepigrapha, Josephus, or elsewhere—mentioned such a significant pool. John described the Pool of Bethsaida as having five porticoes. His report was judged misinformed, because no ancient building resembled a pentagon. It seemed to follow that the evangelist could not have been a Jew who knew Jerusalem.

Archaeologists, however, decided to dig exactly where the evangelist claimed a pool was set aside for healing. Their excavations revealed an ancient pool with shrines dedicated to the Greek god of healing, Asclepius. The pool had porticoes (open areas with large columns): one to the north, one to the east, one to the south, one to the west, and one transecting the roughly rectangular building.[13] The building, dedicated to healing, thus had five porticoes. Hence, the evangelist knew something about Jerusalem that was not mentioned in other sources, composed by individuals, like Josephus, who had lived there.

The discovery of the *Copper Scroll* in Qumran Cave III added to this fascinating research. This Dead Sea Scroll describes where the Temple treasures were hidden before the Roman soldiers surrounded the city. It refers in frustrating detail to some of the topography in and around Jerusalem. One passage of this scroll apparently refers to the Pool of Bethsaida, mentioned by the evangelist, which makes sense in light of the other places in which treasures were hidden; but the reading is far from certain.[14] Conceivably, however, this Dead Sea Scroll helps to prove that the author of John was not ignorant about Jerusalem.[15]

Most commentators, intent on understanding the meaning of the pericope in which Jesus turned water into wine (John 2:1–11), have missed the importance of an oblique aside made by the evangelist: "Six stone jars were standing there, for the Jewish rites of purification, each holding twenty or thirty gallons" (2:6). Now, with the *Temple Scroll,* the longest of all the Dead Sea Scrolls, we possess a pre-70 C.E., firsthand insight into the regulations and specifications for purification. A house and everything within it, especially valuable commodities stored in pottery vessels, become impure when one who is ritually unclean enters:

And if a woman is pregnant, and her child dies in her womb, all the days
on which it is dead inside her, she is unclean like a grave; and every house
she comes into is unclean, with all its furnishings, for seven days. . . . And
all earthen vessels [וכול כלי חרש] shall be broken, for they are unclean and
cannot become clean again forever (11QTempleᵃ 50:10–19).[16]

Excavations in the upper city of Jerusalem have unearthed large stone vessels,
like the ones the evangelist notes in passing; all of them antedate the destruction
of 70 and caused the excavator N. Avigad to report, "we were astonished by the
rich and attractive variety of the stone vessels."[17] Hence, the evangelist, who was
most likely a Jew, and probably his fellow Jews—not only his sources—possessed considerable knowledge about Jewish purification rights. We now know
from other areas of research that the stipulations for purification developed considerably from the time of Herod the Great in 37 B.C.E. until the destruction of the
Temple in 70 C.E.

The Gospel of John should not, therefore, be ignored in the study of pre-70 traditions that may contain history. All pertinent data should be amassed in order to
reconstruct the past; John must not be shelved in attempts to say something about
Jesus, son of Joseph, and his time. As D. M. Smith has demonstrated, the Gospel
of John contains "an array of historical data," which have as good a claim to be
historically reliable as passages in the Synoptics.[18]

DUALISM

The Dead Sea Scrolls have had perhaps the greatest impact upon the study of
Johannine theology. The dualistic thinking so characteristic of John is not to be
traced back to Platonic idealism. It is also appreciably different from that found
in rabbinic literature (and in Sirach and Judith).[19] What scholars could not find
within Judaism before the discovery of the scrolls, beginning in 1947, is boldly
displayed, with surprising clarity, within the most important of the scrolls, the
Rule of the Community (1QS, 4QS, 5QS).[20] In columns 3 and 4 of this document,
we find what the Master (משכיל) taught those entering the sect: the cosmic dualism between two powerful forces (angels), expressed in terms of a light/darkness
paradigm, with humans at the center of the struggle and divided into two lots—
the Sons of Light and the Sons of Darkness.

Some sections of this *Rule* were memorized, and surely that is the case with
columns 3 and 4. The section begins with the words, "It is for the Master to instruct and teach all the Sons of Light" (1QS 3:13). Such an initiate was to know
by heart that "from the God of knowledge comes all that is and shall be" (1QS
3:15). Other scrolls composed in the Qumran community show that these words
were memorized. For example, in the *Angelic Liturgy*[21] we see the effect of the
Master's teaching: "For from the God of knowledge came into being all which is

forever" (4QShirShabb 4; cf. MasShirShabb 1:2). Fully initiated members of the Qumran sect would not have needed to carry a copy of 1QS 3–4 to quote from it. As novitiates they had studied it for a period of at least two years. All Qumranites had been examined in its teachings by leaders of the sect (1QS 6:14–20).[22] This section of the *Rule of the Community* was also probably recited in various cultic settings.

After the burning of their buildings, those Qumranites who survived the attack by Roman soldiers would have been dispersed with cherished memories, including the secrets that had been revealed only to them through the Righteous Teacher (see 1QpHab 7). If they entered any other Jewish group, they would have surely influenced its members with their special insights.

If, indeed, Qumranites or the wider group of which they were members (the Essenes)[23] joined a new group within Second Temple Judaism, the Palestinian Jesus Movement, they would have influenced it with their special "knowledge" (דעת) and "mysteries" (רז). As some scholars have suggested since the 1950s, Acts possibly records the movement of some Essene priests into this group: "And the word of God increased; and the number of the disciples in Jerusalem multiplied greatly, and a great crowd of the priests followed in the faith" (6:7).[24] This statement occurs in one of Luke's little summaries, easily dismissed as devoid of historical worth; but it is never wise to discard data that, in the light of other sources, may preserve vestiges of history.

We know of two major priestly groups in first-century Jerusalem, the Sadducees and the Essenes.[25] It is practically impossible to imagine that Acts 6:7 refers to Sadducees. In stark contrast to the Essenes,[26] they rejected the concept of a resurrection (see esp. Acts 4:1–4), actively persecuted Jesus' group (Acts 1 – 12; see, e.g., 5:17), and probably had no patience with messianism. Even though Acts surely reflects Luke's own tendencies and is theologically slanted to prove that the Spirit has broken forth again in history, we may trust Luke's report that priests joined the Palestinian Jesus Movement in the 30s and 40s. It is also conceivable that Luke was wrong chronologically and was thinking about the Essenes, who joined the Jesus group after the destruction of 70 C.E.

The Book of Acts also refers to the Palestinian Jesus Movement as "the Way": thus, Paul's report, "I persecuted this Way to the death" (22:4). "Way" is a technical term, as becomes clear when studying Acts 9:2: Paul is commissioned by the high priest to bring, bound, to Jerusalem "any belonging to the Way." Where did this technical term come from? It is not typical of the Old Testament, the Septuagint, the Apocrypha, the Pseudepigrapha, Philo, Josephus, or the Jewish magical papyri. It is, however, the self-designation of the Qumran sect: "These are the rules of the Way [הדרך] for the Master in these ages" (1QS 9:21; see also 1QS 9:19; 11:11; 1Q30 2; 1Q22 2:8; 1QSa 1:28; 11QTemple[a] 54:17). The most likely reconstruction of Christian origins thus leads us to postulate that members of Jesus' group were called "the Way" because of the Qumran sect and perhaps because of the larger group of the Essenes. From this it might follow that some, possibly numerous, Qumranites or Essenes had joined Jesus' group by the time Luke wrote Acts, or even earlier. While this scenario helps us catch another insight into the presence of former Essenes within early Christianity, it does not permit us to see Essene influence in such Johannine phrases as that attributed to Jesus, "I am the way" (14:6).

In light of the favorable interest in the Levites in many of the scrolls found in the Qumran caves,[27] and given that we now know that Essenes were probably living in the southwestern section of Jerusalem,[28] it is worth pondering what relation the well-known Barnabas, a Levite from Cyprus, had with Essenes of Levitical descent, living in Jerusalem and its environs (Acts 4:36). If he was a convert and a Levite, then why not others—especially those we call Essenes?

The most reliable indication that Essenes and those familiar with Qumran theology were entering the Jesus group in sufficient numbers to have an impression on the new movement *after the 60s* is the paucity of parallels in works prior to that time. There is virtually no clear Essene influence on Romans, Galatians, and other authentic writings by Paul.[29] In contrast, however, significant links with Essene thought preponderate in works postdating the 60s and especially 70 C.E., namely, Ephesians, Hebrews, Matthew, Revelation, and especially the Gospel of John.[30]

It is in John that we find a dualism that is not paralleled in Greek, Roman, or Egyptian ideology. It is not found in Philo or Josephus, neither in the Apocrypha nor Pseudepigrapha (with the exception of the *Testaments of the Twelve Patriarchs*). Terms and phrases, known for centuries as "Johannine," have turned up in the Dead Sea Scrolls, and precisely in the section of their book of rules that was probably memorized, namely, the *Rule of the Community* 3–4.

Observe John 12:35–36, a passage once cherished as of the evangelist's own creation:

> Jesus said to them, "The *light* is with you for a little longer. *Walk* while you have *the light,* lest *the darkness* overtake you; *he who walks in the darkness does not know* where he goes. While you have *the light,* believe in *the light,* that you may become *Sons of Light.*"

Why did the evangelist use such symbolism, such phrases and terms, and from what source did he inherit the technical term "[the] Sons of Light"? The most probable explanation is that he, and perhaps those in his own group, were influenced by *the light/darkness paradigm,* developed only in the *Rule of the Community.* In that scroll we find an explanation of who are the "Sons of Light" (see 3:13, 24, 25), and we are introduced to the phrase, "and they shall walk in the ways of darkness" (3:21; cf. 4:11). One passage in the *Rule* contains phrases and words that seem "Johannine" to many who do not know that this scroll antedates John by about two centuries:

> In the hand of the Prince of Lights [is] the dominion of all the Sons of Righteousness; in the ways of light they walk. But in the hand of the Angel of Darkness [is] the dominion of the Sons of Deceit; and in the ways of darkness they walk. By the Angel of Darkness comes the aberration of all the Sons of Righteousness; and all their sins, their iniquities, their guilt, and their iniquitous works [are caused] by his dominion, according to God's mysteries, until his end. And all their afflictions and the appointed times of their suffering [are caused] by the dominion of his hostility. And all the spirits of his lot cause to stumble the Sons of Light; but the God of Israel and his Angel of Truth help all the Sons of Light. He created the spirits of light and darkness, and upon them he founded every work (1QS 3:20–25).[31]

While expressions familiar to a Christian seem "Johannine," this passage is certainly not a Christian composition (*pace* those scholars who confuse the distinguishing borders of the Essenes and Jesus' group). The kerygma does not appear in it; Jesus is neither mentioned nor adumbrated in it. The *Rule* is a pre-Christian, Jewish work that emphasizes cosmic dualism, expressed in terms of the light/darkness paradigm, subsumed under the absolute sovereignty of "the God of Israel."

In John 3:16–21 we find the following famous passage:

> For God so loved the world that he gave his only Son, that *all who believe* in him should *not perish* but have *eternal life*. For God sent the Son into the world, not to condemn the world, but that *the world might be saved* through him. He who believes in him is *not condemned;* he who does not believe is condemned already, because he has not believed in the name of the only Son of God. And this is *the judgment,* that *the light* has come into the world, and men loved *darkness* rather than *the light,* because their *deeds were evil.* For *all who do evil hate the light, and do not come to the light,* lest their *deeds* should *be exposed.* But *he who does the truth comes to the light,* that it may be clearly seen that *his deeds* have been *accomplished through God* [lit., "have been worked in God"].

This passage reflects the Johannine christological proclamation that Jesus is God's only Son (3:16; 20:31). No Qumranite could agree—unless, of course, he accepted Jesus as the Messiah and believed in him. A member of the Qumran sect would have needed instruction in this belief, by someone other than the Master. This claim is Christian proclamation, the kerygma; as such, it is distinctly Christian.

The Christology here belongs to the evangelist, but he did not create the symbolism. The *spirit* is definitively Christian and Johannine, but the *mentality* was inherited. The source, or at least one of the major sources, is clearly Qumranian in perspective (as signaled by the terminological links, even technical terms, italicized in the Johannine excerpt, above).

The evangelist refers to Jesus as "the Son." We can no longer report that the Dead Sea Scrolls do not refer to God's Son, or the Son[32] (even though there is no evidence of the apocalyptic title, the Son of Man). The *Elect of God Text* (4Q Mess ar) does refer to a powerful person named the "Elect of God" (בחיר אלהא). Who this person is remains unclear; moreover, it probably is from a pre-Qumran composition.[33] (For the record, none of the over four hundred scrolls mentions or alludes to Jesus of Nazareth, despite the misguided attempts by some scholars to identify some of Qumran's anonymous leaders, like the Righteous Teacher or Wicked Priest, with Jesus, Paul, or other persons prominent in the origins of Christianity.)

Significant data have revolutionized our perception of early Jewish theology. It is clear that the Qumranites knew the concept of being "God's son," as it is well known from scripture (esp. Psalm 2), but now there is evidence that they knew about the apocalyptic title, "the Son of God," which certainly obtained a different meaning. One Dead Sea Scroll, to date unpublished, does contain the title "Son of God." It is an Aramaic pseudepigraphon of Daniel (4Qps DanA[a] = 4Q246). The two-columned fragment has nine lines and is dated by Milik to the end of the first century B.C.E. The document refers to the "Son of God" (ברה די אל) and also to the "Son of the Most High" (ובר עליון). J. A. Fitzmyer interprets this document as "properly apocalyptic." He concludes that these Aramaic titles were "applied to some human being in the apocalyptic setting of this Palestinian text of the last third of the first century B.C.," and that these titles "will have to be taken into account for any future discussion of the title used of Jesus in the NT."[34]

Obviously, the evangelist inherited the title "the Son" from Palestinian Judaism and also from early Christian sources, oral and written, but he placed his own creativity upon them. The 4Q246 fragment warns us of the limits of our knowledge and that we must be careful about arguing what was not known in first-century Judaism. It urges us, further, to ponder how and in what ways the evangelist, and others like him, were influenced by ideas such as the following:

> [But your son] shall be great upon the earth. [O King! All (men) shall] make [peace], and all shall serve [him. (Col. 2) He shall be called the son of] the [G]reat [God], and by his name shall he be named. He shall be hailed (as) the Son of God, and they shall call him Son of the Most High. As comets (flash) to the sight, so shall be their kingdom.[35]

This text is not necessarily messianic; at least, "the Messiah" is not mentioned in what has been preserved and shared so far. However, the phrase "all shall serve him" is reminiscent of another, as yet unpublished text, *On Resurrection* (4Q521), in which we read that the heavens and the earth shall obey (or serve) "his Messiah" (למשיחו).

The Qumran Community (יחד), like the Johannine Community, was exclusive. The word "all" (כול) appears with more frequency in the Qumran scrolls than in any other biblical or parabiblical works. This concept appears twice in the previously quoted pericope from John ("all who believe" [3:16] and "all who do evil" [3:20]), which reflects two distinct opposites in humanity; it is an anthropological dualism. In John the word "all" (πᾶς) appears infrequently—only 63 times, in contrast (for example) with Matthew and Luke, in which it appears 128 and 152 times, respectively. Still, where "all" appears in John, we have possible evidence of Qumran influence.

There are only two main antecedents to the Johannine dualism: Qumranism and Zurvanism, the latter developed in ancient Persia by a group within Zoroastrianism. Zurvanism most likely influenced the Qumran sect, and it probably influenced John's Gospel.[36]

The Qumran concept of final judgment at the messianic end time is reflected in John 3:16–21: those who are not "Sons of Light" will perish; all "Sons of Light" will have eternal life. These thoughts are most likely influenced by Qumran dualism, developed at least two centuries earlier and found again in the passage taught to initiates: Those who are not Sons of Light will receive "eternal perdition by the fury of God's vengeful wrath, everlasting terror and endless shame, along with disgrace of annihilation in the fire of murky Hell" (1QS 4:12–13). In John 3 the evangelist refers to "the wrath of God" (v. 36), which is reminiscent of "by the fury of God's vengeful wrath" in the *Rule* (1QS 4:12). By contrast, the Qumranites believed that the Sons of Light will be rewarded "with all everlasting blessings, endless joy in everlasting life, and a crown of glory along with a resplendent attire in eternal light" (1QS 4:7–8).

Often overlooked when studying John and the Dead Sea Scrolls is the fact that both were very interested in salvation. The evangelist thinks in terms of the world's salvation, a concept very close to the Qumranites' understanding that they were exiled and living in the wilderness in order to atone for the land: The Holy Ones in the Community were chosen by God "to atone for the earth" (1QS 8:6, 10); "they shall atone for iniquitous guilt and for sinful faithlessness" (1QS 9:4). It is conceivable that *from the thought-world of Qumran the evangelist derived words, expressions, and terms to express his conviction* that the world has been saved.[37]

The key that opens up the probability that John 3:16–21 has been influenced by the concepts developed quintessentially in 1QS 3–4 is the appearance of the light/darkness dualism, a paradigm most likely created at Qumran (and, I am convinced, by the Righteous Teacher). Note these *termini technici,* which (except for "Sons of Darkness") are found in the *Rule* (cols. 3–4):

light	darkness
Sons of Light	[Sons of Darkness; see 1QS 1:10]
Angel of Light	Angel of Darkness
Angel of Truth	Spirit of Perversity
Sons of Truth	Sons of Perversity

Sons of Righteousness	Sons of Perversity
spring of light	well of darkness
walking in the ways of light	walking in the ways of darkness
truth	perversity
God loves	God hates
everlasting life	punishment, then extinction

These technical terms form *a paradigm*. It explains the human condition by clarifying that God "created the spirits of light and darkness" (1QS 3:25), that "he founded every work upon them" (3:25), and that all humans, including the "Sons of Light," err because of the Angel of Darkness (3:22).[38] All these terms (except for "Sons of Darkness") are clustered in a focused passage to be taught to and memorized by those who wish to cross over the barrier and into the community; it is the *Rule* 3:13–4:14. For example, "Sons of Light" (בני אור), which is unique to Qumran theology and is the sect's self-designation,[39] is defined in 1QS 3:13–4:26 (3:13, 24, 25; cf. 1:9; 2:16; 3:3) and is found in many other Qumran Scrolls (specifically, 1QM 1:1, 3, 9, 11, 13; 4Q510 11:7, 4QCatᵃ 12 + 1:7 and 1:11; 4QFlor 1 + 1:9).

It is apparent to most specialists that in some way the Gospel of John has been influenced by Qumran's dualism and its terminology. Darkness (σκότος, per John 3:19) is contrasted with light (φῶς), evil (πονηρά) with truth (ἀλήθεια), hate (μισέω) with love (ἀγαπάω), and perishing (ἀπόλλυμι) with receiving eternal life (ζωὴν αἰώνιον).[40]

The probability that the Gospel of John is influenced by Qumran's dualistic terms and conceptions, though not its theology, is enhanced by the appearance of "the Sons of Light" and related Qumranic technical terms, as emphasized here in a later passage in John (12:35–36):

> Jesus said to them, "*The light* is with you for a little longer. *Walk* while you have *the light,* lest the darkness overtake you; *he who walks in the darkness does not know where he goes.* While you have *the light,* believe in *the light,* that you may become *Sons of Light* [υἱοὶ φωτός = בני אור]."

It is possible that the evangelist received from Qumran the idea of "walking in darkness" versus "walking in light," both of which derive not from Greek but from Semitic conceptuality (הלך; cf. 1QS 3:21: "and they shall walk in the ways of darkness"; note also 1QS 4:11).

Nowhere in the ancient world do we find the dualism of light and darkness developed so thoroughly as in Qumran's *Rule of the Community*. As in John's Gospel, it is a cosmic and soteriological dualism, subsumed under belief in one and only one God, and joined with a conviction that evil and the demons will cease to exist. As R. E. Brown observed, "It will be noted that not only the dualism but also its terminology is shared by John and Qumran."[41]

In addition to those already mentioned, several terms and phrases are significantly shared by the Qumranites and the Johannine Christians: among others, "doing the truth" (1QS 1:5; 5:3; 8:2; John 3:21; 1 John 1:6), "water of life" (1QH 8:7, 16; 1QpHab 11:1; CD 19:34; John 4:10–14), "works of God" (1QS 4:4; John 9:3), "light of life" (1QS 3:7; John 8:12), and "knowing the truth" (1QH 6:12; 9:35; 10:20, 29; John 8:32). In Qumran's *Thanksgiving Hymns* God is described "as perfect light" (1QH 4:23); the author of 1 John writes, "God is light and in him is no darkness at all" (1:5).

It is important to stress that the evangelist (like others in his community) probably has been influenced by Qumran's terminology, and in some passages he reveals that his thought and even perception have been shaped by the ideas, phrases, and technical terms of Qumran. There is, however, insufficient evidence to warrant the conclusion that he was a former Qumranite or Essene, or that he was influenced by their premessianic eschatology and peculiar theology.[42] He was a Christian; that is, he took some earlier terms and concepts and reshaped them to articulate the contention that Jesus was none other than the Messiah promised to the Jews (see, for example, John 4:25–26).

In summary, the preceding discussion of excerpts from the Dead Sea Scrolls and the Fourth Gospel helps to clarify a consensus in research. Among all the ancient collections of writings, it is only the Dead Sea Scrolls that disclose to us a type of thought, a developed symbolic language, and a dualistic paradigm with technical terms that are surprisingly close to the Gospel of John.[43] This consensus is clearly articulated by D. M. Smith: "That the Qumran scrolls attest a form of Judaism whose conceptuality and terminology tally in some respects quite closely with the Johannine is a commonly acknowledged fact."[44] J. Painter rightly concludes that "the context in which the Johannine tradition was shaped . . . is best known to us in the Qumran texts."[45] The evangelist's most striking point of contact with the Dead Sea Scrolls, whether direct or indirect, is surely with the dualism developed in two columns of the *Rule of the Community,* probably known by heart to all members of the Qumran sect.

THE JEWISHNESS OF THE JOHANNINE GROUP

Subsequent to widespread recognition that the fourth evangelist had been influenced in some way by the dualism found in the *Rule,*[46] scholars became convinced, thanks to the work of J. L. Martyn and R. E. Brown, that the Gospel of John bears the marks of a major sociological rift.[47] The term ἀποσυνάγωγος appears only in John (9:22; 12:42; 16:2); it means that members of the Johannine community have been thrown out of the synagogue. According to 9:22, the parents of a man who had been blind from birth are said to fear the Jews, "for the Jews had already agreed that if anyone should confess [Jesus] to be Christ, he was to be put out of the synagogue." These words indicate not only the actions by some

Jews in a synagogue, but also that members of the Johannine community had been attending, and wanted to continue to attend, Jewish services and the calendrical festivals in the synagogue. It is hence beyond any doubt that some members of the Johannine community, perhaps many, were Jews who believed that Jesus was the Christ. Many members of the Johannine group (including some who had not been born Jews) saw themselves, as W. A. Meeks explains, "entirely within the orbit of Jewish communities." It also seems evident that the leaders of these "Christian" communities "despised secret believers in Jesus who wanted to remain in the Jewish community."[48] The Johannine community was obviously Jewish, and we have slowly come to recognize that in many ways the Gospel of John is the most Jewish Gospel in the Christian canon.

The Jewishness of John and the crisis created by the Johannine community's exclusion from the synagogue services become readily apparent when the Gospel is studied in light of the Jewish festivals.[49] Chapters 7 and 8, and perhaps also 9, are united by a common setting. Chapter 7 clarifies the setting: it is the "Feast of Tabernacles" (7:2). Being a devout Jew, Jesus makes the required pilgrimage up to Jerusalem for the Feast (7:10) and enters the Temple (7:14). This great feast celebrates at the end of the year (*Tishri,* in early fall) the ingathering of the crops and is sometimes called "the Feast of Ingathering." It is also called the Feast of Booths, when Jews celebrate the period in the wilderness following the exodus from Egypt.

Parts of John 7 and 8 may indicate how some Jews remembered the way this Feast was celebrated when the Temple was still standing, or how it may have been commemorated in the synagogue from which they were later excluded. The fourth evangelist has Jesus stand up in the Temple on the last day of the Feast and exhort those who heard him to "come to me and drink" (7:37). The multiple references to water and to "rivers of living water" may reflect the seven-day water-libation ceremony (*m. Sukk.* 4:9). From the Pool of Siloam, south of the Temple, a priest would bring water in a golden container. The priest would then proceed ceremoniously through the "Water Gate" of the Temple, pour the water into two silver bowls near the altar, from which the water would pour forth from perforated holes. This libation to Yahweh would elicit rejoicing and the playing of trumpets, flutes, and rams' horns. On the one hand, Jews in the Johannine community may have remembered experiencing these celebrations; on the other hand, they may have remembered reliving them in synagogues. In either case, John mirrors the fact that both of these once cherished opportunities are no longer possible to the Jews in the Johannine school.

Jesus' words, "I am the light of the world" (8:12), which are reminiscent of Qumran ideology, have an interesting setting. He is said to have uttered them also during the Feast of Tabernacles, one of whose ceremonies is called the "lighting of lights" (*m. Sukk.* 5:2). The lighting of lights and the dancing that ceremoniously accompanied it in the Temple would have been remembered well after 70 C.E. and perhaps were reenacted in some way in synagogue services. Whether the evangelist is referring to the Temple ceremony of Jesus' time or recalling how Tabernacles was celebrated after 70, it is clear that Jewish festivals play an important, if perhaps only a rhetorical, role in the Gospel. This fact underscores the Jewishness of the Johannine group and helps us to comprehend the pain of their being excluded from the synagogue services.

Another rift in the Johannine community is obvious. The First Epistle of John illustrates that some members of that community have been deceived or misled: "They went out from us, but they were not from [or of] us; for if they had been from us, they would have continued with us" (2:19). They subsequently left the community, and the author denounces them as antichrists. We have only the word of 1 John's author, but according to him these former members of the community could not agree on the reality of the incarnation. They ostensibly would not confess that Jesus was the Christ and denied that he had come in the flesh, as one truly human.[50]

If these Christians read John, it was in light of the Johannine claim that Jesus was one who was from above and had descended to earth. E. Käsemann claimed that John contains some passages that are naively docetic. John can be read to support Docetism (the doctrine that Jesus was not really human), but it is certainly not a docetic text.[51] If this schism is viewed in light of the rift with synagogue Jews, and if both rifts are perceived in light of Qumran influence on John, then it is easy to imagine that former Essenes in the Johannine community would have been less likely than Greek converts to give up the position that the Messiah had been a real human.

It is possible to distinguish different Jewish beliefs in a messiah. Some Jews believed he would be earthly (see, for example, the *Psalms of Solomon*). He could experience exhaustion and be so emotionally torn as to cry, and both human emotions are portrayed in John (see chaps. 4 and 11). Other Jews believed in a messiah who would be heavenly, coming from the sky or out of the sea (thus, *1 Enoch* 37–71 and 4 Ezra). The Qumranites believed in the first concept. They expected an earthly, human messiah who would be sent by God (1QS 9). An unpublished text does mention God's (lit., "his") messiah, who will appear when the Lord restores life to those who are dead (*On Resurrection,* 4Q521).[52] Hence, it is more likely that former Essenes would have agreed with the evangelist and with the author of 1 John against the schismatics.

A third rift, well-known and discussed in most commentaries, is also evident in John.[53] The Gospel's prologue and other passages show us with impressive force the polemic between the Johannine group and the followers of John the Baptist. The evangelist has the Baptist state, "I am not the Christ," and deny that he is Elijah or "the prophet" (see John 1:19–23). These retorts are probably directed against those Jews who believed that John the Baptist was the Christ, or at least Elijah, or the prophet. The function of John the Baptizer in this Gospel is reduced to making straight the way of the Lord, as Isaiah prophesied (1:23), and proclaiming that Jesus of Nazareth is "the Lamb of God who takes away the sins of the world" (1:29) and "the Son of God" (1:34).[54]

These observations cumulatively lead to a reconsideration of the Johannine community. It seems to have been something like a "school"; we should not forget, however, that it was similar to other schools in antiquity and was not simply the Qumran Community revived.[55] The clearest signals that John is from a school are the evidence of its relation to 1 John and the Gospel's apparent writing and rewriting (the addition of chaps. 1, 21, and perhaps 15—17).

Experts on John have begun to agree on a probable solution to a major problem. John 14 ends with Jesus' exhortation to his disciples, "Rise, let us go hence" (v. 31). According to the Gospel's present shape, Jesus subsequently launches into long speeches (chaps. 15—17). Then we come to John 18, which begins, "When Jesus had spoken these words, he went forth with his disciples across the Kidron Valley, where there was a garden, which he and his disciples entered" (v. 1). These words follow chapter 14 much more sensibly than chapters 15—17. Hence, John 15—17 was probably added by the evangelist in a "second edition" of the Gospel.

The clinching argument in favor of this hypothesis is the recognition that chapters 15 through 17 appeal for unity. John 15 uses the image of the vine and urges the reader to remain grafted onto the true vine, which is Jesus. John 17 is Jesus' appeal to God that his disciples be one: "I do not pray for these only, but also for those who believe in me through their word, that they may *all be one*" (17:20). These words make best sense in light of the sociological rift in the community. The fourth evangelist (or a later editor) has Jesus appeal to the Johannine Christians, probably calling on all of them to avoid, or more likely to heal, the schism.

We should note, as Bultmann demonstrated long ago, that the Prologue, John 1:1–18, is probably a hymn once chanted in the community and now added to the Gospel for the purpose of clarifying that Jesus had clearly come in the flesh (1:14). Bultmann noted that the most striking parallels to the Logos-hymn are found in the *Odes of Solomon*.[56] After the discovery of the Dead Sea Scrolls and the recovery of the Greek version of *Ode* 11, M. Testuz concluded that the *Odes* were composed by an Essene.[57] J. Licht, among others, acknowledged the strong links between the *Odes* and Qumran.[58] J. Carmignac and I suggested, with different nuances and insights, that the author was a Christian who may have once been an Essene;[59] conceivably, this Christian author completed his compositions within, or in the environs of, the Johannine school.[60] No other early Christian work except the *Odes* refers so frequently to Jesus as "the Word," which is best known to us from John 1:1–18; but the attempts to prove that the *Odes* depend on John's Gospel have not proved persuasive to most experts. As Smith reported, "The many affinities with the Odes of Solomon, which partly overlap with those of Qumran, are not easily explained as the result of the Odist's use of the Johannine literature."[61] Scholars are likewise almost unanimous in concluding that it is unlikely that the evangelist borrowed from the *Odes*. Hence, it seems most likely the *Odes of Solomon* come to us from the same environment as the Gospel and perhaps were composed within the Johannine community.[62]

The Gospel of John was not written by a philosopher working alone and dependent on the Synoptic Gospels.[63] It is, rather, the product of a group of scholars, most of whom were Jews, who worked independently of the Synoptics.[64] The Fourth Gospel took shape over more than two decades in something like a school. It is intriguing to ponder who may have been members of this school. How many of its early members had been Essenes? Had any of them formerly lived on the marl terrace south of Qumran or in one of the caves just north or west of Qumran?

THE GOSPEL OF JOHN AND SOCIOLOGY

These insights into the Johannine group and their social rifts with John the Baptist's group, with "Judaism," and with "heretical" Christians lead to further sociological reflections. As W. A. Meeks pointed out twenty years ago, the Gospel of John indicates that faith in Jesus demands "transfer to a community which has totalistic and exclusive claims." The Fourth Gospel and its two editions reflect the history of the community and reinforce its isolation.[65]

The Dead Sea Scrolls and the archaeology of Qumran reveal to us an exclusive Jewish sect. Although it had documents used by many other Jews and other Jewish groups, it is cut off from other Jews and vehemently rejects the Temple cult. It sees only its own members as "Sons of Light"; all others, even those heralded as the most pious within Jerusalem, are "Sons of Darkness," who belong to Belial, the devil. It is a sociological group with strong barriers that lives "liminally," between the end time and the messianic age.[66] Only members of the Qumran Community have secret knowledge, understand some of the writing that is encoded (4Q186, 4Q317), and possess the key for unlocking God's word (1QpHab 7). Love is reserved only for "the Sons of Light," those who belong to the Community.

These observations help us to understand Johannine sectarianism, even if one is not impressed by the evidence of direct influence of Qumran thought on the Gospel of John. Like the scrolls composed at Qumran (esp. 1QS, 1QSa, 1QSb, 1QH, 1QM), John is the product of a sect, and in it Jews representing numerous types of Judaism played a significant role. These Jews are being cut off from other Jewish groups and excluded from the synagogue services. The Jews in charge of the local synagogue are in revolt against the Johannine group;[67] in such a setting there is no place for those who are secret admirers of Jesus. Like the Qumran Community, the Johannine group has strong social barriers, and the transition through initiation from Judaism to Christianity was surely the passage from one social status to another, which tended to strain ethnic identities. Johannine Christians also live in a liminal time between Jesus' resurrection and his return (thus, especially 1

John). They too possess secret knowledge, which are major terms in the Dead Sea Scrolls, in the Fourth Gospel, and in 1 John, since Jesus is the only one who knows and reveals God (John 1:18). As H. Leroy demonstrated long ago, the Johannine language and use of rhetoric, especially the rhetoric of misunderstanding, illustrate a community with special speech known only to those who know the truth.[68]

Under the influence of Qumran, the Johannine group more and more delimited the love commandment so that it included only its own members. This development is complete by the time 1 John is written: "We know that we have passed out of death into life, because *we love the brothers*" (1 John 3:14). Those outside the community, even other "Christians," are labeled antichrists (1 John 2:18–25). Once Qumran, or Essene, influence is obvious in ideological terms, it is imperative to perceive the influence of Qumran in sociological issues. Is it possible that earlier rivalries between Essenes and Pharisees were later transferred to the social setting of the Johannine sect?[69]

TRANSLATING THE GOSPEL OF JOHN TODAY

The Greek noun, Ἰουδαῖοι, is almost always translated "Jews." That rendering is, however, sometimes inaccurate. The social setting of John's Gospel, and the rivalry between Jewish groups—the post-Yavnian (Jamnian) Hillelites and the post-70 Christians, who had been born Jews—caused the evangelist to creatively reconstruct the history of Jesus' time.[70] By his own time the opponents of Jesus' group are not the Sadducees and chief priests, who ceased to exist as a social force after 70 C.E. The opponents were the only other group of Jews who survived the destruction of 70: the Pharisees, followers of Hillel and Shammai. It is they whom John sometimes simply labeled Ἰουδαῖοι.

Context is more important than etymology when translating a word that has a wide semantic range. It is, therefore, sometimes absurd to translate Ἰουδαῖοι as "Jews." Take, for example, John 11:54: "Jesus therefore no longer went about openly ἐν τοῖς Ἰουδαίοις, but went from there to the country near the wilderness, to a town called Ephraim; and there he stayed with the disciples." To render Ἰουδαίοις in this verse as "Jews," as do most translations, indicates that Ephraim was not a Jewish town, that the disciples were not "Jews," and perhaps that Jesus was not a Jew. According to John (11:57) and many other passages in the Gospels and Acts, the opposition to Jesus emanated from the priestly circles in Jerusalem. It is sometimes best then to render Ἰουδαῖοι as "Judean leaders." In this way, the meaning of John 11:54 becomes clear: "Jesus therefore no longer went about openly among the Judean leaders."

Research on the scrolls and other Jewish writings, especially the Pseudepigrapha, has increased our sensitivity as translators to the different meanings that words obtained by the first century C.E. One of these multivalent terms is surely Ἰουδαῖοι. As I hope to show in a future publication, there were before 70 C.E.

many Jewish groups, certainly more than twelve (*pace* Josephus). After 70 only two survived with any recognition and influence: the Hillel group, which gave us the Mishnah, and the Jesus group, which gave us the New Testament. The Qumran community was burned and disappeared from view, except for the upper portions of the northern tower, until R. de Vaux excavated what many judged to be a Roman fortress. The Qumranites and other Essene groups were murdered or eventually disappeared.

SUMMARY AND RECONSTRUCTION

Summary[71]

Let me begin by emphasizing a new perspective. Thirty years ago we imagined that Qumran was perhaps an isolated group living in the wilderness. Now we know that only a small percentage of the writings found in the Qumran caves were composed at Qumran. The scrolls contain writings from many other Jewish groups, including at least the *Books of Enoch, Jubilees,* the Jewish substratum to the *Testaments of the Twelve Patriarchs,* earlier versions of the *Temple Scroll* and the *Damascus Document, Qumran Pseudepigraphic Psalms,* the *Prayer of Joseph, Second Ezekiel,* and the *Copper Scroll.* We now take far more seriously Josephus' reference to two types of Essenes, recognizing that Essenes lived throughout ancient Palestine.

In this process we have become much more aware of the unique features of Qumran theology. To be taken seriously is D. Flusser's comment that the Qumran community "is the only group within Second Temple Judaism to develop a systematic theology. . . . The Dead Sea Sect, in the paradoxical restriction of its ideas, created a system which later influenced the history of all mankind."[72] As I have stated repeatedly in my own works, while the Qumranites taught an esoteric wisdom reserved only for full initiates, their ideas, symbols, and technical terms were widely known by other Jews. Indeed, Josephus knew a vast amount about their theology.

These observations lead us to focus on the Gospel of John. Schnackenburg concludes that apocalypticism has not influenced John as much as Qumran thought. He contends that "the frequently recurring concepts of 'truth,' 'reveal' and 'know,' the importance of the divine Spirit, the longing for the heavenly world and also the close brotherly union seem to establish a close affinity between the Qumran community and the circle which one must envisage behind the Johannine writings, from their mentality and diction."[73] Schnackenburg represents the consensus among specialists who have focused on the Dead Sea Scrolls and their relations with John. I am convinced that Essene influence on John can be seen in the following fifteen ways:

Dualism, expressed in terms of two cosmic spirits, explains the presence of evil in the world. Technical terms for expressing this conception were developed in a unique way at Qumran and were inherited from Essenes by the Johannine school. At Qumran and in the Gospel of John, we hear about "the spirits of truth and deceit" (1QS 3:18–19; 4:21, 23; John 14:17; 15:26; 16:13; cf. 1 John 4:6), the "Holy Spirit" (1QS 4:21; John 14:26; 20:22), and "the Sons of Light" (1QS 3:13, 24, 25; John 12:36). The Johannine Paraclete and Jesus himself (the "Light of the World," John 8:12; 9:5) function in many ways as do the spirit of truth and "Angel of Light" at Qumran (1QS 3:25). Note these shared *termini technici:*

Dead Sea Scrolls	Gospel of John
"in the light of life" (1QS 3:7)	"the light of life" (8:12)
"and they shall walk in the ways of darkness" (1QS 3:21; cf. 4:11)	"and who shall walk in the darkness" (12:35; cf. 8:12)
"by the furious wrath of the God of vengeance" (1QS 4:12)	"the wrath of God" (3:36)
"blindness of eyes" (1QS 4:11)	"the eyes of the blind" (10:21)
"in the fullness of his grace" (1QS 4:4; cf. 4:5)	"full of grace" (1:14)
"the works of God" (1QS 4:4)	"the works of God" (6:28; 9:3)

Because of their isolation from the Temple, the priests who followed the Righteous Teacher into the wilderness to prepare the way of the Lord, acting out the prophecy of Isaiah 40:3, perceived reality in stark ways and developed a unique form of dualism with sharply focused, technical terms. The dualism developed in the Dead Sea Scrolls is certainly reflected in John. In some ways the Johannine School and its Gospel have been impacted by Essene concepts and terms. What is new today, after thirty years of research and the ability to study over 430 scrolls, are the discoveries that this dualism is defined, and its technical terms amassed, *only in 1QS 3 and 4;* that the novitiates were forced to memorize this section; and that other Qumran compositions indicate these terms reflect the mindset of the community and overflow into other Qumran compositions.

One should not jump to the conclusion that John is virtually a Qumran composition. As Schnackenburg points out, the "important contrast between life and death, however, which dominates Johannine thinking, has no parallel at Qumran." To him this discovery is the "strongest argument to show that Johannine 'dualism' cannot have been taken over from Qumran." Johannine dualism is certainly influenced by the Essenes, but it was not unreflectively borrowed from them without incorporation into the prismatic Christian kerygma. As Schnackenburg stresses,

"One can hardly say more than that the Johannine 'dualism,' based on Jewish thought, has in many respects its closest parallels in Qumran, especially with regard to 'light–darkness.' But then there are profound differences which stem from the Christian faith and its doctrine of salvation."[74] The uniqueness and brilliance of Qumran dualism and its technical, well-developed terms are stunning in the history of human thought. To proceed by recognizing that they shape the *mentalité*— though not the *esprit*—of John's Gospel is the correct track to follow, as we seek to discern how and in what ways Qumran locutions shaped the presentation of the fourth evangelist's narrative, conceptuality, and terminology.[75]

Dualism of flesh and spirit. As Flusser and W. D. Davies have pellucidly demonstrated, a feature of Qumran theology that distinguishes it from other theologies in Early Judaism is the flesh versus spirit dualism.[76] In Early Judaism the flesh versus spirit dualism denoted far more than merely human weaknesses versus divine strength; it mirrored an eschatological conflict, two spheres of power, and overlapping modes of existence.[77] Thus, we obviously need to explore how this particular terminology shaped John, especially in 3:6: "That which is born of the flesh is flesh, and that which is born of the Spirit is spirit." The cultured articulation of this flesh versus spirit dualism in John is indicative of scholarly reflection within the Johannine School. Could the evangelist have been influenced by this particular dualism, found in the Dead Sea Scrolls? One cannot deny that this shared *theologoumenon* indicates some Essene influence on the Fourth Gospel, but its extent and the reasons for its occurrence raise different issues.

Predestination. M. Broshi rightly stresses that perhaps "the most important theological point differentiating the sectarians from the rest of Judaism was their belief in predestination, coupled with a dualistic view of the world (*praedestinatio duplex*)."[78] Josephus reported that the Essenes' predestinarianism distinguished them from other Jewish groups, like the Sadducees and Pharisees. As J. C. VanderKam states, the Essenes thought that God "not only predetermined all and then proceeded to create the universe in line with his plan; he also chose to communicate with his creatures and to scatter clues throughout his creation to the structure of the cosmos and the unfolding pattern of history."[79]

One way for Qumranites to explain why well-educated and cultured people, like the reigning high priest, were so impervious to the truth was to say that they were not created as "Sons of Light." Predestination is implied in the *Rule* and apparent in the *Horoscopes*. In John there is no thoroughgoing predestination, because of its missiology (see, e.g., 3:16–21),[80] but there are definite strains of predestination in the claims that no one can come to Jesus "unless the Father" who sent him "draws" that person (6:44), that those who do not believe in Jesus have the devil as their father (8:44), and that the Lord has blinded the eyes of those who do not see (that is, believe) that Jesus is the Christ (12:40; see also 1:12–13; 3:31; 4:42–44; 6:45). Predestination is also apparent in the contrast between those "of God" (8:47) and "of the truth" (18:37), on one side, and those "of the world"

(8:23), "of the earth" (that is, "from below" [3:31]), and "of the devil" (8:44), on the other. Flusser rightly stressed that some "connection or affinity" between the Qumran Scrolls and John is "indicated" by the fact that in both "the predestinational ideas are linked with dualistic motifs: 'He that is from God heareth God's words; ye therefore hear them not; because ye are not from God' [John 8:47]."[81]

Pneumatology. In the scrolls and in the Fourth Gospel we find a strikingly similar pneumatology. Most important, the concept of the "Holy Spirit" (רוח קודש = τὸ πνεῦμα τὸ ἅγιον) in the scrolls reflects a development from the Hebrew scriptures.[82] The Spirit is now a hypostatic being, separate from God. As F. M. Cross stated judiciously, "In the Qumran Rule the Spirit of Truth has a 'greater distance' from God; the hypostatized Spirit *of* God has become largely identified with an angelic creature, the spirit *from* God, and their functions combined."[83] If this development was achieved by the Essenes (as I am convinced), then John has been influenced by this idea. We need to allow, however, for the possibility that earlier Jesus had inherited this concept from the Essenes.[84] The unusual term, "Spirit of truth" (רוח אמת = τὸ πνεῦμα τῆς ἀληθείας), also links the scrolls (1QS 3:18–19; 4:21, 23) and the Gospel (14:17; 15:26; 16:13; cf. the variant in 4:24); apparently, the evangelist inherited this as a technical term from Essenes. In John the Paraclete appears mysteriously, without explanation or introduction; thus, it is wise to consider the advice of O. Betz that the Johannine Paraclete is rooted in Qumran theology.[85] The overall mentality that explains human destiny and meaning through angelology, similarly coined and subservient to one Creator, unites the scrolls and the Gospel of John.[86]

Realizing eschatology. As is well known, Qumran theology, in contrast with the Jewish apocalypses, is built upon the presupposition that the present—and not the far-off future—is the end time.[87] The *pesharim* interpret scripture so that prophecies do not point to the future; they explain the past, present, and near future of the Qumranites. In the *Thanksgiving Hymns* we breathe the air of end-time realization. This is singularly important, since only in John—in stark contrast with the eschatology of the Synoptics, Paul, 2 Peter, and Revelation—do we find a shift from the expectation of the eschaton, or the return of Christ, to the exhortation to experience salvation in the here and now. Surely, in light of obvious Essene influence on John, it is not wise to deny that the eschatology of the evangelist has been shaped by the Essenes.

Esoteric knowledge. Both the Essene literature and the Gospel of John stress esoteric knowledge. For approximately two years, and maybe more, the Qumran initiate was instructed in Essene lore. During this time he was periodically tested and examined for moral and mental acceptance. John reflects a school in which teaching, studying, and interpreting the scriptures proceeded in light of special, revealed knowledge. Both the Qumran Scrolls and the Fourth Gospel are first and foremost revelatory compositions. Both highlight the importance of "knowledge," and this emphasis makes them exceptional in early Jewish literature prior to 135 C.E. This shared emphasis may perhaps be because of Essene influence on John's Gospel.

Salvific and eschatological "living water." Both in the scrolls and in John's Gospel we find a technical term, "living water" (מים חיים [1QH 8:7, 16; 4Q504; 11QTemple 45:16];[88] ὕδωρ ζῶν [John 4:10] or τὸ ὕδωρ τὸ ζῶν [John 4:11]). In both writings this expression denotes eschatological salvation. In the *Biblia Hebraica* it means "running" or fresh water; in the New Testament it appears only in John (cf. Rev. 21:6; 22:1, 17). The noun "water" occurs with unusual frequency in the scrolls, and the provisions for purification at Qumran are exceptional. A shared preoccupation with water distinguishes John from the Synoptics: ὕδωρ appears 21 times in John but only a total of 18 times in the Synoptics (Matthew, 7 occurrences; Mark, 5; Luke, 6). Here, surely, one should be open to some Essene influence on the evangelist.

United community. The Hebrew noun יחד is well known, but in the Dead Sea Scrolls it obtains a unique meaning. It is best translated "Community," which reflects the concept of oneness.[89] It is pervasive in the *Rule,* shaping and uniting the disparate works collected into it. After or just before the schism that devastated the Johannine community, the evangelist enlarged the first edition of John, adding chapters 15 — 17. It is impressive to observe therein the repetitive emphasis placed on the concept of unity, expressed through the word "one." The author depicts Jesus praying to the Father, beseeching that his followers be united into one:

> I do not pray for these only, but also for those who believe in me through their word, that they may be one [ἕν], even as you, O Father, are in me, and I in you. . . . The glory that you gave me I have given to them, so that they may be one [ἕν] even as we are one [ἕν], I in them and you in me, that they may become perfectly one [ἕν] (John 17:20–23).

Is it not conceivable that Essenes, living within the Johannine community and perhaps working in the Johannine school, helped other Johannine Christians work through the tragic traumas of their schism in light of a theology of "being one"? Essene influence at the level of the Gospel's redaction, perhaps as a means of rethinking some aspects of the schism with the synagogue and within the community, needs to be explored.

Purity. The Qumranites accentuated in an extreme way the necessity of ritualistic purity. The author of the Fourth Gospel and his Community knew in a special way the Jewish rites for purification and the debates concerning them (see 2:6 and 3:25). The references in John are oblique, suggesting that perhaps the author knew about the Essene obsession with purity.

Messianology and Christology. Only three Jewish groups prior to the destruction of 70 C.E. clearly yearned for the coming of the Messiah: the Jews behind the *Psalms of Solomon,* the Qumranites, and the followers of Jesus. Recently, interest in Qumran messianism has peaked because of discussions of recently published texts in which "the Messiah" is mentioned.[90] Only in John do we find the Greek transliteration for משיח: Μεσσίαν (1:41) and Μεσσίας (4:25). Clearly the fourth evangelist and his community claimed that Jesus was indeed the Messiah promised to Jews. Were discussions with Essenes, living within or contiguous with the Johannine School, responsible for these aspects of Johannine Christology? It cannot be demonstrated, but it seems a likely scenario to me.

A barrier for love. At Qumran the biblical exhortation to love one's neighbor, which elicited deep discussions on defining "neighbor" among Jews prior to 70 C.E., was restricted to the elect ones, "the Sons of Light." Only members of the community were "Sons of Light"; all others were "Sons of Darkness." Concomitant with Essene predestination, a Qumranite was exhorted to love only those in the community and to hate all others (1QS 1 — 4).[91] Surprising in light of Jesus' exhortation to love "one another" as he had loved his disciples (John 13), and especially in light of his instruction to love even enemies (Matt. 5:44 and parr.), is the Johannine tendency to restrict love to one's fellow Christian. This tendency comes to virtually full bloom in the Johannine epistles. It seems wise to consider Qumran influence in the shaping of this Johannine tendency. As M.-É. Boismard contends, it is rather obvious that 1 John "is addressed to a Christian community whose members to a large extent had been Essenes."[92]

Anonymity. In a frustratingly disconcerting manner the Qumranites habitually avoided proper names. The key figures in their history—that is, the Righteous Teacher, the Wicked Priest, and the Man of Lies—remain anonymous in all of the hundreds of scrolls. While a unique phenomenon in early Jewish literature, this anonymity is amazingly present in the Gospel of John. The fourth evangelist never informs the reader of the name of Jesus' mother. The name of the Beloved Disciple is also hidden from the reader, although his identity was known to the Johannine Christians. The Qumran Scrolls and the Fourth Gospel utilize in stunningly unique ways the narrative art of anonymity. Probably the anonymity of the Righteous Teacher has helped to shape the presentation of the Beloved Disciple.[93]

Symbolic language. In the Dead Sea Scrolls, especially in the *Hodayoth,* column 8, we find an unusually refined employment of symbolism and metaphor.[94] Among over five hundred early Jewish writings, some of the scrolls may be categorized with John in terms of their refined, symbolic theology. Both the Qumran Scrolls and John stand out in early Jewish literature (that is, documents composed by Jews prior to 200 C.E.) with regard to the literary skills demonstrated: the employment of paronomasia, *double entendre,* metaphor, and sophisticated language. I am convinced that the best explanation for this phenomenon is that the fourth evangelist was directly influenced by Essenes: that is, he knew Essenes and discussed theology with them. Their highly developed language helped to shape his own reflections and articulations.

A solar-lunar calendar. The Essenes and the communities behind *Jubilees* and the *Books of Enoch* followed a solar-lunar calendar[95] and thus observed festivals, holy days, and the beginning of the year at a time different from that of the Jewish establishment in Jerusalem. This is a remarkable sociological phenomenon whose theological ramifications are profound when one understands how the Essenes perceived the cosmic dimension of the calendar. Because a time different from that in the Synoptics is given in John for the celebration of the Last Supper, it is conceivable that the Johannine community followed, or recorded that Jesus had followed, an Essene calendar. This possibility is weakened by our inability to discern how unique the Essene calendar was, but it is strengthened by the growing awareness that Jesus, according to John, apparently celebrated the Last Supper within the Essene quarter of Jerusalem.[96]

Other features of Qumran theology reappear in the Gospel of John, but our ability to discern the level and extent of Essene influence is hindered by our inability to determine whether such ideas were unique to the Essenes. Under this category we would place a cosmological panorama for the drama of salvation: The Qumranites thought about angels being present in divine services and celebrated with them the angelic liturgy, while thought in the Johannine community was directed to "the one from above." In the scrolls (especially 1QH 8) and in John (especially chap. 21) narrative art is shaped by motifs of paradise and Eden.[97] Both communities experienced isolation from the Temple cult, and both developed theological reflections in light of persecution from the reigning priests. The Qumran Scrolls and the Fourth Gospel are both shaped in paradigmatic ways by Isaiah. In contrast with other Jewish groups, both preserve a belief in resurrection. Both are shaped by schools. Perhaps the *commandment* of Jesus in 13:34 appears only in John because of the Essene penchant for rules and legislations.

Reconstruction

Scholars agree that the fourth evangelist is influenced either directly or indirectly by the Dead Sea Scrolls. The most obvious point of influence is, as we have seen, Essene dualism. There is, however, no consensus on how this influence made its way into John.

I am impressed by five intriguing hypotheses of how the ideas in the Dead Sea Scrolls have influenced John. First, W. H. Brownlee suggested that the influence from Qumran came through John the Baptist, who may have been an Essene (a suggestion supported in part by Bo Reicke).[98] This hypothesis is indeed conceivable. Some influences from Qumran on John the Baptist are evident, and the Beloved Disciple was probably once a follower of the Baptist.[99] But we know so little about the Baptist. Most important, the obvious tension, reflected in John, between the evangelist's Community and Baptist groups diminishes the possibility that this is the best scenario.[100]

Second, Brown stressed the importance of the scrolls for John and concluded that the influence came to the evangelist indirectly: "In our judgment the parallels are not close enough to suggest a direct literary dependence of John upon the Qumran literature, but they do suggest Johannine familiarity with the type of thought exhibited in the scrolls."[101] In his masterly essay, "The Qumran Scrolls and the Johannine Gospel and Epistles," Brown contended that the "ideas of Qumran must have been fairly widespread in certain Jewish circles in the early first century A.D. Probably it is only through such sources that Qumran had its indirect effect on the Johannine literature."[102] This is admirably cautious, and to suggest that Qumran ideas were widespread seems obvious, but what we have been focusing upon are ideas, symbols, and technical terms that after forty years of research are now seen as *ostensibly unique* to the Qumran community.[103] I concur with Brown that there is no evidence that the evangelist had been an Essene or had studied the *Rule,* yet I agree with J. Ashton that Brown has given us a rather obtuse scenario.[104] Surely the influences from Qumran are more important than an ambiguous explanation that concludes with some inexplicable "indirect" influence.

Third, I argued in the 1960s that the influence was direct.[105] I was convinced that the evangelist "did not borrow from the Essene cosmic and communal theology," but we "have seen that John has apparently been directly influenced by Essene terminology."[106] Ashton, I think not unfairly, criticizes my lack of precision:

> [I]t makes little sense to speak, as Charlesworth does, in terms of "borrowing," however right he may be, against Brown and Schnackenburg, to adopt a theory of direct influence. For what *kind* of borrowing is he thinking of? Does he picture John visiting the Qumran library, as Brown calls it, and taking the Community Rule out of the repository, scrolling through it, taking notes perhaps, and then making use of its ideas when he came to compose his own work?[107]

I never concluded that the evangelist had direct access to a Qumran scroll, but I realize that my presentation could have been improved, beyond stressing that the influence can be explained "through the vivid memory of an Essene who had become a Christian, made notes on its contents, perhaps only mental ones, and then composed his Gospel . . . in Palestine."[108] To clarify my position: the Essenes memorized 1QS 3 and 4, and some of them—I am convinced—entered the Johannine school and left their imprint on the Gospel of John.

Fourth, Ashton calls both Brown and me to task for not realizing how significant is the influence from Qumran. He is convinced that the fourth evangelist had once belonged to Essene groups. He contends that "the evangelist had dualism in his bones . . . [and] may well have started life as one of those Essenes who were to be found, according to Josephus, 'in large numbers in every town.' "[109]

Fifth, and in similar fashion, E. Ruckstuhl has suggested that the Beloved Disciple, the Gospel's trustworthy witness (19:35; 21:24), may have been a monk who once lived in the Essene quarter of Jerusalem. He is impressed by how the Qumran calendar helps to explain the time of Jesus' Last Supper, according to John, and he suggests that this meal may have been an Essene Passover supper.[110] It is possible that the Last Supper was celebrated in the guest house of Jerusalem's Essene quarter and that the seat of honor was given to the Beloved Disciple, a leading Essene. Since he would thus be a priest, it is understandable how he was known to the high priest (John 18:15–17). There is impressive evidence that Essenes were living in the southwestern corner of Jerusalem when Jesus celebrated the Last Supper, and it is conceivable that he celebrated the meal in an Essene quarter. Ruckstuhl's suggestion regarding the date of the Last Supper is, however, rather speculative, and I am persuaded that John 18:15–17 is not a narrative about the Beloved Disciple. It is conceivable, nevertheless, that some Essene influence came to the evangelist through him, since it is probable that he had been a follower of the Baptist.

After more than thirty years of work on John and the Dead Sea Scrolls (usually focusing on the Gospel or on one scroll without thinking about the other), I am persuaded that, while nothing can be clearly demonstrated, a scenario is conceivable. Let me now present what I am convinced is the best explanation for the pervasive, profound Essene influence on the Fourth Gospel.

Not all Qumranites died in the attack on their abode in the wilderness in 68 C.E. Some fled southward to Masada and left some scrolls, which archaeologists have uncovered. Other Qumranites were still alive when the Gospel of John was being written. It seems widely, and wisely, acknowledged that some Essenes became Christians.[111]

The most striking and impressive parallels between the Dead Sea Scrolls and the New Testament documents are in those compositions produced by the second generation of Christians; hence, the influence from the Essenes did not come most powerfully through John the Baptist or Jesus, although (as I have shown) the points of contact here are also impressive. Paul was not significantly influenced by the Essenes, but the Pauline school (which produced Ephesians, 2 Cor. 6:14–7:1, and other documents) shows signs of Essene ideology and terminology. Mark is not similar to the Dead Sea Scrolls, but Matthew certainly contains significant affinities—and that leads us to the School of Matthew. It is obvious that scholars are perceiving in the products of the Pauline school and the Matthean school the most impressive links between the Essenes and early Christianity. The same conclusion applies to John.

John's Gospel comes to us from a Johannine School,[112] reveals sources and probably two editions, and discloses a struggle with the synagogue. These and other observations prove that Jews were in the Johannine Community; it does not seem prudent to deny the possibility that some of these Jews had been Essenes. The influences from the Dead Sea Scrolls in the Gospel of John most likely come, therefore, from former Essenes living in the Johannine Community. They had *memorized* portions of the scrolls, certainly some of the *Thanksgiving Hymns* and the *Rule of the Community* (at least 1QS 3:13–4:14). Some of these former Essenes probably labored in the Johannine School; perhaps one of them was the author of the *Odes of Solomon*.

CONCLUSION

Have the Dead Sea Scrolls revolutionized the interpretation of John? Our answer should be an unequivocal "yes." John is not a late second-century Greek philosophical composition. Using earlier writings, it is in its final form a late first-century composition, influenced significantly by the symbolic language found in the Qumran Scrolls, and is probably our most Jewish Gospel.

The Qumran Scrolls help us to perceive how Johannine Christians searched for their own identity in a world that had become increasingly more hostile. The search for identity had been sought earlier by the followers of the Righteous Teacher, who led a small band of priests from the Temple in Jerusalem to an abandoned ruin in the wilderness just west of the Dead Sea. The Johannine Christians founded their faith on the truthful eyewitness of the Beloved Disciple (John 19:35; 21:24). Today many discover their own identity by reading the scrolls, John's Gospel, and often both.

The Dead Sea Scrolls challenge us to think about the source of the fourth evangelist's vocabulary. They help to clarify the uniqueness of the Gospel of John and the evangelist's distinctive anthropology, cosmology, Christology, and theology.

NOTES

1. It is a personal pleasure and honor to think of Moody Smith in writing this work. He and I have been friends, colleagues, and tennis partners for over thirty years. He has been a mentor and a confidant, and has brought considerable happiness into my life. An expanded version of this essay will appear in a forthcoming publication.

2. See the trustworthy, nonsensational introductions of J. C. VanderKam, *The Dead Sea Scrolls Today* (Grand Rapids: Eerdmans, 1994); J. A. Fitzmyer, *Responses to 101 Questions on the Dead Sea Scrolls* (New York: Paulist, 1992); H. Stegemann, *Die Essener, Qumran, Johannes der Täufer und Jesus* (Freiburg: Herder, 1993).

3. See, for example, *Paul and the Dead Sea Scrolls,* ed. J. Murphy-O'Connor, O.P., and J. H. Charlesworth (New York: Crossroad, 1990); and *The Scrolls and the New Testament,* ed. K. Stendahl with J. H. Charlesworth (New York: Crossroad, 1992).

4. Baur pointed to an *Entwicklungsprozess* ("developmental process"), which proved that John could not belong to the apostolic period (*Kritische Untersuchungen über die kanonischen Evangelien* [Tübingen: Fues, 1847], esp. 328, 365, 378, 383). See the insightful discussion by M. Hengel, "Bishop Lightfoot and the Tübingen School on the Gospel of John and the Second Century," *Durham University Journal* (January 1992): 23–51, N.B. 24.

5. A. Loisy, *Le quatrième évangile* (Paris: Picard, 1903), 123–29.

6. J. Weiss, *Das Urchristentum* (Göttingen: Vandenhoeck & Ruprecht, 1917), 624.

7. E. J. Goodspeed, *An Introduction to the New Testament* (Chicago: University of Chicago Press, 1937), 314–15.

8. In the 1960s I remember R. E. Cushman, then Dean of Duke Divinity School, discussing with me why it was clear to him that John was composed by a Christian who was deeply imbued with Platonic philosophy.

9. M. Hengel, *The Johannine Question* (London: SCM, 1989), 111. Note also C. K. Barrett, who contends that "two circumstances have led to a strong reiteration of the Jewish background and origin of the gospel: on the one hand, the criticism, directed against Bultmann and those who follow him, concerning the relative lateness of the comparative material used to establish a Gnostic background of John; on the other, and more important, the discovery of the Qumran scrolls" (*The Gospel of John and Judaism* [Philadelphia: Fortress, 1975], 7–8).

10. Cf. K. Aland, "Der Text des Johannesevangeliums im 2. Jahrhundert," in *Studien zum Text und zur Ethik des Neuen Testaments,* ed. W. Schrage (Berlin: de Gruyter, 1986), 1–10.

11. See J. Ashton, *Understanding the Fourth Gospel* (Oxford: Clarendon, 1991), 199–204.

12. See U. C. von Wahlde, *The Earliest Version of John's Gospel* (Wilmington: Glazier, 1989).

13. See J. Jeremias, *The Rediscovery of Bethesda* (Louisville, Ky.: Southern Baptist Theological Seminary, 1966).

14. In 3Q15 11:12 J. T. Milik reads אשדתין בית and takes the second noun to be a dual construction (*Beth Esdatayin*); hence, the meaning could be "[in] the House of the Two Pools" ("Le rouleau de cuivre provenant de la Grotte 3Q (3Q15)," in *Les 'Petites Grottes' de Qumrân,* ed. M. Baillet, J. T. Milik, and R. de Vaux, DJD 3 [Oxford: Clarendon, 1962], 214, 271–72).

15. See J. Jeremias, *ABBA* (Göttingen: Vandenhoeck & Ruprecht, 1966), 361–64.

16. According to the text and translation in *The Temple Scroll,* ed. Y. Yadin (Jerusalem: Israel Exploration Society, 1983), 2.222–24.

17. N. Avigad, *Discovering Jerusalem* (Nashville: Thomas Nelson, 1983), 176; for photographs and pertinent discussions, see 120–36.

18. D. M. Smith, "Historical Issues and the Problem of John and the Synoptics," in *From Jesus to John,* ed. M. C. de Boer, JSNTSup 84 (Sheffield: JSOT, 1994), 252–67.

19. See G.H.C. Stuart, *The Struggle in Man between Good and Evil* (Kampen: Kok, 1984), esp. 94–100.

20. One manuscript of this document was found in Cave I, ten copies in Cave IV, and one in Cave V. The critical edition of the *Rule,* with apparatus, may be found in the Princeton Theological Seminary Dead Sea Scrolls Project: *The Dead Sea Scrolls—Hebrew, Aramaic, and Greek Texts with English Translations,* vol. 1: *Rule of the Community and Related Documents,* ed. J. H. Charlesworth (Tübingen: J.C.B. Mohr [Paul Siebeck]; Louisville, Ky.: Westminster John Knox Press, 1994).

21. A pre-Qumran origin of the *Angelic Liturgy* is conceivable, but the work was certainly used in the Qumran community and its composition at Qumran is probable, as C. A. Newsom points out (*Songs of the Sabbath Sacrifice,* HSS 27 [Atlanta: Scholars Press, 1985], 2).

22. See E. P. Sanders, *Judaism: Practice & Belief 63 B.C.E.–66 C.E.* (London: SCM, 1992), 349.

23. Despite the dissent of a few authors, a consensus still exists among the best Qumran specialists on the identification of the Qumranites with the Essenes. L. H. Schiffman challenges the Essene origins of the Qumran group, but he has affirmed (at

least to me on several occasions) that the Qumran group in the first century C.E. is to be identified as Essenes. After almost thirty years of teaching and publishing on the Qumran Scrolls, I have concluded that the Qumran group was a sect (deliberately removing itself, sociologically and theologically, from other Jews and, indeed, persecuted by the powerful Temple group), and that we should think about Qumran Essenes, Jerusalem Essenes, and other Essene and Essene-related groups living on the outskirts of most of the Jewish cities, as Philo and Josephus reported. See, further, Schiffman, *Reclaiming the Dead Sea Scrolls* (Philadelphia: The Jewish Publication Society, 1994).

24. The verb ὑπήκουον ("followed") with the dative case denotes full surrender.

25. For evidence of Essenes living in Jerusalem, see the pertinent chapters in *Jesus and the Dead Sea Scrolls*, ed. J. H. Charlesworth (New York: Doubleday, 1992).

26. This statement does not mean that the Essenes affirmed in their own writings the belief in a resurrection. They did not reject it, and they used books in which it was clearly present: namely, Daniel 12, *1 Enoch*, and *On Resurrection* (4Q521).

27. R. C. Stallman, "Levi and the Levites in the Dead Sea Scrolls," *JSP* 10 (1992): 163–89.

28. Both the *Temple Scroll* and Josephus mention a gate, purportedly that of the Essenes, which was located at the southern end of Jerusalem's western wall. Many archaeologists now claim that a gate, below the remains of a Byzantine and probably a Herodian gate, is indeed the "Essene Gate." It is located in the southwestern section of the old wall of Jerusalem (not the present Turkish wall) and appears in the model of first-century Jerusalem near the Holy Land Hotel. For photographs, drawings, and discussion, see R. Riesner, "Jesus, the Primitive Community, and the Essene Quarter of Jerusalem," in *Jesus and the Dead Sea Scrolls*, 198–234.

29. See the pertinent chapters in *Paul and the Dead Sea Scrolls*.

30. K. Stendahl demonstrated that there is a school of Matthew and that scholars within it interpreted scripture in a manner strikingly similar to that found in the Qumran commentaries, or *pesharim* (*The School of St. Matthew and Its Use of the Old Testament*, rev. ed. [Philadelphia: Fortress, 1968]). Also see K. Schubert, "The Sermon on the Mount and the Qumran Texts," in *The Scrolls and the New Testament*, 118–28; and W. D. Davies, *The Setting of the Sermon on the Mount* (Cambridge: Cambridge University Press, 1966), esp. 208–56. Davies argues—and I fully concur—that the Sermon on the Mount "reveals an awareness of the [Dead Sea Scroll] Sect and perhaps a polemic against it" (235). On the links between Essene thought and Ephesians, see *Paul and the Dead Sea Scrolls*, ix–xvi. Essene affinities with John are recognized by the contributions in *John and the Dead Sea Scrolls*, ed. J. H. Charlesworth (New York: Crossroad, 1991).

31. Translation by Charlesworth, *The Rule of the Community and Related Documents*.

32. 4Q381 85 reads הבן, but it means "understand."

33. See F. García-Martínez, "4 Q Mes. Aram. y el Libro de Noe," in *Escritos de Biblia y Oriente*, ed. R. Aguirre and F. García Lopez, Bibliotheca Salmanticensis 38 (Salamanca: Casa de Santiago, 1981), 195–232; also, B. T. Viviano, "Aramaic 'Messianic' Text," *ABD* 1 (1992): 342.

34. J. A. Fitzmyer, *A Wandering Aramean: Collected Aramaic Essays*, SBLMS 25 (Missoula, Mont.: Scholars Press, 1979), 92–93 (see also 90–91, 102–7); idem, "The Aramaic 'Son of God' Text from Qumran Cave 4," in *Methods of Investigation*

of the Dead Sea Scrolls and the Khirbet Qumran Site, ed. M. O. Wise (New York: New York Academy of Sciences, 1994), 163–78. Milik had lectured on this text at Harvard as early as 1972.

35. Fitzmyer's translation; for text and translation, see his *A Wandering Aramean,* 92–93.

36. See Charlesworth in *John and the Dead Sea Scrolls,* xiii–xvi, 76–106.

37. E. Haenchen draws attention to the importance of the Dead Sea Scrolls for interpreting John 4; see *John 1,* Hermeneia (Philadelphia: Fortress, 1984), 223. Compare P. Garnet, *Salvation and Atonement in the Qumran Scrolls,* WUNT 2 (Tübingen: Mohr [Siebeck], 1977).

38. Clearer in the *Horoscopes* than in the Rule is the explanation that each Son of Light has a mixture of darkness along with light (see esp. 4Q186). Each human has nine parts, some of light and others of darkness. Some humans are very evil, having eight parts of darkness and one of light; other humans are nearly perfect, having eight parts of light and one of darkness.

39. The appearance of the technical term "Sons of Light" has been found only in Qumran compositions and in documents influenced by Qumran theology. See D. Flusser, *Judaism and the Origins of Christianity* (Jerusalem: Magnes, 1988), esp. 26; idem, "The Parable of the Unjust Steward: Jesus' Criticism of the Essenes," in *Jesus and the Dead Sea Scrolls,* 176–97.

40. Those who are convinced that John is predestinarian will be impressed by the possibility of additional Qumran influence, because it was at Qumran that predestination was developed in a unique way in Second Temple Judaism. See J. H. Charlesworth, "The Theologies in the Dead Sea Scrolls," in H. Ringgren, *The Faith of Qumran* (New York: Crossroad, 1995). Also see R. Schnackenburg, *The Gospel according to St John,* 3 vols. (New York: Crossroad, 1968–87), 1.132–33, and the discussion of predestination in the "Summary," below.

41. R. E. Brown, *The Gospel according to John (i–xii),* AB 29 (Garden City, N.Y.: Doubleday, 1966), lxii.

42. Brown concludes (ibid., lxiii): "In our judgment the parallels are not close enough to suggest a direct literary dependence of John upon the Qumran literature, but *they do suggest Johannine familiarity with the type of thought exhibited in the scrolls*" (italics mine).

43. Some of the Hermetic tractates and Gnostic codices are strikingly similar to John, but the influence seems to flow from the Fourth Gospel to them.

44. D. M. Smith, *Johannine Christianity* (Columbia, S.C.: University of South Carolina Press, 1984), 26.

45. J. Painter, *The Quest for the Messiah,* 2d ed. (Nashville: Abingdon, 1993), 29.

46. See O. Böcher, *Der johanneische Dualismus im Zusammenhang des nachbiblischen Judentums* (Gütersloh: Mohn, 1965); R. E. Brown, "The Qumran Scrolls and the Johannine Gospels and Epistles," in *The Scrolls and the New Testament,* 183–208; Schnackenburg, *The Gospel according to St John,* 1.108, 128–35, 241, 249, and 402–7; and most of the essays in *John and the Dead Sea Scrolls.* G. Baumbach denies a direct influence from the *Rule* on John; see his *Qumran und das Johannesevangelium,* AVTR 6 (Berlin: Evangelische Verlagsanstalt, 1957), 53.

47. J. L. Martyn, *History and Theology in the Fourth Gospel,* 2d ed. (Nashville: Abingdon, 1979); R. E. Brown, *The Community of the Beloved Disciple* (New York: Paulist, 1979).

48. W. A. Meeks, *The Moral World of the First Christians* (Philadelphia: Westminster, 1986), 109; see also idem, *The Prophet-King,* NovTSup 14 (Leiden: Brill, 1967).

49. See A. Guilding, *The Fourth Gospel and Jewish Worship* (Oxford: Clarendon, 1960), 92–120. I am also indebted to discussions with students, especially with Scott Shidemantle, in my seminars on the Gospel of John.

50. See esp. Brown, *The Community of the Beloved Disciple;* D. M. Smith, *First, Second, and Third John* (Louisville, Ky.: John Knox, 1991); and R. Schnackenburg, *The Johannine Epistles* (New York: Crossroad, 1992), 17–24.

51. See E. Käsemann, *The Testament of Jesus* (Philadelphia: Fortress, 1968), and the counterarguments by Hengel, *The Johannine Question,* 68; R. A. Whitacre, *Johannine Polemic,* SBLDS 67 (Chico, Calif.: Scholars Press, 1982), 127–28; and M. M. Thompson, *The Humanity of Jesus in the Fourth Gospel* (Philadelphia: Fortress, 1988).

52. The rumors that this text has the Messiah raise the dead is based on a dubious restoration and overlooks the fact that, in the immediate context, the governing subject is clearly "the Lord."

53. See W. Baldensperger, *Der Prolog des vierten Evangeliums* (Freiburg: Mohr [Siebeck], 1898); R. Bultmann, *The Gospel of John* (Philadelphia: Westminster, 1971), 84–97.

54. The hypothesis that Qumran influence impinged on the writing of the Fourth Gospel through John the Baptist will be considered in my "Reconstruction," below.

55. R. A. Culpepper, *The Johannine School,* SBLDS 26 (Missoula, Mont:. Scholars Press, 1975). See also G. Strecker, "Die Anfänge der Johanneishchen Schule," *NTS* 32 (1986): 31–47, and E. Ruckstuhl, "Zur Antithese Idiolekt—Soziolekt im johanneischen Schrifttum," in *Jesus im Horizont der Evangelien* (Stuttgart: Katholisches Bibelwerk, 1988), 219–64.

56. Bultmann, *The Gospel of John,* 13–18.

57. *Papyrus Bodmer X–XII,* ed. M. Testuz (Cologne: Bibliotheca Bodmeriana, 1959).

58. J. Licht, "Solomon, Odes of," *EncJud* 15 (1971): 114–15.

59. J. Carmignac, "Un qumrânien converti au christianisme: L'auteur des Odes de Salomon," in *Qumran-Probleme,* ed. H. Bardtke (Berlin: Akademie, 1963), 75–108; J. H. Charlesworth, "Les Odes de Salomon et les manuscrits de la Mer Morte," *RB* 77 (1970): 522–49.

60. See Charlesworth in *John and the Dead Sea Scrolls,* 107–36.

61. Smith, *Johannine Christianity,* 27.

62. See J. H. Charlesworth and R. A. Culpepper, "The Odes of Solomon and the Gospel of John," *CBQ* 35 (1973): 298–322.

63. Even though we have come to realize how different are the *Tendenzen* of Mark, Matthew, and Luke, I concur with the majority that there is still merit in seeing these three Gospels together and in contrast with John, because they tend to see the chronology and teaching of Jesus with (*syn*) the same eye (*optic*). Yet we must be alert to the distortions that also can arise by the assumption that they see Jesus synoptically and with little differences.

64. Although the author of John may have known one of the Synoptics, he was not dependent on them, as Gardner-Smith, Goodenough, Käsemann, Cullmann, Robinson, Smith, and other gifted scholars have demonstrated in different ways. As P. Borgen

pointed out, John seems to relate to the pre-Synoptic tradition that is evident, for example, in Paul ("John and the Synoptics," in *The Interrelations of the Gospels*, ed. D. L. Dungan, BETL 95 [Leuven: Leuven University Press, 1990], 408–37). See now the major study by D. M. Smith, *John among the Gospels* (Minneapolis: Fortress, 1992), and idem, "The Problem of John and the Synoptics in Light of the Relation Between Apocryphal and Canonical Gospels," in *John and the Synoptics,* ed. A. Denaux, BETL 101 (Leuven: Leuven University Press, 1992), 147–62.

65. W. A. Meeks, "The Man from Heaven in Johannine Sectarianism," *JBL* 91 (1972): 44–72; see esp. 70–71.

66. I use the term "liminality" in the sense defined by V. Turner, *Process, Performance, and Pilgrimage* (New Delhi: Concept, 1979), esp. 11–59; see also J. Z. Smith, "Birth Upside Down or Right Side Up?" *HR* 9 (1969–70): 281–303; idem, "A Place on Which to Stand: Symbols and Social Change," *Worship* 44 (1970): 457–74.

67. See J. H. Neyrey, *An Ideology of Revolt* (Philadelphia: Fortress, 1988), esp. 208–9.

68. H. Leroy, *Rätsel und Missverständnis*, BBB 30 (Bonn: Hanstein, 1968).

69. As Painter points out, "This comparison [between John and Qumran] is important because it highlights the sectarian character of both the Qumran community and the Johannine Christians" (*Quest,* 38). See also M.-É. Boismard in *John and the Dead Sea Scrolls,* 156–65.

70. See the studies by Jewish and Christian scholars in *Hillel and Jesus,* ed. J. H. Charlesworth and L. Johns (Minneapolis: Fortress, 1996), and compare the treatment of R. A. Culpepper, *Anatomy of the Fourth Gospel* (Philadelphia: Fortress, 1983), 125–32.

71. Here I am succinctly collecting my own reflections over thirty years; I am not reviewing the research by Qumran and Johannine experts nor merely summarizing the previous discussion. Hence, it is not possible to present an exhaustive report of the best research. For bibliographical assistance, consult B. Jongeling, *A Classified Bibliography of the Finds in the Desert of Judah 1958–1969,* STDJ 7 (Leiden: Brill, 1971), 111–29, and J. A. Fitzmyer, *The Dead Sea Scrolls: Major Publications and Tools for Study,* rev. ed. (Atlanta: Scholars Press, 1990), 173–79.

72. D. Flusser, *The Spiritual History of the Dead Sea Sect* (Tel Aviv: MOD, 1989), 46.

73. Schnackenburg, *The Gospel according to St John,* 1.129.

74. Ibid., 1.131–32.

75. In using these terms I wish to express my indebtedness to R. de Vaux, P. Benoit, and J. Murphy-O'Connor, who during my time at the École Biblique emphasized, under the influence of J. Guitton, that early Christian theology was shaped by the *esprit* of Jesus and in some ways developed through the *mentalité* of Qumran.

76. See W. D. Davies, "Paul and the Dead Sea Scrolls: Flesh and Spirit," in *The Scrolls and the New Testament,* 157–82; Flusser, *The Spiritual History of the Dead Sea Sect,* 52–56.

77. See J.D.G. Dunn, "Jesus—Flesh and Spirit: An Exposition of Romans I.3–4," *JTS* 24 (1973): 40–68, esp. 52–55. It is surprising to see today R. P. Menzies's conclusion that the dualism in the *Rule* is a psychological dualism, pertaining to "human dispositions" (*The Development of Early Christian Pneumatology,* JSNTSup 54 [Sheffield: JSOT, 1991], 80).

78. M. Broshi, *The Dead Sea Scrolls* (Tokyo: Kodansha, 1979), 12–20 (quotation, 15). Flusser concurs: "The great basic idea, which the Teacher of Righteousness apparently

gave the world and which differed from those of similar movements of his age, was the doctrine we call the doctrine of predestination" (*The Spiritual History of the Dead Sea Sect*, 46). I am impressed that the three of us independently came to the startling conclusion that the Essenes bequeathed to western civilization the concept of predestination.

79. J. C. VanderKam, *The Dead Sea Scrolls Today* (Grand Rapids: Eerdmans, 1994), 109.

80. See Schnackenburg, *The Gospel according to St John*, 1.132–33.

81. Flusser, *Judaism and the Origins of Christianity*, 28–29.

82. See F. F. Bruce, "Holy Spirit in the Qumran Texts," *ALUOS* 6 (1966–68): 49–55.

83. F. M. Cross, *The Ancient Library of Qumran and Modern Biblical Studies* (Grand Rapids: Baker, [1958, 1961], 1980), 213 (italics his).

84. See my discussion in *Jesus and the Dead Sea Scrolls*, 20–22.

85. O. Betz, *Der Paraklet Fürsprecher im häretischen Spätjudentum, im Johannesevangelium und in neu gefundenen gnostischen Schriften*, AGJU 2 (Leiden: Brill, 1963). Also see A.R.C. Leaney, "The Johannine Paraclete and the Qumran Scrolls," *John and the Dead Sea Scrolls*, 38–61.

86. Of course, the authors of the scrolls habitually refer to God as אל, whereas the fourth evangelist preserves Jesus' preferred reference to God as Father, πατήρ (e.g., John 14:8–11).

87. One of the best studies is by H.-W. Kuhn, *Enderwartung und gegenwärtiges Heil*, SUNT 4 (Göttingen: Vandenhoeck & Ruprecht, 1966).

88. See J. H. Charlesworth, "An Allegorical and Autobiographical Poem by the Moreh Has-Sedeq (1QH 8:4–11)," in *"Sha'arei Talmon"*, ed. M. Fishbane, E. Tov, and W. W. Fields (Winona Lake, Ind.: Eisenbrauns, 1992), 295–307.

89. P. Wernberg-Møller long ago warned against thinking that the יחד indicated "a monastically organized society of Jewish ascetics." He rightly stressed that the community was "open for membership to any pious Jew of the required intellectual and moral standard" ("The Nature of the YAHAD According to the Manual of Discipline and Related Documents," *ALUOS* 6 [1966–68], 56–81 [quotations, 68]). See also S. Talmon, *The World of Qumran from Within* (Jerusalem: Magnes, 1989), 53–60; J. Maier, "Zum Begriff יחד in den Texten von Qumran," in *Qumran*, ed. K. E. Grözinger (Darmstadt: Wissenschaftliche Buchgesellschaft, 1981), 225–48.

90. Wild and unprofessional claims about the messiah in some Dead Sea Scrolls have been made. For a judicious assessment, see the chapters by Charlesworth, Schiffman, VanderKam, and Talmon in *The Messiah*, ed. J. H. Charlesworth (Minneapolis: Fortress, 1992), as well as the chapters by Collins, VanderKam, and Puech in *The Community of the Renewed Covenant*, ed. E. Ulrich and J. VanderKam (Notre Dame, Ind.: University of Notre Dame Press, 1994). Equally important are Flusser, *The Spiritual History of the Dead Sea Sect*, 83–89, and L. H. Schiffman, *Reclaiming the Dead Sea Scrolls* (Philadelphia: Jewish Publication Society, 1994), 317–27.

91. See Flusser, *The Spiritual History of the Dead Sea Sect*, 76–82.

92. Boismard, in *John and the Dead Sea Scrolls*, 165.

93. See J. Roloff, "Der johanneische 'Lieblingsjünger' und der 'Lehrer der Gerechtigkeit,'" *NTS* 15 (1968–69): 129–51.

94. See Charlesworth, "An Allegorical and Autobiographical Poem."

95. See the authoritative study of Talmon in *The World of Qumran from Within*, 147–85.

96. See the discussions in Charlesworth, *Jesus and the Dead Sea Scrolls*.

97. As Adam, having sinned, knew that he was naked before God, so Peter, having denied the Christ, is described as naked and jumping into the cleansing water before the Lord.

98. W. H. Brownlee, "John the Baptist in the New Light of Ancient Scrolls," in *The Scrolls and the New Testament*, 33–53; idem, "Whence the Gospel according to John?" in *John and the Dead Sea Scrolls*, 166–94; cf. Bo Reicke, "Nytt ljus över Johannes döparens förkunnelse," *Religion och Bibel* 11 (1952): 5–18.

99. See my *The Beloved Disciple* (Valley Forge, Pa.: Trinity Press International, 1995), esp. chapter 12.

100. Thus, Ashton: "The pervasive and deep-lying dualistic structures . . . are scarcely to be accounted for by the suggestion that the evangelist was a disciple of John the Baptist, unless the latter was himself so deeply soaked in Qumranian ideas as to be virtually indistinguishable from one of the community's own teachers" (*Understanding the Fourth Gospel*, 235).

101. Brown, *The Gospel according to John (i–xii)*, 29.lxiii.

102. Brown, rpt. in *The Scrolls and the New Testament*, 206 (originally published in 1955).

103. See, further, my introductory comments in Ringgren, *The Faith of Qumran*.

104. See Ashton, *Understanding the Fourth Gospel*, 235.

105. I was (and remain) influenced by Brown's research, as well as that published by K. G. Kuhn: "Johannesevangelium und Qumrantexte," in *Neotestamentica et Patristica*, ed. W. C. van Unnik, NovTSup 6 (Leiden: Brill, 1962), 111–22; idem, "Die in Palästina gefundenen hebräischen Texte und das Neue Testament," *ZTK* 47 (1950): 192–211.

106. Charlesworth, *John and the Dead Sea Scrolls*, 103–4. This essay was first published in *NTS* 15 (1968–69): 389–418.

107. Ashton, *Understanding the Fourth Gospel*, 236–37.

108. Charlesworth, *John and the Dead Sea Scrolls*, 105. What I omit from this quotation is my attempt to state in the 1990s what should have been presented more lucidly in the 1960s.

109. Ashton, *Understanding the Fourth Gospel*, 237.

110. E. Ruckstuhl, "Zur Chronologie der Leidensgeschichte Jesu, I," *SNTU* 10 (1985): 27–61 (esp. 55–56) + "Zur Chronologie der Leidensgeschichte Jesu, II," *SNTU* 11 (1986): 97–129; idem, *Jesus im Horizont der Evangelien* (Stuttgart: Katholisches Bibelwerk, 1988), 393–95.

111. It is conceivable that none of the Qumranites ever became Christians. That still leaves most of the Essenes to be accounted for—over 3,700 of the 4,000 Essenes living in ancient Palestine, if Philo and Josephus can be trusted. Did none of the Essenes join the Palestinian Jesus Movement? Is that likely when Pharisees are clearly known to have joined it?

112. Perhaps other compositions as well come from the Johannine school, including 1, 2 and 3 John, the Apocalypse of John, and the *Odes of Solomon*. Ignatius probably knew John and the *Odes*, but it is difficult to prove this point.

5

The Gospel of John and Hellenism: Some Observations

THE SITUATION IN RECENT RESEARCH

The Greco-Roman setting of the Gospel of John (= John) is self-evident and obvious. The Gospel is written in Greek and tells about Jesus, who was executed when Pilate was Roman governor of Judea. Its Jewish background is also evident, since it reports on persons and events that took place among Jews and Samaritans in Judea, Galilee, and Samaria. In John 7:35 the question is raised whether Jesus intends to go outside of Palestine to the Diaspora among the Greeks (Έλληνες), and according to John 12:20–21 some Greeks, who were among those who went up to Jerusalem for the Passover feast, wished to see Jesus.[1]

The topic of this chapter is "The Gospel of John and Hellenism." The first question to be addressed is the problem of defining the term "Hellenism." It has been used to designate the period from Alexander the Great (356–23 B.C.E.) to Roman imperial rule (ca. 30 B.C.E.).[2] As far as culture, philosophy, and religion are concerned, the epoch does not end with the establishment of the Roman Empire. In the characterization of these aspects of Hellenism, some scholars place the emphasis on Greek elements, others on Oriental features. Against the background of such aspects, it is relevant to raise the question of John and Hellenism.

In his book *The Interpretation of the Fourth Gospel,* C. H. Dodd emphasized Greek elements and developed a Platonizing interpretation of John. He took his starting point in the thoughts and ideas of the Gospel rather than in the person of Christ. In an appendix he stated, "It will have become clear that I regard the Fourth Gospel as being in its essential character a theological work."[3] The author "is thinking not so much of Christians who need a deeper theology, as of non-Christians who are concerned about eternal life and the way to it, and may be ready to follow the Christian way if this is presented to them in terms that are intelligibly related to their previous religious interest and experience."[4]

Dodd drew largely on parallel ideas in Philo's writings and concluded that whatever other elements of thoughts may be found in John, it certainly presupposes ideas having remarkable resemblance to ideas of Hellenistic Judaism, as represented by

Philo. There is a decisive difference, however. John conceives of the Logos as incarnate, and of the true human as not merely dwelling as reason in all humans. Logos, which in Philo is personal only in a fluctuating series of metaphors, is in John fully personal, standing in personal relation with God and with people and having a place in history. As a result, those elements of personal piety, faith, and love, which are present in Philo's religion but not fully integrated into his philosophy, come into their own in the Gospel. The logos of Philo is not the object of faith and love, but the incarnate Logos of the Fourth Gospel is both lover and beloved: To love him and to have faith in him is of the essence of that knowledge of God which is eternal life.[5]

Against Dodd it should be said that while there is in Philo's writings extensive use of Greek philosophical ideas that largely have a Middle-Platonic stamp,[6] this is not the case in John. Therefore, one cannot use Philo's writings in such a direct way as Dodd does to describe the background of John. However, Philo may exemplify Jewish traditions and thought-categories that are interpreted along different lines by him and by John.

Likewise, Dodd emphasizes that the Johannine ideas show kinship with ideas in some of the tractates of the Hermetic writings: "It seems clear that as a whole they represent a type of religious thought akin to one side of Johannine thought, without any substantial borrowing on one side or the other."[7] One can concur with Dodd's view that some ideas in the Hermetic writings are akin to elements of Johannine thought, but the many other ideas in those writings differ greatly from John.[8] Thus, the question of how the points of kinship are to be understood must be subject to further discussion.

Rudolf Bultmann placed John within the context of a form of Hellenistic syncretism in which Gnosticism was the dominant factor. He took the person Jesus as his point of departure and interpreted Johannine Christology against the background of the Gnostic myth:

> *The Gnostic myth* depicts the cosmic drama by which the imprisonment of the sparks of light came about, a drama whose end is already beginning now and will be complete when they are released. The drama's beginning, the tragic event of primeval time, is variously told in the several variants of the myth. But the basic idea is constant: The demonic powers get into their clutches a person who originates in the light-world either because he is led astray by his own foolishness or because he is overcome in battle. The individual selves of the "pneumatics" are none other than the parts or splinters of that light-person. . . . . *Redemption* comes from the heavenly world. Once more a light-person sent by the highest god, indeed the son and "image" of the most high, comes down from the light-world bringing *Gnosis*. He "wakes" the sparks of light . . . and "reminds" them of their heavenly home.[9]

> [T]he figure of Jesus in John is portrayed in the forms offered by the Gnostic Redeemer-myth. . . . It is true that the cosmological motifs of the

myth are missing in John, especially the idea that the redemption which the "Ambassador" brings is the release of the pre-existent sparks of light which are held captive in this world by demonic powers. . . . But otherwise Jesus appears as in the Gnostic myth as the pre-existent Son of God whom the Father clothed with authority and sent into the world. Here, appearing as a man, he speaks the words the Father gave him and accomplishes the works which the Father commissioned him to do.[10]

Bultmann's characterization of early Gnosticism, which lies behind the later Gnosticism documented in literary sources, is rather hypothetical. Moreover, Bultmann himself admitted that John differs from the Gnostic myth at central points. Thus, it is justified to see if other sources can give us a better picture of the background for the thought-world of John and, at the same time, to look for affinities between Johannine ideas and ideas found in later Gnostic writings.

The only body of writings upon which John with certainty depends is the Old Testament.[11] Thus, John's use of the Old Testament and exegetical traditions needs to be examined to see whether it may reflect Hellenistic features. Other relevant sources of information can be used in a more general way, such as parallel ideas, methods, and forms, as well as social and historical data gleaned from literary and archaeological sources.

Sources from ancient Judaism are of primary interest. One basic observation is the fact that Judaism in antiquity belonged to the Hellenistic world. Raymond E. Brown and Martin Hengel take this broader context of Judaism as background for John but do not regard this as the primary question to ask. Brown writes: "We take for granted, therefore, a Greek strain within Judaism which had an influence on Johannine vocabulary and thought. But the question which we ask here is whether there was another Hellenistic influence on John that did not come through Judaism but come from without."[12] Correspondingly, Martin Hengel stresses the Jewish nature of John: "That does not mean that the Gospel is clearly cut off from the world of 'Hellenism'; certainly not. Rather, it belongs in it to the degree that ancient pre-rabbinic Judaism in its creative multiplicity is also a part of the 'Hellenistic world', in Palestine and the Diaspora."[13]

Instead of looking for direct influence from outside of Judaism, the difficult challenge is, then, to look into the possibility that John has distinctively Jewish and Christian expressions of broader Hellenistic features. Accordingly, the following hypothesis will guide the present analysis of John and Hellenism: On the basis of Gospel traditions and further Jewish and Christian developments, John cultivates ideas and practices that to some extent are distinctively Jewish-Christian versions of aspects and trends present in the larger Hellenistic world. John's Gospel has a distinctive unity of thought in its interpretation of the traditions from and about Jesus. Its various aspects may, nevertheless, show affinities with different ideas and practices in the Hellenistic surroundings.

Before entering into such an examination, one has to realize that the division between Palestinian (or normative) Judaism and Hellenistic Judaism is not basic and does not provide us with an adequate tool for categorization.[14] Thus, both Jewish writings from the Diaspora, such as the writings of Philo of Alexandria,[15] and Palestinian writings, such as the Dead Sea Scrolls, are relevant sources. The rabbinic material is hard to date, but some of the traditions go back to New Testament times or before. When parallels are found in datable writings such as Philo's writings, the Dead Sea Scrolls, Josephus, and the New Testament, then there is a case for judging rabbinic material to have come from the first century C.E. or earlier.

Within the limits of this chapter, only a few ideas can be selected for analysis. Thus, the observations made are, out of necessity, incomplete. This study should then be followed by further discussions about John's "I am" sayings, the theme "to know God/the Son," Docetism or anti-Docetism, elements of predestination, and so forth.[16] The present analysis will thus be limited to the following topics: agency, ascent/descent and vision of God, "birth from above," equality with God, wisdom and logos, internationalization, "the Jews," the cosmos, and light and darkness. The examination will be based upon the Gospel in its present form, without entering into discussion of the question of possible sources.

AGENCY

The idea and practice of agency can serve as a convenient starting point.[17] The Jesus-logion found in John 13:20 ("he who receives any one whom I send receives me; and he who receives me receives him who sent me")[18] has a firm place in the Gospel tradition, as seen from the parallels in Matthew 10:40; Mark 9:37; Luke 9:48; and 10:16, as well as the variants present in John 5:23; 8:19; 12:44–45; 14:7 and 19; and 15:32.[19] The saying, as such, formulates a principle and a rule of agency among persons, as stated in the Halakhah: "an agent is like the one who sent him."[20] Another conventional rule for the practice of agency among persons is formulated in John 13:16: "a servant is not greater than his master; nor is he who is sent [ἀπόστολος] greater than he who sent him." A close parallel occurs in *Genesis Rabbah* 78: "the sender is greater than the sent."

Such rules reflect, of course, the normal conventions for agency and diplomacy in the Greco-Roman world.[21] Philo may serve here as an example. He was the head of a delegation from Alexandrian Jewry to Emperor Gaius Caligula, and he stated as a generally practiced rule that "the suffering of envoys recoils on those who have sent him" (*De Legat. ad Gaium* 369). In general, therefore, the rules of agency and diplomacy demonstrate that Judaism, inclusive of early Christianity, functioned within the wider Hellenistic world. Philo uses the technical Greek terms for an envoy, πρεσβευτής (*In Flac.* 98 and *De Legat. ad Gaium* 182, 370), and for a body of envoys or delegation, πρεσβεία (*In Flac.* 97 and *De Legat. ad*

Gaium 181, 239, 247, 354), in his report on the embassy to the Roman emperor. This embassy consisted of five Jewish envoys who met before Gaius Caligula (*De Legat. ad Gaium* 370). Philo employs the same terminology when he refers to envoys from almost the whole world (*De Legat. ad Gaium* 182). These technical Greek terms are not used in John. Thus, the Johannine language is in this respect closer to Halakhic language than is Philo's. One point in favor of regarding the Jewish Halakhah as being the immediate background for the use of agency in John is the circumstance that the term used in John 13:16, ἀπόστολος ("the one who is sent"), renders the Hebrew word for an agent and an envoy, שׁלִיחַ.

However, the Johannine and the Halakhic language and rules are to be examined against the broader background of the Oriental-Hellenistic world.[22] The Oriental context is sketched by Jan-Adolf Bühner, who refers to a text from Ras Shamra[23] that states that "a messenger has the word of his Lord on his shoulders." Thus, the christological usage of the principle of agency in John presupposes the role of agents and envoys in the Jewish state and in Judaism, an institution that functioned within the broader intercourse between the Jewish people and other nations in the Middle East and in the Mediterranean world.

A COMMON TREND: ASCENT/DESCENT AND VISION OF GOD

Visionary and "mystical" trends in Judaism have contributed to the interpretation of the Jesus-traditions in John. The notions of seeing God and God's glory are central, and epiphanic events in the Bible serve as background and models. John objects to the motif of ascents but keeps the motifs of glory, hearing, and seeing; he ties these ideas exclusively to Jesus, the Incarnate One. Some of these Johannine ideas show affinities with ideas and phenomena in the wider Hellenistic world.

The Old Testament story about the revelation at Mount Sinai played a central role in Judaism. Such a Sinaitic framework is seen in John 1:14 and 18: "we saw his glory, glory as of the only Son from the Father, full of grace and truth. . . . No one has ever seen God . . ." (au. trans.). The disciples saw the glory of the Son, who was "full of grace and truth" (see Ex. 33:18, 22; 34:5–6), and, thereby, the Son mediated the vision of God's glory, while a direct vision of God was denied Moses and human beings in general (Ex. 33:20). The same view is formulated in John 1:18: "No one has ever seen God; the only God ['Son' (mss.)], who is in the bosom of the Father, he has made him known."[24] The brief exposition of Isa. 54:13 ("And they shall all be taught by God") in John 6:45b–46 also draws on features from the theophany at Sinai, as indicated by the ideas of hearing and seeing God: "Every one who has heard . . . Not that any one has seen . . . "[25] Also here in the background is the idea that no one can see God: "you cannot see my face; for man cannot see me and live" (Ex. 33:20, au. trans.). Thus, according to John, those who are taught by God have heard from him without actually seeing him.

By contrast, John writes that the Jewish authorities have neither heard the voice of God nor seen his form, and thus they have no share in the revelation at Sinai: "His voice you have never heard, his form you have never seen" (5:37). It is probable that God's "form" (εἶδος, 5:37) was the (preexistent) Son of God, who is the only one who has seen the Father (6:46). By rejecting Jesus as the Son, the Jewish authorities demonstrate that they did not see God's form at the (anticipatory) Sinaitic epiphany. This interpretation receives support from John's comment on Isaiah's Temple vision (Isa. 6:1–10), in which John seems to identify the glory as the glory of Jesus, seen by the prophet ahead of time: "he [Isaiah] saw his [Jesus'] glory and spoke of him" (John 12:41).[26]

In the story about the Sinaitic revelation, the term "ascend" plays a central role (Ex. 19:20, 23; 24:1, 2, 9, 13, 18). In Jewish exegesis it can be said that Moses entered into heaven when he ascended the mountain (Philo, *De Vit. Mos.* 1.158–59; see also Josephus, *Ant.* 3.96; *Bib. Ant.* 12.1; *Mek. Exod.* 19:20; *Num. Rab.* 12:11; *Midr. Ps.* 24:5 and 106:2). The comment in John 3:13, "No one has ascended into heaven," seems, then, to serve as a polemic both against the idea of Moses' ascent and against similar claims of, or for, other human beings. Philo gives an example of this kind of *imitatio Mosis* in *De Vita Mosis* 1.158. After telling about Moses' entry into the place where God was, Philo concludes, "he has set before us . . . a model for those who are willing to copy it."[27] As an example of a claim made by another human being, one might refer to Philo's own ascent to the heavenly sphere: "I . . . seemed always to be borne aloft into the heights with a soul possessed by some God-sent inspiration" (*De Spec. Leg.* 3.1–6). The Qumran fragment, 4Q491 (frag. 11) 1:12–19, also probably describes the ascent of a human being: "none shall be exalted but me . . . . For I have taken my seat in the [congregation] in the heavens."[28] Thus, John 3:13 probably is a polemic against persons in the Johannine environment who maintained that they were visionaries like Moses.[29] John's Gospel reflects an environment in which Jewish versions of such ascent traditions existed. Its polemic against human beings who claim that they have ascended to heaven is partly due to the conviction that what is to be sought in heaven, such as God's glory, is now in the Incarnate One present on earth. Thus, the ascent motif is put upside down in John's Gospel when it is applied to the Incarnate Logos/Son.

John's polemic against persons' heavenly ascent does not reflect a general attitude among early Christians. Paul reports that he was caught up into the third heaven (2 Cor. 12:3); John the seer heard a voice, saying, "Come up hither," and then he was in the Spirit and saw a heavenly scene (Rev. 4:1–2). These reports of ascents are not understood to challenge the unique revelation in Jesus Christ, however.

In different forms the idea of ascent to heaven was widespread in the wider Hellenistic world.[30] When John reacted against persons' claims of ascent within a Jewish context, he reacted against a Jewish (and Christian) phenomenon that at the same time took place within a Hellenistic context. Two reports illustrate such a context. It was reported that the astronomer Ptolemy told the following about his own experience: "Mortal as I am, I know that I am born for a day, but when I follow the serried multitude of the stars in their circular course, my feet no longer touch the earth; I ascend to Zeus himself to feast me on ambrosia, the food of the gods."[31] In Lucian's *Icaromenippus* (2) Menippus claims to have returned from a visit to heaven. He speaks of a three-stage flight: from moon, to sun, to heaven. The ascent is bodily. Menippus reports, "Here I am, I tell you, just come back to-day from the very presence of your great Zeus himself, and *I have seen and heard wonderful things.*"[32] It is to be noted that here, as in the Sinaitic traditions, the seeing and hearing are central notions in the description of the ascent.

JEWISH AND CHRISTIAN VERSIONS OF A COMMON HELLENISTIC NOTION: BIRTH FROM ABOVE

C. K. Barrett states that the point of departure for the evolution of the terminology of "birth from above" is primarily the Jesus-logion about the need for becoming like children in order to enter the kingdom (Matt. 18:3 parr.), taken together with the belief that the kingdom was not only to be expected in the age to come but had already been manifested, germinally or potentially, in the person and work of Jesus. This belief distinguished primitive Christianity from Judaism and made possible the development of the traditional material in Hellenistic terminology, wherein rebirth and supernatural begetting were not uncommon. John did not plagiarize the notions of salvation and regeneration current in the Hellenistic world or effect syncretism of Jewish and pagan ideas. He perceived that the language of Judaism ("the kingdom of God") and the language of Hellenism (γεννηθῆναι ἄνωθεν, "birth from above") provided him with a unique opportunity of expressing what was neither Jewish nor Hellenistic but simply Christian.[33]

There are exegetical traditions that offer a basis for placing John's idea of rebirth within a Jewish setting, however. Philo says in *Quaestiones et Solutiones in Exodum* (2.46) that Moses' ascent at Sinai was a second birth, different from the first. Philo interprets Ex. 24:16, which concerns God's calling of Moses on the seventh day:

> But the calling above [Greek fragment: ἀνάκλησις] of the prophet is a second birth [Greek fragment: δεύτερα γένεσις], better than the first. For the latter is mixed with body and had corruptible parents, while the former is an unmixed and simple soul of the sovereign, being changed from a productive to an unproductive form that has no mother, but only a father, who is [the Father] of all. Wherefore, the "calling above" or, as we have said, the divine birth, happened to come about for him in accordance with the ever-virginal nature of the hebdomad. For he "is called on the seventh day," in this [respect] differing from the earthborn, first-molded man, for the latter came into being from the earth and with a body, while the former [came] from ether and without a body. Wherefore the most appropri-

ate number, six, was assigned to the earthborn man, while the one differently born [was assigned] the higher nature of the hebdomad.

For Philo, the number seven symbolizes the true nature of an Israelite, who celebrates the seventh day.

There are several agreements between this Philonic passage and John 3:3–13 and 1:13.[34] (a) The ascent at Mount Sinai is interpreted as birth (John 3:5, 13). (b) This birth is from above (John 3:3, 7; Philo: "calling above" = "from ether"). (c) It is a birth with God as father, without a mother (John 1:13). (d) It is a second birth, different from the birth from a woman (John 3:3–7). (e) There is some correspondence between John's distinction of σάρξ ("flesh") and πνεῦμα ("spirit") and Philo's distinction between σῶμα ("body") and νοῦς ("mind").[35]

The question can be raised whether Philo's idea of second birth, expressed here, depends on Hellenistic ideas of rebirth such as those found in Hermetic teachings. The thirteenth tractate of the *Corpus Hermeticum* is entitled, "Concerning Rebirth." According to this tractate, in rebirth the father is the will of God, the womb wisdom, the seed the real good, and the offspring a god—a child of God.[36] One obvious difference between John and this Hermetic tractate should be mentioned: In the Hermetic teaching Wisdom serves as mother-womb, while both Philo and John assert that no mother is involved in the second birth. It is, moreover, important to notice that Moses' rebirth is identified by Philo with his experience at Sinai. The implication is that Philo draws on Jewish exegetical traditions, which he develops further in his interpretation. This understanding is supported by the fact that the experience of the burning bush and the revelation at Sinai are interpreted as birth in rabbinic traditions, as Edmund Stein and Erik Sjöberg have shown.[37]

Sjöberg gives *Canticles Rabbah* 8:2 as an example of the latter point: " 'I would lead Thee, and bring Thee': I would lead Thee from the upper world to the lower. 'I would bring Thee into my mother's house': this is Sinai. R[abbi] Berekiah said: Why is Sinai called 'my mother's house'? Because there Israel became like a newborn child."[38] Sjöberg states that, according to Rabbi Berekiah, the Israelites at Sinai came into a completely new situation. Their relationship to God was rebuilt upon a completely new foundation. Rabbi Berekiah's word about Israel as "a newborn child" was an interpretation of the "mother" mentioned in Song of Songs 8:2, and it is evident, therefore, that the picture of birth is meant here. Furthermore, other parallels exist, such as *Exodus Rabbah* 30:5, where it is said that Torah conceived Israel at Sinai.

For his part, Stein has drawn the attention to *Exodus Rabbah* 3:15 on Exodus 4:12, and *Tanḥuma* (Buber) *Shemoth* 18,[39] about Moses' vision of the burning bush. According to this piece of tradition, God's relationship to Moses was compared with that of a mother who conceives and gives birth to a child, when God dedicated Moses and commissioned him to his high charge.[40] Moses at the burning bush experienced rebirth.[41]

Although the dates of the written forms of *Canticles Rabbah* 8:2, *Exodus Rabbah* 30:5, *Exodus Rabbah* 3:15, and *Tanḥuma* (Buber) *Shemoth* 18 are late, these passages and Philo, *Quaestiones in Exodum* 2.46, illuminate one another mutually: The rabbinic passages support the hypothesis that Philo relies on Jewish exegesis as a basis for his understanding of the Sinaitic ascent as rebirth, and Philo supports the hypothesis that the core of the rabbinic passages goes back to the beginning of the first century or earlier. Moreover, Philo's Jewish background is also seen in the fact that in *Quaestiones in Exodum* 2.46, both kinds of birth, bodily and noetic, are interpreted as caused by God's activity. And in *De Vita Mosis* 2.69–70 Philo makes clear that Moses' ascent of mind penetrated also his body. Thus, for Philo, Moses has significance as a person in history and as a symbol of mind as well.

The conclusion is clear: There is basis for interpreting birth from above in John 1:13 and 3:3–13 against the background of Moses' and Israel's rebirth at the Sinai event. This concept of rebirth has then, in John, been combined with the word from the Gospel tradition about becoming like a child as a condition for entry into heaven. This understanding of John 3:3–13 clarifies Jesus' rebuke of Nicodemus: "Are you the teacher of Israel, and yet you do not understand this?" The idea of discontinuity and new beginning, associated with the Sinai event, is in John transferred to the new beginning in the life and teachings of Jesus, the Incarnate One. Thus, Nicodemus had to face the message of discontinuity from his own background as "the teacher of Israel" as a condition for seeing and entering the kingdom of God. John has drawn on Sinaitic traditions about birth from above and has thereby interpreted a Jesus-logion in a way reflective of the fact that Judaism and Johannine Christianity were part of the Hellenistic thought-world in which the ideas of rebirth were not uncommon.[42]

A DISTINCTIVE EXPRESSION OF A COMMON HELLENISTIC THEME: EQUALITY WITH GOD

In John 5:17 Jewish exegesis is utilized. When it is said in v. 17 that God works up to now, that is, including the Sabbath, a widespread exegetical debate on Genesis 2:2–3 is presupposed and used.[43] The problem lay in the conviction that God cannot stop working. Consequently, the notion of the Sabbath-rest of God, as stated in Genesis 2:2–3, stands in tension with this continuous working of God. Evidence for such exegetical debate on the Sabbath-rest of God is found as early as the second century B.C.E., in Aristobulus,[44] and more material is found in Philo and in rabbinic writings.

According to rabbinic exegesis, the Sabbath commandment does not forbid one to carry something about in one's house on the Sabbath. God's homestead is the upper and lower worlds. Therefore, he may be active within it without coming into conflict with the Sabbath (*Gen. Rab.* 30:6). Philo, relying on the Septuagint rendering, notices that Genesis 2:2–3 reads κατέπαυσεν, not ἐπαύσατο. Thus, the text means "'caused to rest,' not 'rested,' for he causes to rest that which, though actually not in operation, is apparently making, but he himself never ceases making" (*Leg. All.* 1.5–6). Thus, the meaning of the seventh day for Philo is that God, who has no origin, is always active. "He is not a mere artificer, but also Father of the things that are coming into being" (*Leg. All.* 1.18). All created beings are dependent and really inactive in all their doings: "[regarding] the number seven . . . [i]ts purpose is that creation, observing the inaction which it brings, should call to mind him who does all things invisibly" (*Heres* 170).

An interpretation of Gen. 2:2–3 similar to that of Philo seems to be presupposed in John 5:1–18. The Son of God brings the Father's upholding and providential activity to bear upon the case of the healing of a person on the Sabbath. And the healed person is dependent and inactive, even in the carrying of the mat on the Sabbath, because the Son of God told him to do so. This passage illuminates the Johannine perspective that in Jesus, his actions, and his words, the divine and heavenly realm is present on earth. Thus God's "heavenly Halakhah" that he never ceases working, not even on Sabbaths, invalidates the earthly Halakhah about not working on the Sabbath.

When this Jewish exegesis of Gen. 2:2–3 is applied to Jesus and his healing activity on the Sabbath, it leads to the charge, made by the Jews, that he made himself equal to God.[45] The Jews were harsh in their criticism of human persons who claimed to be equal to God, as is reported of Antiochus Epiphanes (1 Macc. 9:12). Nevertheless, there was a debate among them about "two powers in heaven."[46] Philo in several places drew on Ex. 7:1, where Moses is called god to Pharaoh. According to *De Vita Mosis* 1.158 Moses was given the same title as God, in that he was named god and king of the whole nation and went into the darkness where God was (Ex. 20:21).

The theme of claiming equality with God occurs in the Old Testament (Isa. 14:13–14), in Philo (*Leg. All.* 1.49; *De Virt.* 171–72; and *De Legat. ad Gaium* 75), and on various levels in the Greek world. In Greek sources the scale of uses extended *from the positive meaning*, to live a god-like life or do a god-like act, *to the negative and improper claim* that a person is like the gods (Homer, *Iliad* 5.440–41; Philostratus, *Life of Apollonius* 8.5 and 8.7). Thus, in Judaism and in John distinctively Jewish ideas about being equal with God are expressed, but this occurs within the larger framework of a theme that is found, with different shades of meaning, in the wider Hellenistic world.

WISDOM AND LOGOS

The prologue of John ("In the beginning was the Word," 1:1) refers to the story of the creation in Genesis (1:1, "In the beginning God created"). As is commonly recognized, this interpretation of Genesis 1 is developed further on the basis of

Old Testament and Jewish wisdom traditions. Here are some of the relevant wisdom ideas.[47] (a) Like the Logos, Wisdom was an agent in creation. In Prov. 8:27–30 Wisdom tells how she aided God in the creation. She was God's artisan. According to Wisd. Sol. 9:9, Wisdom was present when God created the world, and in 7:22 Wisdom is called "artificer of all" (au. trans.). (b) Like the Logos, Wisdom is life and light for human beings. In Prov. 8:35, Wisdom says, "He who finds me finds life," and Baruch 4:1 promises that all who cling to Wisdom will live. Similarly, Eccl. 2:13: "Then I saw that wisdom excels folly as light excels darkness." (c) The prologue of John says that Logos came into the world and was rejected by people, especially by Israel (John 1:9–11). Likewise, Wisdom came to humankind; for example, Wisd. Sol. 9:10 records Solomon's prayer that Wisdom be sent down from heaven to be with him and work with him. Proverbs 8:31 says that Wisdom was delighted to be with the human race. The foolish rejected Wisdom (Sir. 15:7), and according to *1 Enoch* 42.2, "Wisdom came to make her dwelling place among the children of men and found no dwelling place" (au. trans.). The same idea is found in Bar. 3:12 but here addressed to Israel in particular: "You have rejected the fountain of wisdom." In John 1:14 it is said that Logos set up his tent and tabernacled among us; so also Sir. 24:8–12 says that Wisdom set up her tabernacle in Jacob (Israel).

At the same time there are parallels with the ideas of logos and wisdom in Philo's writings and in Gnostic writings, such as the tractate, *The Trimorphic Protennoia*. For Philo, God was transcendent and could not be identified with the world or any part of it. Platonic and Stoic ideas help Philo to express the relationship between God and the world. Here the Logos is the Mediator. Logos proceeds from God and is the medium of the creation of the world. The higher world, κόσμος νοητός ("noetic world") cannot be thought of in terms of space; it is the Logos of God in the act of creating the world.[48]

Logos is also the medium of the divine government of the world. It is not only transcendent in the mind of God but also immanent in the created universe. "In all respects the Logos is the medium of intercourse between God and this world."[49] By logos, then, Philo means the Platonic world of ideas, conceived not as self-existent, but as expressing the mind of the One God. We find in the prologue of John parallels of Philo's thoughts about logos and world, creation and government and communication.

There are several important observations that can be made on these similarities. Since Philo often uses the terms λόγος ("word") and σοφία ("wisdom") interchangeably, he demonstrates how wisdom categories and ideas can be expressed and further interpreted by means of the term "logos." Moreover, in *De Somniis* 1.75 Philo interprets Gen. 1:3 and moves from the spoken word to Logos as an entity distinct from God, as the model behind the work of creation: "for the model was the Word of his [God's] fullness, namely light, for he says, 'God said, "Let there be light."'" Although Philo's Platonizing idea of a model behind the work of creation is not found in John's prologue, a corresponding exegesis is presupposed, in which the statement in Gen. 1:3, "God said," is understood to mean "Logos."[50] Thus, we see that wisdom categories and wisdom ideas in the Old Testament and in Judaism have had a formative impact on Philo's exegesis and on John's exegetical elaborations on the creation story (Gen. 1:1–5) in the prologue.

There are also parallels in Gnostic writings such as *The Trimorphic Protennoia*.[51] The same vocabulary and world of thought as in the Johannine prologue are found in *Trimorphic Protennoia*: "word," "truth," "light," "beginning," "power," "world," and "reveal." The similarity between John 1:14a and *Protennoia* 47.13–16 is quite striking:

The Word became flesh and set up a tent among us (John 1:14, au. trans.).

I revealed myself to them in their tents as the Word, and I revealed myself in the likeness of their shape. And I wore everyone's garment and hid myself within them (*Protennoia* 47.14–16).

At this point there is also a basic difference. In John's prologue Logos becomes a historical and individual person, while according to *Protennoia* Logos resides in a series of sovereignties and powers, belonging to the various spheres spanning heaven and earth.

The many other differences speak also against any theory of direct influence between the two writings. Carsten Colpe and others see Jewish wisdom traditions behind both *Protennoia* and John's prologue.[52] It should be added that the Gnostic wisdom myth, which one finds in Gnostic systems, is considered by some scholars to be an adaptation of personified Jewish Wisdom.[53]

Thus, it may be seen that the Old Testament and Jewish wisdom ideas were adapted along various lines, such as in Platonizing directions (Philo), Gnostic mythological directions *(Protennoia),* as well as in the direction of Jesus traditions in John's Gospel.

INTERRELATED CONCEPTS

Wisdom ideas have contributed to the descent/ascent motif in John. The most important passages are Prov. 1:20–23; 8:12–36; Sir. 24:1–22; Wisd. Sol. 6–10; LXX Bar. 3:9–4:9; *1 Enoch* 42 and 94; 4 Ezra 5:10–11; and *2 Bar.* 48:36. The aspect of descent is seen, among other places, in John 1:14: Logos, which existed from the beginning and was God (1:1–2), became a human being, "flesh." The theme of ascent is particularly present in John 13–20 as the idea of the return to the Father. In John 1:14 the direct impact of the idea of wisdom is seen in the term "the word," as was shown above. As we have also observed, vv. 14–18 reflect a Sinaitic and epiphanic model, according to which the word of the law was revealed

and the theophanic glory was sought. Thus, the prologue also presupposes the iden-
tification of wisdom and the law, such as Sirach 24 testifies to. The giving of the
Law through Moses at Sinai is even referred to in a direct way in John 1:17, and
John 10:34–36 says that "the word of God" came to the Israelites at Sinai.

Moreover, ideas about the law and wisdom are brought together in the concept
of "bread from heaven," which gives life to the world (John 6:33) just as God gave
life to the world when he gave the law at Sinai (*Tanḥ.* [Buber] *Shemoth* 25;
Mek. on Ex. 15:26; *Ex. Rab.* 29:9). A presupposition is the identification of the
manna with the law, as seen in Philo (*De Mut. Nom.* 253–63) and the *Mekilta* on
Ex. 13:17.[54]

As for the ideas of agency and diplomacy, they are applied in John to Christology.[55] Old Testament and Jewish ideas about Moses, prophets, and angels as
God's messengers have prepared the ground for this interpretation.[56] A frequently
used characterization of Jesus in John is "the one who is sent by the Father" (and
similar phrases), and Jesus characterizes God as "the one who sent me" (and similar phrases).[57] Since Philo's writings were written during the first half of the first
century C.E., they are of special importance. Philo applies the technical term for
an envoy, πρεσβευτής, not only to envoys on the human level, but also to the
personified Logos, who acts as ambassador (πρεσβευτής) of the ruler (namely,
God) to his subjects (*Heres* 205). The term is furthermore used by Philo about angels who are envoys, backwards and forwards, between people and God (*De Gig.*
16), and who as God's ambassadors announce predictions to the (Jewish) race (*De
Mig. Abr.* 115). Here the notion of ascent/descent is evident.

In John 6:31–58 the idea of God's commissioned agent is woven together with
the ideas of wisdom, law, and "bread from heaven." Thus, Jesus identifies himself with that bread and says, "For I have come down from heaven, not to do my
own will, but the will of him who sent me [τοῦ πέμψαντός με]" (John 6:38). Accordingly, by refusing to recognize "him whom he [the Father] has sent," the
"Jews" (understood in John's negative sense) prove that they have no share in the
revelation to Israel, probably referring to the revelation at Sinai (John 5:37–38).

The topic of ascent is a part of the logic implicit in the idea of Jesus as the commissioned agent of God, since one who is sent on a mission is to return and report
to the sender (*y. Ḥag.* 76d).[58] John 13—20 is correspondingly dominated by the
theme of Jesus' return to his Father, and in 17:4 he reports that the charge has been
accomplished: "I glorified thee on earth, having accomplished the work which
thou gavest me to do."

One might ask if this descent/ascent motif is to be understood as a cosmic dualism between the "heavenly," divine realm and the earthly, evil realm. John 8:23
seems to fit into such an understanding: "You are from below, I am from above;
you are of this world, I am not of this world." One possible understanding of this
statement is that Jesus does not belong to the created cosmos, as his audience does.
If so, the distinction between "from below" and "from above" is in itself not the

dualistic principle. In favor of this understanding one might refer to 8:21, where Jesus says that he is going away—meaning, back to his Father. Correspondingly, in 8:26 Jesus, as God's commissioned envoy, declares to the (created) world what he has heard from the sender, the Father. The test of whether those who are from below and are of this world will die in their sins (vv. 21 and 24) is their reaction to God's envoy, Jesus. Thus, there is an ethical dualism and not a spatial one, even here in John 8:21–30, although spatial distinctions are drawn. As background, one might refer to the circumstance that in Jewish sources the realm above may mean the heavenly world, while the realm below may mean the earthly world. Both are created, but they set the stages for different possible actions: "No evil thing comes down from above" (*Gen. Rab.* 51:5). In rabbinic traditions humankind is understood to be a mixture of the upper realm and the realm below. If a man sins, he will die, and if he does not sin, he will live (*Gen. Rab.* 8; see further, Str-B 2 [1924]: 430–31).

In John, humankind, as such, is not seen as a mixture of heaven and earth. Jesus' Jewish listeners were from below, not partly from above and partly from below. John's distinction shows similarity with Gnostic dualism, which distinguishes the lower, psychic world from the upper, pneumatic world. As a parallel *The Hypostasis of the Archons* can be cited: "beings that merely possess a soul cannot lay hold of those that possess a spirit; for they were from below, while it was from above" (2.87.16–20).[59] However, this dualism is cosmic in nature, while the Johannine dualism is of an ethical nature, in spite of its spatial framework. Nevertheless, although John's dualism remains within Jewish and Christian categories, it comes quite close to Gnostic views.

INTERNATIONALIZATION

Another affinity between the Fourth Gospel and trends in Hellenism is internationalization. According to John 2:21, Jesus, as the risen one, takes the place of the Temple in Jerusalem. Correspondingly, in 4:20–24 worship on Mount Gerizim (as performed by "the fathers") and in Jerusalem will be replaced by the worship of the Father in spirit and truth. This statement, made in a dialogue with a Samaritan woman, opens up an international perspective: "As the N.T. people of God, [worship of God] is not subject to the limitations imposed by the history of salvation on the ancient temple of Jerusalem, whose rites it replaces by a worship in Spirit and truth founded on Christ which makes no difference between Jews, Samaritans and gentiles."[60]

This perspective is also expressed in the two references to "the Greeks" in the Gospel. John 7:35 reads, "Does he intend to go to the Diaspora of the Greeks and teach the Greeks?" (au. trans.). The word "Greeks" (Ἕλληνες) may refer to Greek-speaking, Diaspora Jews. However, the genitive expression, "of the Greeks," can be translated as "among the Greeks." This raises the question of whether Jesus will go to the Dispersion, among the Greeks, and will teach the Greeks. The word

Ἕλληνες also occurs in 12:20–21: "Now among those who went up to worship at the feast were some Greeks. So these came to Philip . . . and said to him, 'Sir, we wish to see Jesus.' " Since these Greeks were pilgrims who came to worship at the feast, they were Gentiles who had become Jewish proselytes. In any case, the word "Greeks" refers to persons of Gentile origin.[61] There is also a reference to Gentiles in John 10:16: "I have other sheep, that are not of this fold." "This fold" means Israel, and the "other sheep" are Gentiles. It is also probable that Jewish ideas about the gathering of the scattered children of Israel are transferred in John 11:52 to the Christian community, so that the verse refers to the ingathering of believing Gentiles.

These points in John indicate that the Johannine community comprised both Jews and non-Jews and that it had loosened itself from the Jerusalem Temple by transferring the role of the Temple to Jesus, who died and rose again. Likewise, the story about the healing of the man born blind who was excluded from the synagogue (John 9) implies that there had been a break between the Johannine community and the synagogal community. J. Louis Martyn and Raymond E. Brown have drawn the probable conclusion that the occasion for the writing of John's Gospel was an experience of expulsion of a Christian community from its home in the synagogue.[62]

Thus, John's Gospel reflects a situation where the Johannine community had moved beyond the ethnic Jewish boundaries into the broader world of other nations, as indicated by John's use of the terms "the Samaritans" and "the Greeks." In its own way John represents here the Hellenistic tendency towards internationalization. Against this background, how should one characterize the Johannine community? It has been suggested that it was a sectarian in-group, defending itself against the out-group.[63] John's positive and open use of the terms "Greeks" and "Samaritans" does not fit well into such an understanding. As suggested below, the traumatic experience of the expulsion from a synagogue community has caused the terms "Jews" and "the world" to be used partly as negative terms that express hatred, but no such associations are indicated in the use of the terms "the Greeks" or "the Samaritans." John 3:16, which speaks of God's love of the world, also suggests a more positive and open attitude, a more universal perspective, than that of a sect.

DUALISM: "JEWS," "COSMOS," AND OTHER TERMS

John's dualism may be understood as an interplay between traditional ideas and the self-understanding of the Johannine community in its continuity and discontinuity with Judaism. John's strange use of the term "the Jews" (οἱ Ἰουδαῖοι) illustrates this duality.[64] The continuity is expressed by the fact that Jesus was a Jew (thus, John 4:9 and 18:35), and in Jesus' word to the Samaritan woman, "for salvation is from the Jews" (John 4:22).[65] The discontinuity is expressed in the characterization of the Jewish authorities as being hostile to Jesus (5:10, 15, 16,

18; 7:1, 13; 8:48, 52, 57; 9:18, 22; 10:24, 31, 33; 11:8; 18:12, 14, 31, 36, 38; 19:7, 12, 14, 31, 38; 20:19).

A division took place within Israel. On the one hand, Jesus' Jewish disciples confessed that they had found the Messiah (John 1:35–42). Nathanael, who recognized Jesus as the Son of God, the king of Israel, was the prototype of a true Israelite. Such true Israelites are the sheep who belonged to "this fold" (John 10:16). The "Jews," negatively understood, do not believe and do not belong to the sheep of Jesus (John 10:26).[66]

This movement towards internationalization has a cosmic dimension. It can be seen in the broadening of ethnic concepts into cosmic concepts, as is the case in John's interpretation of the notion that Israel was God's possession, and the notion that God chose Israel out of love. The words, τὰ ἴδια ("[his] own [property]") and οἱ 'Ιουδαῖοι, in John 1:11 refer to the people of Israel, as described in Ex. 19:5: "you shall be my own possession among all peoples."[67] In the cosmic context of the prologue, the concept probably has been broadened to mean human beings as the property of the creator. This is seen in the parallel thought in John 1:10, where it is said that the world, ὁ κόσμος, did not recognize him through whom the world was made. This broadening of the concept has as its background the idea that Israel regarded itself as the center of the world.[68] The same broadening of a national concept is also seen in the parallelism between "the Jews," negatively understood, and "the world," negatively understood, in their hostility against God (see John 15:18–16:4); here, also, "the Jews" represent the world.

Correspondingly, there is also a broadening of positive ideas associated with Israel. The statement in John 3:16, "God so loved the world," has as its background God's love for his people, as expressed, for example, in Deut. 7:7–8: "It was not because you were more in number than any other people that the LORD set his love upon you and chose you, for you were the fewest of all peoples; but it is because the LORD loves you . . . "[69]

The movement from national concepts to cosmic and international concepts is also present in Johannine Christology. Nathanael confesses Jesus to be the king of the Jews (John 1:49), and Jesus tells him that he will see "greater things." These greater things are not specified, but they are connected with Jesus' reference to the "Son of Man," who will be in permanent contact with heaven (1:50–51).[70] Correspondingly, the concept of messiah in 4:25–26 is followed by the broader idea of "the Savior of the world" (4:42).

When this cosmic broadening of national and ethnic concepts is combined with a movement towards internationalization, John may then be seen to represent a distinctively Jewish and Christian tendency, which is parallel to the Hellenistic movement from the perspective of the city-state to more universal perspectives. It may even be said that the cosmic broadening of ethnic ideas in John corresponds to the cosmic broadening of the ideas of the city-state (πόλις) to the view that the whole cosmos is a πόλις, inhabited by gods and men.[71]

In John's pointedly negative and dualistic uses of the concepts of "his own property," "the Jews," and "the world," one might find affinities between John and Gnostic views.[72] Nevertheless, John bases his view on the biblical conviction that God is the creator, positively understood. Thus, the negative reaction is the rejection made by God's or the Son's own possession—the created world, with its center in Israel.

To conclude: The main themes, discussed above, have as their focal point this move from ethnic and synagogal boundaries into the world, represented by the "Greeks" (John 7:35 and 12:20–21) and by the Samaritan town (4:39–42). The revelation at Sinai was a preview of the true revelation of God's glory in the Incarnate Logos (= Wisdom) and Son (John 1:14 and 17), who is the only one who has seen God. Moses was a witness to Christ, about whom he wrote (5:39). The teacher of Israel, Nicodemus, did not seem to understand that the birth from above, associated with the Sinai experience, was, indeed, a birth of the Spirit, to take place for those who believed in God's Son (3:1–17). "The Jews" (negatively understood) had not heard God's voice nor seen God's form at Sinai, since they did not believe in Jesus, God's commissioned envoy (5:38). Thus, as the Johannine community moved beyond the ethnic Jewish boundaries, it understood its identity both in continuity with, and in discontinuity from, the Jewish people and its traditions. God's Son, as the commissioned agent, caused a division to take place between recognition/belief and rejection/disbelief within the Jewish people, and this dual reaction represented what was to happen everywhere (John 15:18–27; 17:20).

DUALISM: LIGHT AND DARKNESS

The first observation to be made here is that John's terminology is drawn from the Old Testament. The word "light" (τὸ φῶς) in John 1:4–9 refers to Gen. 1:3, "'Let there be light'; and there was light." The word "darkness" (ἡ σκοτία) is given as light's contrast in John 1:5, and a corresponding contrast in the external world is found in Gen. 1:18, where it is said that the sun and the moon had the task of separating light from the darkness. However, in John this contrast has been transferred into a dualistic contrast. The word "life" in John 1:4 points back to Gen. 2:7, which concerns God's breath of life and man as a living being. Philo testifies to such an interpretation of the creation story (*De Opif. Mundi* 30): "Special distinction is accorded by Moses to the breath and to light. The one he entitles, 'the breath of God,' because breath is most life-giving and of life God is the author, while of light he says that it is beautiful preeminently [Gen. 1:4]." When life and light are seen together in John 1:4, Ps. 36:9 also provides background: "For with thee is the fountain of life; in thy light do we see light."

Furthermore, in Jewish sources light and life are associated with wisdom and with the Torah. It is of interest to notice that, according to rabbinic sources, the primordial light (Gen. 1:3), which gave Adam universal sight, was removed because of sin. However, the light will come back in the next age (*y. Ḥag.* 12a, *Gen. Rab.* 12:6; *Tanḥ.* [Buber] *Bereshit* 18). Correspondingly, according to John 1:5b, light was not overcome by darkness, but nightfall must have led to a new situation. Since John 1:9 and 12:46 associate the coming of light with the coming of Jesus, it follows from this coming that primordial light, which humankind had according to 1:4, was removed from them. And since the light's coming brought back life (8:12), it follows that the original life, mentioned in 1:4, was lost. John's train of thought thereby follows that of Jewish traditions, which considered light and life among the things lost at the Fall and brought back at a later moment in history, or in the coming aeon. Thus, the idea of light follows to some extent the same line of thought as that of primordial Logos/Wisdom, which became flesh in Jesus (1:1–2 and 14). The weaving together of light and life and Logos is seen, moreover, in 1:4: "In him [the Logos] was life, and the life was the light of men."[73]

In the Dead Sea Scrolls, sin and darkness are also related to creation.[74] God "created the spirits of light and darkness and upon them he established every act" (1QS 3:25). Although both the Dead Sea Scrolls and John represent a modified dualism, there is an important difference. In John, light and darkness are not created as two (almost) equal powers as they are in the Dead Sea Scrolls. In fact, in John 1:4 it is said only of light that it was with human beings in the beginning. On this essential point John is closer to the tradition that let Adam, and thereby humankind, have light as their original possession with the ensuing Fall and darkness.

Both in the Dead Sea Scrolls and in John there is an ethical dualism. In 1QS 4:2–14 the ways of the spirit of light are described by means of righteous attitudes and moral deeds, and the ways of the spirit of darkness or perversity are characterized by means of a list of immoral deeds. John 3:20–21 also pictures an ethical dualism: "For every one who does evil hates the light, and does not come to the light, lest his deeds should be exposed. But he who does what is true comes to the light, that it may be clearly seen that his deeds have been wrought in God." In John this ethical dualism is applied to the coming and role of Jesus—the Son, the preexistent, personified Logos—who existed before creation (John 1:1–3). As a parallel, one might refer to the personal, angelic leaders in the Dead Sea Scrolls, the Prince of Light and the Angel of Darkness, but both of these were created. In John there is no Angel of Darkness pictured, although there is a trace of an angelic antagonist in the figure of "the ruler of this world" (John 12:31). In contrast with the Dead Sea Scrolls, John associates light with Logos and identifies him as the Incarnate One. In that way the historical person, Jesus, is the light. Thus, evil deeds basically mean the rejection of him, and good deeds are people's coming to him, while in the Dead Sea Scrolls the acceptance of the law separated the sons of light from the sons of darkness.[75]

Thus, the dualism of light and darkness in John is primarily to be seen against the background of the Old Testament and Jewish writings, especially as exemplified by the Dead Sea Scrolls. Nevertheless, by emphasizing the contrast between light and darkness, John and the Jewish writings employ a language that was characteristic also of religious and philosophical language in the Hellenistic world. At certain points there are even strong affinities. For example, although the Old Testament can see life and light together, as in Ps. 36:10, this combination is typical in the first and thirteenth of the Hermetic tractates.

The terminology of life and light is also characteristic of the *Odes of Solomon*. In *Poimandres* the formula of life and light is very important. The secret of immortality, in fact, is the knowledge that God is life and light, and that we are his offspring. It is probable that here light is the eternal light, of which visible light is the "copy." The corresponding Johannine term is "the true light" (John 1:9). In *Poimandres* over against the primal light stands the chaotic ocean of darkness; one may compare John 1:5: "The light shines in darkness, but the darkness did not overpower it" (au. trans.). However, this cosmological dualism in the Fourth Gospel is not ultimate as in *Poimandres*.[76] As already stated, in John it is a modified form of dualism, which exists within the context of the created world.

CONCLUSION

1. It is difficult to identify direct Hellenistic influence on John from outside of Judaism. Thus, the hypothesis that has guided the present analysis is: Judged on the basis of Gospel traditions and further Jewish and Christian developments, John cultivates ideas and practices that to some extent are Jewish-Christian versions of aspects and trends present in the larger Hellenistic world.

2. The christological usage of the principle of agency in John presupposes the role of agents and envoys in the Jewish state and in Judaism, an institution that functioned within the broader intercourse between the Jewish people and other nations in the Middle East and in the Mediterranean world.

3. John 3:13 probably is meant to be a polemic against persons in the Jewish and Christian environment who maintained that they were visionaries who ascended to heaven like Moses. This polemic is partly due to the conviction that what is to be sought in heaven, such as God's glory, is now in the Incarnate One present on earth. When John reacts against persons' claims of ascent within a Jewish context, he reacts against a Jewish (and Christian) phenomenon, which at the same time was widespread in the Hellenistic world.

4. Wisdom ideas have contributed to the descent/ascent motif in John. Ideas about the law and wisdom and the motif of descent are brought together in the concept of "bread from heaven." The aspects of descent and ascent are part of the logic implicit in the idea of Jesus as the commissioned agent of God, since one who is sent on a mission is expected to return and report to the sender.

When it is said in John that Jesus is from above while his listeners were from below, this distinction shows similarity with Gnostic dualism between the lower, psychic world and the upper, pneumatic world. This Gnostic dualism, however, is of a cosmic nature, while the Johannine dualism is basically ethical in nature, in spite of its spatial framework. Nevertheless, although John's dualism remains within Jewish and Christian categories, it approaches Gnostic views.

5. Another affinity between John and trends in Hellenism is internationalization. This movement towards internationalization has a cosmic dimension. It can be seen in John's broadening of ethnic Jewish concepts into cosmic concepts. John's Gospel reflects a situation in which the Johannine community had moved beyond the ethnic Jewish boundaries into the broader world of other nations, as indicated by John's use of the terms "the Samaritans" and "the Greeks." It may even be said that the cosmic broadening of ethnic ideas in John corresponds to the cosmic broadening of the ideas of the city-state ($\pi\acute{o}\lambda\iota\varsigma$) to the view that the whole cosmos is a $\pi\acute{o}\lambda\iota\varsigma$, inhabited by gods and mortals.

6. As the Johannine community moved beyond the ethnic Jewish boundaries, it understood its identity both in continuity with and in discontinuity from the Jewish people and their traditions. God's Son, as the commissioned agent, caused a division to take place within the Jewish people between recognition/belief and rejection/disbelief, and this dual reaction represented what was to happen everywhere. In John's dualism the terms, "the Jews" and "the world," have both positive and negative usages.

7. The dualism of light and darkness in John is primarily to be seen against the background of the Old Testament and Jewish writings, especially as exemplified by the Dead Sea Scrolls. Nevertheless, by emphasizing the contrast between light and darkness, John and the Jewish writings employ a language that was characteristic also of the religious and philosophical language in the Hellenistic world. At certain points there are quite strong affinities between Johannine and Gnostic ideas, such as their close combination of life and light.

NOTES

1. Concerning the discussion of the use of the term, Ἕλληνες, in the Fourth Gospel, see below. See also C. K. Barrett, *The Gospel according to St John: An Introduction with Commentary and Notes on the Greek Text*, 2d ed. (Philadelphia: Westminster, 1978), 325–26, 421–22; Raymond E. Brown, *The Gospel according to John (i–xii)*, AB 29 (Garden City, N.Y.: Doubleday, 1966), 314, 466.

2. See Per Bilde, "Hellenismen i nyere forskning," *Religionsvidenskabeligt Tidsskrift* 16 (1990): 3–39 (here, 5–7, with attention to the views of R. Bichler; cf. J. G. Droysen); see also Hans Dieter Betz, "Hellenism," *ABD* 3 (1992): 127–35 (esp. 127).

3. C. H. Dodd, *The Interpretation of the Fourth Gospel* (Cambridge: Cambridge University Press, 1953), 444.

4. Ibid., 9.

5. Ibid., 73.

6. See John Dillon, *The Middle Platonists: A Study of Platonism 80 B.C. to A.D. 220* (Ithaca, N.Y.: Cornell University Press, 1977), 139–83; Peder Borgen, "Philo of Alexandria: A Critical and Synthetical Review of Philonic Research since World War II," *ANRW* 2.21.1 (1984): 98–154 (esp. 147–54); idem, "Philo of Alexandria," in *Jewish Writings in the Second Temple Period: Apocrypha, Pseudepigrapha, Qumran Sectarian Writings, Philo, Josephus*, ed. Michael E. Stone, CRINT 2.2 (Assen and Philadelphia: Van Gorcum/Fortress, 1984), 233–82 (here, 264–74).

7. Dodd, *The Interpretation of the Fourth Gospel*, 53.

8. See Rudolf Schnackenburg, *The Gospel according to St. John*, 3 vols. (New York: Crossroad, 1968–87), 1.136–38.

9. Rudolf Bultmann, *Theology of the New Testament*, vol. 1 (New York: Scribner's, 1951), 166–67.

10. Idem, *Theology of the New Testament*, vol. 2 (New York: Scribner's, 1955), 12–13.

11. See Edwin D. Freed, *Old Testament Quotations in the Gospel of John*, NovT Sup 11 (Leiden: Brill 1965); Peder Borgen, *Bread from Heaven: An Exegetical Study of the Conception of Manna in the Gospel of John and the Writings of Philo*, NovT Sup 10 (Leiden: Brill, 1965; 2d ed., 1981); Günter Reim, *Studien zum Alttestamentlichen Hintergrund des Johannesevangeliums*, SNTSMS 22 (Cambridge: Cambridge University Press, 1974); Maarten J. J. Menken, "The Old Testament Quotation in John 6,45: Source and Redaction," *ETL* 64 (1988): 164–72; idem, "The Provenance and Meaning of the Old Testament Quotation in John 6:31," *NovT* 30 (1988): 39–56; Bruce G. Schuchard, *Scripture within Scripture: The Interrelationship of Form and Function in the Explicit Old Testament Citations in the Gospel of John*, SBLDS 133 (Atlanta: Scholars Press, 1992). On the more controversial question of John's relationship to the Synoptics, see D. Moody Smith, *John among the Gospels: The Relationship in Twentieth-Century Research* (Minneapolis: Fortress, 1992); Peder Borgen, "John and the Synoptics," in *The Interrelations of the Gospels: A Symposium Led by M.-É. Boismard, W. R. Farmer, F. Neirynck, Jerusalem 1984*, ed. David L. Dungan and William R. Farmer, BETL 95 (Leuven: Leuven University Press, 1990), 408–37; Frans Neirynck, "John and the Synoptics: Response to P. Borgen," in *The Interrelations of the Gospels*, 438–50; Peder Borgen, "John and the Synoptics: A Reply," in *The Interrelations of the Gospels*, 451–58; idem, "The Independence of the Gospel of John: Some Observations," in *The Four Gospels 1992: Festschrift Frans Neirynck*, ed. F. Van Segbroeck, C. M. Tuckett, G. Van Belle and J. Verheyden, 3 vols. (Leuven: Leuven University Press, 1992) 3.1815–33.

12. Brown, *The Gospel according to John* (I-XII), AB29, lvi.

13. Martin Hengel, *The Johannine Question* (Philadelphia: Trinity Press International, 1989), 113.

14. The champion of "normative" Judaism is George Foot Moore, *Judaism in the First Centuries of the Christian Era*, 3 vols. (Cambridge, Mass.: Harvard University Press, 1927–30). Correspondingly, Erwin R. Goodenough, *Jewish Symbols in the Greco-Roman Period*, especially vol. 1 (New York: Pantheon, 1953), 3–58, stresses the distinctiveness of Hellenistic Judaism. Among the scholars who argue against this sharp distinction, see esp. Rudolf Meyer, *Hellenistisches in der rabbinischen Anthropologie: Die rabbinsche Vorstellungen von werden den Menschen*, BWANT 74 (Stuttgart: Kohlhammer, 1937); Martin Hengel, *Judaism and Hellenism: Studies in Their Encounter in Palestine during the Hellenistic Period*, 2 vols. (Philadelphia:

Fortress, 1974); Gerhard Delling, "Perspektiven der Erforschung des hellenistischen Judentums," *HUCA* 45 (1974): 133–76. See also Borgen, *Bread from Heaven;* Howard Marshall, "Palestinian and Hellenistic Christianity: Some Critical Comments," *NTS* 19 (1972–73): 271–87 (esp. 271–75); Peder Borgen, "The Early Church and the Hellenistic Synagogue," in idem, *Philo, John and Paul: New Perspectives on Judaism and Early Christianity*, Brown Judaic Studies 131 (Atlanta: Scholars Press, 1987), 207–32; Martin Hengel, *The "Hellenization" of Judaea in the First Century after Christ* (London and Philadelphia: SCM/Trinity Press International, 1989); Aryeh Kasher, *Jews and Hellenistic Cities in Eretz Israel: Relations of the Jews in Eretz–Israel with the Hellenistic Cities during the Second Temple Period (332 B.C.E.–70 C.E.)*, Texte und Studien zum antiken Judentum 21 (Tübingen: Mohr [Siebeck], 1990); *Greece and Rome in Eretz Israel: Collected Essays*, ed. Aryeh Kasher, Uriel Rappaport, and Gideon Fuks (Jerusalem: Yad Izhak ben-Zvi/The Israel Exploration Society, 1990).

15. The following works by Philo are cited in the present chapter: *De Opificio Mundi* (= *De Opif. Mundi*), *On the Creation of the World; Legum Allegoriae* (= *Leg. All.*), *Allegories of the Law; De Gigantibus* (= *De Gig.*), *On the Giants; De Migratione Abrahami* (= *De Mig. Abr.*), *On the Migration of Abraham; Quis Rerum Divinarum Heres* (= *Heres*), *Who Is the Heir?; De Mutatione Nominum* (= *De Mut. Nom.*), *On the Change of Names; De Somniis* (= *De Somn.*), *On Dreams; De Vita Mosis* (= *De Vit. Mos.*), *On the Life of Moses; De Specialibus Legibus* (= *De Spec. Leg.*), *On the Special Laws; De Virtutibus* (= *De Virt.*), *On the Virtues; In Flaccum* (= *In Flac.*), *Against Flaccus; De Legatione ad Gaium* (= *De Legat. ad Gaium*), *On the Embassy to Gaius; Quaestiones et Solutions in Exodum* (= *Quaes. Ex.*), *Questions and Answers on Exodus.*

16. For surveys of research on John, see Robert Kysar, *The Fourth Evangelist and His Gospel: An Examination of Contemporary Scholarship* (Minneapolis: Augsburg, 1975); idem, "The Fourth Gospel: A Report on Recent Research," *ANRW* 2.25.3 (1985): 2389–480; J. K. Riches, *A Century of New Testament Study* (Cambridge: Lutterworth, 1993), 175–97.

17. Peder Borgen, "God's Agent in the Fourth Gospel," in *Religions in Antiquity: Essays in Memory of Erwin Ramsdell Goodenough*, ed. Jacob Neusner, Studies in the History of Religions 14 (Leiden: Brill, 1968), 137–48 (rpt. in Borgen, *Philo, John and Paul*, 171–84, and in *The Interpretation of John*, ed. John Ashton, IRT 9 [London and Philadelphia: SPCK/Fortress, 1986], 67–78). See, further, Jan-Adolf Bühner, *Der Gesandte und sein Weg im 4. Evangelium: Die kultur- und religionsgeschichtlichen Grundlagen der johanneischen Sendungschristologie sowie ihre traditionsgeschichtliche Entwicklung*, WUNT, Reihe 2, 2 (Tübingen: Mohr [Siebeck], 1977).

18. Here and throughout, all biblical translations are from the RSV unless otherwise indicated.

19. See Peder Borgen, "The Use of Tradition in John 12:44–50," *NTS* 26 (1979): 18–35; rpt. in idem, *Logos Was the True Light and Other Essays on the Gospel of John*, Relieff 9 (Trondheim: Tapir, 1983), 49–66. In the Old Testament the principles of agency are present in an embryonic form, such as God's word when the people had rejected Samuel: "they have not rejected you, but they have rejected me" (1 Sam. 8:7).

20. *Mek. Ex.* on Ex. 12:3 and 6; *m. Ber.* 5:5; *b. Metzi'a* 96a; *b. Ḥag.* 10b; *b. Qidd.* 42b, 43a; *b. Menaḥ.* 93b; *b. Nazir* 12b, among others.

21. Margaret M. Mitchell, "New Testament Envoys in the Context of Greco-Roman Diplomatic and Epistolary Conventions: The Example of Timothy and Titus," *JBL* 111 (1992): 641–62.

22. Mitchell ("New Testament Envoys," 645 n. 11) restates my listing of "principles about rabbinic agents . . . : 'Thus there are striking similarities between the halakhic principle of agency and ideas in the Fourth Gospel, as (a) the unity between the agent and his sender, (b) although the agent is subordinate, (c) the obedience of the agent to the will of the sender, (d) the task of the agent in the lawsuit, (e) his return and reporting back to the sender, and (f) his appointing of other agents as an extension of his own mission in time and space' (Borgen, "God's Agent," 143–44). But [Mitchell replies] these elements are found also, for example, in Greco-Roman diplomatic and social relations. . . ." On the whole, Mitchell's comment is to the point, but she does not pay enough attention to some terminological differences as well as to some differences of nuances and of (religious) perspective in the Halakhic principles, as compared with usual Greek principles (cf. Josephus, *Ant.* 15.136). Moreover, she hardly touches on the similarities between the Greco-Roman and the wider Oriental-Hellenistic rules and conventions for agency and diplomacy. See Bühner, *Der Gesandte und sein Weg im 4. Evangelium,* 118–80, 185–91.

23. Bühner, *Der Gesandte und sein Weg im 4. Evangelium,* 120 (on Text 137, ll. 38–42).

24. M.-É. Boismard, *Le Prologue de saint Jean,* LD 11 (Paris: Editions du Cerf, 1953); Nils Alstrup Dahl, "The Johannine Church and History," in *Current Issues in New Testament Interpretation: Essays in Honor of Otto A. Piper,* ed. William Klassen and Graydon F. Snyder (New York: Harper & Row, 1962), 124–42 (esp. 132–33).

25. On the "hearing" at Sinai, see Deut. 4:12; 5:24; 18:16; Sir. 17:13; 45:5; *Mek. Ex.* on Ex. 20:2; 1QM 10:8b–11. See Borgen, *Bread from Heaven,* 150, and Carey C. Newman, *Paul's Glory-Christology: Tradition and Rhetoric,* NovTSup 69 (Leiden: Brill, 1992), 110–13.

26. See Dahl, "The Johannine Church and History," 133; Borgen, *Bread from Heaven,* 133–34.

27. See Peder Borgen, "Heavenly Ascent in Philo: An Examination of Selected Passages," in *The Pseudepigrapha and Early Biblical Interpretation,* ed. James H. Charlesworth and Craig A. Evans, JSPSup 14 (Sheffield: JSOT, 1993), 263–67.

28. Morton Smith, "Two Ascended to Heaven—Jesus and the Author of 4Q491," in *Jesus and the Dead Sea Scrolls,* ed. James H. Charlesworth, Anchor Bible Reference Library (New York: Doubleday, 1992), 290–301; Craig A. Evans, "The Recently Published Dead Sea Scrolls and the Historical Jesus," in *Studying the Historical Jesus: Evaluation of the State of Current Research,* ed. Bruce Chilton and Craig A. Evans, NTTS 19 (Leiden: Brill, 1994), 563–65.

29. Hugo Odeberg, *The Fourth Gospel Interpreted in Its Relation to Contemporaneous Religious Currents in Palestine and the Hellenistic-Oriental World* (Uppsala: Almquist & Wiksells, 1929), 72–94; Dahl, "The Johannine Church and History," 141; Borgen, *Bread from Heaven,* 185. The interpretation of John 3:13 as a whole is difficult; see Peder Borgen, "Some Jewish Exegetical Traditions as Background for Son of Man Sayings in John's Gospel (Jn 3,13–14 and Context)," in *L'Évangile de Jean: Sources, rédaction, théologie,* ed. Marinus de Jonge, BETL 44 (Leuven: Leuven University Press, 1977), 243–45, and Francis J. Moloney, *The Johannine Son of Man,* 2d ed., Biblioteca di Scienze Religiose 14 (Rome: Liberia Ateneo Saleiano, 1978), 54.

30. See D. W. Bousset, "Die Himmelreise der Seele," *ARW* 4 (1901): 136–69, 229–73; James D. Tabor, *Things Unutterable: Paul's Ascent to Paradise in Its Greco-Roman, Judaic, and Early Christian Context,* Studies in Judaism (Lanham, Md.: University Press of America, 1986); Borgen, "Heavenly Ascent in Philo," 246–68; Hans Georg Gundel, *Astrologumena: Die astrologische Literatur in der Antike und ihre Geschichte* (Wiesbaden: Steiner, 1966), 29–30, 180–81, et passim; Martha Himmelfarb, *Ascent to Heaven in Jewish and Christian Apocalypses* (New York and Oxford: Oxford University Press, 1993); idem, "Heavenly Ascent and the Relationship of the Apocalypses and the *Hekhalot* Literature," *HUCA* 59 (1988): 73–100.

31. Quoted from Franz Cumont, *Astrology and Religion among the Greeks and Romans* (New York: Dover, 1960 [rpt. of the English translation of 1912]), 81.

32. Translation by A. H. Harmon in *Lucian,* LCL (Cambridge, Mass.: Cambridge University Press, 1915), 2.268–323 (emphasis added).

33. Barrett, *The Gospel according to St. John,* 206–7.

34. See, further, Borgen, "God's Agent in the Fourth Gospel," 146.

35. John sees humanity as a totality, whereas Philo has a dichotomized anthropology. Philo, however, keeps the Jewish understanding that both body and mind are created, and Moses' ascent included both, as can be seen from *De Vita Mosis* 2.69–70. See also Borgen, *Bread from Heaven,* 182; cf. 118–212.

36. See Dodd, *The Interpretation of the Fourth Gospel,* 44.

37. Edmund Stein, "Der Begriff der Palingenesie im Talmudischen Schrifttum," *MGWJ* 83, N.F. 47 (1939): 194–205; Erik Sjöberg, "Wiedergeburt und Neuschöpfung im palästinischen Judentum," *ST* 4 (1951): 44–85.

38. Translation in H. Freedman and Maurice Simon, *Midrash Rabba,* vol. 9: *Song of Songs* (London: Soncino, 1961), 303.

39. *Midrash Tanchuma: Ein agadischer Kommentar zum Pentaeuch von Rabbi Tanchuma ben Rabbi,* ed. Solomon Buber (Vilna: Romm, 1885 [rpt., Jerusalem: Ortsel, 1963–64]).

40. The exegetical basis for this interpretation is the alternative derivation of the verbal form in Ex. 4:12, from the Hebrew verb meaning "to conceive" (cf. Ex. 2:2).

41. Stein, "Der Begriff der Palingenesie im Talmudischen Schrifttum," 196–97.

42. See Barrett, *The Gospel according to St. John,* 206–7.

43. For the following, see Peder Borgen, "Creation, Logos and the Son: Observations on John 1:1–18 and 5:17–18," *Ex Auditu* 3 (1987): 89–92.

44. Nikolaus Walter, *Der Thoraausleger Aristobulos: Untersuchungen zu seinem Fragmenten und zu pseudepigraphischen Resten der jüdisch hellenistischen Literatur,* TU 86 (Berlin: Akademie, 1964), 170–71; Peder Borgen, "Philo of Alexandria," in *Jewish Writings in the Second Temple Period,* 277; idem, "Aristobulus—A Jewish Exegete from Alexandria," in Peder Borgen, *Paul Preaches Circumcision and Pleases Men and Other Essays on Christian Origins,* Relieff 8 (Trondheim: Tapir, 1983), 179–90 (esp. 180, 184–85); and idem, "Aristobulus and Philo," in *Philo, John and Paul,* 1–16 (esp. 12).

45. For the following section, see especially Wayne A. Meeks, "Equal to God," in *The Conversation Continues: Studies in Paul and John in Honor of J. Louis Martyn,* ed. Robert T. Fortna and Beverly R. Gaventa (Nashville: Abingdon, 1990), 309–21.

46. Alan Segal, *Two Powers in Heaven: Early Rabbinic Reports about Christianity and Gnosticism,* SJLA 25 (Leiden: Brill, 1977).

47. See Brown, *The Gospel according to John (i–xii),* AB 29:522–23.

48. See Dodd, *The Interpretation of the Fourth Gospel*, 67.

49. Ibid., 68.

50. Thus, Borgen, "Logos Was the True Light: Contributions to the Interpretation of the Prologue of John," in *Logos Was the True Light and Other Essays*; see also idem, "The Prologue of John—As Exposition of the Old Testament," in *Philo, John and Paul*, 75–101 (here, 84).

51. See Craig A. Evans, "On the Prologue of John and the *Trimorphic Protennoia*," *NTS* 27 (1980–81): 395–401.

52. Carsten Colpe, "Heidnische, jüdische und christliche Überlieferung in den Schriften aus Nag Hammadi, III," *JAC* 17 (1974): 109–25, esp. 122.

53. See Kurt Rudolph, *Gnosis: The Nature and History of Gnosticism*, ed. R. McL. Wilson (San Francisco: Harper & Row, 1983), 280–82, and esp. George W. MacRae, "The Jewish Background of the Gnostic Sophia Myth," *NovT* 12 (1970): 86–101.

54. Borgen, *Bread from Heaven*, 148–50.

55. See Francis H. Agnew, "The Origin of the NT Apostle-Concept: A Review of Research," *JBL* 105 (1986): 75–96.

56. See Bühner, *Der Gesandte und sein Weg im 4. Evangelium*, 270–385.

57. Borgen, "God's Agent in the Fourth Gospel," in *Religions in Antiquity*, 137–48; see also Bühner, *Der Gesandte und sein Weg im 4. Evangelium*.

58. Borgen, "God's Agent in the Fourth Gospel," in *Religions in Antiquity*, 143.

59. Schnackenburg, *The Gospel according to St. John*, 2.199.

60. Ibid., 1.438.

61. See commentaries, such as Brown, *The Gospel according to John (i–xii)*, 29.314, 318, 466, 470.

62. J. Louis Martyn, *History and Theology in the Fourth Gospel*, 2d ed. (Nashville: Abingdon, 1979 [1st ed., 1968]); Raymond E. Brown, *The Community of the Beloved Disciple* (New York and Ramsey, N.J.: Paulist, 1979).

63. See Ernst Käsemann, *The Testament of Jesus: A Study of the Gospel of John in the Light of Chapter 17* (Philadelphia: Fortress, 1968); Wayne A. Meeks, "The Man from Heaven in Johannine Sectarianism," *JBL* 91 (1972): 44–72.

64. Schnackenburg, *The Gospel according to St. John*, 1.287.

65. Barrett, *The Gospel according to St. John*, 237; Schnackenburg, *The Gospel according to St. John*, 1.435–36.

66. Dahl, "The Johannine Church and History," 136–37.

67. Brown, *The Gospel according to John (i–xii)*, AB 29.10.

68. Barnabas Lindars, *The Gospel of John*, NCB (London: Oliphants, 1972), 90.

69. See Lindars, *The Gospel of John*, 158–59. For such positive use of the term, "the world," see, further, John 3:17; 4:42: 6:33, 51; 10:36; 12:47.

70. See Marinus de Jonge, *Jesus, Stranger from Heaven and Son of God: Jesus Christ and Christians in Johannine Perspective*, SBLSBS 11 (Missoula, Mont.: Scholars Press, 1977), 58–59.

71. Thus, see Araios Didymos in Eusebius, *Praeparatio Evangelica* 15.15.3–5.

72. Rudolph, *Gnosis*, 305.

73. On the textual problems in John 1:3–4, see Barrett, *The Gospel according to St. John*, 156–57.

74. For the following, see James H. Charlesworth, "A Critical Comparison of the Dualism in 1QS 3.13–4.26 and the 'Dualism' Contained in the Gospel of John," in

John and Qumran, ed. James H. Charlesworth (London: Chapman, 1972), 76–106; Raymond E. Brown, "The Qumran Scrolls and the Johannine Gospel and Epistles," in idem, *New Testament Essays* (Milwaukee: Bruce, 1965), 102–31; Borgen, "Logos Was the True Light."

75. Brown, *The Gospel according to John (i–xii),* AB 29.515–16.

76. See Dodd, *The Interpretation of the Fourth Gospel,* 36.

J. Louis Martyn

6

A Gentile Mission That Replaced
an Earlier Jewish Mission?

I

Although different from one another in numerous and important regards, the Johannine labors of Ernst Käsemann, Wayne Meeks, and myself converge in one shared conviction: The Gospel of John originated in a local church—or group of churches—markedly distinct from the types of Christianity that were developing during the same period into the Great Church.[1]

Käsemann's first serious plunge into the Johannine waters came in his inaugural lecture at the University of Göttingen in 1951.[2] A decade and a half later, with some changes, he used the Schaffer lectures at Yale to continue his search for the place of the Fourth Gospel in the history of early Christian thought and life.[3] The major result can be stated in two sentences: To compare John's theology with theologies in other strains of early Christian tradition is to see that the evangelist was heir to the kind of naively docetic, highly enthusiastic strain of Christian thought combatted both by Paul (1 Cor. 4:8–13; 15:12) and by the author of 2 Timothy (2:18). The church in which John lived, then, was a sort of conventicle shoved off into a corner, quite distinct from the emerging catholic church, indeed, in some regards hostile to it.[4]

I myself approached the question of the place of the Johannine church in the history of early Christianity by first investigating that community's relations with its parent synagogue, a line of approach quite different from the one followed by Käsemann.[5] In one regard, however, my work led to a picture of Johannine Christianity similar to that of Käsemann. Convinced that the history of the Johannine community, from its origin through the period of its life in which the Fourth Gospel was composed, forms to no small extent a chapter in the history of *Jewish Christianity,* I concluded that this community stood at some remove not only from the parent synagogue—from which it had been excommunicated—but also from the emerging Great Church.[6]

Bringing to the study of the Johannine question both a penetrating *religionsgeschichtlich* analysis—focused largely on Jewish and Samaritan speculation about

Moses as prophet and King—and an admirable sensitivity to what we might call the in-group nature of Johannine language, Wayne Meeks also concluded, following his own path, that the church reflected in the Fourth Gospel was a "special group of former Jews" in which "we have the very model of a sectarian consciousness."[7] Thus, from 1972 onwards Meeks has repeatedly referred to the Johannine church as a sect, a practice that has elicited sharp disagreement in some quarters.[8]

II

Largely in response to the works of Käsemann, Meeks, and myself, there have been recent attempts—notably by Raymond E. Brown and Martin Hengel—to show that the Fourth Gospel, far from being the maverick product of an essentially sectarian church, originated in or near the streams that flowed together to become the Great Church.[9] As Käsemann, Meeks, and I have ourselves argued the sectarian case in quite different and sometimes mutually contradictory ways,[10] one is not surprised to see that Brown and Hengel have formulated a number of different counterarguments.[11] They share, however, one very important claim: A major mark of the essentially orthodox character of the Johannine community lies in its understanding of its mission. With slight variations from one another, Brown and Hengel hold that, like the emerging Great Church, the Johannine community considered the Gentile world to constitute its mission frontier. Indeed, in Brown's view the Johannine community that is reflected in the Gospel had substituted the Gentile mission for its earlier mission to the Jews, as had the Great Church.[12]

We have, then, a question of some importance in our quest to discern the place of John in early Christian thought and life. What can we say about the history of the Johannine community's vision of the ecclesiological future? Specifically, at the time of the Gospel, had the Johannine community shifted its mission frontier from Jews to Gentiles?

III

We can be confident, I think, that the community was born when Christian evangelists preached their gospel in the synagogue(s) of John's city.[13] With that event, a group of Christian Jews was born in the synagogue. During the immediately following period, members of this group continued what we may call a mission to Jews, preaching the good news of Jesus' messiahship to their fellows in the synagogue.[14]

In time several factors—not least the conversion of large numbers of synagogue members (12:11, 19)—led the Jewish authorities to expel this inner-synagogue group (9:22; 12:42; 16:2).[15] Suffering the deep pain of being separated from their social and theological cosmos, the group of Christian Jews became a discrete community of Jewish Christians, with a common history of suffering and with a shared language system reflecting that history.[16]

One considers seriously the possibility, then, that the Gospel might also reflect a shift in mission frontier corresponding to the pain of excommunication. That is to say, such a painful separation from the parent synagogue might have led members of the Johannine community to shake the Jewish dust off their sandals. Abandoning their Jewish mission, they might have turned to the Gentiles, thus showing that in this regard their community found itself in the midst of the stream that flowed into the emerging Great Church.[17] Do the pertinent data in the Fourth Gospel reflect that development?

IV

Explanations of Jewish Holy Times

> After this there was a festival of the Jews . . . (John 5:1).
> Now the Passover, the festival of the Jews, was near (6:4).
> Now the Jewish festival of Booths was near (7:2).[18]

These and similar explanatory notes have been taken by some to indicate that the evangelist was addressing his work to Gentiles, for it seems that only Gentiles would need to be told that Passover and Booths are festivals of the Jews.[19] We have here, however, an instance in which modern interpreters can easily go astray if they do not trouble themselves to enter into the strange and linguistically dialectic world of the Johannine community.[20] To read through the whole of the Gospel is to see that the expression, "Passover, the festival of the Jews," begs for comparison with the evangelist's numerous references to "the Jews," and even more with the expression, "their Law" (15:25; cf. 8:17; 10:34; 18:31; 19:7), both being locutions stemming, probably without exception, from the evangelist himself.[21] From that comparison one returns to the work of Meeks, thus recognizing that, given the sociolinguistic world of the Johannine community, these locutions reflect a group made up of former Jews, not of Gentiles.[22] In short, the first words of 6:4 can be paraphrased, "Passover, the feast of the Jews who celebrate it, in distinction from the members of our community, who do not do so, being no longer 'Jews' in the sense in which we ourselves use that term."[23]

Translations of Jewish Terms and Names

> They said to him, "Rabbi" (which translated means Teacher) (John 1:38).
> "We have found the Messiah" (which is translated Anointed [χριστός]) (1:41).
> "You are Simon, son of John. You are to be called Cephas" (which is translated Peter) (1:42).
> "I know that Messiah is coming" (who is called Christ [χριστός]) (4:25).

"Go, wash in the pool of Siloam" (which means Sent) (9:7).
"Rabbouni" (which means Teacher) (20:16).[24]

In these passages we have parenthetical, explanatory translations of a sort that would be needed, one may suppose, only by Gentiles. Regarding them, Brown has commented, "The fact that such explanations are clearly parenthetical indicates that this effort towards comprehensibility for non-Jews was made in the last pre-Gospel period of Johannine life."[25] More probable is the suggestion of John Painter that these explanations are glosses, added to the body of the Gospel by the redactor responsible for John 21.[26] That chapter reflects the redactor's concern to baptize the Johannine community and its Gospel into the emerging Great Church by bringing both community and Gospel into an essentially positive relationship with the Petrine line of Christianity.[27] And since the Great Church lived on the Gentile mission frontier, and since the Johannine redactor was intent on making the Gospel of his church compatible with the interests and makeup of that Great Church, he would have had ample reason for adding the instances of translation that are found in the body of the Gospel. On this reading, then, those parenthetical translations are post-Johannine glosses that tell us nothing about the makeup and missionary passions of the Johannine community when the Gospel itself was written.

A Reference to Teaching "Greeks"

The Pharisees heard the crowd muttering such things about him, and the chief priests and Pharisees sent temple police to arrest him. Jesus then said, "I will be with you a little while longer, and then I am going to him who sent me. You will search for me, but you will not find me; and where I am you cannot come." The Jews said to one another, "Where does this man intend to go that we will not find him? Does he intend to go to the Dispersion among the Greeks [τὴν διασπορὰν τῶν Ἑλλήνων] and teach the Greeks [τοὺς Ἕλληνας]? What does he mean by saying, 'You will search for me and you will not find me' and 'where I am you cannot come'?" (John 7:32–36).

The major thrust of this passage has to do with Christ's return to the Father. Allowing the Jews to misunderstand that reference, however, John refers to the possibility that Jesus will leave the Jewish homeland, go into the Diaspora, and teach there.[28] And whom might he teach? Linguistic analysis suggests two major possibilities for translating the expression, τὴν διασπορὰν τῶν Ἑλλήνων, the locution that provides the antecedent for τοὺς Ἕλληνας.

John could mean "the Diaspora *that consists of* Greek-speaking Jews" (an explanatory genitive). On this reading, the prospect is that Jesus (through the Johannine community) might go away from Palestine to the Diaspora of Greek-speaking Jews in order to teach those Jews. This interpretation was advanced in 1959 by

J.A.T. Robinson.[29] It has also been questioned, often by saying that had John intended to refer to Greek-speaking Jews, he would have spoken of Ἑλληνισταί ("Hellenists") rather than of Ἕλληναι ("Greeks").[30]

Alternatively, John could mean "the Diaspora of Jews who live *among* the Greeks" (a genitive of direction), in which case the prospect is that going abroad into the Jewish Diaspora, Jesus (through the Johannine community) would teach Gentiles. A large number of interpreters have elected this reading.[31]

A third possibility emerges, however, when one compares 7:35 with 12:20, for the latter is the only other text in which John uses the word, Ἕλληνες ("Greeks"). There, as we will see below, he employs that word to refer neither to Greek-speaking Jews nor to Gentiles, but rather to non-Jews who have attached themselves to the synagogue and who are, therefore, scarcely typical Gentiles.[32] Thus, one may see 7:35 itself as a reference to a development subsequent to the Johanine community's move away from Palestine. God-fearers come not only to synagogues in the neighborhood of the Johannine community, but also to meetings of that community itself:[33] "Does he intend to go to the Diaspora of Jews who live among the (numerous) God-fearers [τὴν διασπορὰν τῶν Ἑλλήνων; genitive of direction] and there teach the God-fearers [τοὺς Ἕλληνας]?" On that reading this text tells us nothing about a mission to Gentiles themselves.

Weighing all three readings of John 7:35, one sees that this rather opaque text may reflect some kind of openness to non-Jews who have already begun to worship the God of Israel. It scarcely tells us that at the time of the Gospel the Johannine community had a discrete mission to Gentiles. And it certainly does not indicate that the community had shifted its mission frontier from Jews to Gentiles.

"Other Sheep"

> I have other sheep that do not belong to this fold. I must bring them also, and they will listen to my voice. So there will be one flock, one shepherd (John 10:16).[34]

In chapter 10, John employs the word "sheep" fifteen times, using it in ways that reveal both the history of the Johannine community and the community's hopes for the future.[35] Leaving aside for a moment John's reference to "other sheep," we attend both to the parable of 10:1–6 and to its interpretation in 10:7–10 and in 10:11–18.

Noting that 10:1 follows on from 9:41, one sees that the sheep who hear the voice of the Good Shepherd have already been portrayed in the blind man of 9:1–39. He has heard Jesus' voice and has followed him, while refusing to hear the voice of strangers (the synagogue authorities who attempted to snatch him out of Jesus' hands). Thus, just as the blind man of John 9 is the prototypical member of the Johannine community, so the sheep of John 10 stand for that community in four ways:

a. It is they who hear the Good Shepherd's voice, who follow him, and whom he calls by name (10:3, 4, 27).

b. It is they who flee from alternative shepherds and who refuse to listen to them, because they do not recognize the voices of those shepherds (10:5).

c. It is they whose lives are threatened by the wolf when he comes to snatch them away (ἁρπάζω) and to scatter them (σκορπίζω, 10:12; see also ἁρπάζω in 10:28, 29; cf. 16:2). And it is they who, when they are thus endangered, are abandoned by the hired hand, who chooses to protect himself rather than to risk his life for the sheep (10:12; cf. 12:42).

d. And finally, it is they—the members of the Johannine community—who receive the absolute assurance from the Good Shepherd that however threatened they may be, no one will ever be able actually to snatch them out of his hand or out of the hand of the Father (10:28–29).

Clearly then, the parable and its interpretation constitute an allegory, in the reading of which those who were initiates by virtue of sharing both a common history and a language reflecting that history—that is to say, the members of the Johannine community—would easily recognize the following four representations:

a. The sheep stand, as said above, for the Johannine community.

b. Strangers, thieves, robbers, and the wolf stand for the Jewish authorities ("the Pharisees" of John 9), who kill, destroy, snatch away, and scatter members of the Johannine community (16:2).

c. The hireling probably stands for the secretly believing "rulers" (12:42), who avoid the possibility of their own excommunication and death by abandoning the Johannine community when it is endangered.

d. The Good Shepherd stands for Jesus, as he is active through Johannine evangelists who are prepared—in his pattern—to face the most severe forms of persecution for the community, and who both receive and transmit the absolute assurance that, however threatening the Jewish authorities may become, they shall never be able to snatch any member of the community out of the hands of Jesus and the Father.

In light of this reading, who are the "other sheep" of John 10:16? Authors of commentaries are virtually unanimous in the opinion that these other sheep are Gentiles who will be evangelized in what is universally called "the [sic!] Gentile mission." There are good reasons, however, to swim directly against the stream in this instance.[36]

In the reading of 10:16 itself, one notes several points. These other sheep already exist, as Jesus' sheep. Moreover, like "the dispersed children of God" (11:52; see below), they do not need to be evangelized. Being altogether trusted by the Johannine community—they are other sheep *of Jesus*—these persons presumably share with that community a history of persecution at the hands of synagogue authorities. They need to be comforted and assured, then, no less than the Johannine group itself. That shared need is sensitively described by H. B. Kossen:

These people, whose belief was so severely tested because of their expulsion from the Jewish community, had to be confirmed in their conviction that it was precisely their belief in Jesus as the Christ, the Son of God, which gave them eternal life in his name (John 10:31). They must be assured that—like Nathanael who was told by Jesus: "Behold an Israelite indeed, in whom is no guile!" (1:47)—they [were not severed from Israel. They needed to be assured that, on the contrary, they] belonged to the true Israel, that they belonged to Jesus' sheep. "The Jews" did not belong to Jesus' sheep because they did not believe in him as the Messiah (10:24–26). But they—the readers of this gospel—could apply Jesus' word to themselves: "My sheep hear my voice, and I know them, and they follow me: and I give them eternal life; and they shall never perish, and no one shall snatch them out of my hand" (10:27–28).[37]

In John 10:16, the evangelist informs his community that there are other Jewish-Christian communities, whose members need the same comfort and assurance needed by their own. He then adds that these other communities also need to be gathered. Apparently considering his own community to be a sort of mother church to other Jewish-Christian churches, the evangelist looks forward to a unity—one flock, one shepherd—that will ensue when these others are gathered into his church.

On this reading, John 10:16 is very far indeed from reflecting a Gentile mission. The ecclesiological future portrayed there is not the result of a mission of any sort, properly speaking. That future will come with the unification of several Jewish-Christian communities, all of which have an essentially common history of persecution by Jewish authorities.[38]

The Prophecy of Caiaphas

But one of them, Caiaphas, who was high priest that year, said to them, "You know nothing at all! You do not understand that it is better for you to have one man die for the people than to have the whole nation destroyed." He did not say this on his own, but being high priest that year he prophesied that Jesus was about to die for the nation, and not for the nation only, but to gather into one the dispersed children of God (John 11:49–52).

Brown points out the carefulness of Severino Pancaro's exegesis, according to which John hears in Caiaphas' prophecy a reference to "all those (whether Jew or Gentile) who would be united into this new People by the death of Christ."[39] In several regards, such as the analysis of pertinent expressions in the Septuagint, I should agree. As an exegesis of John's text, however, Pancaro's treatment leaves much to be desired. In his conclusion this usually perceptive scholar says, "[Jesus'] death makes children of men [presumably, Pancaro means "makes men children of God"], and it is because they are made children that they are united, but John wishes to insist more on the 'gathering into one' than on the act of becoming a child of God."[40] But in 11:52 John utters not a word about persons being *made* children of God. He speaks, rather, of the gathering of persons who were children of God before they were scattered.

From this observation one returns first to 1:12–13, and second, to 10:16. John 1:12–13 is the only other passage in which the evangelist speaks of children of God. There one learns that in the evangelist's view, neither Jews nor Gentiles are children of God. That identity is given by God only to those who receive Jesus as the Logos.[41] In 11:52 John speaks of the gathering into one of persons who are already Christians.

And which Christians, specifically, does he have in mind? That question brings us back to 10:16. Taking one's bearings from that passage, one sees that in 11:52 John is using the prophecy of the high priest Caiaphas to formulate a reinterpretation of the widespread and classic motif pertaining both to the Jewish Diaspora and to its being gathered in. In John's setting the children of God who have been scattered are the other Jewish-Christian conventicles we have seen reflected in 10:16. In 11:52 John again speaks to his own community about those other conventicles, adding the assurance that the high priest himself "had unwittingly prophesied the redeeming significance of Jesus' death especially for them."[42]

Again, then, we have a passage that fails to reflect a Gentile mission.[43]

"Greeks" Who Have Come to Worship at the Feast Seek Jesus

Now among those who went up to worship at the festival [Passover] were some Greeks [Ἕλληνες]. They came to Philip . . . and said to him, "Sir, we wish to see Jesus." . . . [Then] Andrew and Philip went and told Jesus. Jesus answered them, "The hour has come for the Son of Man to be glorified. Very truly, I tell you, unless a grain of wheat falls into the ground and dies, it remains just a single grain; but if it dies, it bears much fruit" (John 12:20–24).

In an admirable essay, Kyoshi Tsuchido begins by noting that this paragraph shows Johannine style at numerous points, indicating it to be "an editorial creation, freely composed by the Evangelist." To be sure, in his composition John "used some pre-Johannine fragments," but in the text as it stands one finds that he "describes the sayings and the works of Jesus and simultaneously reflects his own *Sitz im Leben*."[44]

In John's own setting, who are these "Greeks"? Since they are identified not only as Ἕλληνες but also as persons who *regularly* come to Jerusalem in order to worship at the time of Passover, they are surely Gentiles who—like the Ethiopian eunuch of Acts 8—had become attached to Judaism before expressing interest in Jesus.[45] Their attachment to Judaism is hardly a matter in which John has no interest. Scarcely typical Gentiles, they worship the God of Israel by observing

Passover, ignorant of Jesus' having replaced that feast.[46] Given that characteristic, their coming on the scene is in John's view a development of considerable import. Jesus responds by saying that the hour has arrived for his glorification, an event that will bear much fruit (John 12:24), demonstrating, among other things, Jesus' replacement of the Jewish feasts.

But if John refers here to God-fearers—persons who are Jewish to the extent of regularly praying to the God of Israel—and if their desire to see Jesus is a move of their own volition, on what reading of the text can one say that it has pertinence to the question of a discrete mission *to pagan Gentiles?* A number of interpreters would answer by saying that John considers these God-fearers to be representatives of the Gentile world.[47] One might endorse that reading if one had already found secure references to Gentiles in 7:35, 10:16, and 11:52. And if one had found references to Gentiles in those earlier texts, one could find further reflections of a Gentile mission in such references as "the savior of the world" (4:42) and "all people" (12:32), clear indications of some kind of theological universalism.[48] Jesus' statement about drawing "all people" to himself would then be particularly revealing, coming as it does shortly after the reference to the God-fearers' request to see him. That is to say, one could read 12:20 as a text in which John—like Luke, the author of Acts—views inquisitiveness on the part of God-fearers as an intermediate step in the direction of a discrete mission to Gentiles.

That last interpretation is especially to be resisted, however, because reading an aspect of Luke's *Weltanschauung* into John is precisely the move to be avoided in pursuing our question (see further, below). Moreover, as we have seen, the case for finding pagan Gentiles in John 7:35 is scarcely convincing, while in 10:16 and 11:52 that case is excluded.

And there is a striking congruity between John 12:20–21, 32 and Isaiah 2:2–3: In each case the motif is that of people *coming to* the established group, rather than that of missioners *going out to* those people. Thus, the interpreter who wishes to see in John 12:20 the reflection of a discrete mission *to* Gentiles must accept the burden of proof.

Jesus' statements about much fruit (12:24) and about drawing all people to himself (12:32) remain indications of an ultimate, theological universalism comparable to that of Isaiah 2:2–3, until they are followed by a story in which—on the contemporary level—a Johannine missioner reaches out to and brings in at least one God-fearer. And on John's landscape, the God-fearers of 12:20 vanish without a trace.

Pondering that fact, one recalls the care with which John included stories in which members of his community could find reflections of themselves. In 9:1–38 he included a dramatic representation of Jews who had been brought into the community from the synagogue. In 1:29–51 he provided an engaging portrait of followers of the Baptist who had been led to make their entry. And in 4:5–42 John furnished the Samaritans in his church with an account of their journey.[49] If, then, there were other members of his community who had been brought into it as the result of a mission to pagan Gentiles—especially if that mission was of such importance to the community as to have replaced the earlier mission to the Jews—one should certainly expect the evangelist to have provided these persons with an account of their journey.[50]

Striking is the fact that a representation of persons being brought into the Johannine community from the pagan Gentile world is found nowhere in the Gospel. Indeed, except for Pilate, whose presence is demanded by the passion tradition, the Gospel has no compelling Gentile actor at all.[51] In reading 12:20, 12:24, and 12:32, then, we are left with a reference to a certain inquisitiveness on the part of some God-fearers who regularly pray to the God of Israel, with a reference to Jesus' death as the event that will bear much fruit—among God-fearers who at one time observed the Jewish feasts?—and with a theologically universalistic statement. Is the result a sequence of texts that reflects the undertaking of a discrete mission to Gentiles, substituting that Gentile mission for the earlier mission to Jews?

Failure to Believe, in Spite of Many Signs

Although he had performed so many signs in their presence, they did not believe in him. This was to fulfill the word spoken by the prophet Isaiah: "Lord, who has believed our message, and to whom has the arm of the Lord been revealed?" And so they could not believe, because Isaiah also said, "He has blinded their eyes and hardened their heart, so that they might not look with their eyes, and understand with their heart and turn—and I would heal them" (John 12:37–40).

Isaiah said this because he saw his glory and spoke about him. Nevertheless, many, even of the authorities, believed in him. But because of the Pharisees they did not confess it, for fear that they would be put out of the synagogue, for they loved human glory more than the glory that comes from God (John 12:41–43).

Jesus then cried aloud: "Whoever believes in me believes not in me but in him who sent me . . . for I have not spoken on my own, but the Father who sent me has himself given me a commandment about what to say and what to speak. And I know that his commandment is eternal life. What I speak, therefore, I speak just as the Father has told me" (John 12:44–50).

Moody Smith has given us fundamental guidance for the reading of this passage.[52] Following him, we can suppose two pre-Gospel stages. (1) Materials attesting to Jesus' mighty signs were probably collected by Jews—the nascent Johannine community—who used that collection to win other Jews to belief in Jesus as the Messiah. At the same time persons in this community collected passion traditions into a coherent form, so that the community had a collection of signs and a primitive passion story, both probably formed in large part for the same audience — Jews who were the objects of the community's mission. (2) As some of those other Jews proved extremely resistant to the Johannine mission, raising in time very sharp questions and objections, members of the nascent community found that neither of their traditions was effective without the other. In response to this development (and perhaps to inner-church factors as well), someone combined these two traditions in the manner proposed by Robert Fortna in *The Gospel of Signs,* forming a primitive gospel by stitching these two traditions together with the threads that we now have as John 12:37–40.[53]

Since Smith assigns the material beginning in 12:41 (or 12:42) to the evangelist, we can speak of a third stage in which the evangelist made his own contribution, expanding on the earlier transition by means of 12:41–50. This analysis leads, then, to the crucial question: Interpreting 12:37–40 by means of his own composition in 12:41–50, does the evangelist leave indications that, faced with Jewish unbelief, his community has substituted a Gentile mission for its earlier mission to its fellow Jews?

There are no convincing grounds for answering that question in the affirmative.[54] Quite the contrary. Having noted the massive Jewish unbelief that played such a painful role in the history of his community, the evangelist does not find a measure of relief by referring to the encouraging development of a Gentile mission. One notes with some amazement that after mentioning massive Jewish unbelief, he leads his reader right back into the synagogue, so to speak. And there he finds authoritative persons who do believe (John 12:42; cf. 7:48), although they are afraid to confess their faith openly. We are doubtless right to sense here a profound ambivalence. On the one hand, these secret believers elicit from John a certain amount of scorn (cf. 12:43 with the portrait of the hireling in 10:12–13). On the other hand, however, John sees them as persons who may yet be drawn (by God; 6:44) fully into his own community.[55] It is for that reason that in 12:44–50 he provides members of his community with arguments by which they can lessen Jewish fears that to join their community is to stand in violation of monotheism (a matter of no general concern to the Gentile world).[56]

V

This redaction-critical interpretation of John 12:37–50 may not be the *coup de grâce* to the suggestion that, at the time of the Gospel, the Johannine community had embraced an openness of some kind to some kind of Gentiles: to God-fearers, that is, who on their own volition seek Jesus (12:21). Taken together, however, with the readings of other texts offered earlier (including some degree of uncertainty about 7:35), this interpretation seems to me virtually to rule out the thesis that the community had already substituted a Gentile mission for a Jewish one.

Moreover, in this reading of 12:37–50, we come to sense the large and significant distance—in regard to mission frontier—between John and Luke-Acts, the major New Testament witness to the emergence of the early catholic church. For a Christian community maintaining a Jewish mission into the closing years of the first century is neither portrayed nor forecast on Luke's canvas.

Brown is right to recall that Isaiah's prophecy about the blinding of eyes and the numbing of minds was used by some early Christians "as an explanation of the Jewish failure to accept Jesus and as the rationale for turning to the Gentiles (Acts 28:25–28; see Matt 13:13–15)."[57] But when one notes that John has interpreted Isaiah's prophecy by means of the motifs struck in 12:41–50, and when one compares the result with the final scene in Acts, one is doubly impressed with the gulf between Luke-Acts and John, as regards mission frontier. That final scene in Acts is artfully constructed:

> After [the leaders of the Jews in Rome] had set a day to meet with [Paul], they came to him at his lodging . . . Paul made one further statement: "The Holy Spirit was right in saying to your ancestors through the prophet Isaiah, 'Go to this people and say, You will indeed listen, but never understand, and you will indeed look, but never perceive. For this people's heart has grown dull, and their ears are hard of hearing, and they have shut their eyes, so that they might not look with their eyes, and listen with their ears, and understand with their heart and turn—and I would heal them.' Let it be known to you then that this salvation of God has been sent to the Gentiles; they will listen" (Acts 28:25–29).

It is also a scene without parallel in the Gospel of John.

Was the Johannine community, then, a sect in the sense of being not only distinct from the synagogue, but also far removed from the streams that issued into the emerging Great Church? That question has not been fully answered in the present chapter. We have simply found that the community's sense of mission—at the time of the Gospel—was significantly different from the sense of mission characteristic of the Great Church. We can add, however, one weighty observation. From a host of early Christian witnesses, we know that no aspect of life was more important to the self-understanding of first-century churches than the definition of mission frontier.[58]

NOTES

1. Regarding the "place" of the Johannine community, Meeks's interest—to some degree like my own—is primarily focused on John and Judaism. Hence, when he introduced the term "sect" into the present-day discussion of that community, he meant, and continues to mean, a sect of Judaism. He has also said things about this sect, however, that bear on the question of its place in early Christian life and thought. (See n.

7 below.) In this chapter "the Gospel of John" refers to the document we have, less chapter 21 and a few other parts of the text that were also added by a redactor. Regarding the literary history of the Gospel, see esp. D. Moody Smith, *The Composition and Order of the Fourth Gospel: Bultmann's Literary Theory,* Yale Publications in Religion 10 (New Haven and London: Yale University Press, 1965); idem, *Johannine Christianity: Essays on Its Setting, Sources, and Theology* (Columbia, S.C.: University of South Carolina Press, 1984), passim; Rudolf Schnackenburg, *The Gospel according to St John* (New York: Crossroad, 1982), 1.72–74; Raymond E. Brown, *The Gospel according to John (i–xii),* AB 29 (Garden City, N.Y.: Doubleday, 1966), xxxiv–xxxix; Robert Tomson Fortna, *The Gospel of Signs: A Reconstruction of the Narrative Sources Underlying the Fourth Gospel,* SNTSMS 11 (Cambridge: Cambridge University Press, 1970); idem, *The Fourth Gospel and Its Predecessor: From Narrative Source to Present Gospel* (Philadelphia: Fortress, 1988).

   2. Ernst Käsemann, "Ketzer und Zeuge: Zum johanneischen Verfasserproblem," *ZTK* 48 (1951): 292–311 = *Exegetische Versuche und Besinnungen,* 2 vols. (Göttingen: Vandenhoeck & Ruprecht, 1960, 1964), 1.168–87.

   3. Ernst Käsemann, *The Testament of Jesus: A Study of John in the Light of Chapter 17* (London and Philadelphia: SCM/Fortress, 1968 [German original, 1966]). Between "Ketzer und Zeuge" and *Testament* Käsemann published a productively provocative study of the Johannine prologue, "Aufbau und Anliegen des johanneischen Prologs," in *Exegetische Versuche und Besinnungen,* 1.155–80 (= "The Structure and Purpose of the Prologue to John's Gospel," in Ernst Käsemann, *New Testament Questions of Today* [London and Philadelphia: SCM/Fortress, 1969], 138–67).

   4. Käsemann, *The Testament of Jesus,* 75–76. Among the numerous reviews of Käsemann's *Testament,* see Günther Bornkamm, "Towards the Interpretation of John's Gospel: A Discussion of *The Testament of Jesus* by Ernst Käsemann," in *The Interpretation of John,* ed. John Ashton, IRT 9 (London and Philadelphia: SPCK/Fortress, 1986), 79–98, and Wayne A. Meeks in *USQR* 24 (1969): 414–21. See also now the critique of Käsemann's work at numerous points in Udo Schnelle, *Antidocetic Christology in the Gospel of John: An Investigation of the Place of the Fourth Gospel in the Johannine School* (Minneapolis: Fortress, 1992 [German original, 1989]).

   5. J. Louis Martyn, "The Salvation-History Perspective in The Fourth Gospel" (Ph.D. dissertation, Yale University, 1957); idem, *History and Theology in the Fourth Gospel* (New York: Harper & Row, 1968; rev. ed., Nashville: Abingdon, 1978); idem, "Source Criticism and *Religionsgeschichte* in the Fourth Gospel," in *Jesus and Man's Hope,* 2 vols., ed. David G. Buttrick and Dikran Y. Hadidian, A Perspective Book (Pittsburgh: Pittsburgh Theological Seminary, 1970, 1971), 1.247–73 = *The Interpretation of John,* ed. Ashton, 99–121; idem, "We Have Found Elijah," in *Jews, Greeks and Christians. Religious Cultures in Late Antiquity: Essays in Honor of William David Davies,* ed. Robert Hamerton-Kelly and Robin Scroggs, SJLA 21 (Leiden: Brill, 1976), 181–219 = Martyn, *The Gospel of John in Christian History: Essays for Interpreters,* Theological Inquiries (New York and Ramsey, N.J.: Paulist, 1978), 9–54; idem, "Clementine Recognitions 1,33–71, Jewish Christianity, and the Fourth Gospel," *God's Christ and His People: Studies in Honour of Nils Alstrup Dahl,* ed. Jacob Jervell and Wayne A. Meeks (Oslo: Universitetsforlaget, 1977), 265–95 approx. = Martyn, *The Gospel of John in Christian History,* 55–89; idem, "Glimpses into the History of the Johannine Community," *L'Évangile de Jean: Sources, rédac-*

tion, théologie, ed. Marinus de Jonge, BETL 44 (Gembloux: Duculot, 1977), 149–75 = Martyn, *The Gospel of John in Christian History,* 90–121.

6. Martyn, "Source Criticism and *Religionsgeschichte* in the Fourth Gospel," in *The Interpretation of John,* ed. Ashton, 117; idem, "Glimpses into the History of the Johannine Community," in *The Gospel of John in Christian History,* 120–21. The kernel of the present essay—doubt that the Johannine community had a discrete mission to Gentiles at the time of the Gospel—was a major motif in a paper I presented at the 1979 meeting of SBL. The case for locating the Johannine community in the history of Jewish Christianity has now been both broadened and deepened in a fascinating and instructive essay by Martinus C. de Boer, "L'Évangile de Jean et le christianisme juif (nazoréen)," in *Juifs et chrétiens au premier siècle: La déchirure,* ed. Daniel Marguerat (Geneva: Labor et Fides, forthcoming).

7. Wayne A. Meeks, "Equal to God," in *The Conversation Continues: Studies in Paul and John in Honor of J. Louis Martyn,* ed. Robert T. Fortna and Beverly R. Gaventa (Nashville: Abingdon, 1990), 309–21 (quotation, 319). This conclusion is already present in Meeks' earlier works. See the classic study in which he successfully introduced the use of the term "sect" into present-day discussion of John: "The Man from Heaven in Johannine Sectarianism," *JBL* 91 (1972): 44–72 = *The Interpretation of John,* ed. Ashton, 141–73. See, further, Meeks, "'Am I a Jew?'—Johannine Christianity and Judaism," *Christianity, Judaism and Other Greco-Roman Cults: Studies for Morton Smith at Sixty,* ed. Jacob Neusner, 4 pts., SJLA 12 (Leiden: Brill, 1975), 1.163–86; Meeks, "The Divine Agent and His Counterfeit in Philo and the Fourth Gospel," in *Aspects of Religious Propaganda in Judaism and Early Christianity,* ed. Elisabeth Schüssler Fiorenza (Notre Dame: University of Notre Dame Press, 1976), 43–67; Meeks, "Breaking Away: Three New Testament Pictures of Christianity's Separation from the Jewish Communities," *"To See Ourselves as Others See Us":* Christians, Jews, "Others" in Late Antiquity, ed. Jacob Neusner and Ernest S. Frerichs, Scholars Press Studies in the Humanities (Chico, Calif.: Scholars Press, 1985), 93–115 (esp. 103). As I have said above (n. 1), Meeks's work—to some degree, like my own—has been focused primarily on the place of the Johannine church in its Jewish context. Prior to its exclusion from the synagogue, this church had been a sect "of Judaism," something socially true of none of the Pauline churches (Meeks, "Breaking Away," 94, 106). Meeks also says, however, that in John there is "hardly a hint of a specifically gentile mission" ("Breaking Away," 97). This statement alone suffices to show that Meeks's sociological use of the word "sect" has implications for the place of John in early Christian thought and life, as Raymond E. Brown correctly senses (*The Community of the Beloved Disciple* [New York: Paulist, 1979], 14 n. 8; see also Meeks, "Breaking Away," 114). Regarding Jewish-Christian sects that were as far removed from the emerging Great Church as they were from emerging rabbinism—something true of the Johannine community, I think, but by no means true of the church reflected in the upper strata of Matthew—see, for instance, Joan E. Taylor, "The Phenomenon of Early Jewish-Christianity: Reality or Scholarly Invention?" *VC* 44 (1990): 313–34.

8. See, for example, Brown, *The Community of the Beloved Disciple,* 14 n. 8. I will turn, below, to the recent works of Brown and Martin Hengel, the latter of whom writes on the Fourth Gospel without making any reference to the Johannine labors of Wayne Meeks later than *The Prophet-King: Moses Traditions and the Johannine Christology,* NovTSup 14 (Leiden: Brill, 1967). Is it because of Moody Smith's irenic

approach to the question of John's place in early Christianity that his labors have kindled no such disagreement (note the comment of Brown in the reference, given above)? I think it wise not to bring Smith directly into the debate at this juncture (see below, the discussion of John 12:37–50), but several of his comments should be cited, not least because he has himself applied the adjective "sectarian" to the Johannine church. In an essay titled "Johannine Christianity: Some Reflections on Its Character and Delineation" (*NTS* 21 [1976]: 222–48 = Smith, *Johannine Christianity*, 1–36), Smith speaks of what he himself dubs the Johannine *Eigenart* ["distinctiveness"]: "It can probably be agreed that on any reading of the Gospel and Epistles there appears a sectarian consciousness, a sense of exclusiveness, a sharp delineation of the community from the world. . . . If this sectarian or quasi-sectarian self-consciousness is not a matter of dispute, its roots, causes, and social matrix nevertheless are. What thereby comes to expression? A Christian sense of alienation or separation from the world generally? From the synagogue? From developing ecclesiastical orthodoxy?" (*Johannine Christianity*, 2–4). Later in the same essay, he begins to give at least a partial answer to these questions by speaking of the place of John in early Christian history: "The relative isolation and independence of the Johannine material in language and conceptuality may militate against the traditional viewpoint [that it originated in Ephesus, although its final form may have been published there]. . . . John's relative isolation from other streams of tradition in the New Testament seems to bear witness to a place of origin somewhat off the beaten track . . . . If the Johannine Gospel or tradition actually originated in a relatively remote corner of the Christian map, its distinctive character as well as its difficulty in finding acceptance in the emerging catholic church become more intelligible. Nor is such an origin incompatible with John's Gospel's having rather early made friends among Christians later branded heretical" (22). Note the reference to these comments of Smith in Klaus Wengst, *Bedrängte Gemeinde und verherrlichter Christus: Ein Versuch über das Johannesevangelium* (Neukirchen-Vluyn: Neukirchener, 1981), 93; 3d ed. (Munich: Kaiser, 1990), 178–79. Note also Robert Kysar, *John, the Maverick Gospel* (Atlanta: John Knox, 1976); Fernando F. Segovia, "The Love and Hatred of Jesus and Johannine Sectarianism," *CBQ* 43 (1981): 258–72; and the comment by John Ashton in *Understanding the Fourth Gospel* (Oxford: Clarendon, 1991), 173: "Finding itself alone and confronting persecution, [the Johannine group] had two choices. It could either look for support elsewhere or huddle self-protectively in a small knot. Perhaps it did both these things, but the evidence is stronger for the latter" (see also 173 n. 23).

9. See Brown, *The Community of the Beloved Disciple;* Martin Hengel, *The Johannine Question* (London: SCM, 1989). As Brown and Hengel are very far from understanding themselves to be, in any significant sense, heirs of Ferdinand Christian Baur, there is perhaps some irony in the fact that—in regard to the issue of the present chapter—the results of their labors largely coincide with the conclusion reached a century and a half ago by the Tübingen giant, for Baur thought the Fourth Gospel to be, along with Luke's volumes, a prime witness to the emergence of the Great Church. See F. C. Baur, *Geschichte der christlichen Kirche*, 3d ed., 5 vols. (Tübingen: Fues, 1863), 1.172: "Auf diesen beiden Punkten [sc. die römische Kirche und das johanneische Evangelium] hat das christliche Bewusstsein in seiner freieren Entwicklung dasselbe Ziel im Auge, die Realisierung der Idee der katholischen Kirche" ("With respect to both [the Roman church and the Johannine Gospel], Christian consciousness in its unimpeded development has the same aim in view: the realization of the idea of

the catholic church"). To the books of Brown and Hengel, one can add some elements in the work of Schnelle, *Antidocetic Christology in the Gospel of John*. In his conclusion Schnelle says, "The labeling of Johannine Christianity as a marginal group, which one so often reads, is probably not accurate, for sectarian flight from the world is far from the intention of the evangelist (see only 17:15, 18, 20; 20:21–22). Moreover, the high level of its theological reflection, as well as its connections to the Synoptics and especially to Pauline Christianity, make the Fourth Gospel appear rather to be located *at the center of the theological history of earliest Christianity*, at a point at which important currents in developing Christian theology converged" (236, emphasis added). A brief assessment of Schnelle's work has been given by M.J.J. Menken, "The Christology of the Fourth Gospel: A Survey of Recent Research," in *From Jesus to John: Essays on Jesus and New Testament Christology in Honour of Marinus de Jonge*, ed. Martinus de Boer, JSNTSup 84 (Sheffield: JSOT, 1993), 292–320 (see esp. 307–8).

　10. As stated earlier, Käsemann argued by making comparisons among lines of Christian tradition, and his portrait is that of a highly hellenized church, presumably one that was pursuing a Gentile mission.

　11. Indeed, Brown and Hengel differ in a number of ways. One notes, for example, that, whereas Brown speaks of the Johannine community as a church drawn both from Jews and from Gentiles (*The Community of the Beloved Disciple*, 82), Hengel finds the founder of the Johannine school (although himself a Jewish Christian) to be "working in a Gentile-Christian milieu," for that founder "presupposes the Gentile mission and the solution of the question of the Law" (*The Johannine Question*, 123). That difference is related to the fact that, whereas Brown accepts the quest for the history of the Johannine community, Hengel does not: "Nowadays we already have all too many attempts to reconstruct a 'history of the Johannine community.' They are all doomed to failure, because we know nothing of a real history which even goes back to Palestine, and conjectures about it are idle" (*The Johannine Question*, 205 n. 85). Brown thinks that when the Gospel was written, the Johannine community had *shifted* its mission frontier from Jews to Gentiles (*The Community of the Beloved Disciple*, 55), whereas Hengel, as noted, thinks the founder himself presupposed the (sic!) Gentile mission. Readers conversant with my own work will not be surprised to hear that, on the whole, I find Brown's argument much more finely nuanced than that of Hengel. Moreover, Brown is admirably willing to note factors that militate against his major argument. One notes, for example, "there is much in Johannine theology that would relativize the importance of institution and office at the very time when that importance was being accentuated in other Christian communities (including those who spoke of apostolic foundation)" (*The Community of the Beloved Disciple*, 87; also see 183–98). See, further, Martinus C. de Boer, "John 4:27 — Women (and Men) in the Gospel and Community of John," in *Women in the Biblical Tradition*, ed. George J. Brooke, Studies in Women and Religion 31 (Lewiston, N.Y.: Mellen, 1992), 208–30.

　12. Brown, *The Community of the Beloved Disciple*, 55. The nature of the communities reflected in the Johannine epistles is a matter left aside in the present chapter.

　13. This view is not held by every Johannine critic, but it is fair to say that it is widespread in contemporary studies. See Robert Kysar, *The Fourth Evangelist and His Gospel: An Examination of Contemporary Scholarship* (Minneapolis: Augsburg, 1975), 147–72; idem, "The Fourth Gospel: A Report on Recent Research," *ANRW* 2.25.3 (1985): 2389–480; idem, "The Gospel of John," *ABD* 3 (1992): 912–31; Smith, *Johannine Christianity*, 62–79 and passim; Teresa Okure, *The Johannine Approach*

to Mission: A Contextual Study of John 4:1–42, WUNT 2/31 (Tübingen: Mohr [Siebeck], 1988), 13; R. Alan Culpepper, "John," in The Books of the Bible: The Apocrypha and the New Testament, ed. Bernhard W. Anderson (New York: Scribner's, 1989), 2.203–28; John Painter, The Quest for the Messiah: The History, Literature and Theology of the Johannine Community (Edinburgh: T. & T. Clark, 1991; 2d ed., Nashville: Abingdon, 1993), passim; Ashton, Understanding the Fourth Gospel, 109 and passim; John Riches, A Century of New Testament Study (Cambridge: Lutterworth, 1993), 180–97; Wengst, Bedrängte Gemeinde und verherrlichter Christus (1990), 75–104. The dominance of this view is also reflected in certain plaintive remarks of Schnelle and Hengel.

14. On the theory of a signs-source or Signs-Gospel, and on the closely related hypothesis that that source or Gospel played a role in the evangelization of Jews, see esp. Smith, The Composition and Order of the Fourth Gospel, 34–44 (Bultmann's analysis); Fortna, The Gospel of Signs; idem, The Fourth Gospel and Its Predecessor.

15. Whether this expulsion was in some way connected with the Birkath ha-Minim is a question that can be left aside in this chapter (see Meeks, "Breaking Away," 102–3). See now the carefully nuanced discussion in de Boer, "L'Évangile de Jean et le christianisme juif (nazoréen)," and the literature cited therein, notably Philip S. Alexander, " 'The Parting of the Ways' from the Perspective of Rabbinic Judaism," in Jews and Christians: The Parting of the Ways A. D. 70 to 135, ed. James D. G. Dunn (Tübingen: Mohr [Siebeck], 1993), 1–25. The thesis that the Johannine group experienced a painful exclusion from its parent synagogue is as close to a simple fact as one can come, whatever the instrument or process by which the leaders of that synagogue effected it. Moreover, seventy-five years of study of the Synoptic Gospels should suffice to teach us that one is obliged to date a given motif at or very near the time of the author of the document in which it is found, unless one can show it to have a significantly earlier origin—something accomplished, with regard to John 9:22; 12:42; and 16:2, neither by Ulrich Luz (with Rudolf Smend, Gesetz, Biblische Konfrontationen/Kohlhammer Taschenbücher 1015 [Stuttgart: Kohlhammer, 1981], 125), nor by Schnelle (Antidocetic Christology in the Gospel of John, 25–31, 120–21), nor by Hengel (The Johannine Question, 114–15).

16. One can compare John 16:2 with 1 Thess. 2:14–15 but not with 2:16a. See Paul S. Minear, John: The Martyr's Gospel (New York: Pilgrim, 1984). Regarding a shared language system, see n. 20 below.

17. See, for example, P. Maurice Casey, From Jewish Prophet to Gentile God: The Origins and Development of New Testament Christology (Louisville: Westminster/John Knox, 1991), 27–31 and passim. See also the review of Casey's work by Leander E. Keck, Interpretation 47 (1993): 413–14; and Thomas L. Brodie, The Gospel according to John: A Literary and Theological Commentary (New York and Oxford: Oxford University Press, 1993), 164–65.

18. To this list one might add John 2:6; 2:13; 4:9; 18:28; 19:14, 40.

19. See, for example, J. W. Bowker, "The Origin and Purpose of St. John's Gospel," NTS 11 (1964–65): 398–408 (408 n. 1); cf. R. Alan Culpepper, Anatomy of the Fourth Gospel: A Study in Literary Design, FFNT (Philadelphia: Fortress, 1983), 219–27 (but see the nuanced statements on 225). Schnelle takes these explanations and the translations, listed below, to show the great distance between the Gospel of John and Judaism (Antidocetic Christology in the Gospel of John, 34).

20. The Johannine language is admirably penetrated in the classic study of Meeks,

"The Man from Heaven in Johannine Sectarianism." See also Meeks, "Equal to God" (above, n. 7), and Martinus C. de Boer, "Narrative Criticism, Historical Criticism, and the Gospel of John," *JSNT* 47 (1992): 35–48.

21. Fortna, *The Fourth Gospel and Its Predecessor,* 311. On "the Jews" in John, see, recently, Ashton, *Understanding the Fourth Gospel,* 131–59. On the expression "their Law" (and similar locutions), see Severino Pancaro, *The Law in the Fourth Gospel: The Torah and the Gospel, Moses and Jesus, Judaism and Christianity according to John,* NovTSup 42 (Leiden: Brill, 1975), 517–22; and de Boer's discussion of "your Torah" in '*Abodah Zara* 16b–17a ("L'Évangile de Jean et le christianisme juif (nazoréen)").

22. See n. 20 above, *pace* Hengel, *The Johannine Question,* 119. Note also the remark of Ashton about recognizing in the Gospel's "hot-tempered exchanges the type of family row in which the participants face one another across the room of a house which all have shared and all [to some degree still] call home" (*Understanding the Fourth Gospel,* 151, modified).

23. Meeks ("Equal to God," passim) is right to suggest that the modern exegete of the Gospel render numerous instances of "the Jews" by the expression "the other Jews," for ethnically the members of the Johannine community were no less Jews than were the persons who remained in the synagogue. As Meeks knows very well, however, members of the separated community did not refer to themselves as Jews. And, as de Boer has shown, that is a point that invites one to compare the Johannine community with the Nazoreans: "Both communities reject the name 'Jews' to describe themselves" ("L'Évangile de Jean et le christianisme juif (nazoréen)").

24. One might add John 11:16 and 20:24, but they are in some regards different from simple translations; note also instances of translation in the other direction: 19:13 ("Gabbatha") and 19:17 ("Golgatha").

25. Brown, *The Community of the Beloved Disciple,* 55.

26. Painter, *The Quest for the Messiah* (2d ed.), 131. Suggesting a line of interpretation that is surely possible, Painter includes in his list of these glosses the passages I have treated above.

27. Regarding the intentions of the redactor in adding John 21, see Rudolf Bultmann, *The Gospel of John: A Commentary* (Philadelphia: Westminster, 1971), 706–18 (*pace* Smith, *The Composition and Order of the Fourth Gospel,* 237), and the cogent comments of Brown: "The themes of Peter's rehabilitation, his role as shepherd of the sheep, his death as martyr, the role of the Beloved Disciple, his death, its relation to the second coming—*these are questions that affected the relation of the Johannine community to the Church at large*" (*The Gospel according to John (xiii–xxi),* AB 29A (Garden City, N.Y.: Doubleday, 1970), 1082, emphasis added). Did the redactor do his work after the Johannine community moved from the east, to Ephesus? Regarding the hypothesis of such a move, see Brown *The Community of the Beloved Disciple,* 56 n. 103, 178–79 (on Marie-Émile Boismard). In light of the arguments advanced later in this chapter, one might also see the parenthetical translations as aids provided for God-fearers who, of their own volition, came to meetings of the Johannine community after it had moved.

28. On the rhetorical use of ironic riddles and misunderstanding in the Fourth Gospel, see especially Herbert Leroy, *Rätsel und Missverständnis: Ein Beitrag zur Formgeschichte des Johannesevangeliums,* BBB 30 (Bonn: Hanstein, 1968).

29. John A. T. Robinson, "The Destination and Purpose of St. John's Gospel," *NTS* 6 (1959–60): 117–31; cf. Painter, *Quest for the Messiah* (2d ed.), 300 n. 45. A

recent comment of Meeks is worth noting. Having cautiously suggested that "there is hardly a hint of a specifically gentile mission in John," he echoes Robinson, saying that in 7:35 and 12:20 John refers to Greek-speaking Jews. He then adds in a footnote, "In any case, if the *hellēnes* in John were meant to refer to a mission to gentiles, the passages in question are a strangely muted way to say so" ("Breaking Away," 97 and n. 10; see also 101).

30. Thus, in effect, Walter Bauer, *Das Johannesevangelium*, HNT 6 (Tübingen: Mohr [Siebeck], 1933), 112; BAGD. In 1935 Hans Windisch also argued for Gentiles in John 7:35 ("Ἕλλην, κ. τ. λ." *TDNT* 2 [1964]: 509–10), but, as Meeks has pointed out, only after noting that Ἕλληναι sometimes refers to "Hellenized Orientals" (Meeks, "Breaking Away," 97 n. 10). On the one hand, then, the assumption that John would have drawn a hard-and-fast distinction between Ἕλληναι and Ἑλληνισταί may be an instance of rushing to judgment (see Meeks, ibid.; and note the comments on John's Greek in K. Beyer, *Semitische Syntax im Neuen Testament* [Göttingen: Vandenhoeck & Ruprecht, 1962], 17, 297–99). On the other hand, the criticism of Robinson's interpretation by C. K. Barrett is to be taken seriously: *The Gospel of John and Judaism* (London: SPCK, 1975), 11–19.

31. See, for example, Brown, *The Gospel according to John (i–xii)*, 29.314; idem, *The Community of the Beloved Disciple*, 57.

32. Josephus uses the word Ἕλλην to speak of God-fearers (θεοσεβέις), "the multitudes of Greeks" (πολὺ πλῆθος Ἑλλήνων) who attached themselves to the Jewish community in Antioch (*J.W.* 7.45). Similarly, in Acts 17:4 (and also other passages) Luke refers to "a great many of the devout Greeks" (τῶν σεβομένων Ἑλλήνων πλῆθος πολύ). About John 12:20 Windisch said that the addition of the clause, "in order to worship at the feast," "definitely excludes the sense of Gentiles" "Ἕλλην, κ. τ. λ.," *TDNT* 2 [1964]: 509).

33. See esp. Martinus de Boer, "God-Fearers in Luke-Acts," in *Luke's Literary Achievement: Collected Essays*, ed. Christopher M. Tuckett (JSNTSup 116; Sheffield: JSOT, 1995), 50–71. See also John MacRay, "Greece," *ABD* 2 (1992): 1092–98, especially 1093: "Luke probably reserves the term 'Greeks' [Ἕλληναι] for non-Jews who worship the one true God (Acts 14:1; 16:1, 3; 17:4, 12; 19:17) [because they are God-fearers] . . . and designates as 'Gentiles' [ἔθνη] those who are polytheistic pagans (4:25, 27; 9:15; 18:6; etc.)."

34. Using the word "gather" rather than "lead," I have given a translation that follows p[66] and Clement of Alexandria. That reading is suggested not only by 11:52, but also by 10:12.

35. The following paragraphs present in amplified and somewhat revised form the interpretation of John 10:16 that I offered in "Glimpses into the History of the Johannine Community" (1975), 170–74 (= *The Gospel of John in Christian History*, 115–19). Regarding the interpretation offered there, my colleague and steady friend Raymond Brown proved his usual accuracy by means of an exception. In *The Community of the Beloved Disciple* (1979) he credited me with the view that in 10:16 John refers to the group Brown himself calls "the apostolic Christians" (90).

36. In 1964 Hans Joachim Schoeps suggested that John 10:16 refers to "the existence of separate Jewish Christian communities" (*Jewish Christianity: Factional Disputes in the Early Church* [Philadelphia: Fortress, 1969], 131 [German edition, 1964]). Without being influenced by Schoeps's suggestion, H. B. Kossen proposed a similar reading in "Who Were the Greeks of John xii 20?" in *Studies in John Presented*

to Professor Dr. J. N. Sevenster, NovTSup 24 (Leiden: Brill, 1970), 97–110. For Kossen, the "other sheep" are "the Christians among [the Jews of the Diaspora] to whom this gospel is particularly addressed" (107).

37. Kossen, "Who Were the Greeks of John xii 20?" 102–3, slightly altered for clarity.

38. If space permitted, we should also consider in detail the fact that after speaking of the hope for one flock and one shepherd, John interprets the pictures of the shepherd and the sheep by means of a disputation (10:22–39) that was developed in the conflict his community *continued* to have with the synagogue (see especially Painter, *The Quest for the Messiah* [2d ed.], 361, and Meeks, "Equal to God," 314). One finds the note of assurance, mentioned above: Jesus' sheep are secure from all threats, because it is impossible for someone to snatch them either out of his hand or out of the hand of the Father (vv. 28–29). One finds also the christological claim that "I and the Father are one" (v. 30). Sensing blasphemy in this claim, the Jews threaten to stone Jesus, for "you, though only a human being, are making yourself God" (v. 33). Jesus finally responds with another and more complicated assertion of his relation to the Father: "I am God's Son . . . the Father is in me and I am in the Father" (vv. 36–38). All of the terms of this disputation are Jewish, producing a text focused on the question whether the Johannine community is in violation of monotheism, an issue bearing no relationship to a Gentile mission or even to the putative presence of Gentiles in the Johannine community. See further Mark L. Appold, *The Oneness Motif in the Fourth Gospel: Motif Analysis and Exegetical Probe into the Theology of John,* WUNT 2/1 (Tübingen: Mohr [Siebeck], 1976), 263.

39. Severino Pancaro, "'People of God' in St John's Gospel?" *NTS* 16 (1969–70): 114–29 (here, 129); Brown, *The Community of the Beloved Disciple,* 56. Contrast the comment of Meeks: "Now because the context makes it clear that these children include more than the *ethnos* of the Judeans, the reader may jump to the conclusion that Gentiles are included" ("Breaking Away," 97).

40. Pancaro, "'People of God' in St John's Gospel?" Pancaro's book, *The Law in the Fourth Gospel* (see above, n. 21), is a significant contribution to Johannine studies.

41. So, rightly, Brown, *The Community of the Beloved Disciple,* 56. Thus, Pancaro is surely correct in saying, "The 'children of God', mentioned in John xi.52, are— contrary to what has been traditionally held—neither the Gentiles nor the Jews of the dispersion as such . . ." (" 'People of God' in St John's Gospel?" 129).

42. Kossen, "Who Were the Greeks of John xii 20?" 107. See also, therein, 106 n. 2; and Martyn, *The Gospel of John in Christian History,* 119. It should be noted that the conclusion to which Kossen comes is different from the one reached in the present chapter: for Kossen, John wrote his Gospel for Christian Jews in the Greek-speaking Diaspora of Asia Minor in order to assure them that they still belonged to the Messiah of Israel, but also in order to call them to fulfill the Messiah's mission by preaching to the Gentiles among whom they lived (110).

43. It is the note of *assurance,* the motif of *gathering the scattered,* and the resultant *unification* that bind John 11:52 and 10:16 to one another, both containing echoes of Zech. 13:7.

44. Kyoshi Tsuchido, " "Ελλην in the Gospel of John: Tradition and Redaction in John 12:20–24," in *The Conversation Continues,* 348–56 (esp. 350, 352, 353; see also Tsuchido, *Tradition and Redaction in the Fourth Gospel* [in Japanese; Tokyo: Sobunsha, 1994]). In addition to providing a comprehensive catalogue of the opinions of other scholars, Tsuchido has penned his own strong argument for finding a reference

to Gentiles in John 12:20. I must confess, however, that I am not persuaded.

45. The participle ἀναβαινόντων ("those who went up") is surely rendered correctly by Walter Bauer as a reference to those "die hinaufzugehen pflegten, um am Fest *anzubeten*" ("who customarily went up there, *in order to worship* at the Festival"; *Das Johannesevangelium*, 160, emphasis added). Note also the comment of Windisch, given in note 32, above.

46. See esp. John 1:29; 19:36.

47. Referring to proselytes rather than to God-fearers, C. H. Dodd remarked, "In the dramatic situation we may suppose [the ῞Ελληνες of 12:20] to be proselytes, but in the intention of the evangelist they stand for the great world at large; primarily for *the Hellenistic world which is his own mission field*" (*The Interpretation of the Fourth Gospel* [Cambridge: Cambridge University Press, 1953], 371, emphasis added).

48. On John 4:42 see especially Craig R. Koester, "'The Savior of the World' (John 4:42)," *JBL* 109 (1990): 665–80, who reaches there and in *Symbolism in the Fourth Gospel: Meaning, Mystery, Community* (Minneapolis: Fortress, 1995) conclusions counter to those given at the end of the present study. Koester sees reflections of a shift in mission frontier in several instances of the Gospel's symbolism, not least that of the three-language sign above the cross. See also Okure (n. 13 above) and Miguel Rodríguez Ruiz, *Der Missionsgedanke des Johannesevangeliums: Ein Beitrag zur johanneischen Soteriologie und Ekklesiologie*, FB 55 (Würzburg: Echter, 1987).

49. See Leroy, *Rätsel und Missverständnis*, 88–99; Kikuo Matsunaga, "The Galileans in the Fourth Gospel," *AJBI* 2 (1976): 139–58; Brown, *The Community of the Beloved Disciple*, 36–40.

50. On characterization in John, see Culpepper, *Anatomy of the Fourth Gospel*, 105–48; idem, "L'application de la narratologie à l'étude de l'évangile de Jean," in *La Communauté johannique et son Histoire: La trajectoire de l'évangile de Jean aux deux premier siècles*, ed. Jean-Daniel Kaestli, Jean-Michel Poffet, and Jean Zumstein, Monde de la Bible (Geneva: Labor et Fides, 1990), 97–120.

51. Cf. Hengel, *The Johannine Question*, 168 n. 48. On the "royal official" of John 4:46, see Brown, *The Gospel according to John (i–xii)*, 29.cxliv. Meeks is right to note that "the boundaries of [John's] story are the boundaries of Israel" ("Breaking Away," 97).

52. Smith, *Johannine Christianity*, 80–93.

53. See esp. Smith, ibid., 93. It is encouraging to see the mutual enrichment resulting from the interchanges between Fortna and Smith; see, for example, Fortna, *The Fourth Gospel and Its Predecessor*, 137 n. 304, 207 n. 492. The argument that lack of detailed agreement among source and tradition critics vitiates their work is well answered in de Boer, "Narrative Criticism, Historical Criticism, and the Gospel of John."

54. Brown answers in the affirmative, but he argues as though John's interpretation of 12:37–40 were given in 12:20–22 rather than in 12:41–50 (*The Community of the Beloved Disciple*, 55).

55. So, rightly, Brown, *The Gospel according to John (i–xii)*, 29.lxxiv.

56. See again Meeks, "Equal to God," passim.

57. Brown, *The Community of the Beloved Disciple*, 55.

58. See, notably, Gal. 2:7, 9; Mark 12:9; 13:10; Matt. 21:43; Acts 28:29. Cf. Justin, *Dial.* 47; and Ferdinand Hahn, *Mission in the New Testament*, SBT 47 (London: SCM, 1963).

Part Two

The Traditions of the Fourth Gospel

Johannes Beutler, S.J.

7

The Use of "Scripture" in the Gospel of John

INTRODUCTION

The question of the degree to which the Fourth Gospel is based on the Old Testament is neither new nor original. In addition to several studies that treat the subject explicitly,[1] there is a host of contributions dealing with aspects of our subject, like the role of "fulfillment" in the Gospel of John[2] or the importance of individual books or traditions from the Old Testament for the Gospel of John.[3] D. Moody Smith, who places the subject along the wider horizon of "The Use of the Old Testament in the New,"[4] has dealt with a number of aspects of the topic.

A careful reading of the literature on our theme and a verification of the results of previous research, made on the basis of the text of John itself, lead to some observations that at first sight seem to be independent of one another but reveal themselves as coherent when we look closer. A first observation we can make is that in the Gospel of John we have to distinguish between explicit quotations of the Old Testament and allusions to it. The fact that there is no consensus on the actual number of explicit quotations of the Old Testament in John[5] has to do with a second observation: Even if we seem to be dealing with an explicit quotation from the Old Testament, often it cannot be decided with certainty which text from the Old Testament is actually quoted.[6] A third observation is that there is as yet no consensus regarding whether John quotes from the Hebrew text of the Old Testament, which he or his source translates, or from the Greek text of the Old Testament (which we used to call the Septuagint), if not from some targumic tradition.[7] Our fourth observation consists in the fact that the texts of the Old Testament to which John refers sometimes seem to form patterns. One famous example is the way that John uses the book of Isaiah in chapters one and twelve of his Gospel.[8] More examples can be given easily.[9]

If we take all these observations together, there seems to be at hand one possible explanation: John is less interested in the "fulfillment" of individual passages of the Old Testament in Jesus than in the "fulfillment" of "scripture" as such. With this thesis we have already formulated our working hypothesis. It is not new, as such, but has been stated already by students of the Fourth Gospel like C. H. Dodd,[10] C. K. Barrett,[11] R. Morgan,[12] C.F.D. Moule,[13] J. Luzarraga,[14] M. Wilcox,[15] and, last but not least, D. Moody Smith himself.[16]

The purpose of this modest contribution consists in showing that the way John uses the expression "scripture" (γραφή, γραφαί) or "writing" (γράφειν) confirms our working hypothesis. Dealing with our subject in this way has two advantages: We can narrow our research to a limited number of texts, and we tread on fresh ground, since this particular aspect of John's use of "scripture" has hardly been dealt with hitherto.[17]

We shall include in our investigation three texts where the fourth evangelist uses the formula "the prophet Isaiah said" (John 1:23; 12:39, 41) or "to fulfill the word spoken by the prophet Isaiah" (12:38). These formulas seem to be equivalent with the expressions using the terms "scripture" or "writing." We shall exclude from our study those instances where John speaks of "writing" in the context of the titulus (John 19:19–22), because they seem to be irrelevant for the question of Holy Scripture.

JOHN'S USE OF "SCRIPTURE" AND "WRITING"

There are twelve instances where John uses the word γραφή in the course of his Gospel, and in all of them the meaning is "Holy Scripture."[18] When he speaks of "writing" (21 instances, plus John 8:8, in the section about the adulterous woman, which we omit), he refers almost exclusively to Holy Writ with two exceptions: the passage about the titulus (John 19:19–22) and some passages about the writing down of the Jesus tradition, proper to the Fourth Gospel (John 20:30–31; 21:24–25). Once John uses the word γράμμα (pl.) for everything that has been written, or "reading and writing," or, more concretely, for the Holy Scripture of Israel, which at the same time served as the schoolbook for young Israelites (John 7:15). We shall include this text also in our considerations. We may add John 7:52, where Nicodemus is admonished to "search [the scriptures]" (cf. 5:39).

Clear References to Individual Texts

There are about nine instances in the Gospel of John where a reference to "scripture" or to a prophet can more or less clearly be identified. We find them in John 1:23; 2:17; 6:45; 10:34; 12:38; 12:39–41; 13:18; 19:24; and 19:37.[19]

In John 2:17 the formula is simply "it is written" (γεγραμμένον ἐστίν). The quotation is taken from Ps. 68:10 (LXX), with the only difference being that the aorist, κατέφαγέν με ("consumed me"), has been transformed into the present, καταφάγεταί με ("consumes me"). What is important for our subject is the fact that John uses a psalm verse as authoritative, as "scripture." Evidently, for him the Book of Psalms already belongs to the canon of Holy Writings of Israel. He joins here a tradition that can be traced back to the Book of Ben Sira, where the

Law, the prophecies, and the wisdom of the elders are placed beside one another (Sir. 39:1), and where these three elements together seem to form the canon of the sacred books of Israel (Sir. Pr.).[20] This development is also reflected in Luke 24:44, where Christ argues for his passion and his resurrection as being foreteold in the Law, in the Prophets, and in the Psalms.

The quotation in John 6:45, "And they shall all be taught by God," seems to be taken from Isa. 54:13 (LXX). The text may allude as well to Jer. 31[38]:31–34 (LXX), but more for the content than for the wording. The Johannine introduction is unique in the New Testament: "It is written in the prophets." Next to our text comes Acts 7:42, "As it is written in the book of the prophets." Evidently in both instances the Prophets are considered to be part of scripture and derive their authoritative power from it, even as they refer to a particular passage from a single prophet. Direct translation of Isa. 54:13 from the Hebrew is improbable.[21]

Likewise, Christ's reference to scripture in John 10:34 can be located with sufficient clarity: "'I said, you are gods'" is taken from Ps. 81:6 (LXX). Direct translation from the Hebrew can be excluded as a possibility, since John does not use the aorist form, $\epsilon\hat{\iota}\pi\alpha$ ("I said"), outside our text.[22] The introduction in John 10:34 sounds unusual for a quotation taken from a psalm: "Is it not written in your law?" It supposes a usage where the "law" is still synonymous with "scripture." This terminology is attested also elsewhere (see John 15:25).[23] It shows that the word taken from the book of Psalms has its authority, not from this individual book, but from scripture as such.

A similar usage of a quotation from the Psalms is found in John 13:18. Here it is qualified as a quotation from "scripture," which had to be fulfilled. The idea of "fulfillment" of scripture occurs first in John 12:38 in the context of Jesus' passion and resurrection, as has often been noted.[24] Both the fact that Jesus had to die for his own, as well as many details of his passion, have been announced in scripture and prove to be part of God's plan of salvation. In John 13:18 the quotation illustrating the betrayal of Jesus by his very friend is taken from Ps. 41:10 (MT), in a rather free rendering due to the redactional tendencies of John.[25]

Another element of the passion of Jesus, foretold in the Psalms, is the division of his garments by the soldiers in John 19:24. The quotation is taken verbatim from Ps. 21:19 (LXX). It is again introduced by the formula that speaks of the "fulfillment of scripture." There is strong external and internal evidence for the shorter reading of the introduction: "that scripture might be fulfilled" (instead of "the scripture saying . . . ").[26] Scripture, as such, had to be fulfilled, and not only this or that individual text. The narrowing of "scripture" to this individual verse seems to be secondary.

The only clear instance where γραφή seems to mean an "individual passage from scripture" is found in John 19:37. In spite of considerable differences in wording, the looking upon the pierced side of Jesus is considered to be foretold by scripture, in this case Zech. 12:10.[27] Scripture, as such, is still in the background since the preceding verse reads: "These things occurred so that the scripture might be fulfilled," with a quotation which cannot be determined with certainty (see below).

In another group of texts, words of the prophet Isaiah are introduced or quoted as such: John 1:23; 12:38; and 12:39–41. In the first case, Isa. 40:3 (LXX) is quoted with some modifications; in the second, Isa. 53:1 (LXX) is quoted literally. Here we find for the first time the idea of "fulfillment" of the prophetic word: We have entered the context of the passion of Jesus in the rejection by his people. In the third text, Isa. 6:10 (LXX) is rendered rather freely.[28] In all these instances a prophetic book points toward Jesus or his important witness, the Baptist.

Unclear or Unspecified References

Besides the clear references to Old Testament texts in the Gospel of John, there are about nine instances where we find an unclear or unspecified reference to "scripture."

1. Already in John 6:31 it is not clear whether the reference to "what is written" points to Ps. 77:24 (LXX)[29] or to some other text, like Ex. 16:4 or 16:15.[30] Even a targumic or midrashic tradition cannot be excluded.[31]

2. The provenance of the word of "scripture" in John 7:37–38 is still more mysterious. The text edition of Nestle-Aland (26th ed.) remarks here laconically, "*unde?*" ("whence?"), and gives a number of possible reference texts. None of them is convincing.

3. We are on slightly better ground with the origin of Jesus from David and from his city, Bethlehem, in John 7:42. But in any case more than one text is referred to. On the one hand some texts like 2 Sam. 7:12, Ps. 88:4–5 (LXX), and Jer. 23:5 speak about an offspring of David to come in the future; on the other, the origin of the coming ruler of Israel from Bethlehem is announced in Micah 5:1. None of these texts alone is sufficient for basing the origin of the Messiah in "scripture."

4. In John 12:14 the basis of the quotation from "what is written" seems to be Zechariah 9:9,[32] but there are elements that cannot be explained by this text. Accordingly, the exhortation in the beginning, "Fear not, daughter of Zion," does not come from Zechariah. Commentators refer instead to Isaiah (40:9) or Zephaniah (3:14f.).[33] Only when taken together do these texts render the wording of John 12:14.

5. The second reference to "scripture" in this text (12:16) may refer to the same traditions of the Old Testament as in verse 14 or to some additional ones, like the announcement of the words of the crowd in verse 13 by Ps. 118:25–26 (117:25–26 LXX). In any case, the disciples seem to "remember" more than one scriptural quotation when they reflect on Jesus' entry into Jerusalem in the light of scripture, after his resurrection and "glorification."

6. The word that the enemies of Jesus "hated him without cause" in John 15:25 is quoted as a word of the "law." We have seen that this expression seems to mean "scripture." The text itself could come from Ps. 34:19 (LXX) or 68:5 (LXX), where we find the same expression, οἱ μισοῦντές με δωρεάν ("those who hate

me without cause").[34] In both cases the participle has been transformed into the verb of a phrase. Jesus appears as the Suffering Just One of the Psalms. The Jews who persecuted him should have known that the Psalms, as part of the "law," speak of him, and they should have believed in him.

7. Even the work of the traitor is considered by John as annnounced in scripture. We have seen this in the detail of the common meal of Jesus and his former friend, in John 13:18 (see above). The reference in John 17:12 is less clear. Possibly this verse refers to the quotation in 13:18. All other texts given as parallels are less convincing (2 Sam. 12:5; Isa. 57:4; Prov. 24:22a [LXX]), since they do not speak of an individual person as "son" or "child" of "death" or "perdition."[35]

8. Another example of an unclear reference is the word of the dying Jesus: "I thirst" (John 19:28). The expression by which it is introduced is unique in the New Testament: ἵνα τελειωθῇ ἡ γραφή ("in order that the scripture might be accomplished"). It may go beyond the usual formula, ἵνα ἡ γραφὴ πληρωῇ ("in order to fulfill the scripture"), which we found in 13:18, 17:12, or 19:24 (see also 19:36), and express a "fulfillment" of scripture to the end.[36] But it remains uncertain which particular text of the Old Testament is referred to. Commentators generally think of psalms like Ps. 68:22 (LXX) (because of the context: the thirst of Jesus is quenched by vinegar)[37] or 62:2 (LXX);[38] but also Ps. 41:3 (LXX) would be possible, given the importance of this psalm for the Gospel of John.[39] In none of these references is the first person singular used. Thus, the quotation remains imprecise and ambiguous.

9. The same holds true in the last Johannine text where the "fulfillment" of scripture is affirmed: John 19:36. The piercing of the side of Jesus, instead of the breaking of his legs, is found in scripture. But there are two possible traditions to which the text could refer. The widely accepted view is that the text speaks of the paschal lamb, of which (according to Ex. 12:10, 46 and Num. 9:12) no bone should be broken. The fact that John seems to parallel the death of Jesus to the death of the paschal lambs on the eve of Passover speaks in favor of this opinion: compare the references in 18:28 and 19:14 to the eating of the paschal lamb and the time of the condemnation of Jesus, the traditional time of the slaughtering of the paschal lambs. On the other side, the quotation of John 19:36 could also come from Ps. 33:21 (LXX). There the context is God's care for the Suffering Just One: not one of his bones will be broken. The use of the third person singular speaks in favor of this suggestion; the context is slightly less convincing. So here also a final decision as to which scriptural tradition the Johannine text refers remains difficult, if not impossible.[40]

References to Moses or the Law in General

In two cases the Fourth Gospel refers to Moses or the law in general as testimony of "scripture" for Jesus. John 5:46 (note v. 47) supposes that Moses "wrote about" Jesus, without any specific scriptural reference. This Johannine text is particularly interesting because it shows clearly that the witness of scripture for Jesus seems to be, for John, independent from this or that particular passage. We shall come back to this observation when we deal with John 5:39 in the following section (see below).

In John 8:17 Jesus bases his claim to be the one sent by God on a principle of the "law," according to which the testimony of two witnesses has to be accepted. We find this quotation in Num. 35:30 and Deut. 17:6; 19:15. The individual passage of the Old Testament seems to be subordinate to the testimony of scripture, as such, to Jesus and his claims. This fits perfectly well with the results we have obtained to this point.

References to the Whole of Scripture

A number of passages, where no particular part or text of scripture is referred to, confirm how much, for John, the whole of scripture points to Jesus. The first example of this kind of witness is found in John 1:45. Philip says to Nathanael, "We have found him about whom Moses in the law and also the prophets wrote, Jesus son of Joseph from Nazareth." It is not clear which christological title is meant by this statement.[41] Earlier Andrew had said to Peter, "'We have found the Messiah' (which is translated Anointed)" (v. 41). Later Nathanael will exclaim, "Rabbi, you are the Son of God! You are the King of Israel!" (v. 49). So the confession of Philip seems to express the christological faith of the Johannine community, as later expressed by Martha (11:27) or the author himself (20:31). As such, it is based in scripture.

In two instances John sees the resurrection of Jesus as announced by scripture. According to John 2:22 the disciples understood only after the resurrection of Christ the witness of scripture about his future resurrection. It is unclear which particular passage could have been referred to. One possible solution to this question could be that John knew the tradition of 1 Cor. 15:4, without caring too much about its detailed basis in scripture. This impression is supported by the second text that bases the resurrection of Jesus from the dead in scripture, John 20:9. The two disciples at the tomb had not yet understood the message of scripture that Jesus had to rise from the dead, and so they could not interpret the empty tomb in the right way. Again, no particular passage or text of scripture is referred to. The reader is supposed to grasp the meaning of the reference without further information.[42]

Again, the whole of scripture is supposed when Jesus tells the Jews unwilling to believe in him, "You search the scriptures because you think that in them you have eternal life; and it is they that testify on my behalf" (John 5:39). The witness of scripture is placed beside the one given by John the Baptist, by the Father, and by the works the Father has given to Jesus (5:31–38). No individual passage of scripture is cited. Scriptures, as such, bear witness for Jesus in his great trial, in his confrontation with "the world."[43] When Nicodemus and some other Jewish officers show beginning belief in Jesus, they are admonished, "Search and you will see that no prophet is to arise from Galilee" (7:52). The "searching" again refers to scripture.[44] For "the Jews," the Bible as such makes clear that a prophet does not come from Galilee.

When "the Jews" wonder how Jesus "is not illiterate, although he has not studied" (γράμματα οἶδεν μὴ μεμαθηκώς, 7:15), the meaning seems to be that Jesus knows scripture.[45] This is clear from the context, where Jesus reveals himself as someone teaching with authority. For John, his education comes not from studies but directly from God. Jesus seems to know Scripture, but it is not the source of his divine knowledge.

Scripture as such is meant in a last text, where it is stated that "scripture cannot be annulled" (John 10:35).[46] The remark refers to the word of scripture, "I said, you are gods" (Ps. 81:6 [LXX]), quoted in 10:34. It serves as basis for an argument a fortiori, proving that Jesus' claim to be the Son of God is justified. Scripture as such has an unquestionable authority. If an individual verse of scripture affirms that all Israelites are gods, then Jesus even more so can claim this dignity for himself.

The Gospel Message in Written Form

John never integrates Christian writings into "scripture," in the sense developed in the preceding sections. In a number of instances, John speaks about the writing down of his message for the benefit of the readers and for their belief, but these references are not directly relevant for the theological question of his concept of "scripture." This perspective is confirmed by the fact that John does not speak of "scripture" (γραφή, γράμμα) where he refers to Christian writings. He only uses the verb γράφειν ("to write") with active or passive forms.

In fact, John 20:30–31 refers to a "book" in which the signs of Jesus are collected and written down for the sake of the belief of the readers. But the change in terminology seems to be significant: John speaks of "this book" (ἐν τῷ βιβλίῳ), instead of the expressions he would use for "scripture." So although the function of the collection of signs of Jesus and of "scripture" is similar, namely to lead to the belief in Christ, their character is different: the Christian witness is going to complement the witness of "scripture" for Jesus, not to make up a part in it. The book to which John refers here is better understood as the whole of his Gospel than as a part of it, like a "signs source." The final text of John does not betray any knowledge of such a document.[47] The fact that the last miracle of Jesus has been reported in 11:1–44, with the resurrection of Lazarus, speaks for the thesis that the passion, death, and resurrection/exaltation of Jesus form the last of the "signs" of Jesus, in the perspective of the fourth evangelist.[48]

That the whole of the Gospel is meant by the "book of the deeds of Jesus" is evident from the second text at the end of the Fourth Gospel, John 21:24–25. It concludes the report about the apparitions of Jesus in Galilee and sums up the whole of his activity. More clearly than in 20:30–31, what has been "written" by the evangelist is his "testimony," which, in a way similar to the one given by scripture, points to Jesus. There remains, however, a stylistic difference that could point to a later time of origin: in the chapters with the great controversies between Jesus and "the Jews" (John 5–10), the "witness" is about Jesus; in John 21:24 it is about "these things" (the words and deeds of Jesus).[49] The interest shifts from the person of Jesus to details of his life, death, and resurrection. An apologetic intention seems to manifest itself (note the same intention in John 19:35).

THE WORDS OF JESUS AND "SCRIPTURE"

There are no reasons for assuming that the words of Jesus are part of scripture for the fourth evangelist,[50] but it may be said that they have a comparable authority. After the resurrection of Jesus, the disciples remembered the word of Jesus concerning his zeal for the house of the Lord and believed in scripture and in the word Jesus had spoken (John 2:22). A similar parallel between the writings of Moses and the words of Jesus appears in John 5:47. Both are meant to cause the Jews to believe.[51] The Jews themselves see a contrast between the law and the words of Jesus (12:34), but this is because of their lack of belief (12:37). As "remembering" is more than once connected with the word of scripture (see 2:17, 22; 12:16), so it can also be referred to the word of Jesus (2:22; 15:20; 16:4).

Finally, the formula of "fulfillment" can be applied to the word of Jesus.[52] This occurs twice in the passion narrative. In John 18:9 Jesus refers to a saying in the discourse on the bread of life (6:39) that he would not lose any of those committed to him by the Father. In 18:32 the announcement of Jesus that the Son of Man would be lifted up (see 3:14; 8:28; 12:32) is fulfilled in his deliverance to the pagan authority.

In all these instances the word of Jesus gains an authority comparable with that of "scripture." The same expressions can be applied to both, but nowhere does his word become formally part of scripture. This development is reserved for later times.[53]

"SCRIPTURE" AND SCRIPTURE

We have seen so far that the fourth evangelist refers to "scripture" often in a general way: either by unclear or unspecified references, or with a reference to a whole book, or without reference to any particular text at all. The impression one gains is that John is more interested in scripture as such than in particular texts pointing to Jesus. In order to verify this impression, we may now try to classify the explicit references to "scripture" or "writing" in John, according to context and speaker. Roughly, we can distinguish between texts with Jesus as speaker and those with comments by the evangelist. The few exceptions will be dealt with in either of the two groups. The references to "scripture" or "writing" with Jesus as speaker are found in two different contexts: the great controversies between Jesus and the "Jews" in chapters 5—12, and the farewell discourse in chapters 13—17. The evangelist's comments are almost exclusively found in the context of the passion narrative.

Jesus' References to "Scripture" in the Great Controversies

In the chapters with the great controversies between Jesus and the "Jews" in Jerusalem, we face especially often the problem of identifying the texts to which Jesus refers or alludes. We remember the very general comment of Jesus in John 5:39, "You search the scriptures . . . ." Scriptures, as such, are a witness for Jesus. In the context Moses is the one who has written about Jesus (5:46), but no particular passage is quoted.

The words about the flowing water (7:38), in the context of the feast of Tabernacles, could not be located in scripture, and likewise the objection of the "Jews" concerning the origin of the Messiah does not lead to any clear scriptural passage. In the same way the principle of the two or three witnesses (8:17) is found more than once in the Old Testament text.

In the controversy about the divine dignity of Jesus at the feast of Dedication (John 10:34–35), Jesus bases his claims on a precise scriptural quotation, Ps. 81:6 (LXX). The text is taken from the "law," as a synonym for scripture. The principle is that scripture cannot be annulled, so the part receives its authority from the whole: The individual text has to be acknowledged as an argument, because it is part of scripture. For the rest it has to be seen that Jesus' reference to Ps. 81:6 (LXX) serves only as a counterargument against Jewish denial of his divine prerogative. It is, therefore, more apologetic than positive. That Jesus is one with the Father cannot be denied, because scripture itself calls the children of Israel "gods." This is an *argumentum ad hominem*, valid so far as it is accepted by the partner in dialogue.

The controversies in the synagogue of Capernaum differ from the preceding ones in their locale and perhaps even in their time of origin,[54] but here also the references of Jesus to scripture remain vague, as we have seen previously. Neither the word about the bread from heaven in John 6:31 nor the one about the divine instruction of the people of God in the time to come according to 6:45 could be located with certainty.

Accordingly, the word of Philip to Nathanael, "We have found him about whom Moses in the law and also the prophets wrote, Jesus son of Joseph from Nazareth" (John 1:45), reads like an introduction to the great controversies. It expresses in a completely generic way the witness of scripture for Jesus.

If we want to sum up this section, we can say that in the great controversies Jesus (and the author) show(s) little concern for the individual passage of scripture as an argument for the claims of Jesus. What counts is scripture as such. If it is "searched" and understood rightly, it bears witness to Jesus (thus John 5:39). Apparently, for the author the "fulfillment" of scripture in Jesus is so self-evident that individual texts have only a limited importance for the argument. What seems to stand behind this perspective is the controversy between church and synagogue at the end of the first century, where the question was no longer whether some isolated texts could be used as proof texts for or against Jesus, but whether scripture as such found its ultimate meaning in a Christian or in a merely Jewish perspective.[55] More than in any other section of the Fourth Gospel, therefore, the great controversies betray the characteristic perspective of the fourth evangelist, as it appears in recent research.

Jesus' References to "Scripture" in the Farewell Discourses

In the farewell discourses of Jesus, the subject of the explicit scriptural quotations is no longer the mission of Jesus but his passion. It is the unjustified hatred of the adversaries of Jesus that has been announced in scripture (John 15:25). We saw that the specific reference is not quite clear, since it leaves open the choice between two different psalms (see above).

In the two remaining instances we find the "fulfillment" formula used more than once by the evangelist in the context of the passion of Jesus (see below). The specific reference to those given to Jesus who were not lost and the one who was lost, in John 17:12, was difficult to locate in scripture, as we saw previously. Still, the whole of scripture seems to stand behind this reference, even if some particular text may have influenced the wording. On the other side, the scene of the common meal of Jesus with the traitor, in John 13:18, leads to a verbal "fulfillment" of scripture insofar as Ps. 40:10 (LXX) is the only text pointing directly to the event reported.

In all these texts, scripture is no longer the common text of Christians and Jews, interpreted for or against the claims of Jesus. It only serves the purpose of introducing the Christian readers into the secret of the passion of Jesus, as announced in the Word of God and rooted in God's plan of salvation. In addition to more general texts, we have also found an example of a very specific one, announcing a detail of the passion of Jesus. This tendency will increase when we turn, as we now do, to the comments of the evangelist that have recourse to "scripture."

References of the Evangelist to "Scripture"

Two texts explaining the resurrection of Jesus on the third day as based in scripture seem to frame the original narrative unity of the Gospel of John (without chap. 21): John 2:22 and 20:9. In both cases the evangelist is the speaker. We have seen that the texts referred to remain uncertain. Rather, it was scripture as such, together with the word of Jesus, that had to be fulfilled.

The nearer we come to the passion narrative, the more precise the quotations and references become. In the framework of Jesus' entry into Jerusalem, the evangelist quotes Zech. 9:9, enlarged and modified by further texts (see above). Here he seems to be dependent on Synoptic tradition, as the parallel in Matt. 21:5 shows. It may be safely assumed that the text from Zechariah forms the basis of the quotation in John, even if John presents the text in a freer way than Matthew.

The remaining references to "scripture" are found in the context of the last hour of Jesus on the cross and the events immediately following his death. This fact alone merits our attention. All the quotations or allusions are introduced directly or indirectly by the "fulfillment" formula (which first occurs in 12:38). The first instance (John 19:24) is particularly interesting. For the division of the garments of Jesus, John quotes Ps. 21:19 (LXX) literally, taking up the allusion in Mark 15:24 (parr. Matt. 27:35; Luke 23:34) and transforming it into a "fulfillment" text. A detail of the passion of Jesus has been announced in scripture and "fulfills" it.

The wording is slightly changed in the next instance (John 19:28). "Fulfillment" is here replaced by "accomplishment" (ἵνα τελειωθῇ ἡ γραφή). Grammatically, it may be linked with the preceding events (everything had been accomplished) or with the following one (Jesus thirsts).[56] In any case, the passion of Jesus comes to its end and completion. The last part of that passion will be the thirst of Jesus, and this too has been preannounced in scripture, as part of God's plan of salvation. Again, not the identity of Jesus or his mission is attested by "scripture," but his departure from this world.

Two events immediately after the death of Jesus, both rooted in scripture, round out our results. The opening of the side of Jesus, instead of the breaking of his bones, and the flowing of blood and water from his side belong as well to the "fulfillment" of scripture (John 19:36–37). As we have seen previously, both quotations are difficult to locate in the text of scripture. Their only function seems to be to show Christian readers that this double event did not happen by chance, but brought God's will to completion. The fact that scripture was fulfilled is again more important than the precise reference to a particular text. Anyhow, the quotation in John 19:37 is relatively clear (Zech. 12:10), and even the choice for John 19:36 is rather limited (the Exodus tradition of Ex. 12:10, 46 [LXX] or Ps. 33:21 [LXX]). We are rather distant from some of the "scripture"-texts of the first half of the Gospel, where the mission of Jesus and his claims as such were the object of the witness of "scripture," and where a global reference to scriptures as such— to Moses or the prophets—could be enough.

If we look back to the evangelist's reference to "scripture" in favor of Jesus, we can see that the evangelist uses the testimony of "scripture" for Jesus, not for his mission as such or for his identity as the one sent by God, but for his departure from this world and his future resurrection. From John 12:38 onwards (that is, from the end of the great controversies between Jesus and the "Jews" in Jerusalem), the evangelist uses the "fulfillment" formula. In all instances "scripture" gives witness to details of the passion and death of Jesus. Some quotations are rather precise. In more than one case, parallel Synoptic tradition can be shown.

CONCLUSION

In his usage of "scripture" and the "written" testimony of the sacred books of Israel, the fourth evangelist shows himself to be at the same time original and indebted to early Christian tradition. He depends on tradition mainly in the context of the passion and resurrection of Jesus. The "fulfillment" formula occurs here, where he draws upon tradition. He himself is usually the speaker, not Jesus. The audience seems to be the Christian readers who had to be introduced to the mystery of the death and resurrection of Christ.

The chapters of the great controversies between Jesus and "the Jews" convey a different picture. The references to "scripture" or "what is written" range from more or less precise quotations to rather vague ones. Moses, the prophets, or the whole of "the law" or scripture frequently bear witness to Jesus. The author seems to be more interested in the fact of the witness of scripture to Jesus than in the details of it.[57] Although the author generally seems to use the Septuagint version, he shows considerable freedom in using it. This observation has been confirmed by more recent research on the scripture quotations in John. The impression conveyed is that John is convinced that scripture as a whole bears witness to Jesus. It is of secondary importance how individual passages of scripture contribute to this conviction.

The reason for this sovereign usage of "scripture" in John seems to lie in the fact that the evangelist writes in a period already remote from the first decades of Christianity, a time of growing familiarity with Old Testament "proof texts." In his documentation of controversies between Johannine Christianity and Judaism, he has reached a kind of "meta-level," where the individual proof text no longer counts, but rather, the whole of scripture is at stake: Does it have to be read with "Christian eyes"—and then every line of it would point to Jesus—or could it be read in a Jewish perspective, refusing to believe in a Messiah Jesus? If this interpretation of John is true, then we have another example that Johannine belief in Jesus is in a sense circular: The individual "proof texts" lead to Jesus, but they can only be understood as a whole when the belief to which they should lead is already presupposed. It is the paradox of Johannine belief that we encounter here.

NOTES

1. See Alexander Faure, "Die Alttestamentlichen Zitate im 4. Evangelium und die Quellenscheidungshypothese," *ZNW* 21 (1922): 99–121; Friedrich Smend, "Die Behandlung alttestamentlicher Zitate als Ausgangspunkt der Quellenscheidung im 4. Evangelium," *ZNW* 24 (1925): 147–50; C. K. Barrett, "The Old Testament in the Fourth Gospel," *JTS* 48 (1947): 155–69; Merrill C. Tenney III, "Literary Keys to the Fourth Gospel," *BSac* 120 (1963): 300–308; Edwin D. Freed, *Old Testament Quotations in the Gospel of John*, NovTSup 11 (Leiden: E.J. Brill 1965); Günter Reim, *Stu-*

dien zum alttestamentlichen Hintergrund des Johannesevangeliums, SNTSMS 22 (Cambridge: Cambridge University Press, 1974); J. Luzarraga, "Presentación de Jesús a la luz del A. T. en el Evangelio de Juan," *Estudios Eclesiásticos* 51 (1976): 497–520; Max Wilcox, "On Investigating the Use of the Old Testament in the New," in *Text and Interpretation: Studies in the New Testament Presented to Matthew Black*, ed. Ernest Best and R. McL. Wilson (Cambridge: Cambridge University Press, 1979), 231–43; Peder Borgen, "John's Use of the Old Testament and the Problem of Sources and Traditions," in *Logos was the True Light and Other Essays on the Gospel of John*, Relieff 9 (Trondheim: Tapir, 1983), 81–91; Martin Hengel, "Die Schriftauslegung des 4. Evangeliums auf dem Hintergrund der urchristlichen Exegese," *Jahrbuch zur biblischen Theologie* 4 (1989): 249–88; Bruce G. Schuchard, *Scripture within Scripture: The Interrelationship of Form and Function in the Explicit Old Testament Citations in the Gospel of John*, SBLDS 133 (Atlanta: Scholars Press, 1992).

2. See Richard Morgan, "Fulfillment in the Fourth Gospel: The Old Testament Foundations," *Int* 11 (1957): 155–65; John O'Rourke, "John's Fulfilment Texts," *ScEccl* 19 (1967): 433–43; C.F.D. Moule, "Fulfillment-Words in the New Testament: Use and Abuse," *NTS* 14 (1967–68): 293–320; F. F. Bruce, *The Time is Fulfilled: Five Aspects of the Fulfillment of the Old Testament in the New*, The Moore College Lectures, 1977 (Exeter: Paternoster, 1978).

3. See the references in Edward Malatesta, *St. John's Gospel 1920–1965: A Cumulative and Classified Bibliography of Books and Periodical Literature on the Fourth Gospel*, AnBib 32 (Rome: Pontifical Biblical Institute, 1967), 25–26; Gilbert Van Belle, *Johannine Bibliography 1966–1985: A Cumulative Bibliography on the Fourth Gospel*, BETL 82 (Leuven: Leuven University Press, 1988), 67, 104–5. For more recent literature see the entries in the annual biblical bibliographies.

4. In *The Use of the Old Testament in the New and Other Essays: Studies in Honor of William Franklin Stinespring*, ed. James M. Efird (Durham, N. C.: Duke University Press, 1972), 3–65.

5. Freed (*Old Testament Quotations in the Gospel of John*) counts 17 explicit quotations; Schuchard (*Scripture within Scripture*) knows 13 (without John 7:37, 42; 15:25; 17:12; 19:28; but with 13:16).

6. For the individual texts see section below on "Unclear or Unspecified References."

7. There seems to be a growing consensus that in many if not most cases, John has recourse to some form of the "Septuagint," that is, the Greek translation of the Hebrew Bible, accessible to us mostly in Christian manuscripts from the third century onward. For this tendency see, particularly, Schuchard, *Scripture within Scripture,* and a number of articles by M.J.J. Menken (see below, notes 25, 28, 29, and 32).

8. See Johannes Beutler, "Greeks Come to See Jesus (Jn 12,20f)," *Bib* 71 (1990): 333–47, especially 345–46.

9. For John 14 and the traditional background of that chapter, see Johannes Beutler, *Habt keine Angst: Die erste johanneische Abschiedsrede (Joh 14)*, SBS 116 (Stuttgart: Katholisches Bibelwerk, 1984); for John 10:1–18, idem, "Der alttestamentlich-jüdische Hintergrund der Hirtenrede in Johannes 10," in *The Shepherd Discourse of John 10 and Its Context*, ed. Johannes Beutler and Robert T. Fortna, SNTSMS 67 (Cambridge: Cambridge University Press 1991), 18–32, 144–47.

10. C. H. Dodd, *Historical Tradition in the Fourth Gospel* (Cambridge: Cambridge University Press, 1963), 31–49, particularly 47–49.

11. Barrett, "The Old Testament in the Fourth Gospel," 156, 169.

12. Morgan, "Fulfillment in the Fourth Gospel," 161, 164–65.

13. Moule, "Fulfillment-Words in the New Testament," 302.

14. Luzarraga, "Presentación de Jesús," 497–501.

15. Wilcox, "On Investigating the Use of the Old Testament in the New," 234–35.

16. Smith, "The Use of the Old Testament in the New," 53–58.

17. See Gottlob Schrenk, "γράφω κ. τ. λ.," in *TDNT* 1 (1964): 742–73; Freed, *Old Testament Quotations in the Gospel of John*, 51–59 (see also below); Hans Hübner, "γραφή, γράφω," in *EDNT* 1 (1990): 260–64; on the "introductory formula," see Schuchard, *Scripture within Scripture*, xv and passim.

18. For the almost complete absence of this term in the New Testament, see Schrenk, "γράφω," 751.

19. As we have seen (above, n. 5), the exact number of Old Testament quotations in the Gospel of John remains disputed among contemporary scholars, and so is the number of clear quotations.

20. For the origin of the threefold "canon" of the Hebrew Bible, see Nahum M. Sarna, "Bible: The Canon, Texts, and Editions," *EncJud* 4 (1971): 816–36, especially 816–26.

21. Cf. Schuchard, *Scripture within Scripture*, 47–57.

22. See ibid., 61.

23. For rabbinic examples see Sarna, "Bible: The Canon, Texts, and Editions," 817.

24. Thus, Smend, "Die Behandlung alttestamentlicher Zitate," 147; more recently, Craig A. Evans, "On the Quotation Formulas in the Fourth Gospel," *BZ* 26 (1982): 79–83.

25. See M.J.J. Menken, "The Translation of Psalm 41.10 in John 13.18," *JSNT* 40 (1990): 61–79.

26. It is supported by א and B, among other manuscripts, and as the shorter reading merits more confidence. The longer reading looks like an interpretation of the shorter one.

27. See Schuchard, *Scripture within Scripture*, 141–47. The text of the Old Testament *Vorlage* seems to remain uncertain.

28. See M.J.J. Menken, "Die Form des Zitates aus Jes 6,10 in Joh 12,40: Ein Beitrag zum Schriftgebrauch des vierten Evangelisten," *BZ* 32 (1988): 189–209.

29. See idem, "The Provenance and Meaning of the Old Testament Quotation in John 6:31," *NovT* 30 (1988): 39–56; Schuchard, *Scripture within Scripture*, 33–35.

30. Freed (*Old Testament Quotations in the Gospel of John*, 11–16) thinks of a combination of Ps. 77:24 (LXX) and Ex. 16:4, 15.

31. Note Peder Borgen, *Bread from Heaven: An Exegetical Study of the Conception of Manna in the Gospel of John and the Writings of Philo*, NovTSup 10 (Leiden: Brill, 1965); Georg Richter, *Studien zum Johannesevangelium*, Biblische Untersuchungen 13, ed. by Josef Hainz (Regensburg: Pustet, 1977), 199–265.

32. Cf. M.J.J. Menken, "Die Redaktion des Zitates aus Sach 9,9 in Joh 12,15," *ZNW* 80 (1989): 193–209.

33. Ibid., 198, with reference to Isa. 40:9; Zeph. 3:16.

34. See Freed, *Old Testament Quotations in the Gospel of John*, 94–95, who considers also possible influence of Psalm 119 (118) and *Psalm of Solomon* 7:1.

35. See Rudolf Schnackenburg, *The Gospel according to St. John* (New York: Crossroad, 1987), 3.182.

36. Ibid., 3.283.

37. Thus, ibid.; also Raymond E. Brown, *The Gospel according to John (xiii–xxi)*, AB 29A (Garden City, N.Y.: Doubleday, 1970), 929. Both authors are skeptical about Psalm 22 (21):16 as possible textual basis for John 19:29.

38. Edwin Clement Hoskyns, *The Fourth Gospel*, ed. by Francis Noel Davey (London: Faber and Faber, 1940), 632.

39. Compare Johannes Beutler, "Psalm 42/43 im Johannesevangelium," *NTS* 25 (1978–79): 33–57 (esp. 54–56), with Hoskyns and Davey, *The Fourth Gospel*, and C. H. Dodd, *Historical Tradition in the Fourth Gospel* (Cambridge: Cambridge University Press, 1963), 42 n. 1.

40. See Freed, *Old Testament Quotations in the Gospel of John*, 108–14; Schuchard, *Scripture within Scripture*, 134–36.

41. Thus Raymond E. Brown: "The 'one described in the Mosaic Law' could well identify Jesus as the Prophet-like-Moses of Deuteronomy xviii 15–18. The 'one described by the prophets' is harder to identify: it could be the Messiah, the Son of Man (Daniel), or even Elijah (Malachi)" (*The Gospel according to John (i–xii)*, AB 29 [Garden City, N.Y.: Doubleday, 1966], 86).

42. That the whole of scripture seems to be intended in both instances has been seen already by Schrenk, "γράφω," 759.

43. See Johannes Beutler, *Martyria: Traditionsgeschichtliche Untersuchungen zum Zeugnisthema bei Johannes*, Frankfurter Theologische Studien 10 (Frankfurt a. M.: Knecht, 1972), 262–64, 353–55.

44. Gerhard Delling, "ἐρευνάω, ἐξερευνάω," *TDNT* 2 (1964): 655–57, gives some examples from Philo (*On the Cherubim* 14; *The Worse Attacks the Better* 57, cf. 141) for this use of ἐρευνάω ("search").

45. See Schrenk, "γράφω," 764, who refers to *Testament of Levi* 13:2.

46. Ibid., 754.

47. Skepticism towards this hypothetical source has increased recently. Those who defend it ascribe to it only two signs of Jesus (thus Hans-Peter Heekerens, *Die Zeichen-Quelle der johanneischen Redaktion*, SBS 113 [Stuttgart: Katholisches Bibelwerk, 1984]) or all of them, including a considerable amount of the Johannine narrative (Jürgen Becker, *Das Evangelium nach Johannes*, 1–2, Ökumenischer Taschenbuch–Kommentar zum Neuen Testament [Gütersloh-Würzburg: Mohn-Echter, 1979–1981]; Robert T. Fortna, *The Fourth Gospel and Its Predecessor: From Narrative Source to Present Gospel* [Philadelphia: Fortress, 1988]). If the latter possibility is assumed, the distinction between John and his putative *Grundschrift* begins to vanish: at the end stands one single author with his school, as presumed by Martin Hengel, *Die johanneische Frage: Ein Lösungsversuch*, WUNT 67 (Tübingen: Mohr [Siebeck], 1993).

48. As has been seen by C. K. Barrett, *The Gospel according to St John: An Introduction with Commentary and Notes on the Greek Text*, 2d ed. (Philadelphia: Westminster, 1978), 78; cf. R. H. Lightfoot, *St. John's Gospel: A Commentary*, ed. C. F. Evans (Oxford: Oxford University Press, 1956), 336, for whom sign and reality merge in the death of Jesus. Brown (*The Gospel according to John (xiii—xxi)*, AB 29A.1058–59) refers the "signs" of John 20:30 less convincingly to the miracles of Jesus and his postresurrection appearances.

49. Thus Beutler, *Martyria*, 223–27.

50. The arguments given by Freed (*Old Testament Quotations in the Gospel of*

John, 51–59) for the opposite position do not seem to be convincing. There is hardly a Christian author before the time of Irenaeus who used Old Testament and New Testament side-by-side as "scripture" (cf. Freed, ibid., 52). The examples given by Freed from *1 Clement* (ibid., 55) all refer back to Old Testament texts, even if transmitted by Hebrews. John 7:42 and 17:12 refer back to imprecise quotations from Amos, rather than to a Christian Gospel or previous words of Jesus, recorded as scripture. In this sense, see Hübner, "γράφη, γράφω," 636–37.

51. See Schrenk, "γράφω," 765.

52. This has been seen, rightly, by Freed, *Old Testament Quotations in the Gospel of John*, 57.

53. See Schrenk, "γράφω," 754, and the texts given by Freed, *Old Testament Quotations in the Gospel of John*, 51–52.

54. Johannes Beutler, "Zur Struktur von Joh 6," *Studien zum Neuen Testament und seiner Umwelt*, series a, 16 (1991): 89 (N.B. n. 2)–104.

55. See Raymond E. Brown, *The Community of the Beloved Disciple* (New York and Ramsey, N.J.: Paulist, 1979), 67.

56. Consult the discussion in Beutler, "Psalm 42/43 im Johannesevangelium," 54–55.

57. The twofold witness of scripture for the mission and the salvific death of Jesus, according to John, has been seen recently by Hengel, "Die Schriftauslegung des 4. Evangeliums," 282.

C.K. Barrett

8

The Parallels
between Acts and John

There is no more profoundly theological work in the New Testament than the
Gospel of John. At the opposite end of the scale, as the most purely narrative work
in the New Testament, is Acts. Certainly the contrast is a matter of degree. John
tells a story, and in the past it has often been read as the most authentic and trustworthy account of the life of Jesus that we possess. Acts contains not only a narrative of things done by the apostles and their contemporaries, but also some of
their speeches, and these contain theological affirmations. But the contrast remains, beyond all qualification, an important part of the variety that marks the
New Testament, and it may therefore seem that little or nothing is to be gained by
comparing Acts with John. One compares like with like, not opposite with opposite. One recalls, however, that Acts is the second part of a longer work, and that
the first volume to which it is a sequel is one of the Synoptic Gospels. It is thus
only one step removed from the question of the relation of John to those Gospels;
this, as no one knows better than Moody, is a complex and disputed question.[1]

A comparative study of two books in the New Testament can hardly fail to be
of some value, even if its main result is an illustration of New Testament variety.
Is it possible that a comparison of Acts and John may do more than this, and by
setting the two-volume work of Luke-Acts in the early Christian tradition as a
whole, give some hints (it will not give more) about the relation of John to the
other strands in the tradition? There is all too little evidence to inform us about
the Christian tradition, oral and written, in the first Christian century, and we cannot afford to neglect any of it. I may perhaps be allowed in this volume to recall,
and with some pride, that Moody and I seem—quite independently—to have
shared this view in the 1990 Colloquium Biblicum Lovaniense, at which he gave
a brilliant paper on "The Problem of John and the Synoptics in Light of the Relation between Apocryphal and Canonical Gospels."[2] In the end this problem will
always involve looking at passages in John and in Mark (and Luke and Matthew)
and comparing them in the greatest possible detail. But when this is done the result is often that A will conclude, "This proves that the two passages are independent," and B, "This shows that the one author made use of the other's work."

It may be that in the end an assessment of John's theological and literary place within the tradition as a whole will prove to be both more achievable and more profitable.

The most recent attempt to bring Acts and John together within early Christian history is Oscar Cullmann's *The Johannine Circle*.[3] In this book, having considered the non-Christian background of John and the Johannine circle, Cullmann turns to the location of the Johannine circle within primitive Christianity. It will be profitable to begin with a brief sketch of his handling of this task.

Cullmann begins his discussion with the question whether there was to be found in the early Jerusalem church a group that shared some of the characteristics of that "nonconformist Judaism" which he has described (as part of the background of John) in an earlier chapter. He answers his question affirmatively; such a group is to be found in the Hellenists who stand over against the Hebrews in Acts 6. These constituted a group "which was more open to foreign influences and adopted a freer attitude to the Jewish Law and the temple cult than the other members of the early church."[4] They must have belonged to the Christian movement from the beginning; they may have included some of those who had followed Jesus during his lifetime. The seven leading Hellenists did much more than serve tables. Stephen's defense against his accusers throws back the charge of unfaithfulness to the law and even claims that the building of the Temple constituted the chief instance of unfaithfulness—a blasphemy that cost Stephen his life. The outcome was persecution that differentiated sharply between the Seven and the Twelve (8:1). The dispersal of the Seven, however, led to the evangelization of Samaria and Antioch, events that awakened the distrust of the Jerusalem authorities, who sent Peter and John to investigate the one region, Barnabas the other.

If now these facts are set beside the characteristics of the Johannine circle, three areas of parallelism appear: (1) theological matters, notably Christology, and the conduct, especially the place, of worship; (2) a strong interest in the mission in Samaria (John 4:31–42); (3) the common roots of Stephen's speech and the Fourth Gospel in "heterodox Judaism."[5] These areas Cullmann proceeds to investigate in detail. Some of them will recur at later points in this paper. For the present it is interesting to note that some of them had appeared long before Cullmann's time in B. W. Bacon's *The Gospel of the Hellenists*,[6] and reappear subsequently in Raymond E. Brown's *The Community of the Beloved Disciple;*[7] and that the existence of "the Hellenists" as a radical group is questionable. Luke uses the word "Hellenist" three times (6:1; 9:29; 11:20),[8] a fact that does not suggest a party label, strictly used. So far from being a radical, Stephen's group was a mediating party.[9]

Taking hints from Cullmann, however, we may consider the following points. In both John and Acts, John the Baptist is mentioned more frequently than in any other book of the New Testament. His role in John and his importance appear at once in the prologue, where the negative statement, "He was not the light," emphasizes the positive, that "he came to bear witness to the light." The Baptist's chronological priority and his secondary status reinforce each other. "He that comes after me is preferred before me"; and even the chronological priority is negated when the pre-temporal existence of the Word is considered: "for he was before me." There is no one with whom John can be identified (John 1:19–22); he is nothing but a voice, resuming and representing the Old Testament (1:23). His baptism has no purpose but to draw attention to an Other (1:24–28), and this John does (1:29–34). The connection and the contrast between Jesus and John are emphasized by the fact that (in the Fourth Gospel, not in the Synoptics) their ministries overlap (3:23–24). This gives John the opportunity to renew his testimony and to compare himself not to the bridegroom but to the bridegroom's friend. "He must increase and I must decrease" (3:25–30). Jesus' greater success is noted at 4:1. Jesus himself returns to the witness of John: He has borne witness to the truth (5:33), but the following verses (5:34–36) keep John in his place. Jesus has the greater witness of the works God grants him to do. And Jesus' return to the scene of John's baptism prompts the comment that sums up the evangelist's own view: "John did no sign, but all the things John said about this man were true" (10:41). John is a highly important and truthful witness to one who is far more important because he is the truth itself.

This is precisely what is said about John in Acts. It is clearest of all when Paul says to the group of disciples in Ephesus, "John baptized with a baptism of repentance, telling the people that they should believe in the one who was coming after him, that is, in Jesus" (Acts 19:4). Baptism into the name of the Lord Jesus, and the laying on of Paul's hands, followed; the result was the gift of the Spirit, of which these disciples had never previously heard.[10] The importance but also the inadequacy of John are stressed throughout, usually in terms of baptism and the gift of the Spirit. "John baptized with water, you shall be baptized in the Holy Spirit" (1:5; 11:16). John provides a framework for the ministry of Jesus (1:22; 10:37; 13:24–25). In the last of these passages, John (as in the Fourth Gospel) will accept only a negative definition of his person: "After John, before his coming, had proclaimed to all the people of Israel a baptism of repentance."[11] Here, however, the view of the Synoptic Gospels that John completed his public ministry before the appearance of Jesus is affirmed.

It is clear, but not perhaps particularly striking, that John and Acts are in agreement regarding John the Baptist as an important figure, the mouthpiece of the Old Testament who sums up the Old Testament's witness to Christ, close to him in time but inferior to him (though to him only: see Matt. 11:11; Luke 7:28) in status. This is not striking, because it is the united witness of the New Testament (that is, of Matthew, Mark, and Luke; there is no mention of John elsewhere). What is striking is the emphasis with which this, and especially the negative aspect of it, is affirmed. It has often been maintained that one purpose of the Fourth Gospel is the refutation of a continuing group or groups of John's disciples, who believed that their master was indeed the true light, that he was the Messiah. The evange-list protests too much to be totally disinterested. R. E. Brown thinks that the Beloved Disciple was a follower of John the Baptist who subsequently, with oth-ers (1:35–37), became a follower of Jesus,[12] and that the Johannine community at a later stage found itself involved in dispute with other disciples of John who had not attached themselves to Jesus; hence the many negative references to John,[13] a refutation of Johannine claims cast in such terms as might have been hoped to win these disciples to Jesus. Brown refers at this point to Acts 18:24–19:7, which (he says) makes the "hope . . . plausible"[14] and, moreover, is located in Ephesus, the traditional origin of the Fourth Gospel. Taken at face value, the mutually sup-portive evidence of Acts and John makes a good case for the continuing existence, well into the Christian period, of a number of disciples of John the Baptist. It must not, however, be overvalued or used with much confidence in the construction of a partly shared traditional background for the Lukan and Johannine writings. There is some—though not conclusive—reason for adopting the traditional loca-tion of the Fourth Gospel; at least there is a better case for Ephesus than for any-where else. There is no case for any location for the editing of Acts—unless, in-deed, we reverse the argument and use Acts 18:24–19:7 as evidence for Ephesus. There is nothing in the events of 19:1–7 to confirm the statement in verse 1 that they happened in Ephesus; in themselves they could have happened anywhere. There is not even any firm ground for describing the group as disciples of John the Baptist; they are simply μαθηταί ("disciples"), and this is a word that Luke commonly uses (27 [25] times) of Christian disciples. If it seems unlikely that Christian disciples should not have heard of the Holy Spirit, the same surely is true of John's.[15] Luke's purpose in including this paragraph is obscure and dis-puted.[16] It is, however, reasonable to note that both Luke and John thought it right to give a proper prominence to John the Baptist but to keep that prominence within bounds, and there is some reason to think that they were aware of the continuing existence of his disciples and considered this a matter to be taken into account in their handling of the Christian tradition. This is far from a claim that the fourth evangelist was aware of what Luke was writing.

The Hellenists of Acts 6:1 were referred to above, with the suggestion that the word was not a current designation of a recognized group but Luke's own inven-tion (serving as a counterpart to "Hebrews"), used by him to describe and at the same time to excuse a Jerusalem party distinct from if not actually opposed to the Twelve. This of course is not to deny—it would be impossible to deny—that there were Jews of the Dispersion who had picked up more than the language of their Greek neighbors, that some of them resided at least temporarily in Jerusalem (Acts 6:9), and that some of them became Christians. It does mean that we should be cautious, more cautious than Cullmann for example, in speaking of "the Hel-lenists" as if they were an organized party exercising a specific and determinable influence in the Jerusalem church of the earliest days. Cullmann sees such an influence in Christology and in the understanding of worship.[17] He finds his material in the speech attributed to Stephen in Acts 7. Here Stephen uses attack as his means of defense. Israel is in error in not recognizing that "the decisive revelations of God are not bound up with a *country* or a particular place."[18] The movable tabernacle provided the true means of worship. Stephen does not oppose the law; on the contrary, he quotes Deut. 18:15 (Acts 7:37) to show that Moses was the prototype of Christ. Jesus is the Righteous One (7:52); he is the Son of Man, who stands at God's right hand, "evidently as an intercessor for Stephen."[19] To all these points there are (according to Cullmann) analogies in John. God is to be worshiped, neither on Gerizim nor in Jerusalem, but in Spirit and in truth (John 4:20–24). Moreover, the glory, the *shekinah*, of God is to be found in the Word who ἐσκήνωσεν ("lived," a play on the word, *shekinah*) among us (John 1:14); and Jacob's ladder (Gen. 28:12), as the link between earth and heaven, is replaced by the Son of Man (John 1:51), in whom God is manifested. "Son of Man" is an important term in Johannine Christology.

The more closely these parallels are examined, the less impressive they become. Cullmann himself recognizes that regarding the Temple, Stephen's speech presents only the negative side of the matter:[20] The Temple is attacked, but no attempt is made to argue that it has been replaced by the person of Christ, the new point of contact between God and humanity. Moreover, Luke uses the reference to the Temple in Stephen's speech to counterbalance a different view, which represents it as continuing to be used by Christians (e.g., 3:1; 21:23–24, 26). Luke's attitude to the Temple illustrates his attitude to Judaism in general.[21] It is doubtful whether he intended to represent one group of Christians as taking a one-sided attitude, though it is of course quite possible that some did. John does not disparage Moses (5:46), but he hardly regards him as the prototype of Christ. The law was given through Moses, grace and truth came by Jesus Christ (1:17). These qualifications are important if we consider Acts as a whole (in which "Son of Man" occurs once only). They do not remove the possibility that some Diaspora Jews may have learned—in part as a matter of necessity—to devalue the Temple as a constituent of Judaism and may have come to think of Moses in terms of the various saviors of non-Jewish religions. However, the fourth evangelist could have become acquainted with such tendencies almost anywhere in the Greco-Roman world.

It is more important to consider the place of the Samaritans. Of two points the first arises out of the account of Jesus and the Samaritan woman in John 4. This shows a positive interest in and concern for Samaritans and knowledge of Samaritan beliefs, and also leads up to the obscure and disputed saying of 4:38: "I sent you to harvest that on which you bestowed no labor; others have labored, and you have entered into their labor." Cullmann thinks that this refers to the claim in Acts 8 that the Samaritans were first evangelized by the Hellenist Philip. Later the Twelve, represented by Peter and John, joined in and completed Philip's work. So put, the observation would form the strongest evidence, if not for a close connection between Acts itself and John, at least for a contact on John's part with a particular—Hellenist—tradition in Acts. Unfortunately, there are several uncertain points in the argument. Alternative interpretations of John 4:38 have greater probability (though Cullmann's cannot be definitely excluded).[22] A mission to Samaria is included among the original agenda for the Twelve (Acts 1:8), and in Acts 8:4–25 Luke seems to be combining two or three pieces of traditional information rather than describing a takeover of a Hellenistic mission by the Twelve.

The second point is that as John 4 shows awareness of Samaritan messianic belief, Acts shows in Stephen's speech awareness of Samaritan interpretation of scripture. I have discussed these matters in some detail, and it will suffice here to quote the conclusion: "It is hard to avoid the conclusion that none of the evidence we have surveyed is sufficient to establish the belief that Stephen (Luke) was in any way connected with Samaria."[23]

It is undoubtedly true that both John and Acts show an interest in Samaritans that is not found in the rest of the New Testament.[24] In John 8:48 Jesus himself is accused of being a Samaritan, which can hardly mean less than the fact that Johannine Christians were accused by Jews of having some special relation with Samaritans. This observation is discussed by R. E. Brown without any clear-cut conclusion: "One may posit that the second group in Johannine history consisted of Jews of peculiar anti-Temple views who converted Samaritans and picked up some elements of Samaritan thought, including a Christology that was not centered on a Davidic Messiah. . . . [T]he evidence of Acts shows that it is not at all implausible to postulate the group which I have reconstructed entering the Johannine community and serving as a catalyst in the break with the synagogue."[25] Even this, however, seems to go further than is justified by the scanty data at our disposal; in particular there is little ground for suggesting any serious contribution of Samaritan thought to the Christology of John. "The Savior of the world," though without parallel in the Gospels, is better explained as part of a general, late-first-century development in Christian theology[26] than as a Samaritanism.[27] The most a cautious student can say is that some strands of primitive Christianity were more sensitive than others to the needs and hopes of Samaritans; that the author of Acts was aware of the existence of such strands, though he did not develop their story beyond the early years represented by Acts 8:4–25 (also 9:31); and that one of these strands contributed to the Johannine tradition, and converted Samaritans may have been one element in the "Johannine circle."[28]

Cullmann finds a further link between Acts and John in a shared relation to what he describes as "heterodox Judaism"—a term that, while criticized in view of the fact that in the first century there was as yet no "orthodox Judaism," bears a clear enough sense, though one that is wide rather than precise. It is necessary "not to limit oneself to Samaritan theology, relevant though that is, but also to consider the simultaneous influence of other groups and conceptions which belong to the same stream of heterodox Judaism: Qumran, the Mandaeans, the baptist movement, Jewish syncretism and gnostic Ebionitism."[29] Of these constituents one that has been held to bind together Acts and John is a shared relation to the Qumran sect. This view turns mainly on the agreement of all three in criticism of the Jerusalem Temple.[30] This agreement is less significant, however, than may at first appear because the rejection of the Temple is based on different grounds in the three sources. At Qumran there is no rejection of the Temple in principle, but as long as it was controlled by apostate priests, those who were faithful to the covenant could play no part in it. The time would come when they would assume control (CD 6:11, 12; 1QH 2:1). Over against this approval of the Temple and rejection of its administration, Stephen argues that the Temple should never have been built;[31] it was like the offering of sacrifice to heathen gods and is a direct contradiction of the express will of God, declared by the prophets. John's attitude is different again. John 4:23–24 could be taken as not greatly different from Acts 7, though worship "in spirit and in truth" has a specifically Johannine ring; but John 2:21, to which Cullmann draws attention,[32] replaces the Temple with the shrine of Christ's body, which goes beyond anything said by Stephen (or by Paul in Acts 17).

So is there little that strikes a bridge between Acts and John, even by way of "heterodox Judaism"? It may be that an examination of considerations, in themselves less particular, less precise, will enable us to go a little further. Four themes, to some extent looked at already, await discussion.

The first is eschatology. John and Acts are the two books in the New Testament where futurist eschatology comes nearest to disappearing. It does not disappear in either. In John we may point to passages that refer to the "last day";[33] there are the ambiguous references to seeing and not seeing (16:19, 20), which were probably intended to have a double reference, to the interval between death and resurrection appearances, and to that between ascension and parousia; and the passage where Jesus speaks of his coming "to take you to myself," to the "many abiding-places in my Father's house." In Acts there is the plainest of references to the return of Jesus, coming as he had gone, with the clouds (1:11; cf. Dan. 7:13); God has appointed a day when he will judge the world (17:31), and the man by whom he will judge will be Jesus, the judge of the living and the dead (10:42); men are urged to repent in order that God may send Jesus, the Christ whom he has appointed for them (3:19, 20). These passages show John and Acts standing within the boundaries of primitive Christian belief, but they are not the passages most characteristic of the two authors. "This is the judgment, that light has come into the world and people loved the darkness rather than the light" (John 3:19). Jesus' hour of suffering and death is also his hour of glory (12:23; 13:31). There is somewhat similar language in Acts (3:13), but the main point is different. In John the future—judgment, for example—is brought into the present. In Acts the future remains future— the day of judgment is still to come—but it becomes sufficiently remote for it to be worthwhile to write the history of the church and its mission, and there will be "times of refreshment"—healings and conversions, for example—to lighten and cheer the period of waiting for the Messiah.[34] Gifts such as speaking with tongues, and the Lord's care for his own, will in the meantime prove that the Lord reigns in heaven and sends his Spirit to those who need his aid.

The two books, different as they are, are alike in this: They represent Christian believers as living without the temporal pressure that is evident in some parts of the New Testament, but as sensitive to an otherworldly pressure conveyed by different means. The other world makes its pressure felt in this world, not by the perception of an impending cataclysm, but by spiritual forces. This leads to a second area of parallelism, or resemblance.

The Holy Spirit plays a more prominent part in John than in any other of the Gospels, and not a little of what is said about the Spirit in John is paralleled in Acts. The relation between the two will be most clearly set out by means of a brief survey of references in the Gospel.

1. Unlike the Synoptic Gospels, John does not say that Jesus was baptized by John the Baptist, but the event seems to be reflected in the Baptist's statement (1:32) "I saw the Spirit descending from heaven like a dove, and it remained on him." This is closely parallel to Acts 10:38, "God anointed Jesus of Nazareth with the Holy Spirit and with power." Here, too, there is no reference to Jesus' baptism, though this is as plainly implied by 10:37 as it is in John; the connection of the negative parallel with the positive is particularly striking. The Baptist goes on to say (in John 1:33) that the descent of the Spirit had been given as an indication that Jesus was the one who would baptize (not with water, or with water only, but) with the Holy Spirit. This corresponds fairly closely with Acts 1:5; 11:16.

2. The next group of sayings (John 3:5–8), especially when taken in the context (see 3:23–30), is also related to Acts 1:5; 11:16. Water alone does not suffice for admission to the kingdom of God. There is a probable reference to John's baptism, though this does not exhaust the significance of the passage.[35] The work of Jesus is needed as a supplement to that of John; his gift of the Spirit is the essential divine operation in both John and Acts.

3. John 3:34 is a difficult verse. It probably means that Jesus is the bearer of the Spirit and there is no limit to the degree to which the Spirit rests upon him. There is no true parallel to this in Acts, but it is hard to think that Luke would have disagreed.

4. The next group of references in John to πνεῦμα, "spirit" (4:23, 24), can be paralleled in Acts but at the same time brings out the distinctiveness of Acts. Again the context is important. Jesus contrasts the true worship of God, which he makes possible, with both Samaritan worship on Mt. Gerizim and Jewish worship in Jerusalem. For the implied criticism of the Temple (and of temples) see above, and compare Acts 7:46–50; 17:24. In Acts true worship is accompanied by manifestations of the Spirit's work (4:23–31; 9:31; 11:28; 13:1–3, [52]; 21:4, 11).

John continues with the proposition πνεῦμα ὁ θεός, "God is spirit." To this there is no verbal parallel in Acts, but it is reasonable to compare Acts 14:15 (θεὸν ζῶντα, "a living God")—God who is alive, that is, real, not a mere material image like that of Zeus (14:13)—and 17:24–29, where the true God is contrasted with those who are confined within temples, made by human art and artifice; he desires to be sought and found, he is not remote; "in him we live and move and have our being." The word is all but used; the true God gives us life and breath (πνοή) and all things.

5. In John 6:63 there are difficult problems that need not be discussed here.[36] The basic proposition, the Spirit is that which gives life, is the fundamental biblical belief about the Spirit (see, e.g., Gen. 1:2; Ezek. 37:1–14; 1 Cor. 15:45; 2 Cor. 2:6). It is the specific New Testament assertion that Spirit and thereby life are communicated through Jesus: the work of Jesus the Word (λόγος) is done through words (ῥήματα). No more than general agreement is to be found in Acts.

6. John 7:39 is John's explanatory comment on the saying of 7:37b, 38. We need not discuss here the question of punctuation; 4:14 is sufficient to show that living water, originating with Christ, wells up in the believer. On this living water John comments, Jesus said this about the Spirit. There are two further propositions: It is believers who receive this gift of the Spirit, and the gift became available only after Jesus had been glorified (in the double act of crucifixion and exaltation). This is precisely the view of Acts, though Luke uses different words to express it. The Spirit is in the gift of Jesus, and he promises it (1:5, 8), but does not give it till after his exaltation (2:33).[37] John and Acts are agreed that the Spirit is the agent of life, that the Spirit is the gift of Christ to believers, but that this gift is not given till after the glorification of Jesus.

7. That there is a special relation between the Paraclete sayings of John 14, 15, 16 and what is said about the Spirit in Acts was argued long ago by W. F. Lofthouse.[38] The core of his argument is given in the words,

> Now, what calls for our notice is that the emphasis of these five passages is precisely that which underlies the conception of the Spirit in Ac[ts] 1 — 15. The Spirit is sent by Jesus and by the Father in Jesus' name; He is given to the disciples as their special possession; He reminds them of Jesus; witnesses of Jesus, as they do themselves; guides them, glorifies Him. "I-ye-He" form a kind of motif throughout. The Spirit is linked as closely to the company of disciples in the life which awaits them as He is linked to Jesus. He is to do for them all that the Master had done on earth. He is to be, so to speak, the Master Himself *en permanence*.[39]

It is hardly necessary to point to the specific verses on which this summary rests, and we need not follow Lofthouse in the view that the Paraclete sayings go back to words spoken by Jesus "in the night in which he was betrayed," though it is fair to add Lofthouse's note that "there is nothing verbally exact about the correspondence; nothing to suggest documentary comparison";[40] and it is useful to add special emphasis to the theme of witness, which as the work of the Spirit and as the work of the disciples is especially characteristic of both John and Acts.

8. The last passage to note is John 20:22.[41] This is the fulfillment of 7:38–39. After his glorification, in death and resurrection, Jesus gives the Spirit to his disciples. There is a promise in Acts (1:5, 8), as there is a promise in John; the promises are fulfilled; but there is no parallel between the fulfillments except that they are fulfillments. In John, Jesus breathes into the disciples. In Acts, there are the public events of the day of Pentecost.

A number of references to the Spirit remain in Acts, such as 4:8, 31; 6:3, 5, 10; 7:55; 8:15, 17, 18, 19, 29, 39; 9:17, 31; 10:19, 44, 45, 47; 11:12, 15, 24, 28; 13:2, 4, 9, 52; 15:8, 28; 16:6, 7; 18:25; 19:2, 6, 21; 20:22, 23, 28; 21:4, 11, which describe Christians as filled with, baptized with, guided by, transported by, and lying to the Holy Spirit—all simply fulfillments of the promise already noted—and 1:16; 4:25; 28:25, where the Holy Spirit is said to have inspired passages in the Old Testament. These are not relevant to this study.

Consideration of the Spirit leads naturally to the church, the community within which the Spirit is at work. That both John and Acts show awareness of this community is only to be expected; they are both Christian books. References in John are clear. In the Prologue, 1:12 and 13 look forward to the existence of those who receive Christ and are born of God. John 4:23 looks forward to a new community worshiping neither on Mt. Gerizim nor in Jerusalem. At 10:16 Jesus, as the Good Shepherd, declares that he has other sheep who are not of the (Jewish) fold; the existence of a church including Gentiles is in mind. John's comment in 11:51–52 (see also 18:14) further shows that, in addition to the Jewish ἔθνος ("nation"), there were other children of God who had to be gathered into one—again the mixed Jewish and Gentile church is in mind. So also 12:20. In 16:2 a time is foretold when believers will be excluded from the synagogue, and even killed. In 17:20 Jesus prays not only for the small group of disciples by whom he is surrounded but also for those who, in the future, will believe "through their word" (διὰ τοῦ λόγου αὐτῶν); this is an Acts of the Apostles in miniature. The following more specific points are more relevant to our purpose.

The theme of witness is important in both books. The Old Testament (Moses and the prophets) bear witness to Christ (John 5:39; Acts 10:43). John the Baptist bears witness: John 1:7, 8, 15, 19, 32, 34; 5:33, 36; similarly Acts (though without the use of the root, μαρτ-): 13:24, 25; 19:4.[42] Most important here, however, is the fact that the disciples are to bear witness as in John 15:27. In the same context (15:26) the Paraclete will bear witness. (See also 4:39; 17:20). In Acts the theme recurs constantly: 23:11 (μαρτυρεῖν, "to bear witness"); 22:18 (μαρτυρία, "testimony"); 4:33 (μαρτύριον, "testimony"); 1:8, 22; 2:32; 3:15; 5:32; 10:39, 41; 13:31; 22:15, 20; 26:16 (μάρτυς, "witness"). Witnessing is primarily the work of apostles, who are not only eyewitnesses of the risen Jesus but have also accompanied him through the whole of his public ministry (1:21–22); others join them without the latter qualification (13:31–32). For both John and Acts, the church, empowered by the Holy Spirit, is a witnessing community.

The response for which the witnesses hope is belief, or faith. This is clear in John 17:20. Response can be inferred from the Paraclete passage in John 16. The world will be put right with regard to sin, righteousness, and judgment, and this includes the element of believing (16:9). The response to the Samaritan woman's testimony is that πολλοὶ ἐπίστευσαν, "many believed" (4:39). In Acts, hearers accept the word that they hear (δέχεσθαι: 8:14; 11:1; 17:11; ἀποδέχεσθαι: 2:41) and believe (πιστεύειν: 4:4; 8:12; 10:43; 11:21; 13:48; 14:1; 15:7; 17:12, 34; 18:8).

Believers live a common life, the distinguishing mark of which is love (John 13:12–17, 34, 35). In Acts this is expressed in κοινωνία, "fellowship" (2:42; see also 2:44; 4:32) and a sharing of the proceeds derived from selling property.

Acts and John are agreed on the scope of the Christian mission. The incorporation in the one flock of other sheep, not of the Jewish fold (John 10:16; see also 12:20–21; 21:11), is a major theme of Acts. There is a similar parallelism between the two books in their attitude to the Jews. Each shows at once an affirmation and a criticism of Judaism. In John, the work of Jesus as a whole is set within a Jewish context; it is only within that context that it can be understood. Salvation is of the Jews (4:22); it is Jews who understand religion, who know what they are worshiping. Yet the same context affirms that henceforth worship will be confined to Jerusalem no more than to Gerizim. The Jews are the children of the devil (8:44); the light has come into the world, and they have chosen darkness. In Acts the Jews are the sons of the prophets and of the covenant (3:25). It is necessary that the gospel should be preached to them first (13:46), but in place after place they reject it, and at the end of the book it is the Gentiles who will listen (28:28). For both John and Acts Judaism is true, but its truth must be rightly interpreted, and again for both authors, the right interpretation is the Christian one.

The favorable position accorded to women in the Lukan writings has often been observed. It is closely paralleled in John.

> In the portrayal of major male and female believers there is no difference of intelligence, vividness, or response. Martha serves as the spokeswoman of a confession of faith (11.27 . . .) that is placed on Peter's lips in Matthew 16.16–17. . . . A whole village comes to believe in Jesus through the word of the Samaritan woman (4.39). In John 20.14 not Peter but Mary Magdalene is the first to see the risen Jesus. . . . If rank in discipleship is set by Jesus' love, as exemplified in "the disciple whom Jesus loved," it is said, "Jesus loved Martha and her sister and Lazarus" (11.5).[43]

It is worth adding that the two books—or rather the two bodies of literature— show the same church organization. Second and Third John (not written by the author of the Gospel but certainly related to it) were written by one who described himself as the presbyter (2 John 1; 3 John 1). It seems that though apostles, prophets, teachers, and an evangelist appear in Acts, presbyters were the ministers with whom Luke himself was familiar (Acts 11:30; 14:33; 15:2, 4, 6, 22, 23; 16:4; 20:17; 21:18).

It may seem paradoxical to include Christology among themes that are to any extent parallel in Acts and John. John is the Gospel of the incarnate Word; λόγος as a designation of Christ does not occur in Acts, and there is nothing corresponding to the σὰρξ ἐγένετο ("he became flesh") of John 1:14. That Acts presents us with, if not a primitive Christology, at least an undeveloped one, and that the Johannine Christology, in contrast, is the most advanced in the New Testament, are propositions frequently heard. These propositions are broadly true. Yet there are resemblances—qualified resemblances, it is true—and these must be considered.

Acts (with Luke 24:53) is the only book in the New Testament to narrate the ascension as an event. But John, far more than any other Gospel, stresses the return of the Son to the Father and to the pre-mundane glory that he shared with him. We have here two different and characteristic ways of stating a conviction that runs through the New Testament as a whole, often expressed by the quotation of Ps. 110:1, one of the earliest and most popular testimonia in the primitive church because it was the clearest prediction of the exaltation and dominion of the Messiah. The truth it was believed to express was particularly emphasized in both John (who does not quote it) and Acts, but in different ways. In Acts it is expressed in narrative terms: Jesus is seen going up to heaven, received by cloudy space; *up there* he will sit at the right hand of God, and *up there* he is seen by Stephen, risen from his seat and about to come to his faithful witness (7:56).[44] John expresses the same emphasis by running down the narrative element implied by the words of the Psalm, and especially by emphasizing that the Son does not rise to some new position of power and glory. Already he was in the beginning πρὸς τὸν θεόν ("with God"). He was never without glory: there was glory that he had before the world was (17:5); Isaiah in the eighth century B. C. E. saw his glory (12:41); he manifested his glory in the course of his ministry (1:14; 2:11; 11:40); the hour is coming when he will be glorified (12:23; 13:31), in the one event which is both death and exaltation; the disciples are in the future to be where he is and to see his glory (17:24), but this glory is something that "thou hast given me because thou didst love me before the foundation of the world." The eschatological chronology and the celestial topography have disappeared; the emphasis on the unique glory of Jesus remains, with just a hint of the old formulation in πρός ("with"; 1:1, 2), παρά ("in [your] presence"; 17:5), and νῦν ("now"; 13:31).

There is similarly diverse emphasis on Jesus as the unique source of salvation. In Acts 4:12 this is stated in the strongest terms: In no one else is there salvation. Luke does not define what he means by σωτηρία. The thought begins, however, from the story of a lame man who σέσωται ("was healed").[45] It is in the name of Jesus Christ of Nazareth that the man now stands in public, cured. Salvation is thus pictured in the restoration of a lame man to full mobility—better, in the perfecting of a physical frame imperfect from birth (3:2). The restoration of all things (3:21, ἀποκατάστασις πάντων) is foreshadowed, that is, a crudely eschatological conception of salvation. Salvation (σῴζειν ["to save"], σωτήρ ["savior"], σωτηρία ["salvation"]) is not of frequent occurrence in John, but when used theologically it is focused on Jesus. If anyone enters through me (δι᾿ ἐμοῦ, in emphatic position) he will be saved (σωθήσεται); he will enter the safety of the sheepfold (10:9). The salvation he brings is all-embracing: 3:17 (ἵνα σωθῇ ὁ κόσμος, "in order that the world might be saved"); 12:47 (ἵνα σώσω τὸν κόσμον, "in order that I might save the world"); 4:42 (ὁ σωτὴρ τοῦ κόσμου, "the Savior of the world"). Salvation proceeds out of a Jewish setting (4:22), but it is for the world. It consists in knowledge of and access to God (17:3), and this knowledge and access are provided in Jesus, whose story is the unique revelation of the invisible God (1:18; cf. 14:6, 9). Acts and John are thus equally concerned to stress the uniqueness of Jesus as the author of salvation, but Acts does this by underlining the old eschatological notion of salvation; John, in language that verges on Gnosticism.

There is a negative parallel between the two books in regard to the death of Jesus: Each almost completely passes by the sacrificial interpretation of the cross. There is one exception in each: Acts 20:28[46] and John 1:29, 36.[47] Apart from these passages, the death of Jesus is in Acts the result of human wickedness and ignorance, an evil deed which God speedily put right by raising Jesus from death, and in John an act of humble love (of which the foot-washing is a sign), which was the occasion of God's defeat of evil and thus of the revelation of his glory. The extent to which there is real similarity here depends upon the degree to which, at the time when John and Acts were written, a sacrificial interpretation had been accepted, and this is very difficult to assess. If it was the generally accepted interpretation, John and Acts were agreed in (for the most part) rejecting it, though they did not adopt the same alternative. If it was not generally accepted, we have two authors who independently went their own ways in supplying (or not supplying) an alternative.

From this comparative sketch of two notable constituents of the New Testament, only modest conclusions can be drawn. In the first place, from all the parallels there must be subtracted what was common Christian belief, shared by all Christians of whatever group or school. This removes a good deal, but not everything, and it is important to place John correctly within the general stream of Christian tradition. Perhaps the evangelist was not quite such a lonely figure as has sometimes been maintained. There is a good deal to be said for the view that Johannine Christianity was an isolated dissenting sect,[48] but not all dissenters are badly informed about the main lines of Christian tradition. I return to the view that though the question of John's knowledge of the Synoptic Gospels can never dispense with the labor of verse-by-verse and word-by-word comparison, it is important to chart John's position as clearly as we can within the Christian history and literature of the first and second centuries. This will never answer such questions as "John's dependence on Mark, or Markan tradition?" But it can hardly fail to be instructive.

NOTES

1. See especially his *John among the Gospels* (Minneapolis: Fortress, 1992). When I first saw this book I feared that I might have lost my subject, but if the index is to be trusted, Acts is referred to only 24 times, and of these 14 fall within three pages.

2. *John and the Synoptics*, ed. Adelbert Denaux, BETL 101 (Leuven: Leuven University Press, 1992), 147–62. I spoke on "The Place of John and the Synoptics within the Early History of Christian Thought," ibid., 63–79.

3. Oscar Cullmann, *The Johannine Circle* (Philadelphia: Westminster, 1975).

4. Ibid., 41.

5. Ibid., 43.

6. B. W. Bacon, *The Gospel of the Hellenists*, ed. C. H. Kraeling (New York: Holt, 1933). Note Bacon's summary paragraph (100): "Of the leaders in the Baptist movement the Samaritan Menander and Elkesai are certainly contemporaries of the fourth Evangelist. If, therefore, the question be asked why the latter devotes a great part of the early chapters of the Gospel to a treatment of the relation between Christian baptism and the baptism of John and declares the former to be the genuine instrument of rebirth, the answer must be sought in the ideas which these Samaritan contemporaries and the 'disciples of John' promulgated. This relationship was evident already to Kreyenbühl, but its explanation cannot be found in the theory he advanced that Menander wrote the fourth Gospel. The true explanation is that as a representative of the Hellenistic Christianity developed on Palestinian soil, the Elder held views analogous to those of the Samaritan Baptists, and employed the imagery of Gnostic sacramentalism to convey a higher spiritual truth."

7. Raymond E. Brown, *The Community of the Beloved Disciple* (New York and Ramsey, N.J.: Paulist, 1979); see 22–23, 48–49, 56, 70, 77, 176–78, 235–40.

8. For the textual problems in these verses, see my commentary, *A Critical and Exegetical Commentary on the Acts of the Apostles*, ICC (Edinburgh: T. & T. Clark, 1994), 1.307–10, 470, 549–51.

9. See C. K. Barrett, "Acts and Christian Consensus," *Context: Festskrift til Peder Johan Borgen/Essays in Honour of Peder Johan Borgen*, ed. Peter Wilhelm Bøckman and Roald E. Kristiansen, Relieff 24 (Trondheim: Tapir, 1987), 19–33 (here, 25–28).

10. In comparison, the story of Apollos is problematical, but the implication of *only* in 18:25 (" . . . *only* the baptism of John") is clear.

11. On the text and construction see Barrett, *The Acts of the Apostles*, 1.637.

12. Brown, *The Community of the Beloved Disciple*, 32–33.

13. Ibid., 69–71.

14. Ibid., 71.

15. Even if John's prophecy was originally that his successor would baptize the unrepentant with the wind (πνεῦμα) and fire of judgment, his followers surely read the Old Testament.

16. See, e.g., Ernst Käsemann, *Essays on New Testament Themes* (Philadelphia: Fortress, 1964), 136–48; Eduard Schweizer, "Die Bekehrung des Apollos, Apg 18,24–26," in *Beiträge zur Theologie des Neuen Testaments: Neutestamentliche Aufsätze (1955–1970)* (Zurich: Zwingli, 1970), 71–79.

17. Cullmann, *The Johannine Circle*, 43; for Cullmann's views of the Hellenists in relation to the Samaritans and heterodox Judaism, see below.

18. Ibid., 43.

19. Ibid., 44.

20. Ibid., 45–46.

21. See my essay, "Attitudes to the Temple in the Acts of the Apostles," in *Templum Amicitiae: Essays on the Second Temple presented to Ernst Bammel*, ed. William Horbury, JSNTSup 48 (Sheffield: JSOT, 1991), 345–67, esp. 366.

22. See my *The Gospel according to St John: An Introduction with Commentary and Notes on the Greek Text*, 2d ed. (Philadelphia: Westminster, 1978), 243.

23. C. K. Barrett, "Old Testament History according to Stephen and Paul," in *Studien zum Text und zur Ethik des Neuen Testaments: Festschrift zum 80. Geburtstag von Heinrich Greeven*, ed. Wolfgang Schrage, BZNW 47 (Berlin: Walter de Gruyter, 1986), 57–69 (quotation, 64). See, however, the article by George Wesley Buchanan, "The Samaritan Origin of the Gospel of John," in *Religions in Antiquity: Essays in Memory of Erwin Ramsdell Goodenough*, ed. Jacob Neusner, Studies in the History of Religions 14 (Leiden: Brill, 1968), 149–75. For Moses in Samaritan belief, see especially Wayne A. Meeks, *The Prophet-King: Moses Traditions and the Johannine Christology*, NovTSup 14 (Leiden: Brill, 1967), 216–57.

24. Except in the Third Gospel; contrast Matthew 10:5.

25. Brown, *The Community of the Beloved Disciple*, 38; see esp. 35–40.

26. Cf. 1 Tim. 1:1; 2:3; 4:10; 2 Tim. 1:10; Titus 1:3–4; 2:10, 13; 3:4, 6; 2 Peter 1:1, 11; 2:20; 3:2, 18; Jude 25.

27. It is more probably of Hellenistic origin; see Rudolf Bultmann, *The Gospel of John: A Commentary* (Philadelphia: Westminster, 1971), 201; Barrett, *The Gospel according to St John*, 244.

28. Meeks, *The Prophet-King*, 318.

29. Cullmann, *The Johannine Circle*, 51.

30. See my discussion, above.

31. Stephen's speech in Acts 7 is the main source, but it is important to have in mind also 17:24, which looks to Hellenistic enlightenment as well as to prophetic criticism.

32. Cullmann, *The Johannine Circle*, 44–45.

33. John 6:39, 40, 44, 54. In *The Gospel according to St John* and in *New Testament Essays* (London: SPCK, 1972), 66–69, I have argued that these belong to the thought of the evangelist, not to an ecclesiastical redactor.

34. Acts 3:20; for the interpretation of καιροὶ ἀναψύξεως, see C. K. Barrett, "Faith and Eschatology in Acts 3," in *Glaube und Eschatologie: Festschrift für Werner Georg Kümmel zum 80. Geburtstag*, ed. Erich Gräßer and Otto Merk (Tübingen: Mohr [Siebeck], 1985), 1–17, esp. 11–13.

35. Barrett, *The Gospel according to St John*, 209.

36. Ibid., 304–5.

37. See Acts 2:38; 5:31–32; and the gift at Pentecost, interpreted in terms of Joel's prophecy (Acts 2:4, 17–21).

38. W. F. Lofthouse, "The Holy Spirit in the Acts and in the Fourth Gospel," *ExpTim* 52 (1940–1941): 334–36.

39. Ibid., 336.

40. Ibid.

41. Some would add John 19:30, but reference here to the Holy Spirit is improbable.

42. Note especially the parallelism between John 1:20, 21 (ἐγὼ οὐκ εἰμὶ ὁ χριστός . . . οὐκ εἰμὶ . . . οὔ, "I am not the Messiah . . . I am not . . . no") and Acts 13:25 (οὐκ εἰμὶ ἐγώ, "I am not he"). The emphasis gives support to the view that both authors have in mind disciples of John who asserted that their master was the Messiah.

43. Raymond E. Brown, *The Churches the Apostles Left Behind* (New York: Paulist, 1984), 94–95.

44. See C. Kingsley Barrett, "Stephen and the Son of Man," in *Apophoreta: Festschrift für Ernst Haenchen zu seinem 70. Geburtstag,* ed. Walther Eltester and Franz Heinrich Kettler, BZNW 30 (Berlin: Töpelmann, 1964), 32–38. Cullmann (*The Johannine Circle,* 44) interprets differently.

45. Acts 4:9. Other analogies could be used; for example, at 27:34 σωτηρία refers to physical well-being in a storm.

46. There are familiar problems of text and interpretation; the important word is *blood.*

47. Here, too, there are familiar problems, but a *lamb* is a sacrificial animal.

48. Ernst Käsemann, "Ketzer und Zeuge: Zum johanneischen Verfasserproblem," in *Exegetische Versuche und Besinnungen* (Göttingen: Vandenhoeck & Ruprecht, 1960), 1.168–87; also idem, *The Testament of Jesus: A Study of the Gospel of John in Light of Chapter 17* (Philadelphia: Fortress, 1968); C. K. Barrett, *Essays on John* (Philadelphia: Westminster, 1982), 126–31.

9

The Tradition History
of the Fourth Gospel

The task entrusted to me for this commemorative volume in honor of Professor D. Moody Smith's sixty-fifth birthday is one with which he himself has been actively concerned during the whole of his scholarly career and research on the Johannine literature, from the very beginning to the recent past. Such concern is evident already at the dissertation stage, in the 1960s, when he takes up a sustained critical analysis of Rudolf Bultmann's theory of sources and composition regarding the Gospel of John;[1] it recurs in a number of articles dating from the 1970s and 1980s, in which he not only continues to pursue the question of pre-Gospel sources but also begins to turn his attention to the relationship between the Fourth Gospel and the Synoptic Gospels;[2] and it comes to the fore once again in the 1990s with his recent monograph on the history of scholarship regarding this Synoptic-Johannine relationship.[3] It is a task that I accepted with pleasure, as a most suitable way of honoring a scholar and gentleman with whose life my own had become curiously intertwined through the years, but also, I confess, with a certain measure of anxiety and trepidation, given a fundamental shift in my thinking with regard to the topic in question.[4]

A word of explanation is in order. Were I writing this study around 1980, my approach and position would be quite different than they are today. The reason is not hard to explain. Not only has the discipline changed, but I too have changed as reader and critic. In effect, the intervening years have witnessed the collapse and displacement of historical criticism as the controlling paradigm in biblical criticism, a position of dominance it had enjoyed since before the century, and the corresponding emergence and development of a number of competing paradigms, which I would describe in terms of literary criticism, cultural criticism, and ideological criticism or cultural studies.[5] This fundamental shift in theory and methodology began in the mid- to late 1970s with the joint appearance of literary criticism and cultural criticism, solidified through the 1980s as both of these paradigms became increasingly popular and sophisticated, and has, I would argue, been undergoing a further expansion and transformation since the late 1980s with the emergence of cultural studies.

Thus, were I writing around 1980 I would still be doing so, by and large, as a practitioner of historical criticism, although very much aware already of certain newfangled developments in the field. Were I writing in the mid- to late 1980s, I would be writing as a subscriber to literary criticism, with an interest in both narrative criticism and rhetorical criticism and the development of a literary-rhetorical approach. Writing as I am in the mid-1990s, I do so as an adherent to cultural studies—with a certain measure of sophistication in historical, literary, and cultural criticism, to be sure, but also with a great deal of interest in the real readers and critics behind all readings and reading strategies.

In effect, I find myself not only having argued different positions at different times but also presently holding a rather minimalist stance regarding the topic as traditionally conceived. While enough to give anyone pause, such a situation also provides a marvelous opportunity for self-analysis as reader and critic. Indeed, given my present theoretical moorings in cultural studies, I propose to deal with the task at hand by way of a hermeneutical reflection: What happens to tradition criticism in the light of this ongoing shift in the discipline, which causes such consternation in me as reader and critic when asked to write about it with reference to the Fourth Gospel? To do so, I find it necessary to engage in metatheory, a theoretical discussion about theory itself and thus about the various competing paradigms. In so doing, I hope to show that any approach to the topic ultimately depends on the reader's own reading strategy and theoretical framework—on how real readers read and interpret the text—thus revealing as much about the text as about its readers and readings. I conclude with some personal reflections on the topic in the light of the preceding discussion.

TRADITION CRITICISM—THEN AND NOW

I begin, then, by examining the practice and discourse of tradition criticism as viewed from three different models and perspectives in contemporary biblical criticism, with special reference throughout to tradition criticism in Johannine scholarship and its resulting view of the tradition history of the Fourth Gospel. I should add that I do so from an autobiographical, and hence, emic perspective: that is to say, from the point of view of an insider, an active participant, at one time or another in these critical paradigms.

Tradition Criticism and Historical Criticism

Tradition criticism was one of several methodological approaches—along with, for example, source criticism, history-of-religions criticism, form criticism, redaction criticism, and composition criticism—comprised by and practiced under the paradigm or umbrella model of interpretation known as historical criticism.[6] As such, it shared in the fundamental reading strategy of historical criticism, characterized by such elements as the following: (1) a view of the text as means, as historical evidence from and for the time of composition; (2) a view of meaning as residing either in the world represented by the text or in the intention of the author of the text, or both; (3) a view of the text as the result of a process of accretion and redaction, with different layers coming from different stages and reflecting/engaging different (theological) situations; (4) a view of the final and present version of the text as problematic, if not altogether unintelligible, given the presence of abundant aporias (any type of perceived unevenness, difficulty, or contradiction, whether of a textual, literary, or conceptual [theological] nature); (5) a view of reading as largely vertical in character, calling for careful separation and reconstruction of the various layers of a text, often at variance if not outright conflict with one another, and a reading of these layers from the ground up.

Within this interpretive framework, it was the task of tradition criticism to trace the various stages of "tradition" present in the text—whether in the form of discrete units, extended passages, or lengthy sections—from the ground to the surface, from the earliest stage of the text to its final and existing version. As such, tradition criticism availed itself of form, source, and redaction criticisms as it sought to tie together the results of these various approaches in some sort of logical, developmental pattern, involving both history and theology. In so doing, tradition criticism set out to shed light not only on the overall process of composition of the text—how it came together as it did, from stage to stage—but also on each stage of composition by means of the text in question at that stage—why it came together in the way that it did.[7] Its overriding concern was thus twofold: What had happened to the tradition in question from stage to stage as it eventually reached its present form? How could this be explained in terms of what was happening in the world behind the text, in the Johannine "community"? The result was a historical-theological reconstruction of the community, as reflected in the text.

In the case of the Gospel of John, critical studies engaged in enormous speculation about the different stages of its formation, yielding an amazing variation of theories revolving around what may be referred to as three main phases of this history: (1) the pre-Gospel stage, involving the oral traditions and written sources behind the Gospel, the earliest version of the Gospel narrative and the various redactions of this early narrative; (2) the Gospel stage, with its focus on a fairly complete version of the Gospel narrative, usually characterized as the stage of the "evangelist"; and (3) a post-Gospel stage, involving a number of later additions to this existing version of the narrative and leading up to its final and present version.[8] Such rampant speculation, it should be noted, could find little grounds for support in the actual textual history of the narrative itself.

Within such an excavative framework of research, my own interests and convictions at that time lay not so much in phase (1) of the pattern, which I regarded as highly unlikely and unpromising, as in phases (2) and (3)—the question of final additions to an already fairly complete Gospel narrative in the light of changing (theological) conditions within the Johannine "community"—no doubt as a result of the influence of redaction and composition criticisms, which by the 1970s had become quite prominent within historical criticism. I argued that as new (theological) problems arose, whether with regard to belief or practice and involving even the interpretation of the existing Gospel itself, certain additions were made in order to address such problems. From the point of view of historical criticism, therefore, I would have undertaken this assignment with the purpose in mind of showing how certain units or sections of the Gospel prove incoherent as they presently stand, because they have in effect been "revised" by a later hand or group of hands with specific (theological) reasons in mind, yielding in the end the present text with all of its attendant problems.[9] I would have attempted to separate the different layers in question, reconstruct the earlier or "Gospel" version, show how the later versions had been incorporated into the text, and explain the need for, and results of, such revisions within the context of the Johannine historical situation. The history of the composition of the text would have functioned thereby as the key to the history of the Johannine community behind the text. Suffice it to say that this I did for several years and with regard to a number of different texts.[10]

Tradition Criticism and Literary Criticism

The advent of literary criticism brought a new paradigm or umbrella model of interpretation—encompassing such different methodological approaches as, for example, narrative criticism, rhetorical criticism, psychoanalytical criticism, structural criticism, and reader-response criticism—with an altogether new mode of discourse to biblical criticism. Its fundamental reading strategy may be summarized as follows: (1) a view of the text as medium, as a message from author to reader with an emphasis on the principles that govern the formal aspects of such communication; (2) a view of meaning as residing largely in the text itself and ranging from a text-dominant pole, with an emphasis on intratextual author-constructs and textual constraints, to a reader-dominant pole, with an emphasis on textual constraints and intratextual reader-constructs; (3) a view of the text as a literary and rhetorical whole, largely bypassing in practice any notion of a process of accretion and redaction but without ruling it out altogether in principle; (4) a view of the final and present version of the text as unified and coherent, with a focus on its artistic and strategic features and its intertextuality, both internal and external; and (5) a view of reading as horizontal in nature, following the order and sequence of the narrative from beginning to end and attentive to the very process of reading itself.

One can readily see how the established discourse and practice of tradition criticism would be directly and severely affected by such a different interpretive framework, given the shift away from textual disruption to textual smoothness, from a problematic and unintelligible text to a unified and coherent text, from a reading in search of stages of composition to a reading in search of arrangement and development, from a text that reflected/engaged the situation of the community to a text that became an object of attention in its own right. Quite simply, the task of tradition criticism would be either sharply curtailed, reduced to those instances of salient and inescapable aporias in the text, or pursued along the lines of intertextual research, by way of textual connections to other parts of the text as well as to other texts. The focus would lie no longer on the historical process of composition and its various stages of formation but rather on the literary process of composition with its artistic devices, strategic concerns and aims, and intertextual echoes or references.

In terms of Johannine scholarship, critical attention turned largely away from redactional theories to an analysis of the Gospel as it presently stood, focusing on what Alan Culpepper aptly characterized as the "anatomy" of the Gospel:[11] reading different units and sections of the Gospel as well as the Gospel itself as unified and coherent, often arguing in the process that the proposed aporias of the past were actually not so at all, either by dismissing them altogether or "revisioning" them as literary devices; and turning to the practical side of reading, the effects of the text on the reader, by way of intratextual reader-constructs such as the implied reader, the informed reader, the ideal reader, and so on. As a result, talk of layers and stages was reduced to a minimum as the present text was subjected to meticulous formal analysis.

Within such an integrative framework of research, my interests and convictions turned to questions of a literary and rhetorical nature. I now sought to show the unity and coherence of the text in question, its spatial design and verbal texture, even with regard to units and sections that I had earlier read as unintelligible in their present form. I spoke of close readings, implied authors and implied readers, narrative world and features as well as strategic concerns and aims. From the point of view of literary criticism, then, I would have pursued the present assignment in one of two ways: first, by focusing on those instances in the narrative where I still failed to see coherence and unity, providing in the process a redactional type of resolution, an explanation in terms of addition and revision, and venturing a rationale in terms of implied authors and readers as well as strategic concerns and aims; second, by exploring the intertextuality at work between the Fourth Gospel and other writings of the period, such as the Synoptic Gospels. Again, this was something that I did for several years and with reference to a number of different passages, including the narrative as a whole.[12]

Tradition Criticism and Cultural Studies

In more recent times a new paradigm or umbrella model of interpretation has begun to find its way into biblical criticism, in part due to certain developments within both literary and cultural criticisms themselves but also, and above all, due to the influx into the discipline of individuals who had never been a part of it before and who were now making their voices heard for the first time: Western women, non-Western readers and critics, and racial/ethnic minorities in the West. On the one hand, therefore, certain theoretical developments were bringing biblical criticism face-to-face with such issues as the polysemy of language, the role of the reader, methodological and theoretical pluralism, and the multiplicity of interpretations. At the same time and on the other hand, certain sociocultural developments were also forcing biblical criticism to deal with the questions of perspective in reading and interpretation, of a multiplicity of readers—real or flesh-and-blood readers—and of the impact of social location on interpreters and interpretation. It is this emerging paradigm, with its twofold focus on texts and readers, that I refer to as cultural studies or ideological criticism.

Its fundamental reading strategy may be described as follows: (1) a view of the text as construction, a reality or world with its own perspective and underlying social location, with an emphasis on the different aspects of such construction; (2) a view of meaning as construction, a "text," the result of an interchange between a contextualized text and a contextualized reader, with the latter as an unavoidable filter in the reading of such a text; (3) a view of the text that neither rules out a process of accretion nor insists on unity and coherence; (4) a view of the final and present version of the text as a construct worth analyzing in its own right, whether ultimately perceived as unified or diffuse; (5) a view of reading as construction, involving a strategy and calling for awareness and analysis of its underlying principles.

Within such a hermeneutical or interpretive framework, the discourse and practice of tradition criticism again take on a very different aspect altogether. In a sense, the question is no longer whether a ground-to-surface reading or a beginning-to-end reading of the text is to be preferred, although to be sure such a decision still remains necessary for any reading, but, rather, why do such different readings of the text—such different "texts"—exist in the first place: Why find rupture rather than smoothness? Why argue for unintelligibility instead of unity and coherence? Why look for historical stages of composition rather than the formal principles of composition? Why opt for one reading strategy instead of another? Such questions ultimately lead to other questions as well: What is the perspective of the reading? What is its underlying social location? Who is the real, flesh-and-blood reader behind it?

With regard to the Gospel of John, critical attention would encompass not only a reading of the Gospel as such—the production of a "text"—but also a reading of other readings of the Gospel—other such "texts." It would also include not only an analysis of the text as a construct, with its own perspective and social location, but also an analysis of such a "text"—such a reading—and other such "texts" in terms of perspective, underlying social location, and the real readers behind them. Indeed, any analysis would be called upon to furnish as complete an account as possible of methodological approach, theoretical orientation, and social location.

Within such a hermeneutical framework, my own interests and convictions have undergone yet another shift. I now speak of texts as I do of readings of texts and readers of texts: as literary or artistic products, rhetorical or strategic products, and ideological or cultural products. I now include within the optic of criticism all three of these dimensions, calling thereby for engagement with interpretation, hermeneutics, and ideology: analysis of texts; analysis of "texts"; and analysis of readers of texts.[13] In fact, I have undertaken the present assignment from the point of view of cultural studies. Thus, I have endeavored to show the discourse and practice of tradition criticism within different umbrella models of interpretation; I have laid bare the theoretical and methodological principles at work in each of the three models; and I have described my own activity vis-à-vis the Gospel of John within the parameters of each model.

TRADITION HISTORY OF THE FOURTH GOSPEL

I would argue, in the light of the preceding hermeneutical reflections, that any account of the tradition history of the Fourth Gospel will largely depend on the one responding to the question and on what interpretive framework and reading strategy such a reader follows in approaching the topic—for example, whether such an approach is predisposed toward aporias in the text, oriented towards unity and coherence, or interested in questions of strategies and "texts." In other words, there is no final, definitive answer but a variety of approaches and stances. What follows is an exposition of my own stance by way of personal reflections.

I cannot begin but with the undeniable fact that I myself have held different positions at different times regarding this question, even with reference to the same narrative units or sections in the Gospel. While I could explain this phenomenon in terms of correct and incorrect readings of the text, due to correspondingly correct or incorrect methods of analysis—as I might well have done in the past—I prefer to speak in terms of different readings or "texts" (different reading strategies yielding different interpretations) by different "readers" within me (different facets of the same, real reader as affected by different intellectual currents at different times). For me, therefore, it is not a question of understanding or misunderstanding the "real" meaning of the text but rather of producing different understandings of the text, different "texts." The situation, as such, is not at all one of profound embarrassment but rather one of creative anagnorisis.

I continue with the further, undeniable fact that I have made choices with regard to reading strategies, adopting some while discarding others along the way. In other words, the lived reality of a plurality of interpretations does not absolve the reader from making fundamental decisions in theory and method, which in turn affect the reading and interpretation of texts. It does force the reader, however, to become quite conscious of the reading strategies involved and the reasons for their adoption.

In this regard I readily avow that I find myself less and less favorably disposed toward those approaches to the Gospel that highlight the disruptive character of the text and use perceived aporias as a key point of departure for reading the text.[14] In fact, the more liberally such a technique is invoked, the less receptive I become. Why? I would respond that by and large I find that the proposed aporias can be readily explained in other—and, I would add, simpler—ways. As such, I tend to see the Gospel at present not so much in terms of a process of accretion and redaction but rather, as a fairly unitary and consistent product. Not entirely, however. I still wrestle back and forth with a couple of sections—specifically, chapters 15—16 and chapter 21—where despite perceived smoothness within their respective narrative contexts, I find myself reluctant to give up altogether on the presence of disruptive aporias.

Such a position clearly indicates that I now see far more unity and coherence in the text, that I can explain the way it has been put together without recourse to the concept of constitutive literary layers. To that extent, it should go without saying that I still remain clearly influenced by the focus on unity and coherence, central to much of literary criticism—up to a point, however. I do not mean to say that aside from the two instances mentioned above, I see no contradictions, no tensions, no dissenting voices in the text. What I do mean to say is that I regard such other "aporias" as neither dismantling the overall unity and coherence of the text—whether at the literary, rhetorical, or ideological level—nor requiring the introduction of constitutive literary layers, but rather as points of tension in the construct.

At the same time, I would hasten to emphasize that while I see such unity and coherence in the text, *I* am the one who is seeing such features in the text. In other words, my argument is not that I have unveiled the real meaning of the text (its actual structure, arrangement, and development) or discovered the intention of the author (whether realized or intended), but that I can advance such a reading of the text in the light of the evidence, the textual features and constraints, that I find in it. Such an interpretation, such a reading or "text," I would add, ultimately reflects my own social location as a reader and critic, and not just in terms of intellectual currents. To this extent the influence of cultural studies upon me should be clear as well: My proposed reading of the Gospel ultimately says as much about me as about the Gospel, if not more.

Finally, with regard to the question of the tradition history of the Fourth Gospel per se, I would respond as follows. First, concerning different stages of the Johannine tradition in the formation of the Gospel, I would limit myself—and reluctantly so—to the possibility of a later redaction of the narrative in terms of chapters 15—16 and chapter 21. Such additions I would explain in terms of perceived changes in the rhetorical situation of the implied readers by the implied author of the Gospel. Second, concerning other texts including the Synoptic Gospels, I would argue for the use of an informed theory of intertextuality, with a focus on modes, kinds, and techniques of intertextual referencing.[15]

In conclusion, I would argue for a minimalist view of the tradition history of the Fourth Gospel in terms of a theory of composition and redaction, and a maximalist view of the use of tradition in the Fourth Gospel, in terms of a theory of intertextuality. I do so, moreover, quite conscious of the fact that this is not the only position I have taken; of the reading strategy and theoretical framework that guide and inform my present position; of the fact that such a position forms part of my own reading or "text," my own construction, of the Fourth Gospel; as well as of the ultimate relationship that exists between this position and my own social location as a flesh-and-blood reader and critic. More than that I cannot argue. Such is, in my opinion, the nature of contemporary biblical criticism, for better or for worse—and with a resounding vote for the former option, on my part.

NOTES

1. Published in slightly revised form as *The Composition and Order of the Fourth Gospel: Bultmann's Literary Analysis,* Yale Publications in Religion 10 (New Haven, Conn., and London: Yale University Press, 1965). For a summary, see D. Moody Smith, "The Sources of the Gospel of John: An Assessment of the Present State of the Problem," *NTS* 10 (1964): 336–51.

2. From the point of view of pre-Johannine sources, see D. Moody Smith, "The Setting and Shape of a Johannine Narrative Source," *JBL* 95 (1976): 231–41, and idem, "The Milieu of the Johannine Miracle Source: A Proposal," in *Jews, Greeks, and Christians: Religious Cultures in Late Antiquity. Essays in Honor of William David Davies,* ed. Robert Hamerton-Kelly and Robin Scroggs, Studies in Judaism in Late Antiquity 21 (Leiden: Brill, 1976), 164–80. From the point of view of the Synoptics as sources, see D. Moody Smith, "John and the Synoptics: Some Dimension of the Problem," *NTS* 26 (1980): 425–44, and idem, "John and the Synoptics," *Bib* 63 (1982): 102–13.

3. D. Moody Smith, *John among the Gospels: The Relationship in Twentieth-Century Research* (Minneapolis: Fortress, 1992). See also idem, "The Problem of John and the Synoptics in Light of the Relation Between Apocryphal and Canonical Gospels," in *John and the Synoptics,* ed. Adelbert Denaux, BETL 101 (Leuven: Leuven University Press, 1992), 147–62.

4. Such intertwining also extends from the beginning of my own scholarly career through the recent past, from a very gracious review of my published dissertation for *Religious Studies Review* in 1982, to a letter of recommendation on my behalf during the process of promotion with tenure to the rank of Associate Professor in 1984, to another such letter during the process of promotion to the rank of Professor in 1991. Let the present study serve, therefore, as a small token of gratitude for such kind and much-appreciated deeds.

5. For an account of the rise and nature of these competing paradigms, see my " 'And They Began to Speak in Other Tongues': Competing Paradigms in Contemporary Biblical Criticism," in *Reading from This Place,* Volume 1: *Social Location and Biblical Interpretation in the United States,* ed. Fernando F. Segovia and Mary Ann Tolbert (Minneapolis: Fortress, 1995), 1–32; see also my "Cultural Studies and Contemporary

Biblical Criticism: Ideological Criticism as Mode of Discourse," in *Reading from This Place*, vol. 2: *Social Location and Biblical Interpretation in Global Perspective*, ed. Fernando F. Segovia and Mary Ann Tolbert (Minneapolis: Fortress, 1995), 1–17.

6. For its background and parameters, see, for example, John H. Hayes and Carl R. Holladay, *Biblical Exegesis: A Beginner's Handbook* (Atlanta: John Knox, 1982), 85–93 (chapter 7: "Tradition Criticism: The Stages behind the Text"), and Robert A. Di Vito, "Tradition-Historical Criticism," in *To Each Its Own Meaning: An Introduction to Biblical Criticisms and Their Application*, ed. Steven L. McKenzie and Stephen R. Haynes (Louisville: Westminster/John Knox, 1993), 53–67.

7. Another task of tradition criticism was to trace the "tradition" in question not only across the different stages of composition of a text but also across a variety of texts, wherever it surfaced. The goal, once again, was to establish some sort of logical, developmental pattern involving both history and theology: How did the tradition change from text to text as it did, and why?

8. From the point of view of tradition criticism across different texts (see n. 7 above), there was also a great deal of speculation regarding extra-Johannine sources, especially with respect to the Synoptic Gospels: Did the fourth evangelist know the Synoptics and make use of them? If so, how?

9. I could have also addressed the question of extra-Johannine traditions, especially the relationship between John and the Synoptics.

10. Among such later additions I included John 6:51b–59; 13:12–20; 15—17; and 21, along with a few other verses here and there. In retrospect, one instance stands out as particularly egregious in this regard. I undertook at one point a study of the theme of discipleship in the Gospel (" 'Peace I Leave with You; My Peace I Give to You': Discipleship in the Fourth Gospel," in *Discipleship in the New Testament*, ed. Fernando F. Segovia [Philadelphia: Fortress, 1985], 76–102) by leaving out a number of crucial texts which I took to be late additions and concentrating instead on what I took to be the original, finished Gospel narrative. In other words, I set out to define discipleship in John not according to the Gospel as it presently stands but rather, according to my view of an earlier, unrevised version of that Gospel! See also idem, *Love Relationships in the Johannine Tradition: Agape/Agapan in 1 John and the Fourth Gospel*, SBLDS 58 (Chico, Calif.: Scholars Press, 1982); idem, "John 13:1–20, The Footwashing in the Johannine Tradition," *ZNW* 73 (1982): 31–51; idem, "The Structure, *Tendenz*, and *Sitz im Leben* of John 13:31–14:31," *JBL* 104 (1985): 471–93.

11. A term that served as the very title of his work: *Anatomy of the Fourth Gospel: A Study in Literary Design*, Foundations and Facets: New Testament (Philadelphia: Fortress, 1983).

12. Three particular instances stand out. First, whereas from my dissertation on I had argued for textual ruptures of all sorts, I would now argue for a clear and comprehensive plot to the Gospel. Second, whereas I had similarly regarded the long farewell discourse of chapters 14—17 as a series of originally independent texts, I would now argue, with reservations, for literary unity and coherence for the chapters as a whole. Finally, whereas I had always looked upon chapter 21 as a late addition to the Gospel, I would now proceed to show how it fit into the narrative as it presently stood. See my studies, *The Farewell of the Word: The Johannine Call to Abide* (Minneapolis: Fortress, 1991); "The Journey(s) of the Word: A Reading of the Plot of the Fourth Gospel" and "The Final Farewell of Jesus: A Reading of John 20:30–21:25,"

in *The Fourth Gospel from a Literary Perspective*, ed. R. Alan Culpepper and Fernando F. Segovia, *Semeia* 53 (1991): 23–54 and 167–90, respectively.

13. See, e.g., Fernando F. Segovia, "Toward a Hermeneutic of the Diaspora: A Hermeneutics of Otherness and Engagement," in *Reading from This Place*, 1:57–74; idem, "Toward Intercultural Criticism: A Reading Strategy from the Diaspora," in *Reading from This Place*, 2:304–31; idem, "The Text as Other: Toward a Hispanic American Hermeneutics," in *Text and Experience: Toward a Cultural Criticism of the Bible*, ed. Daniel Smith (Sheffield: JSOT Press, 1995), 276–88.

14. Although not as plentiful as they once were, such approaches are still very much around: Robert T. Fortna, *The Fourth Gospel and Its Predecessor: From Narrative Source to Present Gospel* (Minneapolis: Fortress, 1988); Urban C. von Wahlde, *The Earliest Version of John's Gospel: Recovering the Gospel of Signs*, Good News Studies 30 (Wilmington, Del.: Michael Glazier, 1989); John Ashton, *Understanding the Fourth Gospel* (Oxford: Clarendon, 1991).

15. See, for example, my own attempt in this regard ("The Journey(s) of Jesus to Jerusalem: Plotting and Gospel Intertextuality," in *John and the Synoptics*, ed. Denaux, 535–41) where I favor the knowledge and use of one or more of the Synoptic Gospels by the Fourth Gospel.

Part Three

Literary Aspects
of John's Gospel

R. Alan Culpepper

10

Reading Johannine Irony

Tracing developments over the past fifteen years in the interpretation of irony in the Gospel of John reminds one of the rapid technological advances we have witnessed during this same period. Although the fourth evangelist had been characterized as a master of irony, at the time I wrote *Anatomy of the Fourth Gospel* there was neither a monograph nor a definitive article on the subject of irony in John.[1] Since the publication of *Anatomy* in 1983, a full-length monograph and various briefer studies have advanced and altered our understanding of Johannine irony. This essay will summarize and comment on these developments, thereby providing a synopsis of the study of Johannine irony. Moody Smith has been for me and for many of his other students a beloved mentor who has encouraged the reexamination of established positions and the exploration of new directions in New Testament scholarship. It is appropriate, therefore, that in honoring him we reassess some of the new directions being taken in this area of Johannine studies. The interpretation of Johannine irony has moved across the spectrum of critical approaches, from the beginnings of Johannine narrative criticism, to reader-response interpretations, deconstruction, and poststructuralism. These developments will be examined, a response to poststructuralist readings of Johannine irony will be offered, and the essay will conclude with suggestions for further research.

A PLACE TO BEGIN

As the basis for understanding irony, I used the works of D. C. Muecke and Wayne Booth, neither of whom had been cited in previous work on Johannine irony.[2] Booth draws a clear distinction between stable and unstable ironies. Stable ironies are (1) intended, (2) covert (they require reconstruction), (3) stable or fixed, and (4) finite, in that they do not mock our effort to find meaning. With stable ironies, "once a reconstruction of meaning has been made, the reader is not then invited to undermine it with further demolitions and reconstructions. That he may choose to do so on his own, and thus render any stable irony unstable, is irrelevant."[3] With unstable ironies, by contrast, "the truth asserted or implied is that no stable reconstruction can be made out of the ruins revealed through the irony. The author—insofar as we can discover him, and he is often very remote indeed—refuses to declare himself, however subtly, *for* any stable proposition."[4] As we will see, the distinction between stable and unstable ironies has become pivotal in the interpretation of Johannine irony.

Drawing upon Muecke and Booth, I interpreted Johannine irony as covert (that is, intended for reconstruction) but stable. It draws the reader into affirming the perspective of the narrator that is sketched by the prologue and that conditions the reading experience of the rest of the Gospel. As with most ironies, John's typically has three participants: the ironist, a victim, and the observer or reader. As basic features of all irony, Muecke identifies "(i) a contrast of appearance and reality, (ii) a confident unawareness (pretended in the ironist, real in the victim of the irony) that the appearance is only an appearance, and (iii) the comic effect of this unawareness of a contrasting appearance and reality."[5] The Johannine Jesus explicitly admonishes his followers, "Do not judge by appearances, but judge with right judgment" (7:24).

Muecke and Booth liken the experience of reading irony to that of being called from a lower level of understanding to a higher one. This leap entails four steps: the reader must "(1) reject the literal meaning, (2) recognize alternative interpretations, (3) decide about the author's knowledge or beliefs, and (4) choose a new meaning which is in harmony with the (implied) author's position."[6] From the higher level, one can also look down on "those who dwell in error," the victims of the irony.[7] Again, such a theory of irony almost echoes the Fourth Gospel itself, wherein the Johannine Jesus is from above and those who are below live in error because they cannot understand: "You are from below, I am from above; you are of this world, I am not of this world. I told you that you would die in your sins, for you will die in your sins unless you believe that I am he" (8:23–24).

Following the pattern of the tragic poets (especially Euripides), John begins with a prologue that establishes the Olympian vantage point from which the reader views the spectacle: The reader is told the true identity of Jesus from the outset. Jesus is the Word that has become flesh. Speaking for the Johannine community, the narrator testifies, "and we have beheld his glory" (1:14). All that Jesus does and says in the course of the narrative serves to confirm the narrator's perspective. In episode after episode the reader watches, secure in this knowledge, while the characters around Jesus stumble and fail to grasp his true identity (for example, "If you knew the gift of God, and who it is that is saying to you, 'Give me a drink,' you would have asked him, and he would have given you living water" [4:10]). Because of the prologue, therefore, the reader is repeatedly able to reconstruct the veiled meanings and to accept the narrator's invitation to move to the higher plane of understanding. Meanwhile, unanswered questions are allowed to hang there, calling for the truth, while the characters make false assumptions, prophesy the truth without knowing it, reason falsely, or naively make statements that convey meanings they do not suspect.[8]

The Gospel of John treats six themes ironically: (1) the rejection of Jesus, (2) the origin of Jesus, (3) Jesus' identity, (4) Jesus' ministry, (5), Jesus' death, and (6) discipleship.[9] The effect of John's irony is to provide a subtle but powerful incentive for the reader to believe "that Jesus is the Christ, the Son of God" (20:31). Reading irony involves the reader in an intellectual dance with the narrator that creates a community of shared perspectives: "Never is the reader the victim of irony."[10] Nor is the reliable narrator ever the victim of John's irony. On the contrary, its strongest effect is inclusion. Irony draws the reader and the narrator together in a community of faith, a whole new (and higher) plane of existence.

JOHANNINE IRONY AS STABLE: AN IRON WHY

Paul D. Duke both informed the section on irony in *Anatomy of the Fourth Gospel* through some of his preliminary work and later amplified it in his dissertation, *Irony in the Fourth Gospel* (1985).[11] Duke's work is still the most detailed and sustained treatment of the subject to date—and it is delightful reading. After introductory chapters on the meaning and functions of irony, Duke examines within John local irony (isolated sayings), extended irony (through ironic characterization, identity, and imagery), and two examples of sustained irony (the man born blind and the trial before Pilate). The concluding chapter comments on the functions of irony in the Johannine context.

Probably the greatest contribution of *Irony in the Fourth Gospel* is its attention to the techniques or devices used to set up irony in John. For example, when the Johannine Jesus uses irony, it usually takes the form of an unanswered question in which word position and repetition are important: "Are you a teacher of Israel, and yet you do not understand these things?" (3:10; see also 10:23, 32). The disciples stand between Jesus and the world. While they are, therefore, occasionally victims of the Gospel's irony, they do not usually manifest the same degree of arrogance as the religious authorities and Pilate. Duke gives examples of the various ways in which the disciples' "innocent unawareness" is exposed: (1) false assumption: "Can anything good come out of Nazareth?" (1:46); (2) misunderstanding: "Yes, now you are speaking plainly, not in any figure of speech!" (16:29); (3) superficial confession: "Now we know that you know all things, and do not need to have anyone question you; by this we believe that you have come from God" (16:30); (4) false promise: "Let us also go, that we may die with him" (11:16).[12] Among the verbal devices used to set up these local ironies one finds questions and repetitions of Jesus' words (either verbatim or with a crucial omission, or repetitions of ἵνα- ["in order that"] clauses that substitute an opposing verb).

"Typical Johannine irony," however, is found in what Duke calls "words from the dark," the words unbelievers say to or about Jesus.[13] Here the irony is set up by (1) false claims to knowledge: "Is not this Jesus, the son of Joseph, whose father and mother we know? How can he now say, 'I have come down from heaven'"? (John 6:42; see also 7:27, 41b–42, 52b; 9:29); (2) false assumptions: "Are you greater than our ancestor Jacob?" (4:12; also see 7:15; 8:53, 57); (3) accusations, whether of demon possession, Samaritan origins, or violation of the law: "Give glory to God! We know that this man is a sinner" (9:24; see also 7:19–20; 8:41; 9:16; 18:30); (4) suggestions of belief: "Can it be that the authorities really know that this is the Messiah?" (7:26; also 7:47–48, 52); "Do you also want to become his disciples?" (9:27); (5) unconscious prophecy and testimony: "If we let him go on like this, everyone will believe in him, and the Romans will come and destroy both our holy place and our nation" (11:48–50; see also 2:10; 7:3–4, 35–36; 8:22; 12:19). Again, the implied author has used questions, declarative statements, and silence to communicate irony. Among the indicators of irony in these contexts, Duke finds repetition, the emphatic pronoun, the derogatory demonstrative, the boastful claim that "we know," and questions prefaced by the negative particle μή. When Jesus' unbelieving interlocutors attempt sarcasm, what the speakers intend as overstatement is perceived by the reader as literal truth or understatement. Another typical tool of irony is the Johannine double meaning.[14] By examining local irony in John, Duke discovers that "different speakers deliver a different type or degree of irony": "form follows theme."[15]

By "extended irony" Duke means the irony that surrounds Jesus' identity throughout much of the Gospel (for example, in the conversation with the woman at the well [chap. 4]) and John's use of ironic imagery (thus Judas "went out and it was night," John 13:30; the soldiers came with lanterns and torches to arrest "the light of the world," 8:12; 18:3). At its heart Johannine theology is ironic, in that it assumes a profound dualism:

> Two worlds have collided in the coming of Jesus, and the inevitable result is the clash of opposition called irony. Human ignorance clashes with divine omniscience, religious institutions clash with "spirit and truth," surface meaning clashes with hidden meaning, appearance clashes with reality. Fundamentally, then, there is irony in John's most basic assertion that "the Word became flesh and dwelt among us" (1:14). . . . Perhaps the most obvious of John's ironic incongruities is summarized in 1:11, "He came to his own and his own received him not."[16]

Among the techniques the Gospel uses for extended ironies, Duke identifies repeating a word associated with a character, "but the second time with a different significance ('the poor' — 12:5; 13:29; and 'charcoal fire' — 18:18; 21:9),"[17] and ironically playing different nuances of a term off one another ("follow," "man," "thirst").

Duke's chapter on "sustained narrative irony" examines two passages in which John's dramatic artistry finds its clearest expression: the healing of the man born blind (John 9) and the trial before Pilate (18:28–19:16, 19–22). Duke's final chapter assesses the functions of Johannine irony in the Johannine context. He perceptively observes that Johannine irony "gives witness to a religious setting shaped by Judaism and a cultural setting influenced by Hellenism. . . . [I]t represents *primarily Hellenistic technique* employed to treat *themes of primarily Jewish concern.*"[18] The unwitting speeches of John's characters are more akin to the techniques one finds in Greek drama than to the use of irony in the Old Testament. John's narrative irony also suggests that the Johannine community was one "particularly shaped by writing": "it reflects far more than do the Synoptics a way of thinking that has been chirographically conditioned."[19] In the context of the Johannine community, irony functions both as a weapon and as a witness. John's irony both assumes and creates a community of understanding and a shared idiom. It calls on those who are "secret believers" to identify publicly with the Johannine community.

Beyond its dramatic power and its developed techniques, however, John's use of irony is "testimony to a unique vision of the Christ-event," a vision that "has perceived in the Christ-event itself something fundamentally ironic" arising from the life and death of Jesus of Nazareth. Consequently, "If John punctuates his witness to Jesus with an occasional wink or grin or tear, if he now and then falls into awesome silence, it is ultimately because there is no better way to tell his story."[20]

For Paul Duke, therefore, John's irony is constructed both on the historical tradition of Jesus' ministry and on the dramatic form of the Greek tragedians. Following the lead of *Anatomy of the Fourth Gospel,* and using the categories proposed by Muecke and Booth, Duke finds Johannine irony to be generally covert, local and sustained, but always stable. In the reading of the Gospel, the reader repeatedly rehearses the leap of faith, ascending from the lower level of perception to the higher until he or she is moved to affirm the narrator's ironic vision of the Christ-event.

Subsequent studies have commended Duke's work while moving in other directions. In *Revelation in the Fourth Gospel* (1986), Gail R. O'Day investigates how the fourth evangelist's use of irony provides "the appropriate vehicle for his theology of revelation."[21] Responding to Culpepper and Duke, O'Day contends that they put too much emphasis on the opposition between the Johannine dualities but neglected

> the ways in which John presents these dualities as *simultaneously* operative in the Gospel. John does not present a simple either/or situation. Through his use of irony, the Fourth Evangelist asks the reader to see the real meaning *in* and *through* the expressed meaning.[22]

O'Day develops this approach to Johannine irony by appealing to Booth and Muecke. With irony there is always conflict between the two levels of meaning, so that passage between them is not smooth: "The correct reading of irony involves a continual awareness of the 'felt presence and felt incongruity of both meanings.' Irony is not 'merely a matter of seeing a "true" meaning below a "false," but of seeing a double exposure on one plate.'"[23] The contradiction or incongruity may be detected in any of three areas: (1) the relationship between text and context (i.e., "the background out of which, in which, and for which the author writes"), (2) the relationship between text and co-text (the literary context created by the author through the use, for example, of comments or asides, parallelism between scenes, and passages in which a character uses irony in a way that the narrator uses it elsewhere), and (3) in the relationship between text and text (i.e., "between one level or aspect of the particular text or passage under consideration and another").[24] O'Day also emphasizes the inclusionary, community-building effect of irony over its exclusionary, victimizing effect.[25] Moreover, "irony is a mode of revelatory language," because it calls for the reader to make judgments about the truth of stated or implicit meanings. Consequently, "the operation of irony as revelatory language suggests that the locus of operation lies *in* the text itself. . . . [T]he literary form in which Jesus is presented as revealer in John is inseparable from the Johannine theology of revelation."[26] O'Day's analysis of irony leads her to regard the locus of revelation, for John, as lying in "the biblical text and in the world created by the words of that text."[27] In an extended analysis of John 4, O'Day demonstrates how the two levels of meaning (ἐν παροιμίας and ἐν παρρησίᾳ, the concealed meaning and the plain meaning) are simultaneously present. Indeed, throughout the Gospel the narrative present and future impinge on each other so that one sees both the earthly Jesus and his future glory.

At the risk of doing injustice to the numerous valuable insights that *Revelation in the Fourth Gospel* offers, for our purposes its primary contributions to the study of Johannine irony are that it calls attention to (1) the continuing significance of the two levels of meaning in narrative irony, (2) the way in which the tension between them leads the reader to participate in the revelatory process, and (3) the coherence between John's narrative mode and its theological claim.

While building on the view (shared by those whose work we have surveyed) that the Fourth Gospel constructs a reading experience that educates the reader in how to read the Gospel and leads the reader to share the perspective of the narrator, Jeffrey L. Staley's *The Print's First Kiss* (1988)[28] takes issue with the claim that "the Johannine narrator is neither unreliable nor deliberately suppressive" and that the reader is never the victim of John's irony.[29] Staley draws from John McKee[30] an understanding of the functions of reader victimization or reader entrapment. Staley, therefore, proposes that John's ironies are not only "stable" but "unstable."[31] The Gospel first creates an implied reader who is an insider by means of the prologue, thereby setting up the reader to make the same error that various characters commit when they assume that they know how to judge rightly but in fact do not. Subsequently, at various points, the narrator leads the reader to make false steps and then supplies a corrective perspective.[32] Through a series of such entrapments, the narrator leads the reader along the path of understanding.

The narrator begins by leading the reader to commit the mistakes of outsiders and gradually leads the reader to identify with the mistakes of the disciples. According to Staley, the tension between John 3:22 and 4:2 forces the reader to share the misperception of the Pharisees. John 4 is a parody of a type-scene, and parody is also a form of irony because it forces the reader to reject the surface meaning and to adopt "another, incongruous, and 'higher' meaning."[33] In John 7:1–10 the reader is led to make the same mistake as Jesus' unbelieving brothers: thinking that Jesus was not going up to Jerusalem for the festival. The confusion created by the narrative's reference to a second Bethany in John 10:40 — 11:18 (cf. 1:28), Staley contends, for the first time places the reader momentarily a step behind rather than ahead of the disciples. Similarly, by means of the surprise introduction of the Beloved Disciple in John 13, the reader is led to raise questions just at the time the disciples are puzzled by Jesus' statements about his betrayal and departure from them. The beginning of a new chapter after the apparent conclusion of the Gospel, at the end of John 20, again catches the reader by surprise: "there is more to his journey of faith than mere confession."[34] With Peter the reader must be taught the importance of joining the content of confession with the course of continual "following." By the end of the Gospel, therefore, the reader has been led to share in the position of the inner group of disciples.

As different as Staley's assessment of the role of Johannine irony is from that in *Anatomy of the Fourth Gospel,* the end result is the same: "with each victimization the implied reader has also been progressing in his journey of faith."[35] One may therefore question Staley's contention that the passages that entrap the reader are examples of unstable irony. Once clarified, the "higher meaning" is still "rock solid," and Johannine irony is still viewed as an important part of the narrative rhetoric by which the implied author leads the reader to share in his faith perspective.

JOHANNINE IRONY BECOMES UNSTABLE:
AN *EIRON* WITHOUT A WHY

By the mid-1980s, developments were well under way in other areas that would lead to a different set of readings of Johannine irony. Several interpreters have seized on the theme of living water and Jesus' thirst as he dies to argue that John's irony is neither as stable nor as constructive as earlier work would lead one to believe. Werner Kelber was the first to claim that the key to John's irony is "not its revelatory power, but its effectiveness in suspending meaning."[36] As an example of how irony prevents meaning from being present, Kelber pointed to the theme of water in John 4; 7:37–39; and 19:28. Although Jesus offers to provide living water, he does not fulfill this promise but rather himself succumbs to physical thirst. "As a result," Kelber comments, "the whole narrative buildup from the literal to the figurative meaning of water has collapsed, and the expected resolution of irony is thereby turned into a stark paradox."[37] Accordingly, irony is prevented from functioning as revelatory language, and the reader is confronted with "the paradoxical collapsing of death with life at the narrative culmination."[38]

In another essay Kelber extended his challenge to the stability of Johannine irony in an interpretation of the metaphor of bread in John 6. As the meaning of the metaphor is repeatedly transformed in that discourse from the material to the nonmaterial to the heavenly and then to the person of Jesus himself, the Jews are scandalized and marginalized. Johannine irony, therefore, creates outsiders as well as insiders: "The more irony is enforced, the more people are marginalized."[39] How much advantage has the reader over the characters when Jesus says, "It is the spirit that gives life; the flesh is useless. The words that I have spoken to you are spirit and life" (6:63)? The words of Jesus are themselves ironic transformations. The irony does not deliver clarity but is fundamentally unsettling; it introduces new conflicts. Consequently, "to focus exclusively on its revelatory aspects forecloses prematurely its narrative operations. In short, readers do not entirely escape irony's victimization."[40] It has often been observed that the basis of Johannine irony is the incarnation, the Word become flesh; Kelber, however, turns the irony of the incarnation in a different direction, contending that the Gospel is less successful than is often claimed in making clear the glory that is "concealed at best and invalidated at worst" by entering the realm of the flesh:

> For in the first place, signs, irony, and metaphor operate less as a "mode of revelatory language," but more as a way of suspending meaning. And secondly, once meaning is deferred, it can become entangled in narratological and grammatological complications without ever seeing the pure light of transparency. John's language, in all its signifying striving after diaphanous purity, reserves a wide margin of uncertainty for the characters in the story, and for the readers as well.[41]

In a brief section near the end of *Literary Criticism and the Gospels*,[42] Stephen D. Moore followed Kelber's lead, observing that in the case of the water imagery, the reader cannot keep the literal meaning separate from the figural meaning. Whereas O'Day insisted that the literal meaning cannot be abandoned once the reader has grasped the higher meaning, for Kelber and Moore "the two levels of meaning are collapsed."[43] Because the two cannot be cleanly separated, irony collapses into paradox. In the death scene the whole structure of Johannine irony collapses, because it is constructed on the distinction between the two levels of meaning. The two elide, annulling the capacity of Johannine irony to deliver a clear, stable vantage point from which the figurative or spiritual sense can be grasped.

Moore subsequently extended his suggestive glossing of Kelber's interpretation in a deconstructive analysis of the water imagery of John 4, 7, and 19.[44] Moore first notes that traditional readings of John 4 have been based on the woman's lack of awareness of her need for living water as well as physical water. Joining with the feminist interpreters who have read John 4 in a nonironic manner,[45] Moore refuses to assume that the woman is less perceptive than Jesus or any more in need. Jesus too has come to the well with both a physical need (thirst) and a figural one (that the woman desire the living water that he would give her). Jesus assumes that the living water is separate from the physical water and can be kept so, but Moore confesses, "For me, however, the real question is whether Jesus himself can keep the living water pure and clear, uncontaminated by the profane drinking water."[46]

When he says "I thirst" (19:28) at his death, Moore suggests that again Jesus has both a physical and a figural need, a thirst for water and a thirst to fulfill the scripture. The physical sense of water, dismissed earlier, now returns. The fulfillment of the higher need, the need to fulfill the scripture, cannot occur apart from the drinking of the ὄξος ("sour wine"; cf. Ps. 69[68]:22 LXX). The two levels of meaning elide: as Jesus dies, he hands over the spirit (his spirit or the Holy Spirit), and when the soldiers pierce his side, water and blood flow out (which is both literal and symbolic)—all of "which is to say that we cannot keep the literal clearly separate from the figurative in the end."[47] Jesus himself, therefore, has become the victim at the cross, not in the traditional sense but in the poststructuralist sense that the two levels of meaning, which he had maintained were separate, have collapsed into paradox.

Jesus would have given the Samaritan woman living water instead of the literal water she had come seeking; if, however, one reads her as a perceptive dialogue partner rather than as an imperceptive victim, she holds the two senses together: "Sir, give me this water, *so that I may never be thirsty* or *have to keep coming here to draw water*" (4:15). Moore concludes, therefore,

> She has insisted, in effect, that earthly and heavenly, flesh and Spirit, figurative and literal, are symbiotically related categories: each drinks endlessly of the other, and so each is endlessly contaminated by the other. To draw a clear line between them, as Jesus attempts to do, is about as effective as drawing a line on water.[48]

In the view of Kelber and Moore, the once stable structure of Johannine irony has collapsed into paradoxical instability. The text undermines its own edifice of meaning, and ultimately it is not just the unsuspecting characters who are victims of Johannine irony but the readers, Jesus, and the implied author as well.

RESPONSE: THE *EIRON'S* WHYS IN THE CRITIC'S EYES

The course of scholarship on Johannine irony has followed the general course of critical theory. It blossomed with the shift of attention from historical to literary issues. The developments we have traced reflect the evolution of critical theory from new criticism to reader response, then to poststructuralist and deconstructive readings of the Fourth Gospel. In spite of the distinctive perspective of each interpreter, two opposing viewpoints have emerged regarding Johannine irony. Culpepper, Duke, O'Day, and Staley find John's irony to be essentially stable, a part of the Gospel's education of the reader, and the "revelatory mode" whereby the reader is led to see who Jesus is and to share the perspective of the Johannine narrator. For Kelber and Moore, on the other hand, the Fourth Gospel eventually undermines such a reading of its irony. At the death of Jesus the distinction between the physical and figural is blurred, so that the reader is prevented from moving confidently to the figural meaning that was offered to the reader earlier in the Gospel.

As we have seen, the linchpin in the argument that Johannine irony ultimately collapses into paradox is Jesus' statement, "I thirst" (John 19:28). This simplest and most primal of statements (one four-letter word in Greek: διψῶ) permits no simple reading. Like all metaphorical, symbolic, and ironic statements, it leads the reader to look beyond its surface meaning. It is entirely plausible that a crucified man would thirst. Both the immediate and the larger context in John, however, suggest further meanings. In John 19:28 itself the narrator comments parenthetically that Jesus said this "in order to fulfill the scripture." Nevertheless, the scripture reference is lacking, in contrast to the quotation of Ps. 22:19 in John 19:24, and the quotation of Ex. 12:46 in John 19:36 and of Zech. 12:10 in John 19:37.

Robert Brawley has called attention to the various ways in which intertextuality may function in the Fourth Gospel's allusion to scripture.[49] The new text does not merely replace its precursor: "Rather, a reference to an old text locates the modern interpreter in a tensive ambiance of echoes between the two texts, and the question is how the two texts reverberate with each other."[50] Brawley observes, in addition, that intertextuality functions in much the same way as metaphors. The echo between the two texts, like the play between words, produces meanings that lie beyond the meaning of either text by itself. As with metaphors, the meaning may be either *epiphoric* (an expanded meaning) or *diaphoric* (a new meaning created by "evoking a new way of construing what we comprehend").[51] In the case of John 19:28, the precursor text is undefined and uncertain. Brawley argues forcefully that the precursor text is Ps. 69:21; nevertheless, the narrator has left the reference undefined so that the reader must make the identification or simply accept the assertion that scripture is being fulfilled. How do the effects of intertextuality differ in situations where the precursor text is not identified? Does the undefined precursor text deconstruct efforts to read the event in the successor text as the fulfillment of scripture, regardless of what the narrator may say? Theoretically at least, the reader is free to read from the perspective of either the precursor or the successor text, to focus on either the correlative or the disjunctive elements of the two, or to elect a third vantage point from which to interpret the intertextuality.

The declaration that Jesus' thirst completed scripture implies that the scripture was previously incomplete, or unfinished. The completion of scripture is a recurring theme in the Gospel of John.[52] A quick check of a concordance shows that there are repeated references to scripture and that the fulfillment formula, "so that scripture may be fulfilled" ($\pi\lambda\eta\rho\omega\theta\hat{\eta}$) also occurs repeatedly in John (12:38; 13:18; 15:25; 17:12; 19:24, 36). What does not occur frequently in John is the verb $\tau\epsilon\lambda\epsilon\iota o\hat{\upsilon}\nu$ ("to complete") in a fulfillment formula; the only such occurrence is in John 19:28. Elsewhere in John $\tau\epsilon\lambda\epsilon\iota o\hat{\upsilon}\nu$ refers to what Jesus does to complete the work given to him by the Father (4:34; 5:36; 17:23). It appears, therefore, that $\tau\epsilon\lambda\epsilon\iota o\hat{\upsilon}\nu$ is used in John 19:28 because of attraction to the similar verb, $\tau\epsilon\tau\acute{\epsilon}\lambda\epsilon\sigma\tau\alpha\iota$ ("[all now] was completed"), in the same verse (and repeated in v. 30, "It is finished"). Indeed, the formula using $\pi\lambda\eta\rho\omega\theta\hat{\eta}$ is so familiar that Codices Sinaiticus, Beza, Theta, and Families 1 and 13 read $\pi\lambda\eta\rho\omega\theta\hat{\eta}$ in John 19:28 instead of $\tau\epsilon\lambda\epsilon\iota\omega\theta\hat{\eta}$. The choice of $\tau\epsilon\lambda\epsilon\iota\omega\theta\hat{\eta}$ in that verse suggests, therefore, that in addition to completing scripture, Jesus' thirst completes the work that the Father had given him to do.

As Kelber, Moore, and many commentators have noted, John 19:28 resonates not only with passages of scripture but also with earlier references to thirst in the Fourth Gospel itself. The connection of $\tau\epsilon\lambda\epsilon\iota\omega\theta\hat{\eta}$ with Jesus' work and with thirst recalls the earlier references to thirst (and hunger) in the Gospel, especially John 4 and John 7:37–39. Scripture plays an important role in both passages. The Samaritan woman recalls "our father Jacob," who dug the well to satisfy their thirst; John 7:38–39 refers to another obscure reference in scripture and forecasts the giving of the Spirit at the glorification of Jesus. Whether or not one reads John 19:28–29 as an echo of Ps. 69:21, any reader who misses the connection in John 19:28–29 with references to thirst earlier in the Gospel will miss much of the figurative, metaphoric, and ironic sense of John's account of Jesus' death.

In several other references to the fulfillment of scripture in John, the precursor text is also left undefined (see John 2:22; 7:42; 17:12; 20:9). In each of these verses, as in John 19:28, there is an explicit reference to scripture or to the fulfillment of scripture, but the reference is not quoted. In most of these cases modern interpreters have suggested that the Gospel may have more than one text in view. In both form and effect these references differ significantly from the references to the fulfillment of scripture in which a specific text is quoted. In John 19:28–29 various elements of scripture are fulfilled: the righteous one thirsts, sour wine is given, a hyssop is used, and Jesus gives up the spirit. The contradictions could hardly be more ironic or more powerful: the giver of living water thirsts, a lack completes, giving is malevolent, and drinking aggravates thirst. Similarly, there is a reference to the fulfillment of scripture, but the verse is not quoted. The scripture is not present but absent in fulfillment.

The issue in dispute between those who read John's irony as stable and those who read it as unstable hinges on whether the narrative context and intertextuality of John 19:28 collapse the distinction between the physical and figurative senses of thirst. Does the text allow the reader to find a vantage point from which the figurative sense is stable, or does the text defy such interpretations? Jesus' response to Peter's intervention in Jesus' arrest has not been given due consideration in this debate. Jesus responded, "Am I not to drink the cup that the Father has given me?" (18:11). When Jesus says that he thirsts (19:28), therefore, the reader has been prepared by the figurative uses of thirst in chapters 4, 7, and 18 to understand thirst as an expression of one's need for that which is essential for life both in the physical sense and in the higher, spiritual sense.

Moreover, Jesus' life is fulfilled only in the doing of what the Father has given him to do. He hungers and thirsts for this fulfillment (see 4:34). When Jesus says he thirsts, therefore, the reader does not imagine that the one who offered living water will not be able to provide it. On the contrary, one grasps the fundamental irony of the passion narrative: that life comes only by death, that Jesus could give living water to others only if he himself thirsts (i.e., for the completion of his mission). The poet Ben Jonson's line, "The thirst that from the soul doth rise doth ask a drink divine" (*The Forest,* ix: "To Celia"), describes Jesus' thirst as well as the thirst of those who seek living water from him. The narrative context, moreover, suggests fulfillment rather than frustration of Jesus' offer of living water: (1) at his death Jesus announces the completion of his work ("It is finished"); (2) he gives up his spirit—and the ambiguity or *double entente* suggests that more is being said than simply that he died; and (3) when his side is pierced, water and blood flow from him (resonating with John 7:37–39).

When Jesus says, "I thirst," he not only points to the fulfillment of scripture and the fulfillment of his offer of living water to those who would come to him; he also figuratively announces his own death. We live in a culture that has commercialized thirst. Thirst is no longer a desperate condition that may threaten one's survival. Instead, the beverage industry has glorified thirst as an occasion for festivity and indulgence: "It's Miller time!" Thirst has become merely the opportunity for refreshment and self-gratification. Only by concentrated effort can we put aside such images and recall that only those who cannot satisfy their craving really know what it means to be thirsty.

Beaten, bleeding, and exhausted, Jesus was unable to meet his most basic needs. By suffering this final thirst, Jesus releases the living water that will become a spring welling up to eternal life (4:14). In his death Jesus joined in fellowship with those who thirst and bleed. To them—and to all who share his thirst for doing the will of the Father—Jesus offers living water. Jesus' thirst was "the thirst that from the soul doth rise," and John affirms that through his death Jesus completes his mission as the provider of living water.

Here as elsewhere, John's irony is stable: "The meanings are hidden, but when they are discovered by the proper reader they are firm as a rock."[53] Although readers may undermine the reconstructed meaning with further demolitions, the implied author does not invite the reader to do so. The irony of Jesus' thirst fits all of Booth's criteria for stable irony. (1) It is intended: The implied author wants the reader to see the essential irony that life comes through death, specifically Jesus' death. (2) It is covert: The meaning is not declared but must be reconstructed. (3) It is stable or fixed: The reader is not invited to undermine it further. (4) It is finite, local, or limited: It does not mock our sense of the significance of Jesus' death.[54] By contrast, it could hardly be said that "the author . . . refuses to declare himself, however subtly, *for* any stable proposition."[55] In a word, Jesus' declaration, "I thirst," has all the watermarks of stable irony.

REFLECTIONS

Perspectives on Johannine irony have changed dramatically in the last fifteen years, allowing readers to appreciate subtleties and to consider nuances that previously went unnoticed. Just as these advances have been the result of the cross-fertilization of insights drawn from literary critics (especially Muecke and Booth), so also we may anticipate that work in other disciplines will continue to enrich Johannine studies. In particular, we may expect that the work being done in speech-act theory,[56] rhetoric,[57] and social science will cast new light on the function of irony in John. As readers move from one level of understanding to another, they are in the process of undergoing a social transformation. Irony speaks to people in a liminal state, to those in process of changing. Perhaps that is one reason why contemporary scholarship has been so fascinated with this subject. The excitement of Johannine studies, so contagiously exemplified in the honoree of this volume, is that it continues to provide fresh insights into the Gospel and new aspects to be considered and evaluated. And in the reading and study of this Gospel we too are changed.

NOTES

1. *Anatomy of the Fourth Gospel: A Study in Literary Design* (Philadelphia: Fortress, 1983), 166. Earlier treatments of Johannine irony can be found in H. Clavier, "L'ironie dans le quatrième Évangile," in *SE I,* TU 73 (Berlin: Academie, 1959): 261–76; George W. MacRae, "Theology and Irony in the Fourth Gospel," in *The Word in the World: Essays in Honor of Frederick L. Moriarity, S.J.,* ed. Richard J. Clifford and George W. MacRae (Cambridge, Mass.: Weston College Press, 1973), 83–96, reprinted in *The Gospel of John as Literature: An Anthology of Twentieth-Century Perspectives,* ed. Mark W. G. Stibbe, NTTS (Leiden: Brill, 1993), 103–13; and David Wead, *The Literary Devices in John's Gospel,* Theologische Dissertationen 4 (Basel: Friedrich Reinhard Kommissionsverlag, 1970), 47–68; and idem, "Johannine Irony as a Key to the Author—Audience Relationship in John's Gospel," in *Biblical Literature: 1974 Proceedings,* compiled by Fred O. Francis (Tallahassee, Fla.: AAR/Florida State University, 1974), 33–50.

2. D. C. Muecke, *The Compass of Irony* (London: Methuen & Co., 1969), and *Irony,* The Critical Idiom 13 (London: Methuen & Co., 1970); and Wayne C. Booth, *A Rhetoric of Irony* (Chicago: University of Chicago Press, 1974).

3. Booth, *A Rhetoric of Irony*, 6.

4. Ibid., 240.

5. Muecke, *The Compass of Irony*, 35.

6. *Anatomy of the Fourth Gospel*, 167, summarizing Booth, *A Rhetoric of Irony*, 10–12.

7. *Anatomy of the Fourth Gospel*, 167; see also Booth, *A Rhetoric of Irony*, 37.

8. *Anatomy of the Fourth Gospel*, 176–77.

9. Ibid., 169–75.

10. Ibid., 179.

11. Paul D. Duke, *Irony in the Fourth Gospel* (Atlanta: John Knox, 1985).

12. Ibid., 53–59.

13. Ibid., 63.

14. Ibid., 91.

15. Ibid., 92.

16. Ibid., 111. Note also Culpepper, *Anatomy of the Fourth Gospel*, 169: "The foundational irony of the gospel is that the Jews rejected the Messiah they eagerly expected."

17. *Irony in the Fourth Gospel*, 115.

18. Ibid., 139–40.

19. Ibid., 148.

20. Ibid., 156.

21. Gail R. O'Day, *Revelation in the Fourth Gospel: Narrative Mode and Theological Claim* (Philadelphia: Fortress, 1986), 3.

22. Ibid., 8.

23. Ibid., 24, citing Muecke, *The Compass of Irony*, 53 and 29.

24. O'Day, *Revelation in the Fourth Gospel*, 26–27.

25. Ibid., 29–30.

26. Ibid., 31–32.

27. Ibid., 47.

28. Jeffrey L. Staley, *The Print's First Kiss: A Rhetorical Investigation of the Implied Reader in the Fourth Gospel*, SBLDS 82 (Atlanta: Scholars Press, 1988).

29. Culpepper, *Anatomy of the Fourth Gospel*, 19, 179–80.

30. John McKee, *Literary Irony and the Literary Audience: Studies in the Victimization of the Reader in Augustan Fiction* (Amsterdam: Ropodi, 1974).

31. Staley, *The Print's First Kiss*, 95 n. 1.

32. Ibid., 95–96.

33. Ibid., 102 n. 38, citing Booth, *A Rhetoric of Irony*, 72.

34. Staley, *The Print's First Kiss*, 112.

35. Ibid., 110.

36. Werner H. Kelber, "In the Beginning Were the Words: The Apotheosis and Narrative Displacement of the Logos," *JAAR* 58 (1990): 69–98 (quotation, 88).

37. Ibid., 88–89.

38. Ibid., 89.

39. Werner H. Kelber, "The Birth of a Beginning: John 1:1–18," *Semeia* 52 (1990): 121–44 (quotation, 137).

40. Ibid., 138.

41. Ibid.

42. Stephen D. Moore, *Literary Criticism and the Gospels: The Theoretical Challenge* (New Haven, Conn.: Yale University Press, 1989), 159–63.

43. Ibid., 163.

44. Stephen D. Moore, "Are There Impurities in the Living Water that the Johannine Jesus Dispenses? Deconstruction, Feminism, and the Samaritan Woman," *Biblical Interpretation* 1 (1993): 207–27; reprinted in idem, *Poststructuralism and the New Testament: Derrida and Foucault at the Foot of the Cross* (Minneapolis: Fortress, 1994), 43–64.

45. Gail R. O'Day, "John," in *The Women's Bible Commentary,* ed. Carol A. Newsom and Sharon H. Ringe (Louisville: Westminster/John Knox, 1992), 295–96 (where the absence of comment on the irony of the scene stands in contrast to her earlier reading of it); Regina St. G. Plunkett, "The Samaritan Woman: Partner in Revelation," unpublished paper cited by Moore, *Poststructuralism and the New Testament,* 46 n. 14; and Sandra M. Schneiders, *The Revelatory Text: Interpreting the New Testament as Sacred Scripture* (San Francisco: HarperCollins, 1991), 180–99.

46. Moore, *Poststructuralism and the New Testament,* 52.

47. Ibid., 59.

48. Ibid., 62.

49. Robert L. Brawley, "An Absent Complement and Intertextuality in John 19:28–29," *JBL* 112 (1993): 427–43.

50. Ibid., 430.

51. Ibid., 431.

52. See the essay by Johannes Beutler in this volume.

53. Booth, *A Rhetoric of Irony,* 235.

54. Ibid., 5–6.

55. Ibid., 240.

56. See esp. Henk Haverkate, "A Speech Act Analysis of Irony," *Journal of Pragmatics* 14 (1990): 77–109; J. E. Botha, "The Case of Johannine Irony Reopened I: The Problematic Current Situation," *Neot* 25 (1991): 209–20; and idem, "The Case of Johannine Irony Reopened II: Suggestions, Alternative Approaches," *Neot* 25 (1991): 221–32.

57. C. Jan Swearingen, *Rhetoric and Irony: Western Literacy and Western Lies* (New York: Oxford University Press, 1991).

Eduard Schweizer

11

What about the Johannine "Parables"?

D. Moody Smith's personal history has revolved around a fascination with the Fourth Gospel and did so as a commitment "to the importance of historical understanding and historical theology."[1] Thus, it may give him some pleasure when I try to deal with that center of his research, though I am not able "to underline certain aspects of John's portrayal which . . . are sometimes ignored or played down."[2] Instead, I revert to a very old problem, one that has been on the table since the publication of the first fascicles of Bultmann's commentary and of my dissertation.[3] Here I try to take up, in a different way, Smith's basic interest in the relation of John to the Synoptics[4] and his dictum, "What is latent in the synoptics is patent in John."[5] I also take up some aspects of the more recent question of how "the world of the Johannine community, and the world of Jesus do, in fact, overlap,"[6] as well as modern research on the parables of Jesus.[7]

THE BEGINNING IN MARBURG

In the spring of 1934 I traveled from Marburg to a meeting near Magdeburg. I was then an enthusiastic railroad traveler and was seriously tempted to look out at the passing scenery instead of at the book I held in my hands. Yet just two or three days before, I had begun Rudolf Bultmann's seminar on the Johannine parables. Therefore, fighting hard against all my temptations, I read all of Adolf Jülicher's *Die Gleichnisreden Jesu*[8] and saw nothing of the picturesque landscape of middle Germany. At the end of the second session of our seminar, I asked Bultmann whether I could still change the topic of my seminar paper from a simple review of a book to the problem of the form, or *Gattung,* of the Johannine parables. Bultmann smiled, indicating that this topic might be a bit much for a fourth-semester student, but agreed. It was a hard battle until I realized that, in John, all the criteria of a genuine parable were lacking: an introduction, such as "the kingdom of God is like . . ."; a phrase like "He who has ears to hear let him hear!" which would indicate that the truth lies behind the seemingly simple wording; a story like that, for instance, of the prodigal son, or of the sower, or of the talents. Were the Johannine parables, then, allegories: the shepherd as a code for Jesus; the sheep, for the believers; the wolves, for the false teachers? This solution seemed more promising; yet, it did not fit either. The main obstacle was the adjective: "the *true* vine," "the *right* shepherd," "the *living* water," or "the bread *of life*." Such terms were not simply additional, qualifying descriptions; nor could the sentence "I am the true vine" be understood as something like the solution of the riddle of an allegory, indicating who was meant by the "vine." That predication qualified the speaking "I" as the only one that was really worth being called such, in contrast to others who were not.

If so, does that formulation really qualify Jesus—that is, explain who or what he was or is? If it were a parable, "I" would be the subject and "vine" the predicate that says something about him. If it were an allegory, it would be the other way around: the mask, namely "vine," would be thrown off by the solution that "vine" is actually a circumlocution for "I," that is, Jesus. What is subject, what predicate? The discourse about the shepherd is introduced by the claim of the Pharisees to be the leaders (or the shepherds; cf. Ezek. 34:1–24) of Israel (John 9:40–41); Jesus answers in his discourse that not they but he is the right shepherd. The discourse on the bread is similarly introduced by the demands of the hearers for a miraculous bread from heaven, like the manna, and they are answered by Jesus that he alone is the real bread from heaven. The discourse on the living water starts from the wish of the Samaritan woman for a spring, which would save her the many trips to the well; and she hears that Jesus himself is that living water. Finally, the discourse on the vine speaks of the coming church over against the Jewish understanding of Israel as a "vine."[9] In all these instances shepherd, bread, water, and vine are the subjects, and the question that the statement of Jesus answers is: "The right shepherd [and so forth] is who?" The question is answered by the predicate "I," Jesus—not the Pharisees, not the manna, not a newly detected spring, not Israel, but Jesus.

Thus, I argued in the Bultmann seminar that the so-called parables in John were neither parables nor allegories, and that their terms ("shepherd," and the like) were neither similes nor, in the strict sense of the word, metaphors; they were, rather, normal qualifications in the category of direct and defining language, which claimed that everything other than Jesus was only in a secondary—indeed, actually figurative—way what it is called. All the shepherds we know on earth are not real shepherds but, at best, shadows of the one shepherd, Jesus. Bultmann agreed totally and asked me to work that out in detail in a future dissertation. He had to wait for another three years, until I wrote my thesis (which, by the way, took me seven months).[10]

THE PARABLES OF JESUS AND THEIR TRADITION
IN THE SYNOPTICS

Ernst Fuchs is said to have declared years ago that in the last fifty years the only fact that New Testament scholarship found out was that Jesus had spoken in parables. Anyone who had been in a good Sunday school would know that. What

Fuchs wanted to say, jokingly, is that scholars had been interested in the contents of the parables but had never reflected on the question *why* Jesus so often used parabolic language. Jülicher still supposed that parables were illustrations. He distinguished the authentic parables, which use similes that should help people to understand Jesus' preaching, from the allegories, developed later, which speak an insider language and use metaphors understandable only to the initiated group of believers. Thus, Mark 4:33 would express the intent of Jesus—"With many such parables he spoke the word to them, as they were able to hear it"—whereas 4:11–12 would reflect the misunderstanding of the later church: "To you has been given the secret of the kingdom of God, but for those outside, everything comes in parables; in order that 'they may indeed look, but not perceive, and may indeed listen, but not understand; so that they may not turn again and be forgiven.' " This distinction is certainly not wrong, but neither is it the pivotal assessment. If Jesus understood his parables as illustrations, helping the hearer to understand his preaching, they would start from or end in a thesis that Jesus wanted to bring home to the people. This is indeed what the rabbis often did: A dogmatic thesis or a legal decision, often chosen from a word in the scriptures, is illustrated by a parable that follows. Not so Jesus: Very seldom is a parable opened or closed by a direct statement that would summarize the message of the parable. Where this does happen, it is very probably the attempt of the later church to "explain" the parable by its interpretation. Luke 16:8–13, for instance, collects various attempts to do so. Why, then, did Jesus speak almost exclusively in parables when not giving ethical advice but expressing his central concern, the mystery of the kingdom of God? Why is it that what Jesus wanted to proclaim could not be formulated without parabolic language?

As the result of intensive research on this problem by many of my colleagues, I see five points. First, Jesus uses everyday language, not a specific religious language. He enters the world of the hearers and picks them up where they live. They do not have to "emigrate" first into another "religious" or "heavenly" world. This is what Jülicher and many others rightly emphasized. Yet, we now must underline at the same time that it is the short introduction, often only implied, which shows that in the stories God himself will come in his kingdom to the hearers, and that it is but the authority of the speaker that vouches for this fact: "It [the kingdom of God] is like leaven . . ." (Luke 13:21).

Second, the everyday language of the parable and, even more, its introduction or summons (like "Listen!" Mark 4:3) reach out to the hearers in order to seize them and draw them into the story. A parable of Jesus can be understood only if we enter it and experience it from inside.[11] The parable does not simply, at least not primarily, convey information. It tries to awaken something in the hearer's experience and to lead him or her to an experience of God, who, in this parable, wills to come and to enter the life of the hearer. The woman who listens to Jesus is reminded of her activity yesterday: "like leaven that a woman took . . . ." This is exactly what she did. Thus, the kingdom of which Jesus speaks is in some way connected with what she often does, has something to do with her and her world, not merely with scribes who can read the Bible, even in Hebrew, and understand what it means. Thus, she gets engaged, and not merely in hearing information that she can know and go home with.

Third, Jesus speaks of things like "three measures of flour." A mixture of around fifty pounds is by no means impossible, but it is amazing and certainly startles the hearers. The woman stops for a moment and probably laughs at the idea that she would have to mix so much flour in her kitchen or before her tent. How could she manage with such an enormous heap of flour? Similar traits are to be found in most of Jesus' parables. They are never speaking of fairy-tale miracles but of very unexpected, surprising facts. What moneylender disposes of fifty million—not dollars, but *day's wages*—and, most astonishing of all, simply tears up the IOU of his debtor (Matt. 18:24–27)? What father acts like the prodigal son's father? What mustard seed becomes a tree, not merely a very big shrub? This shows the principal mistake of Jülicher and many others:[12] Jesus' parables are not illustrations that convince the hearers by matching their common sense, so that they would respond, "Of course, that goes without saying!" On the contrary, the vital and most important part of his parables is the uncommon act or event that startles the hearer. In the parable of the prodigal son the behavior of both sons follows exactly the pattern of modern psychological analysis of adolescence,[13] though in a very pointed way, whereas the behavior of the father is indeed very surprising. So also Luke 13:21: "Fifty pounds of flour," thinks the woman, listening to Jesus' parable. "Is the kingdom of God as big, as great as that?"

Fourth, the parables of Jesus never finish speaking to their hearers or readers. The parable of the lost sheep first emphasized the unspeakable joy of the shepherd. This aspect is part of the text in Luke 15:5–6, as well as in Matt. 18:13; it is even more surprising in the parallel parable of the lost coin in Luke 15:8–10.[14] This seems to be the point that Jesus made. Yet the parable spoke again, when the opponents of the early church derided it for the low status of its members[15] and became, in Matt. 18:12–14, an urgent request to care for other church members that were in danger of going astray. The consequence of these observations is that we can never put a parable aside because we had once understood it. We can never capture it in a statement that would fix its meaning forever, so that we could dispose of the story Jesus told.

Even the one-verse parable of Luke 13:21 spoke again and told its hearer something new: "and [she] hid the leaven under the flour." This is correct wording, but it would have been much more usual to speak of "mixing the leaven with the flour." The unusual term might make the hearer sit up and take notice. It might start a whole train of thoughts: "Indeed, this kingdom of God seems to be a hidden fact! Where is it? The drought kills our harvest, war is threatening, and my husband is still the old drunkard! And yet, the leaven is also hidden and I see nothing of it, but it is still living."

Fifth, the parable ends: "till it is all leavened." Like all the parables of Jesus, it describes a process, not a static, unchangeable object. The kingdom of God is something that lives and grows into a future that is not yet visible.

Hans Weder rightly understood that the "bricks" from which the parables of Jesus are built are not similes but metaphors, and that there is not only one point of comparison. Actually, the whole story follows, in a metaphorical way, the story of the kingdom. One cannot separate the *Bildhälfte* (image) from the *Sachhälfte* (essence), as Jülicher tried to do. The story of the parable is in some way repeated in the story of God, who encounters the hearer. More precisely, the story of the parable is repeated in the story of the kingdom of God, which starts to live in the hearer. Though I disagree with Weder when he sees an authentic parable of Jesus in—or, at least, in the background of—almost every Synoptic parable, he is right, I think, in considering many secondary allegorical additions or reformulations as a necessary development in the time when Jesus was no longer the parable-teller and when, therefore, the christological aspect of the parable—its never negligible dependence on its speaker—had to be made explicit.

THE JOHANNINE "PARABLES": SOME SIMILARITIES

Returning to the "I am" speeches in John, do we detect something comparable there? First, Jesus uses everyday language here, too—so much so that his hearers misunderstand him, thinking that he wants to give them some practical advice for, or some improvement of, their everyday lives. He speaks of living water or bread, of a right shepherd and a true vine, and his audience thinks of a spring instead of a cistern, of bread falling like manna from the sky, of a political and religious leader better than the Pharisees, and of an improved community of Israel. There is but that very strange introduction, "I am . . . ," which suggests a meaning beyond the superficial one, because Jesus is not water or bread or vine in their usual sense and not even a shepherd, either. Again, therefore, Jesus picks up his hearers where they are living, but in a way that exceeds all the Synoptic examples, they remain fixed in their own world, so that Jesus' words baffle them and perplex their thoughts.

Second, in John it is quite clear, too, that getting involved personally is necessary for an understanding of what Jesus speaks. In chapter 4, Jesus' offer of living water brings to light all the sexual problems of the Samaritan woman. In chapter 6, Jesus urges his hearers to come to him and, in a last climax of his discourse, even to eat his flesh and drink his blood, whether verses 51c–58 belong to the original composition (perhaps as a traditional paragraph, taken up by the evangelist from the liturgy of his church, for instance)[16] or have been added by a redactor. In chapter 10, the contrast to other, ostensible shepherds is stated in the introduction and implied by the portrayal of the *right* shepherd, and the involvement of his sheep is described in the second part of the discourse (10:25–30). In chapter 15, the word that points to the true vine makes those who become its branches "clean" (as in 15:3), and listening to the narrator means abiding in him. Thus, the language of Jesus in John is "involving" language, which one cannot understand without getting involved. Differently from the Synoptic reports, however, the often silly misunderstandings of those who do not let themselves become engaged emphasize this necessity through the negative contrast to a fruitful listening.

Third, the unexpected traits of the "I am" discourses of Jesus are, compared with the Synoptic parables, even more exaggerated. Even their wording makes no sense, if one remains within the limits of this earthly world: a "spring of water welling up to eternal life" (4:14), a bread "that endures to eternal life" (6:27), a shepherd who "lays down his life" and "has power to take it up again" (10:17–18), a vine in which people can "abide" and that is identical with "love" (15:4, 9). These things do not exist except in a world "beyond." The fact that all that Jesus promises is totally dependent on the speaker himself and becomes true only through him and through his ministry, a fact still latent in the Synoptics, has become patent in John.[17]

Fourth, in John too the disciple who has been touched, even involved, and who has understood that he finds water and bread, shepherd and vine in Jesus alone, never possesses the truth forever. The water becomes in him a spring welling up again and again, and he experiences rivers of living water that flow on and on (4:14; 7:38[18]). Eating the bread of life is to be repeated time and time again in the eucharist of the church (6:51–58).[19] Accepting the shepherd leads to following him (10:27–28), and knowing the true vine leads to the community of love in the Johannine church, perhaps even to suffering and dying for Jesus' sake (15:9–16:3). Thus, continuing education by the "I am" speeches is clearly offered in John and is equally clearly connected with the relation of the believer to Jesus the speaker.

Fifth, there are some processes described in the Johannine "I am" speeches, too: rivers of water are flowing; bread is and will be eaten; the shepherd brings sheep from other folds, and is and will be followed; the branches of the vine, which are pruned time and again, form a community ready to suffer and to die. These processes take place within the group of believers, however, not in Jesus — except, perhaps, for the case of the shepherd, who fights the wolf and dies. But this exception confirms the rule: the process ends with the death of the shepherd and with his "taking up his life again," with cross and resurrection. Thus, John emphasizes both the ongoing process in the community of the disciples and the permanence of the one who proclaims himself as the "I" (emphasized in Greek) who fulfills all the promises and who is the same yesterday, today, tomorrow, and forever. This is the definitely post-Easter language of John.

THE SPECIFIC JOHANNINE EMPHASIS

In the Fourth Gospel there is but one, very short parable that could be compared with those reported by the Synoptic Gospels: "When a woman is in labor, she has pain, because her hour has come. But when her child is born, she no longer remembers the anguish, because of the joy of having brought a human being into the world. So you have pain now; but I will see you again, and your hearts will rejoice" (John 16:21–22). Even this is not really parallel to the Synoptic examples. The picture of the birth of a child is typical and almost a cliché for the change from sorrow to joy. Its main difference from the parables of Jesus, however, lies in the fact that it is a mere illustration of something that is stated directly in non-parabolic language before the parable ("You will have pain, but your pain will turn into joy," 16:20). As it happens in the world of the parable, so it happens in the world of the implied hearer. Such a reduction of a parabolic story to a statement that is well understandable apart from the picture-world of the parable is lacking in the Synoptic parables of Jesus, as we have seen.

Both the Synoptic parables and the Johannine "I am" speeches know that the normal language of information does not suffice to express what Jesus wants to convey to the hearers. There is, in both, a direct statement that gives information—"The kingdom of God is . . ." and "I am . . ."—but in the Synoptics the statement is followed by "like . . . ," while in John it seems to end not as a comparison but as a clear and direct definition ("I am the right shepherd," "the true vine," and so forth). Nevertheless, the Johannine Jesus is forced to go on in a language that awakens human experiences and emotions. He speaks of a shepherd fighting the wolves, of a vine giving life and fruit to its branches, of a spring welling up, of a nourishing bread. Why then is the introduction of this world of human experiences by the comparative, "like," not just casually lacking, as often in the Synoptics, but made impossible by the claim of Jesus—"I am the *true* vine, the *right* shepherd, the *living* bread"?

The important terms in a Synoptic parable are metaphors. The classic example of a metaphor is the statement, "Achilles is a lion."[20] In fact, Achilles is a man, not a lion, but in one respect the predicate, "lion," describes the subject Achilles better than any other term. When we speak of Mrs. Thatcher as "the iron lady," we do not suggest that she consists of iron instead of muscles and bones; we describe her character, and "iron" fits better than, for instance, "insistent," "uncompromising," or "inflexible." It is better, because it reminds us of experiences we have had of touching iron. It probably evokes some emotions and, in this sense, gets our senses involved. Perhaps one should add that "iron" encompasses a wider field of meaning, without forcing us to decide whether we mean the term in its *sensus bonus,* as "insistent," or its *sensus malus,* as "inflexible." Similarly, the kingdom of God in its faculty and will to permeate the world is depicted in a way that moves our emotions and fetches our old experiences, as "leaven," and this metaphor does not merely strike us but also includes a wide field of possibilities as to how this will happen.

Are terms like "shepherd," "water," and "bread" metaphors in the Fourth Gospel? At first sight, they seem to be so. In fact, Jesus is not a vine but a man. Yet in his relation to the disciples he might very well be called, metaphorically, a vine. But this is not what John really says. He says, "I am *the true* vine." Thus, the principal point John wants to make is obviously the distinction between Jesus and others that are not truly vines, at least not the vine in question. Since "vine" is a traditional picture for Israel (see n. 9), we could say that it is a well-known metaphor, as, for instance, "shepherd" is a metaphor for a leader of Israel. Yet, the point that the Johannine Jesus makes is that he is the true vine. Therefore, the question that John 15:1 answers seems to be: Who is the *true* vine? Who is the genuine Israel? The answer, by implication, is: only Jesus, the Son of Man solely.[21] In chapter 6 Jesus is in the same way presented as the true bread from heaven, in contrast to the manna (John 6:32), and in chapter 10 as the right or real shepherd, in contrast to the self-appointed leaders, the Pharisees (John 9:40–41; cf. Ezek. 34:2–10, 22–30), or to the authorities in the early church who put themselves first (3 John 9) or even to antichrists (1 John 2:18).

In these two examples Jesus is contrasted with a group of people that is metaphorically called "[the] vine [of God]" or "shepherds [of God's people]." Thus, the further description of Jesus as vine or shepherd still uses metaphorical language, but it serves to prove that he is the only one who can give what these terms promise. This becomes more obvious in chapters 4 and 6, where Jesus speaks of the living water and the bread of life. In some way, here also metaphors are used — water and bread for spiritual nourishment, satisfying thirst and hunger — but the "utilization factor" of the picture is very low. Nothing is said about where water and bread come from, how they quench the thirst and still the hunger, what emotions we may have when this happens, and so forth. They are distinguished only as the living water and bread from perishing victuals (even when delivered by "our father Jacob" or fallen miraculously from heaven). Otherwise, the nature or behavior or characteristics of water and bread are scarcely mentioned. All that is said about them serves, again, merely to prove that Jesus is the only one who is in reality what the terms express.[22] Finally, in John 14:6 Jesus proclaims, "I am the way, the truth and the life." "Way" could still be understood as a metaphor, but not so easily "truth" and "life." Even if we might call them, in a broad sense, metaphors, their function is clearly different. When we say "Achilles is a lion," we do not claim that he alone fulfills what the term says, and that all the other lions we know are, in fact, no lions at all. When Jesus proclaims, "I am the way, the truth and the life," he goes on: "nobody comes to the Father but by me."

To be sure, in all these "I am" discourses there are traits that are parallel in the world of metaphors to the world that Jesus wants to convey to his audience.[23] These traits certainly describe Jesus and his ministry. Yet strictly speaking, the terms vine, shepherd, water, bread, way, truth, and life are actually used not in order to depict Jesus and his ministry but rather to show that what we understand by these terms does not fulfill what the terms suggest — neither the vine of God (Israel), nor the shepherds of Israel, nor the manna, nor a spring (compared even with the well of Jacob!), nor all that we call the way or truth or life. In a similar way, Jesus can see "how the fields are already white for harvest" — that is, for the real, the true harvest—whereas human eyes see only "that there are yet four months, then comes the harvest" (4:35). Moreover, the frequent misunderstandings are, for John, means to demonstrate the incapacity of human language, human thoughts, and even human existence (with all that it implies) to comprehend reality as it is revealed in Jesus. Thus, it is no longer the metaphor of the "vine" (or whatever) that helps us to understand who and what Jesus is; it is, on the contrary, Jesus who helps us to understand what a vine is, or a shepherd, or water and bread, or way and truth and life.

How is this related to the parables of Jesus, as the Synoptics report them? We have seen that the earthly Jesus spoke in parables in order to remind his hearers of their experiences (in their everyday lives or in some story they have heard about). He evokes feelings and insights connected with those experiences, and excites some parallel emotions and perceptions that open them to the kingdom of God, which reaches out to them. Thereby they get personally involved in this encounter. When Jesus ceased to be the parable-teller, it became necessary to emphasize explicitly that his parables make sense only because what Jesus tells in them is actually happening in his ministry, including Good Friday, Easter Sunday, and Pentecost. This is what some additional traits or paragraphs of the Synoptics do.[24] John writes decidedly in post-Easter language. In a radical way he proclaims Jesus as the only one in whom all that is promised by terms like "vine" is really fulfilled. Is his message, therefore, merely speculative, something like the Platonic ideology? It might appear so: The real world is, for John, not the bread and water, vine and shepherd, way, life, and truth as we know them in our natural existence on earth, but something beyond all that.[25] Thus, we seem to come close to Plato's cave, in which people see but the shadows of whatever passes by the entrance of the cave (*Resp.* 7.514a–517a). Is an earthly shepherd, for John, the shadow of the real one, earthly bread the shadow of the bread of life, in the same way as for Plato?

For John, earthly persons or things are never shadows of ideas, persons, or things in heaven. They are shadows of Jesus, the Word of God that has become flesh, who is rejected, and who goes to the *cross* to be exalted there to God. This proclamation aims, therefore, at a very earthly engagement of its hearer. The unity of existence in the vine and its branches is described as a mutual abiding in one another, which creates the unity of love in the group of the disciples.[26] The living water becomes a "spring of water," which "wells up" (4:14) in the woman's promulgation of what has happened to her (4:28–29).[27] The care of the right shepherd (10:11) continues in the disciple's "tending and feeding the sheep of Jesus" and in his death for their sake (21:15–19; see also 15:27–16:3).

More than the other Gospels, John speaks the language of the post-Easter church. Yet he writes a Gospel, not a dogmatic treatise about the heavenly Christ. Thus, he puts Christology in the center, perhaps more so than any other New Testament author. Nonetheless, John's Christ is the Word of God that became flesh in a man, Jesus of Nazareth by name, who was sometimes too tired to go on with his disciples (4:6, 8), who was rejected by the majority of his people (6:66; 18:38–19:16), who was betrayed and left alone by his group of disciples (6:64; 18:25–27; 20:19), and who keeps the wounds of his crucified body even as the risen one (20:20, 27). If we do not misunderstand the confession of this one, truly God and truly man, in a static way in terms of substance and nature, but understand that confession in a dynamic way in terms of "existence," John is a good witness to a good creed.

NOTES

1. D. Moody Smith, *Johannine Christianity: Essays on Its Setting, Sources, and Theology* (Columbia, S.C.: University of South Carolina Press, 1984), xiii; idem, *John among the Gospels: The Relationship in Twentieth-Century Research* (Minneapolis: Fortress, 1992), xi.

2. Smith, *Johannine Christianity*, xv.

3. Eduard Schweizer, *Ego Eimi . . . : Die religionsgeschichtliche Herkunft und theologische Bedeutung der johanneischen Bildreden, zugleich ein Beitrag zur Quellenfrage des vierten Evangeliums*, FRLANT 56 (Göttingen: Vandenhoeck & Ruprecht, 1939; 2d ed., 1965), kindly mentioned by Smith (*Johannine Christianity*, 13 n. 27, 44–45).

4. I agree with his position (*Johannine Christianity*, xiii; similarly, but more cautiously, idem, *John among the Gospels*, 177–89, esp. 186–89; and idem, "John and the Synoptics and the Question of Gospel Genre," in *The Four Gospels 1992: Festschrift Frans Neirynck*, ed. F. Van Segbroeck, C. M. Tuckett, Gilbert Van Belle, and J. Verheyden, BETL 100 [Leuven: Leuven University Press, 1992], 3.1783–97 [here, 1796–97]).

5. Smith, *Johannine Christianity*, 191; see also idem, "The Problem of John and the Synoptics in Light of the Relation between Apocryphal and Canonical Gospels," in *John and the Synoptics*, ed. Adelbert Denaux, BETL 101 (Leuven: Leuven University Press, 1992), 147–62 (here, 162).

6. Smith, *Johannine Christianity*, xiii–xiv, referring to R. Alan Culpepper and J. Louis Martyn (see also Smith, *John among the Gospels*, 72, 140, 168–69).

7. See, for instance, Hans Weder, *Die Gleichnisse Jesu als Metaphern: Traditions- und redaktionsgeschichtliche Analysen und Interpretationen*, FRLANT 120 (Göttingen: Vandenhoeck & Ruprecht, 1978), 11–57; and, more recently, Eckhard Rau, *Reden in Vollmacht: Hintergrund, Form und Anliegen der Gleichnisse Jesu*, FRLANT 149 (Göttingen: Vandenhoeck & Ruprecht, 1990).

8. Adolf Jülicher, *Die Gleichnisreden Jesu im allgemeinen*, vol. 1, 2d ed. (Freiburg, Leipzig, and Tübingen: Mohr, 1899).

9. Thus, Psalm 80 and often, also in a specific way, Pseudo-Philo (*Bib.Ant.* 12.8)! With John 1:51 compare n. 21 below; on John 15 as "the *allegory* of the vine," see Smith, *John among the Gospels*, 24, with reference to Hans Windisch.

10. See n. 3 above. Very fortunately, we did not have to deal with mountains of secondary literature in those days and had, therefore, more time to think. D. Moody

Smith, *The Composition and Order of the Fourth Gospel: Bultmann's Literary Theory,* Yale Publications in Religion 10 (New Haven, Conn.: Yale University Press, 1965), 66–71 (et passim), agreed with my thesis. The Jewish background would now have to be taken more seriously than the "Gnostic" one; see, for instance, John Ashton, *Understanding the Fourth Gospel* (Oxford: Clarendon Press, 1991). In my *Ego Eimi* (21–27, 32–33) I pointed to the Old Testament parallels in which God reveals himself in the phrase, "I am . . . ," in the same exclusive sense as the Johannine Christ, and I concluded (ibid., 140) that this claim of Jesus to be the true vine (and so forth) was indeed the central message of the Fourth Gospel, which Jesus himself proclaimed implicitly. Varieties among the "I am" addresses in John are marked by Hans Klein, "Vorgeschichte und Verständnis der johanneischen Ich-bin-Worte," *KD* 33 (1987): 120–36, esp. 121–23.

11. John Dominic Crossan, *In Parables: The Challenge of the Historical Jesus* (New York: Harper & Row, 1973), 13. Compare my studies, *Jesus Christ: The Man from Nazareth and the Exalted Lord* (Macon, Ga.: Mercer University Press, 1987), 86 (and the literature cited there, n. 50); and *Jesus the Parable of God: What Do We Really Know about Jesus?* PTMS 37 (Allison Park, Pa.: Pickwick, 1994), 23–28.

12. I myself summarized Jülicher (*Die Gleichnisreden Jesu,* 66 and 102) in *Ego Eimi,* 114: "Beim Gleichnis [ist] ein Verstoss gegen den Naturverlauf zwar nicht ausgeschlossen, aber Zeichen einer schlechten Komposition" ("In a parable an offense against the normal course of nature is not impossible, but it is a sign of bad composition"[!]). Although I added a critical remark (ibid., n. 11)—"Zu bedenken bleibt freilich, dass das *neutestamentliche* Gleichnis oft Dinge zu sagen hat, die dem logischen Denken enthoben sind" ("However, we should consider the fact that the *New Testament* parables often have to proclaim things that are exempt from mere logical reflection")—I was not courageous enough to go on from there against the venerated authority of Jülicher.

13. Louis Beirnaert, "The Parable of the Prodigal Son, Luke 15:11–32, Read by an Analyst," in *Exegesis: Problems of Method and Exercises in Reading (Genesis 22 and Luke 15),* ed. François Bovon and Grégoire Rouiller, PTMS 21 (Pittsburgh: Pickwick, 1978), 197–210.

14. When I told that story in 1936 in a school class, a boy insisted that this was a very silly woman, because she would have to pay more, for coffee and cookies for all the friends and neighbors, than the silver dollar she had found; and I answered: "Yes, indeed, such a silly woman is God, who lets all his angels jubilate because he has found me—and what a troublesome find he made here!"

15. Or even on another occasion during Jesus' ministry.

16. This is also my suggestion; see, for instance, "Joh 6,51c–58—vom Evangelisten übernommene Tradition?" *ZNW* 82 (1991): 274.

17. Cf. n. 5 above.

18. I think, with Raymond E. Brown, *The Gospel according to John (i–xii),* AB 29 (Garden City, N.Y.: Doubleday, 1966), 320–21, that 7:38 speaks of the body of Christ (not of the believer); cf. Eduard Schweizer, "On Distinguishing between Spirits," *Ecumenical Review* 41 (1989): 406–15 (here, see 412 and n. 14). The latter interpretation would express the continuation of the gift of Jesus in the life of the disciple even more emphatically.

19. Understood as a public confession (Charles H. Cosgrove, "The Place where Jesus Is: Allusions to Baptism and the Eucharist in the Fourth Gospel," *NTS* 35 [1989]:

522–39, esp. 527–29), or as an antidocetic act (Udo Schnelle, *Antidocetic Christology in the Gospel of John: An Investigation of the Place of the Fourth Gospel in the Johannine School* [Minneapolis: Fortress, 1992], 206–8), or simply stating the involvement of the believer.

20. Eberhard Jüngel, "Metaphorische Wahrheit: Erwägungen zur theologischen Relevanz der Metapher als Beitrag zur Hermeneutik einer narrativen Theologie," in *Metapher: Zur Hermeneutik religiöser Sprache,* ed. Paul Ricoeur and Eberhard Jüngel, *EvT* Sonderheft (Munich: Kaiser, 1974), 71–122 (esp. 73); Weder, *Die Gleichnisse Jesu als Metaphern,* 60.

21. I understand John 1:51 (which Smith considers to be in contrast to the Temple [*Johannine Christianity,* 159]) as defining the Son of Man as the true Jacob-Israel (Gen. 28:12; 32:28; see Eduard Schweizer, "σῶμα, σωματικός, σύσσωμος," *TDNT* 7 [1971]: 1024–94 [esp. 1072 n. 457]). Note also John 1:20 as a contrast formula to the "I am" of Jesus; see Boy Hinrichs, *"Ich bin": Die Konsistenz des Johannes-Evangeliums in der Konzentration auf das Wort Jesu,* SBS 133 (Stuttgart: Katholisches Bibelwerk, 1988), iii.

22. Even the proclamation of John 8:12, "I am the light of the world," stands in contrast, in the view of the evangelist, with other claims. In John 1:8–9 he stresses the contrast of the preliminary light of the Baptist to the *true* light (see also 5:35). This speaks, I think, definitely against the thesis of Matthew Fox that the cosmic Christ is the "I am" in all creatures (*The Coming of the Cosmic Christ: The Healing of Mother Earth and the Birth of a Global Renaissance* [San Francisco: Harper & Row, 1988], 154–55, referring to John). One might, perhaps, speak of *analogia fidei,* certainly not of *analogia entis.*

23. The vine creates the fruit on the branches, as does Jesus in his disciples. The shepherd dies for the sheep (also for those who are of another fold), as does Jesus for his disciples and for those who will come from outside. Even in the context of 14:6, Jesus is also speaking of "the way where he is going" (for the necessary counterbalance of the Synoptics to this verse, see Smith, *Johannine Christianity,* 196).

24. Weder, *Die Gleichnisse Jesu als Metaphern,* 95–96, 98.

25. This may be what Seiichi Yagi refers to as "the freedom from conceptual language" (my translation), which is as important for Buddhists as it is for his understanding of the New Testament (*Die Front-Struktur als Brücke vom buddhistischen zum christlichen Denken,* Ökumenische Existenz heute 3 (Munich: Kaiser, 1988), 12; see further, Seiichi Yagi and Leonard Swidler, *A Bridge to Buddhist-Christian Dialogue* [New York and Mahwah, N.J.: Paulist, 1990]). Compare the conclusion of Rudolf Schnackenburg, "Synoptische und johanneische Christologie: Ein Vergleich," in *The Four Gospels: Festschrift Frans Neirynck,* 3.1723–50 (here, 1748–49): the incarnation of the preexistent Logos shifts the emphasis from the resurrection of the crucified Jesus to his origin from God and, thus, to a "high Christology," to an "I am" as the expression of the divine authority of Jesus. Now see also the appendix by Jörg Frey in Martin Hengel, *Die johanneische Frage: Ein Lösungsversuch,* WUNT 67 (Tübingen: Mohr [Siebeck], 1993), 399–402; whether such predicates as "vine" should be called metaphors is more questionable.

26. John 15:9–10, connecting vv. 1–8 and 11–17; see also Smith, *Johannine Christianity,* 216–17.

27. Even if neither John 7:33 nor 4:14 spoke of a current, flowing from the believer towards other people, the context in 4:28–30, 39–42 would do so.

12

"The Words That You Gave to Me I Have Given to Them": The Grandeur of Johannine Rhetoric

Style is the regard that *what* pays to *how*.
—Edmund L. Epstein[1]

Among the many differences between John and the Synoptics that Moody Smith has illumined is the distinctive discourse of the Johannine Jesus. Lacking the other Gospels' pithy sayings (e.g., Luke 9:58–60, 62), parables (Mark 4:3–8, 26–32), and pronouncement stories (Matt. 22:15–22), in John "Jesus speaks in a more elevated, hieratic, even pretentious, style" with "nearer echoes in 1 John than in the other Gospels."[2] Both of Professor Smith's observations are germane to this essay's twofold task. In the first place I shall consider some salient features of John's literary style from the standpoint of particular theories of discourse in antiquity. Secondly, I wish to extend this research to the form and function of the rhetoric in 1 John, which stands alongside the Fourth Gospel as a significant witness to first-century Johannine Christianity. These analyses, in turn, should prompt reflections on the shape of Johannine theology and some challenges presented by its interpretation. In effect the reader is invited to join with me in pondering the report about Jesus, apologetically filed by the temple police in John 7:46: "Never has anyone spoken like this!" To what degree is this assessment true? In what sense is it inaccurate? And what difference should such questions make to an interpreter of the First Epistle of John and the Fourth Gospel?

THE RHETORIC OF THE JOHANNINE JESUS

Investigation of the style of Johannine discourse is hardly novel.[3] The heyday of its exploration may have dawned in the late nineteenth and early twentieth centuries, when the critical paradigm was governed by questions regarding sources: specifically, the origin of the Fourth Gospel in either Semitic or Synoptic tradition, and the unity or disparity of authorship of John and 1 John.[4] While the urgency of some (though by no means all) of these questions may have dissipated, John's peculiar stylistic phenomena and their importance for understanding that Gospel still invite consideration.

Although the Fourth Gospel has been extensively probed with a variety of literary-critical instruments,[5] the theory and practice of classical rhetoric seem to me especially appropriate to the task of appraising Johannine discourse. This decision immediately invites some clarifications. First, although both aesthetics and the social dimensions of language are implied by this study, I am primarily interested in trying, as George Kennedy has encouraged us, to hear John's words "as a Greek-speaking audience would have heard them," which involves an appreciation of rhetoric in antiquity.[6] Second, such an attempt is deliberately limited in its interpretive aspirations. Much as Charles Rosen conceives historical and analytical criticism of music, one may say of rhetorical criticism of biblical texts: "not as the attempt to find new and ingenious things to say about the music of the past, but to account for the way music has been experienced, understood and misunderstood."[7] Third, to warrant this kind of exegetical approach we are no more required to assume that the author of the Fourth Gospel received formal education in rhetoric than we must presuppose the evangelist's enrollment in the Qumran community to account for similarities in thought between John and the Dead Sea Scrolls.[8] Our only a priori is the undeniable: The authors and readers of the New Testament were situated in a culture whose speech and literature were suffused by the norms and techniques of persuasive discourse.[9]

Classical Conceptions of Rhetorical Grandeur[10]

At least by the time of Aristotle (384–322 B.C.E.; see *Rhet.* 3.1403b-1414a), style (φράσις, or *elocutio*) is considered one of the principal components of rhetorical artistry. In fact Quintilian (ca. 40–95 C.E.) highlights the stylistic properties of discourse in his own definition of rhetoric: *bene dicendi scientiam,* "the knowledge of how to speak well" (2.15.38). As theorized by critics such as the celebrated Dionysius of Halicarnassus (*De Compositione Verborum,* ca. 20 B.C.E.), style was subdivided into two categories: diction, or word-selection, and composition, the arrangement of words in various configurations and rhythmic patterns. Not infrequently these categories were broken down into a bewildering array of tropes (verbal "turnings") and figures of speech or of thought (see, e.g., *Her.* 4.19–69 [ca. 85 B.C.E.]).[11] Although the Fourth Gospel is rich in these devices, some of which we shall have reason to note, our study might be more profitably concentrated on the kind of style generally evinced by Jesus' discourse in John.

To get our bearings we begin with *On Style,* produced perhaps in the first century B.C.E. and conventionally attributed to Demetrius. This work offers us the only extant, systematically developed treatment of four primary styles: the plain, the grand, the elegant, and the forceful. Force is the hallmark of Demosthenes (*Eloc.* 5.240–304); in elegance lies charm and wit (3.128–89); trivial subjects invite plain style (4.190–239). The rhetorical style of the Johannine Jesus appears most closely to resemble Demetrius's description of magnificence or grandeur (τὸ μεγαλοπρεπές; 2.38–127). Although it can spring from ornate and unusual diction or word-arrangement, "Grandeur also derives from the subject matter, for example an important and famous battle on land or sea or the theme of the heavens or of earth" (*Eloc.* 2.75, cf. 38–74, 77–113). Demetrius recognizes that diction is plastic and should be suitable to one's subject, like wax that can be molded into various animal shapes (5.296; see also 2.106).

More common among classical theoreticians was the system of three rhetorical styles, which we find in Cicero's *Orator* (ca. 50 B.C.E.): the plain, the middle, and the grand. "The third type of orator is the full, copious, weighty, and ornate. Here surely lies the most power": the *gravis* to storm or to creep into the feelings, to sow new ideas and to uproot the old (*Or.* 28.97). Like Demetrius, Cicero regards style as more than mere ornament; it must be intelligibly conformed to its subject-matter. "Surely [the orator] will be capable of feeling and speaking everything more sublimely and more magnificently when he returns to humanity from the heavens" (*Or.* 34.119).

In his compendious *Institutio Oratoria* (12.10.58–80) Quintilian elaborates Cicero's treatment of three "characters" (χαρακτῆρες) of style. The plain (*subtile,* or ἰσχνόν) is best suited for imparting information; the flowery (*floridum,* or ἀνθηρόν), for charming or conciliation. Emotions are moved, however, by a style that is grand or robust (*grande,* or ἁδρόν):

> The grand style is the sort of river that whirls rocks along, "resents bridges," carves out its own banks; great and torrential, it will carry along even the judge who tries to stand up to it, forcing him to go where he is taken. Such an orator will call the dead to life . . . and cause the state to cry aloud or sometimes . . . to address the orator himself. He will lift the speech high by his amplifications and launch into exaggeration . . . . He will come near to bringing the gods themselves down to meet and talk to him . . . . He will inspire anger and pity; and as he speaks the judge will grow pale, weep, follow tamely as he is snatched in one direction after another by the whole gamut of emotion (Quintilian 12.10.61–62).

The Homeric prototype for this highest eloquence is Ulysses (cf. *Iliad* 3.223; *Odyssey* 8.173), with "strength of voice and force of oratory that in its flow and onrush of words resembled the snows. No mortal, then, can compete with such an orator: People will look to him as a god. This is the force and swiftness that Eupolis admires in Pericles, that Aristophanes compares to thunderbolts. This is the capacity for real oratory" (Quintilian 12.10.64–65).

On Sublimity, an anonymous first-century C.E. treatise customarily ascribed to Longinus, takes up the character and creation of τὰ ὕψη, "a kind of eminence or excellence of discourse [that] is the source of distinction of the very greatest poets and prose-writers. For grandeur produces ecstasy rather than persuasion in the hearer; and the combination of wonder and astonishment always proves superior to the merely persuasive and pleasant" (*Subl.* 1.3–4). True sublimity elevates the orator's audience: it offers intellectual food that bears up under continuous rumination and must be digested over time (7.2–3). Much of *On Sublimity* consists of practical aids in crafting noble diction, figures, and composition (10.1–43.6); for Longinus, however, the primary sources of grandeur are the grasp of great thoughts and strong, inspired emotion (8.1). Greatness of thought inclines toward representation of the gods, though not all discourse about heavenly things excites awe: the *Iliad* blazes with the poet's power at high noon, whereas the *Odyssey* reveals Homer at artistic sunset (9.5–15). Remarkably, for a pagan author, real sublimity is attained in Genesis 1 by "the lawgiver of the Jews—no mean genius, for he both understood and gave expression to the power of divinity as it deserved" (*Subl.* 9.9).[12]

Lastly, Hermogenes of Tarsus (b. ca. 160 C.E.) devotes a large portion of his rambling treatise, *On Types of Style,* to the analysis of grandeur (μέγεθος), one of seven elemental "ideas" or qualities of style. According to Hermogenes grandeur itself consists of various components: solemnity, "things said of the gods *qua* gods" (*Peri ideōn* 242–54); asperity, vehemence, and florescence, which are differently nuanced expressions of criticism (255–63, 269–77); brilliance, "inherent in those acts that are remarkable and in which one can gain luster" (264–69); and amplification (or abundance, περιβολή), the expansion of thought by extraneous ideas (277–96). "Fullness [μεστοτής] is nothing other than abundance taken to an extreme, or what one might call 'abundant abundance'" (*Peri ideōn* 291).[13] By the injection of these properties, discourse that captures great thought may be rescued from the trite or the commonplace (222, 241).

Before turning to John, let us summarize our findings thus far. (1) Reconstruction of positions held by rhetorical theorists of the imperial period amply reinforces a modern reader's intuition of the Johannine Jesus' lofty style. Although the phenomenon is identified in different ways, grandeur or sublimity receives explicit, extensive consideration by classical rhetoricians. (2) Grand style excites within an audience strong if varied responses: powerful feelings, intellectual stimulation, religious wonderment. (3) Like other types of style, grandeur is more than merely decorative: It inheres in thought that was itself conventionally considered to be sublime. (4) Chief among these majestic conceptions, and eminently appropriate for grand stylization, are matters pertaining to divinity. Indeed, the supernatural effects attributed by Quintilian to the ideal orator who speaks in grand style—inciting the state to outcry, raising the dead, calling down the gods for conversation, tossing his judge on a tide of emotion—are fortuitously but nonetheless graphically enacted by Jesus on the stage of the Fourth Gospel (5:18; 7:14–44; 11:43–44; 12:28–29; 18:28–40).

A Sublime Leave-Taking: John 14–17

To consider the whole of John's rhetorical style in the space available to me here is clearly out of the question. As representative of its elevated rhetoric, we may profitably examine selected aspects of Jesus' farewell address and intercessory prayer in John 14—17. When viewed through a classical prism, this longest and largely uninterrupted speech of Jesus in the Fourth Gospel most closely resembles that species of oratory known as epideictic, whose primary concern is the induction or bolstering of beliefs and values held among one's audience in the present (Aristotle, *Rhet.* 1.3.1358b; Cicero, *Inv.* 2.59.177–78). Characteristic of epideictic address (*Her.* 3.6.10–3.8.15), John 14—17 appears not to be a tightly argued exercise in formal logic but rather a ceremonial elaboration (13:1) of topics:[14]

   a.   Jesus' departure and return (14:1–3, 15–17, 18, 27–28; 16:4b–7);
   b.   Relationships that obtain between Jesus and believers (14:15–17, 18–21, 23–24; 15:1–10, 15; 17:6–26), between Jesus and the Father (14:24, 28; 15:9, 10, 15, 23–24; 16:5, 15, 32b; 17:1–2, 4–5), between the Father and believers (14:23; 15:27; 17:3, 11, 17), between believers and the world (14:30; 15:18–25; 16:8–10, 28, 33; 17:9, 14–16), between believers and one another (15:12–14, 17; 17:21–23);
   c.   Peace (14:27; 16:33), joy (14:28; 15:11; 16:20–22, 24; 17:13), loyalty (16:1–4a, 32; 17:6), and glorification (14:13; 15:8; 16:14; 17:1, 4–5, 10, 22–24);
   d.   Knowing (14:4–7; 16:25, 29–30; 17:3, 7–8, 23–25), seeing (14:8–10, 17–19; 15:24; 16:10, 16–22; 17:24), asking (14:13–14; 15:7, 16b; 16:23–24, 26), and loving obedience (14:21–24; 15:1–10, 16a; 17:6).

Jesus' discourse in John 14—17 generally conforms with that subspecies of epideictic later classified as leave-taking (συντακτικός), which expresses a departee's love, gratitude, praise, and prayers for those left behind.[15]

We shall consider two dimensions of Jesus' rhetoric in this chapter. The first and perhaps the most striking stylistic aspect of Jesus' rhetoric in the Fourth Gospel is its circular redundancy of clauses and topics, of which John 17:22–23 is but one concentrated instance that happily embraces most of the topics just tabulated: "The glory that you have given me I have given them, so that they may be one, as we are one, I in them and you in me, [so] that they may become completely one, so that the world may know that you have sent me and have loved them even as you have loved me." How can language that is admittedly so opaque, repetitious, and even monotonous be the vehicle of a discourse that has long been recognized as a religious masterpiece?[16]

Ancient literary critics suggest an answer. The technical term for John's profound yet vertiginous style is *amplification* (αὔξησις, or *amplificatio*), a primary ingredient of grandeur (*De Or.* 3.26.104—27.108; *Her.* 4.8.11; Quintilian 8.4.26–27). While classical theorists differed among themselves on how amplification should be defined—whether "vertically," as a heightening of effect (*Rhet.* 1.9.1368a), or "horizontally," as an extension of thought (*Subl.* 12.1)—its fundamental quality and consonance with sublimity is undisputed: "amplification is an aggregation of all the details and topics that constitute a situation, strengthening the argument by dwelling on it; . . . you wheel up one impressive unit after another to give a series of increasing importance" (*Subl.* 11.1; 12.2). As illustrated by John 17:22–23, the objective of *amplificatio* is not to construct an impeccably logical proof but to wield influence upon one's audience (*Part. Or.* 8.27).

The essence of amplification lies in figures or conventional patterns (σχήματα) of balance and repetition in thoughts and in words (*Eloc.* 2.59–67). The rhetoric of John 14—17 is structurally *balanced* to a fare-thee-well, its thoughts and words characteristically presented in parallel formulations:

> A On that day you will ask nothing of me (16:23a).
> B   Very truly, I tell you, if you ask anything of the Father in my
>   name, he will give it to you (16:23b).
> A Until now you have not asked for anything in my name (16:24a).
> B   Ask and you will receive, so that your joy may be complete
>   (16:24b).

> A   I will do
> B   whatever you ask in my name . . . (14:13a).
> B   If in my name you ask me for anything,
> A   I will do it (14:14).

> A   If I had not come and spoken to them,
> B   they would not have sin (15:22a);
> C   but now they have no excuse for their sin (15:22b).
> D   Whoever hates me hates my Father also (15:23).
> A   If I had not done among them the works that no one else did,
> B   they would not have sin (15:24a).
> C   But now they have seen
> D   and hated both me and my Father (15:24b).

Occasionally the parallelism is honed even to the same number of words and syllables in a clause (technically known as isocolon [*Her.* 4.20.27–28]):

> ἵνα ὦσιν ἕν καθὼς ἡμεῖς ἕν
> so that they be one, just as we are one (17:22b [au. trans.]).

Equally prevalent in John 14—17 is antithesis, the juxtaposition of contrary ideas in parallel structure (*Alex.* 26.25–38; *Her.* 4.15.21; Quintilian 9.3.81–86):

You did not choose me but I chose you (15:16a).

... you will weep and mourn, but the world will rejoice;
you will have pain, but your pain will turn into joy (16:20).

I am asking on their behalf; I am not asking on behalf of the world,
but on behalf of those whom you gave me, because they are yours (17:9).

Repetition, the other main component of *amplificatio,* assumes many different configurations, most of which are conspicuous in John 14—17:

a. Refining (*expolitio*) "consists in dwelling on the same topic and yet seeming to say something ever new" (*Her.* 4.42.54 [trans. H. Caplan, LCL]). This technique takes two forms: simple repetition of the same idea ("A little while, and you will no longer see me, and again a little while, and you will see me" [16:16, 17, 19]; see also 14:1a, 27b; 14:10–11a), or descanting upon the thought ("This is my commandment, that you love one another *as I have loved you*" [15:12; cf. 15:17]; see also 14:2b–3; 14:15, 23).

b. Antanaclasis (*reflexio*), the punning repetition of a word in two different senses (*Her.* 4.14.21; Quintilian 9.3.68), is nicely illustrated by Jesus' (and Thomas's) references to "the way" in John 14:4, 5, and 6.

c. Polysyndeton (the purposeful multiplication of conjunctions) and asyndeton (their deliberate omission) "make our utterances more vigorous and emphatic and produce an impression of vehemence" (Quintilian 9.3.54 [trans. H. E. Butler, LCL]; see also *Eloc.* 2.63–64; *Part. Or.* 15.53–54; *Her.* 4.30.41; *Subl.* 19.1–21.2). Both figures amplify Jesus' farewell address: "Those who love me will keep my word, and my Father will love them, and we will come to them and make our home with them" (John 14:23; see also 14:3–4, 6–7, 12b-13a; 16:22–23a; 17:10–11a); "I am the vine, you are the branches" (15:5a; see also 14:1b).

d. Distribution (*distributio*), enumerating the parts of a whole (*Her.* 4.35.47), describes the analysis of and warrants for the Paraclete's conviction of the world in John 16:8–11.

e. Synonymy (*interpretatio: Her.* 4.28.38), the interchange of different words with much the same meaning, is evident in John's alternations of πορεύομαι ("go") and ὑπάγω ("go away"; 14:2–5, 12, 28; 15:16; 16:5, 7, 10, 17, 28), of λόγος ("word") and ἐντολή ("commandment"; 14:15, 21–24; 15:10, 20; 17:6), of ἀγαπάω and φιλέω, "love" (e.g., 14:15, 21, 23–24; 15:12, 17, 19; 16:27; 17:23, 26), and of λέγω and λαλέω, "say" or "speak" (e. g., 14:29–30; 15:11, 15, 20, 22; 16:4, 6–7, 12–13, 17–18, 25–26; 17:1).

f. Jesus' rhetoric in John, moreover, rings the changes on a hypnotic range of repetitive figures: "Peace I leave with you; my peace I give to you" (14:27 [an example of epanaphora: *Her.* 4.13.19]); "As you have sent me into the world, so I have sent them into the world" (17:18 [antistrophe: *Her.* 4.13.19]); "Believe in

God, also in me believe" (14:1 [epanalepsis: Quintilian 9.3.29]); ". . . that I go to prepare a place for you; and if I go to prepare a place for you . . ." (14:2b–3 [reduplication: *Her.* 4.28.38; Quintilian 9.3.28]); "If you know me [perfect tense], you will know [future] my father also; from now on you [at present] do know him" (14:7 [polyptoton: *Subl.* 23.1–2]); "I am in the Father and the Father is in me" (14:11 [antimetabole: *Her.* 4.28.39]).

Second and beyond amplification, a panoply of other rhetorical devices, regarded by classical theorists as evocative of sublime thought, are displayed by the farewell discourse in John. We need briefly note only a few of them:

a. Some words inherently carry heft, fullness, and sonority (*Part. Or.* 15.53). Strength, like beauty, is indubitably in the beholder's eye. Nevertheless, it is difficult to read or to hear John 14–17 without being impressed by the gravity of such words as "orphaned" (14:18), "abide" (14:10, 17, 25; 15:4–10, 16), "glory" (14:13; 15:8; 16:14; 17:1, 4–5, 10, 22, 24), the portentous "day" (14:20; 16:23, 26) and "hour" (16:2, 4, 21, 25, 32; 17:1), "joy" (15:11; 16:20–24; 17:13), "sorrow" (16:6, 20–22), and "[make] holy" (14:26; 17:11, 17, 19). Of equal force is "I am" (ἐγώ εἰμι), which here, as elsewhere in John (6:20; 8:24, 28, 58; 13:19; 18:6), implicitly asserts Jesus' oneness with God (14:6; 15:1, 5; cf. Ex. 3:14; Isa. 43:10–11, 25; 51:12).[17]

b. Occasionally in John 14–17 Jesus draws comparisons (14:28; 15:13); more frequently he augments the force of his comments (14:12, 18, 21; 15:15, 18; 16:15; 17:4–5). Through expressions of reassurance under particular conditions (among others, see 14:3, 12–15, 21, 23; 15:7; 16:7b–8, 13, 33; 17:7–8), Jesus effectively offers consolation dressed in enthymeme (a proposition with a supporting reason: *Rhet.* 1.2.1356b). By all such formulations discourse on grand topics acquires luster (Quintilian 8.4.3–14; 5.9–11).

c. Rhythmic flow, created by the length of a sentence's constituent phrases (κόμματα) and clauses (κῶλα), is another stylistic trait expansively, if sometimes chaotically, considered by classical rhetoricians. Among them, a rough consensus holds that sentences with long clauses (e.g., John 14:3; 15:19), or the yoking of shorter clauses into longer periods (e.g., John 16:12–15; 17:20–23), is conducive to sublimity (*Eloc.* 1.5; 2.44; *Subl.* 40.1–43.5; *Peri ideōn* 251–54).

d. Notwithstanding the universal esteem in which clarity of expression was held by the ancients (*Rhet.* 3.1404b; *Or.* 23.79; *De Or.* 3.49; Quintilian 8.1.1–2.24; *Peri ideōn* 226–41), most of them acknowledged a place within grand style for purposeful obscurity (ἔμφασις). Hermogenes, for instance, held that discourse about divine subjects depends on "the use of suggestive hints to indicate darkly, in the manner of the mysteries and initiations, something within the sphere of solemn thoughts. By appearing to know, but to be unable to reveal, we give an impression of grandeur and solemnity" (*Peri ideōn* 246; see also *Her.* 4.53.67; Quintilian 8.3.83–86). Such comments may throw light on the more obscure figures (παροιμίαι [16:25, 29]) in John 14–17: its similes (16:21–22) and metaphors (14:6; 15:1, 5, 15; 17:12 [see *Eloc.* 2.77–90; Quintilian 8.6.4–18; *Subl.* 32.1–7]), its allegorical leanings (14:2–3, 23, 30; 15:2–4; 15:6, 8, 16 [see Quintilian 8.6.44–53), and its jarring non sequiturs (14:5/16:5; 14:31b/15:1; 15:15/20). Like others from among his interlocutors in John (3:4, 9; 4:11–12, 15; 7:32–36; 8:21–23), Jesus' disciples can scarcely penetrate his meaning (14:5, 8, 22; 16:17–18); they are attuned to the lower level of discourse whose divine nuances are pitched at a frequency inaudible without a boost from God (cf. John 16:29–31).[18] By its very nature, the sublimity exhibited by Jesus in John "contains much food for reflection" (*Subl.* 7.3), mysterious depths to be plumbed (Quintilian 9.2.65), reverberations of a "dialogue between heaven and earth."[19]

Thus far two claims of our study appear to be mutually confirmatory. (1) Orators and critics, themselves contemporary with the fourth evangelist, meticulously worked out a notion of rhetorical grandeur and expressly associated that style with stirring consideration of divine topics. (2) Jesus' leave-taking in John 14–17, manifestly devoted to transcendent concerns for his disciples, evinces such rhetorical sublimity to an equally explicit and impressively precise degree. Of course, to argue that Johannine style has affinity with modes of Greco-Roman discourse is hardly tantamount to a retraction of Semitic influences on John, much less to a reassertion of C. H. Dodd's thesis that the Fourth Gospel was directed to adherents of "the higher religion of Hellenism."[20] If John now appears to many scholars more Near Eastern in milieu, then its exhibition of Hellenistic rhetoric is no more anomalous than that to be found in the contemporaneous writings of Josephus and Philo.[21] Nor should our results to this point invite preoccupation with sheer style detached from substance, which would distort both John and the rhetoricians. "Magniloquence," as Longinus reminds us, "is not always serviceable: to dress up trivial material in grand and solemn language is like putting a huge tragic mask on a little child" (*Subl.* 30.2; see also *Rhet.* 3.1408a; *Eloc.* 2.114–27). Indeed, before proceeding further, we should ponder the stylistic appropriateness of Jesus' valedictory in John 14–17.

The grandeur of this address, on one hand, is in precise synchronization with the peculiar dialectic exhibited by the Fourth Gospel's presentation of Jesus. To that Christology every reader's port of entry is John 1:1–18, whose conceptual and stylistic similarities with the farewell discourse can scarcely be accidental.[22] And the heart of that Christology beats with the belief that Jesus of Nazareth is "the only [-begotten, μονογενής] God in the bosom of the Father," the incarnate Word whose acceptance confers eternal life (John 1:1, 14, 16–18; 14:9; 20:28). So if one asks why the speech of the Johannine Jesus differs so vastly from that of Jesus in the Synoptics, a *rhetorical* explanation (as distinguished from a tradition-critical estimate) would be that a metahistorical Christology[23] requires for its expression a metahistorical rhetoric. Befitting one who does not merely orate about heaven and earth (cf. *Eloc.* 2.75; *Or.* 34.119) but actually *bestrides* them, the grandeur of

Jesus' discourse in the Fourth Gospel is, in effect, the rhetorical analogue of John's theological paradox: "even when on earth [the Son of Man] is in heaven."[24] That is to say, Jesus *speaks* as Jesus *is:* in flesh, while simultaneously *sub specie aeternitatis* (N.B. John 3:13, 34; 6:63, 68b–69; 14:10, 24; 17:6–8, 14).[25]

The sublimity of John 14–17, moreover, comports with and even transports Jesus' obvious concern for the consolation of his followers, the strengthening of their resolve under fire, and the maintenance of their integrity in love after his departure. These thoughts are expressly developed throughout the discourse (e.g., 14:1–3, 18–21; 15:9–17; 15:18–16:4; 16:19–24; 16:31–33; 17:13–26), as any reader or listener can verify. Less obvious and more subliminal—perhaps for that reason more powerful (see *Subl.* 17.1)—is the effective communication of these values by the style of Johannine rhetoric. Accordingly, Jesus identifies this world (κόσμος) as the theater, not the origin, of his disciples' witness (John 15:19; 17:14–18; cf. 16:28; 17:11), but he *establishes* that distinction by means of sublime discourse that evokes a "wondrous strange," though not perspicacious, response (16:29–30; cf. *Subl.* 1.3–4).[26] Not merely does Jesus say, "Let not your hearts be troubled" (14:1; 14:27c); *the pervasive balance of the rhetoric itself* conveys the steady tranquillity to which the content refers. Not merely does Jesus command that his followers love one another (15:12–17); *the grand reciprocity of John's rhetorical style,* with its ever spiraling repetition and verbal inversions, activates for the Gospel's audience the mutuality that inheres between Jesus and God, among Jesus and his "friends" (15:15; see also 14:20–21; 15:9; 17:10–11, 21–23, 26). "I have given them your word," prays Jesus to the Father (17:14)—and John's sublime stylization of the word, imparted by the Word (1:1) and radiant with glory (17:22), amplifies the divine reality (or truthfulness, ἀλήθεια) in which both Jesus and his disciples are consecrated for mission (17:17–19). And that word is truly a gift: the rhetoric of chapters 14–17, as of Jesus' discourse throughout John, does not arrive at, much less aim for, logical proof of Jesus' claims; rather, it elicits and reinforces that faith in Jesus already active in the listener, activated by God (1:12–18; 3:6–8, 16–21).[27] In that respect the rhetorical style of the Johannine Jesus is no less revelatory than the character of the revelation that he discloses and, indeed, is.[28] All things considered—the speaker's character, the audience's sympathies, the circumstances of the speech—the convergence of style and substance in John 14–17 could hardly be more apposite or, for that matter, more in keeping with the express counsel of classical rhetoricians, for whom suitability to the matter declaimed was the touchstone of stylistic excellence (*Inv.* 1.7.9; *Her.* 1.2.3.).[29]

THE RHETORIC OF A JOHANNINE INTERPRETER

At least as early as the third century, the stylistic as well as conceptual similarities (and differences) between John and 1 John have been perceived by Christian commentators (Eusebius, *H. E.* 7.25.17–26). No less than professional exegetes, many modern readers intuitively recognize that the author of the epistle writes in that repetitive, antithetical, and interwoven style so distinctive in the New Testament yet so typical of Jesus' speech in the Fourth Gospel:[30] "Beloved, let us love one another, because love is from God; everyone who loves is born of God and knows God. Whoever does not love does not know God, for God is love" (1 John 4:7–8; cf. John 17:25–26). Perhaps less attention has been paid, however, to the argumentative functions and persuasive import of grand style in 1 John, as compared with its use in John's Gospel.

The Role of Sublimity in the First Epistle of John

1. We have already noted the Fourth Gospel's use of a metahistorical rhetoric to support its metahistorical presentation of Jesus. A similar though not identical use of sublime style is apparently to be found in 1 John. The avowed objectives of the epistle are the proclamation and assurance to an earthly community of their eternal or indestructible life, which partakes of God's new age (1:2; 5:13, 20). Of related significance are 1 John's repeated assertions that believers who act justly, reject sin, and love their fellows are "born of God" (3:9; 4:7; 5:1, 4, 18) or are "children of God" (3:1–2, 10; 5:2) or more simply are "of God" (3:10; 4:4, 6; 5:19). The theological dialectic implied by these claims—the encouragement of a community whose character is at once historical and suprahistorical—is crystallized in the literary form of 1 John: an epistle that, while avowedly written (1:4; 2:1, 7–8, 12–14, 21, 26; 5:13), lacks salutation and conclusion, addressing its readers as though from beyond time and space in a rhetorical style that, by the conventions of the day, marries the heavens and the earth (*Eloc.* 2.75). When dialectic dissolves into dualism (as is frequent in 1 John), positing a gulf (2:15; 4:4; 5:4–5, 21) or at least ambivalence (2:2; 4:9, 14) between believers and the world, the medium for this message is antithetical parallelism, itself a dimension of sublimity (2:16–17; 4:5–6a; see also 1:6–10; 2:4–5a, 9–11; 4:6–8; 5:10, 12; cf. *Alex.* 26.25–38).[31] Whereas in the Fourth Gospel Jesus personifies the sublime focalization of humanity and divinity, 1 John tends to articulate this convergence with respect to the believing community (3:1–3; 4:4, 6–7, 11–12; 4:16—5:4), whose life flows from God (2:5, 29; 3:1, 24a; 4:13) and whose lodestar nonetheless is Christ (2:1–6; 3:16, 23; 4:2, 9–10, 14; 5:1, 5, 10–11, 20).

2. Another resemblance between 1 John and John lies in their exercise of grand style to accent the mutuality of love and abidance in God that defines Christian community. Possibly owing to the blow inflicted by schism (1 John 2:19; 4:1, 5), the claim of corporate responsibility (2:12–14; 3:17–18) and the demand of love for "the brother" (2:10; 3:10; 4:20–21) or for one another (3:11, 23; 4:7, 11–12) are in fact more thoroughly worked out in the First Epistle than in the Fourth Gospel (John 13:34–35; 15:12, 17). The means for that theological development in 1 John are multiple: substantively, the correlation of unrighteous be-

havior, or "sinning," with failure to love (1 John 3:4–18; cf. John 3:18; 5:24; 8:24; 16:8–9, which associate sin with unbelief); stylistically, the sheer redundancy of "love," noun (ἀγάπη, 17 times) and verb (ἀγαπάω, 28 times); and the balanced reciprocity of 1 John's formulations, which grandly mirror the believers' experience of "abiding" (μενεῖν) in God as God abides in them (2:24, 27; 3:24; 4:13, 15, 16; so also John 15:4, 5, 7, 10).

3. While the Fourth Gospel's priority to, and presupposition by, the First Epistle has not been established beyond all doubt,[32] 1 John obviously draws from a Johannine tradition whose most extensive deposit is John's Gospel. A modern reader of both documents might be tempted to conclude that the style as well as substance of 1 John mimics that of John. In a sense it probably does. Lest that conclusion deteriorate into disparagement of the epistle, we should remember that imitation (μίμησις, mimêsis) had acquired an honorable connotation among many rhetorical theorists of the imperial period.[33] Among them, Longinus associates mimêsis with the attainment of sublimity:

> [Y]et another road to sublimity . . . is the way of imitation and emulation of great writers of the past. . . . In all this process there is no plagiarism. It resembles rather the reproduction of good character in statues and works of art. . . . When we are working on something which needs loftiness of expression and greatness of thought, it is good to imagine how Homer would have said the same thing, or how Plato or Demosthenes or . . . Thucydides would have invested it with sublimity. These great figures, presented to us as objects of emulation and, as it were, shining before our gaze, will somehow elevate our minds to the greatness of which we form a mental image (Subl. 13.2—14.2; see also Quintilian 10.2.1–28).

I would not argue that the author of 1 John aspired to this or to any aesthetic principle, much less consciously aimed at literary effect for its own sake. Given this ancient rhetorical context, we may reasonably surmise, however, that 1 John's grand style not merely ornaments but meaningfully complements the epistle's persistent concern for the community's tradition (1:1–3; 2:7, 24; 3:11) and the coherence of its faith with retrospection of Jesus' sacrificial love (1:5–10; 4:2–3, 7–12). By replicating the linguistic style of Jesus as remembered in the Johannine tradition, 1 John sublimely and subliminally bolsters its exhortation that the church conduct its life in imitatio Christi (2:1–6; 3:16). The rhetoric of the epistle abides, as it were, in the rhetoric of the Johannine Jesus, in a manner compatible with the author's express intention: "This is the message we have heard from him and proclaim to you" (1:5a; cf. John 17:8).[34]

4. Left quite inexplicit in 1 John is a final impression of its mimetic grandeur, which must remain moot. Elsewhere in the excerpt from On Sublimity, quoted above, Longinus muses on the relationship that obtains among mimêsis, inspiration, and artistic achievement:

[Imitation] is an aim to which we must hold fast. Many are possessed by a spirit not their own. It is like what we are told of the Pythia at Delphi. . . . Similarly, the genius of the ancients acts as a kind of oracular cavern, and effluences flow from it into the minds of their imitators. Even those previously not much inclined to prophesy become inspired and share the enthusiasm which comes from the greatness of others (*Subl.* 13.2; cf. 8.1, 4; *Ion* 533c–d; *Phaedr.* 245a; *De Or.* 2.46.194).

Longinus (though to my knowledge not Plato, Cicero, or other ancient theorists) believes that an author may be so steeped in a model's style and thought that the sublime spirit of that mentor is reproducible within one's audience. Without ever advancing an equivalent claim, 1 John does affirm (a) that the gift of God's abiding presence in the believing community is proved by the Spirit (3:24; 4:13), (b) that God's Spirit engenders and bears witness to authentic confession of Jesus (4:2–3; 5:6–8), and (c) that Jesus is the standard by which the church knows the Spirit of Truth and confirms that "We are from God" (4:1, 6).

The backdrop supplied by Longinus brings into relief the First Epistle's stylistic similarity with the Fourth Gospel in a most provocative way. The matter can be posed as an open question: Could 1 John's *mimêsis* of the Johannine Jesus, in sublimity of thought and expression, have been intended or accepted as tacit corroboration of the validity of its author's testimony—a witness whose probative weight was relativized within a church that (a) assumed of every believer an inspired ability to interpret its tradition (2:20, 27) and (b) was riven by the contesting claims of the author and of would-be deceivers (2:26; 3:7; 4:1–6)? Perhaps. Clearly the writer of 1 John is no proto-Montanist, for the only Paraclete mentioned in this letter is Jesus (2:1–2). Just as obviously, the First Epistle chimes with 2 John 7 in emphasizing the salvific importance of Jesus' humanity (most clearly in 1 John 4:2–3; perhaps also in 1:1–4; 4:15; 5:1, 5–8). Nevertheless, the author's insistence that he and his audience are of God and not of the world (3:1; 4:5–6) is consistent with his adoption of a rhetorical sublimity that constantly reminds the reader of the "transworldly" Jesus of Johannine tradition: "God the only Son," who promised those who abide in him the sending of "the Advocate, the Holy Spirit," who would "remind you of all that I have said to you" (John 14:25–26; cf. 1:13, 18; 8:23; 15:19).[35] Throughout 1 John the author cites no external or authoritative warrants to buttress his claims; a rhetorical appeal, expressed in the glorious diction of Jesus, may have been the strongest suit available to him.[36] The proof for this hypothesis is, however, quite beyond reach, since the epistle says remarkably little about the Spirit and absolutely nothing of the Spirit's relationship to kerygmatic style.[37] Much less problematic is the more general conclusion: Theologically and rhetorically—doubtless for both the letter's author and its implied antagonists—the Fourth Gospel describes and circumscribes the field on which the First Epistle plays.[38]

Epilogue as Prologue

At the level of literary analysis, the present essay manifestly challenges the long-standing appraisal of Blass and Debrunner: "The absence of rhetorical art in the Johannine discourses is quite clear."[39] Yet I shall have failed my subject and my readers if the symbiosis of style and substance in John has been neglected. For the evangelist as for the oratorical culture in which he wrote, style was no mere adornment, detachable from the ideas it conveyed.[40] Peculiarly sublime, Johannine rhetoric is at least one mode of thought, indigenous to the Gospel, by which Johannine theology can be appropriately investigated.[41] Furthermore, the loftiness of the Fourth Gospel and the First Epistle corresponds with those aspects of Johannine thought that were evidently intended to consolidate the life of believing communities in the Johannine tradition. Implicit in our results, therefore, is a *constitutive* purpose for John's rhetoric in the ethos of churches within the Johannine circle, a role no less notable than the widely recognized critical and discriminative functions served by John's dualistic language and theology.[42]

A final implication of this study bears on modern appropriation of John for preaching. To comment on this subject does not transgress my assignment, partly because exegesis for preaching has long stimulated the interest of this volume's honoree;[43] partly because preaching provides, for many of this volume's readers, a regular experience of modern oratory; partly because of the overtly kerygmatic tenor of Johannine literature (John 16:13–15; 1 John 1:5). What difference does an appreciation of Johannine grandeur make for those whose interpretation of John migrates from the study into the pulpit?

A sufficient answer to that question entails another essay, which might begin here: The sublimity of John's witness both *confronts* and *elevates* the church (whether ancient or modern) with the core of its own kerygma, conjugated in a mode that is unabashedly grand and inescapably compelling. If ever a New Testament document resisted the homiletical tendencies of liberalized theology—the maceration of biblical myth into moralistic ideals—it is the Fourth Gospel. This is so not because of its dearth of that paraenesis so common in the Synoptics,[44] but because both its theology and rhetoric are driven by a different engine: the living voice of the incarnate Word, whose glory the church has witnessed and in whose love it abides. Likewise, John gains virtually nothing from sermon illustrations in the conventionally mundane sense. A modern congregation, however, would benefit incalculably from the homiletical experience of *being* illustrated—irradiated by "the true light, which enlightens everyone" (1:9) and to which John testifies.

An unrelieved diet of Johannine preaching would give any congregation theological dyspepsia, as Moody Smith wisely cautions us.[45] Nevertheless, proclamation of John and 1 John invites, if not mandates, a rhetoric that completely engages one's listeners with the supernal God who loved the world so much that he gave his only Son for its sins. When the Johannine witness is thus released, "a Bible-shaped word" is communicated "in a Bible-like way."[46] At stake in such

preaching is nothing less than the penetration of this world's brutality and ba-
nality by a confession most sublime: "And the Word became flesh and lived
among us, and we have seen his glory" (John 1:14). Nothing could be more need-
ful for today's church than to be grasped afresh by the grandeur of its own gospel.

NOTES

1. E. L. Epstein, *Language and Style* (London: Methuen, 1978), 1.
2. D. Moody Smith, *John,* Proclamation Commentaries, 2d ed. (Philadelphia:
Fortress, 1986), 4; note also, idem, *Johannine Christianity: Essays on Its Setting,
Sources, and Theology* (Columbia, S.C.: University of South Carolina Press, 1984),
193–95. This point of contrast between John and the Synoptics is implicitly clarified
by several studies in *Jesus and the Oral Gospel Tradition,* ed. Henry Wansbrough,
JSNTSup 64 (Sheffield: Sheffield Academic Press, 1991), particularly David E. Aune,
"Oral Tradition and the Aphorisms of Jesus" (211–65), and Birger Gerhardsson, "Illuminating the Kingdom: Narrative Meshalim in the Synoptic Gospels" (266–309).
3. The most comprehensive study to date is A.-J. Festugière, *Observations stylis-
tiques sur l'Évangile de S. Jean,* Études et Commentaires 84 (Paris: Éditions Klinck-
sieck, 1974). J. P. Louw, "On Johannine Style," *Neot* 20 (1986): 5–12, is a brief but
helpful orientation to the subject.
4. Thus, among others, C. F. Burney, *The Aramaic Origin of the Fourth Gospel*
(London: Clarendon, 1922); C. H. Dodd, "The First Epistle of John and the Fourth
Gospel," *BJRL* 21 (1937): 129–56; Wilbert Francis Howard, *The Fourth Gospel in Recent Criticism and Interpretation,* 4th ed., rev. by C. K. Barrett (London: Epworth,
1955), esp. 213–27, 276–96.
5. A sampler of current strategies is provided in *The Fourth Gospel from a Literary Perspective,* ed. R. Alan Culpepper and Fernando F. Segovia, *Semeia* 53 (1991).
For an incisive critique of some narrative-critical trends in Johannine interpretation,
see John Ashton, *Studying John: Approaches to the Fourth Gospel* (Oxford: Clarendon, 1994), 141–65, 184–208.
6. George A. Kennedy, *New Testament Interpretation through Rhetorical Criticism* (Chapel Hill, N.C., and London: University of North Carolina Press, 1984), 10.
My own essay, "Rhetorical Criticism," in *Hearing the New Testament: Strategies for
Interpretation,* ed. Joel B. Green (Grand Rapids: Eerdmans, 1995), 256–77, surveys
several kindred but distinguishable approaches to biblical rhetoric, examining John
4:1–42 as a test case.
7. In a letter in *The New York Review of Books* 39/7 (9 April 1992), 54, cited in
Ashton, *Studying John,* 161.
8. Thus, the variously inflected conclusions represented in *John and Qumran,* ed.
James H. Charlesworth (London: Chapman, 1972), though contrast John Ashton's
bold, if admittedly unprovable, proposal that the fourth evangelist had been an Essene
(*Understanding the Fourth Gospel* [Oxford: Clarendon, 1991], 232–37).
9. For a reliable overview of vast terrain, consult George A. Kennedy, *A New History of Classical Rhetoric* (Princeton, N.J.: Princeton University Press, 1994), an extensively revised abridgement of his standard, three-volume survey. Graham Anderson, *The Second Sophistic: A Cultural Phenomenon in the Roman Empire* (London

and New York: Routledge, 1993), considers the social dimensions of rhetoric during the era of, and postdating, the New Testament. Stanley F. Bonner, *Education in Ancient Rome: From the Elder Cato to the Younger Pliny* (Berkeley, Calif.: University of California Press, 1977), takes the measure of rhetoric in Roman education.

10. For the discussion that follows, most of the Greek and Latin texts are available in the Loeb Classical Library (LCL): Aristotle, *Peri Poiētikēs* (= *Poet.*); *Technē Rhētorikē* (= *Rhet.*); Cicero, *De Inventione* (= *Inv.*); *De Optimo Genere Oratorum* (= *De Optimo*); *Orator* (= *Or.*); *De Oratore* (= *De Or.*); *De Partitione Oratoria* (= *Part. Or.*); "Demetrius," *On Style* (= *Eloc.*); "Longinus," *On the Sublime* (= *Subl.*); Plato, *Ion*; *Phaedrus* (= *Phaedr.*); *Respublica* (= *Resp.*); *Sophista* (= *Soph.*); Quintilian, *Institutio Oratoria* (= Quintilian); *Rhetorica ad Alexandrum* (= *Alex.*); *Rhetorica ad Herennium* (= *Her.*). For the text of *On Types of Style* (= *Peri ideōn*), see *Hermogenis Opera,* ed. Hugo Rabe (Leipzig: Teubner, 1913); for Augustine's *On Christian Doctrine* (*De Doctrina Christiana* = *De Doct. Christ.*), consult CChr, Series Latina 32 (Turnhout: Brepols, 1962), 1–167. Unless otherwise indicated, English translations of these classical works (herein, occasionally with minor modifications) are those of D. C. Innes (Demetrius), D. A. Russell (Longinus and Hermogenes), and M. Winterbottom (Cicero and Quintilian) in *Ancient Literary Criticism: The Principal Texts in New Translations,* ed. Donald A. Russell and Michael Winterbottom (Oxford and New York: Oxford University Press, 1972).

11. An exhaustive (and potentially exhausting!) inventory of rhetorical figures is compiled in Heinrich Lausberg's magisterial *Handbuch der literarischen Rhetorik: Eine Grundlegung der Literaturwissenschaft,* 3d ed. (Stuttgart: Steiner, 1990), 277–507. Briefer and more sparkling is Brian Vickers, *In Defence of Rhetoric* (Oxford: Clarendon, 1988), 294–339. G. B. Caird angles the discussion toward biblical literature in *The Language and Imagery of the Bible* (Philadelphia: Westminster, 1980), esp. 131–97.

12. Translation by D. A. Russell, in *'Longinus': On the Sublime* (Oxford: Clarendon, 1964), 93–94, who carefully weighs the arguments, lodged since 1733, for this passage's inauthentic interpolation and finds them wanting.

13. This translation and its predecessors are by Cecil W. Wooten, *Hermogenes' On Types of Style* (Chapel Hill and London: University of North Carolina Press, 1987), 33, 51.

14. Kennedy, *New Testament Interpretation through Rhetorical Criticism,* 73–85, extensively develops a similar assessment. Alternatively, in *The Farewell of the Word: The Johannine Call to Abide* (Minneapolis: Fortress, 1991), Fernando F. Segovia proposes that John 13:31–16:33 consists of four discrete units, each with a discernible arrangement of argument tailored to fluctuating rhetorical objectives (see esp. 291–308).

15. *Menander Rhetor* (2.15.430–34), ed. with translation and commentary by D. A. Russell and N. G. Wilson (Oxford: Clarendon, 1981), 195–201. The "farewell address of a departing leader" (*Abschiedsrede*) is a well-attested literary genre in antiquity: see, for instance, Gen. 49:1–33 (Jacob), Deut. 31:1–34:8 (Moses), Plato's *Apology* (Socrates), *1 Enoch* 91–107 (Enoch), and the second-century B.C.E. corpus, the *Testaments of the Twelve Patriarchs.* Useful surveys of the genre are provided by Ethelbert Stauffer, "Abschiedsreden," *RAC* 1 (1950): 29–35; Johannes Munck, "Discours d'adieu dans le Nouveau Testament et dans la littérature biblique," in *Aux Sources de la Tradition Chrétienne: Mélanges offerts à M. Maurice Goguel* (Neuchâtel: Delachaux &

Niestlé, 1950), 155–70; and Segovia, *The Farewell of the Word*, 5–20. William S. Kurz, *Farewell Addresses in the New Testament*, Zacchaeus Studies: New Testament (Collegeville, Minn.: Glazier/Liturgical Press, 1990), offers perceptive exegesis of some specimens.

16. The tension is noted but not resolved by Raymond E. Brown, *The Gospel according to John (xiii–xxi)*, AB 29A (Garden City, N.Y.: Doubleday, 1970), 582. For Rudolf Schnackenburg the "long-pondered theology of John" underlies its "colourless" diction (*The Gospel according to St John*, vol. 1 [New York: Crossroad, 1982], 111–12).

17. Consult Philip B. Harner, *The "I Am" of the Fourth Gospel: A Study in Johannine Usage and Thought*, FBBS 26 (Philadelphia: Fortress, 1970).

18. Whatever may have been the tradition-history of John 14—17 (whose reconstruction was most famously attempted by Rudolf Bultmann, *The Gospel of John: A Commentary* [Philadelphia: Westminster, 1971], 457–631), the disjunctures, scattered topics, and frequent repetition within its canonical form can be appreciably accounted for on rhetorical-critical grounds.

19. Amos N. Wilder, *Early Christian Rhetoric: The Language of the Gospel* (Cambridge, Mass.: Harvard University Press, [1964] rpt. 1971), 50. On the subject of religious obscurity in classical and early Christian discourse, consult George L. Kustas, *Studies in Byzantine Rhetoric*, Analecta Vlatadon 17 (Thessaloniki: Patriarchal Institute for Patristic Studies, 1973), 63–100, 159–99, and Frank Thielman, "The Style of the Fourth Gospel and Ancient Literary Critical Concepts of Religious Discourse," in *Persuasive Artistry: Studies in New Testament Rhetoric in Honor of George A. Kennedy*, ed. Duane F. Watson, JSNTSup 50 (Sheffield: Sheffield Academic Press, 1991), 169–83.

20. C. H. Dodd, *The Interpretation of the Fourth Gospel* (Cambridge: Cambridge University Press, 1953), esp. 3–130.

21. See David L. Balch, "Two Apologetic Encomia: Dionysius on Rome and Josephus on the Jews," *JSJ* 13 (1982): 102–22; Thomas M. Conley, *Philo's Rhetoric: Studies in Style, Composition and Exegesis*, Center for Hermeneutical Studies 1 (Berkeley, Calif.: Center for Hermeneutical Studies, 1987). Likewise, David Daube has persuasively argued for the derivation of rabbinic norms of exegesis, ascribed to Hillel (ca. 50 B.C.E.–10 C. E.), from Hellenistic rhetoric: "Rabbinic Methods of Interpretation and Hellenistic Rhetoric," *HUCA* 22 (1949): 239–64.

22. Note Heinrich Lausberg, "Der Johannes-Prolog: Rhetorische Befunde zu Form und Sinn des Textes," *Nachrichten der Akademie der Wissenschaften in Göttingen, I: Philologisch-Historische Klasse, 1984, Nr. 5* (Göttingen: Vandenhoeck & Ruprecht, 1984), 191–279.

23. Thus, Smith, *Johannine Christianity*, 184–88.

24. C. K. Barrett, *Essays on John* (Philadelphia: Westminster, 1982), 110. This paradox is vividly articulated in John 3:13–14: Of the Son of Man's descent and ascent, Jesus speaks (to Nicodemus) at once retrospectively and apodictically. In the Johannine Jesus time and space intersect, precisely because the Son of Man is the ladder, the means of intercourse between earth and heaven (1:51). To say, "What is being portrayed, therefore, [in John 17] is a Jesus who is not exclusively either on earth or in heaven, but who in some sense is moving from one to the other, who is ascending and is coming closer to the Father" (Thomas L. Brodie, *The Gospel according to John: A Literary and Theological Commentary* [New York and Oxford: Oxford Uni-

versity Press, 1993], 507), seems to me more resonant of Brodie's exposition of John as a kind of map of the stages in human life and belief (31–39) than of the intricate convergence of horizons in Johannine Christology.

25. This suggestion approximates that of Mark W. G. Stibbe, "The Elusive Christ: A New Reading of the Fourth Gospel," in *The Gospel of John as Literature: An Anthology of Twentieth-Century Perspectives*, ed. Mark W. G. Stibbe, NTTS 17 (Leiden and New York: Brill, 1993), 231–47 (esp. 236–39), although Stibbe (following Ernst Käsemann, *The Testament of Jesus: A Study of the Gospel of John in the Light of Chapter 17* [London and Philadelphia: SCM/Fortress, 1968]) stresses more unreservedly than I the unmitigated divinity of Jesus in John (see n. 24 above). Contrast the subtler exegesis of D. Moody Smith, *The Theology of the Gospel of John*, New Testament Theology (Cambridge: Cambridge University Press, 1995), 101–3, who details the merging in John of three distinguishable perspectives on Jesus: the cosmic, the postresurrection, and the historical.

26. Not only for its profundity, but also for its sublime presentation was John characterized as a "spiritual Gospel" (πνευματικὸν εὐαγγέλιον, Eusebius *H.E.* 6.14.7) by early doctors of the church, many of whom were well versed in classical rhetoric. Compare the analyses of Maurice Wiles, *The Spiritual Gospel: The Interpretation of the Fourth Gospel in the Early Church* (Cambridge: Cambridge University Press, 1960), Ronald Dick Sider, *Ancient Rhetoric and the Art of Tertullian*, Oxford Theological Monographs (Oxford: Oxford University Press, 1971), and George A. Kennedy, *Greek Rhetoric under Christian Emperors* (Princeton, N.J.: Princeton University Press, 1983), 180–264.

27. See Smith, *The Theology of the Gospel of John*, 93–99, and compare Kennedy, *New Testament Interpretation through Rhetorical Criticism*, 108–13.

28. "Thus the fundamental question or issue of the Gospel can be stated as the nature of revelation. What God is revealed, and how is God revealed?" (Smith, *The Theology of the Gospel of John*, 75). In a similar vein, see Ashton, *Understanding the Fourth Gospel*, 515–53.

29. For this reminder I am indebted to Beverly R. Gaventa.

30. See especially Amos N. Wilder, "The First, Second, and Third Epistles of John," *IB* 12 (1957): 211–12; Rudolf Schnackenburg, *The Johannine Epistles: Introduction and Commentary* (New York: Crossroad, 1992), 6–11; Duane F. Watson, "Amplification Techniques in 1 John: The Interaction of Rhetorical Style and Invention," *JSNT* 51 (1993): 99–123. In his classes Professor Smith has jocularly dubbed this peculiar style as "Johannese."

31. For this reason great caution is warranted in reconstructing the position of opponents against whom 1 John inveighs and whose assumed theological profile looms large in the masterly commentary by Raymond E. Brown, *The Epistles of John, Translated with Introduction, Notes, and Commentary*, AB30 (New York: Doubleday, 1982), N.B. 47–68, 762–63; see also idem, *The Community of the Beloved Disciple* (New York and Ramsey, N.J.: Paulist, 1979), 93–144. That the epistle's author antithetically contrasts his own position with that of unnamed schismatics (2:18–22; 4:1–6) and deceivers (2:26; 3:7a) can hardly be doubted. Less certain, however, is the presence of secessionist doctrine behind other instances of 1 John's refutatory style (e.g., 1:6–7, 8–10; 2:4–5, 9–11; 3:7b–8, 9–10; 4:7–8, 19–21; 5:10–12; similarly, Pheme Perkins, *The Johannine Letters*, New Testament Message 21 [Wilmington, Del.: Glazier, 1979], xvi–xxiii). Indeed, if 1 John is as relentlessly contentious as some

238 C. Clifton Black

have suggested, one wonders with Judith M. Lieu (" 'Authority to Become Children of God': A Study of I John," *NovT* 23 [1981]: 210–28) why the blade of its rebuttals is so dull, given its author's presumed access to a tradition that could wield polemic with such devastating effect (John 8:21–59).

32. Two recent commentaries proceed from the minority position that 1 John was written before, or alongside, the Gospel in its final form: Kenneth Grayston, *The Johannine Epistles,* NCB (Grand Rapids and London: Eerdmans/Marshall, Morgan & Scott, 1984), and Charles H. Talbert, *Reading John: A Literary and Theological Commentary on the Fourth Gospel and the Johannine Epistles* (New York: Crossroad, 1992).

33. The concept of imitation underwent a complex evolution in antiquity. As a critical term *mimêsis* most commonly refers to an artistic representation of reality, whose epistemological, psychological, and ethical implications vary considerably in the treatments of classical theoreticians (cf., among others, the more negative assessments of Plato [*Resp.* 10.1.595–7.607; *Soph.* 264a–268d] and the more positive though no less diverse presentations of Aristotle [*Poet.,* passim], Cicero [*De Optimo* 3.8; 5.14], and Augustine [*De Doct. Christ.* 4.29.62]). By the late Hellenistic and imperial era, imitation was often understood as emulation of the good and the beautiful, since it was assumed that the orator was an upright Roman of unimpeachable character (e.g., Quintilian 1.Pr.9 et passim). For further consideration of *mimêsis* in the history of rhetoric, consult George A. Kennedy, *Classical Rhetoric and Its Christian and Secular Tradition from Ancient to Modern Times* (Chapel Hill, N.C.: University of North Carolina Press, 1980), 116–19; D. A. Russell, *Criticism in Antiquity* (Berkeley and Los Angeles: University of California Press, 1981), 99–113; and C. Jan Swearingen, "*Ethos:* Imitation, Impersonation, and Voice," in James S. Baumlin and Tita French Baumlin, eds., *Ethos: New Essays in Rhetorical and Critical Theory,* SMU Studies in Composition and Rhetoric (Dallas, Tex.: Southern Methodist University Press, 1994), 115–48.

34. This suggestion echoes, while extending in a more explicitly theological direction, Moody Smith's opinion (following Brown, *The Epistles of John,* 123–29) that John's Gospel has been used as a model in the structuring of 1 John's comments (*First, Second, and Third John,* Interpretation: A Bible Commentary for Teaching and Preaching [Louisville, Ky.: John Knox, 1991], 23–24).

35. With Urban C. von Wahlde I agree that "the author [of 1 John] and the opponents differ in that the author constantly anchors his conception of the Spirit in the ministry of Jesus" (*The Johannine Commandments: 1 John and the Struggle for the Johannine Tradition,* Theological Inquiries [New York and Mahwah, N.J.: Paulist, 1990], 127), while demurring on the fullness and precision with which we can reconstruct the opponents' position (ibid., 105–98; see n. 31 above).

36. For a similar though less speculative estimate, see Judith M. Lieu, *The Theology of the Johannine Epistles,* New Testament Theology (Cambridge and New York: Cambridge University Press, 1991), 23–27.

37. The equation of the voice of Christ, the Spirit's speech, and Christian prophecy is clearer in the Johannine Apocalypse (Rev. 2:1, 7, 11, 17, 29, et passim); for discussion, see Richard Bauckham, *The Theology of the Book of Revelation,* New Testament Theology (Cambridge: Cambridge University Press, 1993), 109–25. Brown, *The Community of the Beloved Disciple,* 138–44, offers an intriguing assessment of 1 John's pneumatological ambivalence.

38. Similarly, Smith, *First, Second, and Third John*, 32, 130–32.

39. Friedrich Blass and Albert Debrunner, *A Greek Grammar of the New Testament and Other Early Christian Literature* (Chicago and London: University of Chicago Press, 1961 [from the fourth German edition, 1913]), 260.

40. Similarly, C. F. Evans, *The Theology of Rhetoric: The Epistle to the Hebrews*, Friends of Dr. Williams's Library Lecture 42 (London: Dr. Williams's Trust, 1988), 3–4.

41. Observe the counsel of Robert Kysar, "The Fourth Gospel: A Report on Recent Research," *ANRW* 2.25.3 (1985): 2389–480 (here, 2464).

42. Thus, among others, Ashton, *Understanding the Fourth Gospel*, 205–37.

43. See his guide, *Interpreting the Gospels for Preaching* (Philadelphia: Fortress, 1980).

44. Consult the discussion in Smith, *The Theology of the Gospel of John*, 146–49.

45. Smith, *Johannine Christianity*, 190–222; Note also C. Clifton Black, "Christian Ministry in Johannine Perspective," *Int* 44 (1990): 29–41.

46. Here I am obviously indebted to Leander E. Keck, *The Bible in the Pulpit: The Renewal of Biblical Preaching* (Nashville: Abingdon, 1978), N.B. 106; idem, "Toward a Theology of Rhetoric/Preaching," in *Practical Theology*, ed. Don Browning (San Francisco: Harper & Row, 1983), 126–47.

Beverly Roberts Gaventa

13

The Archive of Excess:
John 21 and the Problem of Narrative Closure

[C]onclusions are the weak point of most authors, but some of the fault lies in
the very nature of a conclusion, which is at best a negation.
—George Eliot[1]

Really, universally, relations stop nowhere, and the exquisite problem of the
artist is eternally but to draw, by a geometry of his own, the circle within which
they shall happily *appear* to do so.
—Henry James[2]

In the losing battle that the plot fights with the characters, it often takes a
cowardly revenge. Nearly all novels are feeble at the end.
—E. M. Forster[3]

The Gospel writers seem to experience the same difficulties with endings as do
these distinguished modern novelists. The abrupt ending of Mark at 16:8 gives
rise not only to several attempts at repair but to one of the most intransigent problems in Gospel research. If Matthew provides a clear stopping-point with the so-
called Great Commission in 28:16–20, the reader is nevertheless left not knowing
what becomes of the disciples, their commission, or even of Jesus himself. At least
one function served by the Acts of the Apostles is to solve the difficulty inherent
in bringing the Gospel of Luke to an end, although the ending of Acts poses its
own problems.

The Gospel of John appears to many readers to reach a conclusion twice,
prompting Robert Kysar to remark on John's love of endings.[4] Following the resurrection appearances in chapter 20, the narrator provides a brief statement indicating that much remains untold and that the Gospel's purpose is to elicit faith in
Jesus, a statement that might well serve to conclude the Gospel (20:30–31). Chapter 21, with its additional stories and its additional closing comment about the stories that remain untold, disrupts that tidy sense of closure. Chapter 21 is, or at least
appears to be, an excess ending. John 21 is also an ending that is concerned with

excess — an excess of fish, an excess of love, an excess of service, and an extravagant excess of stories about Jesus. Accounting for chapter 21 involves not only explaining the presence of a "second" ending but explaining the content of that ending as well.

ACCOUNTING FOR EXCESS

The excessive ending of the Gospel of John has provoked extensive scholarly discussions.[5] In this century the bulk of critical discussion of John 21 has concerned itself with identifying the origins of this chapter and explaining its relationship to the remainder of the Gospel. That John 21 was either an appendix or an epilogue to the Gospel has come to be a regarded by many as an assured result of historical analysis. As early as 1931, B. W. Bacon announced that even "extreme conservatives" concede that "the original Gospel closes at 20:31, and that chapter 21 as a whole consists of a supplement superadded . . . ."[6] Bultmann's source theory appeared to canonize this view, for as D. Moody Smith put it, chapter 21 is "the key and cornerstone for any redactional theory."[7] Dissenting voices have been raised, particularly in recent years,[8] but much discussion of John 21 continues to assume that it is something like a "supplement superadded," although from what sources and by what means continue to be matters for debate.[9]

By contrast with these investigations, the resurgence of literary approaches[10] has taken up the study of John in its final form, thereby considering John 21 within its literary context. In his landmark study, *Anatomy of the Fourth Gospel*, Alan Culpepper's comments on chapter 21 reflect the tension between the literary and the historical approaches. Culpepper describes John 21 as "an epilogue, apparently added shortly after the gospel was completed," but he goes on to conclude that chapter 21 is also "the necessary ending of the gospel" because it resolves certain tensions in the story and "bridges the gap between the story and the reader."[11] Although Culpepper generally brackets out questions of history and source, they slip back in here and create an interesting conflict. After all, if chapter 21 was added following the completion of the Gospel itself, how can it also be the Gospel's "necessary ending"?[12]

Fernando Segovia examines John 21 within the framework of the genre of biographical writing. He characterizes John 20:31–21:25 as the "final farewell" of Jesus, consisting of an introductory statement about the character and purpose of Jesus' biography (20:30–31), the "final farewell" itself (21:1–23), and a closing statement about the origins and character of Jesus' biography (21:24–25).[13] The relationship between this "final farewell" and the preceding resurrection narratives in 20:1–29 is, on Segovia's analysis, one of "linear and progressive development." The initial discovery of the empty tomb and the appearance to Mary Magdalene (20:1–18) introduce the resurrection itself; 20:19–29 depicts the disciples' change in understanding, grants them the "promised successor" to Jesus, and depicts their new role "in the world"; 20:30–21:25 further develops that role by focusing on mission and the relationship of disciples with one another.[14] Unlike Culpepper, Segovia manages to disentangle himself from questions of the history and origins of chapter 21, but the notion of a "linear and progressive development" from John 20 to John 21 reduces chapter 21 to a commissioning account (thus minimizing the importance of the miraculous catch of fish) and glosses over the repetition between these chapters.

Charles Talbert also treats John 20 and 21 together, but he posits a series of parallels between the two chapters as well as highly structured literary patterns within individual units. An inclusion regarding Peter and the Beloved Disciple marks off the unit (20:2–10 and 21:20–23), which consists of two parts (20:1–31 and 21:1–25), each of which contains two cycles of resurrection narratives and each of which concludes with a statement of the purpose of the Gospel or the grandeur of its subject matter.[15] If Segovia's theory of progression through John 20 — 21 seems vague and reductionistic, Talbert's analysis threatens to force parallels where none exists. To take but one example: Admittedly, Peter and the Beloved Disciple appear both in 20:2–10 and 21:20–23, but they are preceded in 20:1 by Mary Magdalene's discovery and followed in 21:24–25 by the narrator's closing remarks. This makes it difficult to see their presence as forming an inclusion, particularly since both also appear in 21:1–14.

In common with the approaches of Segovia and Talbert, this essay leaves aside questions of source and authorship to ask about the role of John 21 in its present context; whatever the history of the material in chapter 21, it now constitutes the ending of the Gospel and, as such, it merits attention. As distinct from earlier literary approaches to chapter 21, however, this essay draws upon recent discussions of closure in literature, particularly Marianna Torgovnick's work on the shape of narrative endings[16] and D. A. Miller's study of "narratability."[17] What I propose is that 20 and 21 constitute dual endings for the Gospel of John, each of which has a distinct function and focus, and that at least some of the difficulties interpreters have identified in chapter 21 derive from the difficulties inherent in closure (or nonclosure, in this case). John 21 is best characterized, in the elegant phrase of David McCracken, as an "archive of excess."[18]

Before taking up the theoretical discussions, it will be helpful to review John 21, drawing attention to some features that are particularly relevant for this investigation of that chapter and closure. Chapter 21 consists of two scenes narrated in third person (vv. 1–14 and 15–23), followed by closing remarks in first person (vv. 24–25). The narrator both introduces and closes the first scene by characterizing it as a revelation:

> After these things Jesus again revealed (ἐφανέρωσεν) himself to the disciples at the Sea of Tiberias. He revealed (ἐφανέρωσεν) himself in this way (21:1; au. trans.).

> This was now the third time Jesus was revealed (ἐφανερώθη) to the disciples after he was raised from the dead (21:14; au. trans.).

Because φανεροῦν ("to reveal") does not belong to the technical vocabulary of the resurrection appearances, commentators sometimes see in this verb confirmation of the impression that chapter 21 does not belong in its present location or that it constitutes a late addition to the Gospel. What the usage of this particular verb announces, however, is that the story continues the revelation of Jesus, begun in 1:31 (see also 2:11).

The content of the story reinforces the narrator's characterization of it as revelatory, for the movement of the story is movement toward recognition. Initially, the disciples do not know who Jesus is (21:4). Following the miraculous catch of fish, the Beloved Disciple recognizes Jesus with the exclamation, "It is the Lord!" Peter responds by leaping into the sea, and the remaining disciples respond by heading directly for the shore. The second part of the scene (vv. 9–14) completes this recognition with the comment that no one asked Jesus who he was, because "they knew it was the Lord" (v. 12).[19] From lack of knowledge to knowledge limited to the Beloved Disciple to knowledge shared by all, this movement toward recognition dramatizes the revelation of the resurrected Jesus.[20]

The second scene follows but loosely on the first. Here the only disciples involved are Peter and the Beloved Disciple. All reference to setting is omitted, except for the introductory note explaining that Jesus spoke to Simon Peter after they had eaten (v. 15). Particularly because of historical questions about the Johannine community and because of ecclesiastical controversy about the authority of Peter, this scene has prompted enormous debate. Setting that debate aside and admitting the risk of gross reductionism, however, two features of this scene can be identified as important. First, like the one that precedes it, it is concerned with knowledge, although this time the knowledge is that of Jesus rather than that of the disciples. Twice Peter responds to Jesus' question, "You know that I love you" (vv. 15, 16). The third time, Peter extends his comment: "Lord, you know everything, you know that I love you" (v. 17). In addition, Jesus' comments about the future of Peter and the Beloved Disciple provide concrete examples as to the extent of his knowledge.

Second, the scene reaches into the past and the future of both Peter and the Beloved Disciple.[21] Whether or not Jesus' confrontation with Peter is to be understood as Peter's rehabilitation,[22] it surely recalls, at least, that earlier occasion when a charcoal fire burned and Peter three times denied association with Jesus (18:15–27). In addition, Jesus' statement in 21:18 explicitly reaches into the past with the words, "When you were younger, you girded yourself and you walked where you wished . . . ." The end of the same statement anticipates the future: "but when you grow old . . . ." The narrator's explanation in v. 19 likewise looks into Peter's future.

The Beloved Disciple's past is recalled in v. 20 by reference to his presence at the Last Supper and his question about Jesus' betrayal. Commentators occasionally puzzle over the fact that the narrator provides this identification of the Beloved Disciple only here and not earlier, in v. 7, when he is initially reintroduced.[23] That apparent anomaly is resolved, however, once the function of the identification is understood: here it serves to recall the past of the Beloved Disciple, just as vv. 15–18 recall the past of Peter. Similarly, Peter's question provides opportunity for Jesus to say something (however obtuse) about the future of the Beloved Disciple: "If I wish him to remain until I come, what is that to you?" (v. 22). Whatever else is addressed in this scene, it refers both to the past and the future of these two figures.

The narrator's closing remarks in vv. 24–25 shift from third to first person. Once again a central concern is with knowledge, this time the knowledge of the narrator. The narrator points to the Beloved Disciple as the source of the witness and affirms: "We know that his testimony is true" (v. 24). The identity of the "we" remains unclear, but at the very least it refers to some person or persons within the believing community.[24] This assertion shifts the focus from the community of the past and its experience of Jesus to the community of the present. It is not what the disciples knew or even what Jesus knew that stands at the end of the Gospel, but what the community in the present knows. With the final verse of chapter 21, however, another shift is made as the narrator speaks now in first person singular: If everything Jesus did were written down, "I suppose that the world itself could not contain the books that would be written" (v. 25). By contrast with the unequivocal assertion of v. 24, this statement confesses the limitations of knowledge. The Beloved Disciple can be trusted for the testimony of the Gospel, but even he cannot transmit all that Jesus did, for it lies beyond human knowledge.

JOHN 21 AND THE SHAPE OF NARRATIVE

In her study of closure in the novel, Marianna Torgovnick considers variations in narrative shape—the relationship of ending to beginning and middle. She identifies several strategies of closure: circularity, parallelism, incompletion, tangentiality, and linkage. Circularity occurs when the ending "clearly recalls the beginning in language, in situation, in the grouping of characters, or in several of these ways." When language, situation, and character at the end recall not only the narrative's beginning but "a series of points" along the way, it is a parallel ending. Incompletion occurs when the narrative omits some element that is crucial to full circularity or parallelism, either by the author's choice or through some flaw in execution. Tangential endings are those that introduce a new topic, usually deliberately. Linkage exists when the ending of a narrative, rather than recalling its own beginning or middle, anticipates the beginning of yet another narrative.[25] It is important to understand that Torgovnik distinguishes between the terms "closure" and "ending." As is obvious, the end of a narrative is its stopping-place. "Closure," on the other hand, refers to the particular way in which a narrative "reaches an adequate and appropriate conclusion or, at least, what the author hopes or believes is an adequate, appropriate conclusion."[26]

Rather than reading John 20 as the ending of the Gospel and John 21 as an epilogue or appendix, these chapters might better be understood as two separate endings, relatively independent of one another, each of which brings the Gospel to a kind of closure.[27] The independence of chapter 20 from chapter 21 scarcely requires argument, since most students of John assume that chapter 20 provides an adequate ending for the Gospel. It follows readily on the burial at the end of chapter 19 and comes to a clear stopping-place with the narrator's comments in vv. 30–31. The appearances of the resurrected Jesus complete the "lifting up" of the crucifixion, anticipate his ascension, and empower the disciples through the gift of the Holy Spirit.

Demonstrating that chapter 21 can also be construed as an ending to the Gospel independent of chapter 20 is more complicated. Obviously, at least one detail in John 21 assumes that the reader has information supplied in chapter 20: John 21:14 refers to the encounter on the shore as the third time Jesus appeared to his disciples following the resurrection, which of course relies on 20:19–23 and 24–29. In addition, the "again" in 21:1 might be construed as a reference back to the previous resurrection appearances. Those earlier resurrection appearances do not employ the same verb ($\phi\alpha\nu\epsilon\rho o\hat{\upsilon}\nu$), however, and the "again" in 21:1 may link this story back to the earlier revelation stories in John (see 1:31 and 2:11).

Other aspects of chapter 21 are best understood if it is read quite apart from chapter 20, however. The very fact that Peter and others set out on a fishing trip becomes more understandable if they have not yet seen the risen Jesus; the cross having put an end to Jesus, they return to their livelihood.[28] More important, commentators have often struggled with the fact that the disciples do not recognize Jesus when he initially appears on the beach, although they have seen him twice in chapter 20. If chapter 21 provides an ending parallel to chapter 20, however, the anomaly disappears. The disciples have not yet seen the risen Lord, and so they cannot recognize him. In addition, the drama that this scene creates around the recognition of Jesus becomes more convincing if John 21 is a parallel ending for the Gospel.

Apart from the reference in v. 14 to a third resurrection appearance, chapter 21 as a whole follows readily on chapter 19. The phrase $\mu\epsilon\tau\grave{\alpha}\ \tau\alpha\hat{\upsilon}\tau\alpha$ ("after these things"), which introduces chapter 21, connects this scene directly to those similarly introduced in 19:28 ($\mu\epsilon\tau\grave{\alpha}\ \tau o\hat{\upsilon}\tau o$ ["after this"]) and 19:38 ($\mu\epsilon\tau\grave{\alpha}\ \tau\alpha\hat{\upsilon}\tau\alpha$). Although markedly different from the appearances in chapter 20 (see the discussion below), the appearance of the risen Jesus on the beach overthrows the disciples' assumption, enacted in their fishing trip, that the cross was the end of Jesus' story. The conversation with Peter (21:15–19) and the conversation about the

Beloved Disciple (21:20–23) provide the commission necessary to move from the ministry of Jesus to that of the disciples. The narrator's concluding comments about the testimony of the Beloved Disciple and the boundless quantity of Jesus' actions assure the reader of the reliability and extent of this story.

Chapters 20 and 21 provide two endings for the Gospel of John and, in at least a very general sense, they stand in parallel with one another.[29] Furthermore, if read in light of Torgovnik's analysis of closure, these two endings also employ two different strategies of closure, that of circularity in chapter 20 and that of parallelism in chapter 21. The first ending takes readers back to the Gospel's prologue, completing the circle begun there by the appearance of the Logos. Here the ascent of Jesus to the Father (20:17) completes the action begun in 1:10 as the Logos comes into the world, and especially in 1:14 as the Logos becomes flesh. The faith of the Beloved Disciple at the empty tomb (20:8), the reluctant faith of Thomas (20:24–28), Jesus' blessing on others who will believe (20:29), and the final statement of the Gospel's intent to bring people to faith (20:31) take the reader back to the purpose of John the Baptist's testimony (1:7), and more important, to the claim that Jesus gave believers power to become children of God (1:13). Thomas' dramatic greeting of Jesus as "My Lord and my God" (20:28) and the closing identification of Jesus as "the Messiah, the Son of God" (20:31) recall the prologue's identification of Jesus as the one who was with God in the beginning and who is God's "only Son" (1:18).

Of course, some elements in chapter 20 do not fit neatly within this circular movement. The presence of Peter and the Beloved Disciple at the empty tomb echoes their presence in key scenes beginning in 13:21–30. And the Gospel makes frequent reference to Jesus' eventual return to the Father (e.g., 13:1; 14:3, 12, 28; 16:10, 12, 28; 17:3). On the whole, however, the movement in chapter 20 complements and completes that of the prologue.

By contrast, the second ending recalls a number of scenes throughout the Gospel.[30] The testimony of John the Baptist (1:6–8) about Jesus is echoed here in the final words of the narrator, assuring the reader that the testimony of the Beloved Disciple can be trusted (21:24). At the end of chapter 1, Simon Peter, Philip, and Nathanael become disciples by "following" Jesus, and the demand that Peter "follow" Jesus in 21:19 and 22 recalls that scene.[31] John has not previously identified the disciples as fishermen, but the miraculous catch and especially the mysterious meal of fish and bread recollects the miraculous feeding of the five thousand with bread and fish in 6:1–14.[32] The demand that Peter feed the sheep of Jesus may summon up the shepherd discourse in 10:1–18; now it is Peter who must take on the role of the shepherd. Particularly significant is the echo in 21:18–19 of Jesus' statement that "the good shepherd lays down his life for the sheep" (10:11). Similarly, Jesus' words to Peter in 13:36 surely anticipate 21:15–23: "Where I am going, you cannot follow me now; but you will follow afterward."[33] And the threefold question of Jesus to Peter in 21:15–20 recalls Peter's threefold denial in 18:15–27. These particular examples do not exhaust but rather illustrate the extensive network of connections between John 21 and earlier elements in the Johannine story.

Not only do the two endings of John differ in their relationship to the body of the Gospel, but they differ also in their focus. In chapter 20 the narrator places Jesus in the foreground, with the disciples and their responses and responsibilities serving as background for the resurrection of Jesus. The opening scenes in chapter 20, in which the tomb is found to be empty and then Jesus appears to Mary Magdalene (vv. 1–18), sketch the responses of Mary, Peter, and the Beloved Disciple, but always with a view to what has happened to Jesus and what it means. They culminate in Jesus' statement about his ascension and in Mary's triumphant cry, "I have seen the Lord" (v. 18). Similarly, the appearance of Jesus to the disciples in vv. 19–23, even as it grants the Holy Spirit to the disciples, calls attention to the power of the resurrected Jesus, who passes through locked doors and grants the astonishing authority to forgive and retain sin. Admittedly, the doubt of Thomas reveals his reactions to the other disciples' report of the resurrection, but the story culminates in the dramatic confession that Jesus is both Lord and God (v. 28); the story is about Jesus rather than Thomas. Chapter 20 has as its focus Jesus and his resurrection.

Although it would be too much to say that chapter 21 places Jesus in the background, here the narrator moves the disciples and their responses and responsibilities to the foreground.[34] As noted earlier, the story of Jesus' appearance on the beach and the miraculous catch of fish highlights the disciples and their move from lack of recognition to recognition. Peter's conversation with Jesus recalls Peter's denial, reclaims Peter's love for Jesus, and charges him with care of the lambs of Jesus. The saying about Peter's future (v. 18) and the narrator's comment (v. 19) further place him and his particular discipleship in the foreground. The discussion of the past and future of the Beloved Disciple also draws attention to this particular figure (vv. 20–23). The narrator's closing comment about the confidence of believers in the testimony of the Beloved Disciple puts both believers of the past and the present in view, although v. 25 certainly cautions against concluding that Jesus has been moved completely into the background. The shift in focus between the two chapters is analogous to the one that occurs between Luke 24:44–52 and Acts 1:1–11, where the ascension is narrated once with the lens focused on the role of Jesus and a second time with the lens focused on the promises to the disciples.[35]

JOHN 21 AND THE PROBLEM OF CLOSURE

On this reading, therefore, John 20 and 21 are dual endings. Each one follows closely on the end of chapter 19, narrates Jesus' resurrection appearance(s), provides disciples with tasks that continue the work of Jesus, and closes with a strong claim about the "more" that might be told. The two endings differ in their relationship to the story that precedes, with chapter 20 primarily circling back to the prologue and chapter 21 paralleling a number of points throughout the Gospel. They also differ in their focus, with chapter 20 focusing on the resurrected Jesus and chapter 21 on the disciples. If this analysis of John 20 and 21 is persuasive, then the question becomes acute: why provide two endings for this story?

D. A. Miller's study of narrative closure provides a fresh avenue by which to approach this question. In *Narrative and Its Discontents: Problems of Closure in the Traditional Novel*, Miller describes what he refers to as the "narratable" as "instances of disequilibrium, suspense, and general insufficiency from which a given narrative appears to arise." The narratable disrupts the "'nonnarratable' state of quiescence assumed by a novel before the beginning and supposedly recovered by it at the end."[36] In order for narrative to occur, in other words, something must happen that, to one degree or another, disrupts things as they are. To draw on one of the novels Miller discusses, George Eliot's *Middlemarch* is scarcely imaginable without the tension between the idiosyncrasies of Dorothea Brooks and Lydgate, on the one hand, and their community's understanding of what people "ought" to do, on the other. What makes Genesis narratable is God's imposition of creation on the chaos that precedes it. As David McCracken comments: "[I]n all but the most primitive plots, it is hard to imagine story without scandal, if we take *scandal* in a very broad sense to mean something new, anecdotal, and deviant from a general norm."[37]

Whatever form this tension takes in a narrative, it complicates the problem of closure. Closure, to borrow the language of Barbara Herrnstein Smith, "allows the reader to be satisfied by the failure of continuation or, put another way, it creates in the reader the expectation of nothing."[38] If narrative comes into being by virtue of tension or suspense or disruption, then narrative cannot generate *from within* the means to bring narrative to an end. Elements of nonnarratability, of "a world untouched by the conditions of narratability," a world in which nothing is expected, must come into play for narrative to close.[39]

When Miller's insights into the problem of closure are brought to bear on the Gospels, they suggest that the evangelists face the problem in an acute fashion: how can a Gospel possibly come to a close? Surely the dominant principle of the narratives of the canonical Gospels is that, when Jesus bursts on the scene, he shatters the quiescence that precedes him. *He* is the narratable. To bring the narrative to a close requires the restoration of that quiescence or at least the prospect of some new quiescence, but such a development is utterly antithetical to the evangelists' understandings of Jesus. The quiescence presumed by closure is diametrically opposed to the gospel itself.

In the particular case of the Fourth Gospel, it is Jesus' descent from the Father that creates the opportunity for narration. A reasonable form of closure in this instance would be for Jesus to return to the Father and leave behind a stable group of followers, and that is the closure John 20 provides. That quiescence, however, does not and cannot do justice to the ongoing, never-ending character of the disruption created by the descent of Jesus from the Father. Precisely at this point, chapter 21 offers another kind of closure, or perhaps it is anti-closure, one that opens up the futures of Peter and the Beloved Disciple (futures directly connected with Jesus' own will), one in which the community authoritatively asserts the reliability of its traditions, and one that knows that Jesus' story will never close.[40]

The "archive of excess," in McCracken's treatment of John, refers to the claim of 21:25 that the whole world could not contain the books needed to recount all the actions of Jesus, but the phrase aptly characterizes chapter 21 as a whole.[41] This ending deals in excess—the one hundred fifty-three fish, the breakfast waiting even before the fish are hauled to shore, the strength of the nets, the repeated question of Jesus to Peter, the discipleship of Peter and the Beloved Disciple, and, especially, the limitless character of Jesus' deeds. Considered in relation to the Gospel as a whole, the chapter is also a matter of excess, for the Gospel already has an ending in chapter 20. The ending in John 21, however, both recalls a series of scenes throughout the Gospel and signals that this narrative cannot close on a world whose equilibrium is restored or only modestly altered. Following this narrative, nothing can remain unchanged.[42]

NOTES

1. George Eliot, *The George Eliot Letters,* ed. George S. Haight, 7 vols. (New Haven: Yale University Press, 1954–55), 2:324; quoted in D. A. Miller, *Narrative and Its Discontents: Problems of Closure in the Traditional Novel* (Princeton: Princeton University Press, 1981), 189.

2. Henry James, preface to *Roderick Hudson* (Boston: Houghton Mifflin, 1977 [1876]), xv.

3. E. M. Forster, *Aspects of the Novel* (New York: Harcourt Brace, 1927), 95.

4. Robert Kysar, *John's Story of Jesus* (Philadelphia: Fortress, 1984), 91.

5. According to William Baird, debate about the origins of chapter 21 begins at least as early as Hugo Grotius, who argued that John 21 was an addition by the church at Ephesus. See the discussion in William Baird, *History of New Testament Research,* vol. 1: *From Deism to Tübingen* (Minneapolis: Fortress, 1992) 10.

6. B. W. Bacon, "The Motivation of John 21:15–25," *JBL* 50 (1931): 71–80 (quotation, 71).

7. Dwight Moody Smith, Jr., *The Composition and Order of the Fourth Gospel: Bultmann's Literary Theory,* Yale Publications in Religion 10 (New Haven and London: Yale University Press, 1965), 222–38 (quotation appears on 234).

8. See esp. Paul S. Minear, "The Original Functions of John 21," *JBL* 102 (1983): 85–98; John Breck, "John 21: Appendix, Epilogue or Conclusion?" *St. Vladimir's Theological Quarterly* 36 (1992): 27–49; Peter F. Ellis, "The Authenticity of John 21," *St. Vladimir's Theological Quarterly* 36 (1992): 17–25; Willem S. Vorster, "The Growth and Making of John 21," *The Four Gospels 1992: Festschrift Frans Neirynck,*

3 vols., ed. F. Van Segbroeck, C. M. Tuckett, G. Van Belle, and J. Verheyden, BETL 100 (Leuven: Leuven University Press, 1992), 3:2207–221; Timothy Wiarda, "John 21.1–23: Narrative Unity and Its Implications," *JSNT* 46 (1992): 53–71.

9. See Raymond E. Brown, *The Gospel according to John (xiii–xxi)*, AB 29A (Garden City, N.Y.: Doubleday, 1970), 1077–82 for a survey of the debate. In addition, see Rudolf Pesch, *Der reiche Fischfang: Lk 5, 1–11/Jo 21, 1–14* (Düsseldorf: Patmos, 1969), 144–51; Günter Reim, "Johannes 21—Ein Anhang?" in *Studies in New Testament Language and Text: Essays in Honour of George D. Kilpatrick on the Occasion of his Sixty-fifth Birthday*, ed. J. K. Elliott, NovTSup 44 (Leiden: Brill, 1976), 330–37; Robert T. Fortna, *The Fourth Gospel and Its Predecessor: From Narrative Source to Present Gospel* (Philadelphia: Fortress, 1988), 66–79; Frans Neirynck, "John 21," *NTS* 36 (1990): 321–36.

10. I use this phrase because it has become conventional, but it is important to recall Meir Sternberg's sharp criticism of the facile way in which biblical scholars have used the term "literary," as if previous studies were not also literary. He distinguishes, instead, between literary approaches that are concerned with source (that is, the search behind a text for its origins) and those concerned with discourse (that is, the patterns, functions, and effects of the text itself); see *The Poetics of Biblical Narrative: Ideological Literature and the Drama of Reading* (Bloomington, Ind.: Indiana University Press, 1987), 1–57, esp. 15.

11. R. Alan Culpepper, *Anatomy of the Fourth Gospel: A Study in Literary Design*, FFNT (Philadelphia: Fortress, 1983), 96–97.

12. Willi Braun lodges a similar criticism of Culpepper, although Braun's own treatment of John 21 evidences some of the same difficulties involved in combining historical and literary approaches ("Resisting John: Ambivalent Redactor and Defensive Reader of the Fourth Gospel," *SR* 19 [1990]: 59–71, esp. 67–68). See also the review of Culpepper by Richard B. Hays in *Theological Students Fellowship Bulletin* 7 (1984): 20.

13. Fernando F. Segovia, "The Final Farewell of Jesus: A Reading of John 20:30–21:25," in *The Fourth Gospel from a Literary Perspective*, ed. R. Alan Culpepper and Fernando F. Segovia, *Semeia* 53 (1991): 167–90 (here, esp. 175).

14. Ibid., 173–74.

15. Charles H. Talbert, *Reading John: A Literary and Theological Commentary on the Fourth Gospel and the Johannine Epistles* (New York: Crossroad, 1992), 248–64. In this context "inclusion" is a technical term for a passage in which the ending repeats or recalls the beginning.

16. Marianna Torgovnick, *Closure in the Novel* (Princeton: Princeton University Press, 1981).

17. D. A. Miller, *Narrative and Its Discontents* (see above, n. 1).

18. David McCracken, *The Scandal of the Gospels: Jesus, Story, and Offense* (New York: Oxford University Press, 1994), 151.

19. In order to focus on the larger dynamics of this scene, I have omitted discussion of a multitude of detailed exegetical questions.

20. See the insightful analyses of the elusiveness of Jesus in the Fourth Gospel in the recent works of John Painter (*The Quest for the Messiah: The History, Literature and Theology of the Johannine Community*, 2d ed. [Nashville: Abingdon, 1993]) and M.W.G. Stibbe ("The Elusive Christ: A New Reading of the Fourth Gospel," in *The Gospel of John as Literature: An Anthology of Twentieth-Century Perspectives*, ed.

Mark W. G. Stibbe, NTTS 17 [Leiden and New York: Brill, 1993], 231–47; and *John,* Readings: A New Biblical Commentary [Sheffield: JSOT, 1993]).

21. See Culpepper (*Anatomy of the Fourth Gospel,* 58, 67) on the analepses and prolepses in this scene.

22. As is well known, Rudolf Bultmann rejected the view that 21:15–17 should be understood as Peter's rehabilitation, since neither the earlier denial nor repentance is explicitly mentioned (*The Gospel of John: A Commentary* [Philadelphia: Westminster, 1971], 712).

23. See, for example, Brown, *The Gospel according to John (xiii–xxi),* 29A.1109.

24. See the helpful discussion of this problem in Culpepper, *Anatomy of the Fourth Gospel,* 44–46.

25. Torgovnick, *Closure in the Novel,* 13. Robert Tannehill employs Torgovnick's categories constructively in his discussion of closure in Luke-Acts (*The Narrative Unity of Luke-Acts,* 2 vols. [Philadelphia and Minneapolis: Fortress, 1986, 1990] 2.353–57).

26. Torgovnick, *Closure in the Novel,* 6.

27. It is important to underscore that I am not proposing a solution to the problem of the origins or history of these two chapters; what is under discussion here is the literary relationship of the two chapters to each other and to the remainder of the Gospel.

28. Because the disciples have not previously been identified as fishermen, commentators often puzzle over this venture and see this fishing trip as a result of failed faith (e.g., Ernst Haenchen, *John 2: A Commentary on the Gospel of John Chapters 7–21,* Hermeneia [Philadelphia: Fortress, 1984], 222).

29. I use the qualifier ("a very general sense") to distinguish this approach from that of Charles Talbert, discussed above.

30. This feature of chapter 21 may contribute to the critical complaint that the chapter seems composed of a variety of elements that do not necessarily belong together. For example, Bultmann complains that the story in vv. 1–14 "offers such a remarkable confusion of motifs that one can hardly say wherein the real point lies" (*The Gospel of John,* 710).

31. For a more extensive discussion of the connections between chapters 1 and 21, see M. Franzmann and M. Klinger, "The Call Stories of John 1 and John 21," *St. Vladimir's Theological Quarterly* 36 (1992): 7–15.

32. Alan Shaw finds in the similarity between 21:13 and 6:11 an indication that the breakfast in chapter 21 is eucharistic ("The Breakfast by the Shore and the Mary Magdalene Encounter as Eucharistic Narratives," *JTS* 25 [1974]: 12); so also George Mlakuzhyil, *The Christocentric Literary Structure of the Fourth Gospel,* AnBib 117 (Rome: Pontifical Biblical Institute, 1987), 343.

33. See Bishop Cassion, "John XXI," *NTS* 3 (1956–57): 132–36.

34. Alan Shaw notes that Christ is "nowhere the centre of the imagery" in John 21 ("Image and Symbol in John 21," *ExpTim* 86 [1974]: 311); Paul S. Minear identifies as a "major function of chapter 21" its "strong and continuing interest in the disciples of the second generation" ("Original Functions of John 21," 94). I take these observations to be consistent with Brevard Childs's comment that John ends "not with another attempt to create faith in the resurrected Christ, but rather with the issue of how Christ's disciples were to minister to the world in the light of the resurrection" (*The New Testament as Canon: An Introduction* [Philadelphia: Fortress, 1984], 142).

35. Eric Franklin, *Christ the Lord: A Study of the Purpose and Theology of*

Luke-Acts (Philadelphia: Westminster, 1975), 29–41; and Beverly Gaventa, "The Eschatology of Luke-Acts Revisited," *Encounter* 43 (1982): 27–42.

36. Miller, *Narrative and Its Discontents,* ix.

37. McCracken, *The Scandal of the Gospels,* 146 (emphasis in the original).

38. Barbara Herrnstein Smith, *Poetic Closure: A Study of How Poems End* (Chicago: University of Chicago Press, 1968), 34.

39. Ibid., 266–67.

40. Ernst Käsemann rightly comments on John 21:25 that "John's Gospel is and remains an abbreviation . . ." (*The Testament of Jesus: A Study of the Gospel of John in the Light of Chapter 17* [Philadelphia: Fortress, 1968], 54).

41. McCracken, *Scandal of the Gospel,* 151.

42. It is a pleasure and an honor to offer this essay as a token of gratitude to Moody Smith, a cherished teacher, mentor, and friend. I am grateful to C. Clifton Black, Charles B. Cousar, J. Louis Martyn, Paul W. Meyer, and Patrick J. Willson for reading and commenting on earlier drafts of this essay.

Part Four

The Theology of the Fourth Gospel

Paul W. Meyer

14

"The Father": The Presentation of God
in the Fourth Gospel

> The Father and I are one.
>
> —John 10:30

> Whoever has seen me has seen the Father.
> How can you say, "Show us the Father"?
>
> —John 14:9b

In view of such passages as these, one might conclude that there is no such thing as a "presentation of God" in the Fourth Gospel. The unity of Father and Son, a prominent motif in the evangelist's Christology, seems to preclude any talk about God apart from the Son, or at least to render highly problematic any venture to devote a separate chapter on Johannine theology to "the Father." The Jesus of this Gospel frequently claims to say and do and impart only what he has heard and seen and received from the Father (3:11; 5:19; 8:26, 28, 40; 20:21). Furthermore, the evangelist comments that the Father "has placed all things in [the Son's] hands" (3:35). The implications are restrictive: God is known and God's presence felt only because the Son alone "presents" God to the world, is wholly transparent to God, and is the only reliable vehicle for God's presence and action in the world; *"apart from the revelation God is not here and is never here."*[1] The only "presentation of God" in the Fourth Gospel is the self-presentation of Christ in its narratives and discourses.

The disconcerting fact that the Gospel never spells out just what it is that the Son has seen and heard from the Father, except by what Jesus says and does, seems all the more to hide the Father behind the Son. Rudolf Bultmann's reading of this is well known: "Jesus as the Revealer of God reveals nothing but that he is the Revealer. . . . John, that is, in his Gospel presents only the fact [*das Dass*] of the Revelation without describing its content [*ihr Was*]."[2] This seems to cut off even more conclusively any significant talk about God in distinction from the Christ and to signal a collapse of theology into Christology.

It will be well not to dismiss the point too quickly. Bultmann, as is well known, found in this feature of the evangelist's thought sure evidence of his dependence upon the Gnostic redeemer-myth.[3] But others have (more convincingly) seen in this exclusive orientation of Johannine faith around Jesus himself and the evangelist's refusal to spell out some body of esoteric teaching about God, delivered on earth by his emissary, precisely the one feature that most clearly differentiates the Fourth Gospel from the Christian Gnostic literature that was to follow it. The content of the revelation here is not something different from the Christ himself, something (like Prometheus's fire) that he "brings" to earth.[4] "There are no heavenly mysteries revealed to Jesus by God except those disclosed in his own life and death."[5] And the process of the disclosure, the "presentation" of God, takes place for the reader in attending to the Gospel narrative, which fuses historical recollection of the figure of Jesus with theological interpretation. This is far truer to the nature of the Gospel's genre and more satisfying theologically than a notion of revelation that remains empty. But it still means that one may not abstract from the Gospel some detached doctrine of God.

One might, on the other hand, come to just the opposite conclusion: that everything in the Gospel's presentation of Christ is also a "presentation" of God. "When people confront Jesus, they are always dealing with the Father (8:16), and they see the Father (14:7); accordingly, Thomas can address the resurrected one quite directly as 'my Lord and my God' (20:28)."[6] But Thomas's confession is surely not to be interpreted to mean that the evangelist, after maintaining throughout the Gospel a distinction between God and the one he has sent, between Father and Son, has finally abandoned it. The parallelism between the two nominative-vocatives means that in this climactic recognition-confession the fulfillment promised by the departing Christ to Philip in 14:9b has been realized. Does that come down to the same thing, a momentary evaporation of the distinction between the Son and the Father? Does that signal a collapse of Christology into theology? Ashton has remarked that Käsemann's famous characterization of the Johannine Christ as "*der über die Erde schreitende Gott*" (God striding across the earth) "conveys fairly accurately the impression that an unbiased reader would get from a first reading of the Gospel."[7] But a second reading will not rest with such an obviously docetic resolution. It will observe that the confession of Thomas results from recognizing the identity of this risen Lord with the one who was crucified. It will ask why the author has chosen a Gospel form for his message, and why, if Father and Son are simply the same, so much is made throughout of their relationship to each other. Above all, it will continue to be brought up short by the text of the Gospel, in which the term "Father," from whatever social location one might hear it, remains "God-language" that resists being swallowed up in Christology.[8] "There could hardly be a more Christocentric writer than John, yet his very Christocentricity is theocentric."[9]

After such introductory considerations, we may draw back from this fruitless alternative. The "presentation of God" in John's Gospel will not suffer being treated as an independent *locus* in the evangelist's theology, but neither can it be simply suppressed and ignored. Perhaps we will make more progress in understanding if we ask how the references to "the Father" in fact function in the "theocentric Christocentricity" of this complex book.

We may begin by noting the presence of a good bit of incidental "theology," in the conventional and straightforward sense of the term, in the traditions that have come to the evangelist. In this of course the Fourth Gospel does not stand alone. While "the doctrine of God is no longer the thematic center in the NT . . . this doctrine is always and everywhere the NT's most fundamental presupposition, for statements about God form the matrix of the Christian message, conditioning what is said about Jesus. . . ."[10] Not only individual verses in the Gospel of John but often logical and literary transitions as well are intelligible only if one is aware of some of these beliefs and teachings about God that are nowhere spelled out but are simply taken for granted by the writer. An example is the way in which the self-evident axiom of the constancy of the divine activity is presupposed in 5:17 and subsequent verses.[11] Nils Dahl, in discussing discourse about God as "the neglected factor in New Testament theology," has identified as one of the causes for neglect exactly this feature of the New Testament: that its writers, dealing with other themes, presuppose or make only indirect use of some of these basic beliefs about God that are current in their environment, especially in contemporary Judaism. He enumerates several: "God is one"; "The Creator is the giver of life"; "God is the sovereign ruler"; "God is the righteous Judge"; and "God is merciful."[12] He goes on to indicate briefly how some of these traditional formulations acquire new nuances and distinctively Christian focus as they are applied in new settings; the result is "a new articulation of language used to speak about God," in which the traditional and the specifically Christian elements "are combined and interpenetrate one another."[13]

We may thus recognize, just beneath the surface of the text and at many points on it, the presence of a variety of traditional or conventional assertions about God. But because of the lively and creative process of reinterpretation to which Dahl refers, it would be unwise to try to codify these assumed elements into a "Johannine theology" and run the risk of forcing them into an artificial systematic pattern. This is not to say that it is unimportant to be aware of the rich funds of metaphorical language about God on which the Johannine community drew for the shaping of its symbolic world. The wide circulation and very diverse application of the idea of God as "Father" is a particularly striking instance in itself.[14] But this very wealth of material increases the temptation to draw lines of development or influence and to trace genetic relationships that can then take control of the interpretation of the Gospel's text in questionable ways. Two examples of this have special bearing on the present essay.

In the earlier portion of his article on "Πατήρ" (Father) in the *Theological Dictionary of the New Testament*, Gottlob Schrenk devotes a section to "The Influence of the Roman *patria potestas* in the Hellenistic World," an indisputable and important aspect of the legal and social setting of the New Testament.[15] But then the specific appearance of some of these legal details in the parable of the Prodigal Son (Luke 15:11–32) leads to the generalization, "Whenever the NT uses the image of the 'father' it always builds on this concept of patriarchy."[16] The discussion of "Πατήρ in John" then takes its start by making the patriarchal notion of the head of the household (*"Hausvater"*) the controlling image, even to explain "the christological mystery." The patriarchal traits of the language are exploited and emphasized in the subsequent discussion. The Son's love for the Father is interpreted primarily as unquestioning obedience, and the language of Luke 15 is specifically imported to illumine the Johannine text. This can hardly be the way to take the Fourth Gospel on its own terms.

A second example is provided by the almost obsessive desire, running through the literature, to trace the Johannine use of the term "Father" for God to the personal piety and religious intimacy of the historical Jesus. That Jesus referred to God as "[the] Father" is scarcely to be doubted; such usage was not uncommon.[17] What cannot be taken for granted is the extent to which this precedent accounts for the formulations found in John and their frequency. The underlying issue, which can only be mentioned here because it would carry us too far afield, concerns "the specifically Christian usage" and where its roots lie.[18] References to God as the "Father" of Jesus Christ play an important role in the epistolary literature of the New Testament as part of the developing confessional, proto-liturgical, and increasingly stereotypical formulations of the Christian community.[19] But the references are surprisingly scarce in the pre-Johannine gospel traditions.[20] "It is apparent that the earliest document, Mark, has the fewest references [to the Divine Fatherhood], that the latest, John, has the most, and that documents which intervene in date occupy intermediate positions as regards their number of references."[21] This should suggest strongly that the comparatively very high frequency of references to God as "Father" in the Fourth Gospel, indeed the very language itself, has its roots in post-Easter theological development and is part of the community's confessional language, *its* "presentation" of Jesus as the Christ in narrative genre. To appeal to Jesus' own religious usage at this point only stands in the way of examining carefully how this language functions in the evangelist's text.[22]

These two examples serve to demonstrate the importance of focusing on how the language about God as "Father" actually functions in this Gospel before one draws conclusions about its genetic origins or antecedents. But they also serve to recall the point from which this essay began: the close connections between theology and Christology in this Gospel. One can scarcely do justice to the Gospel on its own terms if one does not at the same time account for some of the ways in which the "presentation" of God as "Father" is here related to the "presentation" of Jesus. On this last question there have been some important proposals in the literature on the Fourth Gospel that need to be considered before we can proceed.

In this connection it is useful to recall the striking thematic richness of the Christology of the Gospel. Its opening chapter, with its prologue (vv. 1–18) and its testimonies (of John the Baptist and of the first disciples, vv. 19–51), confronts the reader with this diversity at the very start in the virtual catalogue of titles it contains. These are here taken for granted and woven into the text, but they wait, so to speak, for elucidation as the Gospel unfolds: Logos, Only(-Begotten), Messiah, Elijah, Prophet, Chosen One, Lamb of God, Son of God, King of Israel, and Son of Man.[23] The initial impression is one almost of confusion, or at least of such interchangeability among these terms that it would seem hopeless, perhaps even an act of violence upon the text, to try to break down the evangelist's Christology into some of its component strands and single out some one that concentrates more than the others on Jesus' relationship to God as "Father." Yet on closer examination, that is exactly what the text does seem to allow. Within the overall coherence of the evangelist's Christology, certain constellations of motifs emerge. The titles are not confused with one another. In part at least, they even distribute themselves in different literary layers of the Gospel. Each one that is resumed in the remainder of the Gospel (not all are) is associated with certain recurring phrases, themes, and even topics of potential, and presumably actual, theological debate in the setting of the Gospel during the stages of its composition. This is illustrated clearly by Wayne Meeks's study, "The Man from Heaven in Johannine Sectarianism."[24] Meeks has shown the close connections drawn in the Gospel between the title "Son of Man" and the descent/ascent motif by which Jesus is repeatedly identified as one who has come into the world from heaven and is returning there.[25] This is not to say that the distinctions are watertight or that there is no overlap of one set of ideas or phrases with another. The spatial dualism of "heaven" and "earth" extends beyond the descent/ascent language, for example, but the close connection to which Meeks has drawn attention holds. Statements about the Son of Man and references to God as the "Father," especially as the one who "sent" Jesus, constitute quite distinct strands in the Johannine christological language.[26]

If "Father"-language for God is not closely connected with the Son of Man, there can be little question that the title "Son of God" or simply "the Son" also occupies an important place in this Christology and does at once bring the reader to consider language about God as "Father."[27] It is, in fact, the presence of both terms in the theological vocabulary of the Gospel that resists any easy collapse of the evangelist's theology into Christology or of his Christology into theology. One might even venture to say that the reader is compelled by this language to redefine the term "Christology" itself and to recognize that in its profoundest dimension—not just in this Gospel but in all its variations throughout the diverse traditions of the New Testament—it concerns not the person of Jesus or his identity ("who he is") and the consequences of his life so much as—first, foremost, and always—his open or hidden relationship to God, and of God to him.[28] Without that, there may be a religious hero in the Gospels, but there is no Christology.

Both terms, "Father" and "Son," are of course figures originally drawn from the reciprocal relationships of human life. For that reason—perhaps also because of the long history of Trinitarian debate and the doctrinal and liturgical legacy left by it—the reader of the Fourth Gospel understandably tends to see and hear these words in similar reciprocity of meaning, as if one can never have one without the other. It is plain from the literature on John that the two terms are seen in close coordination with each other.[29] It is characteristic of those treatments of Johannine theology most explicitly attending to its "presentation of God" to do so under a heading such as "The Father and the Son."[30] Even more widespread is an emphasis on the unity of the Son with the Father in the thought of the evangelist.

It cannot be disputed that there is strong support in the text of John for this emphasis on unity. Once again, however, it is the inordinate pressing of this otherwise valid point that threatens to collapse the distinction between Christology and theology. Interpreting the entire Gospel from the motif of unity so prominent in chapter 17, Käsemann not only asserts that "the unity of the Son with the Father is the central theme of the Johannine proclamation," but goes on to say that it follows that "that unity is of necessity also the proper object of faith."[31] It is, indeed, not only 17:11, 22 that assert that Jesus and the Father are "one"; 10:30 does the same. In 10:38; 14:10, 11, 20, as well as in 17:21, Jesus and the Father are said to be "in" each other. Those who respond negatively to Jesus' works "hate" both him and the Father (15:24). To know or not know one is to know or not know the other (14:7; 16:3; 17:3). Behind Jesus' life and activity lie the Father's will (6:40), the Father's life (6:57), the Father's acting (14:10), the Father's word (14:24), and the Father's love (15:10). "My Father" in the mouth of Jesus (ὁ πατήρ μου, 25 times) makes it clear that God is *his* Father as no one else's.[32] Throughout his life on earth, Jesus as the Son is portrayed as remaining in uninterrupted and direct association with the Father (8:16, 29; 16:32b).[33] "The Evangelist no longer perceives simply Jesus, the human being, in the earthly Jesus, but one who has come from God, one who has been identified as God's Son by the exaltation, one who does God's work on earth as if God himself were doing it."[34] The unity of Father and Son is continually set before the reader as a total coalescence of the two in the actual activity of giving life to the world.

Yet a crucial aspect of this unity in action for the evangelist is the "commandment" (ἐντολή, the order, warrant, or charge; cf. 11:57) that Jesus has received from the Father (10:18; 12:49–50), has himself "kept" or discharged (15:10), and passes on to his disciples (13:34; 14:15; 15:10). Because of this term, the correspondence of action between Son and Father has been misunderstood as obedience within a patriarchally structured relationship.[35] But this ἐντολή, in its first appearance in the Gospel (10:18), is the Good Shepherd's act of laying down his life for the sheep, not the surrender of Jesus' own will to yield to God's, as in the Synoptic Gethsemane scene (Mark 14:36; Matt. 26:39; Luke 22:42), but the willing act of Jesus' own initiative and authority (ἐξουσία; cf. John 12:27), which is grounded in the relationship of mutual knowledge and love between Jesus and his Father (10:15, 17). "John himself uses neither the noun 'obedience' nor the verb 'to obey'. Instead he has the formula 'to do the will', which corresponds to the other formula, 'to hear the word'."[36] Jesus' constancy in doing the Father's will (4:34; 5:30; 6:38) or "doing the work[s] of God" (4:34; 9:4; 10:32, 37–38; 14:10; 17:4) does not *produce* unity with the Father—as would be the case if it were understood as obedience—but is grounded in, and springs from, the prior unity of Jesus with the Father.[37]

But how is this prior unity understood? How and in what sense are Jesus and the Father "one" (10:30)? The answer is clear: Jesus is the one who has been "sent" by God.[38] "The origin of his decisions and actions lies outside him; he has been 'sent' and acts on behalf of him who sent him."[39] Such language, while it maintains the evangelist's stress on unity in action, preserves also the distinction between Jesus and the Father—and is a principal reason why the evangelist's theology cannot be collapsed into his Christology.

Because this language about "sending" occupies such an important place in the Gospel, it is not surprising that considerable attention has been paid to the motif of the divine Envoy or Emissary, or to what has been called, in German, the *Gesandtenchristologie* of the Fourth Gospel.[40] However, here once again, genetic considerations have controlled the discussion. For Bultmann, the combination of the commissioning of a divine emissary with the idea of his "coming into the world" from beyond cannot be traced to cultic or eschatological sources or to the precedent of Old Testament prophecy but has its analogues only in Gnostic notions of a Revealer figure.[41] A much larger number of interpreters have sought to illumine the evangelist's language by appealing to the presence in Jewish tradition of the idea of a divinely authorized agent or representative. This can vary all the way from the eschatological "prophet like Moses" (Deut. 18:15–22) to what some have called the "institution" of the שׁליח ("emissary"), the basic principle of which is summarized in such rabbinic texts as Mishnah *Berakot* 5:5 ("The agent of a person is as the person himself") and which some have found perfectly restated in John 13:16b.[42] What is involved in this rather extensive literature is a search for the juridical background that will make intelligible the notion of a divine envoy who does not merely bring information but who mediates a fully authentic and genuine encounter with the God who "sent" him, and nothing less than that. At the same time, however, certain "subordinationist" connotations continue for some to cling to the very notion of an envoy or emissary that is "sent" and so seem to make it irreconcilable with the evangelist's claims for the unity of the Father and the Son. The result has been to stir up again, rather than to settle, a debate about Johannine Christology that pits one reading of the Gospel, one that stresses the mission of Jesus as the divine emissary who has been "sent" into the world, against another that correlates the Father and the Son and emphasizes the unbroken unity between them and the mutual indwelling of each in the other. Genetic considerations continue to play a role, so that the debate turns in part on determining which christological strand is earlier and primary in determining the very structure of the Gospel and which is derivative and ancillary.[43] In an instructive and suggestive essay, Rudolf Schnackenburg has taken note of this discussion and its resulting dilemmas and proposed to show how, in the historical process of its formation, Johannine Christology could bring together such different traditions into a multifaceted whole. The end product of this development is for him perfectly symbolized in the pregnant, recurring phrase of the Gospel, "the Father who sent me."[44]

If one pauses at this point to take stock, the results are far from satisfactory. The issue appears to have become, once again, a matter of refining our understanding of the evangelist's complex *Christology,* and we seem to be no closer to delineating his "presentation of God." The way in which references to God as "Father" function in the Gospel has hardly become clearer. There are several good reasons for pressing the question a step further.

One reason is a consideration of method. Hartwig Thyen has cautioned that genetic inquiries into the history-of-religions origins even of the motifs of Johannine Christology can never take the place of careful observation of the actual use and function of those motifs in their literary and historical contexts in the Gospel itself.[45] That one should not allow the inquiry into the Gospel's presentation of God to be swallowed up in the quest for the origins of its christological motifs is brought home also by James D. G. Dunn's reminder that the primary theological debate that the evangelist was engaged in with his Jewish contemporaries was a debate sooner or later about monotheism, that is, a *theo*logical debate.[46] Dunn has also forcefully argued that to focus on the pre- and post-history of Johannine ideas is to invite anachronisms in interpretation.[47] One form of such anachronism is to project back onto the Gospel a coherence and homogeneity among its diverse christological strands that were attained only in later interpretation and reflection. The fact, as we have already seen in part, is that the materials with which one has to work are not as homogeneous as they have often been taken to be. The Gospel still confronts its reader as a layered document in which the evidence of different traditions and stages in its history has not been completely suppressed in the process of assimilation.[48] John Ashton, who has contributed greatly to understanding the importance of mission and agency in the Christology of John, is clear that these motifs should not be indiscriminately combined. He writes:

> Essentially John saw Jesus' relationship with God in two clearly distinguishable ways, *sonship,* and *mission;* and the two names Jesus has for God ('Father' and 'the one who sent me') though often united in practice ('the Father who sent me') should not be assumed without further proof or argument to have been linked together in the traditions upon which John drew. In chapter 7 the term 'Father' is not used: nowhere in this chapter is there the slightest hint that Jesus regarded himself as the Son of God.[49]

In the second place, the language of "Father" and "Son" requires another look. We observed earlier a powerful tendency among the interpreters of the Gospel always to coordinate closely the Gospel's use of "Father" with that of "Son." Ashton, whose words we have just cited, shares this habit. We propose, however, to carry a step further his care in discriminating one tradition in the Gospel from another and to try to show that the way in which references to God as "Father" function cannot be clearly seen until we break this habit. It is an understandable tendency. Whenever Jesus refers to God as "[my] Father," *we* unconsciously insert the Evangelist's christological identification of him as "Son [of God]" but fail to notice that the resulting coordination is not matched by the evangelist's usage. The Q-logion in Luke 10:22/Matt. 11:27 has long been dubbed a "bolt out of the Johannine blue," because it, along with only one other Synoptic saying, makes this coordination direct and clear;[50] but actually the Johannine usage as a whole is much closer to the Pauline letters. In the undisputed letters, Paul refers to Jesus Christ as "Son of God" or "the Son" or "his [sc. God's] Son" fourteen times but *never* in conjunction with any reference to God as "Father."[51] He refers to God as "the Father" (absolute) nine times (including "the Father of mercies," i.e., "the merciful Father" in 2 Cor. 1:3), as the "Father" of human beings (always "our Father") eleven times, but as "the Father of [our] Lord Jesus [Christ]" only three times (Rom. 15:6; 2 Cor. 1:3; 11:31), and in none of these three contexts is Jesus Christ spoken of as "Son."[52] In the Fourth Gospel, as we have seen,[53] the occurrences of both "Father" for God and "Son" for Jesus are far more frequent. But the actual pairing of these terms as coordinates is surprisingly infrequent. "The Son of God" is linked with "Father" for God only twice (John 5:25; 10:36), while "the Son" (absolute) is coordinated with "the Father" for God fourteen times, with eight of these occurring in a single context.[54] These passages that bring the terms together form a distinct group, which when left to one side leaves the large number of remaining uses of "Father" for God far less susceptible to being subsumed under the Johannine "Christology."

A third reason for pursuing our inquiry is the most telling of all, a matter of basic Johannine usage that is the most surprising in the extent to which it has escaped notice in the literature. We come finally to the "sending" language of the Gospel. The instances have already been enumerated in which God (ὁ θεός) or the Father (ὁ πατήρ) is said to have "sent" (ἀποστέλλειν) Jesus.[55] In these passages the verb is always in the finite active form, in the past tense (perfect in 5:36 and 20:21; elsewhere, aorist).[56] The other verb in this language of sending is, of course, πέμπειν. Several writers have tried to identify a distinction in meaning between πέμπειν and ἀποστέλλειν, with varying conclusiveness.[57] What does appear to be consistent is the formulaic use of the definite singular active participle, always aorist, ὁ πέμψας με/αὐτόν ("the one who has sent me/him").[58] In this formula God is always the antecedent of the participle, the subject of the sending, and aside from the one use of the formula by John the Baptist in 1:33,

Jesus is always the direct object of the participle. The formula can be combined with "Father" ("the Father who has sent me") but more often it stands alone as an epithet for God.[59] It never occurs absolutely (i.e., without a direct object, as though simply "the Sender"). In sum, the point in counting these verb forms is that nowhere in the Fourth Gospel is Jesus ever called the "Envoy" or "Emissary" or "one sent [ἀπεσταλμένος] by God"; only John the Baptist is. There is not so much a *Gesandtenchristologie* in the Gospel as there is a *Sendertheologie*. "The Father who has sent me" or "he who has sent me" is "*God's name*."[60] The language of "sending" is *theo*logical language that undergirds Christology but refuses to be absorbed into it.

We return, finally, to language about God as "Father" in the Gospel. The statistics we have seen are high and the present essay does not pretend to offer a full examination of all occurrences. But it is important to note their distribution. References to God as "Father" and as "the one who has sent [Jesus]" belong very conspicuously to the discourse material; in the few narrative contexts in which they appear, they stand out as editorial insertions of a late stage in the Gospel's composition.[61] Since "the Father" in the absolute appears some seventy-four times and is frequently not coordinated with "the Son," we would expect it to function as a simple equivalent to "God" (ὁ θεός); indeed, the two words do alternate with each other in many contexts.[62] Yet there is a difference of flavor that goes beyond the statistical preponderance of "Father" over "God." For example, the evangelist speaks of "children of God" (1:12; 11:52) but never "children of the Father"; of the "wrath of God" (3:36) but never "wrath of the Father." Contrariwise, we hear of the "house of the Father" (2:16; 14:2) but never the "house of God"; the "will of the Father" (6:40) but never the "will of God"; the "hand of the Father" (10:29) but never the "hand of God." "Father" is the subject of eighteen verbs that never appear with "God" as subject, while "God" appears with only one verb that is not also used with "Father."[63] What is more significant for our purposes is that, while "the Father" and "God" easily and frequently alternate with each other, the formulaic epithet of sending, "the Father who has sent me" or simply "the one who has sent me," belongs strictly to the "Father"-language of the Gospel and with only two exceptions is not even associated with "God" (ὁ θεός).[64] Thus "the Father" and "God" function in many ways synonymously, even though the former is more frequent; "God" and "Father" identify the source from which Jesus has "come" into the world and the goal to which he is "going" or "ascending"; they identify the origin of what Jesus says, of what he does, of the disciples he gathers. But it is the formulaic identification of the "Father" as "the one who has sent me" that gives this "presentation of God" its most characteristically Johannine nuance.

For our understanding of that nuance, we remain deeply indebted to much of the recent discussion of mission in the Fourth Gospel.[65] The problem is that the background materials have focused the discussion as a christological one, on the concept and figure of the one sent, the divine emissary, whereas the Fourth Gospel actually uses this language to point to God, the "Father," as the Sender of Jesus. "When we use the verb 'send' we make clear that God is not simply identical with the [saving] event but transcends it, although he encounters us in it and does so in his totality."[66] Not only does God transcend it; the sending language serves to legitimate and authorize the identity, the mission, and the claims of Jesus *as* the saving event. "His origin establishes his significance."[67]

Early in this essay we referred to Nils Dahl's article, "The Neglected Factor in New Testament Theology."[68] He writes about the New Testament: "The great majority of references to God occur in contexts that deal with some other theme. They serve as warrants and backing for promises, appeals, and threats, or for *statements about Jesus,* the Jews, the church, salvation, moral conduct, prayer, and so forth."[69] It is those *statements* that provide the content of New Testament theology, which today "does not speak about God but about the way in which the New Testament authors talk about God."[70] What we have in the Fourth Gospel, however, is something quite different. Here the evangelist's language about God as "Father" and specifically as "the one who has sent me" points to God as warrant and backing not for what the evangelist says to his readers but, in a second order of theological reflection, for Jesus himself, his words, his deeds, his life. The "presentation of God as Father" in this Gospel is as the Vindicator and Authorizer of Jesus. By contrast, in the letters of Paul, God is the *eschatological* Vindicator, whose act "in power" (Rom. 1:4) in the resurrection provides the *ex post facto* warrant, backing, and justification for Jesus.[71] "The conviction that the crucified 'King of the Jews' was right and had been vindicated by God, who raised him from the dead, forms the basis of the theology of the New Testament in all its varieties."[72] With regard to the historical basis, that remains true. But another stage has been reached in the Fourth Gospel. What is distinctively Johannine about this "presentation of God as Father" is that here eschatology has been replaced by *protology.* Jesus stands in no need of an eschatological vindication. He does not need to come again "in power." He is "right" because God is "the Father who has sent me."

NOTES

1. Rudolf Bultmann, "The Eschatology of the Gospel of John," *Faith and Understanding I* (New York: Harper & Row, 1969), 173; emphasis original.
2. Rudolf Bultmann, *Theology of the New Testament* (New York: Scribner's, 1955), 2.66. For a full discussion of this statement in the context of an examination of the Gospel's concept of revelation, see esp. John Ashton, *Understanding the Fourth Gospel* (Oxford: Clarendon, 1991), 515–53.
3. Rudolf Bultmann, "Die Bedeutung der neuerschlossenen mandäischen und manichäischen Quellen für das Verständnis des Johannesevangeliums," *Exegetica: Aufsätze zur Erforschung des Neuen Testaments* (Tübingen: Mohr [Siebeck], 1967),

57. Again, for fuller discussion and critique of Bultmann's position, see Ashton, *Understanding the Fourth Gospel,* 53–62.

4. Willi Marxsen, "Christology in the NT," *IDBSup* (1976): 155; Hans Conzelmann, *An Outline of the Theology of the New Testament* (New York: Harper & Row, 1969), 340. For a clear summary of the crucial differences between John and Gnosticism, see Hartwig Thyen, "Johannesevangelium," *TRE* 17 (1976): 200–225, esp. 220.

5. Ashton, *Understanding the Fourth Gospel,* 551.

6. Marxsen, "Christology in the NT," 155–56.

7. Ashton, *Understanding the Fourth Gospel,* 72. See Ernst Käsemann, *The Testament of Jesus: A Study of the Gospel of John in the Light of Chapter 17* (Philadelphia: Fortress, 1968), 9 and passim; Käsemann credits earlier such characterizations to F. C. Baur, G. P. Wetter, and E. Hirsch.

8. On the problematic character of the image of "Father" for God in our time, when the brokenness of human relationships has served to make this traditional metaphor not only powerless for many but even destructive and offensive for some, one might well ponder some words of Donald Juel, written about the "Our Father" of the Lord's Prayer in Matthew and Luke but applicable as well to the Fourth Gospel: "Calling God 'our Father' has to do not primarily with traditional or 'natural' imagery. We do not pray to God as 'Male'; we do not speak of God as 'Father' because of some natural necessity—e.g., a 'natural law' according to which the cosmos is ordered according to gender distinctions. The God to whom we are invited to pray is known only in the particular—as the God whom Jesus addressed as 'Father' and who vindicated the crucified Jesus as Christ, Son of God, by raising him from the dead. We experience God as 'our Father' through Jesus. The words must be heard in their Gospel setting. The particularity of that setting . . . is the only promise of deliverance from ideologies of any sort that oppress and enslave and finally undermine the possibility of addressing God as one who cares and can be trusted to listen" ("The Lord's Prayer in the Gospels of Matthew and Luke," *The Lord's Prayer* [*The Princeton Seminary Bulletin,* Supplementary Issue, no. 2 (1992)], 63). "Father" never occurs in the Fourth Gospel with an "our" preceding it; it does not here belong in the community's prayer language. But that does not make it any less theological when used of God, or even confessional. The task at hand is to clarify "the particularity of that setting" in John's Gospel.

9. C. K. Barrett, "'The Father is Greater than I' John 14.28: Subordinationist Christology in the New Testament," *Essays on John* (Philadelphia: Westminster, 1982), 32.

10. Jouette M. Bassler, "God in the NT," *ABD* 2 (1992): 1049.

11. Rudolf Bultmann, *The Gospel of John: A Commentary* (Philadelphia: Westminster, 1971), 246.

12. Nils Alstrup Dahl, "The Neglected Factor in New Testament Theology," *Jesus the Christ: The Historical Origins of Christological Doctrine* (Minneapolis: Fortress, 1991), 158–60.

13. Ibid., 158. See also Bassler, "God in the NT," 1049.

14. "The idea of God as Father and man as his child is found throughout the history of religion from the primitive stages onward" (Bultmann, *The Gospel of John,* 58 [emphasis omitted]). For literature, see the footnotes there; cf. also Gottlob Schrenk and Gottfried Quell, "Πατήρ," *TDNT* 5 (1967): 945–1014.

15. Schrenk, "Πατήρ," *TDNT* 5 (1967): 950–51.

16. Ibid., 984.

17. The literature is extensive. To the article by Schrenk in the *TDNT*, referred to in n. 14 (N.B. 982–96: "Father according to the Jesus of the Synoptists"), one may usefully compare such widely different treatments as T. W. Manson, *The Teaching of Jesus: Studies of Its Form and Content* (Cambridge: Cambridge University Press, 1951), 89–115 ("God as Father"); Bultmann, *Theology of the New Testament* (1951), 1.22–26 ("Jesus' Idea of God"); Conzelmann, *Outline of the Theology of the New Testament*, 99–106 ("The Idea of God"); and Robert G. Hamerton-Kelly, *God the Father: Theology and Patriarchy in the Teaching of Jesus* (Philadelphia: Fortress, 1979). More controversial is the significance of Jesus' use of "Abba"; cf. Joachim Jeremias, *New Testament Theology: The Proclamation of Jesus* (New York: Scribner's, 1971), 61–68; W. D. Davies and Dale C. Allison, *A Critical and Exegetical Commentary on the Gospel according to Saint Matthew*, ICC (Edinburgh: T. & T. Clark, 1988), 1.601–2; and Ernst Haenchen, *Der Weg Jesu: Eine Erklärung des Markus-Evangeliums und der kanonischen Parallelen* (Berlin: Töpelmann, 1966), 492–94, n. 7a.

18. The phrase is used, for example, by Bassler, "God in the NT," 1054.

19. For example, in Gal. 1:1 God is the Father of Jesus Christ by virtue of having performed the essential act of a father, the giving of life. As a consequence, he is the Father also of Christians in vv. 3–4. (This was pointed out to me by J. Louis Martyn.)

20. The presentation of the statistics is often prejudiced by a theological argument. The data are as follows: In Mark, Jesus refers to God as "[the] Father" only three times (in direct address only once, in the Gethsemane prayer, Mark 14:36; once in the apocalyptic discourse in conjunction with mention of "the Son," 13:32; and once as the "Father" of the Son of Man, 8:38). Only once does he speak to the disciples of "your Father in heaven" (11:25). Jesus never refers to God as "my Father" in Mark. In the Q-material as it appears in Luke, Jesus speaks of God as "Father" of human beings four times: in two of these passages as "[the] Father" (once in the Lord's Prayer in Luke 11:2 and again in 11:13, where the text is uncertain [it may read, "your heavenly Father"]) and in two as "your Father" (6:36 and 12:30). To this last-mentioned Q-saying in 12:30 Luke has attached another logion with "your Father" (12:32). The only other references to God as "Father" in the Lukan Q-material are in the much-discussed two verses, 10:21–22, the so-called "bolt out of the Johannine blue," which are closely paralleled in Matt. 11:25–27. Here "Father" is used absolutely of God four times (twice as a vocative and twice closely correlating "the Father" and "the Son") and once as "my Father." Five further examples occur in Luke, all in secondary traditions peculiar to this Gospel: one or two instances of "Father" as a vocative, in Jesus' prayers from the cross (Luke 23:46 and the textually dubious 23:34), and three instances of "my Father" in 2:49; 22:29; and 24:49. It is *Matthew* who has augmented the Synoptic tradition to the level of a representation of Jesus on intimate terms with God as "his" Father and the Father of his disciples. In the Matthean parallels to passages mentioned so far as occurring in Mark and Luke, Matthew adds the possessive "my" in 26:39 and "our" in 6:9 (the Lord's Prayer). To these parallels Matthew adds a single absolute reference to "the Father" in 28:19 (the trinitarian baptismal formula). But he adds another fourteen references in the mouth of Jesus to God as *his* "Father," always with the possessive "my" (7:21; 10:32, 33; 12:50; 15:13; 16:17; 18:10, 19, 35; 20:23; 25:34; 26:29, 42, 53); in six of these fourteen "in heaven" or "heavenly" is added (12:50; 15:13; 16:17; 18:10, 19, 35). Matthew also adds another nineteen references to God as the "Father" of the disciples (always "your" [sg. or pl.], except for "their" in 13:43): 5:16, 45; 6:1, 4, 6 (bis), 8, 9, 15, 18 (bis), 26, 32; 7:11; 10:20, 29; 13:43;

18:14; 23:9); in ten of these nineteen, "heavenly" or "in the heavens" is an added qualifier (5:16, 45; 6:1, 18 (bis), 26, 32; 7:11; 18:14; 23:9). It is especially noteworthy that
in all the Synoptic tradition *only* Mark 13:32 (with its parallel in Matt. 24:36) and the
Q-logion in Luke 10:22/Matt. 11:27 refer to God as "the Father" in correlation with
reference to "the Son." This last point will be picked up below.

21. H.F.D. Sparks, "The Doctrine of the Divine Fatherhood in the Gospels," in
Studies in the Gospels: Essays in Memory of R. H. Lightfoot, ed. D. E. Nineham (Oxford: Blackwell, 1967), 259.

22. After pointing out, in the words just cited, the low frequency of "Father"-
language in the early stages of the pre-Johannine tradition, Sparks disregards his own
findings by reverting to an "explanation" offered by T. W. Manson years ago, before
the impact of form criticism: the statistics do not matter; Jesus' "reticence" in speaking about God as "Father" is due to "the intense reality and deep sacredness of the experience [of the Fatherhood of God]. . . . [W]e cannot speak lightly of the things that
most profoundly move us" (Manson, *The Teaching of Jesus*, 108). Manson thought
"that the only ultimately satisfactory explanation of the authority of Jesus is that which
sets the foundation of it in his unique spiritual experience" (ibid., 106). But Manson's
own immediate appeal to the analogy of the "inaugural vision" of the prophet in ancient Israel destroys at a stroke the category of "uniqueness." More important, what is
missed is the fact that in the Gospel of John those references to God as "the Father
who sent" Jesus function as the evangelist's way of "setting the foundation" of Jesus'
authority outside and beyond the world of human religious experience, even and especially that of the prophets.

23. A recent review of these titles is found in Ashton, *Understanding the Fourth
Gospel*, 253–62.

24. *JBL* 91 (1972): 44–72.

25. Ibid., 52: "There is a curiously close connection throughout the gospel between this title [viz., "Son of Man"] and the descent/ascent language." Similarly,
Rudolf Schnackenburg has observed that the descent/ascent schema is constitutive for
the title, "Son of Man" ("'Der Vater, der mich gesandt hat': Zur johanneischen Christologie," in *Anfänge der Christologie: Festschrift für Ferdinand Hahn zum 65.
Geburtstag*, ed. Cilliers Breytenbach and Henning Paulsen [Göttingen: Vandenhoeck
& Ruprecht, 1991], 275–91, 284).

26. The two strands come together most closely in 5:27 and 8:28. The distinction
is preserved in the difference between 13:31 (God is glorified in the Son of Man) and
14:13 (the Father is glorified in the Son). Of course, both "the Son of Man" in 13:31
and "the Son" in 14:13 refer to Jesus, but there is no evidence in the Fourth Gospel for
the simply synonymous use or interchangeability of "Son" with "Son of Man," or of
"Father of the Son of Man" with the absolute "the Father," both of which Schrenk finds
in the Synoptic tradition (*TDNT* 5 [1967]: 989, n. 278).

27. The statistics of this "Father/Son" language alone compel this recognition.
The following may be mentioned here: Whereas the title "Son of Man" occurs 13
times in the Fourth Gospel, Jesus is called "the Son" 20 times and "the Son of God"
9 times, for a total of 29. In 3 cases of these 29, "only" (μονογενής) is added. (The
reading ὁ μονογενὴς υἱός ["the only Son"] is followed in 1:18, against *UBSGNT*[3],
Novum Testamentum Graece[27], and NRSV; for decisive arguments supporting this
choice, see now Bart D. Ehrman, *The Orthodox Corruption of Scripture: The Effect
of Early Christological Controversies on the Text of the New Testament* [New York

and Oxford: Oxford University Press, 1993], 78–82.) God is referred to as "the Father" (absolute) 74 times; with the possessive "my/your [sg.]" (always with Jesus as the antecedent), another 25 times; with the addition of "who sent me/him," another 7 times; in the anarthrous nominative/vocative of prayer, 9 more times; and as an (anarthrous) predicate, 3 times. This yields a total of 118 occurrences of "Father" for God (cf. the statistics for the Synoptic Gospels in n. 20). For purposes of comparison, one may note that God is referred to with θεός ("God") only 45 times; this count does not include the 31 instances of θεός as a genitive modifier (as in ὁ υἱὸς τοῦ θεοῦ, "the Son of God" [9 times], τέκνα τοῦ θεοῦ, "children of God" [2 times], ὁ ἀμνὸς τοῦ θεοῦ, "the Lamb of God" [2 times], etc.), nor the use of θεός as a predicate (1:1; 8:54) or predicate accusative (10:33), but it does include all uses of θεός with prepositions (22 times) and the one vocative (20:28). Finally, apart from the textually secondary 5:4, κύριος ("Lord") is used of God only in Old Testament citations (1:23; 12:13, 38). But since κύριος is used elsewhere always of Jesus—overwhelmingly in the vocative by those who address Jesus in the narrative, but also in the third person of narrative (whether the narrator is the evangelist or a character in the story) and even indirectly in gnomic statements in Jesus' own mouth (13:16; 15:15, 20)—one may ask whether the reader of the Gospel is not intended to hear even these occurrences in Old Testament citations as referring to Jesus.

28. Though it no longer receives the attention it deserves, a major older presentation of Johannine Christology that presses this point and argues for its applicability to John is Ernst Gaugler, "Das Christuszeugnis des Johannesevangeliums," in *Jesus Christus im Zeugnis der heiligen Schrift und der Kirche,* 2d ed., BEvT 2 (Munich: Kaiser, 1936), 34–67, esp. 49–51.

29. Even the surveys of parallels that can be adduced from the history of religions seem either to presuppose this seemingly self-evident reciprocity or to find it confirmed (e.g., Bultmann, *The Gospel of John,* 58–59; 165–66, n. 1).

30. So Conzelmann, *An Outline of the Theology of the New Testament,* 339–41. Similarly, Rudolf Schnackenburg locates his principal discussion of the Gospel's "Father"-language for God in an excursus devoted to the Johannine "Son-Christology" (*The Gospel according to St John,* vol. 2: *Commentary on Chapters 5–12* [New York: Crossroad, 1987], 172–86).

31. Käsemann, *The Testament of Jesus,* 24–25. Compare ibid., 25: "John's peculiarity [*Eigenart*] is that he knows only one single dogma, the christological dogma of the unity of Jesus with the Father." As is well known, Käsemann concluded that such a strong emphasis on the unity of Father and Son as he sees in the Gospel leads to the danger of Docetism (ibid., 26).

32. John 2:16; 5:17, 43; 6:32, 40; 8:19 (bis), 49, 54; 10:18, 25, 29, 37; 14:2, 7, 20, 21, 23; 15:1, 8, 10, 15, 23, 24; 20:17. Only in 20:17 is God referred to as the "Father" of anyone else (the disciples).

33. Gaugler, "Das Christuszeugnis des Johannesevangeliums," 49.

34. Ibid., 57.

35. So Schrenk, *TDNT* 5 (1967): 984; see also our comments, above.

36. Käsemann, *The Testament of Jesus,* 18. Käsemann goes on to make clear that if this doing of the Father's will is to be called "obedience" as a kind of "paraphrase," "this may not be understood moralistically," nor does it have anything to do with "what we usually mean by humility" (ibid.). See also Bultmann, *The Gospel of John,* 249–50.

37. Very emphatically argued by Thyen, "Johannesevangelium," 221.

38. Greek ἀποστέλλειν (leaving πέμπειν aside for the moment); sent by God (ὁ θεός): 3:17, 34; 6:29; 7:29; 8:42; sent by the Father (ὁ πατήρ): 5:36, 38; 6:57; 10:36; 11:42; 17:3, 8, 18, 21, 23, 25; 20:21.

39. Bultmann, *The Gospel of John*, 249 (German: "handelt im Auftrag," i.e., "acts under commission"; *Das Evangelium des Johannes*, 11th ed., MeyerK [Göttingen: Vandenhoeck & Ruprecht, 1950], 186).

40. Bultmann, *The Gospel of John*, 50, nn. 2 and 3. For a fuller discussion of parallels and background materials, see the excursus, "Jesus der Gottgesandte," in Walter Bauer, *Das Johannesevangelium*, 3d ed., HNT 6 (Tübingen: Mohr [Siebeck], 1933), 58–60.

41. Bultmann, *The Gospel of John*, 50, nn. 2 and 3; 250–51.

42. Karl Heinrich Rengstorf, "ἀπόστολος," *TDNT* 1 (1964): 414–24, esp. 415; Gaugler, "Das Christuszeugnis des Johannesevangeliums," 51–52; Théo Preiss, "Justification in Johannine Thought," *Life in Christ*, SBT 13 (Chicago: Allenson, 1952), 9–31. Peder Borgen ("God's Agent in the Fourth Gospel," in *The Interpretation of John*, ed. John Ashton, IRT 9 [Philadelphia and London: Fortress/SPCK, 1986], 67–78) broadens the discussion of divine agency to include the early stages of Merkabah mysticism. Wayne Meeks (*The Prophet-King: Moses Traditions and the Johannine Christology*, NovTSup 14 [Leiden: Brill, 1967], 301–5) puts it in the context of the question about Mosaic traditions in John. John Ashton (*Understanding the Fourth Gospel*, 312–17) makes it part of a much broader discussion of the "mission" of the Son of God in the Gospel. Jan-A. Bühner (*Der Gesandte und sein Weg im 4. Evangelium: Die kultur- und religionsgeschichtlichen Grundlagen der johanneischen Sendungschristologie sowie ihre traditionsgeschichtliche Entwicklung*, WUNT 2/2 [Tübingen: Mohr (Siebeck), 1977]) provides the most exhaustive investigation of the secular cultural and historical background for the evangelist's "mission-Christology," the key to which he finds in a synthesis of the legate or agent, the שליח, with the prophet. Of special value is his survey of previous discussion of the issue (7–115). A similar treatment, with a sharper focus on the eschatological prophet, is offered by Juan Peter Miranda: *Der Vater, der mich gesandt hat: Religionsgeschichtliche Untersuchungen zu den johanneischen Sendungsformeln: Zugleich ein Beitrag zur johanneischen Christologie und Ekklesiologie*, Europäische Hochschulschriften/European University Papers, Series 23: Theology 7 (Bern and Frankfurt a.M.: Herbert Lang/Peter Lang, 1972); and idem, *Die Sendung Jesu im vierten Evangelium: Religions- und theologiegeschichtliche Untersuchungen zu den Sendungsformeln*, SBS 87 (Stuttgart: Katholisches Bibelwerk, 1977). The sharpest cautions against an anachronistic use of the specific rabbinic terminology (esp. שליח) appear in discussions of the origin of the notion of apostleship in the New Testament, but they need to be heeded in Johannine studies as well (see John Howard Schütz, *Paul and the Anatomy of Apostolic Authority*, SNTSMS 26 [Cambridge: Cambridge University Press, 1975], 27–28 and the literature cited there).

43. See esp. Miranda, *Die Sendung Jesu im vierten Evangelium*, 90–92, and the sharp critique of Thyen, "Johannesevangelium," 221–22. For an admirably clear and balanced discussion of the tensions in Johannine Christology that feed this debate, see Ashton, *Understanding the Fourth Gospel*, 308–29. In the end, like the writers referred to earlier (n. 22), Ashton cannot resist suggesting, even if only by a rhetorical question, that the "original seed" of the "fine flowering" of Johannine Christology is to be found in "Jesus' own sense of the fatherhood of God" (326).

44. Schnackenburg, "'Der Vater, der mich gesandt hat'" (see n. 25), 275–91.
45. Thyen, "Johannesevangelium," 219.
46. James D. G. Dunn, "Let John Be John: A Gospel for Its Time," in *The Gospel and the Gospels,* ed. Peter Stuhlmacher (Grand Rapids: Eerdmans, 1991), 293–322, esp. 318.
47. Ibid., passim.
48. For a finely nuanced discussion of the bearing of this fact upon method in interpretation, see M. C. de Boer, "Narrative Criticism, Historical Criticism, and the Gospel of John," *JSNT* 47 (1992): 35–48.
49. Ashton, *Understanding the Fourth Gospel,* 318. A similar example is provided by the two motifs of Jesus' "coming into the world" and his being "sent." Though Bultmann makes much of their combination (see n. 41 above), the evangelist does not combine them. Not one of the passages in which Jesus (whether himself or as "the light") is spoken of as "coming into the world" (1:9; 3:19; 6:14; 9:39; 11:27; 12:46; 16:28; 18:37) connects this coming with his being sent. The two motifs do lie side by side in 12:45–46, but this is a summary context that recapitulates a variety of themes from the "Book of Signs" (chaps. 1–12), and there is no internal connection between them. On the other hand, the phrase "into the world" does follow the verb ἀποστέλλειν ("to send") in 3:17; 10:36; 17:18; in these cases the context offers clear reasons why the destination of the mission, the κόσμος ("world"), is named.
50. See the concluding remark in n. 20, above.
51. Rom. 1:3, 9; 5:10; 8:3, 29, 32; 1 Cor. 1:9; 15:28; 2 Cor. 1:19; Gal. 1:16; 2:20; 4:4, 6; 1 Thess. 1:10. The coordination begins with the Deutero-Pauline letters (Eph. 4:13; Col. 1:13).
52. Cf. Schrenk, *TDNT* 5 (1967): 1009: "The rule is scrupulously observed that υἱός ["son"] should occur with θεός ["God"] rather than πατήρ ["father"]." For the Synoptics, cf. the comment by Ferdinand Hahn: "Yet on the other hand it must be observed that in all the tradition about Jesus as the 'Son of God' the fatherhood of God and his union [*Bindung*] with the Father do not play any recognizable role; a distinction has therefore to be drawn between 'Son of God' and 'Son—Father' " (*The Titles of Jesus in Christology: Their History in Early Christianity* [London: Lutterworth, 1969], 313).
53. See n. 27 above.
54. John 1:18 (on the text, see n. 27); 3:35; 5:19 (bis), 20, 21, 22, 23 (bis), 26; 6:40; 14:13; 17:1 (bis). The concentration in chapter 5 is striking and has led Jürgen Becker to ask whether this entire group of passages may have its roots in an independent tradition that has left its mark also in Matthew and 1 Corinthians (*Das Evangelium nach Johannes,* Ökumenischer Taschenbuchkommentar zum Neuen Testament 4 [Gütersloh: Gütersloher Verlagshaus/Mohn, 1979–81], 1.239–40). On this tradition see also Eduard Schweizer, "Zum religionsgeschichtlichen Hintergrund der 'Sendungsformel' Gal 4,4 f, Röm 8,3 f, Joh 3,16 f, 1 Joh 4,9," *Beiträge zur Theologie des Neuen Testaments: Neutestamentliche Aufsätze (1955–1970)* (Zurich: Zwingli, 1970), 83–95, and idem, "What Do We Really Mean When We Say 'God sent his son . . .'?" in *Faith and History: Essays in Honor of Paul W. Meyer,* ed. John T. Carroll, Charles H. Cosgrove, and E. Elizabeth Johnson, Homage Series (Atlanta: Scholars Press, 1990), 298–312.
55. See n. 38 above. (In chapter 17, the second person singular pronoun, σύ, is understood to have πατήρ ["father"; vv. 1, 5, 11, 21, 24, 25] as its antecedent.)
56. In addition, Jesus is the subject of the active verb, with the disciples as object,

272

Paul W. Meyer

in 4:38 and 17:18. The verb is used twice of the Jews who sent a delegation to John
(1:19; 5:33) and three more times in straightforward narrative contexts (7:32; 11:3;
18:24), still with at least mild "official" or legatine connotations. The perfect passive
participle (ἀπεσταλμένος, "one sent," "emissary") is used twice of John the Baptist
(1:6; 3:28), once of the Jewish delegates sent to question John (1:24), and once as a
translation of "Siloam" (9:7), but *never of Jesus.*
  57. Rengstorf, "ἀποστέλλω and πέμπω in the NT," *TDNT* 1 (1964): 403–6; Miranda, *Die Sendung Jesu im vierten Evangelium,* 14–15. Schnackenburg sees no difference ("'Der Vater, der mich gesandt hat,'" 277). Bultmann (*The Gospel of John,*
50, n. 2) seems to accept Rengstorf's distinction but to deny that the Gospel observes
it. (The translator's English sentence does not say this, and the original German [*Das
Evangelium des Johannes: Ergänzungsheft,* 11] is ambiguous, but all the passages
Bultmann here cites [1:19, 22; 5:36–37; 20:21] show the two verbs occurring side by
side.)
  58. The finite form of the verb is used once of God's sending the Spirit (future
tense, 14:26), twice of Jesus' sending the Spirit/Paraclete (also future, 15:26; 16:7),
and twice of Jesus' sending disciples (subjunctive, 13:20; present indicative, 20:21).
The participial form is used once in the plural, of the authorities responsible for the
delegation to John (1:22).
  59. With "the Father": John 5:23, 37; 6:44; 8:16, 18; 12:49; 14:24. Without "the
Father": 4:34; 5:24, 30; 6:38, 39; 7:16, 28, 33; 8:26, 29; 9:4; 12:44, 45; 13:20; 15:21;
16:5. There are two gnomic uses of the formula (7:18; 13:16); in both contexts the
sender is still God.
  60. Bultmann, *Theology of the New Testament,* 2.34 (emphasis added). Kendrick
Grobel, the English translator, has inserted here into Bultmann's text the comment,
"Both expressions, as *crystallized participial phrases,* might better be translated with
nouns: 'my Commissioner, the Father,' and 'my Commissioner'" (emphasis added).
For other stereotyped or formulaic participial phrases that serve as epithets or names
for God in the rest of the New Testament, see the important study by Gerhard Delling,
"Geprägte partizipiale Gottesaussagen in der urchristlichen Verkündigung," in *Studien zum Neuen Testament: Gesammelte Aufsätze 1950–1968,* ed. Ferdinand Hahn,
Traugott Holtz, and Nikolaus Walter (Göttingen: Vandenhoeck & Ruprecht, 1970),
401–16.
  61. A word about the procedure on which such generalizations are based is in order, since the identification of "sources" or stages in the composition of the Gospel is
much debated. To stand for "narrative material," in an older edition of the *Novum Testamentum Graece* the text of Robert Fortna's reconstruction of the Signs Gospel (*The
Gospel of Signs: A Reconstruction of the Narrative Source Underlying the Fourth
Gospel,* SNTSMS 11 [Cambridge: Cambridge University Press, 1970], 235–45) has
been highlighted in one color. Other colors have then been used to mark occurrences
of πατήρ ("father") when used of God, υἱός [τοῦ θεοῦ] ("Son [of God]") when used
of Jesus, θεός ("God"), and both verbs ἀποστέλλειν and πέμπειν (both meaning
"to send"), all these instances checked against a concordance to the twenty-sixth edition of Nestle-Aland, *Novum Testamentum Graece* (Stuttgart: Deutsche Bibelstiftung,
1979). The patterns of attribution are thus both clear and striking. In only two passages
(2:16; 18:11) does "Father"-language for God appear in the Signs Gospel. References
to Jesus' having been "sent" by God appear in such contexts only at 9:4, 7b; and
11:41–42, verses that Fortna regards as later insertions into the Signs Gospel.

62. John 1:(14?), 18; 3:35–36; 4:23–24; 5:18, 42–43, 44–45; 6:27 (here very emphatically joined as the twin subjects of one verb), 32–33; 6:45–46; 8:38–40, 41–42, 47–49, 54; 10:29–33; (11:40–41?); 13:1–3; 14:1–2; 16:2–3, 27–28 (v.l.), 28–30; 17:1–5; 20:17.

63. With πατήρ ("father") but never θεός ("God"): ἁγιάζειν ("to make holy"), γινώσκειν ("to know"), δεικνύειν ("to make known"), διδάσκειν ("to teach"), ἐγείρειν ("to raise"), ἑλκύειν ("to draw, pull"), ἐντέλλεσθαι ("to command"), ἐργάζεσθαι ("to work"), ἔχειν ("to have"), κρίνειν ("to judge"), λέγειν ("to say"), μαρτυρεῖν ("to bear witness"), μένειν ("to abide"), πέμπειν ("to send"), ποιεῖν ("to do"), σῴζειν ("to save"), τηρεῖν ("to guard"), and φιλεῖν ("to love"). With θεός but never πατήρ: λαλεῖν ("to speak").

64. The two exceptions are 7:16–18 and 9:4.

65. See n. 42 above.

66. Schweizer, "What Do We Really Mean When We Say, 'God sent his son'?" 310–11.

67. Bultmann, *Das Evangelium des Johannes,* 186, commenting on 5:19 (my translation; emphasis omitted); note esp. his n. 3, attached to these words. (The translation in *The Gospel of John,* 249, is simply wrong, reverses the point, and produces a caricature of Bultmann's theology: "his origin is grounded in what he means for us" [emphasis omitted].)

68. See n. 12 above.

69. Dahl, "The Neglected Factor in New Testament Theology," 156; emphasis added.

70. Ibid., 153.

71. For fuller discussion of Paul on this point, and as representative of a much wider literature, see Ulrich Wilckens, *Resurrection. Biblical Testimony to the Resurrection: An Historical Examination and Explanation* (Atlanta: John Knox, 1978), 1–27.

72. Dahl, "The Neglected Factor in New Testament Theology," 157–58.

Leander E. Keck

15

Derivation as Destiny:
"Of-ness" in Johannine Christology, Anthropology, and Soteriology

Whoever created the Fourth Gospel had the ability to draw its readers into a profoundly different "world" through simple, ordinary language used in extraordinary ways.[1] From the first line onward, one is challenged by arresting assertions that bend out of shape the customary meaning of common words. For example, Jesus claims to be "the living bread that came down out of heaven" (6:51) and that "those who eat my flesh and drink my blood have eternal life" (6:54). To express new thoughts John does not coin new words but combines old ones in such a way that understanding what is said requires not a lexicon but insight. This is true not only of nouns (bread, flesh), verbs (came down, eat) and adjectives (living, eternal) but also of prepositions, as when Jesus says, "I am in the Father and the Father is in me" (14:11). Indeed, this gospel relies repeatedly on one preposition—ἐκ (of, from)—to express not only its Christology but also its anthropology and soteriology. For instance, Jesus tells "the Jews" that "He who is *of* God hears the words of God" (8:47, RSV). Although the whole of Johannine Christology,[2] anthropology, and soteriology does not flow through this one bunghole, enough of it does to justify considering it as an aperture into the Gospel's theology.

In fact, by a particular construal of the Johannine "of-ness," Jeffrey Trumbower's *Born from Above*[3] recently has challenged the predominant interpretation of John since Origen. Trumbower claims that John's "of" language expresses a dualistic anthropology of "fixed origins"; that is, not only do responses to Jesus disclose one's predetermined origin but *these origins cannot change or be exchanged*" (10, italics added). Those who pass from death to life can do so only because they have the right origin to begin with. Thus John's anthropology is protognostic: Like the Valentinians and *The Gospel of Truth* (cited repeatedly), John taught that the saved are predestined by nature, not by election as in Qumran, Paul, and Ephesians (14). "The ability to achieve salvation . . . consistently depends on one's fixed origin. . . . From the author's point of view, all human beings do not start on an equal footing."[4] Given the consequences of such reading, another look at the text is in order, though a full discussion of Trumbower's work cannot be undertaken here.

I

John 1:12–13. It is significant that the Johannine "of" language appears first in the prologue, in what appears to be the evangelist's explanatory comment (v. 12c) on the assertion (in 12ab) about those who receive the Logos, because this puts us in direct touch with his "of" usage. One can expect that clarity gained here will guide one's reading of subsequent usages.

According to the inherited tradition in verse 12a, "to those who received him, he [the Logos] gave the power [ἐξουσία] to become God's children." Clearly, this status is the result of an event in which they became what they had not been before, or apart from, receiving him. That is, by believing in his name they acknowledge his identity and entrust themselves to him. Verse 13 explains this event by contrasting three aspects[5] of ordinary human generation of life ("not of [ἐκ] blood, nor of [ἐκ] the will of the flesh, nor of [ἐκ] the will of [a] man") with being "born/begotten[6] of [ἐκ] God." The point is not that these people were sired by God instead of by human parents. Rather, in receiving the Logos, in believing in his name, they are "begotten of God," so that they are simultaneously their parents' children and God's "children." Those who refused the Logos were begotten by human parents only—of blood, of the will of the flesh, of the will of (a) man— while those who believe were begotten also in an entirely different way—namely, "of God."

Verse 13 provides a fine instance of the evangelist's use of language, for although "begotten" (ἐγεννήθησαν) is used but once, it clearly has a dual meaning: the ordinary generation of human life, and the extraordinary act of God in generating another kind of life, not specified here but which the Gospel will characterize as "eternal."

This passage presents Trumbower with a clear dilemma. With his right hand he grants that the text does imply that this begetting "of God" occurs in conjunction with believing, and that this was also the view of the hymn on which the evangelist comments. In other words, in both tradition and redaction, all persons do "start out on an even footing" but are differentiated by their response to the Logos. But letting this observation stand would vaporize his thesis about "fixed origins." Consequently, what the right hand granted the left hand must take away: He claims that in adding 12c–13 the evangelist really meant to "designate the fixed category and provide an explanation for why certain people believe"—they were "born of God" before Jesus appeared on the scene.[7] However, as an "explanation" this simply self-destructs, for if this divine begetting does not interpret the believing/receiving and instead accounts for a fixed category to which one belongs prior to faith, then "begetting" loses its dual meaning.

More important is noting the import of this passage for Johannine Christology. (1) The act of God in begetting and the act of the Logos-Light in giving power to become God's children are two ways of saying the same thing. The work of the

Son and the work of the Father are identical. This is a major theme in the Gospel. Accordingly, Jesus can say, "I have shown you many good works from [of, ἐκ] the Father" (10:32), as well as, "If I am not doing the works of my Father [τοῦ πατρός μου], then do not believe me" (10:37). (2) Receiving power to become God's children depends on believing in the name of the Logos (accepting his claims for his identity). He is able to give this power because of who he is. In the language of dogmatics, Christology (who Jesus is) makes possible soteriology (what he does); conversely, soteriology makes Christology necessary.[8] (3) Soteriology implies anthropology. Here, what the Logos gives deals effectively with the (unstated) human dilemma at its core—impotence, the inability to make oneself a child of God, and so overcome the limitations of being only "of" human parents.

John 3:3–8. The "begetting" language reappears in the story of Nicodemus's rendezvous with Jesus, who makes it the pivot of the exchange by linking it with ἄνωθεν, which in John regularly means "from above" but which can also mean "again." Jesus, responding to Nicodemus's opening gambit, says, "Unless one is begotten[9] ἄνωθεν one cannot see the kingdom of God." Nicodemus, taking ἄνωθεν to mean "again," protests that it is impossible for a senior citizen to repeat birth from the mother's womb. Jesus now replies, "Unless one is begotten of [ἐξ] water and Spirit[10] one cannot enter the kingdom of God."[11] The fact that one preposition (ἐκ) governs both "water" and "Spirit" suggests that the nouns are not to be separated,[12] so that "water and Spirit" is a hendiadys[13] (two words for the same thing, as in "each and every").

Jesus continues, evidently with an explanation of the necessity of being begotten of water and Spirit, though the paratactic construction does not make this explicit with γάρ (because):

What is begotten of [ἐκ] flesh is flesh
and what is begotten of [ἐκ] the Spirit is Spirit.

This epigrammatic formulation of the principle that like produces like makes the contrast between flesh and Spirit absolute. Here, derivation—one's "of-ness"—determines not only one's "nature" but also one's (future[14]) destiny, for only the Spirit-begotten can enter the kingdom. No provision is made for adding or giving Spirit to flesh, as in the quotation of Joel 2:18 at Acts 2:17. Spirit is not something that flesh lacks, but its antithesis. The problem with flesh is not its behavior but its ontic status—what it is, the phenomenal (the non-Spirit). Consequently, also what flesh begets shares this flaw.

Jesus still is not finished: "Do not marvel because I said to you [sg.], You [pl.] must be begotten ἄνωθεν" (v.7) and proceeds to use the dual meaning of πνεῦμα (Spirit or wind) to assert that the Spirit's work can be recognized but not explained: Just as one does not know the whence and whither of the πνεῦμα (wind) but knows it is blowing because one hears it, "so it is with everyone who is begotten of [ἐκ] the πνεῦμα [Spirit]" (v. 8).[15] The Spirit's action is unexplainable precisely because, being ἄνωθεν, it is not subject to explanations, which pertain to the domain of flesh.

What Jesus tells Nicodemus reformulates and amplifies what was signaled by the prologue in 1:12–13.[16] It is only natural, then, for Trumbower to say that, "when . . . Jesus tells Nicodemus 'unless one is born ἄνωθεν, one cannot see the Kingdom of God,' he means one must belong to a fixed category of persons. . . . Nicodemus does not and cannot belong to this category . . . because they exist as a category before Jesus' coming and their membership list does not grow or shrink with Jesus' advent" (72). Trumbower's exegetical warrants for this interpretation are not convincing. (1) In order to say that in v. 3 Jesus speaks generally instead of addressing Nicodemus ("unless one is begotten . . ."), Trumbower ignores the first part of the verse: "Jesus . . . said *to him*, 'Amen, amen, I say *to you*.'" (2) Trumbower grants that the begetting by water and Spirit refers to a *re*birth, "but it is not a rebirth in which Nicodemus can participate." Why not? Because Trumbower, ignoring John's penchant for paraphrase, distinguishes "seeing" the Kingdom (v. 3) from "entering" it (v. 5). This allows him to infer that "(fixed) birth from above is necessary 'to see' initially; subsequent rebirth from (water and) spirit is necessary to enter." Indeed, "such rebirth accrues automatically to those born from above" (74)—said to be confirmed by Jesus' promise of the Paraclete whom the world cannot receive (14:16–17). But this has nothing to do with rebirth. (3) It may well be that subsequent references to Nicodemus (7:48–51; 19:39) indicate that he "is stuck in the realm of the flesh," but in no way does that confirm the claim that "he is outside the pale; he is not and *cannot be* born 'from above'" (73, italics added).

The function of the stark contrast between flesh and Spirit in verse 6 is not to explain why Nicodemus is in a hopeless situation but rather to underscore the necessity of being begotten ἄνωθεν, because what is of flesh cannot escalate itself into Spirit. In other words, v. 6 is the Johannine equivalent of 1 Cor. 15:50: "flesh and blood cannot inherit the kingdom of God." But whereas for Paul the solution is the ontic transformation of perishable flesh and blood into an imperishable mode of existence, an event expected at Christ's Parousia, John's solution is another "begetting," a categorically different "of-ness" that can occur in the present. While Paul too affirms a decisive change in the believer's present (new creation), he nonetheless distinguishes it clearly from the future transformation; for John, however, this change occurs now in one's positive response to the Redeemer because it is not an ontic transformation but an existential one pertaining to the whence of one's life. Consequently, what is stated formally as a requirement ("unless," vv. 3, 5; "you must," v. 7) actually formulates the gospel, since the requirement implies that the totally different "of-ness" is possible now.

In a word, the exchange with Nicodemus indicates that being begotten of the Spirit = being begotten of water and the Spirit = being begotten from above =

being begotten of God = believing in his (Christ's) name = receiving the Logos-
Light = receiving power to become children of God. Precisely because derivation is destiny, a change in "of-ness" is required—and possible. Were this not the
case, we would expect John 3:17 to say that God sent the Son into the world "so
that those begotten of God would be saved through him."

John 3:31–32a. To a passage concerned with Jesus' superiority over John
(3:22–30) the evangelist appends the narrator's commentary (vv. 31–36),[17] which
concludes this section by looking ahead (cf. v. 34 and 8:26) and back (cf. v. 36
and vv. 16–18). Here for the first time the reader finds that "of" language, used
previously to express Johannine anthropology, is also used to formulate Christology. The passage can be rendered as follows:

> He who comes ἄνωθεν is above [ἐπάνω] all;
> He who exists of the earth [ὁ ὤν ἐκ τῆς γῆς]
> is of [ἐκ] the earth and speaks of [ἐκ] earth;
> He who comes from [ἐκ] heaven is above all
> and testifies to what he has seen and heard [there].

The fact that the passage does not argue *for* the descent-ascent pattern of Christology but *from* it shows that it is taken for granted. It is also assumed that its pattern applies only to Jesus. Consequently, Jesus' coming "from above" (ἄνωθεν)
can imply that he is superior to everyone else. Accordingly, even though John the
Baptist was sent from God to be a witness to the light (1:6–8, 15, 19–34; 3:25–30),
he still was an earthling ("of the earth"[18]), and his testimony was only "of earth"
because it cannot transcend its whence, for derivation is decisive. Moreover, once
derivation (ἐκ) is construed spatially (ἄνωθεν), it can also be used to refer to the
Son's descent from heaven. Consequently, the testimony of Jesus, who is not an
earthling because of his derivation ἄνωθεν (= coming from [ἐκ] heaven), concerns "heavenly things" (3:12), "what he has seen and heard" there (even though
he never conveys privileged information)—namely, "the words of God" (v. 34). In
short, this passage is a commentary on 1:18: Only the Son, who is in the Father's
lap, has made God known because his unique derivation qualifies him to do so.

Although derivation, expressed in "of-ness" language, is used in both Christology and anthropology, it is used in a spatial sense (as in 3:31, "he who comes ἐκ
heaven") only in christological and soteriological statements. The bread discourse
in John 6 shows this usage repeatedly (e.g., "I am the living bread which has come
down from heaven [ὁ ἐκ τοῦ οὐρανοῦ καταβάς]," v. 51; see also vv. 32, 33 41, as
well as v. 38, where some manuscripts read ἐκ instead of ἀπό, printed in Nestle-
Aland [twenty-sixth ed.]). In other words, "of-ness" is combined with the descent-
ascent pattern only in the case of Christ because preexistence pertains only to him.
This is confirmed by the fact that also πόθεν ("from where?") is used in the pregnant sense only of Christ. Thus he says, "I know from where [πόθεν] I have come

and where [ποῦ] I am going" (8:14). In interrogating the formerly blind man "the Jews" admit that they do not know Jesus' "whence," to the man's amazement (9:29–30). On the other hand, it is Johannine irony that has "the Jews" know exactly where he is from; they rely on this knowledge to disqualify him from being the Christ, whose "whence" is unknown (7:27–28; see also 6:24, where knowledge of Jesus' parentage is the basis of their rejecting his claim to have descended ἐκ heaven). It is not accidental that also Pilate asks, "Where are you from?" (πόθεν, 19:9). In other words, Jesus' true "whence" is either not known or used against him, because his claim about his derivation (his ἐκ) is not accepted. This becomes particularly evident in John 8.

John 8:21–24, 42–44a, 47. In chapter 8 Jesus' bitter controversies with "the Jews" repeatedly concern his "of-ness." Moreover, here the anthropological, soteriological, and christological uses reinforce one another. The first controversy of concern here[19] (8:21–24) can be set out as follows:

JESUS:	I am going away, and you will search for me, but you will die in your sin. Where I am going, you cannot come.
"THE JEWS":	Is he going to kill himself? Is that what he means . . . ?
JESUS:	You are from below [ἐκ τῶν κάτω ἐστέ], I am from above [ἐκ τῶν ἄνω εἰμί]; You are of this world [ἐκ τούτου τοῦ κόσμου ἐστέ], I am not of this world [οὐκ εἰμὶ ἐκ τοῦ κόσμου τούτου]. Therefore[20] I told you that you will die in your sins, for unless you believe that I AM, you will die in your sins.

Here Jesus appropriates and interprets the narrator's language in 3:31–32a in order to comment on his death as his departure and return to the Father in heaven.[21] The ἐκ τῶν ἄνω ("from above") here is clearly synonymous with the ἄνωθεν used there. Moreover, "of-ness" (English usage requires that here ἐκ be rendered "from") is first construed spatially (below/above), thereby replacing the narrator's earth/heaven, then is given a distinctly Johannine interpretation as "this world"/not "this world." The text does not simply paraphrase "below" as "this world" (= the earth), as C. K. Barrett says,[22] but interprets "below" anthropologically.

In John, "world" often refers to humanity in need of salvation. It is the skewed and hostile human "world" that God loves enough to send the Son into it in order to save it (3:16–17).[23] The anthropological meaning of "world" is manifest in the fact that frequently it is personified and thus is the subject of verbs normally used of humans: The world "did not know" the Logos (1:10) or the Father (17:25); it cannot "receive" the Spirit (14:17), and the peace that it "gives" differs from that which Christ gives (14:27); soon it will no longer "see" Jesus (14:19) but will "rejoice" when he is gone (16:20). It "hates" both Jesus and the disciples (15:18; 17:14). Nonetheless, the Christ-event occurred so that it would "believe" (17:21) and its sins be "taken away"(1:29).

Here, however, Jesus does not speak simply of "the world" but pointedly of "this world," an expression that reflects "this age" (αἰὼν οὗτος, העולם הזה), frequently found in apocalyptic thought where it is contrasted with "the age to come," as in Matthew 12:32.[24] Like עולם, αἰών ("aeon," "age") in such contexts refers not to a discrete historical period (e.g., the Roman era) but to time-space as a totality, viewed from the standpoint of the future aeon/age from which it differs categorically. The age to come is not the outgrowth of the past and present but the God-given eschatological alternative to it. To speak holistically of all human experience on this side of the divide as "this age" is therefore to disparage it because of its flawed character, as seen in light of its flawless replacement. This devaluation of the present in light of the radically different future is implied in the phrase even if it is not paired explicitly with "the age to come." Thus Paul can speak disparagingly of "the wisdom of this age" (1 Cor. 2:6); he can also substitute "world" for "age" in order to write of "the wisdom of this world" (1 Cor. 3:19). Why neither Paul nor John uses "the age/world to come" need not be probed here. What must be noted, however, is that in John "this world" is so estranged from God that it is subject to a malign power called "the ruler of this world" (12:31; 14:30; 16:11). Evidently, in the Johannine community the somber colors of "this world" have bled into the coloration of "the world."

The foregoing considerations, abbreviated though they are, indicate that when Jesus says, "You are of this world," he is not simply identifying his opponents as earthlings or even as denizens of the known solar system. Rather, he is making an anthropological accusation about the derivation of their real "nature"; he is identifying the hostile "whence" that accounts for their obduracy, for their not knowing either him or the Father (8:9), and for their not understanding that his words about the Sender are about the Father (8:27). Their resistance to him actualizes and demonstrates their "of-ness." They do not realize this, so he makes this disclosure part of his word.[25] At this point Bultmann's famous contention—that as the Revealer Jesus reveals only that he is the Revealer—sells the Fourth Gospel somewhat short.

On the other hand, Bultmann rightly saw that when Jesus amplifies his terse christological assertion ("I am not of this world") by speaking of his relationship to the Sender (8:2, 6, 28–29), he does not provide positive information about his own "of-ness" in order to transmit knowledge about another world but grounds his mission's character and warrant. In John, Jesus is God's Son sent into the world, who during his sojourn in it as an unlettered Nazarene of known parentage was not "of this world." He was a "stranger from heaven."[26] The effectiveness of his mission depends precisely on being "not of this world," for only so could he be simultaneously not part of the human dilemma and truly obedient to the One who sent him into it. Jesus' "of-ness" is as essential to Johannine Christology as his opponents' "of-ness" is for its anthropology.

Especially fascinating in 8:21–24 is the way (a) Jesus interprets the "of-ness" anthropology further and (b) links it with Christology in order to confront opponents with a decision freighted with ultimate consequences. (a) In verse 21, sandwiched between Jesus' two assertions about what will follow his departure ("you will search for me" and "you cannot come") is the dire prediction, "and you will die in your sin." Despite the severity of this promise, "the Jews" ignore it and instead wonder if Jesus is planning suicide (cf. 7:32–36). But Jesus will not be deflected from his prediction (made three times). After interpreting "from below" as "you are of this world," he adds, "therefore I told you that you would die in your sins." Here he interprets their being "of this world" by specifying the resultant destiny. They are "in" sin/sins, not because they are earthlings, but because sin characterizes "this world" that they are "of." In other words, they will die in their sins because, being of this world (= from below), they cannot follow Jesus when he departs for the world he had left.

(b) Jesus' last word, however, states the condition on which the alternative destiny depends:[27] namely, accepting his christological claim—"believe that I AM"—the enigmatic appropriation of God's own self-proclamation in Isa. 43:10.[28] To paraphrase, those who believe what Jesus says about himself—John's "high" Christology—will not die in their sins because believing this makes them no longer "of this world."[29] Accordingly, they will be able to go where he goes—exactly what Jesus promises the disciples (John 13:33, 36; 14:2–3), even if he speaks also of his coming to them (14:18, 23, 28; 16:16).

Given the intimate correlation of soteriology and anthropology with Christology, this passage casts light on "of-ness" because it is by believing a christological assertion that one ceases to be "of this world." Understanding this connection entails grasping what is implied in believing Jesus' claim to be I AM (ἐγώ εἰμι). To begin, it is to acknowledge that Jesus is the phenomenal, temporal mode of the eternal (nontemporal) divine reality itself, so that the response to Jesus is a response to God the Creator on whom all that is is contingent, and who by definition is "not world." Further, one cannot acknowledge that this reality is present without being shaped by it, for to acknowledge its presence is to avow one's contingency on it. To say Yes to this Reality's self-presentation is to place oneself deliberately at its disposal, to open one's existence to its influence; it is to affirm that one's true life is derived from the nonphenomenal, nontemporal Other instead of from the phenomenal and transient. Moreover, it is to see that being "of this world" is likewise a matter of believing, of trusting that its implicit and explicit self-presentation is sufficient, valid and trustworthy enough to obey. Indeed, it is precisely in being confronted by the self-presentation of the Other-as-Jesus that one is confronted also by the extent to which one is "of this world." Given the character and power of "this world," such confrontation is necessary if one is to see the situation clearly enough to grasp the possibility of being free from it.

This analysis of "of-ness" is confirmed in the latter half of chapter 8, which contains Jesus' most drastic polemic against the very Jews who, despite believing in him (vv. 30, 31), nonetheless reject his promise of freedom, claiming that as Abraham's descendants they have never been enslaved. Jesus, however, sets up the following dispute by pointing out that whoever sins is a slave of sin,[30] that their refusal of his word contradicts their claim to be Abraham's seed, and that just as he reflects his Father so also they reflect theirs (vv. 34–38). They respond, "Abraham is our father," but Jesus replies that what they do (seek to kill him, v. 40; cf. v. 59) shows that this is not the case but, rather, exposes who their father really is. It is at this point that the "of-ness" language reappears.

"THE JEWS":   We are not bastards (begotten of [ἐκ] fornication).

JESUS: If God were your Father, you would love me,
                      for I came out from God [ἐκ τοῦ θεοῦ ἐξῆλθον]
                      and now I am here. . . .
                      Why do you not understand my speech [λαλίαν]?
                      Because you cannot hear[31] my word.
                      You are of [ἐκ] your father, the devil,
                      and you want to do the desires of your father. . . .
                      He who is of [ἐκ] God hears the words of God.

Jesus' brutal attack (doubtless reflecting the invective of Jewish-Christian polemic against non-Christian Jews) is based on the previously noted principle that like produces like, here expressed as "like father, like son." Consequently, "of-ness" implies not only the point of origin (derivation) but also the reproduction of its character. In other words, by construing "of-ness" as paternity, one can argue in both directions: One can infer the identity and character of the father from the behavior of the children, and one can attribute the character of the father to the children. Accordingly, since Jesus' opponents' father is the devil, a murderer (v. 44), they seek to kill him (vv. 40, 59). Likewise, because the devil, being "a liar and the father of lies," has "no truth in him" (v. 44), it is inevitable that they do not believe, precisely because he tells the truth (v. 45). Conversely, were he to deny that he knows the Father, he would be a liar too (v. 55). Their claim to have God as their Father is annulled by their refusal to love his emissary, who is "of God" (v. 42). In addition, whereas Jesus always does what is pleasing to his Father (v. 29), his opponents willfully actualize the desires of their father, the devil (v. 44). They are not acting under constraint but as willing servants—the most insidious consequence of their "of-ness."

John 18:36. Jesus' most frequently cited "of" saying was spoken to Pilate:

"My kingdom[32] is not of [ἐκ] this world. If my kingdom were of [ἐκ] this world, my staff [ὑπηρέται] would be fighting so that I would not be handed over to the Jews. But now [NRSV: as it is] my kingdom is not from here [ἐντεῦθεν]." He could just as well have said that it is ἄνωθεν ("from above"); but in this trial, in which the judge is judged by the accused, it is enough to say what Jesus' kingdom is not "of"—"this world," where power is based on might.[33] Consequently, Jesus' supporters do not engage in armed struggle on his behalf, for that would imply that his kingship is contingent on their success—that is, ἐντεῦθεν after all.

II

Several questions will help us consolidate these observations. What, then, does it mean to be "of," whether "of God" or "of the world"? Why is so much emphasis placed on one's derivation? What is implied about the self, and about Christology in John?

To begin with, "of-ness" implies that what is decisive about a person is neither self-generated nor self-defined; to the contrary, one is wholly contingent at the center where the self is constituted. An anthropology based on an autonomous self is precluded. In John, speaking of derivation is itself a way of making an anthropological statement. Indeed, Jesus' repeated insistence that he does not act or speak on his own (5:19, 30; 7:16–18; 8:28, 42) shows that exactly the same holds true of "of" language in Christology as well. This is why Jesus' dictum, "The one who hears the words of God is of God" (8:47), applies to him as well as to those of his hearers who accept his word.

In the juxtaposition of "I am from above" and "I am not of this world," the second claim interprets the first, showing that "of-ness" means more than point of origin. It also determines both what is actualized and the form of the actualized, as noted in the use of "of-ness" in conjunction with paternity. But "of-ness" language appears in other contexts as well because it is based on the principle of replication. Accordingly, it is virtually inevitable that the Jesus who says, "I have come out from God [ἐκ τοῦ θεοῦ ἐξῆλθον] and [now] I am here" (8:42), will also say, "The one who has seen me has seen the Father" (14:9). Nor is it surprising that the one "of God" appropriates the divine "I AM" to assert his identity. So, too, "this world" expresses itself in those who are "of" it: They "judge according to the flesh" (8:15) and so either cannot understand Jesus or reject his claims when they do.

Useful as "of-ness" is for formulating both anthropology and Christology in John, it nevertheless does not dissolve the distinction between the Savior and the saved, because only in the case of the former does "of-ness" refer to a preexistent state. Consequently, when Jesus says he is "not of this world" (17:14, 16) he means that on earth he maintained his unique derivation by not deriving the warrant for his life from "this world" but instead by pleasing the One who sent him.

For the disciples, however, their being "not of this world" is a status acquired. As a result they do not share Jesus' ontic "of-ness" but its consequences: The world hates both the inherently alien Jesus, whose "of-ness" was maintained, and those made aliens by acknowledging the "of-ness" of Jesus. Never does Jesus usurp God's role as the One in whom one's "of-ness" is to be grounded; instead, he is the one through whom this God-grounded "of-ness" is effected.

Instead of imparting his own "of-ness" as the Son (υἱός), Jesus makes it possible for believers to "become" God's children (τέκνα) by being "begotten" of God. Jesus never says they are "begotten of me" or that they are "of me." When he implies that they are "of" his flock (10:26), he refers not to their derivation but to their participation in a community, just as Nicodemus is "of the Pharisees" (3:1). To express Jesus' intimate relation to believers, John uses "in" language (e.g., "I am the vine, you are the branches; those who abide in me and I in them bear much fruit," 15:5).

Jesus is the only character in the Gospel who uses "of" language in the sense reviewed here. The disciples hear it but do not repeat it, nor do his opponents pick it up in order to contest it. It is part of Jesus' distinctive revelatory proclamation, reinforced by the narrator's use in the prologue and at 3:16–21, 31, both of which inform the reader of the transhistorical basis on which Jesus can use this language. Likewise, the narrator's comment at 2:25 signals the mundane basis: Jesus did not entrust himself to those who believed because of his signs, for "he knew what was in everyone" (= he knew that their "of-ness" had not been changed by such faith).

John's relentless dualism, which precludes shades of gray between the black and white alternatives, also makes no allowance either for extenuating circumstances or for oscillation—now more "of" flesh, now more "of" the Spirit. It is either/or, all or nothing, because what is in view is that which defines the existence of the self. Thereby John's dualism is focused on the individual in such a way that what is called for, explicitly or not, is a decision: either to deny the validity of Jesus' construal of one's condition (and thereby to remain determinedly in it) or to affirm that Jesus is right and so have the grounding of one's existence reconstituted, a change so radical that the appropriate metaphor for it is being "begotten of God." What the Gospel, like its protagonist in its narrative, asks from the reader is not the mind's assent to a dualistic worldview but a decision about one's existence, as Bultmann saw in characterizing this dualism as a "dualism of decision." Accordingly, John shows no interest in accounting for the alienation of creation into "this world." Nor does the Gospel encourage the readers (or the characters in the story) to see themselves as victims of fate or as the captives of a malign power, for that would shunt responsibility away from the self who must decide. Nor is Jesus' saying, "You are of this world," either a condescending observation or an explanation[34] voicing the standpoint of an elite. It is, rather, a word whose confrontational character is required if the self's derivation is to be reconstituted and not merely improved.

NOTES

1. See the suggestive study of John's language by Norman R. Petersen, *The Gospel of John and the Sociology of Light: Language and Characterization in the Fourth Gospel* (Valley Forge, Pa.: Trinity Press International, 1993). Petersen contends that John has created "an anti-language" in order to legitimate the community's identity as "an anti-society" (5); thereby Petersen carries forward the work of J. Louis Martyn and Wayne A. Meeks.

2. For a useful overview and assessment of recent studies of John's Christology, see Maarten J. J. Menken, "The Christology of the Fourth Gospel: A Survey of Recent Research," in *From Jesus to Paul: Essays on Jesus and New Testament Christology in Honour of Marinus de Jonge,* ed. Martinus C. de Boer, JSNTSup 84 (Sheffield: JSOT, 1993), 292–320.

3. Jeffrey A. Trumbower, *Born from Above: The Anthropology of the Gospel of John,* HUT 29 (Tübingen: Mohr [Siebeck] 1992). The monograph is a revised version of a 1989 dissertation supervised by H. D. Betz at the University of Chicago.

4. *Born from Above,* 22; see also 30. Trumbower agrees with Meeks's observation that the dualistic picture in John (believers vs. "the world") "is never rationalized by a comprehensive myth, as in gnosticism" (Wayne A. Meeks, "The Man from Heaven in Johannine Sectarianism," *JBL* 91 [1972]: 68). But he undertakes to show that Meeks is wrong in saying that the believers' status "is a *conferred* one, not an ontological one." From Meeks's suggestion that "it is at least as plausible that the Johannine christology helped to create some gnostic myths as that gnostic myths helped create the Johannine christology" (ibid., 72), Trumbower infers that Meeks meant that "the Fourth Gospel may be pushing its inherited traditions in a 'gnosticizing' direction" (*Born from Above,* 55). But this is not Meeks's conclusion but Trumbower's: "The principal author of the Gospel, far from being a 'de-gnosticizer,' was actually interpreting his sources, like the prologue, in a gnosticizing direction" (*Born from Above,* 141; see also 55).

5. Barnabas Lindars, however, suggested that the three phrases "cover the stages of reproduction in reverse order, in an attempt to trace it to its source" (*The Gospel of John,* NCB [London: Oliphants, 1972], 92).

6. Since the point concerns the origin of life rather than the birthing process itself, "begotten" is preferable to the customary "born," retained by NRSV, NIV, and REB.

7. Trumbower, *Born from Above,* 69.

8. For the correlations of theology, anthropology, and soteriology with Christology, see my "Toward the Renewal of New Testament Christology," *NTS* 32 (1986): 362–77.

9. As in 1:13, here γεννηθῇ probably means "begotten" rather than "birth." Dorothy A. Lee's recent defense of "born" is quite unpersuasive (*The Symbolic Narratives of the Fourth Gospel: The Interplay of Form and Meaning,* JSNTSup 95 [Sheffield: JSOT, 1994], 43–48). In making her case she also contends that the "water" in v. 5 "refers metaphorically to the rupture of the amniotic sac in childbirth" (52), and she invents the "labour" of the Spirit in 1:13.

10. Even if the Evangelist originally wrote only of the Spirit, as Bultmann argued, every known text includes the reference to water, which makes it difficult to regard "born of the Spirit" as expressing the truly Johannine point of view before a traditionalist editor added the reference to baptism.

11. According to Matt. 18:3 Jesus said to his disciples, "Truly, I say to you, unless you change [turn] and become like children, you will never enter the kingdom of Heaven" (see also Mark 10:15; Luke 18:17). Barnabas Lindars has reconstructed the Greek form of the saying that came to John (but was not derived from Matthew): "John and the Synoptic Gospels: A Test Case," *NTS* 27 (1981): 287–94.

12. Luise Schottroff, on the other hand, not only regards "of water and" as an original part of the text but also infers from the absence of "water" in v. 8 that the Evangelist takes up the tradition of rebirth through water (Titus 3:5) and quietly reinterprets it as derived from the Spirit (i.e., not sacramentally; "Heil als innerweltliche Entweltlichung," *NovT* 11 [1969]: 300). However, George R. Beasley-Murray is closer to the probable point: "The *whole* expression . . . defines the manner in which one is born from above" (*John*, WBC 36 [Waco, Tex.: Word Books, 1987], 48). Xavier Léon-Defour thinks that the "and" (καί) is epexegetical: water that is Spirit ("Towards a Symbolic Reading of the Fourth Gospel," *NTS* 27 [1981]: 450). On the other hand, Udo Schnelle distorts the meaning when he says that "of water and Spirit" refers to an "all-embracing new creation that is *accomplished* in baptism with water and *leads to* a life filled and determined by the Spirit" (*Antidocetic Christology in the Gospel of John* [Minneapolis: Fortress, 1992], 186 [italics added]). What *Schnelle* says may well be true of the Johannine community, but that is not what the *text* says.

13. So also James D. G. Dunn, *Baptism in the Holy Spirit: A Re-examination of the New Testament Teaching on the Gift of the Spirit in Relation to Pentecostalism Today* (Philadelphia: Westminster, 1970), 192, and Charles H. Talbert, *Reading John: A Literary and Theological Commentary on the Fourth Gospel and the Johannine Epistles* (New York: Crossroad, 1992), 99.

14. Since this is the only passage in John in which "the kingdom of God" is mentioned, it is difficult to discern whether seeing/entering the kingdom occurs now or in the future.

15. The comparison does not imply that "those of the flesh (earth) may indeed have some experience of spiritual things," as Jerome H. Neyrey infers ("John III. A Debate over Johannine Epistemology and Christology," *NovT* 23 [1981]: 115–27 [here, 120]).

16. Neyrey provides a convenient table of parallels between the prologue and John 3 ("John III," 125).

17. That vv. 31–36, like vv. 16–21, are not to be taken, respectively, as the continuation of the Baptist's words to his disciples and of Jesus' word to Nicodemus is generally acknowledged, though there is no marker in the text to indicate this shift. Lee, however, asserts that both passages "make most sense if Jesus . . . is regarded as the speaker" (*The Symbolic Narratives of the Fourth Gospel*, 38).

18. Probably the text uses "earth" instead of "world" in order to avoid saying that John the Baptist was "of the world," a formula with negative meaning (see below).

19. Chapter 8 has three controversies (8:12–20, 21–30, 31–59), which continue those begun at 7:14; they occur during Tabernacles and take place in the temple (7:14; 8:20, 59). For an analysis of the chapter that emphasizes both its function and forensic character, see Jerome H. Neyrey, *An Ideology of Revolt: John's Christology in Social-Scientific Perspective* (Philadelphia: Fortress, 1988), 37–58, 233–36. Neyrey claims that here "Jesus conducts a trial in which some people are formally charged, tried, convicted, and sentenced" (37).

20. NRSV, following p⁶⁶ ℵ a e sy^{s.p}, omits "therefore," and reverses the last two lines. Even without "therefore" the function of the statement remains unchanged.

21. For a discussion of this Johannine way of referring to Jesus' death, see Godfrey C. Nicholson, *Death as Departure: The Johannine Descent-Ascent Schema,* SBLDS 63 (Chico, Calif.: Scholars Press, 1983). Petersen could easily have included "departure" in the following apt statement: "'Exaltation', 'glorification,' 'resurrection,' and 'ascent' all have different meanings, denotations, and referents in everyday language, but in John's special language [sup., n. 1] they refer to the same thing, which is none of the things the words conventionally denote. And for this reason we cannot pin down their Johannine meaning and reference in anything but the minimal structural sense of the Word's return from its incarnation" (*The Gospel of John and the Sociology of Light,* 47).

22. C. K. Barrett, *The Gospel according to St. John: An Introduction with Commentary and Notes on the Greek Text,* 2d ed. (Philadelphia: Westminster, 1978), 341.

23. Paul, too, can use "world" to refer to humanity (2 Cor. 5:19). John, however, shows no interest in the redemption of the nonhuman creation that is in bondage to death, as does Paul (Rom. 8:18–25).

24. While John Ashton rightly notes that the Fourth Gospel prefers "this world" to "this age," strangely he does not see that the former was influenced by the latter, even though the temporal (future) aspect is missing (*Understanding the Fourth Gospel* [Oxford: Oxford University Press, 1991], 207–8). At the same time, Ashton concedes (in another context) that "one is forced to pay attention to a possible apocalyptic background" of John (307 n. 36). His chapter, "Intimations of Apocalyptic" (383–406), limits the two-ages motif to "the age of concealment" and "the age of disclosure" (388)—surely too restricted.

25. Luise Schottroff, on the other hand, insists that in John the dualistic understanding of "world" exists only in connection with the refusal of revelation, that there was no "world" before the revelation. She appeals to 9:41 and especially to 15:22 in support: "If I had not come and spoken to them, they would not have sin" (also 15:24). But her interpretation implies that Jesus' word creates "the world" in the act of his speaking, which overlooks the point that God loved the world so that it might be saved, implying that it needed salvation before the Son arrived (*Der Glaubende und die feindliche Welt: Beobachtungen zum gnostischen Dualismus und seiner Bedeutung für Paulus und das Johannesevangelium* WMANT 37 [Neukirchen: Neukirchener, 1970], 229–30).

26. The phrase is taken from the subtitle of Marinus de Jonge's volume of collected essays, *Jesus, Stranger from Heaven and Son of God: Jesus Christ and the Christians in Johannine Perspective,* SBLSBS 11 (Missoula, Mont.: Scholars Press, 1977).

27. Trumbower recognizes this implicit invitation to believe but appeals to the "above" language in v. 23 to say that the Evangelist has already "stated his ultimate attitude that belief is impossible for them" (*Born from Above,* 87). It is one thing, however, to regard v. 23 as expressing "boundary between Jesus and these Jews . . . in terms of origin"; it is another to say that the boundary cannot be crossed, that their "ofness" is immutable.

28. For a recent, succinct overview of the background of the I-AM formula, see Neyrey, *An Ideology of Revolt,* Appendix 1. This absolute use must be distinguished from that which includes a predicate, as in "I am the bread of life."

29. Given the Johannine penchant for paraphrase, one would not err in inferring that the "ideal reader" (the one who makes all the appropriate moves in reading the

text from the beginning) is expected to see an allusion to the Baptist's identification of Jesus as "the Lamb of God who takes away the sins of the world" (1:29); that is, by believing in Jesus as I AM, one's sins are taken away.

30. Although Trumbower does not actually say so, in his reading of John the saying would mean that one sins because one is a slave of sin, a member of a fixed category. But in that case would not the text say, "Whoever is a slave of sin sins"?

31. NRSV's rendering of "hear" as "accept" is a significant correction of RSV's "bear to hear," for the point concerns their inability to hear (= hearken), not their emotional resistance.

32. Dorothy A. Lee offers no reason for regarding this phrase as another reference to "the kingdom of God" (3:5; *The Symbolic Narratives of the Fourth Gospel*, 45). The two should not be fused without evidence.

33. Petersen uses Jesus' statement to illustrate the point that "anti-languages are not different *languages;* they are languages that differ from an everyday language as a special use of *that* language." Thus Jesus "accepts Pilate's notion of 'King of the Jews' but denies its everyday referent by implying another one that is *opposed* to it. . . . The political referent is displaced by another that is semantically constituted by its otherness—'*not of this world.*' Jesus does not point to a new concrete referent" (*The Gospel of John and the Sociology of Light*, 89).

34. According to Trumbower, the Evangelist appealed to "fixed origins" to explain retrospectively the phenomenon of belief and unbelief (*Born from Above*, 85, 105). At the same time, "by not immediately disclosing the true fixedness and determined quality of the hostile Jews' response, the author has left room for an outsider reading the gospel (perhaps a Jew!) to change his response and join the Johannine community (5:34), but he has also left no doubt in the mind of the insiders who read the gospel that the reason so many reject Jesus has to do with their fixed spiritual origin (8:43–47)" (128). In other words, Trumbower reads the Gospel's statements addressed to outsiders as having the same function as 1 John 2:19 has for insiders: a rationalizing of the fact that the schismatics departed because they were not part of the church in the first place (83). Were that the case, one would expect John 6:66–67 to read differently: there the Gospel not only reports the defection of many disciples but also has Jesus respond to their departure. This would have been an excellent point at which Jesus could have explained that they had not been "born of God" to start with. In other words, Trumbower overlooks a rather elemental point: that nowhere in John does "of-ness" language appear in contexts in which Jesus or the narrator explains to the reader either the acceptance or rejection of Jesus.

Stephen S. Smalley

16

"The Paraclete": Pneumatology in the Johannine Gospel and Apocalypse

The purpose of this article is to explore the fourth evangelist's theology of the Spirit-Paraclete in relation to the pneumatology of John's Apocalypse. I believe this to be a valid and worthwhile exercise because, in my view, Revelation and the Fourth Gospel are subtly but firmly related to each other and emerged from the same community.[1] The nature of that circle and its problems will be considered at the outset, before John's doctrine of the Spirit is examined in a community context.

This chapter is offered to Moody Smith, that doyen of Johannine interpreters, with much gratitude for his friendship and with deep respect for his scholarship.

I

I take it that all the documents in the New Testament bearing the name of John were written for a specific audience. Their content suggests that the authors concerned were sensitive to the needs of a particular church, and that they were addressing problems experienced by the different congregations within it.

If we begin by looking at St. John's Gospel, we find that the heart of the fourth evangelist's message is to be found in his Christology. John is above all concerned with probing the identity of Jesus and with enabling his readers to see and understand that the Son of God is both one with the Father *and* one with us (John 10:30; 14:28; 16:28). In a final way Jesus draws together the spiritual and the material; he makes possible, in both time and eternity, the connection between heaven and earth (1:51). This balanced Christology in John's Gospel is presented to his readers with an appeal for their closer unity and mutual love.

The presence of these elements in the teaching of the Fourth Gospel, taken together, may readily be explained if we envisage a situation of growing conflict in John's community. Some adherents had "seen" who Jesus was and recognized his true origin and nature.[2] But others from a Jewish-Christian background who still felt a loyalty to Judaism may have found it difficult to maintain an ongoing commitment to the *divinity* of Jesus. Still others who had emerged from a Hellenistic

(or even Jewish-Hellenistic) environment may well have become increasingly uncomfortable with the claim that Jesus was fully *human* as well as uniquely related
to God. In the case of the latter two groups, the estimate held of the person of Jesus
was inadequate: for some it was too low, and for others it was too high. Friction
arose, with each side adopting its distinctive stance. If John's Gospel were written at a time when secession from the community, and its possible disintegration,
had become a real threat, then John's balanced Christology, as well as his desire
for love and unity among the members, would have been entirely appropriate.

It is possible, I submit, to discover a similar setting of growing doctrinal tension in the churches addressed by the seer in Revelation, and to discern the outcome—namely, the final dissolution of the Johannine community—in the behavior of the congregations to whom the letters of John were written. As a result, the
history of John's circle can be traced from the Apocalypse, to which I give the
date 70 C.E.,[3] through the Gospel to 3 John.[4]

The reason for spending time in this introductory section on a survey of the back-
cloth against which the Johannine literature came to birth is to make two preliminary points. First, John's volatile church, as it may be discovered especially in his
Revelation and Gospel, experienced problems throughout its life: persecution (both
Jewish and Roman) from without[5] and—most important, in terms of its survival—
doctrinal conflict from within. Second, the community's very setting in life, I would
argue, accounts in general for the equilibrium that is characteristic of John's theology, *including his view of the Spirit,* in both the Apocalypse and the Fourth Gospel.

II

We can now come closer to the subject of this study and investigate the doctrine of the Spirit in John's Gospel[6] before we compare that teaching with the
pneumatology of Revelation.

The fourth evangelist speaks about the Spirit in two ways, although ultimately
these belong together. He tells us about the Spirit in the life of the individual believer, and he also informs his readers about the Spirit in the life of the corporate
church. First, the Jesus of John claims that the Spirit is the agent of regeneration
(3:1–8, whose language of "new birth" is typically Johannine). Since the Word
has become flesh (1:14), the new age of the Spirit has been inaugurated; therefore,
through the agency of the Spirit, believers can be "born again," or "born from
above" (3:3, 7),[7] and share God's life fully in time as well as in eternity.

Second, John describes the Spirit as given to the church at large, to sustain
the common life of believers after the resurrection, as the promised Paraclete
(ὁ παράκλητος). This distinctively Johannine category is used only in the
farewell discourse of John's Gospel (14:16, 26; 15:26; 16:7; cf. also 1 John
2:1), although that material yields a significant amount of information about
the identity and ministry of the Paraclete in John.

The problem remains, however, that the material about the *person* of the Paraclete in the Fourth Gospel is open to different constructions. My own inclination, following Raymond Brown,[8] is to accept the identification of the Paraclete as the Holy Spirit (as in John 14:26), to view this figure in personal terms, and to acknowledge that in the farewell discourse the Paraclete is regarded as the *alter ego* (the "other I") of Jesus. As such, he mediates the spiritual presence of Jesus in the community of disciples.

The possible interpretation of the Paraclete's *activity* is similarly many-sided. The Greek associations of the term παράκλητος are primarily legal.[9] But what is his role in the courtroom? The usual gloss is that the Paraclete acts for the defense, as an "advocate" (the translation used at John 14:6 and elsewhere by the NRSV, for example). In John 14—16, however, the Paraclete becomes a counsel for the prosecution (16:7–11); the only defense he makes is of Jesus, by witnessing to him, rather than at any point coming to the aid of the disciples themselves (15:26). Moreover, other functions appear to belong to the Johannine Paraclete, including the nonlegal activities of teaching and prophecy.[10] In other words, the functions of the Paraclete are too varied to be understood against the backdrop of a single image, legal or otherwise. Equally, his person and work combined are sufficiently diverse in character to mean that no one English translation of the Greek term παράκλητος (not even the popular versions, "Comforter," "Counselor" or "Advocate") can be regarded as adequate.

The actual ministry of the Paraclete, according to John, is exercised in relation to the world as well as to the church. In the church he indwells the disciples (John 14:16–17; cf. Ezek. 2:2); he teaches them and recalls to their memories the instruction of Jesus himself (John 14:26); he bears witness to Jesus and reveals the true nature of their Lord to his followers (15:26);[11] and as the Spirit of truth he guides the church prophetically "into all the truth" (16:13–15).[12] In the world the Paraclete again bears witness to Jesus, especially during times of persecution and conflict (John 15:18–26). He also exercises a ministry of discrimination: "convicting the world of its sin and of its righteousness, and allowing a verdict one way or the other" (John 16:7–11).[13]

The nature and work of the Paraclete in the Fourth Gospel, we may conclude, are consistent with the person and ministry of the Spirit described elsewhere in John and, indeed, in other parts of the New Testament.[14] But the Paraclete is not just the Spirit with another name, for our existing knowledge of the Spirit is expanded by John's special teaching about the Spirit. In particular, the Paraclete reflects Jesus both in his identity and in his activity.[15] As a result, the Spirit-Paraclete exists and works on two levels at once, drawing heaven and earth together (as does the Son of Man in John),[16] in the present as well as in the future.

So the Paraclete, like Jesus himself according to John's Gospel, is by nature at one with both God and humankind. He comes from God when Jesus goes away, and after the resurrection he is "sent" from both the Father and the Son (John

14:26; 15:26; 16:7). The Spirit-Paraclete is thus in union with both God and his glorified Messiah and is able to disclose their natures (16:14–15).

But the Paraclete is also the agent of both God and Christ *on earth*. At every point, it seems, what can be said of Jesus during his earthly ministry may be attributed to the activity of the Paraclete after the resurrection. Both Jesus and the Spirit-Paraclete come from God into the world (John 16:28/15:26a); they both remain with the disciples (15:4/14:17), teaching (7:14–17/14:26), prophesying (14:2–3/16:13–15), and witnessing (8:17–18/15:26b). As the Son glorifies the Father (17:4), so the Paraclete glorifies Jesus (16:14); as believers perceive the true identity of Jesus (1:49–50), so the disciples will recognize the Paraclete (14:17b); as the world rejected Christ (5:43), so it cannot receive the Paraclete (14:17a). In the world itself the Paraclete (again echoing the work of Jesus [5:36]) testifies to the Son (15:26), especially in situations of persecution, and continues his ministry of salvation through judgment (5:22–24/16:8–11).

John's pneumatology in his Gospel is, therefore, akin to his Christology. It is deeply influenced by his understanding that, because the Word has entered history in flesh, earth and heaven have been decisively conjoined; both have become theaters for receiving and acting out God's gift of eternal life (John 1:14, 51). On either side of the resurrection, Jesus and the Spirit-Paraclete, who takes his place in the church and in the world, operate on two levels at once: the material and the spiritual. Indeed, the Paraclete himself bears testimony to the Christ of both time and eternity: a witness to the very words spoken by Jesus during his ministry in Palestine and to his exalted status with the Father (14:26; 15:26; cf. 17:5).

Bearing in mind this understanding of the fourth evangelist's two-level view of the Spirit-Paraclete in relation to Jesus, we may now set alongside it the pneumatology of the Apocalypse. We shall then be in a position to draw some conclusions.

III

At first sight the doctrine of the Spirit in Revelation appears to diverge markedly from that in John's Gospel.[17] For a start, the Spirit in the Apocalypse seems less personal. Thus, the postresurrection nature and activity of the Spirit, as presented by the prophet-seer, do not echo so clearly the person and work of Jesus during his ministry as these are described by the fourth evangelist. Moreover, and perhaps significantly, the term παράκλητος, as such, is not used by John the Divine.

The less than fully personal character of John's pneumatology in the Apocalypse is further illustrated by his reference to the "seven spirits" who, in the opening salutation (Rev. 1:4), appear before the throne of God. We are probably right to identify these spirits with the Holy Spirit.[18] If so, there is an Old Testament quality belonging to these beings, who, in the throne-room scene of Revelation 4, burn like "seven fiery torches" (v. 5) and who are subsequently "sent out" into all the earth (Rev. 5:6).[19]

A second variation between the teaching about the Spirit in John's Gospel and that in Revelation arises from the fact that in the Apocalypse the Spirit seems less personally related to the disciples than he is in the Fourth Gospel (cf. John 14—16). In Revelation (3:3; 16:15) he comes in judgment, not for encouragement, and there is no sense of the Spirit *indwelling* the churches and their members (as in John 14:17; 1 John 3:24 et al.), even if the prophets become his mouthpiece (cf. Rev. 19:10).[20]

A third difference between the pneumatologies of the Gospel and Revelation of John lies in the premise that the ministry of the Spirit in the Apocalypse is less specific than appears to be the case in the Fourth Gospel. In Revelation, for example, the Spirit does not directly teach (cf. John 14:26) or bear witness (15:26; cf. 1:32–33); nor does he seem to renew (John 3:5, 8; 7:38–39), or judge or lead into truth (16:7–13).

The evidence so far marshaled might indeed suggest that the pneumatology of the seer is not only less developed than the evangelist's teaching about the Holy Spirit, but also that, as F. F. Bruce has concluded, "the Spirit appears in the Apocalypse in a different perspective from that in which he is presented in other writings of the Johannine corpus."[21]

Notwithstanding the apparent divergences between the pneumatologies of the two Johns, close parallels may also be observed. First, despite what was said earlier, the Spirit-Paraclete in Revelation, as in John's Gospel, *is* understood as personal, indeed, as a person. The evangelist distinguishes the Spirit-Paraclete from both the Father and the Son. Similarly, the seer refers to God *and* the Spirit in the invocation of Revelation 1:4.[22] He also introduces a demarcation between Jesus and the Spirit in that same prayer of 1:4, as well as in the petition for Christ's advent, offered by the Spirit and the bride (i.e., the church on earth) in Revelation 22:17.

Yet at the same time the apocalyptist, like the fourth evangelist, is well aware of the unity that exists between the Spirit and both God and Christ. The Spirit is God's Spirit (Rev. 3:1; 4:5; 5:6). He is also the Spirit of Christ, who "*has* the seven spirits of God" (3:1) and the "eyes which are the seven spirits of God" (5:6).

Moreover, at the close of each of the seven letters to the churches of Asia, the exalted Son exhorts those who have an ear to listen to what the *Spirit* is saying to the churches (Rev. 2:7 et seq.). The words of Christ are thus described as the speech of the Spirit! In maintaining not only the personality of the Spirit but also his essential unity with both the Father and the Son,[23] the writer of Revelation is expressing a theology of the Spirit which he shares with John the evangelist, and indeed with Paul himself.[24]

In one respect the personal character of the Spirit found in the Apocalypse goes beyond that to be found also in the Fourth Gospel, and in this instance the seer's pneumatology is perhaps even more sophisticated than that of the evangelist. In

Revelation the Spirit, working through the prophets, is immediately *responsive* to the divine will.[25] Thus, when John is commanded by a heavenly voice to write, "Blessed are the dead who from now on die in the Lord" (Rev. 14:13), the Spirit adds his affirmation: "Yes, they will rest from their labors, for their deeds follow them." A similar response is made when the Lord announces his parousia at Rev. 22:12: "See, I am coming soon." In answer, the Spirit and bride say, "Come" (22:17).[26]

A second association between the teaching on the Spirit in the Apocalypse and the Gospel of John involves the concept of indwelling. We noted earlier that in Revelation the Spirit appears to be less personally related to the disciples than is the case in John's Gospel. But even if John the Divine does not develop an understanding of the indwelling Spirit in a manner that is characteristic of the fourth evangelist or of Paul (John 14:17; Rom. 8:14–17; cf. Ps. 51:10–12), we may notice how the Spirit is related to the seer himself. For the purposes of prophecy, the Spirit "comes upon" John in a Hebraic manner; and the result is described by him as being "in [the] Spirit" (ἐν πνεύματι). This is the case in the writer's inaugural vision (Rev. 1:10), in the second ecstasy where he is taken to heaven ("immediately I came to be in Spirit," 4:2), and in two later visions (the scarlet woman, 17:3, and the Lamb's bride in the heavenly Jerusalem, 21:10). In each instance the language echoes strongly that of Ezekiel, where the Spirit is described as lifting up the prophet and carrying him away (Ezek. 3:14; 8:3; 37:1; et al.). The Spirit does for Ezekiel the service that one of the angels performs for John, but the ecstasy and the activity of the Spirit within it are similar.[27]

A third parallel in the pneumatologies of the seer and the evangelist may be discovered in their view of the Spirit's ministry. Although the work of teaching does not feature directly in his activity, the Spirit is heard to declare (prophetically) "what is to come" (John 16:13; Rev. 1:10–11, 19; 4:1–2; 19:10; 22:6). Furthermore, the ministry of the Spirit in Revelation includes witness. Yet the distinctive element in this aspect of the seer's pneumatology lies in his presentation of the Spirit as the Spirit of prophecy, who bears his testimony *through* the witnesses of Jesus.[28] So the two witnesses of Rev. 11:3 are given authority to *prophesy* (in spirit), as they do in vv. 4–10.[29] Similarly, when in Rev. 22:6 John refers to "the God of the spirits [pl.] of the prophets [ὁ θεὸς τῶν πνευμάτων τῶν προφητῶν], who has sent his angel to show his servants what must soon take place," he could be referring to the witness of the Spirit of prophecy, mediated through individual prophetic spirits.[30] As it happens, the statement in Rev. 19:10, "the testimony about Jesus is the spirit of prophecy," is exactly in line with this theology. The Spirit witnesses to the Christian prophets in the early church, and through them to the community at large, just as he had formerly spoken to the prophets of Israel.[31] While the Spirit's activity of testimony takes different forms in the Revelation and Gospel of John, therefore, it may be argued that his work of witness is present in both documents.

Under this same heading—namely, of the nature of the Spirit's ministry as this may be perceived in the Apocalypse and the Fourth Gospel—we can note that the Spirit is associated in the Apocalypse with the image of living water, and that figure is used in the New Testament by the two Johns—of Revelation and the Gospel—alone. Thus, in Revelation 22, the angel shows the seer the river of the water of life, "sparkling like crystal, flowing from the throne of God and of the Lamb" (v. 1). Later, the Spirit and the bride issue an invitation: "Come! . . . let the thirsty come; let whoever wishes accept the water of life as a gift" (v. 17). In the new Jerusalem the flowing water is essentially the symbol of new life, made possible by God's salvific activity in Christ and by the Spirit. Also, as in the Fourth Gospel, it is a gift to be received by faith (John 3:5, 16). The possibilities envisaged in Revelation 22 connect with the prediction of Jesus in John 7:37–39, where he promises to release "streams of living water" to believers after his glorification and by the Spirit, although at that time the Spirit "had not yet been given."[32]

Equally, if the Spirit's work of judgment and leading into truth are more restrained in the Apocalypse than they are in the Gospel of John, these are nonetheless evident. Like the Johannine Paraclete, the Spirit in Revelation exercises a ministry of discrimination.[33] The Spirit is also associated with the message about the "new name" written on the "white stone," in the letter to the church at Pergamum (Rev. 2:17). Such allusions are problematic. But in the end the reference probably has to do with the maintenance, on the part of believers, of truth over and against error, and in this battle for truth the Spirit seems to play a part.[34]

In three directions, then, the nature and activity of the Spirit in Revelation and John's Gospel are found to be clearly proximate: in his person, in his relationship to the church and individual believers, and in his ministry of witness, renewal, judgment and the promotion of truth. The pneumatologies of Revelation and John's Gospel are most closely associated, however, in their constant and distinctive double reference: to this world, and to the life of eternity. This careful balance, which we have already found to be characteristic of the fourth evangelist's pneumatology, is also present in the teaching about the Spirit offered by John the Divine. In Revelation, as in John's Gospel, the Spirit operates on earth *and* in heaven.

Thus, "in Spirit" (ἐν πνεύματι) the seer receives his vision while exiled on Patmos (Rev. 1:10). "In Spirit," also, John is taken from earth up to heaven (4:1–2). In two later ecstasies the same linkage occurs between the temporal and eternal dimensions (17:3; 21:10). Similarly, the seven spirits before God's throne, who, as we have noted, are probably to be identified with the Holy Spirit himself, are sent for purposes of judgment to every part of *earth* (1:4; 5:6).

In the same way, the Spirit in the Apocalypse speaks, from God and through the exalted Christ, to seven specific Johannine churches in Asia Minor during the first century C.E. (Rev. 2—3). The Spirit also communicates with the church in early society through Christian prophets and testifies to the true identity of Jesus

(19:10); while, in the course of that prophetic witness on earth, the Spirit responds to the will of heaven (14:13; 22:17a).[35] The theological balance in John's pneumatology, between earth and heaven, is marked and sustained.

IV

We may now draw together the threads of our discussion and set out some conclusions. First, the situation of the Johannine church itself, as reflected in the Revelation as well as in the Gospel and Letters of John, seems to have accounted for the consistent equilibrium that belongs to all areas of John's theology and especially to his teaching about Christ and the Spirit. The members of his circle needed to be affirmed in the balanced belief that through the Word made flesh, who fully and finally drew together spirit and matter, the salvation of the world has become possible. Such a doctrinal stance carries with it, of course, implications for both faith and life: for the church's attitude to Christ himself, to the Christian community, to the world, to time, to life beyond time, and to the use of power.

I would argue that the readers for whom the Apocalypse was written belonged to a group (or groups) in which tensions were beginning to emerge, particularly over the nature of Christ's person. This means that the christological crisis that may later be detected behind the writing of John's Gospel and letters and, indeed, gave rise to their composition is signaled already in Revelation. In the face of growing theological conflict within his church, as well as threatened opposition and persecution beyond it from God's enemy the Roman state, the seer encourages his followers to embrace a true faith and to pursue moral practice. In so doing he shows his readers that God cares for his world and his people, and that through Christ and by the Spirit, he is intimately involved with them both.

Second, we have observed that while there are close parallels to be noted between the fourth evangelist's theology of the Spirit and that of John the Divine, there are also variations between them. For example, the understanding of the Spirit in Revelation appears at times to be less personal, and the concept of the Spirit's indwelling less developed, than is the case in the Gospel. This might imply that the seer's pneumatology is more primitive; although, as we have seen, these divergences are often more apparent than real. But if they exist, and if we allow that the doctrine of the Spirit in John's Gospel is more evolved than it is in the Apocalypse, the heterogeneity is readily explained by dating Revelation earlier than the Gospel.[36] If that thesis becomes acceptable, we can then go on to suggest that it is precisely in the theology of the Spirit that we discover a progression, from the first document (the Apocalypse) to the second (the Fourth Gospel).

Raymond Brown locates the background of the Johannine Paraclete in three Jewish concepts: the "tandem" relationship belonging to salvific figures, such as Moses and Joshua; the Spirit of God, speaking to people through the prophets; and late Jewish angelology. All these ideas, Brown claims, have been Christianized by

John and drawn into his perception of the Paraclete as the *alter ego* of Jesus: Christ's spiritual presence in the believing community.[37] My own proposal is that while the fundamental background for the Paraclete-figure is undoubtedly to be discovered in Judaism, the Christianizing process, which flowers in the pneumatology of the Fourth Gospel and in the person and work of the Spirit-Paraclete there described, had already begun in Revelation. There, as we have seen, the Spirit advocates, convicts, teaches, prophesies and bears witness, like the Paraclete in John 14—16. Although the term "Paraclete" is not used by John the Divine, the materials used by the fourth evangelist to describe his person and work were already at hand in the Apocalypse, to be taken up and developed in due course.

Third, the balanced doctrine of the Spirit in all parts of the Johannine corpus[38] thus helps not only to link these writings together but also to clarify the order of their composition from the Apocalypse to 3 John. It also reminds us that what the Spirit said to the church in the first century, particularly about God's incarnate presence in his world and thus about the hallowing of all matter, still has relevance for our generation.

NOTES

1. For a detailed defense of the argument that connections exist between the Apocalypse, Gospel and letters of John in terms of both the church situation that lies behind them all and the theology arising from that situation, which they accordingly demonstrate, see Stephen S. Smalley, *Thunder and Love: John's Revelation and John's Community* (Waco, Tex.: Word, 1994), esp. 57–69. For the existence of such a community, see ibid., 17–19. In terms of the authorship of the Johannine corpus, I believe that the Apocalypse was written by John, the Beloved Disciple; that he was the inspiration behind the Fourth Gospel, but that it was composed by some of his followers; and that a senior member of his community, not necessarily involved in the redaction of the Gospel, was responsible for the publication of 1, 2, and 3 John.

2. "Seeing" and "hearing," in the sense of perceiving and understanding, are important concepts in the Johannine corpus. In the Fourth Gospel "sight" and "faith" become virtually synonymous: see John 9:39–41; 12:36–41 (seeing); 20:28–29 (seeing and believing); 5:25; 8:47 (hearing). Note also G. L. Phillips, "Faith and Vision in the Fourth Gospel," in *Studies in the Fourth Gospel,* ed. F. L. Cross (London: Mowbray, 1957), 83–96. Beyond the Gospel, see 1 John 1:1–5; 4:14; Rev. 1:3, 12–13, 17; 2:7; 22:8; et al.

3. So Smalley, *Thunder and Love,* 35–50, esp. 40–50.

4. See further, for this whole area of discussion, Stephen S. Smalley, *John: Evangelist and Interpreter* (Exeter: Paternoster, 1978 [rpr. 1983]), 138–48, esp. 145–48; idem, *1, 2, 3 John,* WBC 51 (Waco, Tex.: Word, 1984), xxiii–xxxii; idem, *Thunder and Love,* 67–69, 134–37.

5. See W.H.C. Frend, *The Rise of Christianity* (Philadelphia: Fortress, 1984), 86–110, esp. 110.

6. On the Spirit in the Fourth Gospel, see, further, Smalley, *John: Evangelist and Interpreter,* 227–33, and the literature there cited.

7. The Greek ἄνωθεν, "[born] anew" or "from above," is doubtless used by the fourth evangelist with deliberate ambiguity. Christian rebirth, that is to say, is divine in origin. However, in context the double meaning is also used as part of John's technique of misunderstanding. Nicodemus (John 3:4) believes Jesus to mean that it is necessary to be born again physically, whereas the primary reference for Jesus (3:3) is spiritual. For parallel usages of ἄνωθεν, see John 3:31; 19:11. See also Raymond E. Brown, *The Gospel according to John (i–xii)*, AB 29 (Garden City, N.Y.: Doubleday, 1966), 130–31.

8. See Raymond E. Brown, "The Paraclete in the Fourth Gospel," *NTS* 13 (1966–67): 113–32.

9. So idem, *The Gospel according to John (xiii–xxi)*, AB 29A (Garden City, N.Y.: Doubleday, 1970), 1135–39.

10. For a study that draws out the hermeneutical role of the Spirit-Paraclete see John Breck, *Spirit of Truth: The Holy Spirit in Johannine Tradition*, 2 vols. (Crestwood, N.Y.: St. Vladimir's Seminary Press, 1991 [vol. 2, forthcoming]). Volume 1 of this work deals with the (mostly Jewish) *Origins of Johannine Pneumatology*. For the link between John's Gospel (together with the Revelation) and Christian prophecy through the Spirit, see David Hill, *New Testament Prophecy* (Atlanta: John Knox, 1979), 146–52, esp. 149–51.

11. Such a testimony would be apposite in a community whose members were divided in their estimate of Christ's person.

12. The expression, "Spirit of truth," appears to rest on the use of a similar phrase in the literature of Qumran (see 1QS 3:13–4:26). Jesus, the Truth (John 14:6), reveals the true way for people to live, aided by his Spirit ("another Paraclete," 14:16), who can therefore be described as "the Spirit of truth." See further Margaret Davies, *Rhetoric and Reference in the Fourth Gospel*, JSNTSup 69 (Sheffield: Sheffield Academic Press, 1992), 90–91.

13. For the exegesis of this baffling passage, on which my translation of 16:8 depends, see D. A. Carson, "The Function of the Paraclete in John 16:7–11," *JBL* 98 (1979): 547–66; also Barnabas Lindars, "ΔΙΚΑΙΟΣΥΝΗ in Jn 16.8 and 10," in idem, *Essays on John*, ed. C. M. Tuckett, Studiorum Novi Testamenti Auxilia 17 (Leuven: Leuven University Press, 1992), 21–31, esp. 25–31 (note, on 31, the paraphrase of this passage).

14. See also Smalley, *John: Evangelist and Interpreter*, 231.

15. See, further, Brown, "The Paraclete in the Fourth Gospel," esp. 127; M. Eugene Boring, "The Influence of Christian Prophecy on the Johannine Portrayal of the Paraclete and Jesus," *NTS* 25 (1978–79): 113–23; Hill, *New Testament Prophecy*, 149–50. For a "lower" view of the Paraclete's identity, in agreement with a less exalted Christology, see Davies, *Rhetoric and Reference in the Fourth Gospel*, 139–53, esp. 145–53.

16. See Smalley, *John: Evangelist and Interpreter*, 92–95.

17. For this section see, further, Smalley, *Thunder and Love*, 152–54.

18. So F. F. Bruce, "The Spirit in the Apocalypse," in *Christ and Spirit in the New Testament: Studies in Honour of Charles Francis Digby Moule*, ed. Barnabas Lindars and Stephen S. Smalley (Cambridge: Cambridge University Press, 1973), 333–44, esp. 333–37, and the literature there cited. See also Revelation 3:1 and 8:2 ("I saw the seven angels, standing before God"). But the status of the seven spirits, judging from the "trinitarian" context in which they are mentioned at Revelation 1:4, is higher than

that of mere angelic beings (so Bruce, "The Spirit in the Apocalypse," 336). John's choice of "seven," apart from his predilection for the number, was no doubt influenced by the fact that in Revelation 2 and 3 the message from God, through the exalted Christ and by the Spirit, is communicated in the first instance to the *seven* churches of Asia.

19. Cf. Ps. 104:4; Isa. 61:1; note also Heb. 1:7, 14. See M. Eugene Boring, *Revelation,* Interpretation (Louisville, Ky.: John Knox, 1989), 75.

20. In Revelation 11:11 we read that the "πνεῦμα ["breath" or "spirit"] of life from God" came into two prophetic witnesses three-and-a-half days after their martyrdom. However, this is not a reference to the Spirit who prophesies, but rather to the breath of resurrection life: the divine power that the Antichrist tries to ape in order to deceive (see Rev. 13:11–18, esp. vv. 14–15). See also Ezek. 37:5, 9–10; note Boring, *Revelation,* 148, and Bruce, "The Spirit in the Apocalypse," 339.

21. Bruce, "The Spirit in the Apocalypse," 337.

22. Note also Revelation 4:5 (the seven spirits *before* the throne of God) and perhaps 14:13 (the declaration by the Spirit *added* to the "voice from heaven"). On this section see, further, I. T. Beckwith, *The Apocalypse of John: Studies in Introduction, with a Critical and Exegetical Commentary* (New York: Macmillan, 1919), 316–17.

23. See, further, H. B. Swete, *The Apocalypse of St John: The Greek Text with Introduction, Notes, and Indices,* 3d ed., Macmillan's New Testament Commentaries (London: Macmillan, 1909), clxiv–clxvi.

24. John 14:26; 15:26; 16:7, 14–15; cf. Rom 8:9–11. Boring ("The Influence of Christian Prophecy," 115–17) suggests that the revelatory "chain of command" with which the Apocalypse begins — God, the exalted Christ, his angel, the prophet, the community, the world (Rev. 1:1–3) — can be paralleled in the Paraclete sayings of the Farewell Discourse: thus John 14:16–17, in which the revelation begins with the Father, goes through Jesus and the Paraclete to the community, and ends in an encounter with the world.

25. Note the parallel responsiveness in Revelation at 16:5 (the angel of the waters) and 16:7 (the altar). See also Rev. 18:20: heaven, with the saints, apostles, and prophets, rejoices over God's judgment on Babylon. For this section see, further, Bruce, "The Spirit in the Apocalypse," 342–44.

26. See also the (early Christian, eucharistic) response of the church at 1 Cor. 16:22; cf. Rev. 22:20 (μαρανα θα ["Come, Lord Jesus!"]). For a study of the use of this invocation in the primitive church, see C.F.D. Moule, "A Reconsideration of the Context of *Maranatha,*" *NTS* 6 (1959–60): 307–10.

27. So Bruce, "The Spirit in the Apocalypse," 339–40.

28. Cf. John 15:26–27: "the Spirit will testify . . . you [disciples] are to testify."

29. For a fuller exegesis of this passage, see Bruce, "The Spirit in the Apocalypse," 339.

30. Cf. 1 Cor. 14:32 and the entry of the Spirit into the prophet at Ezek. 2:2. See, further, Bruce, "The Spirit in the Apocalypse," 339; also Beckwith, *The Apocalypse of John,* 317.

31. See Smalley, *Thunder and Love,* 153–54, and note the further link between John himself and the Spirit of prophecy (Rev. 1:10–11; 4:2; et al.).

32. That moment in John's Gospel occurs after the resurrection, during the fourth evangelist's version of Pentecost (20:22). T. L. Brodie, *The Gospel according to John: A Literary and Theological Commentary* (New York and Oxford: Oxford University Press, 1993), 318–19, argues that the ambiguity in John 7:38 (whether the rivers of

living water flow from the heart of Jesus or of the believer) is deliberate and provides "a rich microcosm of a much larger reality" (319): life flows from Jesus to the believer, and from the believer to others. See also John 4:13–14.

33. Cf. John 16:8–11, and see Rev. 5:6, where the seven spirits of God (= the Holy Spirit; see above) are "sent out into all the earth" in the context of taking the scrolls of judgment.

34. See Smalley, *Thunder and Love*, 127.

35. See further ibid., 152–54.

36. So ibid., 40–50.

37. Brown, "The Paraclete in the Fourth Gospel," 119–26.

38. For teaching about the Spirit in John's letters, see Smalley, *1, 2, 3 John*, xxvii–xxx, 280–87, et passim.

James D. G. Dunn

17

John and the Synoptics
as a Theological Question

INTRODUCTION

The most obvious and striking feature when John and the Synoptics are compared is the difference between the two. For all their individual distinctiveness,
the portrayal of Jesus in the Synoptics is remarkably consistent in content and
character. In contrast, John's portrayal of Jesus seems to move on a quite different plane, as consistently different from the Synoptics in content and character as
they are consistently similar to each other.[1] Throughout most of the twentieth century, this difference has been discussed chiefly as a question of literary relationship: Did John know and use the Synoptics? Resolution of the question has been
sought through comparison of genre and content, with a final judgment of dependence or independence (or somewhere in between) usually regarded as a sufficient
conclusion. This whole dimension of the subject has been thoroughly explored in
recent years,[2] and the history of the debate through the twentieth century has been
most helpfully reviewed by one of the current doyens of Johannine study, Moody
Smith himself.[3] On this aspect of the subject, I have nothing new to add to such
monumental labors.[4]

Too much neglected in recent years, however, have been the theological dimensions of the subject.[5] For the difference between John and the Synoptics is not
merely a historical or literary question. Underlying these questions is a theological issue.[6] At the historical and literary levels the difference in itself may sustain
only academic interest as a historical accident or curiosity. But at the theological
level the difference is a *problem*. The earlier discussions, between (as we might
say) the contributions of Baur and Bultmann, saw the problem clearly but focused
it almost exclusively on the question of whether John counts as history or theology.[7] But the theological ramifications are much more extensive. Does this difference not indicate a fundamental inconsistency in the basic testimony regarding
the central figure of the Christian faith? Does it not indicate the importation into
the earliest Christian tradition of some new and strange elements, which may have
distorted the earliest witness? More fundamentally, what is the significance of this
difference for any Christian claim to a definitive revelation in and through Jesus?

What effect should this difference have on the critical evaluation of the theological claims made by these documents? What are the consequences of this difference for the celebration and expression of the faith that has canonized, and been canonized by, these four Gospels? A finding of literary and historical dependence or independence has far-reaching theological corollaries, and while the theological implications should not be allowed to drive the historical and literary analysis, they cannot be ignored.

It is with such theological ramifications that this little birthday offering in honor of Moody is concerned. There are various aspects to this topic, but here we have space to deal with only three: continuity, development, and diversity.

CONTINUITY

The theological problem posed by the difference between John and the Synoptics is, in the first place, *the problem of discontinuity*. Whereas a clear interrelationship among the Synoptics can be readily discerned and a plausible line of dependence posited from a historically recognizable Jesus to the Synoptic tradition, the quantum leap from the Synoptics to John seems to speak more of discontinuity than of continuity. It is a problem, obviously, because Christian faith is focused to such a high degree on Jesus of Nazareth and on the revelation and redemption he is claimed to have brought, to have embodied, and to have enacted in his ministry, death, and resurrection. That claim ties Christianity—in uncomfortable measure, for the historical critic—to what happened, in word and action, within a specific three-or-so-year span of human history and within a particular social context. That is why the Gospels have always been at the center of Christian faith: the theological rationale being that they guarantee the continuity and consistency between that focal person and period within history, and the ongoing Christian faith and church. When that claim to continuity is challenged, the authenticity of the end product is put under question, explicitly or implicitly, and it becomes a theological imperative to recognize and to address that challenge.

We should not forget that such theological concerns lay behind the emergence and development of the whole enterprise of source criticism, the "invisible hand" that motivated and sustained the Synoptic analysis of documents and pericopes. The quest for sources of the Gospels was, in part at least, an attempt to counter the destructive effects of an Enlightenment criticism that opened up the gap between the Jesus of history and the Christ of faith. One major reason why the hypothesis of Markan priority gained such a sway was that it provided a theological answer to the challenge of F. C. Baur's conclusion regarding the unhistoricity of John's Gospel, the earliness of Mark securing a continuity that could no longer be comfortably affirmed for John. So, too, it is hardly accidental that the Q-hypothesis (namely, that of a primitive source lacking miracle stories) proved so attractive, since it provided a theological response to the problem of miracle so sharply posed by D. F. Strauss by allowing Jesus to be seen primarily as a teacher rather than as a miracle worker.[8] In each case the dominant theological instinct was to get back as closely as possible to Jesus of Nazareth and to the initial impact he made, the assumption being that historical proximity to the *fons et origo* of Christianity was the guarantee of authenticity. To the perceived challenge that foreign elements had entered the tradition at some secondary stage, the only satisfying answer could be the demonstration of continuity between Jesus and the Gospels.

It is the same theological issue that lies behind the twentieth-century preoccupation with the sources for John's Gospel. For if John's Christology has been fundamentally determined by Mandaean sources or by the Gnostic redeemer myth, then that indicates a major element of discontinuity with the earliest traditions about Jesus.[9] Bultmann could live at theological ease with that conclusion by virtue of his Christian existentialist disregard for and distrust in history.[10] But for others a more substantial continuity (*Was* as well as *Dass*) was a theological necessity. It was precisely this concern that motivated the new quest of the historical Jesus, as Ernst Käsemann's famous essay clearly demonstrates.[11] In the case of John, not surprisingly, the theological answer was provided by affirmation of a closer relationship between John and the Synoptics and by the assertion, in particular, that John knew and was dependent on one or more of the Synoptics or on Synoptic-like tradition.[12]

In recent years the debate about John's *religionsgeschichtlich* context and dependency has raised the issue with fresh vigor and with a new twist, particularly in the work of Helmut Koester.[13] At first the issue seems to be the same: whether the Johannine dialogues are fundamentally dependent on Gnostic traditions such as we find in *The Dialogue of the Savior* and *The Apocryphon of James;* that is, whether an originally ungnostic Gospel has been radically altered by importation of foreign elements. But Koester's hypothesis is that these Gnostic documents embody older materials that actually predate John's Gospel, so that the Fourth Gospel in effect brings them into what became the mainstream of Christian tradition by John's modification of them.[14] The twist is that the theological logic of "early = original = authentic" has been radically subverted. Whereas C. H. Dodd's definition of "traditional (Christian) materials" was limited to the Synoptic Gospels, so that his findings could be regarded as a sufficient response to Bultmann's hypothesis of John's dependence on a Gnostic revelation discourse source, with Koester the Synoptics provide only one kind of traditional (Christian) materials.[15] The literary and historical hypothesis thus poses a fresh theological challenge: that the revelation/redemption, perceived in Christ, was from the first grasped and expressed in terms more diverse than those of the Synoptic tradition, so that continuity with primitive source material becomes a questionable criterion of authenticity, and the category of authenticity itself becomes problematic.[16] Once again, it is the theological corollary that gives the historical hypothesis its cutting edge.

In fact, however, it appears that Koester's hypothesis is only a little more credible than Bultmann's; its theological edge may not be so sharp after all, for it has to be said that the postulated links are slender indeed. First, such similarities as there are between *Dialogue of the Savior* 25—30 and John 14:2–12 (Koester's chief example) are open to a variety of explanations, of which the suggestion that the former is more original is hardly compelling. Moreover, the argument that the *Dialogue* is baptismal instruction which is closely related to early Christian documents of about 100 C.E., so that the *Dialogue* itself can be dated to the beginning of the second century, begs too many questions[17] to be worthy of much credence. Second and similarly, the suggestion that John 16:26 ("I do not say that I will ask the Father on your behalf") is a polemical formulation which rejects the more common belief that Jesus intercedes for his own, as expressed in *Apocryphon of James* 11.4–6 (Koester's most explicit claim in this section of his argument),[18] completely ignores the internal dynamic of John's theology at this point.[19] It is true that the *Apocryphon* looks like a dialogue based on traditional sayings of Jesus[20] and is thus like the Fourth Gospel in character (at least in its dialogues), but there is really nothing which gives clear indication that any of the *Apocryphon*'s versions of these sayings, or any of the interpretations given them by the *Apocryphon*, predate the material in John's Gospel.[21]

In comparison with such flimsy and tendentious arguments, the relationship between John and the Synoptics can be maintained on a manifestly much sounder basis. We need only recall that John was able to draw on early narrative material regarding, for example, John the Baptist and the discovery of the empty tomb (cf. John 20:1–10 with Luke 24:22–24), as well as Synoptic-like sayings on which the Johannine dialogues are often clearly based.[22] Moreover, the *religionsgeschichtlich* context of the theology of John's Gospel is much more obviously Jewish apocalyptic and mystical preoccupation with revelation, just as its social context is more obviously that of a recent split with local Jewish synagogues, than anything that as yet properly warrants the title "Gnostic."[23] The point is that the character and content of John's Gospel can be fully and adequately explained in these terms, without any need to resort to a Gnostic hypothesis (à la Bultmann or Koester). As a historical judgment it remains much more probable that the Gnostic documents represent a later reworking of the Jesus tradition, with the detail of the earlier form of individual traditions, thus reworked, difficult if not impossible to reconstruct with any confidence. The relation of those individual traditions to their canonical forms is thus, at best, speculative in the extreme.

In the light of such a historical conclusion, the theological issue becomes less pressing. For if John's Jesus tradition in its earlier form was indeed homogeneous with the Synoptic tradition, then that would confirm that the earliest recollection of and witness to Jesus was of a piece overall. And that would mean both a consistency within earliest Christian self-understanding and a continuity, from earliest to latest, of the canonical Gospel material. The theological corollary, concerning the essentially Jewish character of the earliest gospel and its integral coherence as a criterion of authenticity for Christian self-definition, does not determine the historical conclusion, but it does ensure that the historical debate has a more than merely antiquarian significance.

DEVELOPMENT

If the first issue with heavy theological overtones is the question of continuity, the second is that of *development*. For although continuity between John and the Synoptics can readily be affirmed as we have just seen, the more dominant impression remains one of difference. And if the difference is not to be explained by asserting discontinuity, it has to be explained in terms of development.

The character of that development can be easily instanced. For some reason John has developed the Baptist tradition to reduce the Baptist's role to that of witness to Christ, while enlarging that role itself. For some reason John has developed the tradition of Jesus' miracles by ignoring the exorcisms and focusing the tradition in seven signs. For some reason John has largely excised the tradition of Jesus as a preacher of the kingdom of God. For some reason John has developed the tradition of Jesus' teaching in wisdom sayings and parables into lengthy and convoluted dialogues. Above all, for some reason John has developed the tradition of a Jesus who spoke little of himself into a full-scale self-testimony of one who knows himself to be God's only Son, sent down from heaven to present himself as the revealer of God.

And so the theological problem reemerges, for the development seems to be so extensive and so radical, creating that difference between John and the Synoptics which continues to catch the eye.[24] Even if we cannot say that the development is the result of an internally Gnostic character or tendency already present within the Jesus tradition prior to John, is not the Johannine development itself Gnostic in orientation and direction, as the subsequent use of John by the Gnostics may be said to confirm?[25] In which case, does not John's development of the Jesus of Synoptic tradition actually validate the subsequent Gnostic use of John—with all that that means in theological terms of a dualism between creation and salvation and a docetic Christology? Käsemann, in his description of John's "naive docetism," was not the only one to point up the sharpness of the theological issue posed by John's development of the Jesus tradition.[26] Whatever the historical and literary factors, does the difference between John and the Synoptics not indicate a theological development taken too far?

Here again, however, the relationship between John and the Synoptics helps us to see the theological problem in better focus. For John's portrayal of Jesus, for all its distinctive development, can still be seen as a continuation of various trends already active in the Synoptics. In particular, it is no accident that Mark and John can both be understood as responding to a portrayal of Jesus in too straightforward and triumphalist terms as a miracle worker. On the one hand, Mark continues to play up Jesus as miracle worker in the first half of his Gospel but, in the second, balances that presentation by his emphasis on Jesus as the suffering Son of Man, whereas John, if he did take over a miracle source (the most plausible of the sources postulated for John), took it over critically by warning against a faith too dependent on miracles (2:11, 23–25; 4:48, 53; 6:25–36).[27] Again, John's portrayal of Jesus' divine sonship as already preexisting in heaven can be seen as a continuation of the trend in the birth narratives of Matthew and Luke to push Jesus' sonship back to his beginning.[28] And the transition from Jesus as ambassador of Wisdom (in Q) to Jesus as Wisdom embodied, God with us (in Matthew), is already more than halfway towards John's full-blown incarnation Christology.[29]

Most important of all is the fact that John retains the Gospel format already established by Mark. This is what sets John apart both from the earlier Q-material (assuming that Q did not contain a passion narrative) and from the later Gnostic Gospels.[30] For all the weight that John puts upon Jesus as revealer and as teaching by dialogue, these aspects can never be separated in John from the central fact that Jesus fulfilled his heavenly mission by dying and rising again. This motif is so persistent and so pervasive that it dominates the whole: for example, the persistent, drumbeat references to the hour of his approaching death; the repeated motifs of his glorification, ascension, and uplifting on the cross; the Lamb that takes away the sin of the world; the flesh, given for the life of the world, which must be eaten and the blood, drunk; and so forth. What Mark established as Gospel format,[31] what Matthew and Luke confirmed by their integration of Q-material into Mark's Gospel format, John continued to affirm as fundamental by retaining his development of the Jesus tradition within the same Gospel format.[32]

The theological corollary is clear: From its earliest format a "Gospel" was "a passion narrative with extended introduction" (M. Kähler), the teaching and activities of Jesus set within a framework provided by the story of the cross and resurrection as climax,[33] so much so that it becomes at once questionable whether any "Gospel" lacking that framework deserves the title "Gospel." Insofar as it was a single document, Q, properly speaking, is a collection of Jesus' teaching; it only became a "Gospel" when merged within the Markan Gospel framework in Matthew and Luke. As taken up in an independent trajectory described by the *Gospel of Thomas* and later dialogues, Q is still no "Gospel." And though the later Gospels lay claim to belong to the genre of "Gospel," the climactic character of the passion narrative in the earliest Gospels had already provided a theological criterion of what a "Gospel" is, which proved decisive in the second and third centuries.[34] It is the coherence of the Fourth Gospel with the Synoptics on this vital point that makes it possible to draw out such a definitive theological corollary.

Nevertheless, the difference persists. The fact remains that in relation to the Synoptics, John's Gospel is a considerably developed form of Gospel—a development, it would appear, largely determined by the social and religious context in which it received its definitive shape. We need not pursue the details of that development, since others have offered plausible and fruitful speculation on the basis of what indications there are.[35] The theological point is that "Gospel" was not a static category but allowed quite a substantial development of content. If John's Gospel *format* can be said to validate such a crucial theological definition of "Gospel," then we must acknowledge also that John's developed *content* validates an adventuresome use of that format: in this case, evidently, a portrayal of Jesus angled to catch and satisfy the interest of those eager for genuine revelation from above—and, indeed, to validate even a dangerous use as "Gospel," since that same portrayal seems to have given scope to those who pushed Christology in a docetic direction.[36] At all events, the difference between John and the Synoptics quite quickly gives substance and guidelines to a theology of development.

DIVERSITY

Talk of development among the Gospels leads us already into the final theological dimension to be outlined here: that of *diversity*, or in terms of Cullmann's article, still valuable after fifty years, the plurality of the Gospels as a theological issue.[37] For it remains an astonishing fact, too little appreciated because of its familiarity, that the New Testament canonizes not simply one but no less than *four* Gospels.[38] The immediate parallel that may come to mind, the Pentateuch, is not close enough, since the five books are all attributed in tradition to one and the same author (Moses) and since the differences within the Pentateuch are more equivalent to those within the Synoptics than those between the Synoptics and John.

That the early churches were aware of the theological implications and potential problems of embracing four Gospels is sufficiently indicated by the titles that became attached to the four : not "The Gospel *of* Matthew," and so on, as though there were indeed four different gospels, but the gospel "according to [κατά] Matthew," and so on, indicating that the four Gospels are but four versions of the one gospel. Hengel notes that the κατά-formulation in a book's title was highly unusual for this period,[39] so we may deduce that the choice of terms was deliberate and constituted a deliberate theological assertion.[40] It is true that we cannot be sure of the date when the formulation first appeared (Hengel may be too sanguine on the point); but its very usage and the evidently equally deliberate avoidance of the plural, "Gospels" (εὐαγγέλια),[41] are sufficient to confirm that an issue of theological importance was discerned here more or less from the first. It is true that several of the noncanonical Gospels also used the κατά-formula.[42] That fact, however, simply indicates a claim to "Gospel" status on the pattern of one or more of the canonical four and thus amounts to an affirmation of their already normative status; it is insufficient to sustain a claim that the earliest forms of the one "gospel" in written form were more inchoate and diverse.

Given this emphasis on the oneness of the written gospel, the fact that the one gospel came from the earliest witnesses in four forms is all the more striking. It is a fact of theological weight that any or all attempts to reduce the fourfold Gospel to a single, universal, fixed form (the one gospel definitively formulated in one Gospel) failed to gain widespread acceptance. To be sure, Matthew probably intended to replace Mark; his almost complete absorption of Mark within his Gospel may well indicate an assumption that in consequence Mark was no longer necessary. Luke's initial justification of his enterprise (Luke 1:1) presumably indicates some dissatisfaction with his predecessors. And John no doubt wanted to produce a self-sufficient Gospel, despite his allusion to "many other signs" that he had not recorded.[43] But the fact remains that whereas Q as such was allowed to disappear (assuming it did once exist as a single document), Mark was not, despite its apparent redundancy.[44] Likewise, later attempts, such as that of Marcion to reduce the Gospel to one (redacted Luke) or of Tatian to combine the four into a single form (the *Diatessaron*), also failed to overthrow the pattern, even if its formal recognition only came with Irenaeus.[45]

Equally striking is the fact that the early church as a whole did not perceive the difference between John and the Synoptics as so much of a problem that John had to be sacrificed. It would no doubt have been an attractive option for some to defend the oneness of the gospel by clinging only to the majority, the homogeneous Synoptics. Indeed, we may deduce from the infrequency of reference to John's Gospel in the early Fathers and from the copious use of it by the Valentinians,[46] that John's Gospel was in some danger of being taken over by the Gnostics and thus lost to the emerging Great Church. Here again it was probably Irenaeus who stemmed the tide and demonstrated John's authenticity as a statement of the one gospel. Whatever the precise course of events, the fourfold character of the written gospel was retained, with John's Gospel understood as integral to that fourfold unity.

The theological corollary is once again clear: namely, that within the framework of the written gospel and integral to the Gospel format is an inevitable and necessary diversity. The fact of the fourfold Gospel, and particularly of John's Gospel within the oneness of the gospel, constitutes both a warning against any attempt to freeze the gospel traditions into a single form or to insist on uniformity or close conformity in presentation of the one gospel, and an encouragement to recognize the adaptability of the one gospel to different times and circumstances, to meet changing needs and challenges. The fact that the one gospel is preserved for later generations as "the Gospel according to" four different names is a clear enough indication that no one individual—or church or tradition, for that matter—can reproduce the gospel in its completeness. Such individuals, churches, and traditions can remain faithful to the four-in-one only by recognizing that different forms of the gospel today, even those containing emphases and tendencies divergent from their own, may still be expressions of the one gospel in accordance with the pattern of John's difference and divergence from the Synoptics. The fact that the one gospel is normatively embodied in four diverse Gospels is a standing reminder that the gospel is only expressible and graspable in concrete, contextualized, circumstance-oriented form. To grasp after some more fundamental canonical norm, as though some purer form of the gospel could be abstracted from the four Gospels, would fly in the face of the canonical facts and would amount to transforming the icon of four context-specific Gospels into a humanly contrived idol.[47]

In short, the diversity that John in particular brings into the understanding of the one, fourfold Gospel should be given more recognition in view of its theological significance.[48] Indeed, we may sharpen the point by noting that the character of this fourfold oneness is much clearer (since we have all four Gospels to hand) than the character of the threefold oneness of the Trinity can ever be, so that the four-in-oneness of the gospel can and presumably should have more influence on contemporary expression of Christian faith and theology than the three-in-oneness of God!

CONCLUSION

All aspects of the above discussion require, of course, much more detailed treatment: the meaning of "gospel," the idea of canon and the relation of the canonical Gospels to certain apocryphal and Gnostic texts, various christological issues, and so on. But enough has been said, it may be hoped, to show how the theological dimension in any question of the relation of John and the Synoptics is fundamental. The more that theological questions are ignored, the more pressing it becomes to expose them, since they often provide the hidden agenda behind both radical and more traditional theses regarding the relation of the four Gospels. Indeed, it is an axiom of critical scholarship that theological *Tendenzen* should be exposed to clear view, wherever they are operative. At the same time it is the theological dimensions of such investigations and discussions that give the more focused historical and literary analyses their wider usefulness to both theology and church. In both directions the relation of and difference between John and the Synoptics as a theological question needs further debate and should prove to be of continuing fruitfulness.

NOTES

1. See, for example, D. Moody Smith's outline of the differences in his *John among the Gospels: The Relationship in Twentieth-Century Research* (Minneapolis: Fortress, 1992), 4–6.

2. See particularly *John and the Synoptics,* ed. Adelbert Denaux, BETL 101 (Leuven: Leuven University Press/Peeters, 1992).

3. Smith, *John among the Gospels;* see also his earlier essays collected in *Johannine Christianity: Essays on Its Setting, Sources, and Theology* (Columbia, S.C.: University

of South Carolina Press, 1984). Smith defines the problem thus: "The problem of John and the Synoptics is, then, how to account for John's extensive differences from the other Gospels within a generally similar overall framework" (*John among the Gospels*, 6).

4. My own pennyworth contribution to the debate is contained in "Let John Be John: A Gospel for Its Time," in *The Gospel and the Gospels*, ed. Peter Stuhlmacher (Grand Rapids: Eerdmans, 1991), 293–322; see also "John and the Oral Gospel Tradition," in *Jesus and the Oral Gospel Tradition*, ed. Henry Wansbrough, JSNTSup 64 (Sheffield: JSOT, 1991), 351–79. I remain convinced that the important role of oral forms of the Jesus tradition has been given insufficient scope in discussions on the relationship between John and the Synoptics. We certainly cannot assume that the written Gospels gave the teachers within most churches their first knowledge of many traditions or made redundant the (variant?) oral versions that it had been their responsibility to retain and retell. In "John and the Synoptics: 1975–1990" (in Denaux, ed., *John and the Synoptics*, 3–62, esp. 55–59), Frans Neirynck critiques my essay on "Oral Gospel Tradition" by juxtaposing my individual observations against those of my predecessor at Durham, C. K. Barrett.

5. Compare, in particular, Frans Neirynck, "John and the Synoptics," in *L'É-vangile de Jean: Sources, rédaction, théologie*, ed. Marinus de Jonge, BETL 44 (Gembloux: Duculot, 1977), 73–106; also idem, "John and the Synoptics: 1975–1990" (see above, n. 4).

6. Toward the end of his *John among the Gospels*, Smith notes how the question of relationships opens up as soon as we ask, Why these differences? (185, 188–89), and points to issues (191–93) similar to those discussed in what follows.

7. See Edwyn Clement Hoskyns, *The Fourth Gospel*, ed. Francis Noel Davey (London: Faber & Faber, [2]1947), 17–135; John Ashton, *Understanding the Fourth Gospel* (Oxford: Clarendon, 1991), 9–43.

8. For more details of these developments, see Werner Georg Kümmel, *The New Testament: The History of the Investigation of Its Problems* (Nashville: Abingdon, 1972), 120–205.

9. See, for example, Rudolf Bultmann's *Theology of the New Testament*, vol. 2 (New York: Scribner's, 1955), particularly 10–14.

10. Ashton, *Understanding the Fourth Gospel*, 44–66, gives a sympathetic treatment of Bultmann's own highly theological interpretation of John.

11. Ernst Käsemann, "The Problem of the Historical Jesus," in *Essays on New Testament Themes* (London: SCM, 1964), 15–47.

12. Most important here has undoubtedly been C. H. Dodd, *Historical Tradition in the Fourth Gospel* (Cambridge: Cambridge University Press, 1963). In this context the conclusion that John builds on early Jesus tradition is more important than the suggestion that specific dependence on one or more of the Synoptics as such can be affirmed only for a late stage of redaction of John's Gospel.

13. Helmut Koester, "One Jesus and Four Primitive Gospels," in James M. Robinson and Helmut Koester, *Trajectories through Early Christianity* (Philadelphia: Fortress, 1971), 158–204; see also Koester, *Introduction to the New Testament*, vol. 2: *History and Literature of Early Christianity* (Philadelphia: Fortress, 1982) 178–98, and idem, *Ancient Christian Gospels: Their History and Development* (Philadelphia and London: Trinity Press International/SCM, 1990), 173–271.

14. See, for example, Koester, *Introduction to the New Testament*, 2.185.

15. This is Koester's own observation (*Ancient Christian Gospels,* 256).

16. Ibid., 179–80.

17. See, for example, my *Unity and Diversity in the New Testament: An Inquiry into the Character of Earliest Christianity* (London: SCM, 1977, ²1990), 141–47.

18. Koester, *Ancient Christian Gospels,* 195–96. (Koester cites the reference as *Apoc. Jas.* 9.4–6.)

19. It was well perceived by Bultmann, *The Gospel of John: A Commentary* (Philadelphia: Westminster, 1971), 588–89.

20. Thus Koester, *Ancient Christian Gospels,* 189.

21. Contrast the discussion by Pheme Perkins, *The Gnostic Dialogue: The Early Church and the Crisis of Gnosticism,* Theological Inquiries (New York and Ramsey, N.J., and Toronto: Paulist, 1980), 107–12, 145–56; see also idem, *Gnosticism and the New Testament* (Minneapolis: Fortress, 1993), 122–42. D. Moody Smith, "The Problem of John and the Synoptics in Light of the Relation between Apocryphal and Canonical Gospels," in Denaux, ed., *John and the Synoptics,* 147–62 (here, 147–52), provides a useful review of the debate on that relationship, occasioned by the conversation between Koester and John Dominic Crossan. For additional bibliography, see Richard J. Bauckham, "Gospels (Apocryphal)," in *Dictionary of Jesus and the Gospels,* ed. Joel B. Green and Scot McKnight (Downers Grove, Ill., and Leicester, England: InterVarsity, 1992), 286–91 (here, 291). It is, of course, a methodological non sequitur that absence of evidence of influence from canonical traditions is sufficient proof that the variant tradition is as early as, or even earlier than, the canonical versions (see further Perkins, *Gnosticism and the New Testament,* 130–31). Smith comments appositely: the apocryphal Gospels "are pre-canonical, not in the sense that they pre-date the canonical gospels individually, but in the sense that the apocryphal gospels pre-date the establishment of Matthew, Mark, Luke, and John as an authoritative canon of scripture" ("The Problem of John and the Synoptics," 155) .

22. See Dodd, *Historical Tradition in the Fourth Gospel;* Dunn, "John and the Oral Gospel Tradition."

23. See further, for example, my "Let John Be John"; also idem, *The Partings of the Ways between Christianity and Judaism and their Significance for the Character of Christianity* (London and Philadelphia: SCM/Trinity Press International, 1991), 220–29.

24. Smith can even ask whether John should be called "the first apocryphal gospel" ("The Problem of John and the Synoptics," 156).

25. As is well known, the first commentary written on the Gospel was by Heracleon, a Valentinian; see Elaine H. Pagels, *The Johannine Gospel in Gnostic Exegesis: Heracleon's Commentary on John,* SBLMS 17 (Nashville: Abingdon, 1973).

26. Ernst Käsemann, *The Testament of Jesus: A Study of the Gospel of John in the Light of John 17* (London and Philadelphia: SCM/Fortress, 1968).

27. See, for example, my *Unity and Diversity in the New Testament,* 302–3, and Koester, *Ancient Christian Gospels,* 251–53.

28. See Raymond E. Brown, *The Birth of the Messiah: A Commentary on the Infancy Narratives in the Gospels of Matthew and Luke,* new updated ed. (New York: Doubleday, 1993), 141.

29. See M. Jack Suggs, *Wisdom, Christology, and Law in Matthew's Gospel* (Cambridge, Mass.: Harvard University Press, 1970). It should occasion no surprise that one of the central pieces of Matthew's wisdom Christology is the so-called "Johannine thunderbolt" of Matt. 11:27.

30. Thus D. Moody Smith, "John and the Synoptics and the Question of Gospel Genre," in *The Four Gospels 1992: Festschrift Frans Neirynck,* ed. F. Van Segbroeck, C. M. Tuckett, G. Van Belle, and J. Verheyden, vol. 3, BETL 100 (Leuven: Leuven University Press/Peeters, 1992), 1783–97 (here, 1784). So far as the *Gospel of Peter* is concerned, see particularly Raymond E. Brown, "The *Gospel of Peter* and Canonical Gospel Priority," *NTS* 33 (1987): 321–43.

31. The use of εὐαγγέλιον ("gospel") in Mark 1:1 was probably sufficient to establish this as the title of the book written by Mark and, thus, as the title of the genre; see particularly Robert Guelich, "The Gospel Genre," in Stuhlmacher, ed., *The Gospel and the Gospels,* 173–208 (here, 195); Martin Hengel, "The Titles of the Gospels and the Gospel of Mark," in *Studies in the Gospel of Mark* (Philadelphia: Fortress, 1985), 64–84 + 162–83 (here, 83–84). Otherwise, contrast Koester, *Ancient Christian Gospels,* 13–14.

32. Cf. the conclusion of Udo Schnelle, "Johannes und die Synoptiker," in Van Segbroeck et al., eds., *The Four Gospels 1992: Festschrift Frans Neirynck,* 3.1799–1814 (here, 1814). But *pace* Schnelle and Smith, *John among the Gospels,* 179–80, John's use of what had evidently become a widely recognized Gospel genre does not necessarily imply his knowledge of Mark in particular.

33. *Pace* Koester, *Ancient Christian Gospels,* 45, the buildup to the passion narrative in all three of the subsequent canonical Gospels constitutes "a fundamental structural element" in their composition.

34. Cf. Guelich, "The Gospel Genre," in Stuhlmacher, ed., *The Gospel and the Gospels,* 204–5.

35. Raymond E. Brown, *The Community of the Beloved Disciple* (New York, Ramsey, N.J., and Toronto: Paulist, 1979); J. Louis Martyn, "Glimpses into the History of the Johannine Community," in de Jonge, ed., *L'Évangile de Jean,* 149–75, reprinted in Martyn's *The Gospel of John in Christian History: Essays for Interpreters,* Theological Inquiries (New York, Ramsey, N.J., and Toronto: Paulist, 1979), 90–121.

36. Brown, *The Community of the Beloved Disciple,* 110–20.

37. Oscar Cullmann, "Die Pluralität der Evangelien als theologisches Problem im Altertum," *TZ* 1 (1945): 23–42 = "The Plurality of the Gospels as a Theological Problem in Antiquity," in idem, *The Early Church: Studies in Early Christian History and Theology,* ed. A.J.B. Higgins (Philadelphia: Westminster, 1956) 37–54.

38. Harnack made similar observations nearly a hundred years ago, as cited in Hengel, "The Titles of the Gospels and the Gospel of Mark" (*Studies in the Gospel of Mark,* 64).

39. "[O]nly a few very late instances" (Hengel, ibid., 65, et passim).

40. Ign. *Smyrn.* 5.1; 7.2; *Did.* 15.3–4; and *2 Clem.* 8.5 may provide further indication that written Gospels were already known as "the gospel"; see the discussion in Hengel, ibid., 71, 167 nn. 41–45, and Koester, *Ancient Christian Gospels,* 14–20.

41. Hengel, "The Titles of the Gospels and the Gospel of Mark," 67–72.

42. See, e.g., *New Testament Apocrypha,* vol. 1: *Gospels and Related Writings,* rev. ed., ed. Wilhelm Schneemelcher, ET ed. R. McL. Wilson (Cambridge and Louisville, Ky.: James Clarke and Westminster/John Knox, 1991), 136.

43. Cullmann, "The Plurality of the Gospels as a Theological Problem," 43–44. Cf. Martin Hengel, *The Johannine Question* (Philadelphia and London: Trinity Press International/SCM, 1989), 194 n. 8: "the editors [of John] hardly wanted to 'suppress' the Synoptics but rather to correct them and 'surpass' them."

44. See, for example, C. K. Barrett, "The Place of John and the Synoptics within the Early History of Christian Thought," in Denaux, ed., *John and the Synoptics,* 63–79 (here, 75–79).

45. See, again, Cullmann, "The Plurality of the Gospels as a Theological Problem," 47–52.

46. See Joseph Newbold Sanders, *The Fourth Gospel in the Early Church: Its Origin and Influence on Christian Theology up to Irenaeus* (Cambridge: Cambridge University Press, 1943), 55–66. Smith, *Johannine Christianity,* 4–6, briefly reviews discussion on the point since Sanders.

47. See, further, the conclusion to my *Unity and Diversity in the New Testament,* 376–85.

48. See also Smith, *John among the Gospels,* 193: "The emerging gospel, and New Testament, canon bends to accommodate the Gospel of John and in doing so deepens and changes its character."

Part Five:

Appropriating the Proclamation of the Gospel of John

Wayne A. Meeks

18

The Ethics of the Fourth Evangelist

The topic of this essay, suggested by the editors, either poses a question that cannot be answered, or it is an oxymoron. If we inquire about "the ethics of Kant," the question is about an explicit and systematic discussion of the principles on which moral action is based and the logic by which moral decisions may be made. Obviously the Fourth Gospel contains no such system; whatever it may be, it is not a philosophical treatise. If we inquire about "the ethics of Richard Nixon," we are probably asking for an assessment of the late president's moral character as exemplified in his public life. But the moral comportment of the fourth evangelist was acted behind the curtain of history. Even the identity of this writer is at best uncertain; we have no biographical facts at all on which to base judgments about his or her character. Thus neither of the most natural ways of construing the phrase "the ethics of someone" gets us anywhere when applied to the author of the Fourth Gospel. I choose rather to take the topic as an inquiry about the use of the Fourth Gospel in more or less its final form (hence "fourth evangelist") as an instrument of moral formation.

It is in this latter sense of the term, however, that the phrase may be oxymoronic. The kind of ethos that the narrative of the Fourth Gospel seems designed to reinforce, when taken at face value in its historical rather than its canonical context, is not one that many of us would happily call "Christian" in a normative sense. One could argue that this Gospel has won its secure place in the affections of generations of readers and its profound influence on theological, literary, and moral sensibilities of Western culture only through an endless series of more or less strong misreadings (in the sense that literary critic Harold Bloom gives to the word).[1] I begin, therefore, by trying to state candidly why the Fourth Gospel seems to stand opposed to some of the values that many thoughtful Christians hold. By focusing on what is wrong with the Fourth Gospel as an instrument of moral formation—at the risk that such a focus may seem perverse to many readers—we may be able to sort out some of the complexity that emerges when the historical interpreter of a canonical text meets the ethical interpreter.

I

What is wrong with the Fourth Gospel as a vehicle of moral formation? First, its form is wrong: It offers no explicit moral instruction. Unlike the Jesus of the Synoptic Gospels, the Jesus of John, as Moody Smith points out, teaches in public only about himself. The maxims (gnomes) that are so characteristic of Jesus' sayings in the Q, Synoptic, and Thomas traditions, and which were universally recognized in the ancient Mediterranean culture as the idiom of popular moral instruction, are missing altogether from John. Even in the Johannine Jesus' private teaching of his disciples, "his instructions lack specificity."[2] The only rule is "love one another," and that rule is both vague in application and narrowly circumscribed, being limited solely to those who are firmly within the Johannine circle.

Second, the narrative does not provide a plausible and universalizable model for behavior. It does include actors who exemplify both positive and negative roles, but those roles are so specific to the situation of those small, embattled communities for which this Gospel was written that only by means of careful contextualization and transformation can they help disciples of a different time and place. (That is the nub of the issue, and we must return to it later.) Neither the main character, Jesus, nor his disciples are imitable. The disciples play an almost entirely passive role; their failure to understand Jesus' words and actions frequently casts them as mere foils to Jesus' superior knowledge and his inscrutability. They are hardly more effectual as characters than the equally misunderstanding opponents of Jesus. The Johannine Jesus, on the other hand, is too alien to human weakness to provide a convincing model, too much "the god striding over the face of the earth." Despite the occasional human touch, like Jesus' weeping for Lazarus, and despite the indubitable fact that this Gospel, every bit as much as Mark's, leads up to and focuses on the crucifixion as its dramatic climax, John does not depict a normal human life or a normal death. This narrative celebrates the enigma of the Son of God who lived in human flesh and whose death was victory over the world and glorification with the Father; it does not show *us* how to live or how to die. Although Jesus bids the disciples follow him and predicts Peter's martyrdom (in the added final chapter; whether the fourth evangelist still speaks here I leave open), they do not go as he goes. He has power to lay down his own life when *his* hour has come, and power to take it up again. He alone, with the Father, knows whence he came and where he is going, and when. The old tradition of the quite human agony of decision in Gethsemane is explicitly negated: "Now my soul is troubled, and what shall I say? 'Father, save me from this hour'? But it was for this reason that I came to this hour! Father, glorify your name" (John 12:27–28).[3]

To be sure, the discourses are rich in irony, but nothing like the irony of Socrates touches the master of these dialogues. In its place is an inscrutable series of paradoxes: the one who is "equal to God" and "one with the Father" is at the same time completely subordinate to the Father's will, doing nothing "of himself." It is hard to see how the disciple is to emulate such a master. The one occasion on which he explicitly gives to the disciples an example (ὑπόδειγμα) is his washing of their feet, at the turning point of the narrative, when he knows "that his hour had come" and "that the Father had given all things into his hands" (13:1, 3). Yet there is nothing really humble about this action, any more than there is when the Pope reenacts it in St. Peter's on Maundy Thursday. It is precisely as "Lord and Teacher" that Jesus demonstrates the service that disciples owe one another, for "a slave is not greater than his master nor an envoy than the one who sent him" (13:12–17).

Third, if we take the narrative as supplying neither rules for behavior nor models of character or action but simply as rendering a narrative world to which readers are invited and challenged to respond by imaginatively appropriate performance, this narrative is profoundly troubling to rational kinds of moral discourse. The approach to life embodied in this narrative seems on its face not merely irrational but antirational. "Logos," the loaded word that meets us in the beginning, seems to promise to Greek cultural sensibilities talk of reason and communication, and it was this word that provided the hook for Alexandrian interpreters to anchor this strange book in the familiar theology of Middle Platonism. Yet the Logos who takes flesh in the narrative is not a model of rationality and communication, but one who demands that followers "abide in *my logos*," a logos that overthrows ordinary rationality, and by riddle, metaphor, irony, and double entendre exuberantly eludes straightforward communication. Only to such abiding does this Gospel promise knowledge of "the truth." It would be understandable if a reader heard that requirement as a demand for submission to the sheer occult power of the one from above—though such a perception would place that reader on the side of those who do not hear Jesus' logos, "the Jews" of "this world" who reject the light sent to them and remain in darkness (see especially 8:30–59). The business of the Johannine style is subversion of reality as perceived in the common sense of a certain tradition. Subversion doubtless may have ethical uses in specific circumstances, but it can hardly be the foundation of ethics.

Fourth, the decision that characteristically divides Jesus' audience between those who come to the light and those who remain in darkness, between those who "abide" to eternal life and those who draw back and are condemned, is shrouded in mystery. Only those who are "chosen out of the world" can make the right choice, and therefore this decision on which everything depends in the narrative world of John seems to be predetermined and so not a morally free decision. The way to life is a series of riddles. No one, enemy or disciple, knows the answers; only Jesus does. And "we," the implied audience, are presumed to know (if we belong to the chosen readers who understand), as we look down upon the foolish Nicodemus and the perplexed crowds and even the struggling disciples. The riddles are like that of the Sphinx or those posed by the various tyrants who rule the kingdoms of fairy tales, demanding that anyone venturing into their territory solve the puzzle or die. In this story, however, there is no young, questing hero to outwit the ruler, but only the omniscient One, come from heaven with all truth given him by the King himself. The disciples do not understand any better than the others; they are saved, not because they are clever or right, but because they are chosen. The God who speaks through this Jesus is Kafkaesque; whether we will enter the Castle depends entirely on the choice we make, but the basis of the choice seems entirely arbitrary and beyond our finding out. We can see why Valentinus liked this Gospel. The mystery of Johannine faith cries out for myth to explain its ground. Perhaps, too, that most poetic of second-century Christian writers felt an affinity to this Gospel because it suits the poet better than the moralist. Of Kierkegaard's stages, John may resonate for the aesthete or the knight of faith, but hardly for the ethical person.

To make matters worse, the enemies of Jesus, the ones who can never solve the riddle, who even when they "believe" are rebuffed as children of the devil, are stigmatized as "the Jews." We find it all too easy to forget what the Fourth Gospel itself acknowledges: that Jesus and his abiding followers are themselves all, ethnically, Jews as well. It is hard to keep in mind the historical context that produced the stigmatization of the term. The members of this Jesus sect, who liked to think of themselves as "Galileans" rather than "Judeans" and perhaps included some Samaritan converts as well, were expelled from the synagogues of their town (John 9:22; 12:42; 16:2). We can understand, then, why they condemned those "Judeans/Jews" who put them out as agents of "this world" and of the devil, whose only king was Caesar. In the centuries since their time, however, the phrase "the Jews" has stood in the translated and dehistoricized Gospel as an ever-ready escape hatch by which the Christian reader may avoid the threatening narrative: We may not want to face what this Gospel asks of us, but at least we are not Jews. It would, of course, be unfair to hold the fourth evangelist responsible for the blood spilled and the gas chambers invented by the late readers of his text, but neither may the postmodern reader forget.

II

We have seen so far that the Fourth Gospel meets none of our expectations about the way ethics should be constructed. If, after all, it has some moral lesson to teach us or some ethical challenge to offer, then we must first submit to its own idiom and the coercive voices of its narrator and its protagonist.

The narrative is relentless, driving toward the "hour" when the Son of Man must be glorified by being "lifted up" on the cross. The story has its share of dramatic conflict, yet the inevitability of its climax does not result, as in most modern drama, from psychological conflict in its characters or from social forces embodied in their relationships, although the latter are certainly represented in John. On the other hand, the transcendental necessity at work in John's story is not quite like that of classical tragedy, either. The protagonist here is from the beginning fully conscious of the way he must go and of the "work" that he must complete. For the other characters, none of whom understands what is happening, it is a story of separation and affiliation, of decision and judgment on which their lives depend, but for which no rational basis is apparent.

As in the old traditions about Jesus, the earthly part of the story begins with John the Baptist. But the Baptist's role here is *not* to baptize Jesus but first to "testify" about him, denigrating himself, and then to transfer representative disciples of his own to him. These first disciples, who "abide" with Jesus for a time, begin the chain of connections that brings other disciples as well, culminating in Jesus' encounter with the otherwise unknown Nathanael, "genuine Israelite." These opening episodes thus indicate that one of the principal themes of this Gospel is the question of how one comes to be and to remain a disciple of Jesus.

The matter of discipleship is, of course, closely tied up with the question of "believing." After the general rule of 1:12, it is of Nathanael that the word "believe" is first used (1:50). Then at Cana the disciples see the first of Jesus' "signs" and believe (2:11)—but they are already disciples before they "believe in him." In one key passage, what we might take to be the fundamental ethical question is also answered by reference to faith. "What shall we do," asks the crowd that has followed Jesus from the place of the feeding miracle to Capernaum, "in order to be working the works of God?" He has just chided them with failure to see the "sign" and has warned, "Do not work [to obtain] the food that perishes [like the manna in the wilderness, Ex. 16:20–21] but the food that abides for eternal life, which the Son of Man will give you." To their question in turn he now replies, "This is the work of God: that you believe in the one he sent" (John 6:26–29). It turns out, however, that believing in this one is not so easy. When Jesus explains further what is entailed in receiving the bread from heaven that the Son of Man gives, even many of his disciples abandon him (6:60–66). Only the twelve stick fast, and even of them Jesus says, "Was it not I who chose you twelve?—and one of you is an informer!" (v. 70).

The Fourth Gospel depicts a Jesus who attracts many to his message and his works—but in the end few remain. It is his "signs" and his teaching that stimulate belief in him. What prevents the majority from continuing that belief? Two things principally: the radicalism of his claims about his own identity, and "fear of the Jews." Many of the Gospel's stories of conflict reflect responses to the Johannine community's struggle to enunciate, by a daring reinterpretation of Jewish scripture and tradition, their understanding of Jesus' identity. The incomprehension by Nicodemus, "the teacher of Israel," of the one who has come down from heaven and the righteous anger of those who take up stones against one who "makes himself equal to God" are examples. The struggle has both radicalized the Johannine Christians' interpretation and led to their being ostracized.

The process of separation has also produced fear, which in this Gospel stigmatizes those who dare not speak openly about Jesus (7:13), family members who shrink back from converts (9:20–23), and timorous believers in high places who try to be disciples in secret (12:42; 19:38–39). For the evangelist, the time for hiding is past (20:19): Now one must be courageous in a world that hates believers, yet a world that Jesus has conquered (16:33). The model disciple is the blind person given sight by Jesus in chapter 9. Unintimidated by the Pharisees who interrogate him, he sticks doggedly to his account of what Jesus has done for him and to the simple calculus of his moral theology, which refutes the sophistry of the questioners: "This is the amazing thing, that you do not know where he is from, yet he opened my eyes!" (9:30). This person, who is contemptuously named "a disciple of that one" by his interrogators, accepts his expulsion from the synagogue with equanimity and, given an appropriate title to confess his faith in Jesus, immediately complies (vv. 35–38).

This Gospel does not provide moral instruction, as we have observed, nor does its narrative directly model character to be emulated. Nevertheless, it presents, in the story of Jesus' mission and the mystery of discipleship, the mirror of a community that has been formed in the crucible of conflict. We know nothing about that community except what we can deduce from this document. Yet we may surmise, from the shape of the narrative itself and from Jesus' instructions to those who believe, a set of attitudes toward the world and a pattern of behavior that govern this community and which the evangelist wants to reinforce.

"This world," seen through the eyes of the fourth evangelist, is God's and the Logos's "own" by right of creation and ultimate judgment, but it is presently a realm of darkness that resists the Light, perversely blind and deaf to the messenger from above. The "ruler of this world" is Satan, and he continues to make mischief for the disciples of Jesus, even though, as the story of Jesus' trial makes clear to the discerning reader, the hidden judgment enacted then is "the judgment of this world," when "the ruler of this world is expelled" (12:31; see also 16:11).

Nevertheless, though for the Johannine sect the world is hostile, alien, and perverse, the ethos of the sect is not altogether "otherworldly." While it has many of the characteristics of an "introversionist sect" (in the typology of Bryan Wilson), in some of its dimensions it is more like Wilson's "conversionist" or "revolutionist" types, as David Rensberger has pointed out.[4] While we cannot plausibly speak of this group's having a sense of "mission" to the world in the aggressive and optimistic sense in which modern Christianity has used that word, it does see itself as presenting, by its own very existence and its own countercultural form of life, "testimony" to the world. This countercultural existence and the decisions it entails for each member of the circle when encountering the agents of the larger society, both Roman and Jewish, have quite definite political and social implications.

The social implications of the Johannine form of faith have become fairly clear in scholarship on the Fourth Gospel of the past two decades. As we now understand the history of the Johannine disciples, to be chosen as those who are no longer "of the world" had meant for them to be separated from the organized Jewish communities of their town, which in the scenes of the Gospel (but no longer in the Johannine epistles) *were* their world. "Believing" for them had entailed a social relocation with profound consequences for family ties (like the fearful parents of the healed blind man), for position in the community (like Nicodemus and Joseph of Arimathea, whose anxieties keep them in "the darkness"), and for personal comfort and safety (16:2). "Abiding" in the logos of Jesus entailed for them a steadfast loyalty to the countercultural movement, which had had to find other social forms and locations, outside the synagogues, for its existence. It found them, as we know from the epistles of John, in household-based communities, like those by which other circles of Christianity found a foothold in the more ethnically diverse cities around the Mediterranean.

The "social ethics" of the Johannine Gospel almost boils down to this: resolute loyalty to the community of disciples. That way of putting it, however, misses the Gospel's understanding of what is going on: It is, rather, loyalty to the Son of God that binds together all those whom he "chose" and "sent into the world" as he was "sent from the Father." To abide in Jesus' logos entails abiding in the community, and "to abide" carries the strong connotation of resistance to the dark and hostile world.

It is true that the Fourth Gospel keeps alive the conviction that this alien world was nevertheless created by God through the same Logos that, in Jesus, has called the disciples to their countercultural stance. The evil of the world is not inherent in its existence but is the world's own self-contradiction. The evangelist can still affirm even God's love for this world, but this was doubtless hard to keep in mind for a sect that perceived itself so hated by the world. The writer of First John insists that the disciples must not love the world or anything in it (1 John 2:15–17). Nevertheless, the last discourses and prayer of Jesus in the Gospel remind the Johannine disciples that they do, after all, remain in the world, chosen, sent, and kept there by the Son and the Father. The Son has not prayed to the Father to take them out of the world, but to protect them from the evil one (John 17:15). They are there to bear witness to Jesus, as the Paraclete he sends bears witness (15:26–27). Those readers who follow Clement of Alexandria in calling this Gospel "the spiritual Gospel" should keep in mind that the Spirit of Truth this Gospel describes is a prosecuting attorney who *indicts* the world "in the matter of sin, in the matter of righteousness, in the matter of judgment" (16:8–11). Doubtless the testimony implied here is in part verbal, but the final discourses of the Gospel give the impression that the primary testimony of the disciples is their very existence as a community. Their resistance to the world, their form of life in contradiction of its values, is their indictment of it.

This countercultural stance of a community that sees itself (absurdly, in the world's eyes) as a remnant of healthy tissue in the world's cancerous body inevitably has political consequences. The story of Jesus' arrest, trial, and crucifixion in this "spiritual Gospel" contains more explicitly political motifs than any of the other Gospels. John describes the plot against Jesus as calculatedly political (11:48–50), though as usual he sees another dimension, the politics of God, so to speak, ironically implied by his characters' words (vv. 51–53). A detachment of Roman soldiers accompany the agents of the high priests and Pharisees, led by Judas to seize Jesus (18:3). As in all the canonical versions of the passion narrative, the title "King of the Judeans" is central to the trial before Pilate, but no other Gospel expresses so clearly as John the cynical contempt that the Roman governor shows for Jewish national hopes.[5] To be sure, Jesus says straight out, "My kingship is not of this world: if my kingship were of this world, my followers would have fought to keep me from being handed over to the Jews" (18:36). The Johannine groups may look to us like some modern survivalist sect, but this sect does not stockpile weapons. Nevertheless, Jesus' kingship has "real" world political consequences, and the political decisions of Pilate and the Jewish leaders have "religious" consequences. One has to decide where ultimate authority lies (19:10–11); one must decide whether truth grows out of a Roman sword or from the testimony of the One sent from God (18:37–38); one must decide whether God is Israel's king or Caesar is (19:15). The Johannine Christians know that confessing Jesus as their king is dangerous.

For the internal life of the Johannine sect, there is but one rule expressly given as a "new commandment" from Jesus: "Love one another" (13:34; 15:12–17; see also 1 John 2:10–11; 3:11, 23; 4:7–12). It is this mutual love within the community that is set over against the world's hatred. The model is Jesus' love for those whom he names his friends and for whom he lays down his life (John 15:12–15). There is nothing in John, unlike the Synoptics, about loving the sect's enemies. Indeed, by the time the epistles of John are written, hatred for the world seems implicit in the elder's exhortation. Yet the sect does not seek to do harm to the world; its task remains testimony, by the fact of its own (sectarian) existence, its love-bound unity: "that the world may believe . . ." (17:21). Its mission is the Paraclete's mission: to indict the world, not to carry out the judgment that belongs alone to God and the Son of Man, nor to execute the sentence on a condemned world.

III

Paradoxically, the voice of the fourth evangelist, whose words are so dear to so many Christian readers, becomes perhaps the most foreign of any in the New Testament when we hear it with awareness of its historical and social context and its rhetorical force within that context. This voice is sharply sectarian, and culturally and politically subversive. If it is to exert its full force within the polyphony of biblical voices, we must begin by being resolutely honest about its dissonant qualities. To strive to enable such honesty is, I take it, one of the fundamental jobs of a historical critic. It is precisely when the voice of the fourth evangelist seems most harsh to the churches that they may most need to hear just this voice. When the church is too much "of the world," then the echo of its sectarian origins is needed. David Rensberger, a Mennonite, has put with particular clarity the timeliness of the Johannine witness:

> For, above all, the meaning of John's sectarianism is that *because it was sectarian* it challenged the world on the basis of the love of God and the word of God. No religion that sees itself as the backbone of a society, as the glue that holds a society together, can easily lay down a challenge to that society's wrongs. A cultural religion is all too readily told to mind its own business, because it *has* a business, a well-known role in maintaining society's fabric unmolested. It is the sect, which has no business in the world, that is able to represent a fundamental challenge to the world's oppressive orders.[6]

Ironically, in a time when Christianity has been domesticated into a polite hobby or a cheering section for vested social interests, the sectarian stance may be just what "the world" needs as well. Stephen Carter, an Episcopalian and a professor of law, observes that "the very aspect of religions that many of their critics most fear — that the religiously devout, in the name of their faith, take positions that differ from approved state policy — is one of their strengths."[7]

Still, for the shaping of moral sensibilities, this is not the Gospel for all seasons. Whenever Christians hold power in the world, and when they are tempted to identify the enemies of Jesus and of his Johannine disciples with those whom they dislike and whom they have power to harm, the results are likely to be perverse. Historic Christianity holds, against Marcion and his ilk, that "the Spirit of truth" speaks through the entire polyphony of biblical voices. Hearing that single Spirit among the many requires in each time and place delicate judgment — and therefore humility. Traditionally, the way of correcting the one-sidedness of the Johannine voice has been by treating its imagery as "mystical" and "spiritual," in the warm and foggy sense that alone is left to these words in our degenerate speech. To domesticate the Fourth Gospel in this fuzzy way, however, simultaneously robs it of its power and conceals without disarming its potential dangers. Only a candid and contextually sensitive confrontation between the Fourth Gospel's subversive challenge to "this world" and the more accommodating, conversionist, or transformative modes of engagement with the world, represented elsewhere in the canon, can enable the Bible to guide and usefully to complicate — and not merely to decorate — Christian ethical discourse.

NOTES

1. Ernst Käsemann has expressed a similar view (*The Testament of Jesus: A Study of the Gospel in the Light of Chapter 17* [Philadelphia: Fortress, 1968], 75), acknowledged as a possibility that "cannot be ruled out a priori" by D. Moody Smith,

Johannine Christianity: Essays on its Setting, Sources, and Theology (Columbia, S.C.: University of South Carolina Press, 1984), 180–81.

2. Smith, *Johannine Christianity, 178.*

3. Author's translation, here and throughout.

4. Bryan R. Wilson, *Magic and the Millennium: A Sociological Study of Religious Movements of Protest among Tribal and Third-World Peoples* (New York: Harper & Row, 1973); David Rensberger, *Johannine Faith and Liberating Community* (Philadelphia: Westminster, 1988), 27–28.

5. See Rensberger, *Johannine Faith and Liberating Community,* 92–95.

6. Ibid., 142.

7. Stephen L. Carter, *The Culture of Disbelief: How American Law and Politics Trivialize Religious Devotion* (New York: Basic Books, 1993), 37.

Hans Weder

19

Deus Incarnatus:
On the Hermeneutics of Christology
in the Johannine Writings*

That the New Testament writings were not originally written for the canon as such constitutes a historical insight that enhances rather than diminishes their significance. On the other hand, that these same writings are now collected together in a canon is a historical fact whose significance for understanding the individual writings is still underestimated even today. The present essay, in honor of D. Moody Smith, attempts to move one step closer toward *hermeneutics within the canonical context itself.* One might engage in such hermeneutics by interpreting those particular New Testament passages that *take the process of understanding itself as their theme,* as is the case, for example, in the Johannine farewell discourses, in the concept of ἀνάμνησις ("remembrance") in the Gospel of John, or in the reading guides in the Johannine letters. A compilation of all the pericopes that exhibit this characteristic in the canon would yield a hermeneutics that itself actually occurs within the New Testament canon.

In what follows, however, the topic of hermeneutics within the canonical context will be approached somewhat differently. That is, we will not inquire concerning the explicit hermeneutics of individual texts; rather, hermeneutical insights can probably best be acquired where one can observe the concretely developing process of understanding itself, preferably through several stages of theological development. This we will undertake, using the example of the Christology of the Johannine writings. Christology is the central and decisive process of reflection within the *corpus Iohanneum.*[1] Hence, it is no exaggeration to say that Christology is *the* central theme of hermeneutical reflection in these writings. Furthermore, in the Johannine writings we possess a *corpus* in which, with a certain degree of probability, we are able to say something about the process of theological reflection itself. One must, after all, proceed on the assumption that the Johannine writings originated in a school, which carried forward its theological reflections over an extended period of time.[2] A pre-Johannine stage can be distinguished fairly clearly from the Gospel itself, with an additional distinction (which need not be, necessarily, diachronic) discernible between the farewell discourses and the other sections of the book. Finally, in the letter of 1 John we

*Translated by Douglas W. Stott.

encounter an even later stage,[3] which over long stretches explicitly picks up and clarifies themes of the Gospel itself. We are dealing here with acts of reflection whose association with various stages of tradition is possible but not necessary.

For these reasons, the status of Johannine Christology as an example of a hermeneutical process within the canonical context should be considered seriously, since Christology is the long process of penetrating reflection concerning the coming of Jesus of Nazareth. Christology offers an estimation of just what this coming was really about. One is wont to refer to Johannine Christology as a "high" Christology. If this includes the view that the heavenly Christ touched the earth only fleetingly, however, then it does not represent an adequate estimation of Johannine Christology and would be based on a docetic misunderstanding of the Johannine writings.[4] Reference to high Christology does, however, precisely articulate the characteristic uniqueness and the center of the Johannine writings, if it attributes to that which has actually occurred in the flesh in the foreground of the world, a dignity beyond which nothing higher is conceivable. This is precisely what makes the Christology of these writings hermeneutically interesting. Our investigation—commensurate with the stages of the actual process of reflection—will proceed in four steps. We will consider the pre-Johannine Christology on the basis of the prologue, particularly on the basis of the incarnation statement of 1:14. The assertion that the Logos became flesh will be further interpreted in the Gospel's I-Am sayings, which in their own turn interpret the *semeia* narratives. A further stage of reflection resides in the Paraclete statements in the farewell discourses. Finally, at the end we encounter statements from 1 John that, significantly, can again be characterized as theological rather than christological.

The concept of Christology employed here must be clarified more precisely. "Christology is second-order language about Jesus. John's Gospel is a first-order presentation of Jesus."[5] One can hardly take Moody Smith's hermeneutical observation here seriously enough. If Christology were conceived as a theoretical, secondary language that, as it were, conceptualized what Jesus Christ represents, it would completely miss the point of Johannine Christology. Christology here is *not a theory of the incarnation, but rather an evocation in language of what Christ embodies.* Christology is anything but a theory that replaces Christ. Rather, it is a language with but one goal, namely, to provide access to the event of the incarnation itself. It is the making present—the representation—of something that can never be comprehended theoretically, since its fulcral point is the assertion that the Christ represents the *reality* of God in the world, in the sense of his efficacious presence. The Christ is not information about God, but rather the incarnation of the divine Logos.

THE ONE WHO BECAME FLESH (JOHN 1:14)

The pre-Johannine prologue cannot be understood without reference to the wisdom theology of Hellenistic Judaism. What was once said of Sophia is now said of the Logos, the Christ. Jesus of Nazareth is understood as the embodiment of this Logos, an assertion admittedly no longer attested for wisdom. Nonetheless, in its own turn the figure of wisdom still functions hermeneutically with regard to Jesus: It discloses the depth and significance of that which entered upon the world-stage with Jesus. The one great theme of wisdom theology was the relationship between God and world, between truth and reality. And if one were to character-ize in one sentence the figure of Sophia, one might say—at least with regard to its early Jewish form—that in it the turning of God's love toward the world, the com-ing of God into the world of experience, took on the form of a person. Wisdom theology responded to the question of how God's presence in the world of expe-rience might be conceived and perceived.

It is no accident that the community turned to wisdom in their estimation of Jesus of Nazareth, since his own characteristic feature, after all, was an act of com-ing, an approach to human beings, a turn toward the world itself. This unequivo-cal direction of movement is attested to in a variety of ways in the prologue: The light (of life, which is in the Logos) shines in the darkness (1:5); it illuminates every person who comes into the world (1:9); the Logos was in the world (1:10); it came into its own (1:11) and—as a final answer to its perpetual rejection—be-came flesh (1:14). Thus the hermeneutical accomplishment of wisdom consists, on the one hand, in the fact that it teaches one to understand the fundamental movement of turning that characterizes the being of Jesus as a movement *origi-nating with God*. It teaches one to recognize, in the turning of Jesus, the turning of God's own love toward the world. The Logos hymn admittedly does not orig-inate in the religious speculation of the Johannine community, in speculation (for example) concerning just how a connection between God and world might be con-ceived. The Johannine community was not facing the question of how one might conceive God's presence in the world but rather, the question of how one might appropriately understand the experience with Jesus of Nazareth. The Logos hymn originated in the experiences that were to be had with Jesus of Nazareth and with his own words, as well as words about him.

These experiences are concentrated in the prologue into a single fundamental ex-perience: the experience of reception (ἡμεῖς πάντες ἐλάβομεν ["we have all re-ceived"], 1:16). This experience is, as it were, the reverse side of the fundamental movement of turning. Turning toward (on the one hand) and reception of (on the other) fit precisely together and constitute an asymmetrical relationship in which the qualitative distinction between the two sides comes clearly to expression. The per-son who receives is qualitatively different from the person who gives, although both—each in his own way—are completely oriented toward each other in the process of giving and receiving. At the same time, the correlation of giving and re-ceiving constitutes a relationship in which both sides maintain their own dignity (as opposed, for example, to a relationship of repression, which does not really deserve the name "relationship," insofar as the repressed side has lost its dignity). This *asym-metrical* relationship reflects the fundamental relationship between God and human beings, the relationship between divine creativity and human receptivity.

John 1:16 initially mentions only the act of receiving, without adding an object. Neither does the object have to be added, since whenever we are dealing with reception in the true sense of the word there can be no other object than grace. For only that which comes from grace (χάρις) is that particular gift that allows a person to be a recipient in the pure sense. (All other gifts are bound to conditions: for instance, the gift of the law to the condition of obedience, a condition no longer allowing a person to be merely a recipient but also a perpetrator, worker, payer, and so forth.) This is why 1:16 speaks of grace not directly, as the object of reception, but rather only in an explicative phrase: καὶ χάριν ἀντὶ χάριτος, "grace upon grace." The object appended here merely carries through what is already implied in the process of genuine reception. What is made more precise here is that the object of reception is self-evidently grace: more exactly, grace that in being received actually increases (rather than decreases).

The prologue brings this experience of grace into connection with the origin of the world itself, with the being of God prior to all creation. This reference back to the most primal origin makes good sense, since it serves to facilitate recognition of the real significance of this experience of grace. This experience in the foreground of the world itself demands to be adequately evaluated and appreciated. Whoever experiences grace experiences creative power, the same creator-power present at the origin of the world. Although it is quite possible to discern something like righteousness or requital by referring to the constitution of the world (comparable to the second law of thermodynamics, according to which energy is perpetually maintained), the experience of grace must derive from the God who constituted the world in a creative act. Hence, the prologue must refer to the origin, to the being of the Logos with God, in order to evaluate and appreciate adequately this experience of grace that takes place in the foreground of the world. One might also say that a Christology that associates Jesus completely with God[6] is nothing other than an acknowledgment of the fact that Jesus of Nazareth exercised a creative influence on human beings. Christology is the attempt to understand this reality of Jesus from the perspective of its truth in God.

The hermeneutical accomplishment of wisdom theology consists, on the other hand, in the fact that it makes possible a clarification of the relationship between God and Jesus of Nazareth. Just as wisdom is present in the reality of the world and yet at the same time belongs completely to God, so also does the Crucified, however much he does indeed belong to the world of the flesh, belong completely on the side of God (1:1–2).[7] The Logos that became a human being is without beginning, since—and in this it is like God—it was in the beginning (1:1a). Hence its being—in contradistinction, for example, to wisdom[8]—is primal in the same way as the being of God. The relationship between the Logos and God is no less primal: In the beginning the Logos was oriented toward God (1:1b; this statement is expressly confirmed in 1:2). It is also like God in its essence (1:1c). Although the Logos hymn also seeks to distinguish between the Logos and God (only between differentiated sides is the relationship mentioned in 1:1b possible), it at the same time comes infinitely close to asserting that God and the Logos constitute a unity.

This determination of the relationship between God and the Logos can be explicated with regard both to the Logos and to God. With regard to the Logos, it means that in it God is encountered in his entirety. There is no remnant concealed in God that would not encounter the world in the Logos. This means, further, that it is not merely a particular aspect or part of God that has become flesh in the incarnation. John 1:14 expresses the fullness of the presence of God with the metaphor of the μονογενής ("the only[-begotten]"): The weight and significance of the one who has become a human being, the dignity with which he is equipped, is described as that dignity that he as the first-born has from his Father. Accordingly, the prologue maintains that Jesus of Nazareth is the revealer of God.[9]

One must not, however, understand this revealer as a person who merely supplies information concerning God's essence, his will, and his commandments. In the case of the Incarnate, revelation precisely does not mean information about God but rather, an embodiment of the essence of God. Revelation means God's reality in the sense of efficacious presence. Jesus of Nazareth reveals God precisely in the sense that he becomes an event of God. If an evaluation of the relationship just mentioned is then made with regard to God, it yields an important conclusion regarding the concept of God. If the Logos was itself also in the beginning, then God is no longer conceived apart from his Logos. That means that the turning of God's love toward the world—be it in the creation of the world, in the coming of wisdom, or in the turning of the Christ toward that world—is not conceived as an *accidens* of the divine being; rather, the turning of God's love toward the world is understood as God's primal essence itself. Although, in the view of the world, the incarnation must appear as a chance occurrence, just as the coming of every stranger is a chance occurrence, in the view of God it is given with his very essence itself.

At the same time, this means that God can no longer be conceived apart from the incarnation of the Logos. Whoever would think or conceive of God is directed to the experience of his reality, which in the New Testament bears the name of Jesus Christ. Of course, this may not be misunderstood in the exclusive sense, as if God might be experienced only in the person of Jesus Christ.[10] For it is and remains the Christ who is encountering every person in the light that illuminates every person's life (1:9). The Christ is encountered in that particular vitality bestowed upon every human being, and is encountered in the grace and truth from which every life lives. The Logos, God's word, is equally primal with God himself. The hermeneutical significance of this statement is that God, accordingly, is understood exclusively as the one who speaks—that is, as the God who speaks through his only word, the Christ.

No silence is presupposed from which this speaking might issue, in contradistinction (for example) to Ignatius' notion of the Logos that emerges from silence

(*Magn.* 8.2)[11] and to the independent reality attributed to that silence in Pseudo-Philo (*Bib. Ant.* 60.2).[12] The Logos hymn must be carefully distinguished from this conceptual development, pointing toward gnosis.[13] For a God whose essence is speech cannot fall back into silence, and the notion of a silence from which the Logos emerges at least comes perilously close to a priority of the negative (something actually quite commensurate with later gnosis). Whoever grants this sort of independent reality to silence and darkness is taking a dualistic conception as the basic point of departure, a conception unwilling to refer the whole of reality to God. As frequently as such a conception may well have been entertained in late antiquity, it is in any case not present in the Logos hymn. With that, however, we have made an extraordinarily far-reaching hermeneutical decision.

In summary, one important hermeneutical accomplishment of wisdom theology is that within the experiential world of human beings, something like the turning of God's love yet remains fully conceivable, and it is this possibility that provides the Logos hymn with its point of departure. Despite this, however, a decisive difference should be kept in mind regarding the theological presuppositions. The Logos hymn does not simply represent a type of wisdom theology. Rather, it draws on wisdom theology in order to address its own problem. Whereas wisdom theology primarily responds to the (theological) question of how the coming of God into the world might be conceived, the hymn responds to the (christological) question of how the ministry of Jesus of Nazareth might be adequately evaluated and understood. The hymn does not answer the question of how the Logos comes into the world, but rather, the question of just what significance is to be attributed to the experience of grace and truth[14] that one had with Jesus Christ in the Johannine community.

THE CHRISTOLOGY OF INCARNATION

One important problem attaching to the statement of the incarnation in the hymn is that it might be understood in the formal sense. That is to say, John 1:14 does not associate the Logos's becoming flesh with any information concerning the concrete form of the one who became flesh. Hence, one might understand the incarnation as a kind of tangential contact between heaven and earth, whereby the point of contact itself would have no extension and, accordingly, no form. The humanness of the Incarnate is conceived formally insofar as it is reduced to his mere humanity, quite apart from the concrete form of that humanity. Yet already as regards the prologue, such formalization is quite inappropriate,[15] and the Gospel of John itself, for which the prologue now serves as an overture, made this point perfectly clear. The humanness of the Logos is presented in the story that the Gospel narrates concerning Jesus. With that, the contact between God and world acquires concrete form: namely, the form of the life, ministry, and death of Jesus.[16]

In the transition between prologue and Gospel, the evangelist holds fast to the assertion that the one who became a human being—in constant contact with

God—has made God known in the world (1:18). Neither can this statement be understood in the sense of a communication of heavenly information. In this Gospel, the making known of God through Jesus Christ means that Jesus ministers in God's place, speaks in God's place, and even dies as God. Such exposition means basically a carrying-through of God's essence in the world, the actual presence of God. The giver (God) is present in his gift (Christ) in such a way that he himself is at risk along with that gift. In 1:17 the evangelist already gives us a hermeneutical hint in this direction. Whereas the law was given by Moses and thus represents an object different from Moses, one says of grace and truth that they "*came to be* [mediated] through Jesus Christ" (διὰ Ἰησοῦ Χριστοῦ ἐγένετο). God's grace and truth are not something that—in the form of a text such as that of the law—might be given over. Grace and truth can only come to be; and they come to be in the sense that they occur as a reality in the world. To that extent, it is true that the Christ does not offer grace and truth as something extraneous to himself. Rather, he himself embodies this grace and truth; they came to be with him in that primal beginning, and they enter into human experience through him. The difference between the gift of the law and the coming-to-be of truth derives from the different ontological status of the two entities. The law is a word expressing the will of God in the sense that it charges a person with obedience to that will. The commandment of the law does not actualize itself, but rather, enters into reality insofar as a person acts according to its sense. In contrast, truth and grace belong to the essence of the creative God. Grace and truth have their own reality and enter into reality only insofar as they are *efficacious among human beings.* Whereas the law prompts a person to act, grace and truth exercise their effects on that person quite of their own accord. Thus Christ does not *give* grace and truth but, rather, *is* true, insofar as he leads a person into truth, and *is* merciful, insofar as he heals and delivers.

One should bear in mind that the Gospel of John also engages in Christology that is expressed in titles of majesty, such as Son of Man, Son, Christ, and others.[17] At this point, however, we will follow the above-mentioned suggestion concerning the reality of the Incarnate and concentrate on those statements within the Gospel of John in which Christology is associated with Jesus' ministry. In this respect the I-Am sayings, with which the evangelist christologically interprets the traditions of the *semeia* (σημεῖα, "signs") narratives, are particularly suitable. Hermeneutically, this interpretation accomplishes precisely that which was the center of the prologue's focus: a perception of the reality of God in the ministry of Jesus Christ. The *semeia* narratives ground statements concerning God in the reality of the Christ.[18] Contrary to a frequently defended position within scholarship according to which the Gospel of John represents a view critical of miracles, one must remember that the *semeia* narratives constitute an important part of the Gospel itself, something already evident in the quantity of miracle stories and in the penetrating intensity of their interpretation. The *semeia* narratives are anything but ballast drawn from tradition. Rather, they were quite consciously incorporated into the Gospel because "they aptly put the question of Jesus' identity (and thus create the possibility of genuine faith), not because the author wished to correct their erroneous theology."[19] The signs (*semeia*) are narratives in which the identity of the Christ reveals itself. They express what is intended, concretely, by the making known of God through the one who became a human being, and to that extent they express the glory (δόξα) of the one who became a human being. "The *doxa* of the Son, bestowed by the Father before the foundation of the world (John 17:5bc, 24cd; see also 12:41), visible in the incarnation of the Preexistent One (John 1:14ab), is manifested in the miracles (John 2:11; 11:4, 40) and perfected on the cross, in order to return to the one *doxa* with the Father (John 17:1b, 5, 10b, 22, 24c)."[20] Again, the reality of the sign (σημεῖον) must be taken seriously, since it is not only a reference to the δόξα but also an expression of the same.[21] The *semeia* are thus not events referring or pointing to something extraneous to themselves; rather, in them *the δόξα of the Christ actually takes place*.

The Christology of the incarnation can be observed anew in the *semeia* narratives interpreted by the I-Am sayings, since these narratives—like John 1:14—associate the heavenly truth of the Christ with the earthly reality of bestowed life. The *fullness* of the bestowed goods is a clear indication of the heavenly dimension. This indication seems to come from the same fullness (πλήρωμα) from which "we" ourselves have received grace upon grace (see 1:16). The *semeia* narratives explicate just what this received grace really is by speaking about that which is graciously bestowed. The heavenly dimension also comes to expression in the fact that Jesus expressly identifies his works as works of the Father. "Throughout the Gospel Jesus repeatedly asserts that he works not by his own power and authority, but by God's, and not by his own will, but in submission to that of the Father."[22] Although the σημεῖα are immersed in the material reality of the world, they are misunderstood if taken to be innerworldly phenomena. Thus, for example, the crowd is criticized in John 6:26–27 because in the miracle of the bread they have not perceived any sign pointing to heaven, but rather, seek Jesus out merely because they have eaten their fill. In this respect the σημεῖα are related to the center of Johannine Christology: In them, too, the most important thing is the identity of the Christ, and to that extent the revelation of the Father.[23] Once again, we must emphasize that this revelation does not involve information but, rather, efficacious presence—not merely a showing but, rather, a taking place or substantiating. Precisely these miracle stories make it quite clear that the revelation of the delivering God exists only in the form of an actual deliverance of human beings from sickness and death.

The earthly dimension is secured through the massive materiality characterizing all the *semeia* narratives.[24] It is as if these stories were trying to discourage any merely symbolic interpretation, even though they—precisely as σημεῖα[25]—

culminate in such symbolic meaning. Here, apparently, everything hinges on the symbolic meaning being perceived *within* that massive materiality, and not through it or tangential to it. This is analogous to the incarnation statement, according to which the heavenly glory (δόξα) can be discerned in no one other than this specific one who became human. If one views its connection with the incarnation, there is no need to find an antidocetic feature in the materiality and concreteness of the σημεῖα.[26] One might just as easily understand this peculiarity as a consequence of the incarnation statement. Viewed hermeneutically, the *semeia* exhibit an independent, innovative function within the developmental process of Johannine Christology and are not merely reactions to degenerate manifestations within that Christology. It generally makes more sense to understand Johannine theology as a process deriving from the fact that faith in Christ itself prompted reflection and was not merely the occasion for reacting to external misunderstanding. The *semeia* narratives and their interpretation in the Gospel carry the pre-Johannine Christology conceptually further, insofar as they conceive the coming of the heavenly deliverer (thus, 3:17) together with those particular deeds of deliverance that also affect the materiality of the world. To that extent, they express nothing more than the being of the Christ himself, which has its origin in God and at the same time extends into the most extreme reaches of the world's materiality.

The fulcral point of the interpretation of the pre-Johannine *semeia* narratives in the I-Am sayings consists in the fact that they present Jesus himself as the gift that the miracles bestow. Thus, for example, John 6:35 interprets the miracle of the bread, narrated in 6:1–15, so that the bread of life bestowed there is identical with the person of the Christ. He is the bread of life insofar as he bestows bread in abundance. Or John 8:12 identifies the light, given to the blind through healing, with the person of the Christ. He is the light insofar as he bestows light, illuminating thus the lives of human beings. In this way the Gospel holds fast to the notion that the gift Christ gives cannot be distinguished from Christ himself. Jesus himself is the gift he gives; he is himself the reality he embodies. The person of Jesus is just as inseparable from the bread he gives and the light he causes to shine as is the Christ, in 1:17, from the grace and truth he bestows. The christological assertion in 1:17 is exactly repeated in the interpretation that the *semeia* narratives undergo in the Gospel of John.

Thus, the I-Am sayings secure the fact that the efficacious presence of Jesus in the miracle of deliverance is understood, not merely as a sign for something else, but rather, as the reality of the God who is present. When the Christ identifies himself as the bread of life, this means that the Christ must be perceived in the bread, and, in this, Christ also the giver of all goods necessary for life—namely, God himself. (That God, as the giver, enters completely into the gift is a notion that virtually demands a consideration of trinitarian implications.) Only now does the evangelist realize what the *semeia* really mean. As long as the bread as a gift is distinguished from Christ, the sign is not adequately understood. In that case it is still merely a sign of legitimation. Whoever understands the sign as a (formal) sign of legitimation will only approach the periphery of the Christ. And whoever sees merely bread in the bread will not know who is actually being encountered in this gift. This is why the *semeia* narratives explicate the reality of Christ from the perspective of content; they show the concrete[27] fashion in which Jesus Christ is creatively efficacious in the world.

THE SPIRIT OF TRUTH (THE PARACLETE)

As developed in the Johannine writings, the Christology of incarnation necessarily involves the notion that the Christ is bound to a particular moment in the history of the world. Because he became flesh, he became temporal. But as self-evident as the idea of temporality is with regard to the human being Jesus, it is just as problematic with regard to the assertion that this particular human being represents the reality of God in the world. For the idea of God quite correctly includes the idea of perpetual presence; the turning of God's love toward the world is conceived as perpetual, taking place ever anew and in every age. Thus, the Johannine Christology of incarnation stands before the problem of how it is able to conceive of the Christ simultaneously as the *incarnate* Logos in its entire temporality, on the one hand, and as the incarnate *Logos* in its never-ending presence, on the other. This problem is resolved with the help of the specifically Johannine[28] figure of the Paraclete.[29]

The extent to which the Johannine school was conscious of the problem of temporality can already be seen in the fact that chapters 13 – 17 deal with the farewell of Jesus to an extent unique in primitive Christianity. Because temporal limitation belongs to the essence of the one who became flesh, Jesus' farewell is understood as a necessary presupposition for the coming of the Spirit. Hence, it is said of the Paraclete that he cannot come before Jesus has gone, and that Jesus will send him after he, Jesus, has departed (16:7). This statement makes it clear that the everlasting presence of the Spirit is assured only because of the temporality of the Christ. The Paraclete appears as the fruit issuing from the fact that the presence of Jesus Christ was finite. Any digression from this temporality constitutes a limitation of the idea of incarnation. The Paraclete is something like the eternal presence with his own of the one who became flesh. Thus, it is the goal of his coming to be with his disciples in all eternity (14:16); they recognize him because he abides with them (14:17). It is commensurate with the strictly conceived temporality of the incarnate Logos that the presence of the Paraclete in the world and among the disciples is conceived with equal strictness as eternal presence. The Paraclete is the attempt to bring to expression those experiences of the efficacious presence of the Christ, produced after the death of Jesus.[30] The sending of the Paraclete is completely and exclusively bound to the Christ who was sent. The Spirit is sent by the Father in the name of Christ (14:26). Wherever the name of Christ is spoken, the Paraclete will be present (a local understanding of ἐν ["in"]), or the speaking of Christ's name prompts the sending of the Paraclete (an instrumental understanding of ἐν). However this ἐν is understood, in either case it is clear that the Paraclete remains closely bound to the Christ. (To that extent the church made a fortunate decision with its formula *filioque* ["and the Son"], since it thereby understood the Spirit as proceeding *from the Father and from the Son*.) The Paraclete is, thus, the everlasting presence of that which was once embodied in Christ.

Bound up with this everlasting presence of the Christ in the Paraclete is the unsurpassable character of his presence among the disciples. It is said that the Paraclete will teach the disciples *all things* and will bring to their remembrance *all* that Jesus said to them (14:26). This assertion is commensurate with the fact that this Spirit of truth will lead them into the realm of the *whole* truth (16:13). This consistent emphasis on "all" (πάντα) brings to expression the belief that nothing need be added to the reality of this Spirit; that reality is the whole and, to that extent, needs no complement or completion. This unsurpassable character itself emerges of necessity from Johannine Christology. If Jesus Christ represents the incarnation of the one divine Logos, then the Spirit embodying his presence among his own can be surpassed by nothing more. This unsurpassable character reflects the fullness of God's presence in Christ. It is said that the Paraclete represents the absent Jesus among the disciples and will abide with them eternally (14:16). It follows from this that the presence of the Paraclete can never be surpassed by the coming of a different Spirit.

The Christology of the Gospel is consistently characterized by the unity of Father and Son, and this recurs in the notion of the Paraclete. Thus does Jesus entreat the Father to send the Paraclete (14:16). Christ sends the Paraclete from the Father; at the same time, this Paraclete is the Spirit that has proceeded from the Father (15:26). Finally, the unity of Father and Son explains why the Paraclete takes from that which belongs to Christ (16:14). The Paraclete is the Spirit who proceeds both from the Father and from the Son. This corresponds to the pointed unity of Father and Son, which characterizes the Christology of the rest of the Gospel.

This close relationship with the Christ also manifests itself in the fact that the Paraclete places the Christ completely at the center. He is identified as the Spirit of truth (15:26; 16:13), of that truth that Christ himself is (1:17). The Spirit too is sent (14:26) like the Christ; just as the latter came, so also comes the Spirit (16:13). He will maintain the Christ in remembrance among the disciples (14:26). It is also said that the Paraclete will bear witness to the Christ (15:26); he will bring to all the world's attention that which is the truth of the Christ. That the Paraclete will teach nothing other than the Christ is shown by the summary statement that the Paraclete will glorify the Christ (16:14). In this sense the Paraclete fulfills a hermeneutical function.[31] Just as it is the task of Christology to bear witness to

the δόξα—the significance, the dignity of the one who became a human being—
so also is it the task of the Spirit everlastingly to express precisely this dignity.

One might say that the point of the Christology of incarnation is that it perceives Jesus Christ as the reality of deliverance in the world. Christology ensures
that the Christ never degenerates into mere information. In this regard, too, the
Paraclete constitutes a repetition of the christological point, since he represents,
as it were, the activity of the Christ after his death. The Christ remains active
among the disciples even after his death inasmuch as the "other" Paraclete teaches
the disciples all things (14:26). This teaching (διδάσκειν) is already a comprehensive process of education in the Septuagint, a process only marginally related
to our own theoretical understanding of teaching. Teaching actually means to direct someone's attention to what is essential, to introduce that person to the truths
of life.[32] This introduction to the truths of life, the teaching of the disciples, takes
place through the Paraclete in that he will recall to the disciples everything Jesus
said to them (14:26). The task of the Paraclete is not, however, merely to remind
them of how things were. The Paraclete is not some worldly protocolist. The nature of this recollection, prompted by the Paraclete, can be discerned in the
Gospel of John itself. The Gospel decisively describes—according to its own
self-understanding—the earthly reality of Jesus of Nazareth, but at the same time
it envisions a δόξα ("glory") in the one who became flesh, a dignity comparable
to that particular dignity that an only-begotten son has with his father. One might
say, therefore, that the Paraclete is the form that the Easter recollection of the human being Jesus assumes. That this recollection takes on the form of the efficacious Spirit suggests that the recollection of Christ is not the work of the disciples
but is, as it were, the work of the substance or content of the recollection in them.
This offers a possibility for conceiving anew the efficacious presence of Christ, a
presence secured in Christology, as the efficacious presence of the Spirit at work
in the recollection of Christ. In both cases the Christ is conceived as reality. Precisely this is the fulcral point of Christology.

The Paraclete is admittedly at work, not only among the disciples, but in the
world as well. He will convict the world—which cannot accept him—in matters
of sin, righteousness, and judgment (16:8–11). One might understand this conviction forensically: When the Paraclete comes, he will sit in judgment over the
world by pronouncing sentence upon the condition of the world. This would then
constitute a supplemental final judgment, one that according to John has actually
already taken place with the coming of the Christ (see 3:17–18). In this case, however, the Paraclete enters into a certain contradiction with the Johannine conception of the time of Jesus as the eschatological moment, unless one understands
him strictly as the evocation or making present of that particular eschatological
moment of crisis. One might understand this conviction of the world in a purely
accusatory sense: the Paraclete is transformed from an intercessor into an accuser
of the world by proving to the world itself that it is in the wrong. Yet this under-

standing, too, seems inappropriate. John and his school do not conceive deliverance within the horizon of indictment. Hence, one might understand this conviction of the world in what might be called an existential sense (existential not in the sense of existentialist philosophy, but rather, in the sense of the existence and activity of the Paraclete). Proof of the untruth of the world exhibits the character of an existential confrontation with the truth. Existentially, the Paraclete represents what is true; he causes what is true to come to the world, and only in this form does he convict that world of untruth. One might also say that the Paraclete makes it possible for the world to encounter what is true, and only in this way does it prompt the world to recognize its own untruth.

If one were to characterize the Paraclete in a single sentence, one might say that he is the advocate of Christ among human beings.[33] The Paraclete is the intercessor who recalls the significance of the Christ, the intercessor who prompts human beings to come to a realization of just what they encountered in Christ. The exact counterpart to this notion is found in 1 John 2:1–2, where the Paraclete functions as the advocate for human beings before God. This is a logical development. To the same extent that Christ represented God among human beings, the Paraclete (in the Gospel) represents the departed Christ among human beings. To the same extent that this Christ was the incarnation of the turning of divine love toward human beings, the Paraclete (in 1 John) now becomes in his own turn an intercessor for human beings before God. The turning of that love finds its fulfillment where the divine Spirit itself puts in a good word for human beings before God.

CHRISTOLOGICAL THEOLOGY (1 JOHN)

First John represents the fourth stage in the process of the development of Johannine Christology. Here a noteworthy shift in the direction of theology takes place.[34] Whereas in the Gospel it is clearly Christ who is the light of the world, this statement is now made again—but this time it refers to God, and it is made at a prominent juncture, immediately after the letter's prologue: "This is the message we have heard from him and proclaim to you, that God is light and in him is no darkness at all" (1:5). Of course, this fundamental theological thesis represents something akin to religious common sense. It is a universal truth, like the truths of wisdom taken up in the prologue to the Gospel. What is interesting here, however, is its grounding. This message was heard from Christ. The statement that God is light has its foundation in that which Jesus embodied. This theological statement is based on the christological insight that Jesus Christ is the embodiment of light.[35] The connection with Christ does not consist in the fact that the statement, "God is light," might have been heard in one of Jesus' own statements. Rather, the Johannine school itself perceived its own experience with the Christ as an experience of light, and *that* gives them the right to trace this theological statement back to Christ.[36] It is qualified christologically in the sense that it now brings to pointed theological expression the fundamental experience that occurs with Christ. Christology does not stand for information about God; it stands, rather, for an experience with the Logos,[37] an experience that in its own turn enables one to make statements about God from within one's own experience. The theological statement of 1 John merely draws the logical conclusion from the christological point of departure in the Gospel. If Jesus Christ stands in God's stead, if he embodies God's reality in the world, then precisely his efficacious presence also reveals something about God.[38] The efficacious presence of the Christ as light consisted in the fact that he placed human beings in the light and gave them the light of life. Taking this efficacious presence as its point of departure, 1 John now asserts that the reality of God is light.

In a unique way, the Christology of the Gospel made Jesus unequivocal. That is, it conceptualized his activity and ministry as creating and delivering. He embodied not an admixture of grace and disfavor, but only grace. There is in him not an admixture of truth and untruth, but only truth. He brought into the world not light and darkness, but only light. He did not come both to deliver and to condemn; he came, rather, only for deliverance. First John repeats this christological unambiguousness inasmuch as it designates God absolutely as light and expressly holds fast to the assertion that there is no darkness in him at all. God's unambiguous nature emerges through the fact that he is completely perceived in the coming of the Christ. Of course, this unambiguousness does all the more urgently pose the question concerning whence darkness then comes. It comes from wherever it comes, in any case not from God. It comes probably from the ethical and existential opposition to the light: it is dark where one does not allow the light to shine.

Analogous to the statement that God is light, yet another theological statement is made in 1 John: "God is love" (1 John 4:8b). This statement too must be understood as ripe fruit on the tree of christological reflection. The Gospel understands the sending of the Son as an expression of God's love for the world (John 3:16). First John 4:9–10 picks up this idea. God's love was made manifest in the sending of the Son (v. 9). And again, the term "manifest" (ἐφανερώθη) refers not to a mere showing, or some sort of information about love, but rather, to its emergence as an event. It became an event in the sending of the μονογενὴς υἱός, of the only-begotten and to that extent unique Son. It is a sending in which God comes completely and with no reservations. We must understand this statement as the reverse side of incarnation Christology. It was not merely a portion of God that was embodied here, not merely one of his characteristics or actions; rather, the divine fullness itself became completely efficacious as love. And from this event of love—an event that took place in the foreground of the world and that proves itself in the sending of the only-begotten Son—it follows that God must be understood completely and exclusively as love. This unambiguous nature of

God is comparable to the unambiguous nature of the being of light in 1 John 1:5. The *christological* statement, according to which the divine fullness came into the world in the one who became a human being, corresponds to the *theological* statement that this God is now to be understood completely as that which he became in the Christ. The Christology of the incarnation corresponds precisely to this christological theology, whose understanding of God derives completely from the perception of the Christ.

In this connection the christological interest of 1 John also acquires clear contours. The christological arguments in 1 John are concentrated essentially in the assertion that Jesus Christ really did come in the flesh. The earthly reality of the Christ is thereby maintained, because it is a matter of the reference to reality, attached to the claims concerning God. The direction of the argument is the reverse of that taken by the Gospel. Whereas the latter was concerned with understanding the human being Jesus of Nazareth as the Christ, as God in person, it is now a matter of maintaining the divine Christ as a real human being.[39] What is at stake is the dimension of reality of Johannine theology. And a decision is made regarding the dimension of reality of Johannine theology by holding fast to the worldly reality of the one who came.[40]

CONCLUSION

The point of our reflections has been to observe the process of understanding undertaken by Christology over several stages, with the goal of making a contribution to hermeneutics in the canonical context. The Christology of the Johannine writings is of great hermeneutical interest because it combines in a consistent manner the highest majesty of the Son of God with the deepest humanity of Jesus of Nazareth. The pre-Johannine Logos Christology exploits the hermeneutical potential of wisdom theology in order to comprehend the coming of the human being Jesus as a turning of God's love toward the world. The experience of the graciously bestowed Son, which one had with Jesus Christ, was evaluated and acknowledged in its full import by being traced back to the primal Logos. The one who became a human being becomes conceivable as the reality of God in the world, and God is himself no longer conceivable apart from this turning of his love toward that world. The Gospel reflects further on this pre-Johannine Logos Christology, especially with regard to the concrete form assumed by the Logos that became a human being. He not only gives grace and truth; he *is* grace and truth. The I-Am sayings combine the heavenly truth of the Logos with the earthly reality of Jesus, and they identify Jesus himself as the gift bestowed in the miracles of the *semeia* narratives. The Paraclete represents yet a further stage of reflection. This figure allows us to conceive at the same time the temporality of the Incarnate and his eternal presence in the world. The Paraclete is the fruit of the fact that Jesus' time was finite. He is the advocate of Christ (and, to that extent,

of the God who sent him) among human beings, inasmuch as he maintains the recollection of the δόξα of Jesus Christ; he is the creative power of the substance that
calls itself into recollection. The christological theology of 1 John draws the logical conclusion within the process of reflection undertaken by Johannine Christology. Predications about Christ (such as light and love) are now, as it were, given
back to God himself. With regard to hermeneutics in the canonical context, this
means that the process can be perceived as a whole. If the position of 1 John were
taken on its own, its theology might be problematic. To the extent, however, that
the reality of God was embodied undiminished in the Logos, it is only logical that
one perceive this reality, in its own turn, completely christologically. The Christology of the incarnation corresponds precisely to a christological theology whose
understanding of God derives completely from the perception of the Christ.

NOTES

1. D. Moody Smith correctly observes that "the christological content and emphasis" is "dominant in the Gospel of John" (*Johannine Christianity: Essays on its
Setting, Sources, and Theology* [Columbia, S.C.: University of South Carolina Press,
1984], 178).

2. Most recently this view has been supported by Rudolf Schnackenburg, *Die Person Jesu Christi im Spiegel der vier Evangelien*, HTKNTSup (Freiburg, Basel, and
Vienna: Herder, 1993), 251–54 (ET, *Jesus in the Gospels* [Louisville, Ky.: Westminster, 1995]).

3. Hypotheses have recently resurfaced, according to which the Johannine letters
represent the oldest documents within the Johannine writings (e.g., Udo Schnelle, *Antidocetic Christology in the Gospel of John: An Investigation of the Place of the Fourth
Gospel in the Johannine School* [Minneapolis: Fortress, 1992], 235–36). Such hypotheses, however, create more problems than they solve. Thus, for instance, Schnelle
must interpret the prologue of the Gospel as an antidocetic response to the docetic
Christology of the adversaries in 1 John (this, a criticism of Schnelle's otherwise impressive interpretation of the prologue: ibid., 211–27). The prologue is better understood, however, as a move away from wisdom Christology toward an incarnation
statement, as a step that could later serve as the foundation of docetism rather than as
a response to it. One can doubt that Christ has come in the flesh only when the incarnation statement has already been made.

4. Marianne Meye Thompson (*The Humanity of Jesus in the Fourth Gospel*
[Philadelphia: Fortress, 1988], 121–22) justifiably criticizes the view of "naive docetism," inaugurated by Käsemann. Yet it is no less false to understand the Gospel as
antidocetic (ibid., 122), for in fact it does presuppose that Jesus was a man of flesh and
blood. Rather, its interest is christological: "On this assumption [namely, of the true
humanity of Jesus] it builds its argument that the one who became flesh was indeed
God's Word" (ibid., 122).

5. Smith, *Johannine Christianity*, 175.

6. This is the accomplishment of the prologue over against other, possibly earlier,
drafts, such as the one that specifies the baptism by John as the beginning of the

Gospel. Michael Theobald (*Die Fleischwerdung des Logos: Studien zum Verhältnis des Johannesprologs zum Corpus des Evangeliums und zu 1 Joh*, NTAbh, NF 20 [Münster: Aschendorff, 1988], 477) speaks, in this context, of a "transcending of the question of the *arche* [beginning] of Jesus as the revealer of God out of its historical dimension into that of eternity." It is questionable whether one should speak here of this sort of transcending. In my opinion, the dimension of history is not transcended but, rather, recognized for the first time in its true significance. The origin of that which happened in the concreteness of historical reality resides in the creative origin of the universe.

7. Following Theobald, *Die Fleischwerdung des Logos*, 491: "One the one hand, the Logos is so profoundly bound up with all that has been created that, as the one who became flesh, it belongs *completely* on the side of human beings. *On the other hand, it has always been with God and is of his essence* (θεός), so that it also belongs *completely* on the side of God."

8. Although the assertion is indeed made that there was wisdom before all that is created, it is expressly designated as God's first creation: Prov. 8:22 (in MT as רֵאשִׁית, the first creation of his ways; in LXX as ἀρχή, the beginning of his ways to his works); similarly, Sir. 24:3 ("I came forth from the mouth of the Most High").

9. This is the confession of the "*identity* of Jesus as the revealer of God" (Theobald, *Die Fleischwerdung des Logos*, 493). According to the prologue, "Jesus . . . is not some accidental, contingent 'expression' of God but, rather, his most essential and only word, . . . his self-expression" (ibid., 492). Insofar as one understands all these statements not in the sense of information but, rather, in the sense of the specific form of an event, in the sense of reality, they do express an important christological dimension of the prologue.

10. "In short, the prologue (1:1–18) claims that God can be known only in Jesus Christ" (Thompson, *The Humanity of Jesus in the Fourth Gospel*, 51). This assertion fails to consider that the universal dimension of the Logos (1:1–5, 9–12, based on wisdom theology) is not suspended through the notion of incarnation. One must, rather, reverse this statement: Wherever a person has recognized God, this recognition comes through that particular, experiential reality perfectly embodied in Christ.

11. Theobald addresses this issue (*Die Fleischwerdung des Logos*, 481–83). Even if one assumes a kinship between this notion—one with Gnostic inclinations—and the wisdom theology of Judaism, one must distinguish carefully between the emergence of wisdom out of the mouth of God, on the one hand, and the emergence of the Logos from silence on the other (contra Theobald, ibid., 483).

12. Theobald addresses this issue (*Die Fleischwerdung des Logos*, 486–88).

13. Hence it is inappropriate to assert that "gnostic thinking, though neutralized in the prologue, has nonetheless covertly influenced it" (contra Theobald, *Die Fleischwerdung des Logos*, 486). All of the passages adduced by Theobald (ibid.: John 1:1–2, 5, 18) can be explained effortlessly from the perspective of Hellenistic-Jewish wisdom theology.

14. The incarnation statement and the statement concerning the δόξα ("glory") of the only-begotten son (in v. 14) are grounded (in v. 16) in the experience of having received grace and truth from him in abundance.

15. Thompson justifiably argues that the prologue presupposes the humanity of Jesus (*The Humanity of Jesus in the Fourth Gospel*, 51–52). Its whole thrust is the statement that in this concrete humanity God himself has become reality.

16. Jesus' humanity is absolutely fundamental for the Gospel (thus, Thompson, *The Humanity of Jesus in the Fourth Gospel,* esp. 117–22).

17. Thus, Schnackenburg, *Die Person Jesu Christi im Spiegel der vier Evangelien,* 277–315.

18. Similarly, Boy Hinrichs, *"Ich bin": Die Konsistenz des Johannes-Evangeliums in der Konzentration auf das Wort Jesu,* SBS 133 (Stuttgart: Katholisches Bibelwerk, 1988), 95: "The evangelist succeeds in adequately . . . grounding and mediating theology as Christology" by concentrating on the Word (as it comes to expression in the I-am sayings).

19. Smith, *Johannine Christianity,* 177; see also 179.

20. Schnelle, *Antidocetic Christology in the Gospel of John,* 164.

21. Following Schnelle, ibid.: "It [the miracle] is not only an indication of the *doxa,* but an expression of the *doxa* itself. Certainly, Jesus' *doxa* is more than his miracle working, but at the same time, the *doxa* is fully present in each miracle."

22. Thompson, *The Humanity of Jesus in the Fourth Gospel,* 120.

23. Following Schnelle (*Antidocetic Christology in the Gospel of John,* 168), who refers to the important motif of the unity of Father and Son in the Johannine interpretation of the *semeia* narratives.

24. "At the same time the miracles with their materiality, which is bound up with the earthly and subject to verification in space and time, point to Jesus' humanity" (Schnelle, *Antidocetic Christology in the Gospel of John,* 166).

25. One should bear in mind that the Gospel intends to distinguish these events from mere mighty deeds; it is no accident that they are called σημεῖα ("signs") and not δυνάμεις ("mighty works"; following Thompson, *The Humanity of Jesus in the Fourth Gospel,* 119). In this context it is significant that these events are not merely arbitrary signs whose concrete form has nothing to do with their semantic function (like "the signal," τὸ σύσσημον, of Mark 14:44: the kiss of Judas, a sign that means something quite different from that which it portrays).

26. Contra Schnelle, who ascribes an "antidocetic funtion" to the "powerful deeds of the λόγος ἔνσαρκος ["enfleshed Logos"]" (*Antidocetic Christology in the Gospel of John,* 175). A more persuasive view is the analysis of Thompson, which shows that the Gospel of John is to be interpreted neither docetically nor antidocetically (*The Humanity of Jesus in the Fourth Gospel,* 121–22.).

27. Fundamental significance attaches not only to the "that" of the *semeia,* but also to the fact that Jesus performed precisely these and no other signs (following Thompson, *The Humanity of Jesus in the Fourth Gospel,* 119–20).

28. Following Jürgen Becker, *Das Evangelium nach Johannes: Kapitel 11–21,* ÖTK 4, 3d ed. (Gütersloh: Mohn, 1991), 2.564.

29. Thus, Becker, ibid., 563–68.

30. Following Smith, *Johannine Christianity,* 185: "The Spirit or Paraclete as the mode of Jesus' abiding with his disciples seems to be a felt reality, a presence regarded as given rather than imagined."

31. William Loader views this as the "greater event," mentioned in the farewell discourses (*The Christology of the Fourth Gospel: Structure and Issues,* BBET 23, 2d ed. [Frankfurt and New York: Lang, 1992], 125–26): "The greater event has accordingly a hermeneutical function." Concerning this hermeneutical function, see also Schnelle, *Antidocetic Christology in the Gospel of John,* 231: "The Paraclete actualizes and makes present the witness of the Johannine tradition to Jesus Christ."

32. See Karl Heinrich Rengstorf, "διδάσκω, κ. τ. λ.," *TDNT* 2 (1964): 135–65, esp. 137.

33. So also Becker, *Das Evangelium nach Johannes,* 2.472: "But the Spirit-Para-clete is not the intercessor before God, like the Exalted in 1 John 2:1 (and, in substance, also John 14:14), but is understood above all as the representative among the disciples of him who is now exalted."

34. See also R. Alan Culpepper, *1 John, 2 John, 3 John,* Knox Preaching Guides (Atlanta: John Knox, 1985), 15: "Whereas Christology dominates the Gospel of John, 1 John is theocentric: it explores the nature of God's character." One must be sure to distinguish, however, between a theocentrism untouched by Christology (on the one hand) and a theocentrism that, as it were, brings in the harvest of christological reflection (on the other). We are dealing with the latter type in 1 John.

35. Hans-Josef Klauck speaks of the "christological derivation" of this insight (*Der erste Johannesbrief,* EKKNT 23/1 [Zurich and Neukirchen-Vluyn: Benziger/ Neukirchener, 1991], 1.83).

36. "Jesus lived in an exemplary fashion the self-disclosure of God as light; he makes it accessible to experience; and, above all, he makes it accessible to reenactment" (Klauck, *Der erste Johannesbrief,* 1.83). One would have to ask, however, whether this statement is not composed with too much emphasis on theoretical information ("to live in an exemplary fashion"; "to make accessible to reenactment").

37. The fulcral point is this accessibility to experience, the reality of the divine light in Christ; so also Klaus Wengst, *Der erste, zweite und dritte Brief des Johannes,* ÖTK 16 (Gütersloh: Mohn, 1978), 50, who emphasizes the element of the becoming of an event. It is unclear to me, however, why this statement might not be reversed (as Wengst postulates [ibid., 51]).

38. Following Gerd Schunack, *Die Briefe des Johannes,* ZBK, NT 17 (Zurich: Theologischer Verlag, 1982), 24: "What in the Gospel of John is a (christological) predicate of the revealer, who in concurrence with the Father says, 'I am the light of the world' (8:12), is now similarly transferred and referred to God, such that in its encounter with the revealer faith has acquired insight into the essence, or at least the reality, of God." By "reality" one may—also in Schunack's sense—understand "efficacious presence."

39. Following Thompson, *The Humanity of Jesus in the Fourth Gospel,* 122: "The Gospel declares that in the flesh of Jesus *God* is revealed; the Epistle, that God is revealed in the *flesh* of Jesus."

40. Following Martin Hengel, *The Johannine Question* (London and Philadelphia: SCM/Trinity Press International, 1990), 57–63. The Gnostic thesis that Christ did not come in the flesh turns the human being Jesus into a *quantité négligeable,* thereby annulling the notion of incarnation (esp. 59). See further idem, *Die Johanneische Frage,* WUNT 67 (Tübingen: Mohr [Siebeck], 1993), 170–85, esp. 178.

20

Inclined to God: The Quest for Eternal Life— Bultmannian Hermeneutics and the Theology of the Fourth Gospel

My first encounter with Moody Smith was through the publication of his *The Composition and Order of the Fourth Gospel: Bultmann's Literary Theory* in 1965.[1] At the time I was in the early stages of a Ph.D. thesis on "The Idea of Knowledge in the Gospel and Epistles of John." His work provided an invaluable analysis and critique of Bultmann's literary and source theory. In the preface to his work Moody Smith wrote, "The endeavor to show that Bultmann's literary and source criticism is simply a means of rationalizing and supporting his own theological views was abandoned at an early stage as both tendentious and unprofitable."[2] Bultmann may well have been wrong in aspects of his interpretation of John. The reason for this, however, is not that he was driven to find his own theology in John or, for that matter, in any specific document of the New Testament. He was not embarrassed to admit that Paul had attempted to establish the physical resurrection of Jesus on the basis of a series of "eyewitness testimonies."[3] His conclusion was that at this point, Paul had fallen away from the truth of the gospel.[4]

For the most part it is doubtful that anything is added to Bultmann's theology by his source and literary theory. He has not forced his source and literary theory on John to support his own theology. (Indeed, many scholars have adopted aspects of his source and literary theory without sharing his theological stance.) Perhaps his view of the role of the ecclesiastical redactor is an exception. Here he has identified certain tensions in the Fourth Gospel, attributing them to a later redactor. But the redactor's supposed sacramental views are probably the result of a misreading of some parts of the Gospel in the light of later developments. While the eschatological tension in the Gospel is accurately observed by Bultmann, there is no contradiction of the views of the evangelist at this point. The evangelist was preoccupied with the present fulfillment brought about by the coming of Jesus, but Bultmann wrongly thought that the hope of a future fulfillment was irreconcilable with this view, attributing it to the ecclesiastical redactor. The future fulfillment is unavoidable for those aware, as the evangelist obviously was, of the problem of death that faced believers.

What is important for Bultmann's theology is his view that the evangelist was combating Gnostic influence and a view of signs that treated them as proof upon which to base faith. Bultmann's signs-source theory leads to a more negative view of signs than is justifiable on the basis of the evangelist's decision to *use* the signs in his Gospel. If the evangelist himself was responsible for the portrayal of the works of Jesus as signs, then a positive evaluation of the signs is consistent with the prominence of the signs in the Gospel. In fact, Bultmann's view of signs is not as negative as is sometimes supposed.[5] But even this question is quite peripheral to Bultmann's hermeneutic.

More important for his hermeneutic is his view that, to understand the theology of the Gospel, it is necessary to discern the evangelist's understanding of reality with its central and controlling concepts.[6] What is in view in this study is a focus on Bultmann's hermeneutic and its importance for the theology of the Gospel. This differs from an evaluation of Bultmann's exposition of the theology of John, although the two tasks are not unrelated.

The Gnostic influence in the Gospel is understood in terms of a view of authentic life that, while in itself being a mythical expression, provided the evangelist with the preunderstanding (*Vorverständnis*) upon which he built and which made his own views intelligible. Here there is need to take account of Bultmann's existentialist hermeneutic and the justification of it in relation to the Fourth Gospel. The existentialist interpretation is an aspect of Bultmann's general, *critical* hermeneutic. It finds particular application within the Gospel where it is, according to Bultmann, an aspect of the evangelist's theological outlook. Consequently, Bultmann argues that in this case the hermeneutic is not used against the uncritical outlook of the evangelist but in the service of elucidating the evangelist's critical interpretation of the tradition at his disposal. In particular, the evangelist has historicized the mythical understanding of existence in the Gnostic discourse-source, which is used to provide the preunderstanding for his own understanding of authentic existence.[7] Without preunderstanding there would be no understanding.

THE *WELTANSCHAUUNG*[8] OF THE PROLOGUE

All writings give expression to an understanding of reality. More often than not, this understanding is implicit rather than explicit. When it is implicit, there is greater danger that the reader will interpret what is read from the perspective of his own worldview, with its controlling concepts, rather than from the implied worldview of the author.[9] In a few instances authors actually make their worldviews explicit. This is the case in the Fourth Gospel.

Whether the prologue (John 1:1–18) is a late addition to the Gospel, a completely original composition of the evangelist, or based on an earlier source, we can scarcely doubt that the evangelist himself placed it at the beginning as an appropriate introduction to the Gospel. What this introduction does is signal to the reader the kind of world in which the following story takes place. In some ways the themes that emerge here are more the presuppositions of the story and of the evangelist's theology than the theology itself, though this distinction is something of an oversimplification.

The prologue provides the worldview within which the story, told by the Gospel, *works*. The opening, with its focus on the Logos, gives expression to the theme of revelation.[10] Even though this use of the Logos is restricted to the prologue, it signifies the theme of revelation that dominates the rest of the Gospel, where it is expressed in other terms. In the prologue the motif of revelation is expressed in relation to creation. All things, without exception, were created by the Logos. The prologue is emphatic on this point by repetition and restatement of the motif in positive and negative terms. The world and all that is in it are the creation of the Logos and are consistent with the Logos.[11]

DUALISM

Indeed, the paradox of evil in a good creation is heightened in the Johannine context, where a world made for and by the revealing activity of God rejects that revelation. That heightened paradox is further expressed in terms of the darkness of the world, in which the light of the eternal Logos shines. Thus, the worldview is one involving the presence and power of a prevailing darkness in a world created for and by the power of the light of the eternal Logos. The prologue does not portray a static worldview, either of the way things are or of the way they should be.[12] Rather, it is the view of a world in process.

The revelation takes place in a world created for revelation. Paradoxically, the world is dominated by the darkness, which not only rejects the light but is diametrically opposed to it (1:5; 3:19–21). The story of the Gospel thus takes place in a world torn by the conflict between the light and the darkness, the revelation of God and the forces opposed to that revelation. That worldview, which can be understood in terms of an apocalyptic ideology, forms the framework of the Johannine story. For this reason Bultmann made dualism an essential aspect of the Johannine theology.[13] Later attempts to deal with Johannine theology have rejected the priority given to dualism by Bultmann in favor of a christological focus. Here we might question whether this dualism is a primary element of Johannine theology or, rather, the perception of reality within which the idiom of Johannine theology is to be understood.[14]

THE SIGNS

Against this background the signs are to be understood as revealing expressions of the material creation.[15] Indeed, they can be seen as precursors of the completion of creation. Whereas Genesis gives the impression of a creation completed in seven days, with the completion of each stage declared to be good by God, John sees the creation as still in the process of attaining completion (John 5:17).

The first sign at Cana involved the creative act of turning water into wine (John 2:9), and the healing at the sheepgate pool of Bethzatha made a man "*whole*" (ὑγιής, 5:6, 9, 11, 14, 15; 7:23),[16] as he was *intended to be in creation*. The fact that Jesus did this on the Sabbath, the day that celebrated the completion of God's creative work, was a challenge to the view of the completed creation. According to the rabbis, the creation needed only to be preserved, a work that they allowed was constantly necessary for God, even on the Sabbath. According to Jesus, the creation also needed to be completed, and this was the point of his challenge in 5:17.[17]

The ongoing, creative work of Jesus is again emphasized after the second Sabbath sign (John 9), which picks up the conflict from John 5. But the aggressive conflict in John 9 was concentrated on the once blind man, returning only to focus violent action on Jesus in John 10:31–39. In response to a renewed attempt to kill Jesus, which is a resumption of 8:59 (see also 5:18; 7:1, 25; 8:37, 40), Jesus inquired of the Jews for which of his "good works" (ἔργα καλά) they were seeking to kill him (10:32). Throughout John 9 the man who had been healed of blindness concentrated on the nature of the work Jesus had performed, insisting that it was the work of a man from God.[18] Jesus appealed to his works as "*good* works," the evaluation that God proclaimed at the conclusion of each stage or day of the creation, according to Genesis 1. In this way John has portrayed Jesus as the one who brings the creation successfully to its completion, and the signs are precursors of that completion.

To summarize, the prologue presents us with a dynamic view of creation. All is not *complete* or as it should be. Although all things, without exception, are the creation of the Logos, the prologue reports the rejection of the Logos by the world. That rejection is reported in a context that highlights the paradoxical nature of the rejection.

The world created by the Logos has the potential to bear the Logos, to be an agent of the revelation. Because all things were created by the Logos, they have this potential.[19] The significance of the signs in John is that aspects of the creation, all of which have the potential to speak of God, actually become revealing. This is true only of some aspects of the creation, because the creation is unfinished, in the process of being realized. The signs are those aspects that have become revealing. Yet they are not seen as such by all people, because humanity itself has not attained the fulfillment of God's creative purpose, and the signs themselves have a role to play in transforming human consciousness. The signs proclaim the unfinished creation and point in the direction of its completion. In the ambiguity of the present creation, the signs proclaim the goodness of God and his creative work and participate in making the creation "whole," in bringing it to completion. As communicative actions, the signs invite those who believe, who come to the light, to share in the works of God (John 3:21).

While Bultmann thought that the evangelist was critical of the crude approach to signs in his source, he argued that the evangelist's interpretation involved an interaction of word and sign in communicative action. Thus "the concepts of σημεῖα ["signs"] and ῥήματα (λόγοι) ["words"] both qualify each other: σημεῖον ["sign"] is not a mere demonstration, but a spoken directive, a symbol; ῥῆμα ["word"] is not teaching in the sense of the communication of a set of ideas, but is the occurrence of the Word, the event of the address."[20] Further, "the concepts of σημεῖα and ῥήματα (λόγοι) flow together: The σημεῖα are deeds that speak, and their meaning is developed in the discourses; moreover, the ῥήματα are not human words but words of the revelation, full of divine and miraculous power—they are indeed miraculous works."[21] And "[the evangelist] has on the one hand made plain the meaning of the σημεῖα as deeds that speak, and on the other hand represented the words of Jesus as divinely effected event, as ῥήματα ζωῆς ["words of life"]."[22]

EXISTENTIALIST INTERPRETATION
AND THE UNDERSTANDING OF EXISTENCE

This worldview has as its central and controlling concept that of human *existence (Existenz)*,[23] for which the philosophy of existence[24] provides adequate categories. While Bultmann argues that an understanding of existence is manifest in all writings, especially historical writings, this is the explicit theme of the biblical writings and the key to the interpretation of them.[25] But what understanding of existence is to be found there, and how does this relate to his existentialist understanding? First, in talking of *existence,* Bultmann asserts something uniquely human. It is that freedom with which to choose what from the past will be valued and what choices now shape the present. In keeping with the view of the creation in process is an understanding of the human reality as possibility (*Möglichkeit*); that is to say, *existence* is potentiality to be. Each person himself or herself chooses, in concrete decisions, whatever he or she might be.[26] In those choices potentiality is either realized or lost, and this is understood in terms of the realization of, or the failure to realize, authentic existence. For Bultmann, this is the point of the Johannine dualism: to show that human decision is always between good and evil, authenticity and inauthenticity. This is not a state of being but something chosen anew in each decision.

INCLINED TO GOD

We are to understand that the world, created by God by his Logos, is inclined to God, directed towards God. Bultmann expressed this understanding in words from Augustine[27] that he quoted frequently: "O God, you have made us for yourself [*ad te*], and our heart is restless [*et cor nostrum inquietum est*] until it finds its rest in you."[28]

As written by Augustine, this might be thought of as a statement about the "elect," because the "us"—we who have been created to be inclined to God (*ad te*)—is further elaborated only in terms of "our heart."[29] But for Augustine this statement is to be understood as an anthropological truth. For him, then, the restless heart was a pervasive phenomenon and one that he knew from his own experience. At the same time this means that the restlessness of the heart, understood as a psychological phenomenon and not as a theoretical presupposition, is taken with fundamental seriousness. It is to be understood as an expression of the fact that God has made us for himself (*ad te*), that is, directed towards himself.[30] Because of this direction or inclination, alternative orientations are unsatisfactory, not only in fact but also psychologically. The latter is the point of the reference to the restless heart.[31] This implies that self-awareness is oriented to God and finds its true meaning only in that relationship.[32] Those who orient their lives in other ways find no rest. The restlessness of heart is expressed in unending striving.

The existential inclination to God is a theme to which Bultmann returned time after time. He certainly understood this as an anthropological affirmation. Thus, he interpreted the saying as follows:

> In the same way *the comprehension of records about events as the action of God* presupposes a prior understanding of what may in my case be termed the action of God—let us say, as distinct from man's action, or from natural events. And if this is countered by saying that neither can man know who God is before his manifestation, nor consequently, what God's action may be, then we have to reply that *man may very well be aware who God is, namely, in the inquiry about him.* If his existence were not motivated (whether consciously or *unawares*) by the inquiry about God in the sense of the Augustinian "*Tu nos fecisti ad Te, et cor nostrum inquietum est, donec requiescat in Te,*" then neither would we know God as God in any manifestation of him. In human existence an *existentiell* knowledge about God is alive in the form of the inquiry about "happiness," "salvation," the meaning of the world and of history; and in the inquiry into the real nature of each person's particular "being." If the right to designate such inquiries as the inquiry about God can be attained only from belief in the manifestation of God, the phenomenon as such is the relation of the matter to the manifestation.[33]

The context of this exposition is Bultmann's assertion that "A presupposition for comprehension . . . is a prior understanding of the subject." Here his discussion has much in common with that of Augustine, when dealing with the subject of "happiness" in relation to "memory."[34]

> How then am I to seek you, Lord? When I seek you, my God, my quest is for the happy life. . . . Is not the happy life that which all desire, which indeed no one fails to desire? . . . My question is whether the happy life

is in the memory. For we would not love it if we did not know what it is.
. . . Therefore, it is known to everyone. If they could be asked if they want
to be happy, without hesitation they would answer with one voice that
they so wish. . . . That is the authentic happy life, to set one's joy on you,
grounded in you and caused by you. That is the real thing, and there is no
other. Those who think that the happy life is found elsewhere, pursue another joy and not the true one. Nevertheless, their will remains drawn towards some image of the true joy (*Confessions* 10.20.29; 10.22.32).

This preunderstanding (*Vorverständnis*) is elsewhere explained by Bultmann
as a "not-knowing knowledge," or a way of raising the question. Here it is the
knowledge involved in the *inquiry* about God, and this inquiry is explicitly said
to be "consciously or *unawares*." While preunderstanding may be a consequence
of previous understanding, what Bultmann here has in mind is the fundamental
"life-relation" of all human beings.[35] Human existence is motivated by the inquiry
about God, "consciously or *unawares*." "In human existence an *existentiell*
knowledge about God is alive . . . ."[36] Here we have an ontological statement, "in
human existence," that is the equivalent of *Dasein*. But what here defines *Dasein*
is a concrete, existential (actual or *ontic*) response to life. What makes appropriate the application of a concrete response to an ontological description is that this
is the universal response of all human beings to life. The unfulfilled nature of human life as "potentiality to be" gives rise to the inquiry about happiness, salvation, the meaning of the world and history, and the real nature of each person's
peculiar being, which, *from the standpoint of faith*, are identified with the inquiry
about God. By indicating *the standpoint of faith*, it is clear that Bultmann's intention is not to inform others of the way they should understand their lives.
Rather, it is the way Bultmann, as a believer, understands them, and in this respect
he reveals his positive evaluation of all quests for God in human life.

Again, in *Jesus Christ and Mythology*, following the same quotation from Augustine, Bultmann wrote:

> Man has a knowledge of God in advance, though not of the revelation of
> God, that is, of His action in Christ. He has a relation to God in his search
> for God, conscious or unconscious. Man's life is moved by the search for
> God because it is always moved, consciously or unconsciously, by the
> question about his own personal existence. The question of God and the
> question of myself are identical.[37]

Bultmann was here responding to the objection to his view that human beings
have a *relation* to God prior to knowledge of the revelation of God in the scriptures. That life-relation is explained in terms of the search for God, which is said
to be identical to the quest for authentic existence. Fundamental to a correct understanding of Bultmann at this point is the recognition that his understanding of

existence is essentially relational. From the standpoint of faith, authentic existence (the question of myself) can only be realized in relation to God because "our heart is restless until it rests in you."

Bultmann's existentialist interpretation involved preunderstanding, described as having "in advance a vital relation to the subject matter of the text," here understood to be the revelation of God in the scriptures. He regarded the rejection of such preunderstanding as misguided.

> For the fact is that I have such a relationship to the question about God, a truth to which St Augustine gave classical expression in the words: "*Tu nos fecisti ad te, et cor nostrum inquietum est, donec requiescat in te.*" Human life is—consciously or unconsciously—impelled by the question about God.[38]

Human life is "impelled by the question about God." With the urgency that human life is driven by the question of its own authenticity, so the urgency of the quest for God is to be understood.

Finally, Bultmann responded to John Macquarrie's objection to his view of the exclusive and absolute claim of the Christian kerygma. In response, Bultmann wrote:

> Now I do not deny that there is an understanding outside of Christian faith as to what God is and what grace is. I am convinced that Augustine's words, "Our heart is restless until it rests in Thee," are true of all men. In all men, explicitly or implicitly, the question concerning God is a living one. The exclusiveness of the kerygma consists in the fact that it provides the answer to this question by offering the right to say "God is my God." From the standpoint of faith, it can of course be said that in all human questions concerning God, God reveals himself.[39]

Here Bultmann addressed the question of knowledge of God outside Christian faith. Clearly, he affirms that there is knowledge of God, universally, in the form of the search for God. But outside of faith, the question of God becomes distorted into an answer, because the unanswered question is disturbing, and only an answer provides the security for which all people long.[40] The revelation in which faith finds its rest offers no such fixed security, but only trust in God in the face of the uncertainty of the future. But is there positive knowledge of God outside the Christian scriptures? Here Bultmann says that "From the standpoint of faith . . . in all human questions concerning God, God reveals himself." This goes beyond the preunderstanding that makes the revelation intelligible. It is an affirmation of revelation within the questioning itself. Thus, because the question of God is alive in human life generally, there is a hint in Bultmann's writing that there is also revelation and genuine knowledge of God beyond the Christian revelation.[41]

The revelation encounters human beings who are already in search for God. In the "I am" sayings, as understood by Bultmann, Jesus presents himself as the one for whom all people are searching.[42] This is both an affirmation of all searches and a rejection of all answers that are not found in him. Those who are driven in their search, whether implicit or explicit, are confronted by the word of the Revealer, "I am he, for whom you seek."[43] The revelation resonates in the lives of those who respond to the contradiction and hear the new word that it speaks as a new possibility for human life.

THE QUEST FOR . . .

The First Word of the "Incarnate" Word

The first word of Jesus[44] in John was spoken to the two disciples of John (the Baptist) who, of their own initiative, *followed* Jesus. He asked them, "What are you *seeking*?" (τί ζητεῖτε; John 1:35–38). The first word of the central character of the story in a book like John suggests an impressive and significant pronouncement. In that word we learn that Jesus encountered those who were already seeking him. This point is made even more emphatically when we compare the Johannine account of the gathering of the first disciples with that of the Synoptics (for instance, Mark 1:16–20).[45] In John we are made aware of a widespread anticipation of the coming of the Messiah by a delegation sent to John (the Baptist). The underlying purpose of the delegation was to discover if he, perchance, might be the Christ or some other figure of eschatological significance (John 1:19–28). Three things of importance emerge in the record of this incident:

1. The activity of John raised the messianic question: Could it be that he might be the Messiah?
2. The Messiah, though he might be present, was hidden away and must be sought out. Hence, the questions are put to John.
3. John indicates that the purpose of his activity was to bear witness to the coming one who was hidden, not known even to him, and through a pre-arranged sign he related his baptizing activity to the revelation of the coming one to Israel (John 1:26, 31–34).

The Concentration of the Motif of "Seeking" in John

The concentration of uses of ζητεῖν ("seeking") in John is impressive. The verb is used 34 times in John, as compared with 14 times in Matthew, 10 times in Mark, 25 times in Luke, 10 times in Acts, and 117 times in the New Testament. In John the most frequent use of the verb signals the theme of *quest:* thus, 1:38; 6:24, 26; 7:11, 34, 36; 8:21; 11:56; 13:33; 18:4, 7, 8; and 20:15. Next are the references to attempts ("seeking") to kill Jesus, which, paradoxically, turn out to be essential to the quest theme. The theme of quest is suggested by this motif, and the prominence of it can hardly be doubted in John.[46]

Not only is seeking Jesus a common motif in the Johannine narrative; it is the subject of Jesus' discourse on three occasions (7:33–34; 8:21; 13:33–36), as well as a point of reference in his dialogue with the crowd (6:26). In the discourses the motif is pointed: It is raised in the first instance to those opponents who had been sent to arrest him and is repeated to the Pharisees, who appear as adversaries. There is a slight variation. In the first instance, the arresting officers are told, "You will search for me, but you will not find me," whereas the Pharisees are told, "You will search for me, but you will die in your sin." In each case *the failure to find* is implied. Here the manner of seeking is wrong, because the aim is to destroy the real source and object of the quest.

In the farewell discourses (13:33–36) similar words concerning seeking were spoken to the disciples, and Jesus explicitly mentioned that he had said the same thing to "the Jews."[47] Yet there is a difference in what is said. In all instances Jesus tells his hearers, "You will search for me." The servants are told, "But you will not find me," and the Pharisees, "You will die in your sin." But the disciples are told, "Where I am going you cannot come." Following Peter's question this view is modified by Jesus, "Where I am going, you cannot *follow* me now; but you will *follow* afterward." Consequently, like the Jews the disciples' quest would not be fulfilled immediately. Unlike the Jews, whose quest was ultimately doomed, the quest of the disciples was to be fulfilled in the future.

The taking up of the motifs of *seeking* and *finding* (or *not finding*) into the discourses of Jesus confirms the importance of the theme in John. The complexity of the theme is signaled by the introduction of the conflict with the Jews, who sought to arrest and to kill Jesus. By repeating to the disciples the words that he spoke to "the Jews," Jesus signaled that the quest of the disciples, paradoxically, would be fulfilled only after he had departed. That departure was effected through the quest to arrest and execute him, and those responsible would die in their sins; but the disciples would, in their turn, follow him, and their quest would be fulfilled.

Quest Motifs: Following, Seeking, Finding

In John 1:29–41 John (the Baptist) identifies Jesus through the prearranged sign and reveals him to two of his own disciples who were evidently, like John, searching for the coming one. In all of this, Jesus is presented in passive terms as the one for whom all people are searching. Those who came inquiring to John were in fact in search of Jesus, who is in due course revealed as the Messiah. John came baptizing in order to reveal Jesus as the Messiah to Israel, and John's two disciples were in search of the Messiah.

When John announced that Jesus was the lamb of God, they immediately *followed* Jesus; and when he saw them *following* him, he asked them, "What are you *seeking*?" (τί ζητεῖτε). They asked him, "Rabbi, where do you *dwell*?"

(ποῦ μένεις). He replied, "Come, and you will see." We are then told that they *came* and *saw* and *remained with* him that day. With this we have an indication of the successful completion of the first cycle. We are made aware of the first as leading on to the second when we are told that Andrew, the brother of Simon Peter, was one of the two who heard John and *followed* Jesus. In this way the second cycle goes on, when we are told that Andrew "first found his brother Simon and said to him, 'We have *found* [εὑρήκαμεν] the Messiah' (which is translated, 'the Christ')."[48]

In these episodes an important sequence of motifs is established: *following, seeking, finding*. In addition, the episodes reveal the anatomy of a quest story. The same sequence of motifs appears in the quest story of John 6, where we are told that a great crowd *followed* Jesus, because they saw the signs he performed on the sick. Later, when Jesus had recrossed the lake, the crowd came to Capernaum *seeking* Jesus (ζητοῦντες 'Ιησοῦν) and *finding* him (εὑρόντες αὐτόν) beyond the sea where Jesus told them, "You *are looking* for me [ζητεῖτέ με], not because you saw signs, but because you ate your fill of the loaves."

Quest, Not Call (John 1:19–51)

J. Louis Martyn argued that the tradition used by the evangelist contained a series of episodes moving from traditional expectation to discovered fulfillment and presenting a somewhat passive Jesus.[49] Against this view are the following considerations:

1. The evidence of the "call stories" of the Synoptic tradition. The evangelist is more likely to have modified Synoptic-like tradition than (as Martyn argues) to have retained tradition with which he was uncomfortable. If the evangelist modified one episode into a "call story" for this reason, why did he allow the theme of discovered fulfillment to stand in the majority of the episodes? More likely is the view that the evangelist transformed "call stories" into quest episodes. He did this, not because of discomfort with "call stories," but in order to develop the quest theme.

2. The scope and importance of the quest theme is not restricted to the episodes that deal with the gathering of the disciples. Evidence of the theme is to be found in the spread of the quest motifs (*following, seeking, finding*) throughout the Gospel and especially in the use of ζητεῖν,[50] a motif that Jesus made the subject of his own discourses.

3. The evidence for the importance of quest is not restricted to these motifs, as some critics have concluded.[51] Indeed, more important is the evidence of the formal quest story in the *chreiai* (see below). The concentration of quest stories in John was clearly the work of the evangelist, confirming that the quest themes in the narrative of the gathering of the disciples go back to him and not to an unknown source.

The Quest Stories

The analysis of the anatomy of the quest story is the consequence of the study of the *chreiai* (didactic anecdotes) in Greco-Roman rhetoric and the application of that analysis to the study of the Synoptic Gospels.[52] My own work has applied this analysis to the Fourth Gospel. Initially, I was concerned with socio-rhetorical issues, and only in the latter stages of my work did I become aware of the importance of this investigation for Bultmann's hermeneutical studies and his interpretation of John. His *formgeschichtlich* work of 1921, *Die Geschichte der synoptischen Tradition,* remains the foundation for any work on the *chreiai* in the Synoptic Gospels.

The anatomy of the quest story can be set out briefly as follows:[53]

1. The quester makes an implied or explicit request.
2. The quest dominates the story, and the quester is not simply a foil for Jesus.
3. The quester seeks something crucial for human well-being, and in John something important at a physical level can become important for well-being at a spiritual level.
4. There is an objection or difficulty to be overcome, and this may redefine the direction of the quest.
5. The pronouncement of Jesus (a word or an action) holds the key to the resolution of the quest.
6. The outcome of the quest is of crucial interest and must be indicated in the quest story.

The Two Signs at Cana

The two best examples of concise and discrete quest stories are the two Cana stories of John 2:1–11 and 4:46–54, which are miracle stories and, as such, form the subcategory of *miracle-quest stories.*[54] In many ways they are typical miracle stories:[55]

1. The circumstances are noted. There was no wine, and the boy was at the point of death.
2. The means of overcoming the wine shortage and of healing the child are specified. Jesus' instruction to the servants (2:7–8) and his life-giving word, "Go, your son lives!" (4:50), are portrayed as the instruments of dealing with the problem and the healing.
3. The evidences of the wine miracle and the healing are given in some detail, and there is a stress on the belief that results from the miracles.[56]

Yet these are not straightforward miracle stories. This is noted by Francis J. Moloney,[57] who (following Bultmann) sets out the shape of the typical miracle

story and his own analysis of the two Cana stories in John. The typical miracle
story is set out as follows:

1. The problem is stated;
2. A request made;[58]
3. The manner of the miracle is described;
4. A successful outcome is announced;
5. A response of wonder is described.

Moloney also gives a five-point structure for the two Johannine stories:

1. Problem (2:3; 4:46);
2. Request (2:3; 4:47);
3. Rebuke (2:4; 4:48);
4. Reaction (2:5; 4:50);
5. Consequences (2:6–11; 4:51–53).

In particular, what distinguishes the stories in John from the "normal" pattern of
a miracle story is the *rebuke* of Jesus. This constitutes the objection that, along
with the request, is essential to the structure of the quest story.

The first sign at Cana of Galilee (2:1–11) has all the marks of a miracle-quest
story.

1. The mother of Jesus, the quester in this story, came to Jesus with the statement, "They have no wine." This is no idle gossip but clearly constitutes an implied request. That Jesus is expected to act is shown by his mother's instructions
to the servants.

2. The quest for more wine holds the story together from beginning to end.

3. The quester is important in her own right, not merely as a foil to Jesus, and
her story resurfaces in a later scene (19:25–27).

4. The objection to the quest is expressed in Jesus' response:

   a. He addresses his mother as "Woman," which, while not abrupt or
       rude in itself (see 4:21), is an extraordinary form of address of a
       son to his mother. This tone is reinforced by the remainder of
       Jesus' words to his mother:
   b. "What is there between us?" that is, "What concern is that to you
       and to me?" (τί ἐμοὶ καὶ σοί);
   c. "My hour has not yet come" (οὔπω ἥκει ἡ ὥρα μου; compare ὁ
       καιρὸς ὁ ἐμὸς οὔπω πάρεστιν, John 7:6).

All of this appears to be a definitive, if bewildering, refusal to act. Certainly the
response constitutes an objection, a problem to be overcome if the quest is to suc-

ceed. A similarly bewildering objection is made to the official in the second Cana sign (4:48), and a puzzling objection of a different order is given to the brothers' request in 7:6–8.[59] What unites these sayings is that they constitute objections to the various quests described. One consequence of this reading is that a less negative view of the sayings emerges, for they are to be seen as obstacles to be overcome, and in all cases Jesus actually complies with the request that he seems to reject.

5. But does the quest for wine qualify as a quest for something important for human well-being? At this level the story has constituted a problem, because Jesus appears to be called on to deal with something trivial and hardly important for human well-being. This assessment might fail to grasp the significance of the wedding banquet in the Jewish culture of the time. There is also a symbolic contrast between the old wine of Judaism and the new wine of the kingdom. The sign provides the first in a sequence of contrasts that continue with old and new Temples (2:13–22), and old and new birth (3:1–15). Further, the provision of the wine, in true Johannine style, is explicitly made to point beyond itself, to manifest the glory of Jesus.

6. The pronouncement of Jesus holds the key to the resolution of the quest. In the case of John 2:1–11, the solution is not in his word to his mother, which only expresses the obstacle to success. This was overcome by the mother of Jesus, who persisted in spite of rebuke and told the servants to obey the instructions of Jesus. Jesus then told the servants to fill the water pots, to draw from them, and to take what they had drawn to the chief steward (ἀρχιτρίκλινος; 2:7–8).

7. The success of the quest is attested by the chief steward, who, as an independent witness that is ignorant of the way the wine has been provided, confirms the provision of *good* wine.

8. The interpretation of the miracle goes beyond the provision of wine, because the event is seen as a sign in which the glory of Jesus is revealed with the consequent belief of the disciples. In this instance the memorable saying is provided in the commentary by the evangelist, which did not belong to the traditional story (whose climax is found in v. 10).[60] Verse 11 reveals the evangelist's interest in the progress of the disciples. No account is taken of the response of the mother of Jesus to the sign, even though she is portrayed as a successful quester. At the crucifixion, Jesus again refers to her as "Woman." The repetition of this form of address in 19:26 constitutes a *resumption* of the question of the relation of Mary to Jesus. In both places she is called, not by her name, but "the mother of Jesus." In 2:3 that relationship is specifically put in question. In 19:26–27 she is portrayed, along with the Beloved Disciple, as an ideal disciple. In this way we are left in no doubt of her ultimate response to Jesus. The question of her relationship to Jesus is also now settled by Jesus, who declares the Beloved Disciple to be her son and her to be his mother.

The second sign at Cana (4:46–54) also has all the marks of the miracle-quest story.

1. The circumstances described bring Jesus back to Cana of Galilee and provide the opportunity for the royal official (βασιλικός).[61] He took the initiative
and made a direct approach to Jesus and an explicit request. He asked Jesus to
come down and heal his son, who was about to die.

2. Certainly the quest dominates the story from beginning to end. It is the focus of each episode of the passage.

3. The quester remains important, even though the objection threatens to make
him a foil for Jesus. The objection (4:48) seems out of place, because the request
already marks out the royal official as a believer. His continuing story not only
traces the course of his quest, it takes account of his household.

4. The objection of Jesus (4:48) extends the length of the story, because to overcome that objection the royal official must reiterate and persist in his request. The
objection, like that expressed by Jesus to his mother in 2:4, is somewhat enigmatic
and perhaps seems out of place. In normal terms *this request* appears to express
faith rather than to demand a miracle as a basis for faith . Even so, faith of a new
kind is a consequence of the performance of this sign.

5. The sign is a response to an individual need and certainly concerns an issue
of human well-being. It is the life of the son of the royal official that is at stake,
and this is a matter of concern for both of them.

6. Certainly the pronouncement of Jesus holds the key. This is made clear by:

   a. The words themselves—"Go, your son lives" (4:50);
   b. The way those words are recalled (4:53) and echoed in the report
      of the servants (4:51);
   c. The double stress on belief, which makes clear that it was conse-
      quent to the word of Jesus (4:50, 53). In the first instance the royal
      official believed Jesus' word when he first said, "Go, your son
      lives." Then, when he learned that the healing took place at the mo-
      ment Jesus said, "Your son lives," he believed and so did his whole
      household (4:53).

7. The story goes out of its way to make clear that not only was the boy healed,
but also that the royal official believed and so did his whole household.

8. Because the focus of the story moves from the life-saving word of Jesus,
which saves the son of the royal official from physical death, to the belief of the
royal official and his household, at a symbolic level the life-saving word becomes
the life-giving word of Jesus to that whole household.

Connecting the signs. The evangelist has gone out of his way to ensure that the
reader is aware of the connection of the two signs, explicitly linking them in 4:46
and 54, so that they form an *inclusio,* as is commonly noted.[62] The *inclusio* is of
the evangelist's making. He mentions the location of the marriage in Cana of
Galilee (2:1), and the conclusion of that story (2:11) notes "this, the beginning of

signs," again mentioning Cana of Galilee. The second Cana sign is introduced by reference to Jesus' return "to Cana of Galilee, where he made the water into wine" (4:46), and concludes (4:54) by referring to "the second sign Jesus did, coming out of Judea into Galilee." The *inclusio* is reinforced by the recognition that in these two stories we have the only two concise and discrete *miracle-quest stories* in John. Thus, we have an *inclusio* of the evangelist's making, focused on the theme of quest, using the only two miracle stories in John that are without any dialogues or discourse attached, such as we find in chapters 5, 6, 9, and 11. The evangelist has incorporated these miracle-quest stories into an overarching framework by explicitly relating them to each other as the first and second Cana signs. The *inclusio* implies that the whole section is concentrated on the theme of quest.

The Feeding Sign of John 6[63]

This story begins with the crowd's *following* Jesus (John 6:2) beside the sea of Galilee. In response to their initiative, Jesus fed them. Their response was to declare, "This man is truly the prophet who is coming into the world." Having declared him to be the prophet, the crowd was about to take him and make him king (6:14–15), suggesting an identification of Jesus with the prophet like Moses of Deuteronomy 18:15, 18—the prophet-king. But because Jesus knew that they were about to come and make him king, he withdrew again into the mountain, alone. Later (on the next day),[64] after Jesus had rejoined the disciples, the crowd came to Capernaum, *seeking* Jesus, and *found* him (John 6:24–25) on the other side of the sea.

What we have here fits the anatomy of a quest story and includes the motifs already associated with quest. The crowd takes the initiative in *following* Jesus. His withdrawal (John 6:15) constitutes the objection, or obstacle, to be overcome if the crowd's quest is to be successful. Here the objection signals, as is often the case, a *redirection* of the quest and Jesus' dissatisfaction with their intention to make him king. Thus, when the crowd subsequently comes *seeking* Jesus and *finds* him, the story has all the marks of a successful quest story. The crowd passed the initial test by *seeking* Jesus and *finding* him. What follows, however, shows Jesus' continued dissatisfaction with their quest (6:26–27).

In the ensuing dialogue the crowd continued to compare Jesus with Moses, although he had distanced himself from their conception of his role (6:14–15). The comparison with the feeding story, just narrated, cannot be missed *by the reader*. But it is unclear what the crowd had in mind when they asked Jesus:

> What sign are you going to give us, then, so that we may see it and believe you? What work are you performing? (6:30).

This is somewhat strange, given that Jesus had just performed a notable feeding sign. The incongruity of the demand is accentuated by the crowd's appeal to the tradition of the giving of the manna in the wilderness, as an example of what they have in mind.

> Our ancestors ate the manna in the wilderness; as it is written, "He gave them bread from heaven to eat" (6:31).

In response, Jesus makes three points. He accepts that the testimony "He *gave*" refers to Moses and asserts that what Moses *gave* (the manna) was not the *true* bread from heaven. The one who *gives* the true bread is "my father." The bread of God comes down from heaven and gives life to the world. On the basis of this explanation, the crowd requests of Jesus, "Sir, give us this bread always."[65] Now the quest has been redirected by Jesus, and the crowd has responded positively. It only remains for Jesus to reveal what this bread is, and this is the final test for the crowd to overcome.

> Jesus said to them, "I am the bread of life. Whoever comes to me will never be hungry, and whoever believes in me will never be thirsty" (6:35).

In this quest story the preunderstanding of the crowd, expressed in their expectations about him, is confronted with objections by Jesus. These are not *merely* tests to be overcome if the quest is to be successful—that is, tests of their resolve. The objections mark the point at which Jesus opposes their expectations, even if those expectations are the basis upon which there is the possibility of understanding him. The expectations are met with a correction so scandalous to them that, although they desire life from the true bread from heaven, they are unable to stomach his interpretation of it. The remainder of the chapter emphasizes the scandalous nature of Jesus' self-revelation and the angry murmuring that it caused (John 6:41, 52, 60). One reason for this is that the revelation put in question the human will to self-security.[66]

ALL ARE SEEKERS[67]

Bultmann's existentialist hermeneutic is peculiarly at home in the Gospel of John. Not only is the prologue a basis for understanding the *possibility* of authentic existence given in creation, but the quest stories manifest the quest for life, and the "I am" sayings of Jesus affirm that he is the real fulfillment of all quests. The Logos is the source of the life-giving light, which has within it the possibility of an illumined existence, authentic existence. The positive value of all searching, of all quests, is central to Bultmann's interpretation of John and forms a central plank in his hermeneutical approach, a platform described as the preunderstanding that makes the revelation intelligible. The place of the *genre* and motifs of the quest story reinforces the perception of the appropriateness of Bultmann's insight, at least in relation to John. According to Bultmann, because of the drive for self-security, the human will to life tends to distort the question into an answer that provides self-security in a way that ignores the *possibility* of human life and fails to choose authentic life. In the place of trust in the God of creation is self-reliance, where the self is not open to the challenge of the future, the challenge of the revelation. Yet the revelation encounters all people precisely in the will to life, although the manner of the meeting is at once an affirmation and a contradiction. It affirms the quest but contradicts all self-assuring answers. In the quest-story the objection functions in a way to make this clear, and in the "I am" sayings of Jesus, some of which occur in the quest-stories, there is a clarification and correction of the understanding of that for which all are seeking.

The importance of the *genre* of the quest-story in John is difficult to overestimate. The use of the first of the great symbolic "I am" sayings as the climactic pronouncement of the quest-story of John 6 alerts us to the theological significance of this particular quest story. The use of the symbolism of bread within this quest-story suggests that, although the context implies a contrast being made between Jesus' understanding of bread and the Jewish understanding of the manna as a symbol for the law, a more universal application is in view. That the crowd was fed by Jesus and came again seeking bread confirms this. Bread was, for them, the means of sustaining life. It was for this reason that bread, the manna, became a symbol for the law. The logic of the symbolism is dependent on the perception that "the life is more than food" (see Matt. 6:25–33). Yet food, as that which sustains physical life, has become the symbol of the source of the life that is beyond physical survival. The great religions of the world have all recognized that physical survival does not exhaust the meaning and purpose of human life. The contrast is not between bare existence and the desired quality of life, which today is often invoked in discussions of euthanasia. In such discussions bread is not a symbol, but the desired reality. In other words, physical life is the reality, and bread is the means of supporting this. But for the life of which Jesus speaks, he is himself the bread, that is, the source and means of supporting that life. The viability of this use of language arises from the fact that material possessions do not satisfy the human quest for life, and the fundamental nature of the human quest is well captured in terms of thirst and hunger. These are fundamental drives for survival. Something of the same force is captured by Bultmann when he says, "Human life is—consciously or unconsciously—impelled by the question about God." The words convey the sense that this is not something about which we are free to choose. We are *impelled* by the question about God, consciously or unconsciously. But whether it is conscious or unconscious matters, because we do choose *how* we seek to satisfy our hunger and thirst, and how we seek to direct our lives. How then is this fundamental response to life to be understood?

Death, which terminates physical life, is one reason why this question arises in a critical fashion. More significant, however, is the human quest for some meaning in the context of a world that so often seems meaningless and purpose-less. Yet within the human psyche, there is a drive that refuses to accept a sense of meaninglessness. The signs provide a clue to that meaning in a world whose meaning has not yet become evident; and in the midst of competing ideologies, one of which was the Jewish understanding of the law, John proclaimed Jesus as the bread of life, the source of true life.

The evangelist himself was responsible for the development of many of the tra-ditions into quest-stories, because he perceived the turmoil of human life as a quest and Jesus as the fulfillment of that quest of all who were searching. At the same time, the evangelist depicts the quest as a consequence of the unfulfilled nature of human life, apart from the revelation of God brought by Jesus. According to Rudolf Bultmann, it is a fundamental assumption of the evangelist that the universal quest for life has God as its goal, and that the quester meets the goal of the search in the revealer. Because of this, the revealer presents himself in the "I am" (ἐγώ εἰμι) revelatory formula, in which he identifies himself with whatever it is for which the people are searching. Naturally, the fulfillment has the power to transform the na-ture of the quest. If this perception is true to the evangelist's point of view, it is sig-nificant that quest-stories should be an important feature of the Gospel.[68]

Because human life is unfulfilled, the Johannine Jesus was able to present him-self as the fulfillment of the human quest. This is the force of the ἐγώ εἰμι say-ings. Naturally, it is the evangelist who presents Jesus in this way, even when he does so by using the words of Jesus. The diversity of questers seeking Jesus, as portrayed in John (the Baptist, disciples of the Baptist and their associates, the mother of Jesus, Nicodemus, a Pharisee, a ruler, Samaritans, a nobleman, a Galilean crowd, Mary and Martha, Greeks, and Mary Magdalene), reveals the uni-versality of the quest: that all are questers, until they come to Jesus.

NOTES

1. Dwight Moody Smith, Jr., *The Composition and Order of the Fourth Gospel: Bultmann's Literary Theory,* Yale Publications in Religion 10 (New Haven, Conn.: Yale University Press, 1965).

2. Smith, *The Composition and Order of the Fourth Gospel,* vii.

3. Rudolf Bultmann, "New Testament and Mythology: The Problem of De-mythologizing the New Testament Proclamation," now in *New Testament and Mythology and Other Basic Writings,* ed. Schubert M. Ogden (Philadelphia: Fortress, 1984), 1–43 (see esp. 9, 37); idem, *Theology of the New Testament* (New York: Scrib-ner's, 1951), 1.45, 295 (see also the note on that page), and 305; idem, "Johannes-evangelium" in *RGG*[3] 3 (1959): 840–50; and idem, *Jesus Christ and Mythology* (New York: Scribner's, 1958), 32–33.

4. See my *Theology as Hermeneutics: Rudolf Bultmann's Interpretation of the History of Jesus,* Historic Texts and Interpreters in Biblical Scholarship 4 (Sheffield: Almond, 1987), 111, 154–56.

5. In the Synoptics (Mark 8:11–13 and parr.) the opponents of Jesus demand that he offer a sign to justify his claims to authority (a use also to be found in John), and Jesus predicts that false prophets and false Messiahs would perform "signs and wonders" (Mark 13:22 and parr.). The latter is not found in John, who alone of the Gospel writers depicts the "miracles" of Jesus as signs.

6. See *Karl Barth—Rudolf Bultmann: Letters 1922–1966,* ed. Bernd Jaspert and Geoffrey W. Bromiley (Grand Rapids: Eerdmans, 1981), 38, 96. See also my *Theology as Hermeneutics,* 57.

7. See Rudolf Bultmann, *The Gospel of John: A Commentary* (Philadelphia: Westminster, 1971), 61–62, 149, 182.

8. Here, *Weltanschauung* ("worldview") needs to be distinguished from *Weltbild* ("world-picture"), which has a more restricted range of meaning. When the modern, scientific *Weltbild* is spoken of, this includes the assumption of the causal nexus but contains no comprehensive vision of the nature of reality. Bultmann elsewhere wrote that "When this picture of the world [*Weltbild*] is completed by the inclusion of man, it is customary to call it a world-view [*Weltanschauung*]" ("What Does It Mean to Speak of God?" in *Faith and Understanding* [London: SCM, 1969], 58). He questioned whether a comprehensive vision was possible on the basis of the modern scientific *Weltbild.* Thus, *Jesus Christ and Mythology,* 38: "Certainly it is a philosophical problem whether the scientific world-view [*Weltbild*] can perceive the whole reality of the world and of human life. There are reasons for doubting whether it can do so." Indeed, today, questions about the meaning of life are frequently considered to be meaningless.

9. Other kinds of confusion are also possible where, for example, the conflict between dominant concepts of the text and the interpreter's own worldview go unrecognized.

10. See Bultmann, *The Gospel of John,* 13, n. 1, where he says "that the 'Logos doctrine' of the Prologue gives expression to the idea of revelation which dominates the whole Gospel."

11. Bultmann stressed the evangelist's view of the possibility of revelation in the creation (*The Gospel of John,* 44, 52–53).

12. Cosmologies often provide the basis for an ideal view of the world. Such is the case in Genesis 1. See my "Theology, Eschatology, and the Prologue of John," *SJT* 46 (1993): 27–42.

13. Rudolf Bultmann, *Theology of the New Testament* (New York: Scribner's, 1955), 2.15–32. After setting out the historical situation of John (2.3–14), Bultmann gives first place to "Johannine Dualism" in his statement of Johannine theology.

14. See Jürgen Becker, "Beobachtungen zum Dualismus im Johannesevangelium," *ZNW* 65 (1974): 71–87 (here, 80).

15. Bultmann emphasizes the way that material creation is able to express the revelation (*The Gospel of John,* 182, 364).

16. In John 5:13 the man whom Jesus made "whole," *who does not know who Jesus is,* is described simply as ὁ ἰαθείς, which is in contrast to the repeated description of him as the one whom Jesus had made whole.

17. Naturally, Jesus' claim to participate in God's creative work was also a point of contention.

18. See John 9:31–33, and compare 9:16. The same conclusion concerning Jesus' signs was drawn by Nicodemus (John 3:2).

19. See the first edition of my *The Quest for the Messiah: The History, Literature and Theology of the Johannine Community* (Edinburgh: T. & T. Clark, 1991), 274–85. Bultmann refers to this as the possibility, given in creation, because the light of the Logos contained the possibility of illumined existence, that is, authentic existence (*The Gospel of John*, 44, 52–53).

20. Bultmann, *The Gospel of John*, 114.

21. Ibid., 452.

22. Ibid., 698.

23. For Bultmann, as for existentialist philosophy generally, the term *Existenz* is specific to the human subject.

24. *Existenzphilosophie*: that is, existentialist philosophy; see Bultmann, *Jesus Christ and Mythology*, 45, 55.

25. Ibid., 51–59.

26. See Rudolf Bultmann, "Polis and Hades in Sophocles' Antigone," in *Essays Philosophical and Theological* (London: SCM, 1955), 22–35 (here, 30–33); idem, "The Significance of 'Dialectical Theology' for the Scientific Study of the New Testament," in *Faith and Understanding*, 145–64, esp. 149–50; idem, "The Eschatology of the Gospel of John," in *Faith and Understanding*, 165–83, esp. 170; and my *Theology as Hermeneutics*, 19–43.

27. Augustine, *Confessions* 1.1. Except where quoted by Bultmann, quotations from the *Confessions* are from *Saint Augustine: Confessions*, trans. and ed. Henry Chadwick, World's Classics (Oxford: Oxford University Press, 1992).

28. The saying was quoted by Bultmann in *Essays Philosophical and Theological*, 257–58; *Jesus Christ and Mythology*, 52; *Kerygma and Myth: A Theological Debate*, ed. Hans Werner Bartsch, 2d ed. (London: SPCK, 1964), 1.192; *The Theology of Rudolf Bultmann*, ed. C. W. Kegley (London: SCM, 1966), 275. The earliest of these is the essay, "The Problem of Hermeneutics" (1950), in *Essays Philosophical and Theological* (234–61); then, the lectures of *Jesus Christ and Mythology*, which were delivered in 1951 though not published until 1958; followed, in 1952, by "On the Problem of Demythologizing" in *Kerygma and Myth*, 1; and finally, Bultmann's "Reply" (1966) in the volume edited by Kegley. In *The Gospel of John* (61, 149, 181–82, 296, 317, 530), Bultmann raises the question of the role of preunderstanding in relation to revelation, independently of the quotation from Augustine.

29. The context makes quite clear that this is meant to be an anthropological statement, even though, for Augustine, only the elect ultimately find rest.

30. In the *Confessions* Augustine interpreted this to mean that *humanity* was created to praise God and was unsatisfied, unfulfilled, outside this purpose.

31. Here, in the opening of the *Confessions*, we note the two distinctive perspectives of the work that have made it a genuine classic: the depth of the psychological insight achieved and the ability to combine this with genuine anthropological analysis.

32. Bultmann's assertion that self-understanding and the understanding of God are bound together also strikes a chord in Augustine. See esp. *Confessions*, book 10, on "Memory," in particular paragraphs 1 and 2 (chapters 1 and 2), 35 and 36 (chapters 24 and 25).

33. Bultmann, "The Problem of Hermeneutics," in *Essays Philosophical and Theological*, 257–58.

34. For Augustine's discussion of the quest for happiness, see *Confessions*

10.20.29–23.33. While Augustine's discussion of "memory" owes more than a little to Neoplatonic sources, it is also driven by an anthropological application of the analysis of his own experience.

35. See Bultmann, *Jesus Christ and Mythology*, 50.

36. The German term, *existentiell,* denotes the actual response in a concrete situation, while *existential* describes the philosophical analysis of existentialist philosophy. In English the former is frequently, though not uniformly, translated as "existential" and the latter, as "existentialist." The same distinction is sometimes made by using the terms *ontic* and *ontological.*

37. Bultmann, *Jesus Christ and Mythology*, 52–53.

38. Bultmann, *Kerygma and Myth*, 1.192.

39. Bultmann, "Reply," in *The Theology of Rudolf Bultmann*, 275.

40. On this theme, see my *Theology as Hermeneutics,* 120–26, and esp. Bultmann, *Essays Philosophical and Theological,* 98, 115. See also Bultmann, *Faith and Understanding,* 264, 318–23; *The Gospel of John,* 530.

41. See my *Theology as Hermeneutics,* 220–25.

42. Bultmann, *The Gospel of John,* 225.

43. Ibid., 364 (also 107 n.2). The revealer answers all human questions (189) and "outside the revelation man is always a seeker" (378), because what is myth and dream is reality here (530). See also his contribution to "ζάω, κ. τ. λ.," in *TDNT* 2 (1964): 832–75, esp. 871–72.

44. Noted by Bultmann in *The Gospel of John,* 100.

45. The Synoptic accounts are based on Mark, where the first disciples were called by the authoritative "Follow me" of Jesus. There is no suggestion that any of these disciples had any prior knowledge of Jesus. The impression is given of the authoritative word of Jesus shaking these five men out of the complacency of self-satisfied lives. For the different approach of John, see the second edition of my *The Quest for the Messiah: The History, Literature and Theology of the Johannine Community* (Nashville: Abingdon, 1993), 179–82.

46. See my *The Quest for the Messiah,* 2d ed., 183 n. 53.

47. Reference here to "the Jews" covers both the Pharisees of 8:21 and their servants in 7:33–34.

48. See Painter, *The Quest for the Messiah,* 2d ed., 169–77, 182–85.

49. Martyn's views are to be found in his essay, "'We Have Found Elijah': A View of Christ Formulated Very Early in the Life of the Johannine Community," in *The Gospel of John in Christian History: Essays for Interpreters* (New York and Ramsey, N.J.: Paulist, 1978), 9–54. For a critical discussion of his views, see my *The Quest for the Messiah,* 2d ed., 179–82.

50. See Painter, *The Quest for the Messiah,* 2d ed., 183 n. 53 and 184 n. 57.

51. See ibid., 178 n. 38.

52. See especially *Pronouncement Stories,* ed. Robert C. Tannehill, in *Semeia* 20 (1981).

53. For a fuller statement, see my *The Quest for the Messiah,* 2d ed., 177–78.

54. Tannehill (see n. 52) recognized the miracle-quest story as a subtype of quest story, noting that a minority of Synoptic quest stories fall into this category. It is notable that the miracle stories of John 5 and 9 are *not* quest stories. In those stories the healings are initiated by Jesus, and they become the basis for conflict stories, which conclude with the rejection of Jesus or his follower.

55. See Rudolf Bultmann, *The History of the Synoptic Tradition* (Oxford: Black-well, 1968), 209–43 (esp. 221–26), and his discussion in *The Gospel of John*, 115–18 and 204–8.

56. See John 2:11 and 4:50–53. Having returned home and having discovered and made known the exact correspondence in time of the word of Jesus and the actual heal-ing of his son, the official and all the members of his household also came to believe.

57. Francis J. Moloney, *Belief in the Word. Reading the Fourth Gospel: John 1 – 4* (Minneapolis: Fortress, 1993), 90, 189–90.

58. Not all miracle stories involve a request. Those that do might well be classi-fied as miracle-quest stories. The request is not essential to the anatomy of a miracle story, though it is essential to a miracle-quest story.

59. The incident between Jesus and his brothers is generally taken as straightfor-ward evidence of their unbelief (7:5). Read in the light of the quest-story genre, the story reads somewhat differently. In addition, the belief of the disciples is put in ques-tion at the end of the farewell discourses by Jesus' question ("Do you now believe?"), and the evidence of the scattering of the disciples implies a negative answer (16:31–32). Read in this light, the unbelief of the brothers in 7:5 indicates that they do not *yet* aspire to faith, as understood in this Gospel. But, then, neither did the disciples at this stage! The quest of the brothers is, nevertheless, successful. After the brothers have left, as instructed by Jesus, he also went up to Jerusalem, where his disciples saw his "works."

60. See Painter, *The Quest for the Messiah*, 2d ed., 185–91.

61. In each of the Cana miracles, there is an official with a title that remains some-what enigmatic (today, at least): chief steward (ἀρχιτρίκλινος) and royal official (βασιλικός).

62. See for example Francis J. Moloney, "From Cana to Cana (John 2:1–4:54) and the Fourth Evangelist's Concept of Correct (and Incorrect) Faith," in *Studia Biblica 1978 II: Papers on the Gospels: Sixth International Congress on Biblical Studies*, ed. E. A. Livingstone, JSNTSup 2 (Sheffield: JSOT, 1980), 185–213.

63. For a fuller treatment of John 6, see Painter, *The Quest for the Messiah*, 2d ed., 253–86.

64. The expression, τῇ ἐπαύριον, signals that the events on the succeeding day are part of a connected sequence with those of the previous day; see John 1:29, 35, 43.

65. Compare the request of the Samaritan woman in 4:15, which, like 6:34, lacks comprehension but must be taken as a positive response to Jesus. In the case of the Samaritan woman, the response was the beginning of a chain of events that concludes with the climactic confession of 4:42. In this respect the sequence resembles the chain of events recorded in 1:19–51, and esp. 1:35–51. Therefore, the echo of her response in 6:34 sets up a positive resonance, leading to the expectation of a positive conclu-sion in the quest of the crowd. Such, however, is not to be. In the finished Gospel the crowd was unable to overcome the final offense of Jesus' self-revealing words.

66. See Bultmann, *The Gospel of John*, 327; idem, *Theology of the New Testa-ment*, 2.27–28, 67–68.

67. Idem, *The Gospel of John*, 378.

68. On this theme see Bultmann, *The Gospel of John*, 61–62, 182, 378–80, 530–32; and Painter, *Theology as Hermeneutics*, 120–26.

Index of Scripture and Other Ancient Sources

Old Testament

New Testament

Ancient Jewish Literature

APOCRYPHA

PSEUDEPIGRAPHA

RABBINIC LITERATURE

Greco-Roman Literature

Early Christian Literature
APOSTOLIC FATHERS

PATRISTIC LITERATURE

NAG HAMMADI TRACTATES

Index of Ancient Terms

Greek

Hebrew and Aramaic

Latin

Index of Modern Authors

DATE DUE